# KAREN ARMSTRONG
# HOLY WAR

Karen Armstrong, one of the foremost commentators on religious affairs, is the bestselling author of *A History of God* (1993), *The Battle for God* (2000), *Islam: A Short History* (2000), and *Buddha* (2001), among many other books. Having spent seven years as a Roman Catholic nun, she left her order in 1969 and took a B.Litt. at Oxford, taught modern literature at the University of London, and headed the English department of a public girls' school. She became a freelance writer and broadcaster in 1982, and in 1983 she worked in the Middle East on a six-part documentary television series on the life and works of St. Paul. Her other television work has included "Varieties of Religious Experience" (1984) and "Tongues of Fire" (1985); the latter resulted in an anthology by that name on religious and poetic expression. In 1996 she participated in Bill Moyers' television series "Genesis." She teaches at the Leo Baeck College for the Study of Judaism and the Training of Rabbis and Teachers and was awarded the 1999 Muslim Public Affairs Council Media Award. She regularly contributes reviews and articles to newspapers and journals.

ALSO BY KAREN ARMSTRONG

*Through the Narrow Gate*

*Beginning the World*

*The First Christian: St. Paul's Impact on Christianity*

*Tongues of Fire: An Anthology of Religious and Poetic Experience*

*The Gospel According to Woman:*
*Christianity's Creation of the Sex War in the West*

*Visions of God: Four Medieval Mystics and Their Writings*

*Muhammad: A Biography of the Prophet*

*A History of God:*
*The 4000-Year Quest of Judaism, Christianity, and Islam*

*Jerusalem: One City, Three Faiths*

*In the Beginning: A New Interpretation of Genesis*

*The Battle for God*

*Islam: A Short History*

*Buddha*

# HOLY WAR

# HOLY WAR

*The Crusades and Their Impact*

*on Today's World*

# KAREN ARMSTRONG

ANCHOR BOOKS

A Division of Random House, Inc.

New York

SECOND ANCHOR BOOKS EDITION, DECEMBER 2001

*Copyright © 1988, 1991, 2001 by Karen Armstrong*

All rights reserved under International and Pan-American Copyright Conventions.
Published in the United States by Anchor Books, a division of Random House, Inc.,
New York. Originally published in hardcover in Great Britain by Macmillan,
London, in 1988, and subsequently published in hardcover in a revised edition in
the United States by Doubleday, a division of Random House, Inc., New York, in
1991, and in trade paperback by Anchor Books, a division of Random House, Inc.,
New York, in 1992. This Anchor Books edition contains a new preface.

Anchor Books and colophon are registered trademarks of Random House, Inc.

Library of Congress Cataloging-in-Publication Data
Armstrong, Karen.
Holy war : the Crusades and their impact on today's world / Karen Armstrong.
p.   cm.
Includes bibliographical references and index.
1. Crusades.   2. Crusades—Influence.
I. Title.
(D157.A76   1992)   91-35560
909.07—dc20   CIP

Anchor ISBN: 0-385-72140-4

www.anchorbooks.com

Printed in the United States of America
10

For my dear friends
Abdul Halim Zoabe of Nazareth, his Jewish-Israeli wife, Anat,
and their sons, Salah Adam and Nizar Amir,
who by making me a member of their family
have been a crucial influence in my developing
the "triple vision" that I have tried
to articulate in this book.

# CONTENTS

# PREFACE

On September 11, 2001, in an attack that changed the world forever, Islamic extremists destroyed the World Trade Center in New York City and demolished a wing of the Pentagon. As he planned a new campaign against international terrorism, President George W. Bush explained that this would not be a war against Islam; indeed, he hoped to enlist the support of such Muslim states as Iran, Egypt and Syria. But it was perhaps unfortunate that he called his riposte a Crusade, because he could not have chosen a word more likely to antagonize his potential Muslim allies. To understand why this should be so, we need to think again about these medieval wars of religion, not least because there is a sense in which we can trace the roots of the present conflict to November 25, 1095, when Pope Urban II summoned the expedition that would become known as the First Crusade.

*Holy War* was first published in the United Kingdom in 1988. I had recently spent a good deal of time in the Middle East making a television series about the Crusades, and the parallels between those medieval holy wars and the current hostilities in the region had intrigued me. These modern wars may have begun in a secular spirit, but they seemed to be acquiring an increasingly religious momentum. Since then I have written two other books on related subjects: *Jerusalem: One City, Three Faiths* and *The Battle for God,* which have developed and expanded some of the themes explored in these pages. But I still believe that it is important for Western people to consider these contemporary holy wars in connection with the Crusades, because they remind us of our own input, involvement and responsibilities.

Since 1988 we have seen extraordinary changes in the Middle East, some of which I could not have predicted. There have been two Western-led offensives against the regime of Saddam Hussein in Iraq, and it was significant that as soon as the first bombs dropped on Baghdad, the attack was condemned in the Arab world as "*al-Salibiyyah!*" "A Crusade!" The memory of the medieval holy wars, initiated by the West, has been rekindled in the Middle East by the present troubles, and the study of the Crusades is certainly not an arcane discipline in either Israel or in the Muslim world. In the territories that had been occupied by Israel in 1967, a popular uprising known as the *intifadah* broke out in 1987. Its leaders and ideology were secularist, but the emergence of the Islamic militant group Hamas brought a religious dimension to the Palestinian resistance for the first time. The *intifadah* was a watershed; it convinced Yitzak Rabin, Prime Minister of Israel, that peace was the only viable option, and in 1993 the signing of the Oslo Accords gave hope of a resolution to the Arab-Israeli conflict. But the assassination of Rabin by a young Jewish fundamentalist in 1995 showed that far from being a pacific force in the region, religion was a potent weapon in the struggle. Religious extremists were as opposed to peace as they had been in 1981, when a Muslim fundamentalist had shot President Anwar al-Sadat for signing the Camp David Accords. As I write this new preface in the autumn of 2001, the peace process in the Middle East seems doomed, and the Israelis and Palestinians appear to be on the brink of a potentially disastrous all-out war. On both sides the leaders are secularists, but each faces potentially murderous opposition from religious zealots in its own camp. The suicide bombers of Hamas believe that they are fighting a *jihad* of self-defense in the spirit of Saladin, as discussed in this book. On the Israeli side, the Jewish settlers in the West Bank and Gaza Strip, many of whom come from the United States, are inspired by a religious Zionism, which, in its passionate adherence to the Holy Land, is strongly reminiscent of the crusading ethos.

It is also remarkable that the holy shrines of the Western Wall and the Haram al-Sharif are so often flashpoints in the conflict. A second *intifadah* erupted in the autumn of 2000, when the former Israeli general Ariel Sharon marched onto the Haram with a large entourage of right-wing supporters in what appeared to the Palestinians and to the Muslim world as a whole to be an aggressive and provocative manner. In the summer of 2001, Palestinians stoned Israeli worshipers at the Western Wall, after a Jewish fundamentalist had attempted to lay the foundation stone for a third Jewish temple to replace the Muslim shrines on the Haram, the third holiest site in the Islamic world. We often believe that we have abandoned such ancient religious enthusiasms as the devotion to sacred space in our predominantly secularist and scientific world, but it seems that a fierce loyalty to the holy places can still inspire aggression and violence, just as it did at the time of the Crusades.

Before the Crusaders arrived in Jerusalem in July 1099 and savagely butchered some 40,000 of its Jewish and Muslim inhabitants, Jews, Christians and Muslims had lived together there under Islamic rule in relative harmony for 460 years—almost half a millennium. Saladin achieved the reconquest of Jerusalem for Islam in 1187, but relations between the three religions of Abraham were never as good in Jerusalem again. Henceforth, the members of each faith eyed one another warily, constantly fearing assault or the expropriation of their shrines and homes. The Crusades had effected a tragic sea change in Jerusalem, where the coexistence that once prevailed now seems an impossible dream. In the West, the Crusades were also decisive. The Crusades made the hatred of Jews an incurable disease in Europe, and Islam would henceforth be seen as the irreconcilable enemy of Western civilization. These Western prejudices have certainly played their part in today's conflict, and affect the way Western people view the Middle East today in highly complex ways.

In *Holy War* I tried to show that the Crusades were not a fringe movement in the Middle Ages; they were central to the new Western identity that was forged at this time and which persists to the present day. The Crusades also show religion at its very worst. After writing *Holy War* I was so saddened by the conflict between the three Abraham traditions that I decided to embark on the research for my book *A History of God*. I wanted to demonstrate the strong and positive ideals and visions that Jews, Christians and Muslims share in common. It is now over a millennium since Pope Urban II called the First Crusade in 1095, but the hatred and suspicion that this expedition unleashed still reverberates, never more so than on September 11, 2001, and during the terrible days that followed. It is tragic that our holy wars continue, but for that very reason we must strive for mutual understanding and for what in these pages I have called "triple vision."

# INTRODUCTION

In England we usually learn about the Middle Ages when we are quite young children and it seems a rather magical time. We are taught about great moments in our own history (the Battle of Hastings in 1066 and the signing of Magna Carta in 1215) and also some of the important events in Europe. We learn that this was a great age of religious faith, the period of the monasteries and St. Francis of Assisi. It was a time when magnificent cathedrals were built for the glory of God and when exquisite manuscripts were illuminated. It was also a time when heroes like Richard the Lionheart fought unequivocal villains like his brother King John. It all sounds rather glamorous and so far in spirit from our own time that the events become surrounded with a legendary aura. This is the time when we first hear about the Crusades, and they seem as magical and impractically poetic as the rest of the period: for two hundred years the brave Crusaders sewed red crosses on their clothes and marched off to Jerusalem to rescue Christ's tomb from the villains (a people vaguely known as "the infidel" or "the Saracen"). Unless we go on to specialize in medieval history when we are older, it is likely that most British people retain a rather vague and confused impression of the Crusades. They keep their old glamour and that may be enhanced by the reading of authors like Malory, Sir Walter Scott, Alfred Lord Tennyson and the Pre-Raphaelites. The extraordinary story of the Crusades becomes merged with medieval legends about King Arthur, the Holy Grail and Robin Hood. On the other hand, as we grow older we become aware that our first childish impressions of the Middle Ages were inevitably oversimplified: we gather that King John seems to have been a better king than his more romantic brother Richard the Lionheart. We also become aware that the brave and noble Crusaders actually butchered thousands of "infidels" during their holy wars.

Until relatively recently I was myself rather confused about the Crusades. The old glamorous associations remained and they still seemed rather dashing events that were larger than life. But I was also aware that the Crusaders committed violent atrocities against many thousands of innocent Muslims and Jews and this seemed wicked and perverse. Yet I also noticed how frequently we used the word "crusade" in a positive context. We often talk about crusades against poverty or injustice and praise a "crusading journalist," who is bravely uncovering some salutary truth. We would all condemn the cruelty of the Crusaders out of hand but paradoxically we call any campaign of principle a "crusade": could it be that at some level the idea of a crusade had found a strong acceptance against all logic and reason?

In 1983 I spent some time in Israel researching and making a television series about early Christianity for the British Channel 4. While I was there I found myself confronted with the Crusades time and time again. It is quite possible to live in England without giving the Crusades a thought for months at a time, but this was simply not possible in Israel. There you constantly come across churches, castles and whole cities built by the Crusaders, and for the first time crusading became a historical reality to me: this was no vague legend. Nearly a thousand years ago, when Europe was still a barbarous and uncivilized place, thousands of Christians had struggled all the way to the Middle East and established states and kingdoms there. They were our first colonies. It seemed an extraordinary thing to have happened. I was particularly struck by the Crusaders' massive castles and fortresses and discovered that they were built all along the borders of their states: there was a chain of Crusader castles in Israel, Lebanon, Syria and Jordan. Not surprisingly, Israelis and Palestinians both seemed quite knowledgeable about the Crusades. Israelis pointed out that their own huge building developments on the hills around Jerusalem looked remarkably like Crusader castles: the people who lived there saw themselves as defending Jewish Jerusalem from the Arabs. In order to attack Jerusalem, an invading Arab army would have to fight its way through these densely populated civilian settlements in the firing line. I discovered that crusading studies flourished in the Hebrew University at Jerusalem. It was hardly surprising. The ruins of the Crusader castles were powerful reminders of another Western state which had established itself in a hostile Muslim world and seemed to have been just as worried about national security as the state of Israel today. It had never occurred to me to link the exotic and dubious crusading project of the Middle Ages with the violent conflict in the Middle East today, but in Israel it seemed very easy to do so.

My visit to Israel in 1983 was also the date when the Arab-Israeli conflict became a reality to me. Until that time my ideas about it had been just as vague and unfocused as my ideas about the Crusades. I had been shocked by Palestinian terrorism and by Israeli brutality in Lebanon but had never felt that any of this tragic violence had anything to do with me personally. I was aware, of course, that Britain had played an important part in the creation of the state of Israel, and during my first visit to the country I was aware that the British had left a great deal of resentment behind. This was not a new idea to me: I was acutely aware of the distress British colonial policy had caused in places like Africa and India. But in Israel this became a personal reality to me: nobody discussed the events that led up to 1948 in very much detail but, although everybody was very warm and welcoming to me personally, I found that I was constantly having to listen to violent diatribes against the British national character by my new Israeli and Arab friends. This was very disturbing. I could see that this portrait of the British as complacent, patronizing hypocrites, pickled in an-achronistic habits of formality, was an exaggeration and therefore a distorted stereotype. But when I tried to argue about it, neither the Arabs nor the Israelis wanted to listen. They seemed to need to think about the British in this way; it was an essential part of their world view that they were anxious to preserve at all costs. It gave me much food for thought. It was years since Britain had played any active role in the Middle East but clearly we had hurt both the Arabs and the Jews at a fundamental level and were still bound together with them somehow, in a three-sided relationship of pain. Further, as I listened to Israelis and Arabs arguing their own case in the conflict against that of the "other" side, I found myself becoming involved and aware for the first time of the complexity and pain of the issues.

I was also very surprised at the strength of my own reaction to the country which I had been brought up to call the "Holy Land." Even though I was no longer a believing or a practicing Christian, I found it very moving to be living and working in Jerusalem, a city which had been imaginatively and emotionally present to me since I was a small child. The film we were making examined the Jewish roots of the Christian faith, and naturally we spent some time filming at the Wailing Wall, the last remaining relic of the ancient Jewish Temple. There Judaism, too, became a reality for me for the first time. I was moved to see the passion and fervor with which Jewish pilgrims kissed the stones of the Wailing Wall and astonished to see tough young Israeli soldiers, carrying heavy submachine guns, binding their *tefillin* to their foreheads and swaying devoutly in prayer. I had been brought up to see Judaism as a superseded religion, and even though later I realized that this was a Christian distortion, I had still never really considered it as anything but a prelude to Christianity. Now I saw its immense emotional power, something quite independent of my Christian vision of the world. Further, I could not quite imagine a British soldier praying so devoutly and openly, but in Jerusalem religion seemed to be in the very air and stones.

Yet there was another fact to be absorbed. When I looked up above the Wailing Wall, I saw the great mosques of the Dome of the Rock and al-Aqsa and was told that Jerusalem was the third most holy city in the Islamic world. I knew, of course, that Islam was one of the great world religions but now realized that to my shame I knew next to nothing about it. My thoughts about Muslims had in fact advanced very little from my early vague notions of "the infidel" and "the Saracen" derived from those early history lessons on the Middle Ages. In my free time I visited the mosques and again was struck by the fervor of the Muslims praying there. I was surprised to find myself deeply drawn to the peace and spirituality of al-Aqsa, with its great space and silences—light-years away from the popular, journalistic view of Islam as the violent religion of the sword. In the Dome of the Rock, however, I saw the rock on which Abraham was believed to have bound Isaac to sacrifice him to God. I learned that, like Jews and Christians, Muslims regard themselves as children of Abraham, and I recalled that the Jews had deliberately built their Temple on the site where Abraham was commanded to sacrifice his son. Later, in the Holy Sepulchre Church, I met Abraham again in a huge mosaic depicting Isaac's sacrifice on the spot where Jesus, the Son of God, was said to have died to save the world. On the opposite wall was a giant crucifixion: God, like Abraham, had been prepared to sacrifice his own son. It seemed that in all three of the religions of Abraham there is a fundamental image of extremity. This was underlined by the fact that the actual Church of the Holy Sepulchre had been built by the medieval Crusaders, who had killed so many Muslims during their conquest of Jerusalem that the blood was said to have come up to the knees of their horses.

The crusading theme seemed to me to be somehow germane to both the modern conflict and the uneasy relationship that has existed over the years between Judaism, Christianity and Islam, the three religions of Abraham. When I began to research the topic, I expected to find some similarities and analogies between the medieval conflict and the modern situation but over the years I have discovered that the connections are deeper. I now believe that the Crusades were one of the direct causes of the conflict in the Middle East today. I know that this is a startling statement and I welcome the opportunity to explore it in depth.

In order to do so I shall try to establish the habit of what I call triple vision. Usually when we strive to be objective we say that we want to see "both" sides of the question. In this long conflict between the three faiths, however, there are three sides. At each point I shall try to consider the position and point of view of Jews, Christians and Muslims. Since the Crusades, all three have been implicated in different ways in the holy wars between them, and the original relationship that they bear to one another has been shot through with cruelty and pain. The greatest tragedies have occurred when one tradition has sought to eliminate the other two or when two of the traditions have joined forces and completely ignored the third. In the Middle East one becomes acutely conscious of the strong connection between the three religions and also, perhaps for that very reason, of their acute alienation from one another. I realize that my argument is complex but I hope that the reader will bear with me because I have found that when you have mastered the habit of triple vision you can never see things in quite the same way again. It has radically altered my view of the Middle East and has given me a new appreciation of the mechanics of prejudice.

It is triple vision that makes this book rather different from other books about the Crusades. I am not a professional historian and I am certainly not attempting to rival the medievalists who have devoted their lives to a study of the Crusades. Quite the contrary: I am entirely in their debt. I acknowledge my indebtedness to Sir Steven Runciman, the father of crusading scholarship in Britain, and also to the insights of Professor Jonathan Riley-Smith. But I have also been indebted to Norman Daniel, Francesco Gabrieli and Amin Maalouf for their work on the Muslim view of crusading and to Schlomo Eidelberg and Eliezer Schweid for their insight into the Jewish angle. What I have attempted to do is bring the work of all these scholars together, so that we see a three-sided picture of Christians, Muslims and Jews engaged in a deadly conflict. In much the same way, in the modern period we have an inevitable polarization of interest. I cannot hope to rival Amos Elon's compelling account of the strange history and deep dilemmas of Zionism and the state of Israel. Nor will I equal the passionate erudition of Edward W. Said in *Orientalism: Western Conceptions of the Orient*, in which he traces the history of Western hostility to the East. I have needed the insights of these and many other writers and scholars. Again, I have attempted to consider the Jewish case alongside the Arab and the Muslim and—most important—to include the contribution made by the Christian West in today's conflict. In order to develop a clear knowledge of any tradition, it is obviously important for scholars to isolate and examine things separately. Sometimes, however, it is important to put things back together again.

My own training has been in theology and in literature and this means that my book on the Crusades is bound to be different from the book of a professional historian, but I think that my particular disciplines are especially appropriate to the subject. Theology and literature both teach one to connect the like with the unlike and to see that this can make a new truth. Both disciplines provide an alternative to a purely rational view of the world and both are concerned with mythology: they take fiction very seriously indeed. Literature in particular teaches us the power of emotion as a force in the world and shows that our thoughts are never entirely cerebral. The Crusades, like so much of the modern conflict, were not wholly rational movements that could be explained away by purely economic or territorial ambition or by a clash of rights and interests. They were fueled, on all sides, by myths and passions that were far more effective in getting people to act than any purely political motivation. The medieval holy wars in the Middle East could not be solved by rational treaties or neat territorial solutions. Fundamental passions were involved which touched the identity of Christians, Muslims and Jews and which were sacred to the identity of each. They have not changed very much in the holy wars of today.

I shall not be dwelling on weaponry or on the economic or military aspects of the holy wars, medieval and modern. This is a history of myths, emotions and religious passions that were tied to practical, violent policies. Because I want to develop this triple vision, I have not discussed the holy wars being fought in Northern Ireland or South America today. I am concentrating on a long struggle between Jews, Christians and Muslims that began over a thousand years ago and has led to tragic and catastrophic events in our own century.

It is hard to have one's old prejudices shattered and it is distressing to examine the sins of one's own culture. It is particularly difficult to enter into another culture—it might even be impossible to do so. Certainly I have tried to enter into the minds of the Crusaders, so that we can understand what they thought they were doing when they slaughtered Muslims and Jews as an act of the love of God. I have also tried to come to a greater understanding of Judaism and Islam. It has been difficult to shed my Christian-formed notions of religion and I hope that Jews and Muslims will forgive any mistakes that I have made. The journey toward understanding and peace will take all of us a long time.

# AUTHOR'S NOTE

I shall have to use rather technical terms sometimes, some of them Hebrew or Arabic words. To help the reader I have compiled a Glossary at the end of the book, but these preliminary terms might be useful at the outset.

**Eretz Yisrael** (Hebrew). The Land of Israel. This is a vital concept in the ideology of the Jewish holy war, which centers on the land that God promised to Abraham and to his descendants, the Jewish people. Abraham's grandson Jacob had his name changed to Israel, as a sign of God's special favor. Jacob had twelve sons, who were all born in the Promised Land, but who later emigrated to Egypt during a famine. These twelve sons of Jacob founded the twelve tribes of Israel, and when Moses and Joshua led the tribes back to the Promised Land and established the children of Israel there, each tribe lived in a specially designated area in the land of Israel. Jews regard Eretz Yisrael, therefore, as the land of their fathers, and religious Jews from the time of Joshua until the present day believe that their right to return there is authorized by God.

**Crusade** (from the French *croix*: cross). The term did not become common to describe the Christians who fought a holy war for the Holy Land until relatively late in the movement. As we shall see, the Crusaders usually called themselves "pilgrims." But from the start they were associated with the Cross. They sewed crosses on their clothes and felt that they were literally obeying Christ's command to his followers to take up their cross and follow him to death, if necessary. At the time of the First Crusade, people from England who came to France to join one of the crusading armies there but who did not know a word of French were able to show that they were Crusaders by making a cross of their fingers, and so received directions and help. The Cross and the Crucifixion were central to the movement from the beginning. The Crusaders were going to liberate the Church of the Holy Sepulchre, which they believed contained the site of Golgotha and the tomb of Christ, but which was at that time in the hands of the Muslims.

**Jihad** (Arabic). The word literally means "struggle" and is used in the Koran (the sacred book of Islam) usually as a verb: Muslims are urged "to struggle mightily in the way of God." The idea of struggle and achievement are crucial in Islam and the word *jihad* has always retained this connotation. But most frequently the "struggle" referred to is the war Mohammad was forced to wage against the non-Muslim Arabs of Arabia. Later, by extension, it came to mean "holy war" and in that sense is discussed in the Sharia (Islamic law) in the century after Mohammad's death.

# MAPS

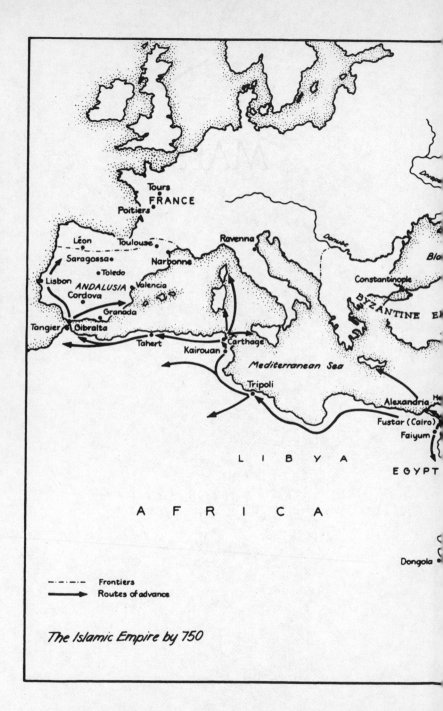

The Islamic Empire by 750

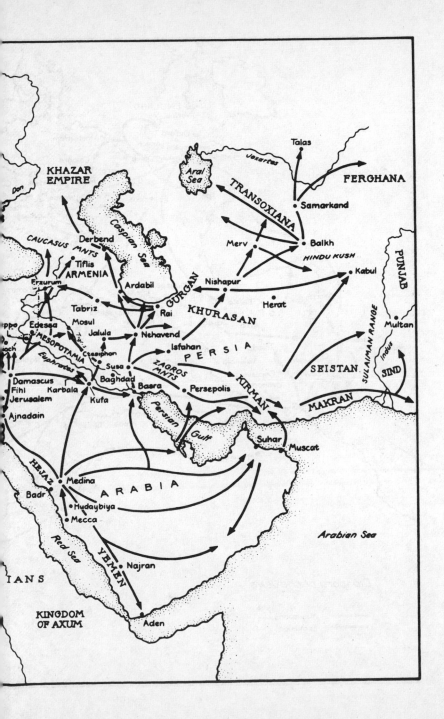

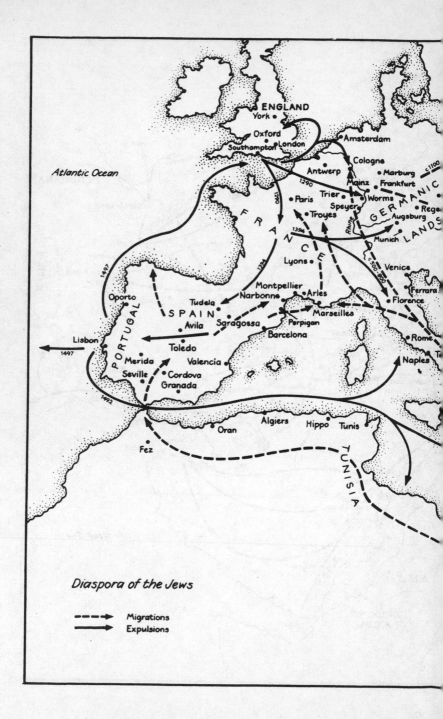

Diaspora of the Jews

- - - → Migrations
——→ Expulsions

Europe at the time of the Crusades

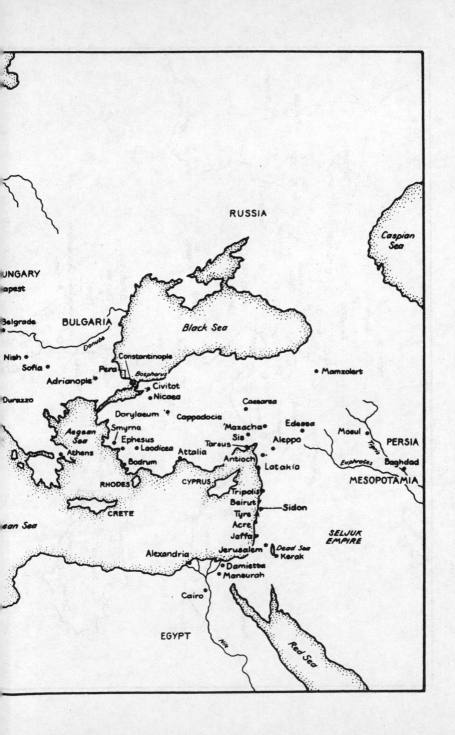

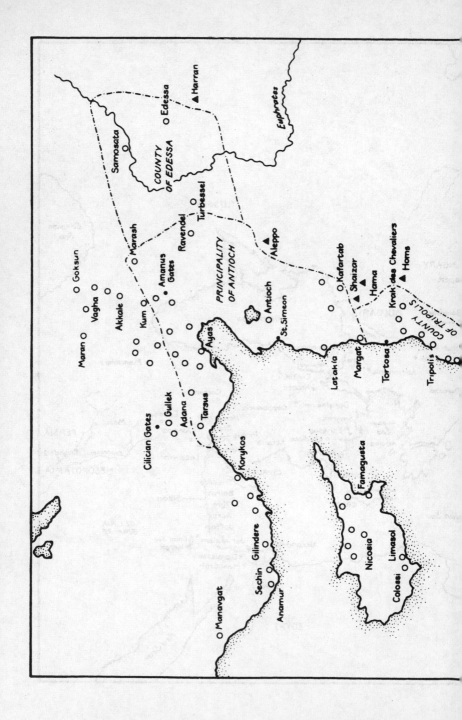

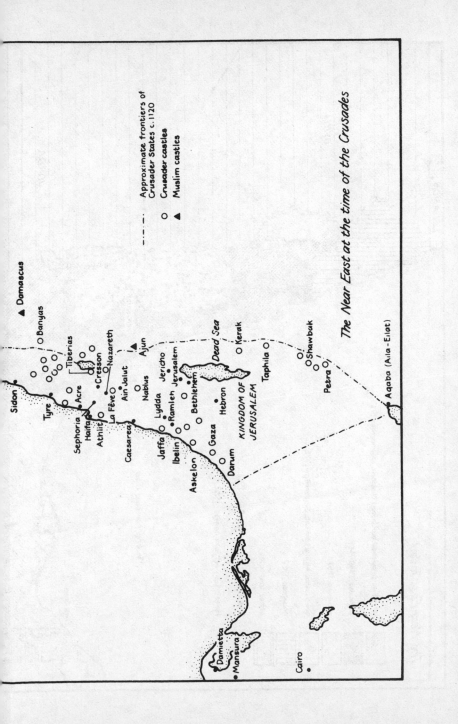

The Near East at the time of the Crusades

Approximate frontiers of
Crusader States c.1120
○ Crusader castles
▲ Muslim castles

▲ Damascus

○ Banyas

Tiberias

Nazareth

Cresson

▲ Ajun

Sidon

Tyre

Sephoria

Haifa

Acre

Athlit

La Fève

Ain Jalut

Caesarea

Nablus

Jericho

Jerusalem

Dead Sea

Kerak

Lydda

Ramleh

Bethlehem

Jaffa

Ibelin

Hebron

Gaza

Taphila

KINGDOM OF
JERUSALEM

Askelon

Darum

Shawbak

Petra

Aqaba (Aila-Eilat)

Damietta

Mansura

Cairo

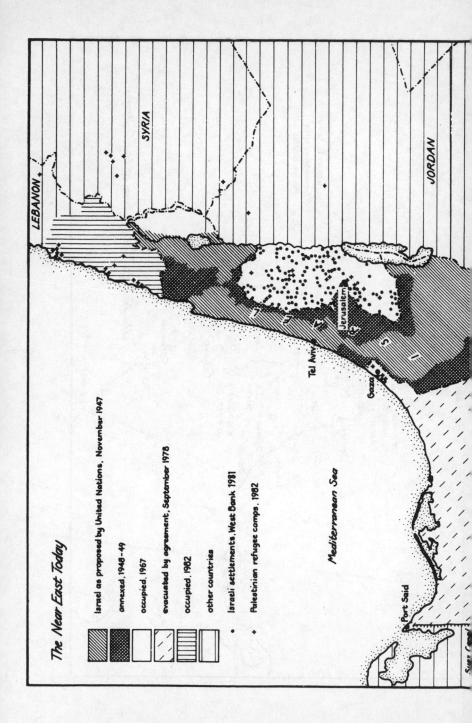

The Near East Today

Israel as proposed by United Nations, November 1947

annexed, 1948-49

occupied, 1967

evacuated by agreement, September 1978

occupied, 1982

other countries

• Israeli settlements, West Bank 1981

✦ Palestinian refugee camps, 1982

LEBANON

SYRIA

JORDAN

Jerusalem

Tel Aviv

Gaza

Mediterranean Sea

Port Said

Suez Canal

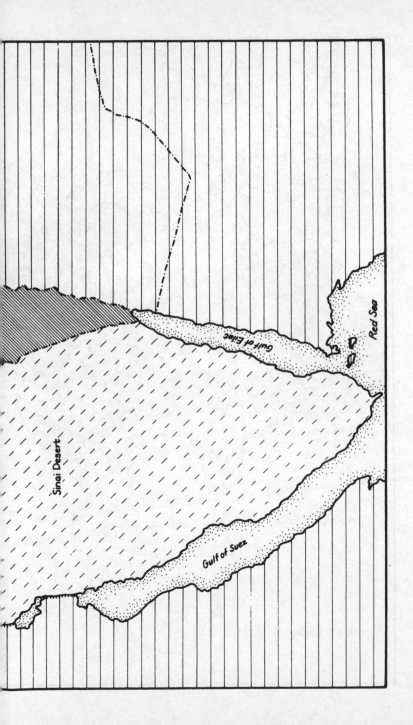

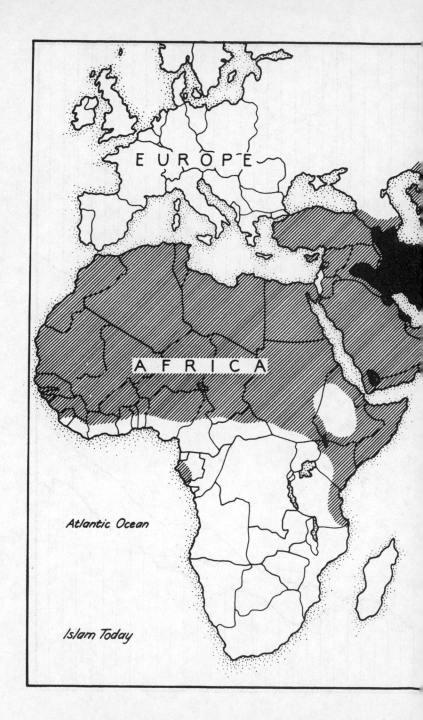

EUROPE

AFRICA

Atlantic Ocean

Islam Today

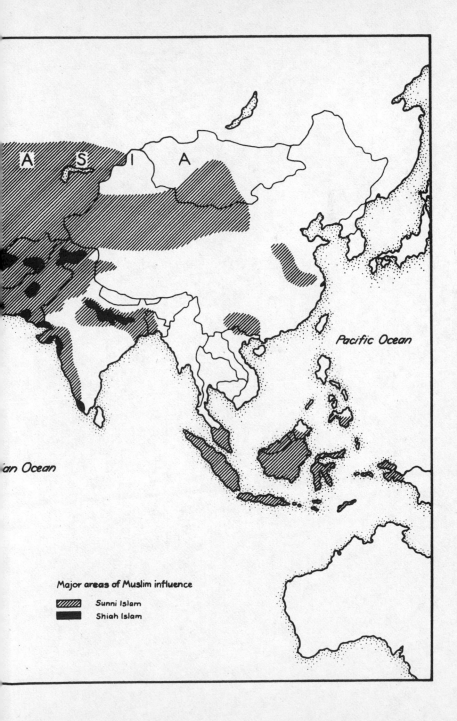

A S I A

Pacific Ocean

ian Ocean

Major areas of Muslim influence

Sunni Islam
Shiah Islam

# PART ONE

## Journey to a New Self

# In the Beginning

## There Was the Holy War. Why?

On November 25, 1095, at the Council of Clermont, Pope Urban II summoned the First Crusade. For Western Europe it was a crucial and formative event and it is having repercussions today in the Middle East. Addressing a vast crowd of priests, knights and poor people, Urban called for a holy war against Islam. The Seljuk Turks, he explained, a barbarian race from Central Asia who had recently become Muslims, had swept into Anatolia in Asia Minor (modern Turkey) and had seized these lands from the Christian empire of Byzantium. The Pope urged the knights of Europe to stop fighting each other and to make common cause against these enemies of God. The Turks, he cried, are "an accursed race, a race utterly alienated from God, a generation, forsooth, which has neither directed its heart nor entrusted its spirit to God."[1] Killing these godless monsters was a holy act: it was a Christian duty to "exterminate this vile race from our lands."[2] Once they had purged Asia Minor of this Muslim filth, the knights would engage in a still more holy task. They would march to the holy city of Jerusalem and liberate it from the infidel. It was shameful that the tomb of Christ should be in the hands of Islam.

There was an extraordinary response to Urban's appeal. Popular preachers like Peter the Hermit spread the news of the Crusade and in the spring of 1096 five armies of about 60,000 soldiers accompanied by a horde of noncombatant pilgrims with their wives and families set off to the East. They were followed in the autumn by five more armies of about 100,000 men and a crowd of priests and pilgrims. The numbers were astounding for this time.[3] As the first armies approached the Byzantine capital of Constantinople, it seemed to the appalled but fascinated Princess Anna Comnena as though "the whole West, and as much of the land as lies beyond the Adriatic Sea to the Pillars of Hercules [Gibraltar]—all this, changing its seat, was bursting

forth into Asia in a solid mass, with all its belongings."[4] To the sophisticated Byzantines it looked like a great barbarian invasion, similar
to those which had destroyed the Roman Empire in Europe. The
West was invading the East for the first time in the modern period,
filled with the aggressive righteousness of a holy war, a righteousness
that would characterize its future dealings with the Orient. This Crusade was the first cooperative act of the new Europe as she crawled
out of the Dark Ages. It appealed to all classes of society: to popes,
kings, aristocrats, priests, soldiers and peasants. People sold all they
had to equip themselves for this long and dangerous expedition, and
for the most part they were not inspired by lust for material gain.
They were gripped by a religious passion. They sewed crosses on their
clothes and marched to the land where Jesus had died to save the
world. It was a devotional pilgrimage at the same time as it was a war
of extermination.

Clearly crusading answered a deep need in the Christians of Europe.
Yet today most of us would unhesitantly condemn the Crusades as
wicked and unchristian. After all, Jesus had told his followers to love
their enemies, not to exterminate them. He was a pacifist and had
more in common with Gandhi, perhaps, than with Pope Urban. Yet
I would argue that the holy war is a deeply Christian act. Like Judaism
and Islam, Christianity had an inherent leaning toward violence, despite the pacifism of Jesus. All three religions are historically and
theologically related and all worship the same God. All three traditions
are dedicated in some way to love and benevolence and yet all three
have developed a pattern of holy war and violence that is remarkably
similar and which seems to surface from some deep compulsion that
is inherent in this tradition of monotheism, the worship of only one
God. The pattern is as regular as a Jungian archetype. For over a
thousand years European Christians tried to hold out against this
violent tendency and to keep Christianity a religion of love and peace,
yet when Pope Urban called the Crusade they responded with a sigh
of relief and reproduced the pattern of holy war with an uncanny
accuracy. It is as though they felt that at last they were doing what
came naturally. In order to understand the Crusades, therefore, as well
as the holy wars of today, we need to examine this pattern of violence
and try to discover why each of the three religions felt that they needed
a holy war.

In about 1850 B.C.E. a man called Abram left his home in Ur of
the Chaldees and journeyed to the land of Canaan, the modern Israel.
He had been summoned to emigrate by a Divine Being who revealed

that he had decided to be the special God of Abram and his offspring. Abram should change his name to Abraham as a sign of his new status, and should make a covenant agreement with God, who in return would bless him and his descendants. The children of Abraham would become a great people and God promised that he would give them the land of Canaan. This event, as it was told centuries later in the Bible,[5] changed the world. It is not only the Jews, Abraham's physical descendants, who see this as the beginning of their history—Christians and Muslims also regard themselves as children of Abraham, as we shall see later in this chapter. Christians and Muslims have persecuted or fought holy wars against Jews at different times in their history, but both claim the Jewish past as their own and see themselves as the recipients of the promises God made to the Jews. This revelation to Abraham was a revolution in the history of religion. Gradually the Jews came to realize that their God was not just one god among many. He was the *only* God and all other "gods" were just human inventions. This was an extraordinary idea in the pagan world, where people worshiped many gods and had developed some religions of great power and beauty. The Jews themselves were often unable to believe that there truly was only one God and often lapsed naturally and easily into paganism, but eventually monotheism, the worship of only one God, was firmly established in Judaism, and later in Christianity and Islam, the two religions that derived from Judaism. These three religions are all deeply related, yet at different times they have fought each other in savage holy wars. The seed of much future strife is found in the original revelation to Abraham. Almost the first words that God spoke when he revealed himself to Abram were: "To your descendants I will give this land" (Genesis 12:7). To make this promise good Abraham's descendants had to fight the first of many savage holy wars for this land, which many Jews today still see as essential to the integrity of Judaism. After all, God spent more time promising Abraham that he would give this land to his descendants than making any further theological revelations about himself. The Holy Land will be a key factor in our story.

Jews, Christians and Muslims all believe that God has revealed himself intervening directly in human affairs in events that become a history of salvation. One of the most crucial of these events was the Exodus, the mythical story of the Jews' liberation from slavery. The Israelites, Abraham's descendants, had emigrated to Egypt in about 1700 B.C.E. Their position there deteriorated so much that by 1250 they were mere slaves. Then God intervened. He told his prophet

Moses that he had to act and save his people; he must force Pharaoh to let the Israelites go free and then lead them home to the Promised Land of Canaan. Moses was very reluctant to do this, because it seemed a hopeless task, but God promised to help him. He terrorized the Egyptians by sending cruel plagues, and when Pharaoh remained obdurate in his refusal to free the Hebrew slaves, God sent the most terrible plague of all. The Angel of Death passed over the houses of the Jews and killed the firstborn son in every Egyptian family. Every year Jews celebrate this saving event in the feast of Passover, for it was a graphic demonstration of their status as the chosen people: God had drastically discriminated between themselves and the Egyptians. After this catastrophe, Pharaoh decided to let the Israelites go and Moses led his people out of Egypt. But before they had got very far Pharaoh changed his mind. He and his army pursued the Jews and caught up with them at the Reed Sea (usually misleadingly translated Red Sea).[6] It seemed that the Israelites would be herded back to slavery or even exterminated, but God intervened once more. He parted the waters of the sea so that his people could cross dry-shod, but drowned the whole Egyptian army when they tried to follow. This story of violent miracles was obviously a mythical version of the Hebrews' escape from Egypt, but the myth was crucial in forming the Jews' view of themselves. It shows what is involved in their view of salvation. God's people have to act to save themselves, even though their position seems hopeless or dangerous. God will always help them in miracles that suspend the normal course of nature, and the salvation of the chosen people means the annihilation of their enemies as two sides to a single coin. Salvation is the violent separation of the just and the unjust. The next stage in the story of the Exodus reveals the archetypal paradigm that has recurred in all three of the monotheistic religions, when a holy journey or a migration becomes a holy war.

The Israelites were now an independent people, but their salvation was not yet complete. They were still only a collection of tribes who had been unused to controlling their own destiny and they had to learn how they were to live as God's chosen people. They did not journey directly to the Promised Land, but for forty years they lived as nomads in the Sinai Peninsula. It was a holy journey during which, the Bible tells us, they were deeply dependent upon God, who fed them with manna and guided them step by step. Most importantly, on Mount Sinai God gave Moses the Ten Commandments, the basis of the Torah or the law.[7] This was God's greatest gift to his people, because it imposed the divine order on the world and was a revelation of God's will. By observing the 613 commandments of the Torah, which governed the smallest details of everyday life, the Jews naturally acquired a unique identity, which they believed to have been directly inspired and shaped by God. Throughout their history Jews have revered and studied the Torah, which they believe God gave to Moses during the forty years in the wilderness. That this formation of a new Jewish self should have begun during a journey was significant. Traveling and migration are evocative symbols of spiritual passage. The Israelites were traveling away from shame and oppression to dignity and freedom, from desolation to intimacy with God, from helplessness to self-determination. Journeys and migrations have also been crucial and formative events for Christians and Muslims.

One of the Ten Commandments given to Moses on Mount Sinai was "Thou shalt not kill." Indeed most of these commandments are concerned with an absolute respect for the inalienable rights of others, and this is one of the greatest legacies of Judaism to the rest of the world. But, as they prepared to enter the Promised Land, God told his people that they would have to engage in a ruthless war of extermination. By taking his people back to Canaan, Moses was taking them back to their roots because of God's original promise to their father Abraham. They believed that the land was theirs, but there were other people living there already who had made it their home for centuries, and naturally they were not going to hand over their country without a fight. These people were in the way of the divine plan; they were also essential enemies of the new Jewish self. Because they opposed values and plans that were "sacred" to the Jews and essential to God's plans for them, they had to be annihilated. The normal human rights that Jews were commanded to extend to other people did not apply to the Canaanites, who had become the enemies of God. This absolute hostility is a characteristic of the holy war. Because the Canaanites were obstacles to Jewish fulfillment they had to be exterminated and there was no possibility of peaceful coexistence. "I shall exterminate these," God told his people, "they must not live in your country" (Exodus 23:23, 33). It was not simply a territorial matter. The Canaanites had achieved a more advanced culture than the Israelites and their lifestyle would be very attractive to the weary nomads. They could destroy this newly emerging Jewish self and the new religion of monotheism, which was still so revolutionary that it was a fragile plant. The Israelites could very easily be seduced by the Canaanites' fertility cults and idolatrous faith. Therefore God gave Moses very clear instructions, frequently repeated in the Bible, about how these new enemies and their religions were to be treated:

When Yahweh your God has led you into the land you are entering to make your own, many nations will fall before you: Hittites, Girgashites, Amorites, Canaanites, Perizzites, Hivites and Jebusites, seven nations greater and stronger than yourselves. Yahweh your God will deliver them over to you and you will conquer them. You must lay them under a ban. You must make no covenant with them nor show them any pity. You must not marry with them: you must not give a daughter of yours to a son of theirs, nor take a daughter of theirs for a son of yours, for this would turn away your son from following me to serving other gods, and the anger of Yahweh would blaze out against you and soon destroy you. Instead, deal with them like this: tear down their altars, smash their standing stones, cut down their sacred poles and set fire to their idols. For you are a people consecrated to Yahweh your God. It is you that Yahweh your God has chosen to be his very own people out of all the peoples on the earth.                                   (Deuteronomy 7:1–6)

In a Jewish holy war, there was no question of peaceful coexistence, mutual respect or peace treaties. The little Jewish kingdom was an island of true religion in the ocean of Middle Eastern paganism. There was a religious siege and naturally a deep insecurity. Until the Israelites felt more confident, they could only fight their enemies to the death. When God had saved his people from the Egyptians the ordinary laws of nature had been suspended; so too when the Jews had to establish themselves in the Promised Land, ordinary morality ceased to apply. This is a crucial element in the holy wars of both Jews and, later, Christians.

Moses died before reaching the Promised Land. It was Joshua who in about 1200 B.C.E. led the Israelites into Canaan and established the twelve tribes of Israel in the Promised Land by means of a long and utterly ruthless military campaign. He fulfilled the commands of God perfectly. When a town was conquered, it was duly put "under a ban," which meant total destruction and extermination. Men, women, children and even the animals were massacred and the cities reduced to rubble:

When Israel finished killing all the inhabitants of Ai in the open ground and where they had followed them into the wilderness, and when all to a man had fallen by the edge of the sword, all Israel returned to Ai and slaughtered all its people. The number of those that fell that day, men and women together, was twelve thousand, all people of Ai. . . . Then Joshua burned Ai, making it a ruin for evermore, a desolate place even to this day. (Joshua 8:24, 25, 28)

Then Joshua came and wiped out the Anakim from the highlands, from Hebron, from Debir, from Anab, from all the highlands of Judah and all the inhabitants of Israel; he delivered them and their towns over to the ban. No more Anakim were left in Israelite territory except at Gaza, Gath and Ashdod.          (Ibid., 11:21, 22)

The holy war continued for another two hundred years, under the judges and heroes of Israel like Gideon, Deborah and Samson. As they exterminated their foes, the Israelites also tried to build up their own faith. As the pagan towns and shrines were destroyed, temples to Yahweh were built at Shiloh, Dan, Bethel, Bethlehem and Hebron.

A turning point in the holy campaign was King David's conquest of the Jebusite city of Jerusalem in about 1000 B.C.E. From this point Jerusalem, the "City of David," would be consecrated to the one God, and because of this originally Jewish occupation the city would later become holy to Christians and Muslims too. Jerusalem will be crucial in our story. But it is important to notice that it did not become "holy" to the Jews until quite late in its own history and in the history of the chosen people, even though the Jews would later see it as essential to the integrity of Judaism. It is also true that its sanctification had certain ironies. David departed from Joshuan practice when he conquered Jerusalem. He did not massacre the Jebusites, though he had shown no squeamishness about massacring *goyim* or the non-Jews in their hundreds elsewhere. It seems that he wanted to make the Jebusites his own personal followers, whose loyalty was assured because their survival depended totally upon him. Jews were beginning to feel more confident and able to exploit the people of Canaan instead of seeing them as absolute and therefore deeply disturbing enemies. David wanted to make Jerusalem the capital of his kingdom and the center of Judaism, so he had the Ark of the Covenant, a precious relic of the years in the wilderness, brought into the city in triumph. He then wondered whether he should build a temple for the Ark, which in some mysterious way localized the Presence of God (the *Shekinah*). But God forbade David to build a temple in Jerusalem and there are two versions of this story. In one version God said that he had always been a nomadic God who had never been associated with one particular shrine.[8] It may be that David, a passionately religious man, realized the danger of identifying the *Shekinah* with one temple, built by human hands. It could lead to an idolatry, which lifted an earthly place and a human building to the same level as God himself. In a later version, God forbade David to build the temple because he had shed too much blood, albeit at the divine command.[9] This shows the first sign of worry about the morality of the holy war. In this version, God tells David that the building of the temple has been assigned to his son Solomon, the man of peace. (The name Solomon comes from *shalom*, the Hebrew word for peace.)

Solomon did indeed build a temple. This man of peace was in a very different position from his predecessors. The kingdom of David had been torn apart internally and had modest borders, but Solomon established a strong state with significantly broader frontiers.[10] The new Temple was just one aspect of a building project that was actually part of his war effort. Besides the Temple, which was a magnificent building, Solomon rebuilt the ancient towns of Hazor, Megiddo and Gezer, as military bases for his new chariot army. Thousands of laborers were conscripted into the building force as a form of national service. Like all conscription, it was fiercely resented, particularly as it lacked the dignity of military service and seemed to reduce the conscripts to the level of slaves. Was their position very different from the position of their fathers in Egypt, who had been forced to build Pharaoh's pyramids? There was, therefore, a rather dubious element in the building of the Temple from the very beginning. When the Temple was completed there was a further irony. When they entered this wonderful new building to pray in the Presence of the one God, the Israelites would have been inescapably reminded of the Canaanite cults that they had been told to destroy. When they entered the sanctuary, they would have seen an enormous basin called the "molten sea" standing upon the figures of twelve brazen oxen. This was a giant bath for purification, but its imagery was identical with the Canaanite myth of Yam, the primeval waters. The tall free-standing pillars would have reminded them of the "standing stones," the fertility symbols of Canaanite cults that they had been commanded to tear down. The whole building was designed like a typical Canaanite temple and, instead of expressing the pure monotheism of Moses, the Temple had strongly pagan elements.[11] It seems to have been part of Solomon's policy of assimilation with the surrounding culture. He had established himself as an all-powerful despot, like other Middle Eastern kings, although hitherto God and the prophets had insisted that this was an un-Jewish institution, for only God could command his people. Solomon also married foreign wives, which was anathema to the spirit of Judaism and directly opposed to God's specific instructions to Moses.[12] Solomon was a confident monarch and his empire was powerful and secure. He did not feel threatened by the surrounding paganism and felt that a degree of assimilation was acceptable in

Yahwism. Violent and absolute rejection was unnecessary to a king who felt that the chosen people had reached a new era of security.

But such assimilation was dangerous. Solomon was a wise and religious man, but ultimately God condemned and punished him for this syncretism. How could the Jews retain their unique identity if they absorbed an alien culture? But later kings also flirted with paganism and assimilation, and the common people were fatally attracted to the pagan fertility cults of Canaan. When drought threatened their harvests, the Israelites found it natural to turn to the worship of Baal like their neighbors, who believed that they could manipulate their gods to force them to send rain. Prophets like Elias and Elijah demonstrated that this was a useless and unreligious attitude and waged a passionate war of words and violent deeds against this pervasive paganism.[13] The Temple of Solomon was not the only sanctuary in the Promised Land; the older temples continued to function and frequently the priests brought aspects of pagan worship into the rituals and liturgy of Yahwism. They were naturally influenced by the prevailing local religious climate and were not yet ready for the austere monotheism that the prophets and sages were developing. This religious strife in the Holy Land was paralleled by a political division. The northern tribes broke away from the southern kings in Jerusalem and formed their own kingdom which they called the Kingdom of Israel and which opposed the smaller Kingdom of Judah in the south. Never again would the Jews experience the unity and security they had known under Solomon. Further, their independence was constantly threatened by powerful neighbors who were building mighty empires in the Middle East. Finally in the year 722 there was a catastrophe. The Kingdom of Israel was conquered by King Tiglath-Pileser III of Assyria. The ten northern tribes of Israel were deported, forced to assimilate and were, in religious terms, annihilated. These ten lost tribes disappeared from history forever.

The Kingdom of Judah was naturally appalled by this tragedy and the kings of Jerusalem desperately sought to protect themselves from such a fate. Some of them, like Kings Ahaz and Manassah, thought that syncretism and assimilation were the answer, as many Jews have thought since. But in the year 622 King Josiah sought a religious answer to the problem of Jewish survival. While repair work was being done in the Temple, the high priest Hilkiah discovered an ancient manuscript. It may have been a manuscript of the whole of the Pentateuch or it may simply have been a manuscript of Deuteronomy that finished with the series of terrible curses that filled Josiah with horror, because they seemed already to have been partially fulfilled. The Lord had told Moses that occupation of the Holy Land depended upon a scrupulous observance of the Torah. If the Israelites disobeyed God they would lose their land:

> Just as Yahweh took delight in giving you prosperity and increase, so now he will take delight in bringing you to ruin and destruction. You will be torn from the land which you are entering to make your own. Yahweh will scatter you among all peoples, from one end of the earth to the other; there you will serve other gods of wood and stone that neither you nor your forefathers have known. Among these nations there will be no repose for you, no rest for the sole of your foot; Yahweh will give you a quaking heart, weary eyes, halting breath. Your life from the outset will be a burden to you; night and day you will go in fear, uncertain of your life. In the morning you will say, "How I wish it were evening!" and in the evening, "How I wish it were morning!" such terror will grip your heart, such sights your eye will see. (Deuteronomy 28:63–67)

Millions of Jews in our own time have experienced the terror of exile. Josiah had already seen the ten tribes disappear and after reading this manuscript he felt that the only way for the Kingdom of Judah to survive was by a return to religion and an absolute rejection of syncretism.[14] He made the Jerusalem Temple the center of this revival of the religion of Moses and Joshua, and for the first time Jerusalem and the Temple became essential to the Jewish religious experience. Worship in the Temple now became obligatory for every Jew in Judea. All the other shrines were destroyed and their priests were invited to serve in the Temple of Jerusalem, where they could be supervised to make sure that they were not bringing pagan practice into the pure religion of the Jews. On the great feast days all Jews were obliged to make a pilgrimage to Jerusalem and attend the sacrificial liturgy. Only in the Temple was it permissible henceforth to make a sacrifice to God. Pilgrimage, later to become an important practice in both Christianity and Islam, now became central to the Jewish faith, and from the start it was linked with a new offensive against paganism, which seemed more threatening to the Jewish people than ever.

Josiah's reform can be said to be fundamentalist, because it was a return to ancient ideology, at the same time as it was innovatory. It was inspired by a fear of losing the Holy Land and saw the religion of Judaism as essentially linked to the physical occupation of the land of Israel. This was a return to the religion of Abraham. But another view of Judaism was slowly emerging which was making the Jewish faith a religion of the heart. Prophets like Amos and Isaiah insisted that Temple sacrifice was not enough. A good Jew must take care of the poor and the needy; the Lord loved mercy and compassion more than sacrifice and pilgrimage to the Temple. In this view, external and liturgical conformity could not take the place of morality and justice.[15] The political outlook was bleak. The new Babylonian empire threatened to destroy the tiny Kingdom of Judah and the prophet Jeremiah foretold this ultimate disaster. Yet, despite his proverbial lamentations, Jeremiah also taught the Jews that the chosen people could still survive even in exile. Provided they remained faithful to the Torah and observed the covenant with Yahweh, God would still be their God as he had pledged to Abraham.[16] In this prophetic view, Judaism did not depend upon the physical possession of the Holy Land.

The disaster struck in 589 B.C.E. Babylon destroyed Jerusalem, and most of the inhabitants of Judea were deported to Babylonia, leaving behind only a few peasants and poor people. The trauma of exile had entered the Jewish experience for the first time. During the exile in Babylon, exile came to have rather the same connotations as the concept of Original Sin in Christianity.[17] Exile became a metaphor for sin, as well as a punishment. It meant a state of shameful weakness, of vulnerability unto death, apparent desertion by God and banishment from one's best self. In exile a Jew could not be what God had intended him to be: a member of a fiercely independent and autonomous people, "set apart"[18] from all other nations in the Promised Land. Undoubtedly the exile to Babylon was traumatic, but very often trauma can lead to a new religious insight. These Jewish deportees did not disappear like the ten northern tribes. They were not forced to assimilate with the pagan population but were permitted to live in separate Jewish communities, the first ghettos. Here they could still be "set apart" and observe the commandments of the Torah. Some of the exiles lived in Babylon itself and others lived in a settlement on the banks of the Cheder in an area which they called Tel Aviv. In these communities Judaism came of age. When the people had lived independently in their own land, they had constantly been seduced by paganism. In exile, paganism lost its attraction forever and the Jews learned a deeper level of religious commitment. A new individual element entered Jewish practice. Instead of renewing the covenant collectively and being herded along to the Temple for compulsory worship, the Jews of Babylon became personally responsible for their own religious life. Each Jew renewed his own covenant to Yahweh. He had to learn the Torah himself and absorb it into his heart and mind so that it became his own. Without the Temple, the Book became more important and study of the Torah and the Prophets led many of the exiles to a deeper understanding of monotheism and Judaism. Personal accountability has become a hallmark of Judaism and in exile the importance of the individual was emphasized in quite a new way.

But a minority group were unable to adapt fully to life in Babylon. All Jews certainly mourned the loss of Jerusalem, but to some Jerusalem had become more precious because of its loss. They felt quite a new hatred of the *goyim* who had made it impossible for them to live a full Jewish life:

> Beside the streams of Babylon
> we sat and wept
> at the memory of Zion,
> leaving our harps
> hanging on the poplars there.
>
> For we had been asked
> to sing to our captors,
> to entertain those who had carried us off:
> "Sing," they said,
> "some hymns of Zion."
>
> How could we sing
> one of Yahweh's hymns
> in a pagan country?
> Jerusalem, if I forget you,
> may my right hand wither!
>
> May I never speak again,
> if I forget you!
> If I do not count Jerusalem
> the greatest of my joys!
>
> Yahweh, remember
> what the sons of Edom did
> on the day of Jerusalem,
> how they said, "Down with her!
> Raze her to the ground!"
>
> Destructive daughter of Babel,
> A blessing on the man who treats you
> as you have treated us,
> a blessing on him who takes and dashes
> your babies against the rock!
>
> (Psalm 137)

This psalmist felt that the physical land of Israel was essential to his Jewish identity, and because the Babylonians had destroyed Jerusalem it was as if they were destroying his Jewish self. The amoral vengeance he plans springs from a desperate insecurity.

Yet the new inner confidence felt by the majority led some Jews to wait hopefully for a return to Zion. In Babylon, the prophet Ezekiel and the anonymous prophet who is usually called the Second Isaiah promised the Jews that God would restore them to the Promised Land. They would return to Jerusalem, rebuild the Temple and build Tel Aviv again in the land of their fathers.[19] God had only wanted to punish the people for their sins, but he would reward their fidelity by a glorious return. The pre-exilic prophets had already begun to look forward to a day when the chosen people would rule the whole world in a new era of cosmic peace, when the wolf and the lamb could lie down together.[20] World dominion was a natural development of the Jews' belief in the one God and the idea has also been important in Christianity and Islam. If there is only one God, there can be only one solution for the world and this must lead to the triumph of the one true faith. The prophets in exile linked this final cosmic triumph with the return of the Jews to Jerusalem, which they often called Zion.[21] Not only would the Israelites rebuild Jerusalem, but they would also inaugurate a new era of peace and justice. All their former enemies would be forced to come to Jerusalem in a penitential pilgrimage to acknowledge Jewish sovereignty. The Second Isaiah called to Jerusalem:

> Arise, shine out, for your light has come,
> the glory of Yahweh is rising on you,
> though night still covers the earth
> and darkness the peoples.

> Above you Yahweh now rises
> and above you his glory appears.
> The nations come to your light
> and kings to your dawning brightness.

> Lift up your eyes and look around:
> all are assembling and coming towards you,
> your sons from far away
> and your daughters being tenderly carried.
> And your gates will lie open continually,
> shut neither by day nor by night,
> for men to bring you the wealth of the nations
> with their kings leading them;
> for the nations and kingdom that refuses to serve you shall
>     perish,

such nations shall be utterly ruined.
The glory of the Lebanon will come to you,
with cypress and plane and box,
to adorn the site of my sanctuary,
to glorify the resting place of my feet.

The sons of your oppressors will come to you bowing,
at your feet shall fall all who despised you.
They will call you "City of Yahweh,"
"Zion of the Holy One of Israel."

(Isaiah 60:1–4, 11–14)

This return to Zion would result in the salvation of the whole world, because the *goyim* would be forced to worship the one God. From the very beginning there had been a universal message in Judaism. God had promised Abraham that "all the tribes of the earth shall bless themselves in you" (Genesis 12:3). Fantasies of this final redemption have inspired Jews through the centuries and they are still inextricably linked to a return to the land of Israel.

The confidence of the exilic prophets was shown to be justified just sixty years after the deportation to Babylon. The Medes and the Persians had conquered the Babylonians and in the year 538 B.C.E. Cyrus, the King of Persia, gave the Jews permission to return to their homeland and rebuild the Temple. The Jews naturally hailed Cyrus as the anointed one of God, but Cyrus was not motivated solely by compassion for the Jews. He believed that, by allowing the subject peoples of his empire religious autonomy, he would ease the burden of rule and administration. Throughout his empire he encouraged the reconstruction of ancient shrines, hoping that their gods might bless him and further his reign.[22] This suggests an essential difference between monotheism and polytheism. In general, pagan rulers did not initiate religious persecution. A pagan like Cyrus believed in many gods and therefore could envisage many solutions and possibilities and this led to tolerance and to religious coexistence. The Jewish monotheists, however, had hitherto been unable to accept the presence of neighboring shrines to gods other than their own. When Cyrus issued the edict of return, they naturally saw him as inspired by their God for their greater glory. Some 42,360 Jews left Babylon and Tel Aviv and began the long journey home.

Yet—and this is an important point—most of the Jews remained behind in exile. They no longer saw physical possession of the Holy Land as essential to the Jewish identity. Furthermore they saw certain religious problems in the return: was it likely that their brothers would create the New Jerusalem of peace and justice foretold by the Second

Isaiah? In this view, a physical return to Zion actually endangered the shining religious ideal. It was surely more religious to look forward to a divine intervention in history that would establish the full redemption than to create an imperfect Jewish state. Keeping the return and the redemption in the future tense would ensure that a yearning for salvation did not become muddied by the squalor of politics. The year 538, therefore, marked an important parting of the ways in Judaism that still persists. There are Jews who see the land of Israel as essential to Judaism and consider that living in the physical land is obligatory for all Jews. There are other Jews who think that secular and political hegemony in Israel is dangerous and unreligious, and most Jews have remained in the diaspora. After 538 Babylon remained an important center of Judaism for centuries. There the Jews prayed facing Jerusalem, but kept it as a distant ideal. They were confident enough to develop a very different attitude toward the Gentiles. The Scriptures composed in the diaspora sometimes show the influence of Gentile culture. The Book of Ecclesiastes, for example, has been fruitfully inspired by Hellenic Stoicism. The diaspora Book of Jonah shows real compassion to non-Jews. When Jonah warns the pagan people of Nineveh that unless they repent God will destroy their city, they do repent and the city is spared. Jonah is furious about this and goes off to sulk, but God gently teases him out of this absurdity. The Jewish prophet is to save the Gentiles as well as the chosen people: "Am I not to feel sorry for Nineveh," God asks, "the great city, in which there are more than a hundred and twenty thousand people who cannot tell their right hand from their left, to say nothing of all the animals?" (4:11). The lessons of the Book of Jonah have been important to Christians and Muslims as well as Jews; the *goyim* have learned far more from this compassionate Judaism than from the Scriptures written in the land of Israel after 538, like the Books of Maccabees, which speak mainly about new and violent holy wars there. In the diaspora a humanism developed in Judaism that would ultimately enter Christianity through the Jewish Jesus and St. Paul and help to shape the tradition of Western humanism.

The Jews who returned to Jerusalem in 538 had originally no intention of fighting a holy war. They had peaceful ideals, and the return of 538 could be seen as a nonviolent version of the Exodus. God had destroyed Pharaoh, but the Persian King Cyrus had cooperated with him. The journey home was intended to lead to a constructive rebuilding of the land, instead of a holy war. But sadly the return led to new Jewish intolerance. When the exiles reached the Promised Land they discovered other people living there, as Joshua had done before them. In the north were pagans who had settled there when the ten tribes had been deported in 722. In Judea and Samaria dwelt the descendants of the Jews who had not been deported to Babylon; they seemed very strange to the returning exiles, who rejected both sets of people, calling them the *am ha'aretz*, the people of the land. They insisted that only those who had experienced the exile were true Jews.[23] They thus began the bitter debate about who really was a Jew, which still continues today. Naturally the People of the Land were angry. When the native Jews offered to help to rebuild Jerusalem, they were told that they had no place in the new Jewish kingdom. This led to hostility and warfare, and the building work was constantly threatened by the military attacks of the People of the Land. As Nehemiah, who led this rebuilding, explained, each builder "did his work with one hand while gripping his weapon with the other. And as each builder worked, he wore his sword at his side" (Nehemiah 4:18). In our own time the rebuilding of Jewish Israel has led to a similar hostility from the current People of the Land.

In the first century of the Christian Era, the Jewish people were once again divided in their approach to the Gentile world. Many Jews in both the diaspora and in the Holy Land were strongly attracted to the Hellenic culture of the Roman Empire. They did not feel they had a duty to oppose Roman rule and they had an open, accepting attitude toward the *goyim*. Philo, the great Jewish philosopher of Alexandria who died in about 40 C.E., actually wrote about God in terms of Greek philosophy and interpreted the Scriptures allegorically in a way that pagan philosophers could understand and appreciate. Indeed, many pagans were attracted to Judaism, which was at that time a deeply respected religion in the Roman Empire. Some became converts but most were content to be "godfearers," worshiping in the synagogue but not observing the whole of the Torah. Ethical monotheism was seen as the great idea of the age and the Romans' respect for antiquity drew many pagans to the ancient religion of the Jews. Indeed it has even been suggested that one of the Flavian emperors might well have converted to Judaism as Constantine later converted to Christianity.[24] It is fascinating to reflect how very different history might have been had this happened.

Other Jews deeply distrusted this positive approach to the world of Rome. Many were attracted to the Jewish apocalyptic writings that had started to appear at the end of the second century B.C.E. Because there no longer seemed any hope of the Jews having an independent kingdom of their own, some began to look forward to a cosmic triumph at the end of time. Scriptures like the Book of Daniel or apocryphal works like the Book of Jubilees foretold great battles in which the armies of God would defeat his enemies. All the nations of the world would gather at the Mount of Olives opposite Jerusalem and there would be a battle in which God himself would lead the Jews into the fray and cruelly exterminate their enemies. Then the Kingdom of God would be established, the Jews would rule the world and the redemption would have been accomplished. Jews of this persuasion began to look forward to a Messiah, the anointed one of God, who would prepare them for this final cosmic triumph.[25] They believed that he would be a Jew of the house of David. In the Holy Land, which was now occupied by the Romans, several people came forward claiming to be this Messiah: they undertook to wage a holy war against the Romans in order to eject them from the land as a first step to the final redemption.[26] These apocalyptic ideas flourish in Israel today, where many radical Jews expect the imminent coming of the Messiah.

Various sects in Palestine were dedicated to these apocalyptic ideals and denounced those Jews who seemed ready to assimilate with the *goyim*. Thus in the first century C.E. the Essenes continued a well-established Jewish practice, pioneered by sects like the Rechabites and the Nazirites, of making an exodus into the wilderness in order to build communities of true Jews. The Essenes believed that the Jerusalem Temple was contaminated by the priestly party, the Sadducees, who cooperated with the Roman authorities. The famous scrolls discovered at Qumran by the Dead Sea contain some ideas of the Essenes. They speak of two Messiahs, one a king and the other a priest who would rebuild the Temple. They also speak of a coming holy war against the Romans, the *kittim*, which would ushen in the Last Days. The Essenes were deeply respected and are mentioned with reverence by Philo and by the contemporary Jewish historian Josephus. They believed that they had a mission to convert their fellow Jews: some were ready to fight them, others to engage in a polemical war. John the Baptist, whose blistering sermons are preserved in the New Testament, may well have been an Essene.[27]

The Essenes left their secluded communities to fight alongside the other Jewish zealots who rose up against the Romans in the Great Jewish Revolt, which broke out in 66 C.E. Incredibly, the Jews were able to keep the Roman army at bay and to hold their own until the catastrophe of 70 C.E. when the Romans finally conquered Jerusalem and burned down the Temple. The chosen people had lost their land for the second time and began a new exile which would last for nearly two thousand years. The Romans made Jerusalem into a pagan city which they called Aelia. Jews like the Pharisees did not see the destruction of the Temple, horrific as it was, as fatal to Judaism. Rabbis known as the *tannaim* began work on what would ultimately become the Talmud to ensure the survival of their religion. They accepted the Roman occupation of Palestine, cooperated with the Roman authorities and condemned any further conflict with Rome. Other Jews remained true to the apocalyptic ideals and could not accept this attitude. They continued the struggle against Rome to the death, feeling that the Roman contamination of the Holy Land threatened the integrity of Judaism. In 73 C.E. the last remaining Jewish rebels gathered in the mighty fortress of Masada by the Dead Sea and were finally forced to surrender. In a passionate speech their leader, Eleazar ben Yair, urged the 960 men, women and children to commit suicide rather than submit to Rome. When the Romans finally entered the citadel they found only a "dreadful solitude" and heard the awe-inspiring story from some women who had hidden while their fellows had done themselves to death. The Romans at first were skeptical but

> when they came upon the rows of dead bodies, they did not exult over them as enemies but admired the nobility of their resolve and the way in which so many had shown in carrying it out without a tremor an utter contempt of death.[28]

In their new exile, the Jews gradually came to terms with the loss of Jerusalem. But they still awaited a Messiah who would one day lead them back to their land. They felt that the loss of their homeland was a rent in the nature of things. Some developed a tradition that the *Shekinah*, the Presence of God, had gone into exile with the Jews, and this implied a metaphysical displacement in the very ground of reality. The loss of Jerusalem naturally meant the end of any Jewish rapprochement with the pagan world of Rome. Jews preferred the study of Torah to the study of the pagan philosophers: after 70 C.E. there could be no new Philo. Gradually, too, the pagans stopped flocking to the synagogues. Instead they were attracted by a new sect, which claimed to be a universal form of Judaism.

Years before the fall of Jerusalem, in about 27 C.E., Jesus had presented himself to the Jews of Palestine as the Messiah. He began his preaching with the announcement "The Kingdom of God is at hand!" and he urged the Jews to prepare for this great event.[29] He began his mission in his native Galilee in the north of Israel and quickly attracted a large following. He seems to have devoted himself particularly to converting the poor and the "sinners" of Israel, who either collaborated with the Romans or who did not observe the Torah.[30] These sinners were aggressively spurned by the establishment, but Jesus insisted that they had to be brought back into the fold and healed before the redemption. Eventually he went to Jerusalem as the Messiah. He started his triumphal procession into the city on the Mount of Olives, where the Messiah was expected to appear; he rode on an ass, as the apocalyptic prophet Zechariah had foretold, and the crowds hailed him as the Son of David, crying, "Blessings on the coming Kingdom of our father David!"[31] Then he seems to have occupied the Temple and preached of the coming Kingdom for a week.[32] It is not clear what Jesus intended to do about the Romans, but eventually he was arrested by the authorities and the governor Pontius Pilate sentenced him to die by the Roman punishment of crucifixion, which might indicate that he was worried about Jesus' political activities. Yet it seems clear that Jesus was a strict pacifist. He told his followers to turn the other cheek when attacked and when he was arrested he refused even to defend himself verbally.[33] It has been suggested that he was expecting the Kingdom of God to arrive in a great cosmic miracle, without his having to fight the Roman occupation.[34] When this miracle failed to happen, Jesus' despair and bewilderment echo in his cry from the cross: "My God! my God! why have you deserted me?" (Mark 15:34).

Yet even after his death his disciples refused to despair. They had visions of him and believed that he had risen to a new kind of life. Very shortly, in their own lifetimes, he would return and establish the Kingdom of God, so they devoted themselves to preparing for the redemption. Like Jesus, they had no desire to found a new religion. They saw themselves and were seen by their fellow Jews as a perfectly legitimate Jewish sect. The only thing that distinguished them was their belief in Jesus as the Messiah and their expectation of his Second Coming. Otherwise they were fully observant Jews, worshiping daily in the Temple and living according to the Torah.[35] Certainly they had no desire to preach to the *goyim*, and when one of their number started to bring Gentiles into the Jewish sect, telling them that they had no need of the Torah, they disowned him and his converts after a very bitter dispute in about 50 C.E.[36]

It was the Jewish Paul who took Christianity to the Gentile world of the Roman Empire and who made it a Gentile faith. He believed that Jesus had saved the whole world, not just the Jews, and that when he returned in glory to establish the Kingdom this would not just be a Jewish triumph. His death and resurrection had ended the days of the Jews' special mission, and Christianity was a universal religion. In Pauline Christianity there was no longer any possibility of a holy war, because Christians must show charity even to enemies, as Jesus had enjoined. Christianity was a spiritual religion: salvation now meant a liberation from sin and death, not an extermination of the enemies of God. Because the normal world was passing away and the Second Coming was imminent, fighting for a stake in this world was meaningless. A Christian's only duty was to prepare for the redemption.[37] Yet, though Paul rejected essential Jewish teaching, he remained deeply Jewish in spirit and stamped Christianity with the imagery and mythology of Judaism. He taught Christians that they were the fulfillment of Jewish history and that they were the New Israel. God had been preparing the world for Christ ever since he had first revealed himself to Abraham, who was therefore the father of all those who believe in Jesus, not just the father of the Jews. He taught Christians that Jesus was their "Passover," leading them from death to a new spiritual life. They were now in "exile," not from the Holy Land but from Christ and the imminent Kingdom of God. They already belonged to the next world. The holy men of the Jews like Abraham, David and Moses were models for the Christians too because they had been waiting for Christ without realizing it.[38] Paul formed an important Christian attitude toward the Jews, which has had political consequences in the present conflict, as we shall see in Chapter 11. Christians were taught to appropriate Judaism for their own purposes and would ultimately find it difficult to read the Jewish Scriptures except in a Pauline, and therefore distorted, way; they would find it difficult to recognize that important elements in their faith were really Jewish and would ultimately view the Jews as renegades, who had stupidly failed to recognize Jesus and had therefore lost their special vocation.

By the end of the first century the apocalyptic Judaism that had always been important to Jesus and his first followers brought a new violence into the peaceful religion of Jesus and Paul. This is particularly clear in two of the later books of the New Testament, which were both written at least fifty years after St. Paul's death. The author of Revelation was probably a Jewish convert to Christianity, and when he looked forward to the Second Coming of Christ he naturally saw it in terms of the Jewish apocalyptic tradition. In his book the cosmic battles foretold by the Jewish prophets herald the final triumph of Christianity, when God would send down from heaven the New Jerusalem and a new and perfect world. The Crusaders would be deeply affected by this vision. He also spoke of God's enemies as frightening monsters. In particular he wrote of a great Beast who would crawl out of the abyss and take up residence in the Temple. This would be one of the signs of the approaching end.[39] This probably had a contemporary reference that is now completely lost to us, but later generations of Christians found their imaginations haunted by this Beast, and naturally they made their own interpretations of the strange image. The Beast was conflated with another enemy of God, whose arrival, it had been said, would herald the Last Days. The author of the Second Epistle to the Thessalonians was not St. Paul but was writing years after his death and using Paul's name as a sign of discipleship. He was struggling with a very great problem. In the First Epistle to the Thessalonians, written in about 52 C.E., Paul had promised that Jesus would arrive very soon, certainly within Paul's own lifetime. Why had he not appeared? The author of Second Thessalonians explained some fifty years later that Jesus could not return until the "Great Revolt" or the "Great Apostasy" had taken place.[40] A Rebel would appear just before the Second Coming, who would set himself up as the enemy of God and would even claim to be God himself. He would establish himself in the Temple in Jerusalem and deceive many Christians and lead many people astray. The author of Second Thessalonians implies that this was a widely held Christian belief, and again it probably had a meaning that is now lost to us. Later generations of Christians naturally identified this Rebel with the Beast who would occupy the Temple before the Last Days. As a new Christian apocalyptic tradition grew, which had to cope with the uncomfortable fact that Jesus had not returned as quickly as had been promised, Christians developed a belief in a figure whom they called Antichrist. By the time of the Crusades, European Christians firmly believed that before the final apocalypse Antichrist would appear in Jerusalem, would set himself up in the Temple and fight the Christians there in the great battles foretold by Revelation. These terrible wars would herald the Last Days and the Second Coming of Christ. Some people saw Antichrist as a diabolic monster, like the Beast in Revelation; others saw him as an ordinary but absolutely evil human being like the Rebel in Second Thessalonians. Political and heretical leaders were often identified with Antichrist, and what we might call "Antichrist-spotting" became a habit in Western Europe. Belief in Antichrist was very important in the ideology of crusading.

By the end of the first century, therefore, the peaceful religion of Jesus and Paul was being invaded by more violent and martial ideas. Alongside the pacifism of Jesus, there grew a religion of battles and horrors. Jesus had preached a Jewish humanitarian religion, which has been very formative of many Western ideals, but the more violent, apocalyptic strain of Christianity would be equally influential. The aggression of Christianity surfaced quite early in the history of the Church in the two movements of martyrdom and monasticism, which would later be very important in the ideology of the Christian holy war.

The Roman Empire had destroyed the Jewish homeland and during the second and third centuries it sometimes seemed as though it would also destroy Christianity. From time to time the Roman authorities persecuted Christians who refused to sacrifice to Caesar and seemed a potential political threat. Thousands of Christians were put to death in the Roman stadiums and this trauma stamped itself on the Christian consciousness. It gave to Christians a strong sense that "the world" was against them and would overwhelm the true religion.[41] This deep insecurity led to an aggressive cult of voluntary martyrdom that was not very dissimilar to the spirit of the Jewish martyrs at Masada. The martyr was seen as a perfect Christian, because Christ had said that giving one's life for the beloved was the greatest act of love. The martyr was imitating Jesus perfectly in his death. But this love acquired an aggressive dimension. Christians started to denounce themselves to the authorities, in order to force the Romans to put them to death. This was not because they had a masochistic yearning for pain and for death, nor was it because they wanted to prove their love for Christ. These voluntary martyrs believed that they were taking part in a continuing cosmic battle with evil. The death of every martyr brought the final victory and the Second Coming of Christ nearer and was part of the Last Battle foretold by the prophets. The martyr seemed to be passive in that he allowed violence to be inflicted upon him, but he believed that he was a "soldier of Christ" and that his death was a "victory."[42] The Church tried to stop this passion for voluntary martyrdom, but it never completely died out; it surfaced later in Europe, when Christians felt their identity threatened by the enemies of God, and the martyr impulse would be important during the Crusades.

When the persecutions stopped and Christianity became the official religion of the Roman Empire, there was a gap in the Christian life. How were you to be a perfect Christian when there was no longer any possibility of martyrdom, voluntary or otherwise? The answer that some fervent Christians found was very similar to the solution of the Jewish Nazirites or Essenes. Radical Christians fled "the world," which they felt was destructive of the Christian life, and took refuge in the wilderness. They were inspired to make this exodus in order to witness to true Christian values, and just as the Jewish sectarians saw themselves as the only true Jews, so too these monks, who had escaped from the contaminating world, persuaded other Christians to think that they were the only perfect Christians. Jesus and Paul had never envisaged this kind of asceticism but had seen Christians as living in the world and waiting for the Second Coming, but many of their sayings were reinterpreted and applied to the monastic life. Jesus had said that a disciple had to be prepared to leave his home and family, and follow him even unto death,[43] and the monks believed that they were the only Christians who did this as they struggled to "die to themselves" in the desert. St. Paul and St. John had spoken disparagingly of "the world" and now monks and their fellow Christians believed that it was impossible to preserve a truly Christian identity in the world. Monasticism began in the Middle East and did not reach Europe until the late fifth century, but once it had arrived Western Christians soon saw the monasteries as fortresses of Christianity in a Godless world. Benedict of Nursia introduced a less masochistic and more temperate version of monasticism into Europe than that which had been practiced by the original Eastern Fathers of the Desert, but there was still an aggression in Western spirituality. The monks were regarded as taking part in a holy war. In the frightening world of the early Middle Ages, Europe was a very dangerous place. Christianity was threatened first by the barbarian invasions that destroyed the Roman Empire in Europe and then by invasions of Norsemen, Muslims and Magyars in the ninth and tenth centuries which constantly threatened the precarious establishment. Just as the knights fought these earthly enemies of God and of Christians, the monks fought their spiritual enemies. This was written into the charters and deeds of gift to monasteries:

> The abbot is armed with spiritual weapons and supported by a troop of monks anointed with the dew of heavenly graces. They fight together in the strength of Christ with the sword of the spirit against the aery wiles of the devils. They defend the king and clergy of the realm from the onslaughts of their invisible enemies.[44]

At an early date the insecurity of Western Christians brought an aggressive element into the peaceful religion of Christianity.

Yet still Christians tried to keep this violence in check and remain pacifist. In the Greek Orthodox Church of the Byzantine Empire war was always regarded as unchristian and during a campaign a soldier was denied the sacraments.[45] The Byzantines preferred to use mercenaries in their wars rather than allow Greek Christians themselves to fight. But Byzantium was less vulnerable than the Church of Western Europe, which was exposed to one invasion after another. In the West, Latin theologians developed the concept of a just war, which would enable Christians to fight and defend themselves without guilt. In the early fifth century the great St. Augustine of Hippo in North

Africa watched the destruction of the Western Roman Empire with horror. He decided that, while wars against other Christians were always sinful and unjustified, God could sometimes inspire a Christian leader to wage war against pagans as he had inspired Joshua and David to massacre their enemies in the Old Testament. What must distinguish Christian from pagan violence was that it had to be inspired by love. When he used violence, a Christian must be full of love for the enemy he was fighting, and see his violence as medicinal, used in rather the same way as a parent who chastises a child for its own good. Jesus had used this kind of violence when he drove the moneylenders out of the Temple and blinded St. Paul on the road to Damascus. Sadly this medicinal Christian violence would sometimes result in the death of the enemy. Although Christians needed to defend themselves, Augustine insisted that self-defense alone could not justify violence, because self-defense could be inspired by hatred.[46] Augustine's arguments were tortuous and paradoxical and show how difficult he found it to justify a war of Christians, but, without fighting, Christianity could not survive. When the barbarian tribes sacked the great city of Rome in 410, Augustine saw this as the triumph of evil over good. Civilization and culture had been overthrown and the existence of Christianity itself seemed in danger. Yet Augustine's church in North Africa, where there were many thriving Christian communities, was destroyed not in the sixth century by the barbarian tribes that overturned the Roman Empire but by a new religious menace that appeared in the deserts of the Hejaz in the Arabian Peninsula during the seventh century. The third religion of the monotheistic tradition had been born, and from the start Islam threatened the vulnerable Christians of the West.

If most Western people were asked today which of the three monotheistic religions was the most violent, they would probably unhesitatingly reply: "Islam." For hundreds of years, Western Christians have described Islam as "the religion of the sword" but this is inaccurate, one of the prejudices we have inherited from the period of the Crusades. It is just one example of the distorted picture that many people in the West have of Islam, about which we are generally rather ignorant. It will therefore be important to give some account of the rise of Islam to show how Muslims see themselves as part of the divine plan for the world. It is certainly true that the holy war played its part in the establishment and spread of Islam, but it is not correct to see Islam as a bloodthirsty and essentially aggressive religion. When the first Muslims converted to Islam, the idea of the holy war was far from their minds. Like the ancient Israelites, who had responded to the trauma of slavery in Egypt by building a new identity, Islam arose from the urgent need of the Arabs of the peninsula to solve the very grave problems of the Hejaz in the early seventh century and to build a new and proud Arab self. At this time Arabia was in crisis. Trade had brought a new prosperity to the Hejaz, especially to the city of Mecca, but this meant that the old tribal values were breaking down, and people felt confused and lost. In the harsh life of the desert, where there were not enough of the necessities of life, a sharing of resources had been essential to the survival of the clan. People who were rich were expected to be generous to those who were not, and a tribal leader won power by his largesse. Such generosity was prudent: a famine or a drought could easily reduce a rich man to poverty over-night and who would be generous to him if he had denied others? But in the new wealthy cities Arabs were losing this sense of respon-sibility and adopting alien, elitist lifestyles. It seemed as though the old Arab way of life was being destroyed and that the rich were separating themselves from the poor. At the same time as the social order was torn apart, the Hejaz was rent by a seemingly incurable tribal warfare, where Arab fought Arab. This meant that they could not unite against their powerful neighbors, the Persians and the Byz-antines, and the Arabs were frequently exploited by these great powers. If they were to make use of their new wealth and not fall into an ignoble and servile dependence on others, they had to find a way of taking their destiny into their own hands, revive the true values of Arabian society and enter history in their own right. That they were able to do this was due to Mohammad, the founder of Islam, who did for the Arabs what Moses had done for the Israelites.

As well as a social and political crisis, there was a crisis of faith, and by the seventh century the Arabs felt a strong sense of religious in-feriority. There were some Jews and Christians living in the peninsula and they looked down on the Arabs as barbarians, who had received no revelation of their own and who practiced a primitive pagan idol-atry. In the old tribal days, life was such a struggle that there had not been much time for religion, but there had been a pantheon of Arab gods. One of these was Hubal, whose curious boxlike shrine at Mecca, called the Ka'aba, was an important place of pilgrimage. From all over Arabia people gathered in Mecca. In obscure ancient ritual, they pro-cessed round and round the Ka'aba, and also venerated the Black Stone, a meteorite set in the wall of the shrine. There were also other rites to other gods which the pilgrims performed in the desert outside Mecca, and these ceremonies were collectively known as the *Hajj*. But by the seventh century this paganism no longer satisfied all the Arabs.

People were beginning to think that monotheism was a more developed faith, but most did not want to convert to Judaism or Christianity because this meant adopting yet another alien ideology. One group of Arabs, whom the pagan establishment called *hanifs* or infidels, sought an essentially Arab solution.[47]

In the old pagan pantheon, the chief God was Allah, whose name meant *the* God. Allah had not been able to exert much control over his fellow gods in the old myths, but now the *hanifs* decided to worship Allah alone and they claimed that he was the God of the Jewish-Christian tradition. They developed a belief which inserted the Arabs into God's plan from the very first days of his revelation to the world. The Jewish Scriptures tell us that Abraham's wife Sarah had seemed barren, so to ensure that Abraham had descendants she encouraged him to take her Egyptian slave girl Hagar as his concubine, a common practice at that time. Hagar bore Abraham a son called Ishmael and had a very uneasy life with Sarah, who was very jealous, despite her earlier acquiescence. But God promised Hagar that he would protect her child, whose name meant "God has heard." Finally, when Sarah had her own son Isaac, she made Abraham send Hagar and Ishmael away, which grieved Abraham very much, but God consoled him, saying:

> Do not distress yourself on account of the boy and your slave girl.
> Grant Sarah all that she asks of you, for it is through Isaac that your
> name will be carried on. But the slave girl's son I will also make
> into a nation, for he is your child too.          (Genesis 21:12)

The Bible says that God watched over Hagar and Ishmael in the desert, preserved their lives and repeated his promise that Ishmael would be the father of a mighty nation.[48] The Arab *hanifs* maintained that Ishmael had lived in the deserts of Mecca and that the Arabs were his descendants. There was a story that when Ishmael had grown up Abraham visited him in the desert and that together they had built the Ka'aba, which had been the first shrine to Allah in Arabia. Later the pagans had desecrated the shrine and given it over to idolatry.[49]

In 610 one of these *hanifs* began to have revelations which he believed came from Allah and which developed this early Arab monotheism. It also fulfilled the ancient biblical prophecy, for because of this revelation Ishmael's "descendants" did indeed become a mighty nation. Mohammad ibn Abdullah had been born in Mecca in about 570. He was a member of the Qureish clan, which ruled the city, but was orphaned early in life and was brought up outside Mecca. Even though he was a young man of great promise, he was only a minor member of the clan and could exercise very little influence in the affairs of the city. This early impotence made him acutely aware of the new social inequality in the Hejaz, which he felt to be immoral and against the Arab spirit. He was deeply disturbed by the plight of the poor and became known for his generosity and kindness in relieving their sufferings in very practical ways. This would become an important feature of the religion he founded. Mohammad was rescued from his early poverty by marriage to a wealthy woman considerably older than himself. Khadija was probably the first person to recognize the genius of her young husband and she would become his first convert when the revelations began. It was a fortunate marriage for Mohammad but it would be a mistake to see it as wholly mercenary. He loved Khadija all his life. During her own lifetime he remained faithful to her and took no other wives; after her death he used to infuriate his later wives by constantly extolling her virtues. Managing his wife's property, Mohammad became a successful merchant, but as he approached his fortieth year he began to spend more and more time in solitary meditation. One day, without warning, he heard a voice which said, "You are the Messenger of God," and which then commanded him to recite these words:

Recite in the name of thy Lord Who created: Created man from clots of blood!
 Recite! Your Lord is the Most Bountiful One, who by the pen taught man what he did not know.                    (Koran 96:2–4)

These first words of the revelation told Mohammad that God had chosen him to convey his message to mankind in the name of the transcendent but beneficent God who is the creator of the universe. The revelation stresses the original insignificance of man but promises that this mighty God is concerned with his progress and development and will reveal himself to all mankind in a great book.

Mohammad was overwhelmed, like other prophets who have experienced a revelation. "I was standing," he is reported to have said, "but I fell on my knees and dragged myself along while the upper part of my chest was trembling. I went in to Khadija and said, "Cover me! Cover me!" until the terror left me."[50] He was also very apprehensive about his ability to discharge the enormous responsibility that God had laid upon him. Khadija's words of comfort not only give us some insight into Mohammad's character, but they also tell us much about the social and moral values of Islam:

Surely, God will never suffer thee to fail. Thou art kind and considerate toward thy kin. Thou helpest the poor and forlorn and bearest their burdens. Thou strivest to restore the high moral qualities that thy people have lost. Thou honourest the guest and goest to the assistance of those in distress.[51]

Like many of the Jewish prophets, however, Mohammad was sometimes very cautious about the Voice and the Presence that came to him more and more frequently. Was this really God or the product of his own imagination? Finally he was convinced of their divine nature. The revelations were always a painful, wrenching experience. "Nevèr once did I receive a revelation without thinking that my soul had been torn away from me,"[52] he said at the end of his life. His face would be covered with sweat: he lay unconscious for an hour or so afterward, was seized with violent shudderings or heard strange noises like the sound of bells and rushing wings. "Revelations come to me in different ways," he said. "Sometimes the words strike directly at my heart like the ringing of a bell, and this is physically hard on me. Sometimes I hear the words as if spoken from behind a veil. Sometimes I see a Presence that speaks the words to me."[53] These mental experiences quite often accompany the productions of genius, when someone makes a real breakthrough to a hitherto undiscovered idea or solution to a problem. Mohammad conveyed each new revelation to his disciples, who immediately learned it by heart, and those who were educated wrote it down. Mohammad himself, like many people in the Hejaz, was illiterate. These collected revelations of God became the Koran (or the Recitation), the holy book of Islam.[54]

Mohammad insisted that his was not a new religion but the ultimate revelation of the Jewish-Christian tradition. He called his religion "Islam," which means "submission" (to God), and his followers became "Muslims," which means "those who submit." Abraham, he taught, had been the first "Muslim" because he had submitted so perfectly to God: he had been neither a Jew nor a Christian because he had lived long before the Torah and the gospels (Koran 3:66–69). Mohammad had never read the Bible, of course, but from the Jews and Christians living in the peninsula he learned some of the stories and teachings of these earlier religions and repeated them, reinterpreted according to the revelations, in the Koran. This makes them rather different from the Biblical version and they probably also reflect the simple, apocryphal beliefs of the Jews and Christians of Arabia, who were so far from the main centers of their religions. The Koran, therefore, venerates Jewish figures like Abraham, Noah, Lot, Joseph and Jonah. It also venerates Jesus, whom Muslims call the Messiah. Mohammad did not believe for a moment that Jesus had been God; this seemed as blasphemous a claim to the Muslims as it had always seemed to the Jews. Jesus was a prophet, like the other Jewish prophets, not the incarnate Son of God. Though Islam was the supreme revelation, the Koran taught Muslims that they must respect Jews and Christians, the People of the Book: "Be courteous when you argue with the People of the Book, except with those who do evil. Say 'We believe in that which is revealed to us and that which is revealed to you. Our God and your God is one' " (Koran 29:46). Indeed one of the greatest Islamic values is liberty of conscience and freedom of thought, to which every individual has an inalienable right.

The first Muslims learned the importance of this ideal by bitter experience. At first Mohammad had only three disciples besides Khadija: his freedman Zaid, his friend Abu Bakr and his cousin Ali ibn Talib, who was only eleven years old. But gradually the new religion attracted other converts in the city. The teaching of Islam was at first very simple. First and most important was the revelation of monotheism: there was no God but Allah and Mohammad was his Prophet. This formed the entire profession of faith. Second, Muslims must prepare for the imminent Last Judgment, and third, they had a duty to care for the poor and oppressed and work to create an equal, just society that truly reflected God's will. Like Jesus, Mohammad identified with the poor and outcast and in this respect his faith was essentially revolutionary and was protesting against the unjust rule of the Qureish in Mecca.[55] Indeed revolution and commitment to social justice are important values in Islam, as we shall see throughout this book. The Koran taught that there could be no distinction between religion and politics but that Muslims must engage in a practical struggle (*jihad*) to create a perfect community (*umma*). Not surprisingly, the first Muslim converts came from the ranks of the weak and underprivileged people of Mecca. In particular slaves, who were treated very cruelly, and women, who were considered little better than animals in pre-Islamic Arabia, both felt that in Islam they would find a means of achieving a human dignity and self-respect. But the cause of Islam made a breakthrough when Omar ibn al-Khattib, a prominent and respected citizen, unexpectedly became a Muslim. The people of Mecca began to realize that they had to take this religion seriously.

At first the Qureish had been patronizing and scornful about Islam but gradually they began to see that it constituted a political threat to their regime. For how long would a man who claimed that God spoke to him and who condemned their rule as unjust and corrupt be prepared to submit to their government? Mohammad also condemned the pagan cult of Hubal and the idols in the Ka'aba and insisted that it be restored to the faith of Abraham and Ishmael. This would ruin the pilgrim trade and could even mean that trade caravans would no longer converge upon Mecca: it threatened the whole Meccan wealth and way of life. The Meccans began to persecute the Muslims. In particular those Muslims who were slaves and women were subject to torture and to inhuman treatment. At one time the Qureish confined Muslims to their houses and imposed a blockade, which cut off their food supplies, and, even though the blockade was eventually lifted, the Muslims had suffered greatly and Khadija and Abu Talib, the young Ali's father, both died. There were also frequent attempts on Mohammad's life and it became clear that the Muslims needed a new home, where they had the freedom to think and to worship as they chose.

They found this home in the year 622. Some *hanifs* of the settlement of Yathrib, which would later be called Medina (the city) and which is about 240 miles north of Mecca, invited the Muslims to settle there. Yathrib was settled by two tribes of Jews and three tribes of Arabs and there was a struggle for the leadership. The Jews had recently been expecting a prophet, who had been promised in their Scriptures (Deuteronomy 18:18), to lead them to new power. When the *hanifs* heard about Mohammad during their annual pilgrimage to Mecca, they assumed that he must be this prophet and they decided to win him over to the Arab side. Some seventy *hanifs* converted to Islam and urged the Muslims to emigrate to Medina and to take on the leadership. This seemed a good solution, though it meant that Mohammad had to abandon his own tribe in Mecca. God, however, promised him that he would one day return to his home (Koran 28:86). Secretly, in twos and threes, the Muslims slipped out of Mecca and made the journey to Medina. Mohammad was the last to leave with Abu Bakr, and left just in time to forestall a serious attempt on his life. For two days he and Abu Bakr hid in a cave outside the city while the Meccans scoured the countryside hunting for the rebellious Prophet. Eventually the fugitives were able to escape to Medina, where they were joyfully received by the Muslim community and Mohammad eventually took over the leadership of the city. This *hijra* or migration of 622 marks the official beginning of the Muslim calendar, and this journey north would be as formative for the Muslims as the Exodus had been for the Jews.

In Medina the Muslims had the chance to build the first Islamic society and, as Judaism came of age in the exile of Babylon, so did Islam come of age in Medina. The Muslims accepted five pillars of the religion. All Muslims had to make the simple profession of faith: "There is no God but Allah and Mohammad is his Prophet." They had to pray at stated times, facing first toward Jerusalem and later toward the Ka'aba in Mecca; they had to give alms to the poor and fast during the month of Ramadan. Finally they had to make the pilgrimage to Mecca, but in the present state of hostility between Mecca and Islam they were unable to do so. Islam was an anti-elitist religion. The prayers and requirements were the same for everybody and there was to be no hierarchy, as there was in Christianity, which made people first- and second-class Christians. Eventually a clergy emerged, who led the prayers and were expert in Islamic law, but they were never priests like Christian priests, who intervened between God and man. Almsgiving was meant to iron out material inequalities and to ensure the even distribution of wealth. Even the fast of Ramadan was a realistic fast that was within everybody's scope. Indeed we shall see that realism is a hallmark of Islam. These years in Medina were hard years. Mohammad had to struggle against the hostility of the non-Muslim Arab community in Medina, who had hoped to get the leadership, and of the Jews, who also fought against his rule. Besides the inevitable difficulties that were involved in setting up a wholly new social order in Medina, the Muslims had to worry about a possible invasion by the Meccans, who now saw Medina as an enemy because the people there had taken in the Muslims. But Mohammad urged his Muslims to take every possible practical precaution and at the same time to pray and foster their knowledge of God, in order to make this a joyful experience. What made Islam a successful and strong faith was its realism and practicality. Constantly in the Koran the Muslims are exhorted to expend every possible *human* effort in the cause. God had promised that he would help them, but he would not do so unless they had worked hard to save themselves. He would not save them by a miracle.[56] This realistic approach, established from the very beginning, is one of the distinguishing characteristics of Islam that, as I hope to show, makes it very different in spirit from both Judaism and Christianity, where the possibility of miracles is not always ruled out.

One of the precautions that Mohammad took was to establish friendly relations with neighboring tribes. There was no attempt to force conversion upon them, for that would have meant that the Muslims were denying others the freedom of belief that they had been denied in Mecca. But more and more Arabs did convert to Islam of their own choice. The religion was very attractive. It was essentially Arab and a marvelous tonic to the Arabs' battered sense of self-esteem: as recipients of God's ultimate revelation, the Arabs were now God's new chosen people. Further, Islam had all the attractions of monotheism, without the complications of practice and belief that Jews and Christians had evolved and which were alien to the Arab way of life. Conversion to Islam was becoming an irresistible trend in the peninsula, though as with all mass movements there were people who joined for unworthy reasons. Mohammad and his most committed converts were constantly worried during these first years about a party of Medinan Arabs who had converted but were not wholly loyal. In the Koran they are called the *munafiqeen* or the hypocrites.

The Meccans were trying to spread hostility against Muslim Medina and were using their trade caravans as a means of inciting the neighboring tribes and the Jews to fight against the city. These caravans were economically crucial to the Meccans and were usually accompanied by an army, so they were a threat to the security of Medina. Mohammad realized that the Muslims would have to fight them if they wanted to survive. He had a revelation that justified the use of violence as a means of self-defense (22:40–42). The Meccans had persecuted the Muslims and were now pursuing them in exile. Unless right-minded people fought tyrants and oppressors, all decency and beneficence would vanish from the earth: "Had Allah not defeated some by the might of others, the earth would have been utterly corrupted" (2:252). Muslims were forbidden to open hostilities: "Fight for the sake of Allah those that fight against you, but do not attack them first. Allah does not love the aggressors" (2:191). The ancient Israelites had been commanded by God to attack and exterminate the Canaanites living in the Promised Land, as a holy initiative, and Christians had denied that violence could be justified by self-defense. But the concept of self-defense was central to the Islamic view of warfare from the very beginning. This was the only way the Koran could justify the military action that Muslims now undertook against the Meccans.

The practice of making a *razzia* (raid) on an enemy tribe was well established in the Hejaz and was deemed normal and acceptable. It was often a necessity in an area where there was not enough for everybody if a tribe lacked the essentials of life. The raiders usually captured cattle, animals and booty but were careful to avoid killing people. This was not for humanitarian reasons but because killing would mean a long and bloody vendetta. The code of the *razzia* meant that you attacked only your enemies, which was again sensible in the

Hejaz, which was torn apart by tribal wars. The Muslims in Medina began to make *razzia* against the Meccan caravans. One day in 624 a small band of 313 Muslims made the hundred-mile journey to Badr in the southwest, to attack a particularly important caravan traveling to Mecca, which was accompanied by most of the Qureish leadership. They had not realized that, in order to protect them from the Medinan Muslims, the leaders of the caravan had asked for a relieving army from Mecca to come to their assistance. When the Muslims attacked the caravan, therefore, they found that they were vastly outnumbered and were fighting nearly a thousand Meccans. It was too late to withdraw, but against all the odds the Muslims won. Their victory was probably due to their tactical superiority and to the fact that they were more firmly united under their military leaders than the more undisciplined Qureish. At the end of the battle the flowers of the Qureish were dead on the battlefield and the Muslims were euphoric.[57] They had fought as hard as they could and because they had done their part God had stepped in and helped them. The success of the Battle of Badr, as it was called, seemed a proof of Mohammad's divine mission. Mohammad himself called it a *furqan*, a word which means both salvation and separation.[58] He had instinctively interpreted Badr in the way that the Israelites had interpreted their victory at the Red Sea; it was a separation of the just from the unjust.

Allah revealed his will to the angels saying "I shall be with you. Give courage to the believers. I shall cast terror into the hearts of the infidels. Strike off all their heads, maim them in every limb."

It was not you but Allah who slew them. It was not you who smote them: Allah smote them so that he might richly reward his faithful. He hears all and knows all. He will surely thwart the designs of the unbelievers.                                                         (8:12, 18)

During our story we shall often find that an unexpected success gives rise to a belief in God's special intervention and stronger sense of divine mission. The unexpected success of Badr meant that, although this had not been the original intention of the Prophet, the migration from Mecca to Medina had in fact been a prelude to a holy war or a *jihad*. Islam had reverted to the archetype.

Yet this still did not make Islam the religion of the sword. Indeed the word "Islam" comes from the same Arabic root as the word "peace"[59] and the Koran condemns war as an abnormal state of affairs opposed to God's will: when the enemies of the Muslims "kindle a fire for war, Allah extinguishes it. They strive to create disorder in the earth, and Allah loves not those who create disorder" (Koran 28:78).

Islam does not justify a total aggressive war of extermination, as the Torah does in the first five books of the Bible. A more realistic religion than Christianity, Islam recognizes that war is inevitable and sometimes a positive duty in order to end oppression and suffering. The Koran teaches that war must be limited and be conducted in as humane a way as possible. Mohammad had to fight not only the Meccans but also the Jewish tribes in the area and Christian tribes in Syria who planned an offensive against him in alliance with the Jews. Yet this did not make Mohammad denounce the People of the Book. His Muslims were forced to defend themselves but they were not fighting a "holy war" against the religion of their enemies. When Mohammad sent his freedman Zaid against the Christians at the head of a Muslim army, he told them to fight in the cause of God bravely but humanely. They must not molest priests, monks and nuns nor the weak and helpless people who were unable to fight. There must be no massacre of civilians nor should they cut down a single tree or pull down any building.[60] This was very different from the wars of Joshua.

But though Islam does not glorify war it is still true that the paradigm of the *hijra/jihad* has been important and formative in Islam. It has constantly inspired groups of fervent Muslims to withdraw from the community when they feel that the Muslims there are no longer faithful to Islam. In this exodus they have much the same instinct as Jewish groups like the Essenes or the Christian monks. The radical Muslims have made a migration away from the main body of the Muslims into the desert and have sought to build an ideal, Islamic society dedicated to justice. Then they have fought against the establishment in a *jihad* or a holy war in order to bring about a reform and an end of corruption. They see themselves as having been persecuted by the current establishment and feel it their Muslim duty to act in order to end a period of oppression. The first group to do this, in the mid-seventh century, was the radical Kharaji sect, who have been the only Muslims who have maintained that the *jihad* is a "pillar of Islam." Perhaps the most recent example is the sect known as the *takfir w'al hijra* group, which withdrew from the Egypt of Anwar Sadat, built an alternative, independent community upon Muslim lines and finally waged a terrorist war against the regime. People who have had recourse to the *hijra/jihad* archetype believe that God will not help them unless they make every human effort to solve their own problems, even if this means fighting other Muslims.

The Battle of Badr was not the end of Mohammad's war with Mecca. Inevitably the Meccans sent armies against Medina and for the next four years there were battles, in which Medina finally emerged as the

stronger power. Many tribes of the peninsula had been delighted by
the downfall of the haughty Meccans and were willing to become
confederates of Medina, even if they did not wish to convert to Islam,
and Medina was gradually being transformed into a powerful city-
state with an exciting and dynamic new Arab ideology. It was now
time for Mohammad to conquer Mecca and fulfill the prophecy of
God that he would one day return home. This way he did this is
instructive, especially in the terms of the archetype. Mohammad was
not only a religious man, who deplored unnecessary war, but he was
also a shrewd politician. He knew that the last thing Medina really
needed was a long, wasteful war. Instead he decided to conquer Mecca
by means of a peaceful pilgrimage.

At the traditional time for the *hajj* pilgrimage to Mecca in 628
Mohammad and a large company of Muslims with their pagan confederates set out from Medina. Accounts of this give different numbers,
ranging from 700 to 1400 men. But it was an unusual army, because
the soldiers were virtually unarmed and carried only swords, which
Mohammad had ordered to remain sheathed. As the Meccans watched
this huge army approaching they expected Mohammad to attack, but
instead Mohammad halted at Hudaybiyya, just outside the Sanctuary
(the twenty-square-mile area around the Ka'aba where all violence was
forbidden). The Meccans sent envoys and Mohammad asked simply
to be able to perform the pilgrim rites at the Ka'aba, which was the
right of every Arab. At first the Meccans demurred, but eventually to
ward off an attack they agreed to make a treaty with Medina that was
to last ten years. Many of the Muslims thought that this treaty was
one-sided and humiliating. Any Meccan who converted to Islam and
migrated to Medina without the permission of his father, for example,
was to be returned forthwith, yet this did not apply to a Medinan
who apostasized from Islam and migrated to Mecca. But Mohammad
had made an important point. The Koran insists that whenever the
enemy wants to make peace Muslims *must* enter into a treaty, provided
that the terms are not dangerous to Islam. Furthermore they must
observe the terms of the treaty scrupulously, however inconvenient
they are.[61] Mohammad pointed out that Muslims had gained by the
Treaty of Hudaybiyya. They were now permitted to make the pilgrimage to Mecca each year, as peaceful pilgrims, carrying only
sheathed swords; Mecca had accepted the right of Muslims to exist
and they could now concentrate on building up the *umma* without
fighting unnecessary wars.

The following year the pilgrimage journey to Mecca was repeated.
In accordance with the treaty, the Meccans evacuated the city to avoid

a clash with the Muslims and from the surrounding hills they watched with fascinated horror as Mohammad and his huge Muslim army solemnly circled the Ka'aba according to the ancient ritual. But instead of venerating the idols in the Ka'aba, the Muslim muezzin climbed onto the roof of the Ka'aba and issued the call to prayer to Allah, the only God. Thus they had returned the shrine to the religion of Abraham and Ishmael. Their devotions completed, they marched peacefully back to Medina, while the awed Meccans crept back into the city.

In the following year the Meccans foolishly broke the Treaty of Hudaybiyya just before the *hajj* and thus relieved Mohammad of his obligation to keep the peace. Mecca had attacked the tribe of Khuza'a, which was confederated to the Muslims. Yet again Mohammad and his scantily armed pilgrim army set out for the pilgrimage to Mecca, but this time they were accompanied by huge numbers of confederates. The Meccans once again sent envoys to try to make peace, in order to ward off a bloody attack. Mohammad promised that if they accepted him as their ruler there would be no bloodshed and no reprisals. No Meccan would be forced to convert to Islam. He would only smash the idols in the Ka'aba. The Meccans agreed and the Muslims honored the conditions of the agreement. Mohammad went straight to the Ka'aba and smashed the idols himself and his army circled the shrine, which was now dedicated to the religion of Islam. He was now the ruler of the city. Not a drop of blood was shed and nobody was forced to convert. Mohammad had turned his peaceful pilgrimage into a conquest. He called the event *al-Fatah*, which is a familiar term to us because it is the name of Yasir Arafat's liberation movement. *Fatah* means "opening," "salvation," "conquest."[62]

Mohammad and his Meccan Muslims had literally returned home when they entered the city, but in an important sense *fatah* was a homecoming for the Muslims of Medina also because it was a return to the origins of the Islamic faith in the one God of Abraham and Ishmael. In 632, two years after his conquest, Mohammad decided to Islamize the pagan shrines around Mecca, which made up the full pilgrimage known as the *hajj*. At each of the shrines he and his Muslims performed and reinterpreted all the old pagan, Arab rites. They threw pebbles at the pillars of Mina, as though they were fighting evil and immorality. They ran seven times between the hills of Safa and Marwa, recalling the distress of Ishmael's mother Hagar when she had run desperately seeking water during her first days of exile in the desert. They drank from the spring that God showed to Hagar, in answer to her prayer. The Prophet also made the *ifada*, the Onrush, mounting his finest camel and charging with his Muslims in a body to Muzdalifa, the lowest point between the mountain of Arafat and Mecca. There he prayed to Allah and made an animal sacrifice to him.

Performance of the *hajj* was the fifth pillar of Islam. If he can afford it and his health and circumstances permit, each Muslim must make the *hajj* once in his lifetime. Mecca is the holiest city in the Muslim world because of its connection with Abraham, Hagar and Ishmael. The very first Muslims had followed the example of the Jews and the Christians and turned in the direction of Jerusalem when they prayed, but in Medina, they started to pray facing Mecca. Mohammad had turned the Muslims back to their Arab roots and given them a distinct and independent identity. But Jerusalem was still important to Muslims, not only because it was connected with so many of the great prophets, but because of its connection with Mohammad. In 620, two years before the *hijra*, Mohammad was said to have made a mystical flight to Jerusalem by night. He had alighted on the site of the old Jewish Temple and had thence ascended to heaven,[63] where he had spoken with Moses and Jesus. This vision of the Night Journey shows the Muslim connection with the two older religions and has made Jerusalem the third most holy city in Islam, after Mecca and Medina.

When Muslims make the *hajj* today, performing all the ancient rituals as Mohammad did, they feel that they are making an emotional and dynamic connection with the roots of their religion. Naturally they think about Mohammad, but they principally remember Abraham, Ishmael and Hagar. Even if Muslims are not Arabs, they are taught that Ishmael and Abraham are their ancestors, in the same way as St. Paul taught Christians to see Abraham as the father of all believers. Islam began as a religion for the Arabs, but from the very first revelation it had also been a message for all mankind. When he made the *hajj* in 632 Mohammad made what has been called the Farewell Address to the *umma*, because he felt that his death was near. In addition to reminding them of the values of Islam, he is said to have looked forward to the time when Islam would have spread to other peoples and told them that all men were equal before Allah, without distinction of social class or racial origin.

O people, your Lord is one and your ancestor is [also] one. You are all descended from Adam and Adam was [born] of the earth. *The noblest of you all in the sight of Allah is the most devout. Allah is knowing and all-wise* [Koran 49:13]. An Arab is superior to a non-Arab in nothing but devotion.[64]

When the Muslim pilgrims make the *hajj* to Mecca today they come
from all over the world. All dress in the ritual white garment, so that
all distinctions of race and class are obliterated. The pilgrimage is
supposed to be an expression of the unity of all Muslims, the children
of Adam and Abraham, and the identical clothes are an important
symbol of this. Together they cry, "Here we are, O Lord," as they
approach the Ka'aba, crying to Allah with one voice. Peace and unity
are the hallmark of the *hajj* and pilgrims are commanded to respect
the holiness of the Ka'aba and the Sanctuary, just as Mohammad did
when he conquered Mecca without bloodshed. Throughout the *hajj*
the pilgrim has to abstain from the smallest hint of violence. He may
not kill game [Koran 5:95] nor take part in a quarrel (2:197). Until
the late 1980s pilgrims observed these prohibitions scrupulously: they
insisted that a pilgrim must not speak in a cross voice, kill even an
insect or uproot a plant. While on the *hajj* a pilgrim must be at peace
not only with all other Muslims but with the whole world. In Chapter
8 we will see how some radical Muslims today have turned the *hajj*
into a violent declaration of war.

Shortly after making the final pilgrimage, Mohammad died and the
shock of his death threatened to break the new Arab unity. In the ten
years since the *hijra* of 622, Mohammad had managed to unite nearly
the whole of the Hejaz under him and most of the tribes were either
confederates or else they had converted to Islam. The caliphs, Mohammad's successors, realized that if the old habits of tribal warfare
were not to surface again Muslims had to expend their aggressive
instinct upon non-Muslims instead of upon one another and make
sure that Islam kept expanding. There was a very similar situation in
Europe at the time of the First Crusade. After the death of Mohammad, Arab armies began to invade the surrounding countries with
such astounding success that just a hundred years after the *hijra* the
new Islamic empire stretched from the Himalayas to Gibraltar. The
soldiers were urged to fight humanely, as the Koran enjoined, but
what had happened to the Koranic condemnation of aggressive warfare? To justify this apparent violation of Mohammad's principles,
Muslim jurists began to develop a theology of the *jihad*. They taught
that because there was only one God there should be only one state
in the world that must submit to the true religion. It was the duty of
the Muslim state (the House of Islam) to conquer the rest of the non-
Muslim world (the House of War) so that the world could reflect the
divine unity. Every Muslim must participate in this *jihad* and the
House of Islam must never compromise with the House of War. At
best a truce could be signed with a non-Muslim people, which must

not exceed ten years. Until the final domination of the world was accomplished, therefore, Muslims were in a perpetual state of war.[65] It is this early doctrine of the *jihad* which has given Islam its reputation of being the religion of the sword and, had Muslims remained committed to this warlike theory, Islam would indeed have become a militaristic and imperialist religion.

But this did not happen. The theory had been developed when it looked as though Islam really *would* conquer the whole world, but by the beginning of the eighth century the *jihad* effort had burned out. The House of Islam had serious internal difficulties, which made any further wars of expansion impossible, and Muslims accepted that, despite the doctrine of the *jihad*, the reality was that there would be no more "holy wars" of conquest. Muslims now realized that the Islamic empire had frontiers that were permanent and, like the Christians and the Jews, they believed that their final world victory was to be postponed until the Last Judgment. They abandoned the doctrine of the *jihad*, which became a dead letter. Instead of seeing non-Muslim countries as enemies they developed normal trading and diplomatic contacts with them. Certainly some Muslim rulers did attack non-Muslim countries, but these were not part of the *jihad* but ordinary secular wars. The caliphs employed a few dedicated men of war who, once in a while, would invade the House of War in a sort of token *jihad*, but in reality Muslims had learned to live side by side with other religions. This new attitude can be seen very clearly in Spain, the last of the great Islamic conquests. The Muslim land of al-Andalus was certainly an Islamic state. Almost as soon as they established their capital at Cordova they began to build the great mosque there, which, with its fortresslike exterior and contemplative interior, shows the great spirituality that was possible within this apparently warlike new religion. Yet the Sultan and his amirs governed al-Andalus in a far more secular style than would have been acceptable seventy years earlier when the Muslims made their first conquests in the Middle East. In Spain, for example, the Sultans at once recognized the existence of the Christian kingdom of León in the north and had diplomatic and trade relations with their Christian neighbors—something that directly contradicted the theology of *jihad* propounded by the jurists in the Sharia, or Holy Law of Islam. The Arab holy war had become Arab imperialism, and no longer entailed a branding of the non-Muslim world as the perpetual enemy.

Muslims may have forgotten the *jihad* but the Christians found it less easy to forget. The Christian world had watched aghast as this new religion swept through the Middle East and North Africa, con-

quering countries which had been strongly Christian with such ease
that people began to ask themselves whether God was on the side of
these "infidels." It was very threatening to the Christian identity to
see this younger, energetic religion that claimed to have superseded
Christianity actually transforming the map and absorbing Christians
into its empire. The *jihad* remained a bogey in the West for centuries.
When, for example, Sultan Abd al-Rahman of al-Andalus made a raid
into southern France in 732, he was defeated by Charles Martel at
the Battle of Poitiers and this has been seen as a turning point of
world history. Gibbon contemplated the consequences of an Arab
victory with a shudder:

> the Rhine is not more impassable than the Nile or the Euphrates,
> and the Arabian fleet might have sailed without a naval combat into
> the mouth of the Thames. Perhaps the interpretation of the Koran
> would now be taught in the schools of Oxford, and her pulpits
> might demonstrate to a circumcised people the sanctity and truth
> of the revelation of Mahomet. From such calamities was Christen-
> dom delivered by the genius and fortune of one man.[66]

This is a distorted and exaggerated view. The Sultan was not continuing the *jihad* and had no intention of conquering Europe. He had
been invited into Christendom by Eudo, Duke of Aquitaine, who
wanted his help against Charles Martel. Muslim historians scarcely
mention "the Battle of Poitiers" except in passing, where they refer
to it as an unfortunate but unimportant little raid. They had no designs
on Europe, which they saw as an undesirable place, with a dreadful
climate and primitive, backward inhabitants who were on a level with
the black barbarians of Africa. Indeed Muslims spoke of a statue in
Narbonne which bore the inscription: "Turn back, sons of Ishmael,
this is as far as you go, and if you do not go back, you will smite each
other until the day of Resurrection."[67] Yet Gibbon's view of the Battle
of Poitiers is not unusual. Centuries after the theory was abandoned
as a practical project by Muslims, it continued to be a buried phobia
in Christendom and still affects our attitude to the Islamic world.
There was a good deal of this kind of fear in the air during the OPEC
oil crisis in 1973: the Arabs seemed to want to "take over the world."

The people who had been conquered by the Muslim armies, however, had quite a different view of the *jihad* and they did not regard
the conquests of Islam as a catastrophe. Quite the reverse was true;
it was the start of a new and exciting phase in their history. This seems
strange to us in the twentieth century: if a foreign power conquered

our country, we would naturally be dismayed. But we have to recall that people of the seventh century did not think about their country as we do today. The people of the Middle East had belonged to one vast empire after another for over a thousand years. They had no aspirations to national independence and the Muslim victories merely meant that they had exchanged one distant world power for another. The Christians of North Africa had long been part of the Roman Empire. Certainly their new masters had a different religion but many found that Islam was extremely attractive.

When the Muslims conquered a people, they did not attempt to force conversion on their new subjects. Mohammad had given an eloquent example of the Islamic principle of the sanctity of the individual conscience when he conquered Mecca without bloodshed and put no pressure on the Meccans to convert. The Koran taught that the People of the Book were to be respected, and within the Islamic empire Jews and Christians were allowed full religious liberty, as were the Zoroastrians, Buddhists and Hindus. This policy was not only the result of religious ideology; it also made sound political sense. When the Muslims first conquered a country, they were naturally only a tiny minority and in no position to enforce conversion, even if they had wished to do so. The Arabs long remained a minority group: the caliphs did not permit the Muslim soldiers and generals to colonize the countries they conquered. Instead of settling down to enjoy the fruit of their labors in a comfortable life, the army set off to conquer new territory, leaving behind just enough soldiers to enforce Muslim rule and to run the administration. In these circumstances, it would have been madness for them to force their religion on the majority. Further, the Middle East had long been an area of religious pluralism and the Arabs were used to religions existing alongside one another. When the Byzantines or the Zoroastrians of Persia had attempted to impose religious conformity on their subject peoples, the result had been politically disastrous for them. The Muslim system was, therefore, rather more acceptable to many people than the policies of their predecessors.

The system was that the Christians, Jews and other religious groups were allowed to practice their religion freely but they had to accept that Islam was the state religion and supreme in the land. These groups were called the *dhimmis* or protected minorities. They paid a tax in return for Muslim military protection—a common enough measure at this time. They were not allowed to bear arms themselves and there were rules that emphasized their subjection to Islam: *dhimmis* had to wear distinctive dress; they had to bow to the Muslims when they paid their tax, the *jizya*; no church, synagogue or temple building was permitted to be higher than the mosque. But scholars point out that these rules were not rigidly enforced and sound more humiliating than they actually were in practice. There was no tradition of religious persecution in the Islamic empire. Occasionally prohibitive measures and even massacres occurred but these usually followed a Jewish or Christian revolt against the Muslim rule. The Muslims were putting down an uprising, not refusing to accept the existence of a rival religion. Within the Islamic empire, there was never any persecution that matched the Christian treatment of the Jews in Europe, for example. If Muslim territory was invaded by Christians or by Jews, then the position of the *dhimmis* tended to deteriorate: thus the Christian *dhimmis* experienced new hostility during the Crusades, when Christians from the West seized Muslim lands and treated the inhabitants cruelly. Life for Jews only became intolerable in Islamic countries after the creation of the state of Israel. On the whole, Islam was a tolerant religion in practice, despite its warlike theology. It encouraged a peaceful coexistence and found it quite possible to live side by side with other religions.[68]

But in fact many of the subject peoples wanted to convert to Islam. Again, this seems strange to us but we must try to look at the matter in seventh-century terms. It must be emphasized once more that there was no pressure to convert. Indeed for one brief period in about 700, the caliphs actually forbade conversion by law: because new converts no longer had to pay the *jizya* tax, the whole economy was in jeopardy! Why was Islam so attractive? Ethical monotheism was the great, dynamic ideology of the day. It was seen as the progressive religion of the more advanced peoples and, for many people of the Orient and North Africa, Islam offered this religion in a form that was more acceptable to them than Christianity. For one thing, its theology was far simpler. Christian doctrines like the Trinity or the Incarnation were beautiful and inspiring if you had been brought up in the tradition of Greek philosophy, which had a triad view of the personality and unique ideas about the human person which contributed to the formulation of those two dogmas. But if you were an oriental Christian with quite different traditions, they were simply baffling. So-called heresies that centered on the knotty problem of how Jesus could be both God and man were rife throughout the Middle East and had, on occasion, been persecuted by the orthodox Christians of Byzantium. The Muslim view of Jesus as a great and privileged prophet made far more sense, as did their policy of toleration to these long-suffering and puzzled Christians. Again, in Spain, this Koranic view of Jesus greatly appealed to many of the Visigoths, who had been converted to Arianism, which had much the same view of Christ. In Islam many people found a form of monotheism that they could really understand and they also discovered that it had a dynamism and excitement of its own. Similarly, the Jews much preferred Islam to Christianity. They did not want to convert but many of the Jews of North Africa fought alongside the Muslim armies and others saw the dramatic rise of this world power whose religion was so close in spirit to Judaism as a sign of the imminent arrival of the Messiah.

Today in the West we tend to see Islam as a religion that is opposed to progress. This is because Western culture has overtaken traditional Muslim cultures and is also a legacy of the colonial period when Islam was often described as a fatalistic religion that is opposed to change. But, as we shall see later, Islam is in essence a dynamic religion that demands action: Muslims have to act in order to put God's will into practice and many Muslim terms are essentially dynamic concepts, expressive of movement and struggle. When the Arabs left the Arabian Peninsula after the death of Mohammad at the start of their *jihad* they were semibarbarians. A hundred years later they were a world power and were creating a new culture of great power and beauty. Islam is in one sense a syncretic religion: it had built on the two older religions of Judaism and Christianity and combined the two with Arabian traditions. In the seventh century Muslims showed that they were quite able to build upon other cultures and to absorb the wisdom inherent in foreign traditions. Again, this is surprising to many Western people today, since the Ayatollah Khomeini declared war on the cultures of the West and the Soviet Union. But in the early Middle Ages the Arabs were quite ready to learn from the people they had conquered: they were eager to absorb the learning, the science and the philosophy of the ancient traditions of Persia or Egypt or to sample the excitement of some Greek thought. In this they were aided by the subject peoples themselves, especially by those who had converted to Islam. These converts wanted to review their own rich traditions in the light of their new religion; they wanted to see how their past fitted their present and how their traditional culture could be assimilated with this foreign, Arabian tradition. It was, therefore, a two-way process. On the one hand the Arabs were seeking to learn from the ancient cultures that had preceded them, and on the other the new Muslims sought to integrate these cultural traditions with their own religion. The result was the dramatic rise of a unique and distinctive Muslim culture that developed a style of scholarship, art and architecture all its own. Just one hundred years after the death of the Prophet, Muslims were founding great universities and were ready to build the Great Mosque of Cordova.

The Muslims were also to build two other important mosques that are vitally connected with our story. One of the first countries to fall to the Muslim armies was Palestine. Jerusalem was forced to open her gate to the Caliph Omar in 638. When Christianity became the official religion of the Roman Empire, Palestine had become Christian too and Jerusalem became a holy Christian city. The pagan temples erected by the Romans after 70 C.E. were pulled down and Christian pilgrims began to visit the site of Christ's death and resurrection. In 638 the magistrate of the Holy City was the Greek Patriarch Sophronius and he had the sad task of escorting the Caliph Omar, who rode triumphantly into Jerusalem on a white camel. Omar asked to be taken immediately to the Temple Mount and there he knelt in prayer on the spot where his friend Mohammad had alighted after his Night Journey to heaven. The Patriarch watched him in horror: this, he thought, must be the Abomination of Desolation that the Prophet Daniel had foretold would enter the Temple; this must be Antichrist, who would herald the Last Days. Next Omar asked to see the Christian shrines and, while he was in the Church of the Holy Sepulchre, the time for Muslim prayer came around. Courteously the Patriarch invited him to pray where he was but Omar as courteously refused. If he knelt to pray in the church, he explained, the Muslims would want to commemorate the event by building a mosque there, and that would mean that they would demolish the Holy Sepulchre. This must not happen, because the Christian shrines must be preserved.[69] Instead Omar went to pray at a little distance from the church and, sure enough, directly opposite the Holy Sepulchre there is still a small mosque dedicated to the Caliph Omar. The other great Mosque of Omar was built on the Temple Mount to mark the Muslim conquest, together with the mosque al-Aqsa which commemorates Mohammad's Night Journey. For years, the Christians had used the site of the ruined Jewish Temple as the city rubbish dump. The Caliph helped his Muslims to clear the garbage with his own hands and there Muslims raised their two shrines to establish Islam in the third most holy city in the Islamic world. The Dome of the Rock and al-Aqsa will be important in our story and are a perfect expression of the position that Islam adopted toward the older religions. On the one hand they are a symbol of a dominant, victorious Islam rising out of the ruins of a superseded faith; on the other, they show a need to root the identity of this new religion deeply in the ancient Jewish religion.

It should be clear, therefore, that the holy-war pattern that developed in all three religions does not reveal an atavistic blood lust nor does it reveal an inherent intolerance. Holy war was a response to trauma. The Hebrews experienced the trauma of slavery in Egypt and the Muslims the culture shock of a changing Hejaz. Both undertook migrations each of which was a journey toward a new self. They wanted to achieve liberated, dignified and independent new identities. But there were other people in the way of these goals and inevitably these people became the enemies of the newly emerging identities. The Hebrews were threatened by the Canaanites, who lived in the land that they believed had been promised by their God to them. They were also deeply threatened by the superior culture and attractive religion of these pagan peoples and felt that their new Jewish identity was in jeopardy. Later Jews would feel threatened by the *am ha-aretz* or by the Romans, and this led them to fight desperate holy wars against these essential enemies. The violence and rejection were seen to be holy because they were inseparable from the Jewish identity that they had been commanded by God to establish. Other Jews, however, gained a new confidence in the diaspora and felt secure enough not to need to root their identity physically in the Holy Land. They were able to adopt more open and tolerant relations with the *goyim* because of this confidence and found that this was enriching. The Muslims achieved this confidence far more quickly than the Hebrews because of their early success, which was in itself perhaps due to wiser management. The Muslims could afford to be more tolerant of the people they conquered and this enabled them to build a rich, new and distinctively Islamic culture and achieve a stronger Muslim identity that did not need to rely wholly on force. Confidence and a sense of security, therefore, led to toleration and peaceful coexistence. When the Jewish or Muslim identity has been gravely threatened, as it has in our own day, Jews and Muslims are very likely to turn to the archetypal holy war in their search for a solution.

There were no "holy wars" in Christianity, however, until Pope Urban summoned the First Crusade, and even then it was another two or three years before the Crusaders really conformed to the archetype of the classic holy war. In the eleventh century Western Christians were beginning to recover from the trauma of the Dark Ages and were trying to create a new Western identity which would enable them to shake off their sense of inferiority toward their more powerful and cultured neighbors. They were trying to achieve a new self and were beginning to feel a new confidence. The Crusades were an essential part of this process and perfectly expressed the new Western spirit. So deeply had Christianity been affected by the Jewish traditions she had inherited that these Gentile Europeans found themselves automatically moving toward the classic solution.

# Before the Crusade

## The West Seeks a New
## Christian Soul

The period known as the Dark Ages might have destroyed orthodox Christianity in Europe. The barbarian invasions of the fifth and sixth centuries had destroyed the Roman Empire there and Europe became a primitive backwater where people gazed at the crumbling ruins of the Roman period as belonging to a bygone race of giants, whose achievements now seemed incredible. The culture of the Empire was lost together with most of the wisdom of the ancient world. People could not even farm the land adequately and their frail settlements were wiped out by an apparently endless cycle of famine, flood and disease. It looked as though the true faith really would be destroyed by "the world" because the new barbarian inhabitants of Europe were either heretics or pagans. In the south of Europe the old Christianity of late antiquity managed to survive and in the fortresses of the monasteries the monks had managed to conserve the writings of some of the Fathers of the Church and a few classical texts. But in the northern provinces of the old Empire, which had always been far from the main centers of power, it seemed that the people would slip hopelessly into godlessness and error. Yet the Western Church not only managed to survive but enabled the West to rise to new power during the period of the Crusades. The popes sent missionaries out to the barbarian kingdoms north of the Alps and achieved some notable success. They managed to convert the Anglo-Saxons in Britain and the Franks of Gaul to "true" Roman Christianity but these were for the most part illiterate and uneducated people. Their faith was often a confused jumble of Christian and pagan ideas and it was clear that there was much to be done before Europe fully recovered from the loss of the Empire.

Europe had a powerful Christian neighbor, however. Although the Empire had been destroyed in the West, the Eastern part of the Empire which had its capital at Constantinople had remained intact and was now known to the Europeans as Byzantium and to the Muslims as *Rum* (Rome). The Emperor of Constantinople, head of church and state, was the descendant of the Roman emperors. He still ruled a powerful and centralized state and fought a shrewdly skillful diplomatic and military campaign to keep the armies of Islam at bay. As the only emperor left, he was now the ruler of Italy, which the barbarians had not yet wholly penetrated, and he had his administrative center at Ravenna. The Greek empire of Byzantium, therefore, had enjoyed unbroken continuity and was the only place in the world where the old Christianity of the Empire survived. The great churches of Jerusalem, Antioch, Alexandria and Rome had either been swallowed up by the Islamic empire or gravely weakened by the invaders. Constantinople, Constantine's imperial city, was now the last powerful bastion of the faith and the guardian of theological purity against the twofold threat of Islam and the ignorant Western barbarians. The Patriarch of Constantinople acknowledged the spiritual primacy of the Pope, but the Emperor's court was felt to mirror the imperium of heaven and the Byzantines liked to depict Christ as Pantocrater, the cosmic Emperor of the universe.[1] This triumphant image of Christ reflected the confidence and serenity of the Greek Church with its deep spirituality and its imaginative intellectual tradition. In the traumatized West the human image of the suffering Jesus would become more popular. But in Byzantium the icons and mosaics of Christ and the saints also reveal the contemplative wisdom of the Eastern Church, whose approach to theology and the holiness of God had developed a tradition that was in many ways different from that developed by the Latin Church of Rome.

There was as yet no doctrinal quarrel between Eastern and Western Christianity: the difference was more psychological than theological. But after the destruction of the Western Empire, the unscathed Eastern Church naturally felt responsible for the vulnerable Latins, who, in their turn, were anxious to preserve their own Latin traditions and identity. The Latins did not want to be swamped by the Greeks. Even though most of the popes of the early Middle Ages were either Greeks or oriental Christians who were refugees from the house of Islam, the Romans were on their guard against too much Greek influence.

Interestingly, the new barbarian converts to Christianity among the Anglo-Saxons and the Franks were particularly strong champions of the Latin rite and were very anxious that the West should not become a mere outpost of the Greek Orthodox Church of Byzantium. They resented the way the Greeks obviously looked down upon them and they hated the fact that Rome, the only glory left in Europe, should be dominated by Byzantium, that more Greek than Latin was spoken there and that the Pope was a Greek. They wanted the Pope to be a Westerner. When St. Wilfred, a leading British Christian, visited Rome in 704 to appeal to the Pope against the Archbishop of Canterbury, he was most distressed, after he had finished his speech in Latin, when the Greek Pope spoke to his advisers in a foreign tongue and when the court patronizingly "smiled and said things that he did not understand."[2] The Western converts did not want to create a separate Church; they simply wanted to be treated with dignity and respect. The popes for their part were finding that the emperors of Byzantium were tending to rival their claim to be the supreme head of the Church. When in 729 the Emperor actually dared to send Pope Gregory II instructions about doctrinal matters, the Pope was furious and mobilized, at least in spirit, these new Western churches against their venerable Greek brother: "The whole West has its eyes on us, unworthy though we are. It relies on us and on St. Peter, the Prince of the Apostles, whose image you wished to destroy, but whom all the kingdoms of the West honour as if he were God himself on earth." He declared that he would send new missionaries to "the most distant parts of the West" and vowed that he would go himself to baptize these barbarian converts whose devotion to the papacy was such that they wished to be baptized by the Pope alone.[3]

In fact, Gregory did not make this journey but twenty years later a pope did cross the Alps when Stephen II made an alliance with Pepin, the new King of the Franks and the son of the famous Charles Martel. Pepin in effect stepped into the shoes of the Greek Emperor as the Pope's chief secular protector. Although Pepin was not yet an emperor himself but only the Pope's client, it was natural that the Byzantines saw Stephen as a traitor and Pepin as a barbarian upstart. But, in the West, people were very pleased at this new assertion of Western power and watched with admiration as Pepin built up a powerful Frankish empire, forcing more pagan peoples into the Church at sword point, in a mighty struggle to make Europe a strong and united power once more. These holy wars of expansion were continued by his son Charlemagne, who eventually succeeded Pepin in 771 and pushed back the frontiers of Christendom even more dramatically. In the year 800 Pope Leo III crowned Charlemagne Holy Roman Emperor of the West on Christmas Day.

This was a deliberate affront to Byzantium, as both Charlemagne and Leo were well aware. It seemed preposterous that Charlemagne, who could neither read nor write, should array himself in the imperial regalia and consider himself the equal of the learned Greek Emperor.

It was also painful that a descendant of those barbarians who had destroyed the Empire in the West was now sitting on the imperial throne. But to many people in Europe it seemed as though the West was now ready to take its destiny into its own hands and assert its independence of the haughty Greeks. Charlemagne's great Cathedral of St. Mary in his imperial capital at Aachen was modeled on the Byzantine imperial basilica at Ravenna: he was quite consciously setting himself up as the Western counterpart to the old Empire of East Rome. But he also inspired another comparison. His throne was built according to the measurements of Solomon's throne in Jerusalem and his biographers constantly compared him to the kings and heroes of Israel: he fought as bravely as Joshua; he was a lawgiver like Moses; he was as dignified and saintly as King David and as great a builder as Solomon.[4] In this new burst of confidence, the Franks were beginning to see themselves as a new chosen people. His biographers liked to present Charlemagne's Aachen as the New Jerusalem, where all the nations came to pay tribute to the great Emperor of the West. It is interesting that they showed no particular hostility to the Muslims: they relished the embassy of Harun al-Rashid, the Caliph of Baghdad, and these "Persians" as they were vaguely called, were treated very sympathetically. The Sultan was said to have made Charlemagne the guardian of the Christian holy places in Jerusalem.[5] At this point the enemy of the West was not Islam but Byzantium. The Byzantine envoys were depicted as crafty but stupid and certainly no match for the Franks. The extravagant chronicler known as Notger the Stammerer, who was writing in about 885, is quite vitriolic in his tales of the Greeks at Charlemagne's court and shows them to be crushed and overwhelmed by the majesty of their Western rival.[6] As Europe asserted its new, fragile independence, it set itself up aggressively against the Eastern Church and saw Byzantium as the natural enemy of the Western identity that was struggling to be born.

Charlemagne's empire and his achievements disintegrated after his death, and during the ninth and tenth centuries Europe experienced new invasions which halted her progress. The Vikings invaded from the north, the Magyars from the east and Muslim pirates raided in Italy and the south of France. But despite this distress, Europe never forgot Charlemagne; people looked back to him nostalgically as a symbol of Western dignity and independence. During the tenth century the Franks lost the leadership of Europe to the Germans, whom Charlemagne had conquered, and in 962 Otto I became the Holy Roman Emperor and initiated an exciting new renaissance of art and letters in his German empire. Yet again this was fiercely resented by the Byzantines, and there was a new hostility and contempt for the Western upstarts. The sensitivity on both sides is clear in the account Bishop Liudprand of Cremona wrote of his embassy to Byzantium on Otto's behalf six years after the imperial coronation. Liudprand had hitherto been a champion of Byzantium. He spoke fluent Greek and when he had made a previous embassy to Constantinople in 649 he had been at pains to explain Byzantine practice to Western people. But now that he went as Otto's envoy he got very different treatment and his account simmers with bitterness, anger and resentment. The climax came as he was leaving the country, when a customs official confiscated the purple silk that he was hoping to take home with him because, the official explained, the Emperor of Constantinople had decreed that the imperial purple could be worn only by the Byzantines, "who surpass other nations in wealth and wisdom." It was a great insult to Otto, the Emperor of the West, and Liudprand wrote furiously to him of his new hatred of the Byzantines:

> So you see, they judge all Italians, Saxons, Franks, Bavarians, Swabians—in fact all other nations—unworthy to go about clothed in this way. Is it not indecent and insulting that these soft, effeminate, long-sleeved, bejewelled and begowned liars, eunuchs and idlers should go about in purple, while our heroes, strong men trained to war, full of faith and charity, servants of God, filled with all the virtues, may not! If this is not an insult, what is?[7]

The Byzantines were seen as the antithesis of the Western identity. There was a new polarization at a time when the West was making a new attempt to revive the old glories of the Roman Empire, and as Europe defined herself anew the Greeks became everything that the Westerners were not. This stereotype of "the Greeks" persisted throughout the Middle Ages. Their elegance and refinement (which the Westerners in fact deeply envied and knew was quite beyond them) have been distorted into an image of weak effeminacy. This scurrilous portrait, as fictional as the ninth-century Cordovan portrait of "the Muslim," was a crooked mirror image of Western deep-rooted feelings of inferiority and a projection of Western envy. The Westerners for their part were already cultivating an image of tough aggression and presenting it as virtue. They were opposing their brute brawn to the Byzantines' brains. It was still not a case of a religious split between the two churches and both Greeks and Europeans would have found the very idea of a divided Christianity a shocking state of affairs, but there was an ever increasing tension between the two. From this point, as Europe really did begin to recover from the Dark Ages, this tension increased.

At about the same time as Otto was reviving the Holy Roman Empire in the West, the Church began an even more effective effort to reform the spirit of Europe. This reform started in the late tenth century in the Benedictine monastery of Cluny in Burgundy and in its many daughter houses. The Cluniac monks wanted to Christianize the people of Europe and educate them in the ways of true Christianity. There was always a difference between what the Cluniacs intended and what the laity understood, but the reform was very successful. Many of the most powerful and successful popes of the eleventh century were Cluniacs who helped to spread the ideals of the reform and made it official Church policy. Slowly Europeans became Christians in spirit as well as in name, but Christian in the spirit of Cluny. Pope Urban II was himself a Cluniac and his Crusade can be seen as one of the most dramatic results of the reform movement.

One of the ways in which they gave Europe a new Christian identity was their ambitious building project, whose achievements have been compared to the building of the Romans.[8] This is very impressive when we remember how poor Europe was at this time. Hundreds of churches were built throughout Christendom, even in quite small villages or settlements. These impressive stone buildings in the Roman style towered over the humble shacks of the people and could be seen for miles around, giving a unified appearance to Europe that suggested a unified Christian spirit and, perhaps, a revived Rome. Inside these churches the people heard Mass and were instructed in the faith. They learned important lessons in the Romanesque sculptures that depicted demons struggling with the soldiers of God. Life seemed to consist of an endless battle with the forces of evil and this reflected the spirit of the Benedictine monasteries, which had always seen themselves as fortresses, waging a holy war against the demons as the knights had fought against the Magyars, Muslims and Vikings who had invaded Europe. There was no thought of offering Christians reassuring or peaceful images, for life was still far too violent and dangerous in Europe and the churches were literally fortresses for the common people in time of war. During the eleventh century the invasions had ceased but there was a bitter and violent internecine feudal warfare. The knights were no longer the defenders of Christendom but, in the absence of an external foe, had turned against one another. During a battle, when the poor were caught between the armies of warring knights, they could barricade themselves in the church and find safety there. The Church was telling them very graphically that not only was she fighting a spiritual war on their behalf but she was also protecting them far more effectively than the knights, who had no concern for their welfare. The common people should look to the Church for help and guidance, not to the barons and their soldiers.

Yet though this building project was undoubtedly very important, the people still had a great deal to learn about the basic facts of the Christian life, and the Cluniacs sought to provide a more spiritual guidance and succor to the people than the purely physical sanctuary of the new churches. They believed, of course, that they were the only people in Europe who were living according to the spirit of the gospels, so naturally when they tried to Christianize the people of Europe they tried to teach them to live like monks. At first sight it seems that the Cluniacs in Europe were living very differently from the way Jesus and his disciples had lived in the land of Israel but the Cluniacs could argue their case effectively. Jesus had, for example, lived a celibate life and monks also lived lives of chastity. Part of the Cluniac reform was directed to enforcing celibacy on the secular clergy, who at this time were free to marry if they chose. The clergy put up a good deal of resistance, and it was not until 1215 that the Church was able to make celibacy obligatory for her priests. Again, Jesus had lived a poor life and the first Christians in Jerusalem had lived in community, holding all things in common, so poverty was considered an essential monastic virtue. It is true that the Cluniac monks lived more comfortably than most poor people at this time and that the Cluniac monasteries were rich and powerful establishments, far removed from that early community in Jerusalem. But at least the Benedictines possessed no personal property and they lived communal lives, with the monks sharing everything equally. A Benedictine monk also took a vow of stability, which meant that he promised to stay in one monastery for the whole of his life. Stability was an important value in the insecure world of the Middle Ages, where the primitive conditions made the whole of life seem fleeting and transient. In a world where agriculture was inadequate, people frequently died of starvation or malnutrition; beauty and health disintegrated very quickly; friends continually died and the community was very vulnerable to natural disasters like famines or floods. Life therefore seemed full of arbitrary change and disaster, which was seen not merely as the punishment for sin but also as the experience of sin itself, in rather the same way as exile was seen by the Jews. By contrast, the monks in their walled fortresses which enshrined the gospel values permanently[9] seemed already to enjoy something of the safety and stability of heaven. Ideally, people believed, everybody should be monks, but this was impossible. The Cluniacs therefore encouraged lay men and women to live like monks as far as they could.

How could this be done? One way was an attempt to regularize the sex lives of Western Christians. Tenth-century penitentials, guides for the priests about how to judge sins in confession, seemed to try to make married people as chaste as monks. Intercourse was forbidden during Lent and Advent, during menstruation, pregnancy and breast feeding, on ember days, on holy days, on Mondays, Wednesdays, Fridays and Sundays.[10] We have no idea whether the laity put these formidable requirements into practice and it seems likely that this attempt to make Europe chaste was resisted by the lay people as steadily as it was resisted by the clergy. A far more popular way of forming the monastic character was the penitential pilgrimage, which became an extremely important part of the Christian life in Europe during the eleventh century.

Christians had always made pilgrimages to their holy places, but in the ideology of the pilgrimage promoted by Cluny it was the journey, not the arrival, that counted. This holy journey would be a journey to a new Christian self because, while he or she was traveling to the shrine, the pilgrim would be living according to the ideals and practices of the monks. The journey to the shrine was therefore a kind of novitiate that formed and shaped the pilgrim and taught him what being a Christian really meant, according to the ideals of Cluny. At first sight, it might seem that nothing could be more different from life in a monastery. Instead of living a life of holy stability, the pilgrim was traveling from one place to another, exposed to the flux of the sinful world, so for the layman the religious life was essentially mobile. But in other respects the pilgrimage did mirror monastic ideals very accurately. Benedictine monasticism depended upon a conversion of life, whereby the monk turned his back on the sinful world and returned to God. Even when a monk was given to the monastery as a young child, he was expected to make that interior decision. Christ had said that nobody could be his disciple unless he was prepared to give up his family and friends and follow him to the ends of the earth, and to fulfill that command the monk made the exodus into the monastery. Similarly, the pilgrim literally turned his back on his old life for a time, leaving family, friends and everything with which he was familiar. In fact during the eleventh century spiritual writers frequently compared the pilgrim's decision to migrate to a new life to Abraham's migration from Ur to the Promised Land or to the Exodus of the Israelites from Egypt.[11] At the outset of his journey, a pilgrim made a vow to pray at the holy place and he donned special clothes at the altar, just as the monk did at the outset of his religious life when he made profession of vows. Like the monk, the pilgrim joined a community dedicated to monastic ideals, for during the eleventh century the pilgrimage became a communual devotion. During the pilgrimage a pilgrim was expected to lead a celibate life, like the monk. Because the journey was often a harsh one, the austerities imposed the practice of monastic asceticism on the pilgrims. If the pilgrim was a rich man, he laid aside the comforts that cushioned him from the sufferings of cold, fatigue and weariness that beset the poor. If he was a poor man, the pilgrim discovered that his poverty was not a shameful state but could have a spiritual value. During the pilgrimage rich and poor lived side by side in a community that, ideally, broke down the distinctions between them. Most importantly for our purposes, during the pilgrimage a pilgrim was forbidden to bear arms or to fight, just as the monk was. This holy journey became immensely popular during the eleventh century and it does seem to have changed the mentality of many European laymen. At the time of the First Crusade, many of the knights and poor people who answered the call to arms were imbued with these monastic ideals and lived fairly devout lives, whereas a hundred years earlier such ideals would have been entirely foreign to them.

But if the Cluniacs were more interested in the journey, for most of the laymen who took part in the pilgrimages it was the arrival that counted. The shrine or the holy place had been very important in the old Latin Christianity of late antiquity. During the fourth century, when Christianity had become the state religion, new churches and basilicas had been built to house the bodies of the martyrs. Christians had come from far and wide to pray at their tombs, because they believed that physical closeness to these friends of God brought them nearer to heaven itself. They believed that the bodies of the martyrs were still imbued with a holiness that was felt to manifest itself physically. When the stories of their martyrdom were read aloud at the tomb, a sweet smell seemed to fill the basilica and the sick and crippled people who had gathered there cried aloud in ecstasy as they felt the power of the saints enter their bodies so strongly that their ailments were healed.[12] This fourth-century devotion to the holy place continued after the barbarian invasions in the new Christian kingdoms and naturally blended with the common pagan belief that certain places were instinct with godhead. Most laymen in Europe felt that "holiness" was not a spiritual or moral state so much as a power that manifested itself physically like a holy radioactivity.[13] When the pilgrim finally entered the shrine at the end of his journey and prayed before relics of saints or at their tombs, he was exposing himself to a power that could kill a wicked man or heal a sick person. Relics were the most important element in the religious experience of Europe during the early Middle Ages. The establishment and the educated Cluniacs found this devotion highly dubious because it reduced religion to pagan magic but they could do nothing to change it. In the frightening world of the eleventh century, the relics gave to lay people some of the stability and security that the monks enjoyed. Because the relic was linked to a man or woman who was now in heaven, it was a tangible bond with the next world. When, therefore, pilgrims prayed at the tomb of St. Peter in Rome they felt an enormous safety in being so close to the man who opened the gates of heaven. People believed that the divine power was channeled to men through relics and so they were carried into battle, to help the army, and were used to bind oaths and treaties with the permanence of heaven.[14] The cult of the pilgrimage during the eleventh century necessarily also cultivated this devotion to the holy place, even though this had not been the original intention of the Cluniac reformers.

It follows that holiness was very local. A saint was only effective in the region where he had lived and died or in the place where he was buried. This is why people often stole the bodies of saints from a city; they wanted to appropriate this power for themselves. But the local character of holiness was problematic for Europeans because all the holiest shrines were obviously in the East, where Jesus had lived and died. This was why legends developed which maintained that after his death many of Jesus' friends had come to Europe and were buried there. St. Peter was firmly believed to have come to Rome, even though there is not a shred of evidence for this. Similarly Mary Magdalene was said to have settled in the south of France and Joseph of Arimathea was believed to have brought the faith to England and to have been buried at Glastonbury.[15] Above all St. James, who was called the brother of the Lord, was believed to have come to Spain and to be buried at Compostela. There was an ancient legend that said that James was Jesus' twin brother, so clearly having his body was the next best thing to having the body of Jesus himself. Compostela became the most holy place in Europe and during the eleventh century pilgrims traveled there in thousands to fill themselves with the holiness of St. James.[16] Along the main pilgrim routes the Cluniacs built churches which housed other relics where the pilgrims could pray during their long journey to Spain, which was the end of the known world.

But obviously there could be no more holy place than Jerusalem, where Jesus had died and risen again to save the world, and during the eleventh century there was a new passionate enthusiasm for Jerusalem and the Holy Land, which was seen by the lay people as the holiest relic of all because of its physical link with the Son of God. The very soil of the land was believed to be pregnant with divine power, because Jesus had walked on it during his life. The Holy Sepulchre Church, which was believed to house the site of Golgotha and which contained the tomb of Christ, was filled with the immense holiness of the events that had redeemed mankind.[17] More pilgrims than ever made the arduous and dangerous journey through Muslim territory to the Holy Land. In Europe more Christians than ever before made donations to the Holy Sepulchre Church and dedicated the churches they built to the Holy Sepulchre. One of the earliest of these churches was at Loches in the Loire Valley. It was built by Count Fulk of Anjou, who had made the pilgrimage to Jerusalem in 1009. When he had knelt to kiss the tomb of Christ he was said to have miraculously bitten off a chunk of stone. He had thus captured some of the holiness of Jerusalem for Europe, which he enshrined in his new Church of the Holy Sepulchre back home. This legend tells us two things. First, a desperation had entered the European devotion to the Holy Sepulchre. More and more Western people felt acutely deprived of the holiness of the East.[18] The story is an excellent example of the literal-mindedness of Western Christianity and its obsession with the holiness of the physical relics of Jesus and the saints. This frantic and irrational love of the Holy Land was quite alien to the piety of the Byzantines, who found it typical of the primitive religion of the Western Christians. Second, Fulk's descendants would become very important Crusaders and in the twelfth century another Fulk of Anjou became King of Jerusalem. A passionate devotion to Jerusalem was one of the results of the Cluniac cult of the pilgrimage and was central to crusading. Though Urban II would have dismissed Count Fulk's passion for Jerusalem as superstitious and excessive, he did call the Crusade a pilgrimage and Crusaders would always call themselves pilgrims. In fact the word "Crusade" did not become common until very late in the crusading movement.

But the pilgrimage was not the only element in crusading nor was it the only way the Church managed to transform the Western soul during the eleventh century. Before any real progress could be made in Europe it was essential that the internecine feudal warfare that was tearing society apart come to an end. The two centuries of invasion had militarized Europe and the knightly aristocracy had become extremely important as a defensive force. They had formed their identity on violence and warfare, which they saw as a glorious activity. But after the invasions ceased and there were no more legitimate external enemies, the system of defense that had evolved collapsed and turned in upon itself. Knights and barons started to fight each other. The country was devastated and property and crops vandalized. To counteract this the Church initiated a peace movement which was called the Peace of God. This began in the south of France at the end of the tenth century. Crowds of priests, knights and poor people gathered in huge "councils" and proclaimed a peace which they called the Truce of God. During this Truce all fighting was forbidden for a definite period and a group of knights volunteered to police the Truce and fight any of the knights and barons who broke it. All swore to keep the Truce in the presence of the relics, and the emotion at these gatherings was intense. They were similar to modern revivalist meetings and the people would cry, "Peace! Peace!" as they begged God to send them peace in their time. Slowly the movement spread and began to form public opinion. War and violence were depicted as unchristian and the common people felt that their hatred of the violent knights was justified. The knights themselves were taught that to fight other Christians was deeply sinful. During the Truce a knight adopted monastic practices, just as he might do if he went on a pilgrimage. He did not bear arms and did not fight, like a monk. To some degree he also lived a life of holy poverty during the Truce. The poor could not carry arms to defend themselves because they simply could not afford the very expensive equipment that made the knights a formidable fighting force. This made them frighteningly vulnerable and, by sharing this vulnerability for a time, the knights became poor men, as it were, and shared some of their problems.[19]

In the year 1033 there was a widespread famine, and an apocalyptic terror spread throughout Europe. As the Burgundian annalist Raoul Glaber wrote: "Men believed that the orderly procession of the seasons and the laws of nature, which until then had ruled the world, had relapsed into eternal chaos; and they feared that mankind might end."[20] They believed that God was about to destroy the world because of their sins, just as he had destroyed the world by flood in the time of Noah. The apocalyptic fear may have been enhanced by the fact that people believed that it was exactly a thousand years since the Crucifixion of Christ. To stave off this catastrophe the lay folk and the clergy marched in huge penitential processions, begging God for forgiveness, and this new terror entered the Peace of God, which suddenly spread that year all over France. At the Peace Councils, there was a new desperation. When they cried, "Peace! Peace!" people were no longer simply asking for an end of war. They were asking God to send a new and better world, free from plague, famine and flood. Glaber tells us that the peace movement now raised enormous hopes, which the Cluniacs and the establishment Church had not intended. The people now felt that they could change history and exercise some control over their own destiny. It was a pathetic glimmering of the concept of self-determination and, when the peace movement seemed to have failed them, Glaber says that thousands of people took a different and desperate course. First the peasants, then the more established classes of society and finally the rich nobles began to march in vast companies to Jerusalem in a mass pilgrimage: "An innumerable multitude began to stream towards the Saviour's Tomb in Jerusalem," says Glaber and was convinced that this meant a new apocalypse.[21] "This vast crowd of people in the Holy City, of which no other century had seen the like, presaged nothing else than the coming of the miserable Antichrist, which must indicate the coming end of the world." These pilgrims seemed to have believed that if they congregated in Jerusalem in large enough numbers Antichrist would have to come and fight them and the battle with Antichrist would bring about the Last Days and the final redemption.[22] God would send down a New Jerusalem, which meant a new and better world. The pilgrims, therefore, were trying to force God to save them by acting themselves, and this will prove to be a crucial element in the holy war.

As in any time of stress, there was a great deal of apocalyptic fervor during the eleventh century. In about the year 1000 an old myth revived that would prove to be very important during the Crusades. The old Sibylline prophets of the late Roman period had said that, before the end of the world, an Emperor from the West would be crowned in Jerusalem and would fight Antichrist there,[23] and people began to look around for an emperor who would fulfill this mission. There was a new feeling of purposefulness. Instead of waiting to be wiped out by another famine or pestilence, people were beginning to feel that they should try to save themselves by fulfilling these ancient prophecies. It was an initiative for self-determination. Thirty years after the great pilgrimage to Jerusalem in 1033, there was another massive exodus from Europe, when 7000 pilgrims left Europe for the Holy Land, probably with the same apocalyptic desire to force Antichrist to declare himself. When Pope Urban made his famous crusading speech in 1095 it was almost thirty years later and time for another such pilgrimage. When people heard that the Pope had urged the knights of Europe to march to liberate Jerusalem, many of them were probably inspired to join the Crusade in order to save the world and bring down the New Jerusalem. Urban himself, of course, would have had no truck with this kind of thinking, but he was unable to control the movement he started, for Jerusalem had been acquiring such rich and complex associations during the eleventh century.

But after the terrors of the first half of the century, the quality of life in Europe began to improve dramatically. There was an agricultural revolution and people felt that they had greater control over their circumstances. There was a new confidence in the air, which toward the end of the century began to express itself aggressively. Instead of cowering passively in land that they could not cultivate properly, Europe started to expand. The Normans had long challenged Roman and Byzantine power in the south of Italy, and in 1061 Count Roger invaded the Muslim stronghold of Sicily and eventually conquered it for Christendom in 1091. In 1066 William of Normandy invaded the Anglo-Saxon kingdom of Britain and in 1085 Spanish Christians, with the help of Frankish knights, managed to conquer Toledo from the Muslims and pushed back the borders of al-Andalus. Although she was against war officially, the Church was still anxious to harness this useful aggression and make it Christian. For many years monks had been encouraged to build monasteries in the no-man's-land on the borders of Christendom and to push against the darkness of paganism and Islam that lurked outside the realm of Christ. Now that the knights were beginning to conquer the Muslims and push forward the frontiers of Christendom even more dramatically, the popes were anxious to keep control of the newly confident laymen.

Yet this involved an obvious inconsistency. Christianity had always been against violence and in the Peace of God the Cluniac reformers had been encouraging the people to see war as unchristian and to hate the knights. How could the Church now bless these new wars of aggression, as in fact she did? But for many years the popes had been preaching a double message. Some of the reformers had wisely felt that to antagonize the knights was foolish. In the Peace of God, knights had policed the Truce by means of violence, which in the interests of peace the Church had been prepared to sanction. In France and Italy other Cluniac reformers began to try to reform the institution of knighthood itself. Instead of harrying the poor and helpless, they taught that the Christian knight should come to the defense of the poor and needy and fulfill a Christian vocation. Other churchmen went further. They encouraged the knights in their diocese to form a militia to defend the local Church and the Christian populace in time of war. One of these bishops was the Bishop of Toul, who became Pope Leo IX in 1049. Two months after his consecration he formed a Roman militia to fight the Normans who were threatening to invade his lands, and in 1053 he actually led his troops into battle himself.[24] Some of his contemporaries felt that this was too extreme, but the popes continued to encourage these ecclesiastical companies. Twenty years later the Cluniac Pope Gregory VII invited the laymen of the whole of Europe to form a militia which he called the Knights of St. Peter, bound to the Pope as its head and dedicated to the defense of the Church. In 1071 and 1074, in response to Turkish victories against Byzantium, Gregory called upon the Knights of St. Peter to march to the East and liberate the Greeks from the infidels. Anybody who died on this expedition would gain an "eternal reward," so that this would be a meritorious war, not sinful violence. Once the knights had conquered the Turks in Asia Minor they would march on to Palestine and liberate Jerusalem. Gregory promised to lead the militia himself.[25] There was very little difference between Gregory's proposals and Urban's Crusade, but during the 1070s nothing came of Gregory's project. Very few knights actually joined the Knights of St. Peter and so there were no Crusades to the East. But when Urban made his appeal to the knights of Europe twenty years later, many of the Cluniac ideas had taken effect in a new way and there were other enthusiasms linked with the pilgrimage to Jerusalem as well.

The Church was, therefore, preaching a very confused message, and many of the knights were perplexed about their careers. Warfare was their life but they also wanted a Christian vocation. Tancred, one of the leaders of the First Crusade, was particularly worried, as his biographer Ralph of Caen recorded:

> Frequently he burned with anxiety because the warfare he engaged in as a knight seemed to be contrary to the Lord's commands. The Lord, in fact, ordered him to offer the cheek that had been struck together with his other cheek to the striker; but secular knighthood did not spare the blood of relatives. The Lord urged him to give his tunic and his cloak as well to the man who would take them away; the needs of war impelled him to take from a man already despoiled of both whatever remained to him. And so, if ever that wise man could give himself up to repose, these contradictions deprived him of courage.[26]

Tancred was obviously not convinced about the Cluniac vision of a reformed Christian knighthood, for he did not see it as the answer to the basic dilemma of Christian warfare. Other knights found their own solutions to the problem in their search for a new identity. Toward the end of the eleventh century the Franks in particular were seeking a new identity and a new Christian vocation. They wanted to regain the leadership of Europe and build themselves anew, and as was natural they looked back to their past. But unlike the Anglo-Saxons or the Germans, who recalled their heroic pagan past in songs and poems, the Franks looked back no further than Charlemagne. In this respect, they had absorbed the message of Cluny: they wanted to be a Christian people, but they were also a warlike and violent people and they needed an aggressive religion.[27] In their search for a solution, they rewrote the history of Charlemagne, that great Christian warrior, to make him relevant to the very different world of the eleventh century. In an age which was passionately attached to Jerusalem, it was important that the founder of the Frankish dynasty should himself have a physical bond with the Holy City, so a new story developed that Charlemagne had made a pilgrimage to Jerusalem in the eighth century. Then Frankish poets and minstrels started to compose the *chansons de geste*, the songs of deeds, to celebrate the holy wars of Charlemagne, and again they made an important innovation. Charlemagne had considered his wars against the Saxons to be holy wars, because they had brought the Germans into the Church. But although he had fought in Spain, these were certainly not holy wars. He had merely gone to help one Muslim leader against another. Yet in the *chansons de geste* Charlemagne's Spanish wars became holy wars, because they provided the Franks with an enemy that could be attacked with impunity.

The creation of an enemy is very important as a foil to a developing new identity. The Muslims or Saracens provided a perfect "enemy," even though it is quite clear that at this point the Franks had nothing personally against the Muslims and knew nothing at all about the religion of Islam. First, they knew that the Saracens of Spain were not Christians. This meant that they must be "pagans" and the *chansons* ludicrously present the Muslims worshiping idols of Mohammad and Apollo. In the Bible, the crime of idolatry had justified Joshua's very savage holy wars and the poets of the *chansons* imagine Charlemagne and his Franks slaughtering Muslims with a real Israelite zeal. Fighting pagans was seen as a Christian duty, therefore: "Never to paynims may I show love or peace," Charlemagne says at the end of *The Song of Roland*.[28] But these "paynims" are not inhuman monsters. The second thing that the Franks needed from their enemy was that he should be a brilliant soldier. The Muslims were known for their military prowess, for their vast empire and advanced civilization. To conquer the Muslims would greatly enhance the reputation of the Franks. Thus in the *chansons* the Muslims are often sympathetically imagined. They are brave soldiers, "worthy and renowned." Their only fault is that they are not Christians: "Were he but Christian, right knightly he'd appear!"[29]

In the character of Roland we see the developing ideal of the new Frank. At the end of Charlemagne's campaign in Spain in 778, the Franks had been crossing the Pyrenees on their homeward march and the rear guard had been separated from the main army. It was ambushed and massacred at Roncesvalles by an army of Basques. Among the slain was Roland, Duke of the Marches and Brittany and the hero of the famous *Song of Roland*. In the poem, his history has been completely transformed, for the people who attack him are Muslims, not Basques. In Roland we see the kind of Christian the Franks wanted to become. He has extraordinary physical courage and massive strength, is very aggressive but not particularly intelligent. The Franks did not want to be wise or intellectual Christians; they saw themselves as men of action above all. In the poem, the rear guard could have been saved if Roland had blown his horn to summon Charlemagne and the main army, but Roland steadfastly refuses to do so. His friend Oliver begs him to blow the horn, and, as they watch their men being slaughtered, Oliver bitterly tells Roland that this carnage is all his fault. He is undeniably right and Roland's refusal to call for help is in fact a suicidal stupidity and irresponsibility. But the poet is on Roland's side: "Roland is fierce and Oliver is wise,"[30] he says and makes it clear that Oliver's common sense is not quite the thing. Roland's most valued possession is his sword Durendal, and when he dies he bids farewell to Durendal before he commends his soul to God. He describes the relics on the hilt, which have made it a weapon of supernatural power: holiness has been put to the service of war.[31] With Durendal Roland had killed hundreds of Muslims, and the poet dwells on this slaughter in delighted but gruesome detail. Yet by means of this violence Roland had hacked his way into heaven, and during the Middle Ages he was venerated as a saint and martyr. At a time when the Byzantines still refused communion to a soldier during a campaign because of the blood he had been forced to shed in battle, Western Christians had taken the old cult of aggressive, suicidal martyrdom to its logical conclusion.

When Urban II summoned the First Crusade he was said to have addressed his appeal particularly to the Franks: in one version of his speech, Urban is made to call them "a race chosen and beloved of God" and tells them to look back to Charlemagne for inspiration.[32] But Urban's ideal of the Crusade would be very different from the holy war of the *chansons de geste*. The ideal of "liberation" had been

very important in the Cluniac reform but it was a very specialized
form of freedom: it meant "freedom from secular control and freedom
under the pope." It was, therefore, synonymous with the expansion
of the power of the Western Church. Urban had already spoken about
"wars of liberation" which had extended the power of the Church into
Muslim territory in Spain and Sicily.[33] In 1089 he suggested that
anyone who wanted to make a penitential pilgrimage to Jerusalem
should commute this into a period of work for the Spanish Wars of
Reconquest.[34] He had already linked the idea of a pilgrimage to Jerusalem, therefore, with a holy war of liberation which would push
back the frontiers of the infidel and extend the power of the Roman
Church. Early in the year 1095 a new opportunity presented itself
which would enable him to link these ideas far more dramatically. The
Emperor Alexius Comnenus I of Byzantium asked Urban for military
help against the Muslim Turks.

Some twenty years earlier, the Seljuk Turks, a barbarian people who
had converted to Islam, had poured into Asia Minor, which was part
of the Byzantine Empire, and had seized a great deal of Christian
territory. Since that time the power of the Turks had waned and their
empire had been torn apart by internal quarreling and dissension
among the emirs and princes. Alexius had been making good progress
in both war and a clever diplomacy, which played one Muslim leader
off against another. A few vigorous campaigns might finish the Turks
completely, but he simply did not have enough soldiers and he appealed to the Pope for help. Clearly it was a project after Urban's
liberating heart. It would certainly expand the power of the Western
Church dramatically, even though Alexius insisted that all lands conquered by Western soldiers should be returned to him. There had
been a serious and official breach in the relations between the Eastern
and Western Churches ever since a dispute about the nature of papal
power in 1054, and Urban saw this request for military aid as a chance
to extend the power of the papal Church more firmly in Byzantium,
which had for so long had insufficient respect for the rising Western
Church. It should also make for better relations between Rome and
Constantinople. He agreed that he would encourage the knights of
Europe to take an army of soldiers to the East, and when in November
1095 he spoke at the Council of Clermont, a council of the Peace of
God movement, he summoned the First Crusade.

We have no contemporary account of Urban's speech, but it seemed
that he began by calling for the Truce of God. Then he called upon
the knights of Europe to stop fighting one another and to band together against the Turks in a twofold war of liberation. First they

should liberate the Christians of Asia Minor from the Turks; then they should march on to Jerusalem to liberate the Holy Land. There would be the Peace of God in the West and the War of God against Islam in the East—a perfect solution to the problems of Europe! Urban seems to have called this expedition a pilgrimage, not simply because of the destination of Jerusalem, but because a large collective pilgrimage was the only model adequate for the massive offensive he had envisaged. The small feudal armies of Europe traveling only short distances could not compare with an army of thousands of Christian soldiers traveling three thousand miles to the Holy Land. Certainly Urban saw it as a Cluniac pilgrimage, on which the soldiers would live like monks. He used the words of Jesus which had hitherto summoned monks into the cloister: "Everyone who has left houses, brothers, sisters, father, mother or land for the sake of my name will be repaid a hundred times over" (Matthew 19:29).[35] He also seems to have reminded them that Christ had urged the Christians to be ready to die for his sake, as a Crusader would have to do. The Crusade would therefore demand a conversion of life and would be a dramatic journey to a new self. But hitherto the pilgrim had always been forbidden to bear arms during his pilgrimage. By giving these "pilgrims" to Jerusalem a sword, Urban had made violence central to the religious experience of the Christian layman and Western Christianity had acquired an aggression that it never entirely lost.

As soon as Urban had finished speaking, there was an explosion of enthusiasm and the crowd shouted with one voice "*Deus hoc vult* [god wills this]!"[36] Yet this apparent unanimity was deceptive because the people seem to have had very confused and different views of the Crusade. Not all the laymen would have understood Urban's sophisticated Cluniac view of the Crusade. Some of the Franks would see it in the light of the *chansons de geste*, others would see it as an apocalyptic pilgrimage for a better world. Others certainly brought secular feudal ideas to the Crusade and saw themselves as fighting for the land of Christ their Lord just as they were bound to fight for the rights of their lord in Europe. Others would see it as a duty to fight for their fellow Christians who had been conquered by the Turks, just as knights were bound to come to the aid of their kinsfolk in a vendetta. One of the very early medieval historians of the Crusades makes a priest ask his listeners during a crusading sermon: "If an outsider were to strike any of your kin down would you not avenge your blood relative? How much more ought you to avenge your God, your father, your brother, whom you see reproached, banished from his estates, crucified; whom you hear calling for aid."[37] All these other lay ideas were very far from Pope Urban's vision of the Crusade, but the idea of a war for the Holy Land had unlocked a powerful complex of passions which he would not be able to control once the laymen responded to his call. This would lead the Crusaders to actions that horrified the Pope.

He had advised the knights to wait until after the harvests of 1096 so that the armies could be properly provisioned, but thousands of Crusaders were too impatient. Popular preachers spread the news of the Crusade, bringing non-Cluniac and popular motivation to the fore, and thousands of lay men and women volunteered to join their armies. The most famous of these preachers was the extremely charismatic Peter the Hermit, who inspired respect from people of all classes of society. "Whatever he did or said it seemed like something half divine," wrote the sophisticated monk–historian Guibert of Nogent, who knew him personally.[38] Peter wandered through France, attracting followers from all classes of society. Wherever he preached, his listeners were spellbound and reduced to tears, even when he reached Germany where nobody could understand a word he said. In Germany, two priests, Folkmar and Gottschalk, also stirred up some enthusiasm and in Germany, too, Count Emich of Leiningen, a robber baron with a reputation for cruelty, proclaimed that he was the Last Emperor of apocalyptic myth, and began to gather an army, which joined up with other crusading armies from England and Flanders.

In March Peter the Hermit led eastward a band of about 10,000 nobles, knights and foot soldiers, which was accompanied by a large crowd of pilgrims. At the same time Walter Sansavoir of Poissy, a French nobleman, led an army of about the same size consisting entirely of foot soldiers. Shortly afterward Emich set out with his huge army of 20,000 men, and two other armies led by Folkmar and Gottschalk started their journey through Eastern Europe toward Constantinople. Pope Urban was still preaching the Cross in France, while these armies began their journey, and five more armies were making their preparations at home, but it seems likely that these first Crusaders considered themselves an advance guard of the whole Crusade, not separate from their fellow Crusaders who would leave Europe in the autumn. Walter Sansavoir's beautifully disciplined troops marched straight through Eastern Europe and arrived in Constantinople in late July. The other Crusaders were not so fortunate. Because they were not adequately provisioned, these vast bands depended on local gifts of food. If this was not available, they had to resort to plunder and raiding. The people of the countries through which they were marching could scarcely provide enough food for their own population, let alone feed these thousands of soldiers and pilgrims. Fighting inevitably broke out and at the end of June, Folkmar's army was destroyed at Nitra in Hungary by the angry Hungarians and very shortly afterward Gottschalk's army was forced to surrender to the Hungarians at Pannonhalma. The Hungarians were so incensed by the Crusaders that they would not even allow Emich's army to enter their country. Emich's Crusaders tried to force their way in and they besieged the city of Weisenberg for six weeks. But they could make no headway and were at last forced to disband and return home in ignominy. Peter the Hermit's army was more successful but suffered greatly during the journey. At Nish, in Byzantium, fighting had broken out in the markets where the Crusaders were trying to buy food and the army was badly mauled, but the survivors managed to reach Constantinople at the beginning of August. The Emperor Alexius, who had asked Urban for a conventional army, gazed at these huge masses of Crusaders and pilgrims with horror and swiftly conveyed them out over the Bosphorus and into Asia Minor. There, however, there was more looting because of famine and because discipline broke down in this alien country. Later in August nearly all Peter's and Walter's troops and pilgrims were massacred by the Turks.

The chroniclers did not approve of these first Crusaders and either omitted all mention of them in their account of the First Crusade or dismissed them as a mob of fanatics and peasants. It is very important for a holy war to be successful and the disastrous failure of these first Crusades called the whole movement into question. If a crusading army was the will of God, how could it fail? This terrible defeat at the hands of the Eastern Europeans and the infidels in Turkey was not the prestigious victory that the West was looking for. The Crusaders were disowned and a popular legend of a "Peasants' Crusade" grew up, quite at variance with the facts;[39] that these Crusaders were all fanatical peasants and that, while the barons and knights made their sensible preparations for the official Crusade, crowds of peasants simply wandered off to the East in a haphazard fashion, crazed by wild dreams of apocalypse and the New Jerusalem. Yet to dismiss these Crusaders simply because they failed is not entirely just. Providing food for the armies would be a major and frequently insoluble problem in the story of the Crusades. As many people would die of malnutrition during the journey as died in battle. The Crusaders who followed in the autumn benefited by their example and were careful to stop any plundering and raiding which would provoke the inhabitants of Eastern Europe. Later Crusaders would forget this lesson and meet with the same tragic fate as befell the first Crusaders in Turkey. In one sense the arrival of Walter and Peter was a great achievement. It was the first united and cooperative act of the new Europe and, for that time, a feat of organization and dedication. It showed that the West was now ready to organize itself and act as a united whole to change history.

In another sense, however, the *legend* of the "Peasants' Crusade" has an important message. Peter's army included some very important lords indeed and yet it was prepared to accept an impoverished hermit as its leader. We do not know much about Gottschalk and Folkmar, but they were not likely to have been rich, and Walter Sansavoir's name clearly indicates his impecunious material status. Crusading was from the start seen as a poor man's movement. Peter the Hermit survived the tragedy in Turkey, joined the First Crusade at Constantinople and became a very important leader of that campaign with a special responsibility for the poor. During the First Crusade the poor would be very important and would be able to influence policy dramatically—I will explain this more fully in Chapter 4. Crusading gave to the poor of Europe their first means of self-expression and their first practical power. It had sprung from monasticism, the pilgrimage and the Peace of God, which had all asserted the value of holy poverty. Even though Urban certainly had no thoughts of including the poor in his Crusade, he had spoken from within the framework of Cluniac movements, which did include and foster the poor, so it was natural and inevitable that the poor would respond. In the popular mind, the Crusade would be the invention of Peter the Hermit, not Pope Urban.[40]

Despite their failure, these first armies of the Cross were the first sign of the expansion of the new West. These ambitious expeditions showed dramatically that the Western world now felt ready to enter the international scene once again. We have seen that Islam rooted the monotheistic religion of the Jews and Christians into Arab pagan traditions and that this unleashed such reserves of energy and confidence in the Muslim Arabs of the backwater of the Hejaz that they found a new identity and became a great world power. A similar process in Europe before the first Crusaders left for the Middle East was creating a new Western identity by rooting the same old monotheistic religion into the distinctive chivalric and pagan traditions of the Christians of Europe. This process, as we shall see, unlocked new reserves of power. The Middle Ages founded the Western spirit and bequeathed to us many of our major preoccupations, passions and prejudices, for good and for ill. We shall see that crusading was not an eccentric hobby of a minority but that it was central to the building of this new Christian identity, touching the new Western institutions in fundamental ways. In the period of the Crusades, the West found its essential soul and would soon become a great world power, would discover a new world and conquer a major part of the globe. If we look at crusading from the point of view of the West, it can seem a positive and glamorous activity, but looked at from the viewpoint of its victims, we see the shadow side of the confident, thrusting Western spirit.

One of the passions that crusading would bequeath to the Western world was a long and shameful tradition of hatred for the Jewish people, and it is here that we begin to find a link between the medieval and modern struggle in the Middle East. The Jews were considered to be the enemies of our society and of all that was sacred to it. The consequences of this history of irrational prejudice have been seen catastrophically in our own century, and Hitler's attempted destruction of the Jewish people was fueled by many submerged crusading myths, as I shall discuss in later chapters. At the beginning of their journey to the East toward a new self, rooted in the birthplace of their faith, the Crusaders slaughtered the Jewish communities of France and Germany in the first pogroms of Europe.

This had certainly not been part of Urban's original intention when he summoned the First Crusade. It is important to be clear that at *this* point the Church was horrified by such blatant persecution of Jews. The official Christian tradition concerning the Jews was that they were undoubtedly a wicked people who had lost their holy vocation because they had crucified Christ. They should be shunned by Christians and must accept an inferior position in Christendom. They were condemned to eternal servitude *but* their lives were to be spared. This was the view of the popes and most bishops in the eleventh century: during the Crusaders' pogroms, the bishops in Germany actually tried to protect the Jews, giving them sanctuary in their churches and palaces to protect them from the mobs of Crusaders, who burned the scrolls of the Torah, tore down synagogues and threatened Jewish men, women or children with a terrible choice: baptism or death. Professor Jonathan Riley-Smith has suggested that the reason why these first Crusaders were disowned by the Church and why churchmen and historians propagated the myth of the "Peasants' Crusade" was shame and embarrassment about these pogroms.[41] The Church continued to oppose the forced conversion of the Jews and violent persecution, and its official teaching was confirmed and enshrined in the thirteenth century in the *Summa Theologica* of Thomas Aquinas. It was not until the sixteenth century that popes supported pogroms against the Jews of Europe. But official Church condemnation of the pogroms was useless. Urban could not control the Crusade he had summoned, which developed its own remorseless dynamic. There was the usual gap between what the Church intended and what the people understood.

Why then did the Crusaders attack the Jews? They had taken the Cross and vowed to fight Muslims, who were a very shadowy reality to them. They were fired by their own visions of glory rather than by a blind hatred of Islam. By the time they had reached their goal, their attitude to Muslims would change drastically, as I shall show in Chapter 4. But the first enemy that the Crusaders created, as a foil to their own new and glorious identity, were the Jews beside whom they had lived in relative harmony for generations.[42] There had always been sporadic violence against Jewish communities in the Gentile world. The Jews lived apart in their own quarters and with a clearly defined foreign identity and so incurred the distrust and fear that are often inspired by an out-group. But there had never been mass organized attacks which were a concerted effort on the part of society. Indeed the Jews in Germany felt quite at home there, so much so that, when they established their cemetery in Worms during the eleventh century, the graves did not face Jerusalem in the normal Jewish manner. They had developed their own rich and unique Jewish tradition, which was widely respected throughout the diaspora and which had produced great scholars who are still studied by Jews as major authorities today. They were already called "Ashkenazim," which may have been a corruption of "Allemagne." They themselves referred to German Jewry as SHUM, after three of the Rhine cities where they had communities: Speyer, Worms and Mainz. They enjoyed good and profitable relations with their Christian neighbors. All this changed forever in the spring of 1096 when the Crusaders decimated SHUM; after this date Jews would never be wholly safe in Europe again.

The only thing we know for certain about the content of Peter the Hermit's sermons was that it was anti-Semitic, because in March 1096 his large army of Crusaders attacked the Jewish communities of France and Lorraine. There are no eyewitness accounts of these first pogroms, but it seems that the Jews were not simply massacred. They were given the choice of baptism and many chose death rather than deny their own religion, without which life was meaningless. We have seen that Peter's vision of the Crusade was quite different from Urban's and that he rather than the Pope was seen as the inspiration of crusading in the popular mind. It seemed frankly illogical to most of the Crusaders to march thousands of miles to fight Muslims in the Middle

East, about whom they knew very little, when the people who had actually killed Christ—or so they believed—were alive and well on their very doorsteps. They said to one another:

> Look now, we are going to seek out our profanity and to take vengeance on the Ishmaelites for our Messiah, when here are the Jews who murdered and crucified him. Let us first avenge ourselves on them and exterminate them from among the nations so that the name of Israel will no longer be remembered or let them adopt our faith.[43]

This account comes from the eyewitness account of a German Jew. The French Jewish communities sent messages to SHUM, warning them of the approaching danger as Peter's Crusaders marched eastward, leaving desolation in their wake. But the German Jews simply could not believe that anything would happen to them, because they felt so established along the Rhine. In our own century, German Jews were equally confident that Hitler would not attack them, and, like their eleventh-century ancestors, they were proved disastrously wrong. When the leaders of SHUM heard the horrifying tales of the Crusaders' pogroms in Lorraine, they wrote back to the French Jews:

> All the communities have decreed a fastday. We have done our duty. May the Omnipresent One save us and you from all the trouble and affliction. We are greatly concerned about your well-being. As for ourselves, there is no great cause for fear. We have not heard a word about such matters, nor has it been hinted that our lives are threatened by the sword.[44]

In the event, when Peter and his army arrived in German territory, they agreed to spare the Jews and Peter promised to speak kindly of Israel there in return for money and provisions.[45] But the scourge of SHUM was a German Crusader, whose motivation looks forward to future German crusading myths that have a terrible resonance for us today.

Count Emich of Leiningen persecuted the German Jews of SHUM for quite different reasons. He believed that he had a special, apocalyptic and imperial destiny. He was that mythical Last Emperor foretold by ancient prophecy.[46] He would fight Antichrist in Jerusalem and be crowned there and his reign would last for a thousand years. These dreams of imperial glory and of a thousand-year Reich continued to haunt German Crusaders and, as I shall show in Chapter 11, became absorbed into popular mythology long after Crusaders stopped marching to the Holy Land. Ever since Charlemagne had dragged Germany into his Christian empire at sword point, the Germans had been obsessed with visions of empire and massive political dreams of world conquest. This myth of the Last Emperor gave Emich a special view of the Jews. St. Paul had said that before the Second Coming of Christ all the Jews would be converted to Christianity,[47] so, as Emich marched east to bring about the Last Days he proceeded to make sure that Paul's prophecy was fulfilled. In May and June of 1096 he systematically attacked all the Jewish communities in Speyer, Worms, Mainz, Regensburg, Cologne, Trier and Metz. His massive army must have looked like the terrifying armies of the apocalypse. The Jews were given the option of baptism or death. A few submitted to baptism but most chose death. Fathers killed their wives and children rather than allow them to abandon the precious faith of their fathers. In each community, synagogues and Torah scrolls were destroyed so that all visible signs of Jewry were erased before Emich marched east toward what he firmly believed would be a glorious destiny and a major step in the salvation of the world. Jews as Jews could have no part in these glorious events: they had to be destroyed in order to bring about Western dreams of fulfillment and world conquest.

The Crusaders had turned Urban's sophisticated Cluniac war of liberation into a vendetta: they hounded the Jews as they would have hounded any other people who had killed their feudal lord. They believed that they were avenging the death of Christ, their lord, and that they were marching east to recover the Holy Land, which was his fief, his patrimony. Their aggressive religion was rooted firmly in their old chivalric traditions. Despite the Church's disapproval, hatred of the Jews continued to be an essential element in crusading. Every time a Crusade was preached there was a fresh outbreak of pogroms. Sometimes people who could not go to the East felt that they were taking part in the expedition by killing Jews at home. The Crusades were the first cooperative and collective act of the new Europe in their struggle for a new soul, and the first thing that the Crusaders did, whenever they set out in one of these massive, international expeditions, was to kill Jews. The Crusades made anti-Semitism an incurable Western disease, which persisted long after the Middle Ages, as I shall show in Chapter 11. The only change in this terrible tradition was to greater intransigence: the Jews of SHUM could have saved themselves in 1096 by becoming Christians, but Hitler sought to kill all the Jews, whatever their religious beliefs. He could not have done this had not Christians in Europe become accustomed to seeing Jews as absolute enemies in a tradition that had lasted for nearly a thousand years.

It should be clear how Crusading is directly linked to the conflict in the Middle East today. At the beginning of their journey to a new identity, the Crusaders slaughtered Jews; at the end of their long and frightening campaign, they massacred the Muslim community in Jerusalem with appalling savagery, as I shall show in Chapter 4. Hatred of Jews and Muslims had been planted deeply in the Western identity. Had there been no European anti-Semitism, it is most unlikely that there would be a Jewish state in the Middle East today. The Arabs and the non-Arab Muslim people of the Middle East encountered the new West for the first time during the Crusades. They now see the Crusades as the start of a long history of Western aggression against the Islamic world of the Middle East. Before the Crusades, Jews and Christians had lived together in Europe in reasonable harmony and Muslims had been vague and exotic figments of the Western imagination, not real live enemies whom it was a duty to slaughter. Since the Crusades such peaceful coexistence has been impossible and the long history of tragic violence between the people of the three faiths began in a vicious Western initiative. It will be one of the arguments of this book that it is not enough to condemn the behavior of either the Israelis or the Arabs in today's conflict; the West must also bear a good deal of responsibility for what has happened.

As yet crusading had not achieved a clear ideology. It was a mixture of popular, monastic and secular motives. It would take three years and the experience of the First Crusade to imbue the Crusaders with the spirit of Joshua, and the Crusade would not become a true holy war, according to the old paradigm, until 1099. I will now, therefore, leave the story of the First Crusaders, who were preparing for their expedition during the first armies' disastrous march to the East and who would not leave Europe until the autumn of 1096. Their story will continue in the second half of this book, which discusses the holy wars of the Middle Ages and today. I now want to look at the origins of the modern conflict, which began as a deliberately secular struggle. There was, on both sides, a search for a new identity that differed from the ideology of the Crusaders because it was not religious but, in some cases, a defiant rejection of religion. Yet in all these secular ideologies that sought to build new selves, Arabs and Jews were still inspired by passions that were not wholly rational but which were fired by old religious myths. Ultimately, and tragically, the conflict would lead to a revival of the old habit of the holy war.

# The Present Conflict
## Jews and Arabs
## Seek a New Secular Identity

### THE JEWS

On May 14, 1948, in the Tel Aviv Museum, David Ben-Gurion held the ceremony of the proclamation of the state of Israel. It was the end of a long struggle by dedicated Jews to give their people a new home and a new identity. Instead of being despised aliens in the diaspora, threatened with persecution and extermination, they wanted the Jews to be proud and strong. They would shake off the weakness of their exile and create a new type of society in the land of their fathers which would be an example to the rest of the world. The new Jewish state had the backing of the United Nations, and within the next few days its right to exist was acknowledged formally by the United States and the Soviet Union. The surrounding Arab states, however, refused to grant a similar recognition. They argued that for over a thousand years Arabs had lived in Palestine and that the great powers had no right to give their land away to another people, to assuage their guilt about anti-Semitism and to plant a Western-backed state in the Middle East. They vowed to annihilate the new state and on May 15, when the British mandate expired, five Arab armies invaded Israel.[1] It looked as though the little David would be devoured by the Arab Goliath, but the Israeli army was stronger and more efficient and was able to push back the invaders. During the hostilities and the "cleaning up" afterward some 750,000 Palestinians left their homeland and have never been allowed to return.[2] The Wandering Jew had been replaced by the Wandering Palestinian and the salvation of the state had, in the time-honored fashion of the holy war, led to the destruction of another people. The Jews who had been persecuted for nearly a thousand years in the Christian West had now made new enemies in the East, and Arabs and Jews have been engaged in a deadly conflict ever since.

But this had not been the original intention of the first Zionists, who had begun to work for the return of the Jews to Israel in the late nineteenth century. The first Zionist settlers had no particular hatred of Arabs when they left their homes in the diaspora to settle in the land of their fathers. In this they were rather similar to the first Crusaders, who had been more preoccupied with their Western visions and problems than with hatred of the Muslims when they set off for the same land to make it their own. The first wave of Jewish settlers arrived in Palestine in 1882, the year after Tsar Alexander III had inspired a new bout of pogroms. Russia and Eastern Europe had had a long tradition of Christian anti-Semitism, but these new pogroms were especially severe; they seemed to subside only to break out again in April 1903 when a brutal pogrom at Kishinev in Bessarabia shocked the world.[3] Despite the anti-Semitic habit, Jews had still expected that eventually in the enlightened twentieth century it would die away, even in Russia, but the Kishinev pogrom showed that these hopes were futile. What was worse, there was a fresh outbreak of anti-Semitism in Western Europe where the Jews had long been emancipated. In countries like France and Germany the Jews had thought that their problems were over and many sought to assimilate with Gentile society. If they felt a lingering anti-Semitism in their Gentile neighbors, they looked forward hopefully to the new century when misguided Christian habits would be superseded by rational secularism or by a saner approach to religion. But these hopes were rudely shattered. In France, the first European country to emancipate the Jews after the Revolution of 1789, there was a hysterical outbreak of anti-Semitism when the Jewish officer Alfred Dreyfus was (wrongly) convicted of treason in 1895. That same year the anti-Semitic Karl Lueger was elected Mayor of Vienna. The reasons for this renewed persecution of the Jews in Europe will be discussed in Chapter 11. Now it is sufficient to say that since the Crusades Christians had made an enemy of "the Jew," just as they had made enemies of "the Muslim" and "the Greek" in the early Middle Ages, producing a series of mythical stereotypes of the Jews which were shadow selves of Europeans, reflecting their own fears and desires in a distorted mirror image. The habit was too deeply entrenched to die away completely, even when Christianity seemed to be losing its sway in Europe. The European anti-Semitism of the late nineteenth century was a secular version of the old Christian hatred of Jews. Instead of hounding the Jews to death for their alien religion, the Jews were now persecuted because they were of an alien race.

One of these anti-Semitic myths should be briefly discussed here because it had an important effect on Zionism. The late nineteenth century was a period of intense nationalism, and Zionism could be described as Jewish nationalism. As the new nation-states were created in Europe, people sought to create a new national identity for themselves and in so doing they made "the Jew" the enemy of this national character. People who were fired with patriotism now blamed the Jews for having no country of their own. In Germany, for example, there was a new cult of the *Volk*⁴ (the people) which linked the soul of the Germans to their land. This soul, people believed, was formed by the German landscape and this meant that the German spirit was alien to the city and to "civilization" (the culture of the city). This led Germans to see the Jews as the essential enemy of the German soul: they had no landscape of their own and so their souls could not develop naturally and this made them deformed human beings. Further, because Jews lived and worked in the cities, they were seen as the epitome of "civilization." The new *völkische* craze created a youth movement, which roamed the countryside soaking up the German soul there. Naturally Jews were not allowed to join these, even if they regarded themselves as more German than Jewish. It also took over student society and students turned the Jews out of their clubs and refused to fight a duel with a Jew because he had no honor to lose. It appeared in many important novels, essays, scientific theories and philosophical works of the time. In this nationalistic climate it was natural for Jews to seek a national solution for themselves, and many of the early Jewish settlers believed that only by reestablishing a physical contact with the land of their fathers could Jews discover their true selves.

But Zionism appeared first not in Western Europe but in Russia, and here many of the Jews sought quite different solutions. Many of them turned to religion to give them strength to bear the pogroms. Others tried to flee. Thousands poured into Western Europe and inadvertently increased the anti-Semitism there. These refugees from Russia and Eastern Europe were different from the European Jews. Their strange clothes and manners and their apparently archaic beliefs reinforced the conviction that the Jews were essentially "other" and horribly different from any other people in the world. Sadly the refugees found that they had not escaped anti-Semitism and many of them and their children would perish in the Nazi Holocaust. Other Jews fled to the United States, where some of them were very successful, but they would be very much aware of anti-Semitism and even today, when American Jewry is very strong indeed, Jews there do not rule out the possibility of persecution. Other Russian Jews decided that more radical answers were needed and those who had received a secular education joined the revolutionaries who were conspiring to overthrow the tsarist regime, which had brought such suffering to their people. Some of these Jewish revolutionaries like Leon Trotsky and Rosa Luxemburg dissociated themselves from their people, following the example of Karl Marx himself, who wrote two frankly anti-Semitic essays.[5] Trotsky and Luxemburg and their like believed that anti-Semitism was simply the result of a corrupt economic system that would disappear like a bad dream after the revolution.

But some of the Jewish revolutionaries were unable to accept this. They suspected that their fellow Gentile revolutionaries were actually anti-Semites and feared that Jews would fare as badly under the Communists as they had under the tsars. In the event, they have been proved right. These secular Jews sought an entirely new solution in Zionism and began to believe that Jews would find no rest until they had a land of their own. In 1882, the year after the first pogroms, Leon Pinsker wrote *Autoemancipation*, which quickly made a great impact on young secular Jews. Pinsker insisted that the Jews had to acquire a country of their own if they were ever to be dignified and free. Before the pogroms, Pinsker had been an assimilationist, but after them he was convinced that assimilation was impossible. A Jew would always be "the Other" for the Gentiles: "for the living, the Jew is a dead man; for the natives, an alien and a vagrant; for property holders, a beggar; for the poor, an exploiter and a millionaire; for the patriot, a man without a country."[6] It was a firmly established Gentile tradition to make Jews the epitome of all that Gentiles were *not* and this meant that Jews could not live in countries ruled by the *goyim*. They had to take their destiny into their own hands and establish themselves in a country of their own, where they were not vulnerable to the passing anti-Semitic whims of their fellow countrymen.[7]

It seemed a compelling solution and Pinsker strongly influenced a new Jewish organization formed in Kharkov in 1882 which called itself the Lovers of Zion. Pinsker had had no decided views about where this Jewish state should be but eventually the Lovers of Zion convinced him that it must be in Eretz Yisrael, the Land of Israel.[8] Although they had usually had a secular education and were not religious people, the members of the Lovers of Zion had grown up in the *shtetls*, the all-Jewish towns and villages. As children they had sat in the synagogue and listened to the psalms and prayers which centered round the ancient land of their fathers. Maurice Samuel, who is an authority on the *shtetl*, has clearly shown the importance of Eretz Yisrael there:

Half of the time the *Shtetl* just wasn't there: it was in the Holy
Land, and it was in the remote past or the remote future, in the
company of the Patriarchs and Prophets or of the Messiah. Its
festivals were geared to the Palestinian climate and calendar; it celebrated regularly the harvests its forefathers had gathered in a
hundred generations ago; it prayed for the Soreh and Malkosh, the
subtropical [early and late] rains, indifferent to the needs of its
neighbors, whose prayers had a practical, local schedule in view.[9]

In a time of crisis it is natural for people to look back to their roots.
We have seen that this is what the Hebrews had done when they made
the Exodus to the Promised Land and what the Muslims had done
in seventh-century Arabia, and the Lovers of Zion naturally thought
of Eretz Yisrael when they wanted to make a new start. Because the
Gentile world seemed committed to rejecting them, it was important
that the Jews rise up to save themselves.

But many of the Lovers of Zion were not content with theory: about
6000 of them simply packed their bags, left their homes and families,
and settled in pioneering communities in Palestine. These first Zionist
settlers showed others what to do, and they would be known as the
First Aliyah (the first immigration). They made many mistakes, which
later Zionist settlers would correct, but their courageous initiative
made an indelible mark on Zionism. It was this practical faith and
pragmatic activity in the pursuit of a quixotic idea that helped to make
the State of Israel an established fact. The practical, pioneering element
has remained a hallmark of Zionism, right up to the present day.

Yet it is also true that without political validation, Zionism would
never have achieved its end. The man who made Zionism a factor on
the international scene was not a Russian. Theodor Herzl was a sophisticated and charismatic Viennese Jew, who at the time of the
Dreyfus affair was an established playwright and a correspondent in
Paris for an Austrian newspaper. As a pressman he was present at
Dreyfus' court martial and left the École Militaire as the crowds were
beginning to scream "Death to the Jews!"[10] Herzl had been a firm
believer in assimilation, but the shock of this new wave of anti-Semitism converted him to Zionism. He was convinced that there would
shortly be an even more terrible anti-Semitic catastrophe and he decided that the Jews must find a refuge, any refuge, where they could
find shelter and safety. In 1896, just six months after the Dreyfus trial,
he published *Der Judenstaat* (The Jewish State), which argued that
the Jews must have a land of their own. He was by no means convinced
that this should be in Palestine, however. Herzl had had an entirely

secular upbringing. The Holy Land simply did not have the same emotional pull for him as it had for the Russian Zionists, who had been brought up in the religious atmosphere of the *shtetl*. Nor did Herzl have any patience with the rough pioneering ethos of the settlers. He saw himself as the Jewish Cecil Rhodes, bringing progress and Western civilization to the Middle East: the Jewish state would be "an outpost of civilization as opposed to barbarism."[11] His colonial vision has left as deep a mark on subsequent Zionism as the practical ethos of the pioneers. Even though most of the first Zionists had their roots in the revolutionary socialism of Russia, the State of Israel still sees itself as the vanguard of the capitalist West, a beacon of civilization in the Islamic wilderness.

For eight years Herzl literally worked himself to death to put Zionism and the Jewish state literally on the map, convinced of an impending holocaust which made a Jewish state a matter of the utmost urgency. He began to meet the great statesmen of the world to interest them in the idea of the Jewish homeland, and was prepared to consider Africa or the Sinai Peninsula as well as Palestine. He looked for allies everywhere. He even talked to the Russian anti-Semite V. K. Plehve, the Czar's Minister of the Interior, who had masterminded the pogroms: after all, it would be in his interests to get rid of the Jews. Herzl was, however, convinced that in the end Britain would establish the Jewish state as part of her colonizing effort. "England the great, England the free," he wrote, "England with her eyes fixed on the seven seas will understand us."[12] He was proved right and without Herzl's political Zionism there would have been no state of Israel. At this time, when the great powers were carving up the world between them, the support of one of them was vital.

But just as crucial was Herzl's work within Zionism. In 1897 he gave the scattered Zionist groups a platform when he convened the First Zionist Congress in Basel and this gave the movement a vital coherence and focus. At the Congress, Herzl's own charisma aroused deep feelings. Mordechai Ben-Ami, the delegate from Odessa, described the emotion when Herzl took the platform:

Many eyes filled with tears . . . Herzl mounted the rostrum calmly . . . Not the Herzl I knew, the one I had seen only the previous evening. Before us was the splendid figure of a son of kings with a deep and concentrated gaze, handsome and sad at one and the same time. It was not the elegant Herzl of Vienna, but a man of the House of David, risen all of a sudden from his grave in all his legendary glory. . . . It seemed· as if the dream cherished by our people for two thousand years had come true at last, and Messiah, the son of David, was standing before us.[13]

This description is significant. The delegates at Basel had no time for religion. They felt that religious Judaism had encouraged the Jews to sit back passively and wait for the Messiah, accepting in the meantime their intolerable situation. Yet, despite this rejection of religion, at almost every turn these secular Jews expressed their Zionism in religious terms. The Zionists wanted to create a new kind of Jew but it was essential that there should be a continuity: the new Judaism had to be rooted in the passions of the past or it would be un-Jewish, superficial and artificial. It would have no roots and would wither away. Ben-Ami was not entirely wrong to see Herzl as the Messiah: he was a *Zionist* Messiah and dramatically expressed in his person and dignity the Zionist principle of self-determination. Instead of abdicating their responsibility and leaving everything to God, the Zionists must take full human responsibility for their own fate and initiate their own secular salvation. But, as we shall see, religion is a powerful force. Seculars who use it, however symbolically, often find it difficult to keep within bounds.

The following year at the Zionist Congress this symbolic and psychological Zionist link with their past led to a fateful decision. Herzl triumphantly announced that there was a real chance that they would be allowed to build a Jewish state in Uganda. He was bewildered by his colleagues' absolute refusal to consider the idea. The Russian delegates actually walked out: they could see no alternative to Eretz Yisrael. They could not articulate their objections logically because it was so fundamental and essentially emotional that it had the authority of a self-evident fact.[14] This made them inaccessible to reason and practical arguments. This inarticulate passion for the Holy Land will be a key factor in our story, modern and medieval. Herzl was forced to accept that Palestine was the only place for a Jewish state. He stood before the delegates, raised his right hand and quoted the words of the psalmist-exile in Babylon: "Jerusalem, if I forget you, may my right hand wither!"[15] From that moment, Zionism ceased to be a purely defensive movement concerned solely with finding a refuge for the Jews and became officially committed to the return to Eretz Yisrael.

When Herzl died at the age of forty-four in 1904, worn out by his labors, the Russian Zionist Chaim Weizmann continued his political activities[16] and in 1917 secured the firm support of the British, for reasons that I shall discuss more fully in Chapter 11. Foreign Secretary Arthur Balfour hoped to enlist international Jewish support for Britain in the war against Germany, and Britain was also looking covetously at the Middle East, hoping to found colonies there after the Great War. There were also more complex reasons why he and his colleagues issued the important statement that would thereafter be known as the Balfour Declaration on November 2, 1917:

> His Majesty's Government views with favour the establishment in Palestine of a national home for the Jewish people, and will use their best endeavours to facilitate the achievement of this object, it being clearly understood that nothing shall be done which may prejudice the civil and religious rights of existing non-Jewish communities in Palestine, or the rights and political status enjoyed by Jews in any other country.[17]

Weizmann was disappointed.[18] The Declaration was deliberately vague about the nature of this "national home": was it to be a political state, a colony or a Jewish reservation? Further, it spoke only of a homeland "in" Palestine, which could mean only a small part of the country, and there was that worrying phrase about the native inhabitants of the country, euphemistically called "non-Jewish communities" as though to disguise the fact that Palestine had a huge Arab majority.[19] But despite Weizmann's disappointment, the Balfour Declaration was crucial to the establishment of the Jewish state. In 1920, after the demise of the Ottoman Empire, Britain and France did indeed establish colonies in the Middle East which they somewhat disingenuously called mandates or protectorates. Britain took Palestine and the mandate there was pledged to implement the Balfour Declaration. Although, as we shall see, the British mandate later had reservations about the Balfour Declaration, finding it difficult—if not impossible —to put into practice, without this British support at that crucial moment the Zionist enterprise would probably have failed.

But in the early years of the twentieth century yet another form of Zionism had developed, which would prove to be vital. Like some of the earlier Zionist ideas we have discussed, this also had its roots in the Jewish religious tradition. It is also reminiscent of some of the early Crusading ideology discussed in the last chapter, because Christianity inherited these religious passions from Judaism. We have seen that all three of the religions of historical monotheism have a strong apocalyptic theme: all believe that God will finally impose his kingdom or his justice upon the world. All three religions have also developed ideologies that we might today call socialist. Indeed, in the Jewish diaspora in the Roman Empire, the Jews had developed what could be described as the first welfare system. Jesus and Mohammad could both be described in their various ways as revolutionaries: they were on the side of the poor and oppressed and fought an unjust or corrupt establishment. It might be the case that, in all three religions, this concern with justice and equality derives from a sense of the overwhelming majesty of the one God, whose might and compassion makes human power and oppression ridiculous and offensive. All three religions, therefore, have an inherent revolutionary strain: from time to time, all three have sought to create a just society on this earth, combining their compassion for the poor and oppressed with apocalyptic ideas of a brave new world. It is not surprising that this strain should enter Zionism and make it, in a deep sense, a revolution.

We have seen already that, in Russia, Zionism sprang from the ideals of revolutionary socialism in which many young Jews were involved. Indeed, despite his anti-Semitism, Karl Marx himself was deeply influenced by these Jewish ideals of equality and a final messianic era, which, in his thought, became the socialist utopia. His friend, the Jewish socialist Moses Hess (d. 1875), made this connection clear in his great book *Rome and Jerusalem*, which has been called the first Zionist classic. Like Marx, Hess drew on the Jewish messianic tradition but put the people of Israel in the center of the picture. He called the Marxist idea of the fulfillment of history "the Sabbath of History." Just as nature has its Sabbath which sanctifies its creation, so too does history, when the historical process is completed. Hess was living at a time of intense nationalism: he saw the rise of the new nation-states as dialectically related to the rise of socialism, but what would give meaning to all the rest was the regeneration of the Jews in their own land. Years before Herzl, Hess had asked why there should not be a Jewish state in Palestine. God's first words to Abraham had assured him that in his seed "all the nations of the earth should find a blessing" (Genesis 12:3): the Jews must rediscover this vocation. Once more the light should go forth from Zion to the Gentiles; then history would be redeemed and the aims of all the other revolutions achieved.

Marx and Engels were both rather scornful of this intensely Jewish vision but other Marxists found a natural affinity between Marxism and Zionism. Thus in 1904 Ber Borochov, a young Russian Jewish intellectual, published *The Jewish National Question and the Class Struggle*, which dwelt less on Marx's messianic ideas than with his economic thesis. Because they had no land of their own, Borochov argued, the Jews were inevitably pushed out of the "primary" economic fields like agriculture into "secondary" fields like commerce and light industry. This meant that they were essentially unproductive and unable to take part in the class struggle. It was their poor economic status that caused anti-Semitism and pogroms. It was no use emigrating to Gentile countries like America, because there would be the same problems. The Jews needed to renew themselves in a land of their own, in an "empty" or undeveloped country like Palestine, which was underpopulated— or so Borochov believed.[20] Throughout Russia and the Ukraine, Marxist Zionist groups were springing up with similar ideas, and some were quick to apply to Zionism the Marxist vision of a final struggle over tyranny, when all peoples would be renewed and history brought to completion. In this new and idealistic "Labor" Zionism, the Jews' reunion with their fatherland would be a crucial step toward the final world victory of socialism.

Thus in 1903 the young David Ben-Gurion wrote that in Palestine the Jews would create "a model society, based on social, economic and political equality." First, the Jews would save themselves. Zionism was not just a flight from persecution but the creation of a new Jewish identity. It was a revolution,

> a revolt against a tradition of many centuries, helplessly longing for redemption. We substitute a will for self-realization, an attempt at reconstruction and creativity in the soil of the homeland. We call for a self-sufficient people, master of its own fate. Instead of a corrupt existence of middlemen, hung up in midair, we call for an independent existence as working people, at home on the soil and in the creative economy.[21]

Work or labor was to be the keynote of this Marxist Zionism. Ben-Gurion and the others who emigrated at about this time in what has become known as the Second Aliyah also believed that they were on the brink of a new world. To his wife Paula, Ben-Gurion wrote to console her for her present sufferings: "Dolorous and in tears you will arise to the high mountain from which one sees vistas of a New World, a world of gladness and light, shining in the glow of an eternally young ideal of supreme happiness and glorious existence."[22] The impact of this new socialist Zionism was well described by David Horovitz, who would later become an Israeli capitalist and president of the Bank of Israel: "In the Labour Zionist youth movement we created for ourselves an ideal world, new, free and noble. We dreamed of Utopia—the Labour Zionist movement was the gate that led to it."[23] It is easy to condemn these ideas as naive or even presumptuous, especially in the light of subsequent history, but this type of idealism has effected many major social and political changes. Without this early faith that they would save the world, many of the early Jewish settlers would not have found the courage to endure the sufferings ahead.

The Second Aliyah began in about 1902. From all over Russia and the Ukraine, Zionists packed bags and made the exodus to Palestine. Nobody organized this but, while political Zionists like Weizmann worked to set up a Jewish state officially, others just got up and left to settle in pioneering communities that reflected their socialist ideology. These settlements that ultimately became the *kibbutzim* were experiments in collective living. They were not unique to the Second Aliyah. An early charter of the Lovers of Zion had expressed this idealism in its vision of the new Israel: there would be "one fortune for the entire society. No man has private property. Also his things, his clothes and whatever he may bring with him or receive from his home belong to the entire society."[24] When the Zionists of the Second and later of the Third Aliyah made this ideal concrete in the *kibbutzim*, they were picking up an old trend in the Judeo-Christian tradition and creating secular monasteries, where a voluntary "poverty" was practiced. If crusading was an offspring of medieval European monasticism, then the new Israel was to be the child of the *kibbutzim*, and both movements were dedicated to the ideal of poverty. The Jewish settlers lived a very frugal life. They wore the clothes of Russian peasants or their old Russian student uniforms until they were quite literally in rags. Food was very simple and there were no luxuries like alcohol and cigarettes. It seemed a first sign of the approaching socialist millennium.

Herzl, as we have seen, had no time for this socialist ideal but had more colonial ideals for the state of Israel. Indeed, in the early days, Ben-Gurion and his fellows in Labor Zionism did not want to create a Jewish *state*; they saw the state in Marxist terms: it was part of the old bourgeois corruption that would wither away when the socialist utopia arrived.[25] They saw the new Israel as an entirely new kind of socialist society and they held on to these ideals until the dark anti-Semitic days of the late 1930s and 1940s clouded these hopes and made them more realistic.

Herzl was not alone in his dislike of this pioneering Zionism. To Orthodox religious Jews the whole movement seemed a denial of religion and an impious aping of messianic redemption. Over the centuries the Jews had come to believe that they must stay in the diaspora until they were spiritually renewed. When the Jews were ready in religious terms, then the Messiah would appear to bring them back home and found a religious kingdom in Eretz Yisrael, based on the Torah. To establish a secular society there without the Messiah seemed blasphemous to the rabbis, who roundly condemned the whole Zionist dream. Some rabbis even refused to make a pilgrimage to Jerusalem lest they condone Zionism. Thus Zadok of Lublin (1823 –1900) wrote:

> I fear lest my departure and ascent (*aliyah*) to Jerusalem might seem like a gesture of approval of Zionist activity. I hope unto the Lord, my soul hopes for his word, that the Day of the Redemption will come. I wait and remain watchful for the feet of his anointed. Yet though three hundred scourges of iron afflict me, I will not move from my place.[26]

But there were religious Jews in Eretz Yisrael, who for centuries had lived a devout life there according to the Torah, often depending upon the alms of Jews in the diaspora. They believed that by this pious activity they were performing a religious service, maintaining a Jewish presence in Jerusalem in readiness for the Messiah. They also were horrified by the Zionists, claiming that when Herzl entered the Holy Land "evil entered with him."[27] The Zionists were just as horrified to find these pious Jews in Eretz Yisrael and turned from them in disgust. For Marxist atheists, these religious people, clinging to the Wailing Wall in their archaic clothes and long beards, dependent on alms, symbolized everything that was wrong with the Jews. They wanted to liberate their people from anachronistic religious traditions that shackled them to the past in attitudes of hopeless dependence.

The Zionists of the Second and Third Aliyahs were also dismissive of a form of religious Zionism that had established itself in the Holy Land. This movement called itself "Mizrachi" or spiritual center. Under the leadership of Orthodox Jews like Rabbi Abraham Kook, they sought, as their name implies, to create a religious focus for Jewish aspiration. They did not want a modern democratic state, as Herzl did, nor did they want Ben-Gurion's socialist society. They wanted to rebuild the ancient Temple and to create a religious society, based on the Torah. Religious Zionists like Rabbi Kook, however, did not recoil in disgust from Ben-Gurion and his followers. He saw that, without knowing it, they were in fact working for the religious Messianic redemption. He and his Orthodox followers were convinced that once the Jews were living again in their own land they would of necessity return to the Torah and abandon their inferior secular dreams. When that had happened, the Messiah would surely come. For their part, Ben-Gurion and the Labor Zionists tolerated the Mizrachi settlers; they were convinced that these religious Zionists were anachronisms who would, like those corrupt institutions religion and the state, also disappear in the clear light of the socialist millennium. Both Ben-Gurion and Rabbi Kook felt that they were in the grip of a providential destiny larger than themselves. The Mizrachi were only a minority but in their religious settlements, side by side with the *kibbutzim*, they were nursing quite contradictory visions of the New Israel. Because the Mizrachi seemed so insignificant and outmoded, the Labor Zionists ignored them. But, as we shall see in Chapter 7, this was short-sighted, for religion seems to be a tougher plant than socialist philosophy allows.

Even though the Labor Zionists of the *kibbutzim* rejected religion and any theistic ideas, they approached the rebuilding of their home-land with truly religious feelings and attitudes. They were indeed creating a new socialist religion, which they called the Conquest of Labor. Their work was a secular prayer. Thus in about 1927 the young pioneer Avraham Shlonsky, who worked as a road builder, wrote this poem:

> Dress me, my own right mother, in a magnificent cloak of
> many colours
> And at the hour of the morning service carry me to work.
> Light wraps my head like a prayer shawl.
> The houses stand upright like frontlets.
> And the roads, paved by labouring hands, run down like the
> straps of *tefillin*.
> Thus shall the fine city offer her morning prayer to her
> creator;
> And among the creators, your son Avraham, paving poet in
> Israel.[28]

The redeemed Zionist does not need God; he himself is the creator.

This religion of Labor enabled the Zionist to redeem himself, to realize his full potential and to liberate him from the humiliation of the diaspora. It is, therefore, not surprising that they tended to ex-perience Zionism and to express its ideals in terms of a religious vocation. A classic example here is Itzhak Ben-Zvi, who became the second President of the state of Israel, and who experienced a real conversion to Zionism in 1905, which took the form of a vision. He had been speaking at a Jewish revolutionary rally when suddenly "there appeared in my mind's eye the living image of Jerusalem, the holy city with its ruins, desolate of its sons.

> At that moment I asked myself: *whom am I addressing*? Will my listeners here at Poltava understand me, will they believe? Are we, the Jews, *real partners* in this revolution and in this victory? Will

this revolution, which promises salvation to the Russians, bring salvation for us Jews too? Why am I here and not there? As these questions arose in my mind I could no longer free myself from them; and as I finished my speech I no longer thought of this demonstration and of the victory of the Russian Revolution but of *our Jerusalem*. That very hour I reached the absolute decision that my place is in the Land of Israel, and that I must go there, dedicate my life to its upbuilding, and as soon as possible.[29]

The Zionists not only experienced Labor Zionism like a religion but, like the earlier Zionists whom we have considered, they expressed their movement in traditionally Jewish religious terms. Part of their revolution was to revive the ancient language of Hebrew for daily use, so that the Jews could speak their own tongue in their newly built land. Naturally, they turned to many old religious terms to express their ideals. The word *aliyah*, for example, did not originally mean "immigration," it also meant "ascent," the word traditionally used for the pilgrimage to Jerusalem. In other words, like the Crusaders, they saw this migration to the Holy Land as a pilgrimage. Just as the Crusaders had been returning to their religious roots and the birthplace of their faith to establish a new Western identity, the Zionists were returning to their collective roots in an attempt to create a new Jewish self. Indeed, they called immigrants *olim* or "pilgrims," just as they do today. When the *olim* arrived at the port of Jaffa they frequently knelt down to kiss the soil of Eretz Yisrael like religious pilgrims. Frequently, the *olim* spoke of their *aliyah* as a "rebirth," just as a religious person will often say that he has been "born again" since his conversion. Often they changed their names after making *aliyah*, a common religious habit after conversion or vocation. Thus David Grien became David Ben-Gurion (son of lions). Frequently these new Hebrew names reflect the sense of strength and mastery that the Zionists wanted the new Jews to have. Thus we have *Tamir* (towering), *Oz* (strength) and *Lahat* (blaze). Some people named themselves after a part of Eretz Yisrael in order to tie themselves more firmly to the land: Sharon, Golan, Karmi (Carmel) and Galil. The name the settlers gave to the pioneering movement as a whole was *chalutzism* and in Hebrew the biblical term *chalutz* had strong religious connotations of salvation, liberation and rescue.[30]

The *chalutz* or pioneer who expressed the new religion of the Conquest of Labor most eloquently may well have been the Russian settler A. B. Gordon. He had formerly been an Orthodox Jew and a Kabalist, but also greatly influenced by the nature mysticism of Tolstoy. He saw the Jews' reunion with their land in mystical terms. Eretz Yisrael was, he thought, superior to all lands, having a spiritual power that was accessible only to the Jews and that was creative of the Jewish spirit. In describing the power, physically inherent in the land itself, Gordon used traditional phrases from the Kabala:

> The soul of the Jew is the offspring of the natural environment of the land of Israel. *Clarity*, the depth of an infinitely clear sky, a clear perspective, *mists of purity*. Even the divine unknown seems to disappear in this clarity, slipping from *limited, manifest light* into *infinite, hidden light*. The peoples of this world understand neither this clear perspective nor this luminous unknown in the Jewish soul.[31]

This was a secular but mystical interpretation of the old religious belief in the "holiness" of the land. Gordon had found the diaspora painful and his *aliyah* did come to seem like a liberation and a reunion with a deeper self. But at first Palestine was not like home at all; he found himself longing for the northern landscape of Russia, his "real" fatherland. How could he make this land his own? By conquering it for himself by labor. Interestingly, the Hebrew word for labor (*avodah*) also means religious worship. By working on the land, the Jews would conquer it for themselves and thereby win their own souls back from the darkness of exile and homelessness. Physical work connected Gordon and his fellows with Eretz Yisrael in a tangible and realistic bond. By means of *avodah*, Gordon learned to appreciate the spiritual power of the country. It was a rebirth of his Jewish soul, a liberation of universal love:

> To the extent that my hands grew accustomed to labour, that my eyes and ears learned to see and hear and my heart to understand what is in it, my soul too learned to skip upon the hills, to rise, to soar—to spread out the expanses it had not known, to embrace all the land round about, the world and all that is in it, and to see itself embraced in the arms of the whole universe.[32]

When the Labor Zionists called their settlement movement "the Conquest of Labor" or "the Conquest of the Land" they did not at first imagine that this would turn into a bloody struggle. They saw farming as a peaceful, creative way of establishing a valid claim to the land of their fathers. But as we know only too well, the Arab inhabitants of Palestine also felt that they had a claim to their homeland. It soon became clear that conflict was inevitable.

The settlers had usually established their colonies and *kibbutzim* on land that they had bought from Arab landlords, who often lived far away and felt little compulsion about making a quick, easy profit. It damaged the Palestinian tenants, who had farmed the land for them, because they had to leave their smallholdings when the Jewish settlers moved in. But this did not at first worry anybody unduly, least of all the landlords: Palestine had long been a neglected province of the Ottoman Empire and for some considerable time nobody had thought that the Palestinians merited much consideration. But only about 6 percent of the land was sold in this way and the Jews remained a small minority until 1948. In December 1918, for example, the year after the Balfour Declaration, the population was estimated as follows:

| Muslim Arabs: | 512,000 |
| Christian Arabs: | 61,000 |
| Jews | 66,000[33] |

The Jewish settlements and *kibbutzim* were islands, surrounded by a substantial Arab majority who were living in cities, towns, villages and farms that had been their homes for centuries. At first the Zionists had not taken the Arab threat very seriously. In fact they had a slogan: "a land for a people for a people without a land."[34] A colonially-minded Zionist like Herzl would have seen Palestine as an "empty" country; the desires of the native inhabitants must fade into insignificance before the will of the great powers. A Zionist like Ben-Gurion believed at first that, because the socialist millennium was approaching, Arab resistance to Zionism would fade away; any such resistance was due to a prerevolutionary consciousness. But they soon became aware that they were up against an enemy who refused to abandon their claim.

On both sides of the Arab-Israeli conflict people have commented that the Zionists were unfortunate in that they tried to establish themselves in Palestine just a hundred years too late. The idea of an "empty" country that was ripe for colonial expansion and development had long been axiomatic in countries like Britain and France. It was this idea which had prompted Herzl to seek the help of the great powers. Given that the Zionists had the support of the British, it would not *once* have been impossible for them to build a homeland in Palestine against the will of the native majority. Well-organized and dedicated colonialists had long been able to appropriate a country in the name of progress. There had been no great outcry when the Australian aborigines or the American Indians lost their land in this way. The Palestinians had a well-educated aristocracy but, even though there had been considerable agricultural and economic development in Palestine during the nineteenth century, they were not as politically aware

or, in Western terms, as educated as the Zionists. In the old colonial
ideology, the Zionists with the backing of a great power could easily
have overcome any native opposition. But after World War I there
was a new spirit abroad. The foundation of the League of Nations
and President Woodrow Wilson's Fourteen Points were creating a
new climate, which insisted upon a people's inalienable right to self-
determination and was protesting against the exploitation of weak
countries by the strong. Further, the recent European dream of national independence had spread to subject peoples. In the colonies,
people were beginning to demand independence as a right. This new
spirit was alive among the Arabs of the Middle East.

During the last days of the Ottoman Empire young groups of Arab
nationalists had begun to plan for their eventual national independence. In 1909 the first meeting of the Young Arabs took place in
Paris and by 1915 Ben-Gurion became aware that nationalism had
spread to the Arabs of Palestine. "It came upon me like a blow," he
recalled years later. "I said to myself 'So there *is* an Arab national
movement *here* (and not just in Lebanon and Syria).' It hit me like a
bomb. I was completely confounded."[35] The Zionists realized that
they had to confront a people who, like themselves, were seeking a
new independence and dignity.

Further, the colonial powers themselves seemed uncertain about
their policy in Palestine at this period. Between 1915 and 1918 Britain
and France had issued a series of completely conflicting pledges and
promises in relation to the fate of the country. The Hussein-McMahon
correspondence had promised the Arabs independence in return for
their support of the British against the Turks in 1915; this independence had generally been considered to apply to Palestine as well as
to Syria and Saudi Arabia. In 1916 the secret Sykes-Picot agreement
divided the Middle East between Britain and France; France took
Syria, of which Palestine was considered a part. The following year
Britain modified Sykes-Picot and awarded Palestine to itself; later in
1917 came the Balfour Declaration; finally in 1918 the Anglo-French
Joint Declaration appeared to promise self-determination and independence to Syria, Iraq and possibly to the Palestinians. At this time
no less a person than Arthur Lord Balfour himself made this famous
statement: "so far as Palestine is concerned, the powers have made no
statement of fact that is not admittedly wrong, and no declaration of
policy which, at least in the letter, they have not always intended to
violate."[36] With these conflicting plans for Palestine, it was inevitable
that both the Jews and the Arabs should regard the land as having
been promised to them at some stage; both could claim to have had

their desire for independence sanctioned by the powers-that-be and neither could place very much reliance on the British, who established their mandate in Palestine in 1920.

Because Zionism was a highly idealistic and moral movement, the Palestinians created a deep moral problem. We can sense this in Ben-Gurion's response to the Palestinian nationalism he discovered in 1915. Hitherto, perhaps, the Zionists had repressed their deepest worries but, once the Palestinians had revealed that they regarded the country as inalienably theirs, it was no longer possible to bury these fears. We see how deep these could be in the account of a very eminent settler of the First Aliyah. Eliezer ben Yehuda could be described as a fanatical Zionist. A brilliant philologist, he was almost solely responsible for the creation of modern Hebrew. When his mother came to visit him in Palestine, he refused to speak to her because she did not know Hebrew and he believed that a Jew must speak only Hebrew in his own land.[37] Yet as early as 1882, when his ship had approached Jaffa, he had had grave doubts about his rights to Eretz Yisrael. He found himself watching the Arab passengers on board and suddenly he realized that they were far more at home in the East and in the Promised Land than he was. Whatever he might be in Zionist theory, he was in fact a foreigner there without political or national right whereas they seemed to belong naturally in the country. The Arabs, he wrote, were "tall, strong young fellows, dressed in the style of the country, but in expensive, elegant attire, and they were all merry and joyful, jesting and riotous."[38] Without warning "an oppressive feeling of dread, as though I were confronting a fortified rampart, suddenly filled my soul." It drained the moment of his arrival in the land of Israel, to which he had so long looked forward, of any meaning:

> Yes! this was the coast of the land of our fathers! And the feeling of dread grew yet stronger within me. Nothing else did I feel, no other thought was in my mind! I am afraid! After about a quarter of an hour my feet were standing upon the holy ground, the land of our fathers—yet in my heart was no feeling of joy, and in my head no thought, no idea whatsoever! My mind seemed to have emptied itself or turned to ice; it would not budge. Only one thing filled my heart—that same feeling of dread. I neither rent my garments, nor fell upon my face, nor embraced the stones, nor kissed the ground. I just stood there in astonishment. Dread![39]

Ben Yehuda experienced the Arabs as a shock, which he could not articulate but which threatened him at a very deep level. They were not merely in the way of the Zionist hope, they were in the way of his new self and were an implacable obstacle—a "fortified rampart" —to all that he held to be most sacred. Eventually he left Eretz Yisrael and became a Territorialist, believing that the Jews should have a homeland but not in Palestine. We should perhaps bear Ben Yehuda's "dread" in mind when we read of the atrocities and irrational behavior of many of the participants on all sides of the holy wars medieval and modern. This kind of shock and inarticulate dismay can easily trigger an extreme reaction. Even Zionists who have no doubt at all about the Jews' right to Eretz Yisrael often have complex feelings about the Arabs, and this is due to the high moral tone that, at least in its early days, Zionism encouraged in the *chalutzim*: they were not to be "pioneers" in the tough, go-getting American tradition but rather vanguards of a new moral order.

What was the attitude of the Palestinians? At the time of the British conquest of Palestine from the Turks in 1918 they had not been told officially about the Balfour Declaration. There were doubtless rumors but many believed the other pledges that had been made, seeming to promise them independence along with the other Arabs of the Middle East. Many greeted the British hopefully, feeling that better days were ahead. Thus the poet Sheikh Ali al-Rimawi described the long Turkish period as a dark one and hailed the British victory as the triumph of justice over oppression, in a poem written in 1918. The Arabs, he said, had high expectations of the British:

> You, as we know, have been a great defender of the oppressed. That is why you gained the victory. You, as we know, have a high opinion of Islam. You worship prosperity and beneficence.[40]

Naturally this rosy—and highly idealized!—view of Great Britain was tarnished when the implementation of the Balfour Declaration became official British policy. The Arabs felt betrayed. As Wadi al-Bustani, who was a civil assistant to the military administration, said in a poem on the Balfour Declaration:

> We opened our hearts to you, extended our hands; but I suspect that you may turn your back on us. I perceive an increasingly widening gulf separating us, you being on one bank and we on the other. In a room in this "Government House" I see concealed a rising palace of the "National Home" [for the Jews.][41]

Despite their natural dismay about British support for the Jewish National Home, there was at first little exaggerated hatred of the Jews. Indeed there was a strong sense that Jews and Arabs were related to one another. In a poem written in 1920 on the occasion of the arrival of Sir Herbert Samuel as High Commissioner, Ma'ruf al-Rasafi protested against the accusation that the Arabs were unfair to the Jews:

> We are not hostile to the Israelites as some accuse us, neither
> secretly nor publicly.
> How can we be while they are our paternal uncles, and while
> the Banu Fihr are related to Ishmael?
> But evacuation is what we fear, and to be ruled by force is
> what we try to avoid.[42]

He urged Samuel to govern the Arabs tactfully and fairly if he wanted to win them over. Al-Rasafi's fears of eviction from Palestine were common, even at this early date.

Although the Palestinians had not owned their land politically during the long Turkish period, they were passionately attached to it and referred to it proudly as *Falastinuneh*: our Palestine. Even those who farmed land as tenants of feudal overlords felt that they had a valid claim to land that they had cultivated for generations, just as the Zionists felt about the land that *they* were farming in Eretz Yisrael. Naturally they had simpler feelings about their land and had not developed the same kind of ideology as the Zionists, who were, as we have seen, attaching themselves to a country that was not their fatherland. The distinguished Palestinian poet Mahmoud Darwish explains this:

> We excavated this land neither in mythical dreams nor in the illustrated page of an old book, nor did we create it in the way companies and institutions are established. It is our father and mother. We did not, either, buy it through an agency or shop, and we have been under no pressure to love it. We identify ourselves as its pulse and the marrow of its bones. It is therefore ours, and we belong to it.[43]

Indeed, many Palestinians found the Zionist attachment to Eretz Yisrael to be artificial compared to the natural love that they felt for the land where they and their ancestors had dwelt for centuries. Their attachment to *Falastinuneh* was not, Darwish says in the poem "Homeland," "a bundle of tales, nor is it only a memory."[44] As Samih al-Qasim puts it in "The Land After My Death":

> Who built the stone barriers at the mountain foot?
> Who taught the breeze
> to be kind to the trees?
> Who but my good-natured grandfather?
> Who taught the plain
> to be a generous giver of crops?
> Who but my father and his old brother?

Who carved the names of relatives, one by one,
on every tree trunk in our groves?
Who but this adorer and worshipper?[45]

I quote these Palestinian writers to show that the Palestinians also had their own developed patriotism. They felt that they had a right to national independence and believed that the colonial powers had promised this and had reneged on that promise. It was inevitable, therefore, that there would be a bitter conflict between the Palestinians and the Zionists, who soon began to fear that the British were about to renege on the Balfour Declaration and give Eretz Yisrael to the Arabs.

It is impossible to give a detailed account of the tangled events that led up to the creation of the state of Israel in 1948. The issues are most complex. Whole books have been devoted to the subject and, to do justice to the point of view of all three participants in the struggle, a whole book is really needed. All that is possible here is a brief account of the main attitudes of the British, the Palestinians and the Jews during the period of the mandate. All three behaved well and badly at different times during the thirty-year conflict; all three made mistakes; all three sometimes committed grave wrong. All three, therefore, contributed to the creation of the conflict that still continues to escalate today.

First, let us look briefly at the point of view of the British. These were difficult days: it was the end of a long and horrific world war; it was also the beginning of the end of empire, though many people were unable to realize or accept this fully. It was the idealistic era following the Treaty of Versailles, which had such high hopes of the brotherhood of man and of a new period of international justice for all. It was also a period of cynicism, as we can see clearly in the astonishing remark of Lord Balfour that I have just quoted. Both the idealism and the cynicism were in evidence in the matter of Palestine. Thus at the end of the war with Germany, Prime Minister Lloyd George, an ardent Zionist, was discovered in his study weeping and reading the Book of Psalms: he explained that the only interesting thing to have come out of the war was the Balfour Declaration. But far away from the idealists in Whitehall, the soldiers and administrators who had to put these ideals into practice naturally had a rather more realistic and world-weary view of the problems involved. The Jews and the Arabs have both accused the British of siding with the "other" side. The fact is that the British, who were in a period of transition themselves, veered uneasily from one side to another. The Balfour

Declaration was committed to guarding the interests of Jews and Arabs and, in trying to be fair to both sides, the British managed to offend both and often behaved mischievously and irresponsibly.

Thus during the period of the military administration between 1918 and 1920 it seemed that the British were inclined to ditch the Balfour Declaration. The Zionists naturally suspected some of the personnel of being anti-Semites and they were right in this assumption. It has sometimes been suggested that the British idealized the Arabs in the Lawrence of Arabia manner but this does not seem to be correct: there was nothing romantic about the Palestinians. What did seem to be present was the British tendency to side with the underdog, though this sometimes came across in an objectionable manner. As one young British officer in Palestine put it: "The Jews are so clever and the Arabs so stupid and childish, that it seems only sporting to be for the Arabs."[46] The situation in Palestine was unfamiliar to many of the officials: they were used to defending the rights of the British against a colonial majority and that seemed somehow "right" but in Palestine they were asked to enforce the wishes of Russian Jews and many found this hard to understand.[47]

Thus the British began in 1918 by restricting Jewish immigration and withholding transfers of land to the Jews, on the grounds that this was a breach of the status quo. They also forbade the public singing of the "Hatikvah" (the Zionist anthem) and refused to recognize Hebrew as an official language. Naturally this gave the Arabs hope that the days of the Jewish National Home were numbered; their confidence may have led to the outbreak of Arab violence against Jews in the Old City of Jerusalem in the early months of 1920. During these pogroms Sir Ronald Storrs, the Governor, did not send the army in nor did he permit the Jews to organize their own defense. But the pogroms led to a resurgence of sympathy for Zionism in Whitehall and the government reaffirmed British commitment to the Balfour Declaration, which it had shown signs of abandoning. The British now officially supported a National Home for the Jews but *not* a Jewish state: that would only be allowed when the Jews had become a majority in Palestine. Given that the Jews were a small minority at present, that could take a very long time indeed. Despite the constant Jewish immigration during the mandate, the Jews remained only a very small percentage of the whole population of Palestine, for the Arabs' birthrate was much higher. From this point, the British remained faithful to the Balfour Declaration for several years, giving the Jews a time of relative peace in which to start constructing their National Home.

During this time their commitment to Zionism, which was not a convenient policy, was remarkable.

By 1928, however, the British attitude had changed. This became clear on the Jewish feast of Yom Kippur that year, when the Governor, with astonishing insensitivity, removed the screen that separated the men from the women at the Wailing Wall. The Wailing Wall is also a Muslim holy place, though not as important to Muslims as it is to Jews: it is where Mohammad was believed to have tethered his horse during the Night Journey. The British claimed that the small screen was a violation of the status quo that they were pledged to preserve. The Jews rioted; this incited the Arabs, who were also encouraged by the British attitude. There were more pogroms in Jerusalem and the following year horrible massacres of Jews by Arabs in Safed and Hebron. This time, however, Arab violence did not work well for the Jews. Times were changing in Britain: it was a period of economic depression and the Balfour Declaration seemed to belong to another era, when Britain had been a mighty colonial power.

During the 1930s the British continued to cool toward Zionism. It was a time of deliberate pacifism as the government strove to stave off the terrible prospect of a world war. It could be that this desire to appease Hitler led to a renewed anti-Semitism. Even when the Arab revolt against the British broke out in Palestine in April 1936, there was no swing in public opinion in favor of the Balfour Declaration. It was generally thought that if the Jewish homeland was causing all this trouble, then the idea was unworkable and should be abandoned. There was a new desire to appease the Arabs. In July that year, the British welcomed the Arab princes of Saudi Arabia and Iraq, whom they had hitherto regarded with colonial contempt, when they appeared as mediators between the Palestinians and the British. They urged their fellow Arabs to trust the British, who had promised not to abandon them. As part of an attempt to appease the Arabs, the Peel Commission, convened to look into the question of Palestine, recommended the partition of the country between Arabs and Jews. The Jews could have a small state in the Galilee and on the coastal plain, which they had been cultivating: the Arabs could take the rest and 250,000 Arabs would be transferred out of the Jewish area in order to accommodate more Jews. Even when the Arabs refused to accept this, in contrast to the Jews who *did* accept partition, the British did not warm toward Zionism. In 1939 a white paper repudiated partition and envisaged the setting up of an independent Palestinian state.

The British remained opposed to Zionism and committed to guarding the rights of the Palestinians to the end of their mandate. Even after the hideous revelations of the Nazi Holocaust, Britain continued to oppose Jewish immigration. President Truman's public demand in 1946 for the immediate admission of 100,000 Jewish refugees to Palestine was refused by the British. On June 29 of that year the British government ordered the arrest of the Jewish leaders and, harried by Jewish terrorism in Palestine, Foreign Secretary Ernest Bevin declared the British intention of referring the mandate back to the United Nations on February 18, 1947. In July that year came the distressing incident of the steamer *Exodus*, which was carrying 4500 survivors of the Holocaust to Palestine. The British refused them entry and sent the ship back to Germany. The British mandate expired on May 15, 1948, the day after Ben-Gurion proclaimed the state of Israel, with the support of the United Nations.

If the British often appeared to be stubborn and one-sided on the question of Palestine, so too did the Arabs. In contrast to Zionism, their movement seemed negative, perhaps inevitably. The Jews had an inspiring ideology and were committed to making the desert bloom. The Palestinians, who knew that they were necessarily excluded from the Zionists' grand scheme, seemed always to by saying no to all this wonderful progress. Sometimes, as we have seen, their negativity broke out in violence that proved harmful to their cause. Thus during the pogrom of April 4–8, 1920, 9 people died (5 of them Jews) and 244 were injured (211 were Jews).[48] The result of this was the renewed British commitment to Zionism at the San Remo Conference at the end of April. Again, in October 1920, the Arabs missed a chance to nip the whole Zionist idea in the bud when they refused to participate in the legislative council which the British proposed to set up. This would have been a predominantly Arab body. The Zionists, headed by Weizmann, took a calculated risk and accepted the proposal, even though it would have been injurious to them. But the Arabs at this stage did not understand the way representative institutions worked; there had been no chance to participate in government under the Ottoman rule, and to them political freedom meant a vociferous and uncompromising adherence to an absolute position. Further, the attitude of some of the British officials as well as the British press was extremely anti-Zionist at that time, despite the San Remo decision. This led the Arabs to think that the idea of a Jewish National Home could easily be quashed without compromise on their part.[49] Their refusal of the legislative council was a disastrous mistake, and unfortunately the cult of the absolute has remained a durable and harmful element in Arab opposition to Israel to the present day. The refusal demonstrates the Arabs' political inexperience at that point: in 1935, when a similar proposal was made by the British, the Arabs showed a cautious interest and it was the Jews who turned it down. By that time a new generation of Western-educated Palestinians was emerging, who were more amenable to the ideas of compromise and representation.

The following year the British made a serious mistake. The Palestinians needed a leader and it was decided that the Mufti of Jerusalem would become a Grand Mufti and the representative of the Palestinians. In 1921 the post became vacant and the young Hajji Amin al-Husseini was one of the contenders for the position. He was in his mid-twenties and ill qualified for the post: he had neither the experience nor the appropriate learning. He was also a fanatical enemy of both the British and the Jews. The Arab electoral college voted sensibly and when the votes came in Hajji Amin was at the bottom of the list. Sheikh Hisam ad-Din, a moderate and learned man, who would have been an excellent leader, was the new Grand Mufti. The Hajji's family, however, one of the most powerful in Palestine, was furious and began a vicious and violent campaign against the result in Jerusalem. During the disturbances, one E. T. Richmond, adviser to the Commissioner for Muslim Affairs and rabidly anti-Zionist, persuaded Governor Sir Herbert Samuel to make Sheikh Hisam stand down and to put the Hajji in his place. Sir Herbert was anxious to appease the Arabs and followed this advice. It was a tragic decision because from that moment there was no hope of a moderate leadership. The Hajji pursued an extreme policy and had a disastrous influence. At the San Remo Conference, which had adopted the Balfour Declaration, the Arab and Jewish delegates had shared a table at a celebration of this event. But by February 1939, when a conference was convened in London to try to settle the problem of Palestine, the Arabs refused to sit with the Jews under any circumstances.[50] This absolute refusal to negotiate with Jews was fatal to the Arabs' cause and was due to nearly twenty years of the Hajji's leadership. The kind of man the Hajji was can be shown by the fact that he sought an ally in Adolf Hitler and thus discredited the Palestinian cause by linking it with the fascist regime.

Yet the Palestinians did not always react violently; even in provocative circumstances they were capable of restraint. From 1921 to 1928 there was no Arab violence against Jews. The year 1925 was particularly testing. In 1924 the United States had closed its doors to Jewish immigrants. This had fatal consequences for the thousands of Jews who would seek asylum from Hitler and would make Palestine even more of a necessary refuge. In 1925 there was a massive flood of Jewish immigrants into Palestine, mainly from Poland. It was the beginning of the wave of immigration known as the Fourth Aliyah, which made Tel Aviv into a relatively populous city. Yet there was no Arab protest. That same year Lord Balfour came to Palestine to preside over the opening of the Hebrew University. This could have been seen as a deliberate provocation and the Arabs could have demonstrated violently but again nothing happened. There are indications that at this point some of the Arabs saw the Jews in a newly vulnerable light: they were the outcasts of the nations and in time Britain would cast them out too.

We have seen that Arab violence did not always damage their cause with the British. The horrific pogroms of 1929 seem almost certainly to have been orchestrated by the Hajji: they seemed to various observers to be too organized to be the eruption of spontaneous violence.[51] The incident at the Wailing Wall on the feast of Yom Kippur the previous year may well have shown the Hajji that there was a definite change in British attitudes and that he could now get away with more extreme measures. The incident also suited his policy, which was Pan-Muslim, based on the theme of protecting the holy places in Jerusalem from the Jews and the Christians. The violence in Hebron in August 1929 left indelible marks on both sides of the conflict: 133 Jews had been killed by Arabs and 339 were injured. In the repression of the attack by the British police, 110 Arabs were killed and 232 wounded.[52] These horrible events did the Arab cause no harm with the British but it naturally hardened the Jewish opposition to the Arabs. It convinced even the most moderate Zionists that there was no hope of any peaceful settlement and that the Arabs could never be trusted.

The Arabs were badly led. During the 1930s other groups sprang up to defend the homeland, independent of the Hajji. There was the Istiqlal (Independence) Party, founded by Awni Abd al-Hadi in 1932; the National Bloc Party, formed and led by Abd al-Latif Salah; the Islah (Reform) Party, founded in 1933 by Hassayn Fakhri al-Khalidi; and the National Defense Party, founded the following year by Raghib al-Nashashibi. In fact these various parties split the opposition to Zionism, and personal and selfish motives had tended to inspire the proliferation of these groups. There was constant bickering between them, based on family interests, and they came in for a great deal of bitter criticism. Thus the poem "Angry Assembly" by Muhyi al-Din al-Hajj Isa, written in 1932:

They met but failed to come to terms. How often they went
   into the attack and talked a lot; but liars and useless beings
   they were.
Among them the hatred and evil intent which they had sucked
   at since babyhood came to light.
Some set traps for others to walk into; some made fun of
   others' dreams. New ideas were invented.
Others pretended to be faithful while they were liars and
   greedy.
Such things cause great grief. If only they had not met.[53]

With such an unprofessional leadership and an undisciplined spirit
which, al-Hajj Isa points out in another poem, makes everybody want
to be a leader and nobody content to be led, there was no way that
an effective opposition to Zionism could be mounted.[54] The rising,
critical younger generation would blame their fathers for the stupidity
which helped them to lose Palestine. The Arab revolt against the
British, for example, was an absurd struggle and seemed to be biting
the hand that was concerned to feed them. Certainly it dissipated their
energies and resources. But it still has to be emphasized that the British
gave them strong grounds for hope that their cause would prevail and
that their violent negative policies sometimes seemed to strengthen
British opposition to Zionism.

Against this hostile background, the character of Zionism had to
change. It could no longer remain a purely mystical, peace-loving
movement. In 1923 the Russian writer Vladimir Jabotinsky founded
the Union of Zionist Revisionists and it was he more than anybody
else who was responsible for militarizing Zionism. "We ought not to
be deterred by this Latin word 'militarism,' " he argued; it was "the
natural defence of a people that had no homeland and faced extinc-
tion."[55] Jabotinsky had no time for Labor Zionism. He was an admirer
of Herzl and shared his aristocratic vision of the new Jew. But in his
own way he was just as idealistic as Ben-Gurion. Revisionist youth
who joined his organization Betar strove for the virtues of *hadar*
(chivalry). Jabotinsky did not want the Zionists to be peaceful peasants
farming the land but proud Crusaders, displaying an unflappable confidence, dignity, a sense of honor and *noblesse oblige*. When the *Betarim*
arrived in Eretz Yisrael, they did not join the Conquest of Labor on
a *kibbutz*; instead they did two years' military service. Jabotinsky had
no socialist dreams of a model society; he wanted a nation-state on
both sides of the Jordan. He was strongly affected by the nationalism
of his day, which had a racist tinge. In later years Ben-Gurion used
to call him "Vladimir Hitler." In Jabotinsky's view, the Jews needed

a state so that they could preserve their racial purity and hence their unique creativity and integrity.

The future state of Israel, he argued, would need an army. It was no use hoping that the Palestinians would meekly acquiesce in the Zionist plan. "They are not a rabble but a nation," he pointed out, "perhaps somewhat tattered but still living. A living people makes such enormous concessions only when there is no hope."[56] Whether the Laborites liked it or not, Zionism was a colonial activity and no colony had ever managed to impose itself against the native majority without force, so the Jews must now build "an iron wall of Jewish bayonets" instead of *kibbutzim*, "which the native population cannot break through."[57] That, he insisted, was the only possible Zionist policy toward the Arabs. There was, he said in the relatively peaceful year 1927,

> an iron law of every colonising movement, a law which knows of no exceptions, a law which existed in all times and under all circumstances. If you wish to colonise a land in which people were already living you must provide a garrison on your behalf. Or else—or else, give up your colonisation, for without an armed force which will render physically impossible any attempts to destroy or prevent this colonisation, colonisation is impossible, not "difficult," not "dangerous," but IMPOSSIBLE. . . . Zionism is a colonising adventure and it therefore stands or falls by the question of armed force. It is important to build, it is important to speak Hebrew, but unfortunately, it is even more important to be able to shoot—or else I am through with playing at colonisation.[58]

The Revisionists quickly became very popular in Eretz Yisrael and the diaspora. Volunteers flocked into Betar and Jabotinsky defiantly trained them on the Mount of Olives under the very noses of the British. Zionism was acquiring the militant image that it would never lose. Even the Laborites now had their defense corps, the Haganah, which would develop its commando wing, the Palmach. Under Jabotinsky's influence, the Haganah became more professional, and after his death in the diaspora in 1941, it would, as we shall see, be his disciples who would play a key and ruthless role in the creation of the state of Israel. Jabotinsky used to say that Judea had fallen in blood and fire and in fire and blood it would rise again. His disciples fulfilled that prophecy.

But Revisionism had other negative effects. During the 1920s, when a relative peace did give the Yishuv, the Jewish community in Palestine, a chance to build their national home, a good deal of time was lost in internal disputes. There was conflict between Weizmann and Ben-Gurion and great conflict between the Laborites and the Revisionists. Jabotinsky accused Ben-Gurion of kowtowing to the British and declared that Jews could not afford idealism; the Laborites called the Revisionists fascists. Just how bitter the conflict was became clear in 1933 when Chaim Arlosoroff, the head of the political department of the Jewish Agency, was murdered on the sand dunes in front of Tel Aviv; two Revisionists were suspected and even arrested, though the case was never proved.

During the 1930s, however, the terrible news from Europe made even Ben-Gurion and his Laborites take a harder line. The situation was becoming desperate, especially in view of the British abandonment of Zionism. The Jews seemed to have no friends left and dreams of a model socialist society gave way to a vision of Palestine as a refuge for as many Jews as could possibly be saved from the approaching calamity. Even the Laborites were now for a Jewish state with a Jewish majority. This meant that the Arabs became more of a threat than ever: "There is no hope that this new Jewish state will survive to say nothing of develop, if the Arabs are as numerous as they are today,"[59] said the veteran Zionist Menachem Ussiskin, who thirty years earlier had been afraid that settlements in Eretz Yisrael would provoke fresh wrath from the *goyim*. The Laborite propagandist Berl Katzenelson was more tolerant about Arab presence in the future state: "I am willing to give the Arabs equal rights," he said, "if I know that only a small minority stays in the land."[60] He proposed a plan for a new state that included a provision to force the Palestinians to leave. "Development means evictions," said Joseph Weitz, the director of the Jewish National Fund. If the land was full of Arabs, how could they possibly accommodate the millions of Jewish refugees whom they hoped to rescue? Weitz wrote in a report that the deportation of the Palestinians from a Jewish state "does not serve only one aim—to diminish the Arab population. It also serves a second purpose by no means less important, which is to evacuate land now cultivated by Arabs and thus release it for Jewish settlement."[61] Weizmann dreamed of buying a lot of land over the border in the Arab countries and pushing the Palestinians into it. He wanted Britain and America to put pressure on the Palestinians to go quietly, but if necessary, he wrote in his diary, "we must be prepared ourselves to carry it out."[62]

When the Peel Commission suggested the partition plan in 1937, many people in Britain objected to the forcible transfer of 250,000 Palestinians from the proposed Jewish state: they argued that there was not enough arable land for many of these peasant deportees in the less fertile area proposed for the Palestinian state. Where the Arabs refused partition outright, one of their reasons was their objection to this forcible deportation. The Jews, however, agreed to the partition plan, even though the tiny state was far too small for their needs. There are indications that the leaders had dreams for the aggrandizement of this very skimpy state of Israel. When Weizmann was asked if he were really satisfied with the very modest little state proposed in the partition plan, he replied: "The Kingdom of David was smaller, under Solomon it became an empire. Who knows? *C'est le premier pas qui compte.*"[63] Ben-Gurion spoke more bluntly at a Zionist meeting: "I favour partition of the country because when we become a strong power after the establishment of the state, we will abolish partition and spread throughout Palestine."[64] The following year he wrote to his son:

> We shall organise a sophisticated defence force—an elite army. I have no doubt that our army will be one of the best in the world. And then I am sure that we shall not be prevented from settling in all the other parts of the country, whether through mutual understanding with our Arab neighbours or by other means.[65]

An unexpurgated text of this letter, only recently made available, adds: "We will expel the Arabs and take their places."[66] Zionism was becoming a tougher and more ruthless movement. Already it was looking forward to an expulsion that would have shocked the young idealists of the Second Aliyah. But it was having to adapt to a world that none of them had envisaged in the early years of the movement. The endless adaptability of Zionism was one of its great strengths. When war broke out between England and Germany in 1939, the same year as the white paper which abandoned the partition plan and proposed an independent Palestinian state, Ben-Gurion gave further evidence of its flexibility: "We shall fight the war as though there were no White Paper," he said, "and the White Paper as though there were no war."[67]

A new type of Zionist arrived in Eretz Yisrael during the early 1940s. Menachem Begin, who was to become Prime Minister of Israel in 1977, had experienced the new anti-Semitism in Poland and the Soviet Union. His whole family had been murdered together with the entire Jewish community of his hometown, Brest Litovsk—some 30,000 souls. Begin was one of the few people to survive an interrogation by Stalin's NKVD unbroken; he survived a slave camp in the Arctic Circle, was released and walked to Eretz Yisrael through Central Asia. He was a tough, desperate man, committed to revenge. He was also intensely religious. In 1943 Begin, an admirer of the late Jabotinsky, took command of the Irgun Zvai Leumi, the Revisionists' military army, and two months later began terrorist activities against the British administration. Begin repudiated the terrorist label himself, but, even though he condemned "murder," he blew up CID offices, tax centers and the Immigration Building, planted bombs and led raids in which Britons and civilian Arabs were killed. Another terrorist organization was Lehi, led by Avraham Stern and called the "Stern Gang" by the British. Stern had been killed in 1942 but Yitzhak Shamir, who would become Prime Minister of Israel in 1986, continued the work of the organization. Begin despised the Stern Gang for its crude methods: he would have nothing to do with such Lehi operations as the killing of six British paratroopers in their beds in 1946. However, the two groups were flung together following the assassination in 1944 by the Stern Gang of Lord Moyne, the British Minister for Middle Eastern Affairs. Ben-Gurion and the Haganah were appalled and started a campaign against both terrorist groups, capturing members and handing them over to the British. During this period underground, the Irgun and Lehi became more desperate than ever.

The bitter war between the Haganah and the terrorist groups came to an end when the British raided the Jewish Agency on June 29, 1946, arresting 2718 Zionists. Begin was now determined to get rid of the British: on July 22 of that year the Irgun blew up a wing of the King David hotel, which housed the British administration, killing 91 people. The British were now determined to hand the problem of Palestine over to the United Nations but were afraid that, if they left, the Arabs would move in and exterminate the Yishuv. The following year, in retaliation for the execution of three Jewish terrorists, Begin hanged and mined the bodies of two British sergeants a few hours later. In Britain there were anti-Jewish riots in four major cities and in Derby a synagogue was burned down.

Up to this point, neither the Stern Gang nor the Irgun had ever attacked an Arab village or town; their campaigns against Arabs had been small and retaliatory in nature. The village of Deir Yassin near Jerusalem had made a nonaggression pact during the winter of 1947–48 with the Jewish suburb of Givat Shaul. When two Jewish settlements nearby were overrun and destroyed during the fighting which had broken out between Arabs and Jews in Palestine, the Irgun and Stern decided to take revenge. The object was to raise Jewish spirits and to break Arab morale. The attackers were supposed to warn the villagers with a loudspeaker so that the women, children and old people could be evacuated, but the loudspeaker van got stuck in a ditch and was abandoned. The Arabs put up a strong resistance, so the Irgun had to ask for help from the Haganah. A squadron of commandos was dispatched and the village subdued. When the Haganah went home, Irgun and Lehi avenged their comrades who had fallen in the battle and began looting and massacring for most of the following day. Two hundred and fifty men, women, children and old people were massacred and their bodies mutilated. The nightmare scenes were described by Meir Pa'il of the Haganah, who had been sent along as a spy. He told his story of the atrocity in 1972. Begin sent his congratulations "on this splendid act of conquest. . . . As at Deir Yassin, so everywhere, we will attack and smite the enemy. God, God, thou hast chosen us for conquest."[68]

The story of Deir Yassin is important because it did terrify the Arabs. On April 25, 1948, the Irgun attacked Arab Jaffa. Again the Arabs fought bravely at first but had not enough ammunition to counter the Irgun's mortars and, with the memory of Deir Yassin fresh in everybody's mind, nearly all the 70,000 inhabitants abandoned their city and fled. There followed scenes of looting, pillaging and destruction. Begin himself has commented that the story of Deir Yassin did a great service to the Jewish state: it got rid of the Arabs.[69]

In 1948, as we have seen, five Arab armies invaded the newly established state of Israel and were repulsed. During the fighting and the cleaning-up operations that followed, some 750,000 Palestinians fled the country and became refugees. They have never been allowed to return. The official Israeli explanation of this mass exodus is that the Jews invited the Arabs to stay but that the Arabs preferred to listen to the advice of their leaders, who urged them to flee. The Palestinian refugees themselves, however, say that they fled because of their fear of Irgun cruelty. The memory of Deir Yassin was still fresh. The Palestinians also claim that Israeli soldiers terrorized many Arab villages, rounding up hostages and shooting them in villages like Safsaf and Sa'sa; that some Arabs were driven from their villages and forbidden to return: the villages were either mined or guarded by soldiers. Some Arabs stayed on as refugees in their own country until they were finally rounded up and sent over the border.[70]

However one chooses to interpret these events of 1948, it is true that the creation of the state of Israel has meant a long history of subsequent suffering for the Palestinian people. It has also added a deep complexity to the new Israeli identity. Zionism had done great things for the Jewish people. It had proved that the Jews were not timid weaklings, religious anachronisms or hopeless aliens. The Israeli Jews were tough pioneers, brave soldiers and creative farmers. The state of Israel had brought the Jews firmly back into the family of the nations and, instead of being seen by anti-Semites as relics of the ancient world, the Jews were now vanguards of progress in the Middle East. The state of Israel must be one of the most extraordinary achievements of the twentieth century, a monument to dedication and resolution. The Zionists had turned an abstruse theory into an established fact. But entwined with this positive Israeli image was the image of the suffering, homeless Palestinians, who to this day claim that they have a right to their own land. The two peoples have been bound together in a history of suffering and violence which continues to escalate.

The Zionists who actually uprooted themselves from the diaspora and made *aliyah* to Eretz Yisrael have never had any doubts about the validity of their claim to the land. They found Zionism a liberating force in their lives and many of them were able to pass this confidence on to their children. They had imagined that the Sabras, the Jews who were born in Israel, would feel much more at home there than their parents. Indeed, because they had been convinced that a physical and spiritual contact with the fatherland was vital for the new Jewish identity, the founding fathers decided that their children should be formed and nurtured by the land of Israel itself. Their souls were to be shaped by it, just as the souls of their fathers had been liberated from the trauma of the diaspora by lovingly cultivating its soil. The settlers decided that the land itself would educate the Sabras. Eretz Yisrael was to be the pivot upon which all educational activity turned and the child's senses, emotions and intellect were to be stimulated and shaped by his native landscape. The homeland would become an essential part of his integrity and identity. The young Sabras toured the country as much as possible, studying its geography and its flora and fauna. These field trips gave Sabras a formative and creative contact with the land. The children made excursions to important historical sites like Masada, where the Jewish resistance fighters had committed suicide rather than submit to the Romans in the year 73. A field trip or a trip to Masada was—and still is—a kind of secular pilgrimage. The Israeli scholar Eliezer Schweid has written of these excursions:

Anyone sensitive to the ambience of these trips can see that they are not merely another form of entertainment. There is something ceremonial, serious and elevated about the way the participants go about their preparations and about the trip itself, a kind of psychological attitude and devotion that give it an almost ritual character. In other words, the field trip is an act of symbolic significance; by means of it one accomplishes a higher purpose. It is the culmination of a process, the fulfilment of a hope. It embodies something of the whole meaning of life.[71]

It was a journey to the roots of the Jewish people and a way of taking possession of the homeland. Each new generation was to establish the land of Israel in its mind and heart more deeply. The pilgrimages, excursions or hikes were complementary to the peaceful Conquest of Labor. This becomes clear when it is recalled that an annual march of citizens to Jerusalem has taken the place the place of a military parade on Independence Day.

But this education did not work infallibly for all Sabras. Eliezer Schweid points out that a significant number of Sabras in each generation cannot share the absolute certainty of the early pioneers. Israel is a garrison state; since 1948 she has existed in a state of siege, rather as the Crusader states had done during the Middle Ages. Israel, like the Crusader states again, is a military state, constantly prepared for war. It is not surprising, therefore, that some Sabras should question Israel's position in an effort to understand a most complex situation. In 1948 the young Sabras were given a wonderful gift: a whole country to explore. But wherever they went there were reminders of danger and of enemies: there were barbed-wire borders, mines, warnings. They would see the ruins of the old Arab villages. Some remember playing with Arab children in their villages before 1948; suddenly those villages—and the children—disappeared and they speak of the profound shock they experienced.

In fact Israelis have contrasting attitudes to these old Arab villages. Thus the eminent Israeli scholar Israel Shahak is outraged that some four-hundred Arab villages were razed to the ground after the 1948 war, "destroyed *completely* with their houses, garden-walls, and even cemeteries and tomb-stones so that literally a stone does not remain standing and visitors are passing and being told that 'it was all desert.' "[72] He finds such an attempt to eliminate the Arab past of his country, together with some uneasy memories perhaps, unethical and he has devoted his life to a critical understanding of the problems of Zionism and Judaism. On the other hand, Moshe Dayan had absolutely no problem about the Arab past:

We came to this country which was already populated by Arabs, and we are establishing a Hebrew, that is a Jewish state here. . . . Jewish villages were built in the place of Arab villages. You do not even know the names of these Arab villages, and I do not blame you because these geography books no longer exist; not only do the books not exist, the Arab villages are not there either. Nahalal arose in the place of Mahalul, Gevat—in the place of Jibta, Sarid —in the place of Haneifia and Kefar Yehoshua—in the place of Tell Shaman. There is not one place built in this country that did not have a former Arab population.[73]

One can see Dayan as an excellent representative of the Zionist struggle. He was brought up on a *kibbutz* and liked to say that he had been intended for a farmer but had turned out to be a soldier instead: he combined the love of the soil of the Laborites with the martial virtues of Jabotinsky. A military hero and for years a leading politician, he was an epitome of the new Jew: tough, brave and absolutely dedicated to his people and to his country. Indeed the army, to which he had given his life, definitely reflects the old Labor ideals. It is a people's army; officers and men are on informal, first-name terms; there is no emphasis on rank and hierarchy; no cult of parades or smart uniforms. In some respects it is reminiscent of the military order of the Templars in the Crusader states, which had a similar cult of tough asceticism and equality.

One of Dayan's favorite pursuits was amateur archaeology. He had a fine collection of antiquities which he had found himself. He once nearly died during a dig when the hole he was in caved in and buried him: he had broken his ribs, injured his spine, and when they dug him out he was unconscious and near suffocation. This did not deter him. He told an interviewer shortly after his accident that his obsessive archaeological digging was a quest for

the ancient Land of Israel. Everything that ancient *Eretz Israel* was; those who lived there then, their way of life. You sometimes feel that you can literally enter their presence. They are dead to be sure. But you can enter the homes of silenced people and sometimes feel more than when you enter the homes of the living. I like to stick my head into a hole in which the people of Bnei Brak lived 6,000 years ago . . . to have a look at their kitchen, to finger the ashes left there from long ago, to feel the fingerprints which that ancient potter left on the vessel.[74]

It is no accident that Israel's two most famous archaeologists were also eminent soldiers. The other is Yigal Yadin, who was a general and chief of staff. If the Israeli army is a living symbol of Zionist ideals, archaeology is a passion that is unique in Israel. This passion, which strikes professionals and amateurs alike, has been given the Hebrew name *bulmus*, an old Talmudic term which denotes a ravenous hunger or mania. Unpaid voluntary work on archaeological sites is one of the two main social services for which Israelis volunteer in great numbers. The other, significantly, is for dangerous duty in crack army units and for service in exposed border settlements.[75] It is not difficult to understand why this should be so. Freud himself compared archaeology to the process of psychoanalysis:[76] in both pursuits people dig for hidden but important roots in the past and gain a new insight and new lease of life in the process. Zionism itself had initiated just such a rebirth by means of a creative encounter with the past, and it is clear that many Israelis find reassurance in discovering in the soil of Eretz Yisrael evidence that their forefathers really were there. Yigal Yadin, who was in charge of the great excavations at Masada, has explained that this journey to the past has a quasi-religious element, and has claimed that it inspires the young Sabra to fight for his country: "Through archeology they discovered their 'religious values.' In archeology they find their religion. They learn that their forefathers were in this country 3000 years ago. That is a value. By this they fight and by this they live."[77] In digging deep in order actually to touch their roots (touching and handling are particularly dwelt upon by Dayan) Sabras are finding certainty. Archaeology is a quasi-religious activity which replaces the old faith and makes Sabras absolutely sure that they have a right to their land.

The same can be said of the cult of hiking in Israel. This again tends to be more intense than in other countries. Clearly it is related to the theme of secular pilgrimage described by Eliezer Schweid. After the 1948 war a young boy called Meir Har-Zion became a living legend in the country by means of his extraordinarily brave hikes. He would often go over the border into Jordan, taking his little sister with him, and explore places like Jericho or the source of the river Jordan. On one occasion he and his sister were taken prisoner when they strayed into Syrian territory and were only released by the kind offices of the Red Cross. These jaunts were extremely dangerous: it was a capital offense for an Israeli—be he Jewish or Arab—to go into Arab territory. On one occasion Har-Zion had to kill an Arab soldier. The reason he became a popular hero and part of the mythology of Israel was surely his refusal to be hemmed in by enmity and hostility. He wanted to prove that the Jews could transcend these boundaries and difficulties. Later, as one might expect, he became a famous commando in the Israeli army. Moshe Dayan wrote that his "fighting instinct and courage set an example for the entire Israel Defence forces." His courage in the face of danger, indeed his disregard of danger, seemed superhuman. It has been said that he was an Israeli version of the Indian fighters in the American Wild West, as he laconically killed

Arabs in the course of his duty, cold-bloodedly, without hatred, but in a kind of fury of efficiency. As Amos Elon points out, the myth of Har-Zion has its worrying aspects but people who become legends in their own lifetime do so for good reason.[78] Israelis are living in a dangerous situation, surrounded by enemies, and Har-Zion's early playful disregard of this danger was a liberating myth.

Obviously not all Israeli hikers go to the lengths of Har-Zion! But it was noticeable before the Palestinian uprising of 1987 how popular hiking and camping expeditions were on the West Bank. This was potentially dangerous. Quite often hikers would be killed by Arabs in the occupied territories. But hiking was a way of laying claim to the territories, of asserting that they belonged to Israel. Israelis are very proud of the beauties of their country, and when they show a foreigner around they do so in a way that is quite different from the way we, for example, in England show visitors famous historical sites. In London we have a joke that we never think of going to the Tower of London or the British Museum unless we have to escort a guest there. Quite the opposite is true in Israel. Both the Sabras and the Israeli Arabs display their country with a fervor that is reverential and emotionally intense.

There are, however, Sabras who question the situation deeply. This is especially true in the new Israeli literature. It has been pointed out that there is not a single good Israeli novel that exalts the glory of war, which must surely make Israel unique. Instead the mood of the best writers is deeply questioning and explores the dilemmas of the Jewish state at a profound level. The fact that they are read so enthusiastically by their fellow countrymen shows that they are fulfilling a real need. Even though some criticize them for their pusillanimous, defeatist spirit, many more must need to work these problems through by reading about them. One of the first of the great Israeli classics is *Days of Ziklag* by S. Yizar, which deals with the 1948 war. Yizar is clearly attached to his country: the book is full of powerful descriptions of the landscape. All these writers in their own way are convinced Zionists but feel that Zionism has problems that people must explore. Repression is too dangerous. The heroes of *Days of Ziklag* feel that their love of their country is a burden, that Zionist rhetoric is a millstone around their necks and that the sacred term "homeland" is demanding, ambiguous and insufficient for the sacrifices they are expected to make. Similarly in the *Tale of Khirbat Khisa*, which was written just after the war of independence, a soldier describes the cold-blooded expulsion of the Arab villagers from their homes and their inhuman dispatch to the "other side." It is a horrible revelation to the young hero. In words that recall the "dread" of Ben Yehuda, he says: "I felt within me a stupefying collapse."[79] When he contemplates the Arab village being absorbed into an exemplary Jewish settlement, he can find nothing positive about this "rebuilding" of the land:

> We'll open a co-op grocery, a school, perhaps a synagogue. There'll be political parties. They'll all discuss lots of things. The fields will be plowed and sown and reaped, and great feats will be accomplished. Bravo Hebrew *Khisa*! Who'll remember that there was once a *Khirbat Khisa* which we drove out and inherited. *We came, shot, burned, blew up, repelled, pushed and exiled. What the hell are we doing here?*[80]

The last question is not rhetorical. It is more of a challenge. The fact that S. Yizar was eagerly read in the years that followed the 1948 war, when people were trying to assimilate what had happened, shows that people needed to work through the issues he raises. Israelis have a lot of impossible things to come to terms with. They have made a point of making the Nazi Holocaust central in the Jewish state. The Holocaust Memorial at Yad Vashem is a secular national shrine. On Holocaust Day each year, everything stops for two minutes and even cars come to a standstill and blow their horns in memory of the six million killed by Hitler. Israel has wisely understood the importance of bringing this tragedy out into the open, so that it does not fester in the depths of the psyche. It is public mourning. Similarly, in allowing these critical voices of her writers and indeed in encouraging them, she is performing a similar service.

The leading Israeli novelist A. B. Yehoshua is similarly obsessed by the Arab past that lies beneath the rebuilt land and shows constant doubts about the rights and wrongs of Zionism. In his first novel *Facing the Forests* (1963), the hero, who, interestingly for our purposes, is writing a thesis on the Crusades, takes a job as a caretaker of a newly planted forest—one of the showpieces of the Zionist enterprise. He finds himself increasingly haunted by the Arab village that the forest had obliterated and finally helps one of the former villagers to burn the forest down in an orgiastic ecstasy of liberation. Yehoshua's heroes and heroines often feel a nagging guilt and constant worry and are frustrated in their attempts to make amends to one another or to Arabs they encounter. When Yehoshua digs below the surface of the Jewish state he does not find the certainty that Dayan did, when he dug for archaeological remains. He finds that the roots of Zionism are tangled with the pain and destruction of the ruined Arab villages.

Amos Oz, who is perhaps Israel's finest writer, is also a staunch

Zionist. He would certainly not wish the state of Israel to disappear. He is a dedicated *Kibbutznik* and proud of the achievements of his country, dwelling particularly on the creation of the *kibbutz*, the resurrection of the Hebrew language, the Hebrew University and, interestingly, the Israeli army. Israelis are very proud of his international reputation and his books are always best-sellers. His articles are read very widely and discussed compulsively. He is a national figure. Oz is, however, very concerned that Israel remain true to the whole of the Jewish tradition and not lose essential Jewish values by a false patriotism or chauvinism. He feels concerned to maintain the humanism that was Judaism's gift to the world and therefore he insists that Zionists must examine their position carefully. In particular they should try to see things from the Arabs' point of view. The Jews, of all people, must beware of the temptation to deny the identity and rights of others.

In his novels and stories we find a love of the landscape but there is often something sinister and threatening about the land of Israel. There is a constant sense of dread, of siege, frontiers. There is barbed wire; there is the danger of Arab terrorism; infiltrators raid on both sides of the borders; jackals howl in the hills outside the *kibbutz* and enemy arc lights search the skies. *My Michael*, Oz's most famous novel, was published in 1968 and became a cult book after the Six Day War, as Yizar's *Days of Ziklag* had been read compulsively after the 1948 war. It was written before 1967 and reflects the situation before the war, however. The picture is bleak. To Hannah, the heroine, Jerusalem is not a holy place but dangerous and threatening. Indeed, she cannot feel safe or at home anywhere in the country and she feels distant from the Zionist hope and confidence. When she visits her mother for a Passover party in a *kibbutz* in the Galilee, she feels at first a wonderful sense of freedom and escape. A trip north means escape from the enemy, who seems to lurk at the gates of Jerusalem. The bus speeds through the rebuilt land; the passengers eat Jaffa oranges and admire the landscape with Zionist reverence; Hannah's companions talk about the War of Independence and the government irrigation works; Hannah smiles prettily and affirms her faith in "all the great works of irrigation."[81] At the *kibbutz*, she whirls around in the hora in a classic evening of Israeli togetherness. For a moment she feels at home and at one with her environment: "I revelled. I was swept away. I belonged."[82]

But towards dawn I went out and stood all alone on the balcony of Emmanuel's small house. I saw coils of barbed wire. I saw dark bushes. The sky lightened. I was facing north. I could make out the silhouettes of a mountainous landscape: the Lebanese border. Tired lights shone yellow in the ancient stone-built villages. Unapproachable valleys. Distant snow-capped peaks. Lonely buildings on the hill tops, monasteries or forts. A boulder-strewn expanse scarred with deep wadis. A chill breeze blew. I shivered. I longed to leave. What a powerful yearning.[83]

The Zionist yearning for the return to Eretz Yisrael seems to have become a yearning to leave it. But we have seen that Oz himself has no desire to see his people leave the country. What he is attempting here is an examination of some of the more frightening aspects of the Israeli experience.

In Part Two of this book we shall see that the Crusaders were inspired by the "holiness" of Palestine to make efforts that often seemed superhuman. We shall find that many of their ideas about the manner in which this land was "holy" are very similar indeed to Jewish ideas discussed in this chapter. But Crusading was not a glamorous experience: it was desolate and terrifying. In their states, the Christians from the West were foreigners and aliens, constantly besieged by a hostile, Islamic world. Oz is pointing to a very similar aspect of the Israeli experience in the Middle East. Hannah does not feel at home there and it is true that the Zionists are foreigners in the region; it is a state of mind powerfully symbolized by Hannah's vision of the Arab world that is so near and yet so far. This has always been part of the Zionist experience; like crusading, Zionism was often a desolate and traumatic experience. We have seen how deeply committed Zionists like Ben Yehuda and A. B. Gordon felt themselves to be in an alien world. Many of the early settlers felt this desolation acutely: it has been estimated that 70 percent of those who made *aliyah* could not bear it and went home.[84] New settlers arriving at Jaffa would see a crowd waiting for the boat at the harbor and assume that it was a reception committee; instead they found that these people were waiting to get on the boat to go home. In this chapter we have been considering the ways in which the Zionists made the land of their fathers "holy" to them. Without this ideology they could not have endured the experience, and the fact that so many settlers left Eretz Yisrael speaks volumes for the courage of the people who persevered. It must also be true that the reason why *My Michael* is an Israeli classic is because Israelis can still relate to Hannah's sense of desolation and of being a stranger in an alien land.

Oz also feels that it is vital for Israelis to consider the problem of the Arabs and that, as victors, they have a duty to look at the matter from the Arabs' point of view and try to understand *their* experience. Throughout *My Michael* Hannah has fantasies of the Arab twins, Halil and Aziz, who were her playmates when she was a child, but who she now imagines have become terrorists. In her dreams she sees them training in order to destroy the land of Israel. But instead of seeing their terrorism as horrific she sees it as an act of love, love of the country that they still consider to be theirs. She sees them at home in the land in a way that she is not and can never be and their activities are presented as an act of union that is deeper than the hectic and self-conscious togetherness of the *kibbutz*. The bombing is an affirmation of their love for one another and for *Falastin* and is an act of harmony:

> Four lithe arms reach out. Matching as in a dance. As in love. As if all four spring from a single body. Cable. Timing Device. Fuse. Detonator. Igniter. Bodies surge down the hill and away, softly padding. And on the slope beneath the skyline a stealthy run, a longing caress. The undergrowth flattens and straightens as they pass. Like a light skiff edging through still calm waters.[85]

Hannah knows very well that the twins are her creations, her fantasy: "I sent them. To me towards dawn they will return. Come battered and warm. Exuding a smell of sweat and foam."[86] The Israeli has created the Palestinian terrorist and is locked together with him in a close union that is almost sexual. Indeed Oz has pointed out elsewhere—and it is a common theme in Israel—that the Israelis and the Palestinians are deeply bound together. One of these bonds is a bond of violence: but it is also true that the Palestinian experience of nationalism has been very close to the Zionist experience. This nationalism is quite different from any other Arab nationalism and, Oz and others argue, is in some deep sense the creation of Zionism.[87]

Some Israelis condemn the work of writers like Oz and Yehoshua but others see them as powerful voices in the peace process. They are preparing their people to make peace, to sympathize with the Arab point of view and to try to understand the part that Israel has herself played in creating this tragic state of affairs. Indeed during the first twenty years of the state of Israel these views were in the ascendent. Ben-Gurion and his successors remained true, in the main, to the high ideals of Labor Zionism. They made mistakes, some of them serious. But before the June War of 1967 there was a spirit of détente in the country. Politically, Begin and his Herut Party were in the wilderness: the government had no time for this extremism, which they considered dangerous and negative. Younger people were beginning to relax; it seemed that the grim struggle of Zionism was over and some of the young tended to mock the high-minded ideals of the Founding Fathers. While none of them seriously doubted basic Zionist principles, they didn't want to be talking about it all the time: *tsionut* (Zionism) was becoming synonymous with "blah-blah." It was a climate of opinion in which people were ready to consider the Arab point of view and in which peace was possible.

Since the 1967 war, however, there has been a pronounced swing to the right. We shall see in Chapter 7 that a new spirit entered Zionism; that in 1977 Begin became Prime Minister and that his party, led today by Yitzhak Shamir, is now the center party. The left is led by Shimon Peres, who in Ben-Gurion's day was considered a young hawk. Most worrying of all, to Israelis of right and left, is the new far right, which seems to be trying to make the conflict with the Arabs a holy war. The far right has a strong religious element, which in itself disturbs many Israelis, who remain true to the deliberately secular ideology of the old Zionism. The new right insists that it is returning to the old pioneering ideals but the *chalutzim* of the Second Aliyah would have been bewildered and horrified by the parties of the far right. They would have seen them as unethical and fanatic.

The Zionists made many mistakes but before 1967 it seemed that the inherent decency of the Laborites and the *kibbutzim* might prevail. The desire to create an equal, just society; to bring a light to the world; to fight against tyranny and oppression had been important ideals and they were not abandoned. There are still people today who hold to them. Most significant is the conversion of former extremists and right-wing Israelis to a more pacifist position. One of these converts is the writer and politician Uri Avnery, who was once a Revisionist and a member of Lehi but is today the head of one of the peace parties in the Knesset. He is an outspoken and courageous critic of any anti-Arab measures taken by the government. He has helped to organize highly dangerous and controversial meetings between leading Israelis and PLO officials in order to create a spirit of détente. Israelis and Arabs must stop seeing each other as monsters, is his perennial cry. Another convert to peace is Professor Y. Harkabi, the former head of the Israeli secret intelligence, who now sees no hope for the Jewish state unless the Israelis are prepared to make important concessions to the Palestinians. There was a dynamic within the ideology of the old secular Zionism which could impel even former extremists to try to see the problem from the Arab point of view as well as their own. Unfortunately, the new spirit abroad in Israel is making a climate where people like Oz, Avnery and Harkabi feel that they are isolated and increasingly ineffectual. In particular the religious aspect of today's far right is felt to be dangerous. There are always two sides to a conflict and peace is possible when both sides are prepared to acknowledge this. But once you believe that you are fighting for God against his enemies, there can only be one point of view and anything that opposes this becomes monstrous and evil. This we shall examine in more detail in the second part of this book.

In the next section of the chapter we shall look at the problem in more detail from the Arab point of view. I have said that the new swing to the right in Israel dates from the Six Day War. But some have seen the very first signs of this aggression to have entered Israeli policy much earlier, when Israel decided to join in the disreputable plan to reconquer the Suez Canal.

## The Arabs

On July 26, 1956, President Gamal Abdel Nasser was due to address the nation and Egyptians turned on their radios with excited anticipation, certain that something dramatic was about to happen. During the two years that he had been in power Nasser had openly defied the imperialist West. He had denounced the Baghdad Pact of 1955, when Britain and America had made anti-Soviet alliances with Turkey, Iraq and Iran, as a thin device whereby the West sought to control the East. Nasser had retaliated by concluding a large arms deal with the Soviet Union to equip him in his struggle against Israel, which had launched a major raid against Egyptians in Gaza earlier that year. The following year, the United States curtly canceled promised aid for the building of the Aswan Dam, and now Egyptians waited for their President to respond. They were not disappointed. Switching from classical Arabic into the fiery Egyptian dialect, Nasser laughed at the West and declared Egyptian independence. He announced that he was going to nationalize the Suez Canal; was it not "our Canal," he asked, paid for at the cost of 120,000 Egyptian lives? Egypt did not need Western aid with such a major source of revenue. He would pay the shareholders full compensation, so that the transaction would be entirely legal, and the Egyptian canal would pay for the Aswan Dam. Nasser could scarcely have made a more significant point; even his more cautious opponents in the Arab world were enthralled.[88] The Suez Canal was a classic symbol of Western exploitation of the people of the Middle East. It had been built by Europeans during the 1860s at quite a low cost but only 7 percent of the shares were owned by the Egyptians, who scarcely benefited from this asset. By nationalizing the canal, Nasser was clearly telling the Egyptian people that they were now going to take control of their own fate and their own country. Britain and France were aghast, and the British Prime Minister Anthony Eden was reduced to incoherent, helpless rage.[89] Not only had this dynamic young President challenged the entrenched British belief that the Egyptians were a stupid race, incapable of self-rule. He had actually dared to deny that the Arab world was merely a subordinate part of the Western system and must, by the very nature of things, serve Western interests. Eden vowed to destroy Nasser and looked around for allies.

Suez, of course, was Nasser's great triumph. Later that year Britain, France and Israel formed a secret pact to effect a joint, concerted attack on Egypt. On October 29, according to plan, Israel attacked Egyptian territory in Sinai. On the following day the United States' resolution in the UN Security Council calling for Israeli withdrawal was vetoed by Britain and France, who then attacked the Canal Zone on November 5, ostensibly to separate the combatants. But this initiative collapsed completely under pressure from both America and the Soviet Union. Israel, therefore, was left isolated and was threatened by both superpowers. In March she was forced to withdraw from the Sinai, having learned how perilous her situation was in the Middle East without the support of at least one friendly superpower. The whole shameful business was a diplomatic victory for Nasser: Britain, France and Israel had been humiliated, the canal now belonged to Egypt.

The Suez victory has to be seen against a long, painful history of colonization. For over a hundred years Britain and France had been establishing colonies in the Middle East. This had begun in 1830 when the French took Algiers, and nine years later the British colonized Aden. As the Ottoman Empire declined, this colonial expansion continued inexorably: Tunisia was occupied in 1881, Egypt in 1882, the Sudan in 1889 and Libya and Morocco in 1912. In 1915 during the First World War, the British responded to the Arab revolt against the Turks by promising the Arabs independence after the war, but the following year the notorious Sykes-Picot agreement divided the Middle Eastern lands of the Ottoman Empire between them, as we have seen. We have also seen the cynical attitude behind the pacts and pledges made at this time to the Arabs. Not surprisingly, when Britain and France marched into the Middle East and set up their mandates and protectorates, many Arabs saw this as yet another colonial venture. They often call 1920 the *am al-Nakba*, the year of the disaster.

It is perhaps difficult for Western people to understand the problems left behind in the Third World by the colonial experience. Surely the colonies were positive creations in many ways, because they brought progress to a backward, primitive world? The colonials not only brought material comfort and goods but decent, progressive values to the people whose land they ruled. It is true that the colonial policies often exploited these countries and that the administration was often deeply contemptuous of "the natives" but it is also true that many of the colonialists were dedicated to the mission of bringing the light of progress to a world darkened by superstition and disease. But in Europe we have had to re-examine our role in our former colonies and this has produced a widespread recoil from these colonial dreams. Historians have compared the crisis of confidence in postcolonial Europe to the collapse of morale in Europe that followed the failure of the crusading project. Many Europeans have become aware of the havoc they have left behind them, together with the superior technology and modern standard of living. The people of the so-called Third World want this progress but they often hate the people who brought it to them because this infrastructure is felt to be somehow alien. Many of these countries have been rushed to progress too quickly, skipping the long development that made the people of Europe ready for these major changes of lifestyle. Europeans are also having to examine the way they often behaved in the colonies and to reappraise these old values. In Britain the film *Gandhi* and the excellent television series *Jewel in the Crown* painted a very painful picture of the way the British behaved in India but the popularity of both films shows that people wanted to look at their old selves and come to terms with this unedifying phase of their history.

We tend to use the phrases "culture shock" and "being cut off from one's roots" too frequently, so that the force is lost and cannot adequately describe what is a very real problem in many countries of the Third World which have been through the colonial experience. Being cut off from one's roots, after all, describes a kind of death and many people in the former colonies feel that they are hanging helplessly between two cultures, at home in neither their ancient native culture nor in the world of Western values. I have stressed this point because I believe that it is crucial in any approach to the Arab response to the role of the West in its recent history and also to the creation of the state of Israel. We have seen that the holy war is often a response to a trauma. The Crusaders were just beginning to recover from the frightening impotence of the Dark Ages and, in an important sense, crusading was a journey toward a new self. It was an attempt to find themselves again in a new and more effective way. Similarly Zionism was an attempt to create a new kind of Jew and was a response to anti-Semitism. In much the same way, perhaps, many of the recent political and religious movements in the Arab and Muslim world have been similar attempts to recover from the distressing experience of colonialism and to rediscover a self that is not in shock, cut off from the past and humiliated by being exposed to contempt.

It must also be remembered that the new climate of opinion created by the League of Nations, the Fourteen Points and the spread of Western nationalism directly encouraged weaker nations to resist exploitation and humiliation. They were told that they had an inalienable right to govern their own destiny. Indeed France and Britain were well aware, when they established their mandates in 1920, that they would shortly have to give these countries independence. But at the time the Arabs who called this new Western intervention in their affairs *al-Nakba*, The Disaster, could only feel their impotence before the powerful world of Europe.

Indeed their crushing defeat at the hands of Israel in 1948 could only increase their sense of humiliation. Finally, when 750,000 Arab Palestinians were forbidden to return to their country and had to live in crowded, hastily constructed refugee camps, the indifference of the rest of the world seemed insulting. It was not easy for the very young Arab states to cope with these thousands of refugees. Egypt, for example, had horrific economic problems and could not feed or accommodate its own poor; Lebanon had potential political problems of its own; the Bedouin regime of King Hussein of Jordan felt precariously unwilling to absorb these thousands of Palestinian refugees. They are not the only people who have found the absorption of refugees and immigrants difficult. Indeed, at the very same time as the Palestinian refugees fled to the Arab countries, the hostility aroused in Arab countries by the creation of the state of Israel made it necessary for nearly 600,000 Jews to flee their homes there and take refuge in the Jewish state. The Israelis received their fellow Jews from the Arab countries and tried to absorb them, and there is no doubt that they made a better job of it than the Arab countries made of assimilating the Palestinians. But it is also true that the way the European Jews in Israel treated these oriental Jews has left a bitter legacy of hatred behind so that there is today a deep rift between the Ashkenazic Jews from Europe and the Sephardim from the Arab world. The Sephardim claim that the Ashkenazim poured scorn on their particular Jewish traditions, tried to force the alien ideology of Zionism upon them and made them into second-class citizens.[90] It is easy to condemn both the Jews and the Arabs for their treatment of these unfortunate refugees. It must seem incomprehensible to the people of the United States because America has a splendid tradition of assimilating refugees and leading them to a new, rich life, though even the United States tragically failed Jews who sought to escape Nazi Germany. To our shame, we in Britain have also treated refugees and immigrants badly and cannot afford to point a derisory finger at either the Jews or the Arabs in this respect.

Yet it still has to be said that the Arab states could have done far more than they did to help the Palestinians. In the next chapter we shall see that there was a very similar situation at the time of the Crusades. When the Crusaders created their states, many of the local Muslim people fled to the surrounding Arab and Muslim cities. But although the Arab leaders were loud in their sympathy for these medieval Palestinian refugees, they did little to help them in practical terms. Similarly today, the Palestinians feel betrayed by the Arab leaders, who have either ignored the problem or have actually made life intolerable for the Palestinians in their midst. All too often the Palestinians have been used in the propaganda war and much rhetoric has been spent bewailing the plight of the refugees. But little effective aid has been forthcoming. Indeed, some of the Arab leaders themselves are opposed to a Palestinian state in the Middle East: Syria, for example, has always regarded Palestine as Syrian territory. As in the Middle Ages, the leaders are often too involved in the pursuit of their own rather selfish political aims to give any real attention to the Palestinian problem.

Nevertheless, it is the case that the loss of Palestine assumed great symbolic importance in the Arab world. It was not just a territorial matter; it was seen as yet another colonial humiliation. The Arabs either see Zionism as a colonial movement or see Israel as the tool of Western imperialism. This is very difficult for people in the West to understand. We can see that, while some Zionists like Herzl or Jabotinsky did have a colonial vision of the Jewish state, such ideas would have been quite abhorrent to an early Laborite of the Second Aliyah. But the Arabs see the state of Israel as an alien, Western presence in the Middle East. It is seen as the representative of the United States in the region. There is some truth in this, in view of the immense amount of aid given to Israel by America. But the idea does not fill us with horror, because in the West our experience of colonialism has been entirely different. The horror which the very idea of Israel inspires seems exaggerated and hysterical to us but if we are to begin to understand the Arab point of view we must make some imaginative effort to enter into the humiliating colonial experience.

The Palestinian disaster is also called *al-Karitha*, a word which denotes a terrible group catastrophe of near cosmic dimensions.

In the Arab world, this colonial humiliation has assumed the importance to the Arabs that the Holocaust has in the spiritual life of Israel.[91] I do not, of course, mean that the two experiences, considered objectively, are equivalent. But we all know that what might seem trivial to one person is a huge internal catastrophe to somebody else. For the Arabs, the creation of the state of Israel has been seen as the ultimate colonial humiliation. Just as the Holocaust became the subject of learned debate in the Jewish world, so too did the Palestinian catastrophe. In 1948 Constantine Zurayk published his classic work *Maana al-Nakba* (*Lesson of the Disaster*), which began a tradition which has become known as the *Ilm al-Karitha* (the Science of the Catastrophe). In this tradition, the Jewish state is seen as a crime against nature, as a "cancerous growth" in the Middle East and an alien intrusion of unspeakable evil.[92] We shall see that during the Middle Ages people in Europe used exactly this kind of imagery to describe heretics living in their midst. Of course such a reaction is irrational, but in our story we shall frequently find that we are not dealing with reasonable and logical states of mind but with emotional states that are just as real but far more difficult to deal with and far more difficult for an outsider to understand.

As usual, the poets and writers give us some indication of the depth of the distress in the Arab world in 1948. From their work we can understand the terrible shock inflicted on the Arabs by their crushing defeat by the Israelis. They show clearly that the Arabs knew full well that their own policies and defects had contributed toward the Israeli victory. The shame was overwhelming throughout the Arab world. The Sudanese poet Abdullah al-Tayyib, who was living in London in 1948, recalls that life lost all its meaning because of the defeat.[93] Those of us who have not been on the losing side of a major war may well underestimate the immense humiliation of defeat. The Iraqi poet Umar Abu Risha makes it clear that he feels that the Arabs as a nation had lost all respect in the world community in his poem "After the Catastrophe."

> O my nation! is there any place left among
> the nations where you can wield your swords
> or pen?
> I think of you with my head bowed down,
> feeling ashamed to face your past.
> O my nation! many a time agonized shrieks

> killed words in praise of you on my tongue.
> How could the flag of Israel be raised in
> the shelter of the Holy Sepulchre and the
> shade of the Haram [the Dome of the Rock]?[94]

The Iraqi poet Adnan al-Rawi mourns the 1948 defeat in "I Ask Forgiveness of God," insisting that "I will not believe in this world any more" and that "I will forget that I am living in a home that was once Arab":[95] the Arab nation has lost its name and nature. Of particular interest, however, is the poem "Men on the Road" by the Egyptian poet Badr Tawfiq, because I think he offers us a clue that might help us to understand the Arabs' apparent callousness to the Palestinian refugees. He describes for us a refugee of 1948: he is a man who is completely helpless, bowed down with "self-blame and regret" and "on the run from both himself and others." Then the Egyptian suddenly recognizes that he is looking at himself:

> I asked him about his identity.
> —False, like yours.
> isn't my picture yours also? he answered.
> Then he insisted I should look in the mirror
> and there I saw my picture on his identity card.[96]

Perhaps the Arabs were unable to accept the refugees because they offered too distressing an insight into the plight of the whole Arab nation. We shall constantly be considering this type of projection. During the period of the Crusades, the Christians of Europe produced monstrously distorted fantasies of both Muslims and Jews that bore no relation whatever to the human reality but were actually projections of buried Christian worries and anxieties. The same process might well be at work in the Middle East today. Badr Tawfiq has not made his Palestinian refugee an inhuman monster but he certainly identifies with him at a deep level and also sees the Palestinian problem as an image of Arab loss of identity. It seems that in the Arab world even those Palestinians who have excellent jobs are regarded as "other," as alien.[97] It may be that some kind of projection is still at work.

But the Arabs have in fact produced a distorted fantasy of "the Jew" and it could be that this new Arab anti-Semitism is also the product of projection. There was no anti-Semitism in the Arab world before the creation of the state of Israel.[98] Until 1948 the Sephardic Jews had lived peacefully in Arab countries and Muslims had never seen the Jews as monsters of human evil in the way that the Christians did. But now Israel was being seen as a cancer and its creation as a catastrophe. It could be that Israel has become an irrational but powerful projection of Arab shame and loss of identity. It was inevitable that, once this distorted view of Israel became current, anti-Semitism would follow. Those Muslims who read the Koran daily and almost knew it by heart suddenly looked with new eyes at those passages which speak slightingly of the Jews as the enemies of Islam. These were composed at a time when Mohammad was having trouble with the Jews of Medina and have an entirely different attitude from those passages which command Muslims to treat the Jews with respect as one of the Peoples of the Book. Now Jews were being seen as the very first enemies of Islam and its essential enemies.[99] This Koranic anti-Semitism, which is as alien to Islam as the Western hatred of Jews was to Christianity, became common among the ordinary people. Scholars and intellectuals preferred to take Western texts like the infamous *Protocols of the Elders of Zion*.[100] It is deeply regrettable that the Arabs have adopted this shameful Western habit. It discredits the Arab cause and makes it impossible for the Israelis to imagine the possibility of peace with the new anti-Semites.

The new anti-Semitism is part of the *Ilm al-Karitha*. Another significant part of this "Science of the Catastrophe" is the new Arab interest in the Crusades. The Crusades were central to the European experience and so have always fascinated historians there, but in most Muslim countries they were regarded as trivial border incidents. But the creation of the state of Israel has inspired Arab historians to look at the Crusades with fresh eyes. The Crusades gave the Arabs their first taste of the Western world. Without any provocation, the Christians of Europe had declared war upon Islam and had mounted a deadly campaign against the people of the Near East. They had massacred, defiled the holy places and driven the medieval Palestinians from their homeland. The *Ilm al-Karitha* sees the Crusaders as the first Western imperialists and the Zionists as either neo-Crusaders or else tools of Western imperialism. Cruel crusading exploitation seems all that the Arabs can expect from the Western world.[101] In this view, the Israelis are surrounded by a nimbus of evil that by rights belonged to the crusading West, but when Israel actually joined Britain and France, the two colonial powers, in the Suez crisis, this must have seemed a clear proof of her expansive colonial intentions.

Against this background of hopeless defeat and humiliation, the victory of Suez was intoxicating. Nasser seemed to have discovered a way to defeat the colonial powers and the dreaded state of Israel, and throughout the Arab world Nasserite ideologies were developed that were strongly anti-Semitic and anti-Western. Egypt, which had hitherto been concerned mainly with Egyptian nationalism, now became the leader of the "Arab nation." It had not been easy to formulate an ideology that was acceptable and emotive enough to mobilize the Arab world against the West. Arabs were used to the religious polity of Islam, where politics was inseparable from religion, and found the Western, secular idealisms alien and difficult to assimilate. The first "nationalist" leader, Jamal ad-Din al-Afghani (d. 1897), had proposed a pan-Islamic solution to the problem of colonial occupation. He had wanted to use religion to cause a mass uprising and his ideas were still very popular during the twentieth century. But later movements for independence opted for the Western ideal of a secular nation-state, which was alien to people brought up in the tradition of a united Islam. In 1908 the Young Turks had successfully staged a revolution in the Ottoman Empire and immediately afterward the Young Arabs held their first meeting in Paris. Arab nationalism had reached Palestine by 1915, when Ben-Gurion first became aware of it. This secular nationalism reminded the people that they had been Arabs before they had been Muslims and urged all the people of the Arab world to unite together to form a solid front against the West. Arab nationalism was extremely strong in Syria and during the 1940s became associated with a vision of a great Arab renaissance (*ba'ath*). Nasser's Suez triumph encouraged the Syrian ba'athists in February 1958 to invite Nasser to form an immediate and comprehensive union between Syria and Egypt, which should be known as the United Arab Republic. In July of the same year a revolution in Iraq toppled the strongest and most effective Western bastion in the Arab world. It looked as though the Arabs were indeed rising powerfully against their enemies and that Israel was being surrounded by strongly united and hostile forces.

Nasser had his own formula for Arab nationalism, based on the unique strategic position of Egypt. He saw Egypt as the center of three circles of power: the Arab circle, the African circle and the Islamic circle. The first two circles of power are self-explanatory, given Egypt's position between Africa and the Arab countries. The third needs some explanation. Nasser's ideology was secular and in 1954, following an attempt on his life, he suppressed the extremist Muslim Brotherhood. He had no wish for an Islamic republic. But Nasser was a sincerely practicing Muslim and was convinced that Islam was crucial to the Arab identity. He felt strongly that Arabs had to create their own distinctively Arab revolutionary ideology and should not borrow alien, foreign ideologies like Communism or Western socialism. There was no need to turn to the Communist East or the imperialist West, for in Islam the Arabs had their own distinctively revolutionary creed.[102] The idea came to him in 1953 during a visit to Saudi Arabia and centered on the pilgrimage. As he stood in front of the Ka'aba, reflecting on the vastness of the Islamic world, he became convinced that the pilgrimage must be politicized and should become "a great political power":

> The press of the world should resort to and follow its news, not as a series of rituals and traditions which are done to amuse or entertain readers, but as a regular political congress wherein the leaders of Muslim states, their public men, their pioneers in every field of knowledge, their writers, their leading industrialists, merchants and youth draw up in this universal Islamic parliament the main lines of policy for their countries and their cooperation together until they meet again.[103]

To this end, with the approval of the Saudis, Nasser established the Islamic Congress, with Anwar Sadat as the first chairman. It was a bold and potentially powerful vision, but the Congress died as Nasser adopted a more revolutionary stance, which the more traditionalist and cautious Muslim leaders were not prepared to follow. This only made it all the more necessary for Nasser to emphasize the revolutionary aspect of Islam. Mohammad had been essentially a revolutionary, and in Nasser's Egypt Islam was presented as a religion which was implacably opposed to despotism and dedicated to the creation of a just and equal society.[104]

In the late 1950s, therefore, Nasser looked all set to form a powerful confederation of united revolutionary Arab states, but in fact the achievement of such a federation was too difficult at this particularly turbulent stage of Middle Eastern development. The Iraqis felt that, having made their own revolution, they had no need of Nasser; and the Syrians, feeling oppressed by Egypt, seceded from the United Arab Republic in September 1961. By the middle of the 1960s, therefore, Nasser was isolated from the rest of the Arab world, though he was still unquestionably a world figure. The traditional and conservative states like Saudi Arabia felt threatened by his plans to modernize the Arab world, and Iraq and Syria, themselves in a state of turmoil, were against him. In 1966 the militant left wing of the Ba'ath Party effected a successful coup in Syria under Hafez al-Assad and Syria became a client state of the Soviet Union. During that year Syria backed guerrilla activity in Israel and taunted Nasser with cowardice. Jordan, Saudi Arabia and Iraq joined in and, to retain the leadership of the Arab world as well as to retain credibility in Egypt, Nasser was under great pressure to make at least a gesture of defiance against Israel. He had been anxious to avoid this, being quite aware of Egypt's military inferiority. But eventually the gesture of defiance that he was expected to make led to the Six Day War of 1967 and another crushing Arab defeat.

The Six Day War was the obverse of Suez. This time it was the Arabs who were humiliated by Israel. This time Israel was not deserted by the great powers but had made sure of the support of Britain and the United States before launching the attack. This time Israel did not withdraw from the territory she had won but occupied the Sinai Peninsula, the West Bank of the Jordan and the Golan Heights. The Arabs were powerless once more. In the years since Suez, the United States and Israel had formed a special relationship, in which Israel was not so much a client state as the representative of American influence in the Middle East and would ultimately come to dictate American policy there. Backed by this superpower, Israel was invulnerable to Arab attack, and the United States guaranteed to make her stronger in military terms than all the Arab states put together. If the influence of Britain and France had waned in the Middle East, their place had been taken by the United States, and the Arab world seemed further from independence than ever. Besides Israel, America had a client state in Iran, and the Iranians had also felt their impotence before the American Goliath. When Mohammad Mossadeq had attempted to nationalize Iranian oil and had overthrown the Pahlavi dynasty in 1953, Shah Mohammad Reza was swiftly replaced by a CIA-organized coup. Mossadeq, a hero of independence, died in prison and Nasser, the onetime hero of the Arab world, was disgraced and discredited by the defeat of the Six Day War, even though the people of Egypt continued to love their charismatic leader. If the people of the Middle East wanted to assert their independence they would have to find a stronger weapon than secular nationalism would prove to be. Some of them would later discover that religion was precisely the weapon they needed and would revive the *jihad*. But in 1967 the Arabs found a new secular hero in Yasir Arafat, the leader of the newly organized Palestine Liberation Organization, and it is important to give some account of this new form of secular revolution in the Arab world, which sought a solution for the peculiarly appalling difficulties of the Palestinian Arabs.

Naturally the Palestinians had suffered far more than any other Arabs from the 1948 catastrophe. Those who had fled from Israel suffered the emotional dislocation of exile. "In twelve hours," one of the refugees recalled, "we had been changed from dignity to humiliation."[105] This was the case with those Palestinians who were able to find lucrative employment and a comfortable life in the Arab world as well as those in the refugee camps. Again, exile and homelessness are traumatic experiences, whatever the circumstances. The Palestinians found themselves scorned by their fellow Arabs in their diaspora. At a time of fierce nationalism in the Arab world, the Palestinians were derided for having sold their land to the Jews and for having run away. The Palestinians had always been a proud people but now they found that they had a new, shameful identity. One woman recalled the meager food rations they were given at the beginning of their exile as a symbol of this humiliation:

> I thought of our rations, this small quantity of flour we needed so as not to die of hunger. *This* was the Palestinian, a refugee, a person without respect, whom others summoned by gesture instead of by name, whom others portrayed as cowardly, though the opposite was the truth.[106]

Fawaz Turki, a refugee from Haifa, also had a bitter memory concerning the food ration that was such an obvious statement of dependency and of the loss of self-determination. He remembered joining a crowd in Beirut to watch a street entertainer with his performing monkey. The monkey was told to " 'show us how a Palestinian picks up his food rations.' I was a rough boy of fourteen, hardened to steet life, but I could not suppress an outburst of tears."[107] It was especially hard to accept the constant accusation of cowardice. The local people would jeer at the refugees and depict them as people who had first "sold their land" and then "fled." They would shout after them in the street, "Where are your tails?" which is apparently a joke about cowardice (turning tail). "I was a Palestinian," wrote Fawaz Turki, "and that meant I was an outsider, an alien, a refugee and a burden."[108]

In these humiliating conditions, it was natural that the refugees should look back on their life in Palestine with deep nostalgia. In the camps the refugees from the same village naturally grouped themselves together in such a way as to recreate the lost village in Palestine as perfectly as possible. They would sit recalling their lost country with such vividness that even those refugees who had left Palestine as tiny children or who had been born in exile were familiar with every detail of village life before 1948. "In Palestine we were in Paradise," one refugee declared.[109] Of course many of these memories were idealized and perhaps even naive. But we are not dealing with reason and logic; moreover these golden accounts of Palestine were probably no more naive or idealized than the dreams of the early Jewish settlers about the wonderful model society they were going to build in Palestine.

Exile is not simply a geographical description of a person's where-
abouts; it has long been recognized to be a state of mind, often a
trauma. A young schoolgirl in Lebanon remembered watching the
Palestinians talking about their home:

> The conversation changed to the past, and how they used to live.
> And when they spoke, they wept, because of the attachment to their
> country. Whoever sits with them can understand more about Pal-
> estine than from going to meetings, because they lived the life. . . .
> But what affected me most was their weeping because the land was
> so dear to them.[110]

When they spoke about returning to their land, this was obviously
not a realistic hope. They spoke of returning to a Palestine that was
exactly the same as it had been before 1948, yet they knew perfectly
well that the country was daily being transformed into the modern
Jewish state and that their villages had been razed to the ground.[111]But
knowing something logically is one thing; accepting it emotionally
quite another.

The profound psychological shock of exile is clear in the writing of
the Palestinian poets, for whom the lost land is a constant theme.
Even those who have a comfortable, prosperous life in the diaspora
see their life in exile as an unnatural state and yearn to return home,
not for material reasons, but with a strong spiritual aspiration. It will
be recalled that in their diaspora some Jews developed a belief that
the *Shekinah*, the Presence of God, had gone into exile with the Jews.
This suggests a fundamental displacement or a metaphysical homelessness in the very ground of reality. I do not wish to compare the
Palestinians' exile to the Jews', but it seems that the myth of the exile
of the *Shekinah* is a very powerful expression of that psychological
dislocation felt by an exile that affects the ground of his being. In
"The Lake of Olive Trees," written in 1957 by Yusuf al-Khatib, the
poet sends messages to his village by means of the birds, the winds,
the stars. He is already depressed that it has become Israeli property
and the wind tells him that the olive tree in the courtyard has wilted
and the house itself has sunk into despair since they left. The poet
then sees his exile to be in some sense a living death and writ large
in the heavens:

> O our village! I swear by your soil
> we have not tasted sleep,
> wakeful through remembering you,
> tearful because of our separation from you.
> And all the time we gaze at the sky

> observing your sad face.
> Oh, how sad your face has become.[112]

His enforced separation is seen as against the nature of things: it is impossible to live cut off from the place of his earliest memories; because of his enforced exile, the homeland itself is, in a real emotional sense, sad and dying.

Jabra Ibrahim Jabra, who was born in Bethlehem, settled in Iraq after 1948 and has a pleasant life there. He is regarded as a leading poet, novelist and critic. But he sees life outside Palestine as a desert. Thus in "Deserts of Exile" (1953) he sees all the Palestinians, however settled and comfortable they are in exile, as wandering perpetually in a life that has become a spiritual wilderness:

> O land of ours . . .
> remember us now, wandering
> among the thorns of the deserts,
> wandering in rocky mountains,
> remember us now,
> in tumultuous cities across the deserts
> and oceans.
> Remember us with our eyes full of a dust
> that never clears in our ceaseless wanderings.[113]

Tawfiq Sayigh, who has taught at prestigious universities in England and the United States, was only sixteen in 1948 but a longing for Palestine is one of the major themes in his poetry:

> My feet are torn,
> and homelessness has worn me out
> Park seats have left their marks
> on my ribs.
> Policemen followed me
> with their suspicious looks.
> I dragged myself from place to place,
> destitute except for
> day-long memories of a home
> that yesterday, only yesterday,
> was mine,
> and except for evening dreams
> of my dwelling there again.[114]

The Palestinians have discovered that physical exile is also a spiritual displacement. It is not true that they would gladly settle in other countries were it not for the dishonest schemes of their leaders, as their enemies maintain. Deprived of their rightful place in the world, they are aliens and outsiders. Even those born in exile inherit this unnatural condition. Thus the poet Radi Sadduq, who was born in 1938, says that the new generation of Palestinians are as deprived and wounded as their parents. Addressing his new-born daughter Rula, he says:

> My little baby! you are a whole world here,
> but with no colour, downtrodden and vagrant.
> O Rula! Stranger you are,
> and the daughter of a stranger who
> is humiliated and a fugitive.(1963)[115]

Not all Palestinians were forced into exile, however. Today Palestinians make up seventeen percent of the population of Israel, where they live as second-class citizens. Where the poets in exile hear their land calling them to return, the Israeli Arab poets see it constantly but see it as possessed by somebody else. The well-known poet Mahmoud Darwish (born in 1942) addresses his country as his lover or as an obsession that he cannot shake off:

> You are my grief and joy,
> my wound and my rainbow,
> my prison and freedom.
> You are my myth
> and the clay from which I was created.
> You are mine with all your wounds,
> each wound a garden. . . .
> You are my sun at its setting,
> and my lightened night.
> You are the death of me and the kiss of
>   life.[116]

In a poem written during the late 1960s, Darwish gives perhaps the most telling insight into the Palestinian loss of identity after the disaster. It is a short poem called "Identity Card," which is addressed to an imaginary Israeli official. Darwish speaks for all Palestinians, who by this time had politically been reduced to a name on an identity card, which hid a much more complex human reality. An Israeli Arab's identity card is marked with the letter "B," a significant indication of his inferior status. The whole poem is governed by the imperative "*Sajil* [Record]!", as the Palestinian demands that the Israeli take note that the impoverished language on the card cannot express the full reality of the Palestinian condition:

> Record!
> I am an Arab

> And my Identity Card
> is number fifty thousand.
> I have eight children
> and the ninth
>     is coming in midsummer.
> Does this anger you? . . .
>
> Record!
> I am an Arab
> without a name—without title,
> patient in a country
> with people enraged.

This last is an important point. Where the best Israeli writers are longing for a peaceful solution, Palestinian poets call their people to war. Their situation does not admit that they accept it without protest. Complaints and yearning for the homeland are not enough. Darwish's poem concludes:

> Record!
> I am an Arab.
> You stole my forefathers' groves
> and the land I used to till,
> I and all my children;
> and you left us nothing but these rocks
> for us and all my grandchildren.
> Yet, will your government take them too,
> as is being said?
> Then write down . . . at the top of page one:
> I neither hate others
> Nor do I steal their property,
> but if I become hungry
> the flesh of my usurper shall I eat.
> So beware . . . beware of my hunger
> and of my anger.[117]

The younger generation was impatient with the passivity of their parents, who had loved their land but who had lost it in some measure through their own mistakes. They were sick of all the talk about Palestine in the camps and wanted action, not words. Many of them began to form nationalistic groups that aimed to win Palestine back. Some of these became *fedayeen*, freedom fighters, and made raids into Israeli territory to attack the settlements. In the first seven years of the existence of the Jewish state 1300 Israelis were killed in Arab raids.[118]

In retaliation, Israeli commandos, led by generals like Moshe Dayan or Ariel Sharon, made retaliatory raids into Arab territories. Dayan explained the new doctrine of retaliatory strikes against civilian targets across the border: Arab governments would only restrain the *fedayeen* when they realized that the "theft of one cow from Ramat Ha-Kovesh will hurt Kalkilia (across the Jordan border) and that the murder of one Jew at Ruhama will endanger the population of Gaza."[119] In the bitter warfare of strike and counterstrike, Israel and the Palestinians were caught in a spiral of violence that became brutal on both sides. The Israeli retaliatory raids had the effect of making the Lebanese, Jordanians and Syrians, whose people also suffered, come down heavily on Palestinian nationalism. They felt that the Palestinians were forcing the Arab states into the kind of confrontation with Israel that some of their leaders were anxious to avoid. With the exception of Syria, the host countries started to police the camps ruthlessly. Palestinians were told to stop all actions to liberate their land and to "leave it to the Arab armies."[120] But the new stern measures were so humiliating that they led to a hardening of Palestinian resolve. A refugee who attended a camp school in Lebanon remembered how armed Lebanese patrols would surround the camps on days commemorating national Palestinian events.

> On those days they would make the school children walk in single file three or four metres apart, and we were forbidden to talk together. When we reached our street each one of us had to go straight to his home and stay there. We weren't allowed to listen to the Voice of the Arabs from Cairo or Damascus. Soldiers filled the camp all the time and used to listen at the windows to hear which station we were listening to. People used to put blankets over their windows to stop the sound going out.[121]

At the Arab summit at Cairo in 1964, the Arab leaders tried to appease the Palestinians by forming the Palestine Liberation Organization in order to muzzle Palestinian nationalism and keep control of the movement. They elected a chairman, Ahmed Shukairy, who would almost certainly prove ineffective and inefficient. It has been said that his unsuitability was the very reason Nasser chose him. Most Palestinians regarded this PLO as useless and continued to join the older organizations, in particular Fatah, founded and led by Yasir Arafat.

In the West, Arafat is often seen as a terrorist, *tout court*. In the Arab world itself, he has a very mixed image. Some Palestinians regard him as a fox, wily and skillful in politics, but lacking the absolute charisma possessed by other Palestinian leaders like the late Issam

Satawi. Certainly, like other revolutionary leaders, Arafat suffers from his connection with terrorism, even though he personally thought that individual acts of terrorism, like the raids of the *fedayeen*, were useless. They merely united the Israelis even more strongly around their leaders. At the time of writing, Arafat has made the PLO repudiate terrorism, against the advice of some of his colleagues. In the early days of Fatah, Arafat was inspired by the liberation of Algeria by committed guerrilla warfare. Instead of attacking civilians, Fatah would skirmish with Israeli troops on the borders, to weaken Israel's formidable war machine. Second, Arafat intended to rebuild the damaged Palestinian identity by means of educational and political programs. He did not expect a quick result but foresaw a long, patient struggle.

There were, however, other Palestinian groups beside Fatah which sprang up spontaneously and quite independently of one another, rather as the first Zionist groups had sprung up in Russia. Two of these should be singled out for special discussion. Like the Labor Zionists, these two groups sought a Marxist solution to the problem of the Palestinians. They believed that Arafat's simple nationalism was inadequate, ignoring problems in the Arab world that desperately needed a solution. The Palestinian disaster was not the fault of the Jews alone. It was also due to deep flaws in the structure of Arab society. George Habache, who founded the Popular Front for the Liberation of Palestine, argued that the liberation of Palestine had to be part of a revolution throughout the Arab world and that the PFLP had to fight the Arab regimes as well as Israel. Nayef Hawatmeh broke away from the PFLP to found a still more extreme and ambitious group. The Popular Democratic Front for the Liberation of Palestine saw the Palestinian struggle as part of the worldwide revolution against capitalism and imperialism. The Jews were not just lackeys of imperialism, they were themselves the victims of bad social structures. This was precisely the conclusion that Zionists like Ben-Gurion and Ber Borochov had reached fifty years earlier. The revolution of the PDFLP was the first Arab organization to recognize the state of Israel, albeit the recognition was a negative one. These two groups obviously found it difficult to get any support at all in the Arab world. The only state that would support them was Syria, whose fiercely anti-imperialist socialism closely resembled their own. Syria encouraged the *fedayeen* to make raids on Israel from Syrian territory, even though this meant that she was herself subject to Israeli reprisal raids. Syria maintained that this was the only possible position for an Arab regime and chided the more moderate states for their hypocrisy. In 1967, although Nasser was initially reluctant, Syria put so much pressure on Egypt that these countries were forced into the war that they had been seeking to avoid, in order to retain their leadership.

The Six Day War was an even greater humiliation for the Arabs than their defeat in 1948, and after the Israeli army's victory there was a new desperation in the Arab world. Israel had not only driven back their armies in a mere six days. She had also occupied strategic land belonging to Syria on the Golan Heights; from Jordan (which had also joined Syria's offensive) she had seized the West Bank and from Egypt she had taken the Gaza Strip and much of the Sinai Peninsula. Despite clear instructions from the United Nations in Resolution 242[122] that these lands should be returned to the Arabs, Israel showed absolutely no sign of retreating and set up a military occupation in these large areas. This confirmed the Arabs in their view of Israel as an expansive and aggressive colonial power which seemed to be able to defy the rules that the rest of the world was supposed to obey. Yet again the world did nothing. Yet again there was a new exodus of Palestinian refugees: 400,000 Palestinians left the West Bank and settled in camps in Jordan; some had fled their homes in the 1948 disaster. Not surprisingly, there was a new determination in the Palestinian revolutionary groups. The Arab leaders had demonstrated beyond a doubt that it was quite useless for the Palestinians to wait for the Arab armies to liberate their homeland. They would have to act for themselves. When Ahmed Shukairy was forced to resign from the leadership of the PLO in December 1967, completely discredited by his association with the Arab states, the Palestinian groups took control of the movement themselves. Henceforth the PLO would be an association of different groups with avowedly different ideologies. Yet, though this meant that the movement was weakened by its diversity, it would have one great strength that would make it essential to the Palestinian people after their long humiliation. It was now their own movement. At last they had their own, autonomous leadership and had taken the first step in their process of emancipation from the Arab world.

In August the following year, the Arab world found a new hero. A squadron of special Israeli troops crossed the river Jordan and entered Arab territory in order to make a reprisal raid against the *fedayeen* in Jordan. There, however, they were opposed by a united group of Fatah men and Jordanians, who managed to resist the invaders for twelve hours and force them to return. They also destroyed some Israeli vehicles and aircraft. The Arabs were led by Yasir Arafat. It is easy to understand how this partial victory was an event of extraordinary importance to the Arab world and to the Palestinians, even though Israelis do not rank the Battle of Karameh (as the encounter became known) as a particularly important incident. For the Palestinians the Battle of Karameh was as crucial and formative as the Battle of Badr had been to Mohammad and the first Muslims in 624. Because of it, the prospect of return, which had hitherto been only a myth, acquired a new reality. Yet it was also crucial in developing the ideology of the new PLO. It is worth pondering on the comparison with Badr. After the Battle of Badr, the prospect of the return to Mecca became a reality; after Badr, Islam adopted the *jihad*, convinced by their success that God had been on the Muslims' side. Yet when Mohammad conquered Mecca he did so by means of a peaceful pilgrimage and no blood was spilled. In 1968 the PLO issued its charter, which committed all its members to a war with Israel that would not cease until the whole of Palestine had been liberated. Yet the Battle of Karameh led the PLO to abandon the old Arab solution to the Middle East problem. There was no talk in the PLO charter of throwing the Jews into the sea. The battle had ended not with a bloodthirsty dogmatism but with a question. Dr. Issam Satawi explained the experience like this:

Until Karameh we were living a dream, the dream of "return": return to the old Palestine, to our houses, our fields, and so on. We looked to the Palestine of the past. Karameh gave back the dimensions of hope to the Palestinian people; after Karameh, victory once again became possible for the Palestinians and then we (I am speaking from a collective point of view, of group psychology) saw the Israelis for the first time. And we asked ourselves, what are we going to do with them?[123]

In the PLO charter the Palestinians explained what they would do with the Israelis when they had liberated their homeland. They would be allowed to remain in the new secular democratic state of Palestine. They could not conscientiously expel the Jews. Instead, the new PLO under the leadership of the hero of Karameh would return to the old Muslim solution of peaceful coexistence. In January 1969 a Fatah leader put the position of the PLO very clearly in a statement to the *Tribune Socialiste*:

There is a large Jewish population in Palestine and it has grown considerably in the last twenty years. We recognise that it has the right to live there and that it is part of the Palestinian people. We reject the formula that the Jews must be driven into the sea. If we are fighting a Jewish state of a racial kind, which had driven the Arabs out of their lands, it is not so as to replace it with an Arab state which would in turn drive out the Jews. What we want to create in the historical borders of Palestine is a multi-racial democratic state . . . a state without any hegemony in which everyone, Jew, Christian or Muslim, will enjoy full civic rights.[124]

This secular vision made a very important distinction that was also a positive innovation in the science of the disaster. The PLO was careful to distinguish in its charter and in its public statements between Zionism and Judaism. The Palestinians said Zionism was racist, so they could not be racists themselves. "We are not the enemies of Judaism as a religion, nor are we the enemies of the Jewish race," Arafat explained. "Our battle is with the colonialist, imperialist, Zionist entity which has occupied our homeland."[125] The PLO, therefore, maintained the Arab view of Israel as a colonial venture but abandoned the anti-Semitism that attacked *all* Jews, as Jews, which was so damaging to the Arab cause.

There was, however, a flaw in the PLO charter. It argued that Judaism was a religion, a matter of private conviction but not a nationality. "Jews do not constitute a single nation with an identity of its own; they are citizens of the states to which they belong."[126] Fifty years ago that had been true but it had not been true since the creation of Israel, which *had* created a nation with a Jewish identity of its own, and the PLO charter, while careful to avoid other distortions of its enemy, had denied that it existed in political terms. The following year, Golda Meir returned the compliment in her famous but ill-judged statement which was a tempting of fate: "The Palestinians do not exist."[127]

The Israelis soon discovered to their cost that the Palestinians did indeed exist. Fatah drew the Israeli army into a dragging war of attrition on the Sinai borders, with the result that Israeli casualties there soon exceeded those in the June War of 1967. They also found that the PLO had become a neighbor. With Syria's approval and King Hussein's agreement, Arafat moved his headquarters from Damascus to Amman. At that point the King needed to dissociate himself from the catastrophe of 1967 and he actually called himself a *fida'i*. But ultimately the establishment of a semiautonomous Palestinian entity in his Bedouin kingdom was a threat to his sovereignty that he could not afford. Nor could he afford the Israeli reprisal raids that killed Jordanian civilians. Accordingly he expelled the PLO from Jordan in what has become known as Black September 1970. The incident revealed an inescapable difficulty in the Palestinian revolution. They were not conducting their movement *in situ*. They had no territory—that was precisely their problem—and they would inevitably involve their fellow Arabs in the host countries in Israel's reprisal raids, which were as ruthless as any of the activities of the *fedayeen*. The next home the Palestinians found was Lebanon and this led to the Israeli invasion of Lebanon in 1982 and the immense suffering that this brought to the Lebanese people, as well as to the Palestinians themselves. The massacres of the Palestinians in the camps of Sabra and Shatilla in September 1982, in which Israel connived, shocked the whole world.

But other more radical groups in the PLO were impatient with Arafat and wanted a speedier solution. Members of the PFLP and the PDFLP were discontented and launched a campaign of international terror which also shocked the world. People were outraged by the spectacle of innocent people being murdered. There were obscene actions like that of the so-called Black September group during the Olympic Games of 1972 when eleven Israeli athletes were murdered. It seemed particularly disgusting that this happened in Germany, the scene of Nazi atrocities against Jews, and also because the games were supposed to be an image of the peace that should exist among nations. The terrorization and murder of elderly tourists on the *Achille Lauro* cruise ship is just one of the many other terrorist enterprises that discredited the Palestinian cause. These acts even alienated many Palestinians, and though they were committed only by some extreme PLO groups, they made the PLO synonymous with terrorism. People began to forget the terrorism of the Irgun and Lehi and began to see Israel as leading the struggle against terrorism. But the Israeli MOSSAD sometimes seemed a very dubious organization: on July 8, 1972, to cite just one example, a car bomb in Beirut killed Ghassan Kanafami, a leading member of the PLFP. It also killed his young niece.

But it is also true that, in however ambiguous a way, these terrorist acts made people conscious of the existence and distress of the Palestinian people. Nobody would ever be able to say again, with Golda Meir, that they did not exist. Similarly the atrocity of Sabra and Shatilla made the world realize that the Palestinians were not only terrorists but also victims. The suffering of the Palestinians in their camps did inspire some sympathy. Thus in the early months of 1987 the Shiite Amal troops in Lebanon tried to get rid of the *fedayeen* in their country by besieging the camps and refusing to let food in to the predominantly civilian refugees within. They began to starve to death and the world was horrified to see Amal militiamen shooting a woman through the head if she tried to escape from the camp to get food for her children.

The British press, for example, was impressed by the fact that the Palestinian people refused to abandon the *fedayeen*, despite the immense suffering. During some particularly serious Israeli air raids which killed civilians and children in Lebanon at the same time, observers noted that all the young Palestinians in the area were members of the PLO; they noted also that the *fedayeen* slept away from the camps to try to protect the civilians and that sometimes the raids attacked targets that were far from any PLO military base. All this showed that the Palestinians were not welcome anywhere. What could happen to a people who had no home?

The new Palestinian identity therefore was deeply ambiguous. Yet despite its association with ruthless terrorism, most Palestinians have found it impossible to dissociate themselves entirely from the PLO. It is too deeply bound up with the Palestinian struggle and too deeply implicated in the Palestinians' desperate building of a new identity. Rosemary Sayigh has shown how for the camp Palestinian the PLO has become a symbol of the people and its destiny. The word *thawra* or revolution "is used as a symbol of the life and destiny of the Palestinian people, reaching back into the past to cast new light on uprisings in Palestine, and pointing out a path into the future. Its reasons go far beyond the situation of the moment to a core of permanent identification."[128] Without the PLO, where is this revolution? How else can the Palestinians hope for a better world? "The revolution gave me the answer to who I am,"[129] one young boy said after the camps had been liberated in Lebanon in 1969. Another said, "With the revolution we broke our handcuffs. Before I was living in a refugee camp, now I feel that it is a training camp."[130] Even Palestinians who have been successful in exile have found the revolution helpful in maintaining a positive Palestinian identity. As the Palestinian scholar Edward W. Said has explained:

> What all Palestinians refer to today as the Palestinian Revolution is not the negative distinction of being unlike others, but a positive feeling of the whole Palestinian experience as a disaster to be remedied, of Palestinian identity as something understandable not only in terms of what we lost, but as something we were forging—a liberation from nonentity, oppression, and exile.[131]

Though it is a flawed movement, the PLO has been an outward sign of this inner grace.

The poem "Men on the Road" by Badr Tawfiq, which I quoted earlier, gives a dramatic expression to the difference made by the new PLO to the Palestinians. It will be recalled that the 1948 refugee was pictured as a shamed, hopeless man. In the part of the poem, however, which deals with the aftermath of the 1967 war and the creation of Arafat's PLO, there is a sudden change in this defeated Arab:

> His face, his way of walking and
> his way of greeting show friendliness.
> His inner being complains of alienation
> and his body suffers from exhaustion.
> He is defiant even with his hands tied.
> He raises his body so as to be seen by all others
> and walks in confidence, unveiled.[132]

Again, Samih al-Qasim has a poem in which he describes the Palestinian refugee as a pathetic creature, dressed like a scarecrow in an old coat. All the doors of the houses in the street were slammed in his face. But

> Then one day, it happened that
> he started walking.
> His cry reverberated in the yards of the
> lifeless houses.
> So all men and women, young and old,
> crowded into the yards of the lifeless houses.
> Seeing him setting fire to the old coat
> they were all alarmed.[133]

The PLO has conveyed a very negative image to the outside world. But it has been remarkably effective in building a new, proud Palestinian identity and helping the Palestinians to overcome their disastrous experience.

After the October War of 1973, when the Arab armies put up a much better showing and there was a new confidence, the PLO was declared to be the sole legitimate representative of the Palestinian people, at the Arab Conference at Rabat in 1974. That year, too, the PLO abandoned the principle of all or nothing and the Palestine National Council declared that they were now ready to establish a mini-state in the occupied territories. This was an important concession. It was a tacit recognition of the state of Israel, though it was not a clear enough recognition to be of any use in negotiations about territory. The PNC also made the decision to meet with the United Nations in Geneva. On November 13, 1974, Yasir Arafat addressed the General Assembly, carrying an olive branch in one hand and a gun in the other. It was a moderate speech that set forth the Palestinian case according to the PLO charter without rhetoric. There was no talk of conquering the whole of former Palestine. Referring to the

PLO vision of a secular democratic state in the whole of Palestine, he called it a "dream." It was simply a vision and inspiration for the future. He hoped that the United Nations would recognize the wrong done to his people. He understood that the PLO was associated with terrorism and that his own reputation had been tarnished. But he also reminded the delegates that some of their own number had once been terrorists and *fedayeen* in their struggle for independence. For the Palestinians too, terrorism was not an end in itself but a sad phase in a difficult journey to freedom and self-determination. At the end of his speech he made a desperate plea:

> I appeal to you to enable our people to establish national independent sovereignty over its own land.
> Today I have come bearing an olive branch and a freedom-fighter's gun. Do not let the olive branch fall from my hand. I repeat: do not let the olive branch fall from my hand.[134]

After the speech Arafat received a standing ovation but there were two states that did not participate. The representative for Israel was not present and the representative of the United States remained seated. On November 22 the General Assembly proclaimed the "inalienable rights of the Palestinian people in Palestine including (a) the right to self-determination without external interference, and (b) the right to national independence and sovereignty"[135] (Resolution 3236). In January 1976 the PLO was actually invited to take part as a full member in a meeting of the Security Council to discuss the question of Palestine. At the meeting the PLO expressed its demand for a Palestinian state alongside the state of Israel but the document put forward at that meeting came up against the veto of the United States, which would not admit the Palestinians' right to establish an independent state. Still, Arafat had taken an important step forward in bringing his people into the family of nations.

Arafat had proved that he was ready to compromise. Although the Palestinians are often labeled terrorists and their movement has indeed been marred by unacceptable violence, there have also been other, more peaceful activities. In particular there were the secret peace talks between Israelis like Uri Avnery and PLO officials, headed by Issam Satawi. These talks with leading members of the PLO, including Arafat himself, were very valuable to everybody who took part in them. Avnery describes their effect:

> One does not make peace except with enemies and one does not make peace with enemies who are despised or who are conceived

of as inhuman monsters. After four generations of war between the Jews and the Palestinians, the enemy—the PLO and its leaders—are regarded by Jewish Israelis as demons, as abominations. In exactly the same way Palestinians regard the hated Zionists, not as normal people with their everyday hopes and cares but as the new Nazis, beyond the pale of humanity. Our dialogue had helped to shatter these diabolical images. It has de-demonized each side in the eyes of the other. Arafat sitting between an Israeli General and an Israeli Member of Parliament is not the same "captain of murderers" he was before; and Zionists cannot be all devils if they sit next to Arafat.[136]

Issam Satawi in particular was aware that these peace talks were an urgent priority; a peaceful solution must be found or there was the danger that the conflict of escalating violence could explode in a final nuclear holocaust. The secular leaders of Israel and the Arab states must talk together while there was still time to find a solution, and a solution meant compromise on both sides. The danger was that the present secular leaders could be replaced by extreme Jewish or Muslim religious leaders, who would refuse any compromise in the name of God.

Once, in a moment of discouragement, Satawi said, "We are fools. All of us working for peace in the Middle East are fools. If we had been working for war we would be respected, macho, adored by the masses. We, the peaceful ones, are fools."[137] On April 10, 1983, he was shot by a Palestinian extremist for being an agent of Israel, the CIA and British intelligence.

The great compromise that Arafat was always being asked to make was that he recognize the state of Israel. Until he had agreed to do this there could be no progress and no way out of the deadlock which people like Satawi and Avnery were trying to break. At the time of writing, however, there has been a major change. In December 1987 an uprising broke out in the West Bank and in the Gaza Strip in protest against the Israeli occupation. This *intifada*, as the uprising has become known, was masterminded by young Palestinians, who were sick of the old PLO and wanted to take the initiative away from its "old" men. Violence was to be kept to a bare minimum. Palestinian children threw stones at Israeli soldiers and at cars bearing the Israeli number plate. There was to be no use of firearms. The uprising has proved to be remarkably enduring. There have been a very large number of Palestinian casualties, many of whom have been babies, children and old people. Very large numbers of Palestinians have been arrested

and in May 1989 Amnesty International issued a report that claimed
that the Israelis were depriving those imprisoned of their human right
to protest peacefully. At about the same time the Red Cross issued a
report, complaining about Israeli treatment of children. The *intifada*
has won the Palestinians many friends and has lost Israel a good deal
of international support. It has also done a great deal for the morale
of the Palestinians of the occupied territories. Observers there speak
of a post-*intifada* identity. Before the uprising, the Palestinians in the
territories had been convinced that they had little hope. The PLO
largely excluded them from its activities and was centered in the Palestinian diaspora. There was a passivity and fatalism. But since the
*intifada* there is a new confidence that expresses itself not in noisy
rhetoric but in quiet determination.[138] They know that their action is
taking effect: it has gravely damaged the Israeli economy and has been
even more devastating to Israeli morale.

The PLO had to respond to this young initiative. On November
15, 1988, at a meeting of the Palestine National Council, the PLO
accepted the existence of the state of Israel. It abjured terrorism
once again. It envisaged the peaceful coexistence of the state of Palestine alongside the state of Israel. The deadlock had apparently been
broken.

Many people remain skeptical, particularly in Israel. Shamir has
absolutely refused to negotiate with the PLO but David Levi, the
Deputy Prime Minister, has argued that Israel has no other choice.
The United States has declared its readiness to talk with the PLO and
Arafat is beginning to be on calling terms with heads of state. He is
frequently seen in the United Nations. The onus now lies with the
PLO to prove its sincerity by continuing in its resolution to abandon
terrorism. But the ball of peace has now landed firmly in the Israelis'
court.

Arafat is continually on the move. He knows that he is in danger
of meeting the same fate as Issam Satawi for his historic act of compromise. It seems, however, that at last there is a tiny chance of a
solution: one of the main obstacles has been withdrawn. A solution
is a vital priority because the danger is great. Those who fear the
influence of religious extremists on both sides of the conflict have
grounds for their anxiety. There are those who wish to turn this
originally secular conflict into a holy war. It is important, therefore,
that we understand what this escalation of religiously inspired violence
could mean for the Middle East, and here the story of the Crusades
and the Muslim retaliation they inspired can give us some valuable

lessons, not because history repeats itself but because the Jews and Muslims who are fighting one another today have many of the same preoccupations and passions as the soldiers of God who fought for their religion when the Crusaders marched to Jerusalem to liberate the tomb of Christ.

# PART TWO

## Holy War

# · 4 ·

# 1096–1146

# The Crusade Becomes a Holy War
## and Inspires a New *Jihad*

In September 1096 Count Bohemund of Taranto saw an army of
Norman Crusaders marching to the port of Brindisi to sail for the
East and he was instantly inspired to join them. Although he was
no longer a young man he was extremely handsome and master of
the grand, flamboyant gesture that so frequently appears in the history
of crusading. Immediately after taking the Cross in the cathedral at
Amalfi he strode down the great steps, tearing his scarlet cloak into
ribbons, which he thrust to left and right into the eager hands of the
captains of his army, so that they could make Crusader crosses for
themselves. "Are we not Franks?" he cried. "Did not our ancestors
come here from Francia and liberate this land with arms? What a
disgrace! Will our blood relatives and brothers go to martyrdom and
indeed to paradise without us?"[1] A few weeks later Bohemund and
his nephew Tancred set sail for Constantinople with a well-equipped
and efficient army. Bohemund had pressing, worldly reasons for becoming a Crusader. His father Robert Guiscard had hoped to leave
him a kingdom in the East, but his invasion of Byzantium had failed,
so Bohemund had only a very small fief in the Duchy of Apulia. The
Crusade was an obvious way for Bohemund to acquire an Eastern
kingdom and it would be easy to dismiss Bohemund's typical Frankish
piety as hypocrisy, which covered naked territorial ambition with the
religious cant of the day. But this would be too modern a view, for
in the Middle Ages people were less self-conscious about motivation
than we are. For Bohemund, as for most of the First Crusaders, secular
and religious motives existed quite easily side by side, and indeed the
First Crusade was able to succeed only because of this fusion of strong
piety and practical good sense.

Bohemund's claim to be a Frank is important, because he was really
a Norman, a descendant of the Vikings who had terrorized Europe
and then subsequently settled there, adopted a Frankish identity and

converted to Christianity. They had their own duchy and had spear-headed the new expansion of Christendom of recent years. The Normans had made a conscious decision to ally themselves with the Europeans and in recent years Europe had acquired an exciting and dynamic self-confidence. This was largely the creation of the Church, and Bohemund therefore would not have seen Christianity as a purely spiritual religion and a private affair, as we do today. He would have seen it as an ideology that led to progress and development, in rather the same way as revolutionaries embraced Marxism in Russia at the time of the 1917 Revolution. Bohemund seems also to have been conscious that the Norman "Franks" were in the vanguard of the new expansion of Europe, because conquest and exploration were in their Norse blood, and it was easy for him to embrace this new Christian aggression because it coincided so perfectly with his own needs and desires. He would become one of the most able leaders of the Crusade and was a shrewdly practical soldier, but he could quite simply tell his men that "This is not a carnal war but a spiritual one."[2] Bohemund's view of the holy war was not the Cluniac vision of Pope Urban but looked to *The Song of Roland*. In the Crusades the Franks would find a perfect way to unite their love of God with the love of war, and thousands of them would fight their way to paradise and to martyr-dom. Certainly Tancred saw crusading as the answer to his long per-plexity. His biographer wrote that as soon as he heard about the Crusade all his energies were released and doubts resolved in what amounted to a religious conversion of life: "at last as if previously asleep, his vigour was aroused, his powers grew, his eyes opened, his courage was born."[3] Everything suddenly came together for him in such a way that he literally had a new vision of life.

But Tancred had a practical problem. Crusading was a very expen-sive enterprise: a knight had to equip himself with horses, servants, armor and weapons for a very long campaign and Tancred could not afford it. His richer uncle Bohemund equipped him and helped him out financially and this would be an important feature of the First Crusade. Rich Crusaders felt it their duty to help poorer knights and everybody felt it a duty to give alms to the poor pilgrims. In this way the Crusade did express the Cluniac vision of the pilgrimage where rich and poor lived in community together and where the reformed Christian knights cared for the poor and the weak. The Cluniac ideal of holy poverty was very important to many of the Crusaders and showed how effectively Cluny had penetrated the consciousness of the West. Most Crusaders had to sell or mortgage property and land in order to be able to afford to go on the Crusade.[4] In Urban's terms they had been prepared to sell all they had in order to follow Christ. Godfrey of Bouillon, whose army was the first to leave Europe in August 1096, had sold his estates of Rosay and Stenay on the Meuse. He would become the first ruler of Christian Jerusalem and was felt to epitomize the ideals of the First Crusade. He had been born heir to the Duchy of Lorraine and was a descendant of Charlemagne, something that he and his fellow Crusaders took very seriously. He embodied the ideals of the *chanson de geste* in being a man of enormous physical strength and indifferent intelligence: the Emperor Henry IV had confiscated the Duchy of Lorraine from his family but had made Godfrey its administrator, a job that he so mismanaged that Henry was about to dismiss him. Like Bohemund, Godfrey had practical reasons for going on the Crusade, as there was no future for him in the West. But he was also a man of strong piety and in particular he lived a very frugal, simple life, showing that he had absorbed the value that Cluny set on holy poverty. In Godfrey too, the hero of the Crusade, we see a mixture of motive and ideology.

His brother Baldwin was a very different sort of man and was frankly secular in outlook. He had been destined for the Church and so had inherited none of the family estates, but he had proved to be quite unsuited for the life of a churchman and returned to the lay state. There was, therefore, no future for him in Europe and he took his wife and children with him to the East, clearly never intending to return. He was a great contrast to his brother in both manner and appearance and they were a dramatic and striking pair. Where Godfrey was tall, blond and of an equable, easy temperament, Baldwin was also tall but dark and autocratic in manner. He had none of Godfrey's austerity and enjoyed luxurious living. He was also by far the more intelligent of the two. His education in the cathedral school at Reims had given him a taste for culture that was unusual in a layman at this time and during the Crusade he proved that he was a very able and shrewd soldier and politician. He was largely responsible for making the Christian Kingdom of Jerusalem an established state in the Middle East. For all its piety, the Crusade would need and value secular pragmatists like Baldwin.

Shortly after Bohemund took the Cross in September 1096 another group of Normans led an army to the East, and here again we see a mixture of motives and ideals. Robert of Normandy, the eldest son of William the Conqueror, was a very pious man and was genuinely moved by Urban's summons. He was a Crusader who certainly gave up everything to follow Christ on the Crusade. His father favored his younger brother William Rufus and the two were constantly at war, and yet Robert was prepared to pledge his duchy to William in order to raise the necessary money to equip his army. It was because of the Crusade that he lost the throne of England and also his life and liberty. William seized the throne when his father died while Robert was still in the East, and when Robert got back he was thrown into prison, where he died, probably murdered, many years later. His brother-in-law, Stephen of Blois, on the other hand, had absolutely no desire to go crusading, and eventually deserted the army. In his family, however, his wife Adela made the decisions and she forced him to go. When he returned in disgrace, she made him take a second expedition to the East in 1100 which was massacred in Asia Minor and the reluctant Stephen died with his men. The third Norman of this group was Robert of Flanders, a good Cluniac. His father had made the pilgrimage to Jerusalem in 1086 and had then stayed on in the East until 1093, helping the Emperor Alexius to fight the Turks in Asia Minor and Anatolia. His son wanted to carry on the family tradition.

Raymund of St. Gilles was also a Cluniac. He had been one of Gregory VII's Knights of St. Peter and had fought the Muslims in Spain. It seems that Urban may have discussed his plans with Raymund before Clermont, because after the speech Raymund was the first noble to offer himself for the expedition. He was simply inspired by religious motives: he had no problems at home but was prepared to give up his rich and comfortable life forever. At the time of the Crusade he was sixty years old and he vowed that he would spend his remaining years in the East. Yet Cluny would not have approved of all Raymund's piety. During the Crusade he showed that he was very credulous about relics and his army was accompanied by a large crowd of poor pilgrims who certainly affected his policies in ways that the papal legate, who traveled with Raymund, did not approve. Adhémar, Bishop of Le Puy, was committed to Cluniac ideals and was a man of wisdom and moderation. While he lived he was a valuable influence for good sense and made sure that the army observed the ideals of the Cluniac reform.

The leaders of the Crusade, therefore, were men with very mixed motives and ideals. Apart from the deserter Stephen of Blois and Hugh of Vermandois, second son of the King of France who got separated from the main army, they all fought bravely to the end under extremely frightening conditions. Even when the enterprise seemed hopeless, they persevered and finally managed to achieve an astonishing success. They were all dedicated men. Yet at this stage the Crusaders were not fighting a holy war in the classical sense and they were not yet imbued with the spirit of Joshua. They all had hopes of the Crusade and were making a journey to a new destiny, but they had very mixed ideas about what that destiny would be. They had Cluniac, Frankish, worldly ideals and ambitions and in some cases a strong personal piety. During the Crusade their practicality and their piety operated together very easily and they seemed sincerely to have believed that working for their own worldly success was quite in accordance with the will of God. The Crusaders were enthusiastic, but they had not yet created a clear crusading ideology that all the soldiers in the army could share. The common soldiers had very different hopes and ideals. Some saw the Crusade as a religious vendetta, others had apocalyptic hopes for a new world and some would have been attracted by the lure of the Holy City of Jerusalem. Many may have believed that they would improve their lot and become rich and famous or they might simply have wanted an adventure, as well as having a strong piety. But all these mixed motives were transformed by the experience of the Crusade itself. Crusading turned out to be quite different from what anybody had expected and the terror and wonder of the campaign gave birth to an ideal of a distinctively Christian version of the holy war.

The First Crusaders had learned from the tragic fate of the five armies that had marched East in the spring. Some of the armies avoided the dangerous journey by land and went by sea. Godfrey and Baldwin, however, deliberately went by land, following the road that they believed that Charlemagne had taken when he had made his (legendary) pilgrimage to the Holy Land. They were consciously following the footsteps of their great ancestor as they sought a new solution, rooting their new selves firmly in the past.[5] But they did not abandon the practical realities of life in a filial dream. The armies that chose the land route had taken care to provision themselves adequately and the leaders were very strict indeed about forbidding looting and pillaging. They thus avoided arousing the hostility of the inhabitants and managed to arrive in Constantinople unscathed and in good order. Here the great armies camped around the city, ready to fulfill the first part of their mandate, which was to help the Emperor Alexius to recover the territories he had lost to the Turks in Asia Minor and Anatolia.

In Constantinople the Crusaders entered a different world and they gazed in astonishment at its palaces, churches and gardens, for there was as yet nothing as sophisticated and advanced in Europe. The city also housed the greatest collection of relics in the world and the Crusaders must have felt surrounded on all sides by the power and holiness of God. But they must also have felt jealous and resentful of the Greeks, who did not seem worthy of this spiritual treasure. The warlike Franks simply could not understand a people who thought war was unchris-

tian and preferred to make treaties with the Muslims and seek a diplomatic solution rather than shed unnecessary blood. Nor could they
respect Alexius, Emperor of Byzantium, who had let himself be
trounced by the Turks. They lacked the political dimension to understand the skillful way in which the Byzantines had held Islam at
bay for centuries, and could only see their policy as cowardly and
dishonorable. For their part the Greeks were horrified by the Franks
and their talk of the holiness of war. They found the massive crusading
armies encamped in the suburbs threatening and could only see these
Western Christians as ignorant barbarians. Alexius certainly did not
trust the Crusaders and was worried that if they did succeed in re-
conquering any of his former territories from the Turks they would
refuse to return it to him and keep it for themselves. He had heard
that in Europe people bound themselves to one another by taking a
feudal oath and he therefore suggested that while they were in the
East the Crusaders should make such an oath to him and accept him
as their overlord. But this sensible solution seemed shocking to the
Crusaders. They saw it not only as a betrayal of their own overlords
in Europe but as against the whole Frankish spirit. Their glorious
ancestor Charlemagne had bequeathed to them an aversion to the
Greek Emperor and their Frankish identity had therefore been founded
on a defiance of the Eastern empire. Alexius found that he had struck
against something that was very deeply buried in many of the Crusaders and which exercised the power of an absolute veto. Godfrey,
the heir of Charlemagne, felt so strongly about it that he attacked the
suburbs of the city on Good Friday. This naturally seemed a blasphemy
to the Byzantines, and Anna Comnena, Alexius' daughter, was even
more horrified to see a priest, who handled the Eucharist daily, wield-
ing a sword and shedding blood.[6] There could scarcely be a clearer
example of the essential difference between the Greek Church and the
Western Christian spirit. While the official Western Church would
have disapproved of violence on a holy day, Godfrey would have seen
nothing wrong with it. His piety was strongly colored by the spirit
of *The Song of Roland* and he would, therefore, have seen fighting for
the honor of his people to be quite compatible with religion. This is
also a very telling instance of the way that different levels of religion
could exist in a Western Christian, who had not yet fully absorbed all
the Cluniac ideals, though he certainly exemplified some of them.
Godfrey understood the Cluniac teaching about holy poverty, but, as
we have seen, the Church had given the knights a confused message
about the Christian use of violence. Godfrey, a simple-minded man,
preferred the clarity of *The Song of Roland*.

Eventually their common sense and the hard facts of the situation led the Franks to accede to Alexius' demands. Leaders like Bohemund, who had fought in the East before, knew that unless they had the cooperation of the Greeks they would be unlikely to succeed in this war in unfamiliar terrian. The Greeks had promised to provision the armies as long as they were within reach of Byzantium and to come to their aid in a crisis. Eventually the Crusaders took the oath, but in the event showed little scruple about breaking it at the earliest opportunity. Urban had partly summoned the Crusade to heal the growing rift between the Eastern and Western churches but in fact the Crusades would destroy any hope of a reunion. The Europeans had long hated the Greeks from afar, but when the Crusaders were actually confronted with the splendors of Constantinople and the elegance of its advanced culture, they felt inferior and this made them defensive and belligerent. During the ceremony of the oath taking one of the knights sat on Alexius' throne and refused to vacate it when the Emperor entered, until Baldwin sharply rebuked him. Alexius then engaged the knight in courteous, if condescending, conversation and let him brag about his prowess in single combat. The Emperor then calmly advised him not to attempt any of those tactics when fighting the Turks, as he would find himself severely worsted.[7] The Franks constantly revealed themselves to the Byzantines as ignorant and uncouth poor relations, who fiercely resented their dependence upon Alexius and resented even more his mastery of a situation that left them floundering.

Once they had taken the oath, the armies were shipped across the Bosphorus and, "at the gates of the land of the Turks,"[8] the Crusaders all received the sacrament. At every important stage of their campaign and at each moment of crisis, the army turned to public prayer. These soldiers ranked liturgy on the same level as war councils and listened to sermons as carefully as they listened to military instructions. The Crusaders were soldiers who understood enough about the importance of nutrition to give their horses double rations before a battle, but would themselves fast for three days before an important offensive, even when they were already weakened by starvation.[9] At times of stress Adhémar would urge them to give alms to the poor, even when most of the soldiers were themselves suffering gravely from want.[10] The prayer, processions, preaching, fasting and almsgiving gave this Crusade a distinctly monastic character; the armies seemed to their contemporaries to be vast military monasteries on the move[11] and gave the campaign the devotion of the pilgrimage that had given birth to it. It made this war different from all their other feudal wars.

In May 1097 the Crusaders and the Byzantines besieged the Seljuk capital at Nicaea. Alexius was probably aware that the Sultan Kilij Arslan I was far away at his eastern border and that this was an opportune moment for an attack. Kilij Arslan had heard about the Crusaders but had not taken them very seriously. It was his troops who had massacred the armies of Peter the Hermit and Walter Sansavoir the previous year and he judged that this next Western assault would be just as easy to deal with. By the time he realized his mistake it was too late. He rushed back to defend his capital, Nicaea, which was manned only by a small garrison, and was soundly defeated by the Christians. He could do no more and sent word to his soldiers telling them to surrender as soon as their situation became intolerable. Eventually the Muslim garrison did surrender but they very wisely surrendered directly to Alexius, knowing that he would offer them acceptable terms. In the agreement, he promised that the city should not be looted. The leaders of the Crusade probably agreed with him that looting would be wasteful and dangerous to the Greek Christians of Nicaea, but their soldiers were furious and their resentment of Alexius grew. They watched incredulously as the Turkish nobles in the garrison were escorted to Constantinople with honor and heard in horror that they had been housed in one of the imperial palaces while awaiting ransom. But this was nothing to their fury when they heard that they had been forbidden to plunder the city. Their desire to loot did not spring entirely from greed. The army was already beginning to feel the pinch of want and some of the poor pilgrims had actually starved to death during the siege. Looting and pillaging would be the only way that the Crusaders would be able to sustain themselves once they were in Muslim territory. Even though Alexius tried to compensate them with very generous gifts of money—more gold than they had ever seen and ample to provision themselves—they still murmured angrily about his "treachery," feeling deprived of an enjoyable raid and manipulated by an effete foreign power.

Nevertheless morale was high. The Crusaders had liberated a Christian city that had had a distinguished history; they had defeated the infidel in their first encounter and had redeemed the disgrace of the Crusaders' defeat the previous year. Their Crusade certainly seemed to be á viable enterprise. They were now ready for the next stage of the campaign, and at the end of June they set off on their long journey south through Asia Minor toward Palestine. Their objective was to liberate the pilgrim route to the Holy Land across Asia Minor, which had been infested with the Turks since the Seljuk victories in 1071, and to liberate former Byzantine territory around Antioch and in Armenia, and they had sworn to return these lands to Byzantium. It was important that there should be a strong Christian presence there and in northern Syria to support the Latin state that they intended to set up in Palestine. From this point they were on their own. The Emperor could not provision them so far from his capital, though he did send guides and advisers with them. The Crusaders were therefore entirely alone, surrounded by the hostile world of Islam, enclosed, as Professor Riley-Smith has said in a memorable phrase, "in an alien, suffering world of their own."[12]

The suffering and terror began on July 1, days after they had left Nicaea. To ease the problem of supplies and provisions, the leaders had decided to march in two companies, and the vanguard set off one day ahead of the others, led by Bohemund, Stephen of Blois and Robert of Flanders, with Bohemund's army of Italian Normans and the armies from the north of France. The second army of southern French and the Lorrainers was led by Raymund of St. Gilles. When the vanguard reached the plain outside Dorylaeum it pitched camp and thus fell into the ambush prepared by the Sultan, who had been lying in wait for them. At daybreak the Turks rushed out of hiding and fell upon the camp; at once Bohemund got the Christians organized. The poor and the noncombatants were put in the middle of the camp and the women were given the job of carrying water to the front line. Runners were dispatched to tell the rear guard to hurry to the rescue and Bohemund sternly commanded his troops to remain on the defensive and not to attack the Turks. Yet the horde of Turks seemed invincible and Fulcher of Chartres describes the paralysis of despair which fell on the Christians who sat in the center of the camp expecting massacre. "We were all indeed huddled together like sheep in a fold, trembling and frightened, surrounded on all sides by enemies," he recalled. "By now we had no hope of surviving."[13] Instantly and as one, they turned to prayer. They decided that God had abandoned them because of their sins and, in the middle of a battle, there was a spontaneous liturgy of penance that could only have happened during a Crusade:

> We then confessed that we were defendants at the bar of justice and sinners, and we humbly begged mercy from God. The Bishop of Le Puy our patron and four other bishops were there, and a great many priests also, vested in white. They humbly besought God that he would destroy the power of our enemy and shed upon us the gift of his mercy. Weeping they sang and singing they wept. Then

many people fearing that death was nigh ran to the priests and confessed their sins.[14]

Suddenly, when all seemed lost, the rear guard arrived. Kilij Arslan had believed that he had managed to trap the whole crusading army and the arrival of a huge army of fresh Christians caught him completely off guard. The Turks fled, hotly pursued by the Crusaders, who razed their camp to the ground. The Sultan had felt able to survive the loss of his capital at Nicaea, for his real capital was his tent, and the destruction of the camp was a far greater blow. He would not feel able to attack the Crusaders again and the hitherto unbeatable Turks had to recognize that they had a powerful new enemy.

The peril of the Christians had been so extreme that their sudden deliverance seemed "a great miracle," as Fulcher put it: the Turks were put to flight because "our comrades reinforced us *and* as divine grace was miraculously present."[15] The sentence perfectly sums up the piety of these First Crusaders, who prayed as though everything depended upon God but fought as though they depended on themselves alone. The shock of Dorylaeum transformed their view of their mission. In Raymund's army, which had been with the rear guard and not present during the attack, an extraordinary rumor circulated. As the chaplain and chronicler Raymund of Aguiles recorded, the Crusaders had been protected by heavenly beings: "Two knights clad in shining armour and of wonderful appearance advanced before our army and so threatened the enemy that they granted them no chance to fight in any way. Indeed when the Turks wanted to strike them with their lances they appeared invulnerable to them."[16] As they continued their journey, the Crusaders excitedly asked each other who these warriors could have been, and finally decided that, as they were so far from their own patron saints, God had sent the local soldier-saints George and Demetrius to help them in their hour of need. From this point other pilgrims and soldiers began to have dreams and visions of these saints; they would also see St. Andrew, the patron of the Greek Church, and the Eastern St. Mercury. No Westerner had had a great devotion to these Eastern saints before, but now that they were in their territory and needed their protection they decided that God had sent them new patrons and protectors. St. George would become the patron saint of the whole Crusade and a very popular saint in the West.[17]

The Crusaders desperately needed this reassurance: it was a way of acclimatizing themselves to the frightening world in which they found themselves. The countryside was alien and filled them with terror: when they reached the Anti-Taurus range of mountains between Goksun and Marash, for example, the precipice they had to surmount filled them with utter despair. As the knights watched the horses and pack animals hurtling over the edge, wrote the author of the *Gesta Francorum* ("The Deeds of the Franks," an eyewitness account): "they stood about in a great state of gloom, wringing their hands because they were so frightened and miserable, not knowing what to do with themselves."[18] The Crusade became a chronicle of terror and suffering. The Turks destroyed the countryside so that the Crusaders could not find food, and men and animals began to die like flies. The poor pilgrims suffered particularly heavy casualties, as always, and depended totally on the alms of knights and soldiers who were themselves dramatically impoverished. As the horses died, more and more knights were reduced to the ranks because without a horse they could not perform their military function; others resorted to riding oxen, goats and sheep and to using dogs as pack animals.[19] They were experiencing a deprivation that went far beyond the secure holy poverty of the monk or the pilgrim back home and were moving into a terrifying new world where the bonds of society seemed to be breaking down. To comfort themselves they instinctively turned to religion and created the myth of the angelic warriors who were fighting on their side. The journey to Palestine had always been holy because it had been a pilgrimage to Jerusalem, but as they progressed the Crusaders felt themselves to be holy in their own right. They had a strong sense that God was, quite literally, marching with them: "As we advanced we had the most generous and merciful and most victorious hand of the Almighty Father with us,"[20] wrote Raymund of Aguiles. He was leading them and preserving them just as he had led the Israelites during their long journey to the Holy Land. At the time of Charlemagne, the Franks had begun to see themselves as God's new chosen people and now the salvation they had experienced at Dorylaeum led them gradually to see themselves as taking up the vocation which the Jews had lost. Slowly too the Crusaders were being drawn together to see themselves as one people as they struggled through the desolate countryside. As Fulcher of Chartres said: "Though we were of different tongues we seemed, however, to be brothers in the love of God and to be nearly of one mind."[21] The Crusaders were being taught by their suffering to see themselves as the united people of God and this holy pilgrimage was forming an entirely new identity. The Franks in particular had been in search of a new vocation and crusading had given it to them.

Yet though they were beginning to see themselves as the chosen people they had not yet developed a Joshuan hatred of their enemy. Their image of the Turks was virtually the same as the portrait of the

Saracens in *The Song of Roland*, except that they seem to have realized that they were not idol-worshipers. The Norman author of the *Gesta Francorum* admired them and considered them to be excellent soldiers; their only failing was that they were not Christians. He also felt a strong sense of affinity with them, and indeed the Turks and the Normans were very much alike. Both were barbarian peoples who had very recently fought their way through to the centers of an ancient civilization and converted to the dominant religion. As the Normans and the Franks were at this time seeking a new Christian identity, the Turks were trying to build a new Islamic identity for themselves and were challenging the Arab establishment, which looked down on them with a certain disdain. After the Battle of Dorylaeum, the author of the *Gesta* wrote:

> What man, however experienced and learned, would dare to write of the skill and prowess and courage of the Turks, who thought that they would strike terror into the Franks as they had done into the Arabs and Saracens, Armenians, Syrians and Greeks, by the menace of their arrows? Yet, please God, their men will never be as good as ours. They have a saying that they are of common stock with the Franks and are naturally born to be knights. This is true and nobody can deny it, that if only they had stood firm in the faith of Christendom and been willing to accept One God in Three Persons . . . you could not find stronger or braver or more skilful soldiers; and yet by God's grace they were beaten by our men.[22]

The Norman author is making the Turks the foil of Frankish eminence and greatness, just as the author of *The Song of Roland* had tried to do with the Spanish Muslims. The Norman author is still very vague about his enemy: he still calls them "pagans" throughout his history, as do the other chroniclers. He appears to think, mistakenly, that the Turks had been Christians at one time. He seems to think that the Arabs and the Saracens are different from one another. Had he known more about Islam, he might have mentioned another affinity. When fighting a *jihad*, Muslims combined piety with practicality, in very much the same spirit as the First Crusaders, and have continued to do so in the holy wars of today.

In September 1097 the Crusade split into two again. Before they went to the Holy Land they had to liberate northern Syria from the Muslims and restore these lands which the Turks had conquered to Byzantium as they had sworn to Alexius. They also needed to establish a Christian bulwark in this area to protect the pilgrim routes and the Christian state they planned to establish in the Holy Land. The main army, led by Bohemund and Raymund, marched to Antioch and encamped aggressively outside this powerful and strategically important city. A splinter group, led by Baldwin and Tancred, headed west toward Cilicia. On September 21 they took the city of Tarsus, and Tancred went on to conquer Adana and Misis while Baldwin briefly rejoined the main army and then set out east on his own toward Edessa.

Baldwin was probably the most secular of all the leaders: he was determined to get a kingdom for himself in the East and had no guilt about his oath to Alexius. He was careful to present himself to the Armenian inhabitants as a Christian liberator and in this he was supremely successful. As he marched toward the city of Edessa the Armenian Christians rushed forward to greet him ecstatically. In the face of this sudden Christian enthusiasm the Muslim garrisons either fled or were brutally conquered and massacred by the Armenians and Franks together. On February 20, 1098, he arrived in Edessa and was welcomed most warmly by the Armenian King Toros. Toros was anxious to get rid of the Turks but had no desire to return to the Byzantine Empire. The Greek Orthodox had always despised the Armenian Christians and thought that they were heretical. Sometimes they had actually tried to suppress the native faith and the Armenians deeply resented them. They had no dreams of independence (they had been part of empires for so long) and had long thought that a Latin Western hegemony would be preferable. Baldwin seemed an answer to Toros' prayer and he adopted the imposing Frank as his son in a strange ceremony: he passed a huge shirt over Baldwin's head and, within its folds, the two men rubbed chests. Baldwin was now coregent and heir to the throne. Yet, under most suspicious circumstances,[23] Toros was murdered on March 10 and Baldwin became head of state. At once he set about endearing himself to the Armenians and conquered the Turkish garrison of Samosata. There was no thought of returning this new territory to the Emperor, of course, and Baldwin had at a stroke greatly increased the size of his principality. In Samosata he discovered many Armenian hostages whom he returned to their families, greatly enhancing his popularity. Baldwin had established the first Western colony in the Middle East in circumstances that were as manipulative and ambiguous as most later colonial adventures in the area.

In the meantime the rest of the Crusaders were in extreme distress at Antioch; their experience here would be crucial to the Crusaders' understanding of the special nature of their mission. Despite the dreadful march, the army arrived at Antioch at the end of October 1097 in reasonable shape. Here they were replenished by supplies brought them by the Genoese fleet and there was, initially, a fair amount of food in the region. The Crusaders knew that they should try to take the city because Antioch had been one of the most important Christian cities in the early centuries of Christianity; St. Peter had been its first bishop and it was here that the disciples of Jesus had been called "Christians." But the ancient Christian Church of St. Peter had now been converted into a mosque; it was obviously the Crusaders' duty to liberate such a holy city, which would have been a major cult center in Europe. To take the city and the country surrounding it would also consolidate the gains that Baldwin would make in Edessa. Yet there were grave doubts among the leaders. With winter coming on, would the army realistically have the strength to besiege such a powerful and well-defended city? Some of the leaders thought that they should wait for help from the Byzantines and for reinforcements from France. Others, however, including Raymund of St. Gilles, had been powerfully affected by the new view of the Crusade:

> We have come here by the inspiration of God; through his mercy we obtained Nicaea, a very strongly fortified city, and through the same clemency we have obtained victory and security from the Turks. . . . Thus we should commit our lot to him. We ought not to fear Kings, or the chiefs of Kings, nor yet places or times, when God has snatched us from so many dangers.[24]

The first part of that speech could be seen as conventional rhetoric, but the final sentence shows a willingness to put the crusading army outside the limitations that affect ordinary mortals. If God was fighting for the Crusaders why should they worry about the perils of winter or the impregnable walls of Antioch?

The decision to besiege Antioch almost finished the Crusade. To keep such a vast army of 50,000 soldiers with its crowd of poor pilgrims in one place for months at a time inevitably meant that the food available in the region was quickly exhausted. The country was stripped bare and severe famine set in. The efficiency of the siege was impaired because men were sent out further and further afield on raiding and foraging expeditions, sometimes as far as fifty miles away. Knights and poor people all started to die of starvation in great numbers. By January 1098 the famine reached its peak:

> The starving people devoured the stalks of beans still growing in the fields, many kinds of herbs unseasoned with salt, and even thistles which because of the lack of firewood were not well cooked and

therefore irritated the tongues of those eating them. They also ate horses, camels, dogs, and even rats. The poorer people ate even the hides of animals and the seeds of grain found in manure.[25]

In January Peter the Hermit himself deserted the army. He was caught, brought back and the affair was quickly hushed up. It seems that Peter lost no real prestige among the leaders because he would soon be seen heading important missions to the Turks and preaching major sermons. The Crusaders were far more tolerant of deserters than the people back home because they knew what they had been up against. That same month even Bohemund thought that he ought to go home. He could not bear to watch his men and horses dying all around him when he himself was too poor to alleviate their sufferings. It was not only the rank and file who were dying; the leaders themselves had become poor and many important knights had been reduced to the ranks. By June 1098 there were only about 200 horses left in the entire army. Men who were wealthy and powerful in Europe were now riding donkeys and mules. The Crusaders really were shut off from everything they had known before in a strange, self-enclosed world of suffering.

If doughty Crusaders like Bohemund and Peter the Hermit lost faith for a time, why did the majority of the Crusaders decide to continue squatting before Antioch, watching their companions dying like flies of hunger and disease? We get some insight into what was going on in the minds of the Crusaders from a letter written by the bishops in the army: "How one against a thousand? Where we have a count, the enemy has forty kings; where we have a regiment the enemy has a legion; where we have a knight they have a duke; where we have a footsoldier they have a count; where we have a castle they have a kingdom." The bishops naturally felt that they were a tiny Christian island surrounded by a mighty Muslim ocean. The Crusaders stayed because they were deeply convinced that God would ultimately rescue them. The bishops continued their letter: "We do not trust in any multitude nor in power nor in any presumption, but in the shield of Christ and justice, under the protection of George and Theodore and Demetrius and St. Blaise, soldiers of Christ truly accompanying us."[26] This was not a pious figure of speech. It was "truly" a fact. Crusaders at Dorylaeum had seen these celestial warriors fighting for them. They now felt surrounded by an unseen heavenly army. To desert would be stupid; the deserter would be deserting Christ and his special friends. When the Crusaders started to refer to themselves as the "army of God" or "soldiers of Christ"[27] they meant this literally, and this meant that desertion was the ultimate apostasy. The malnutrition disposed the Crusaders to hallucinate and not surprisingly they began to "see" more of these celestial warriors of God watching over the army, or else they dreamed of receiving heavenly messages of comfort which assured the Crusaders that "the Lord is with you."[28] This was not a pious fancy nor was it rousing rhetoric: they believed it was the literal truth.

The author of the *Gesta Francorum* shows the Crusaders fighting very hard indeed and making sensible stratagems; at the same time he shows us how they used to make a conscious effort to work up in themselves a sense of God's protection. After a particularly strong attack of the Turks outside Antioch, we see the Crusaders in his army gathered around their leader Bohemund:

> Angry at the loss of our comrades, we called on the name of Christ and put our trust in the pilgrimage to the Holy Sepulchre and went all together to fight the Turks, whom we attacked with one heart and mind. God's enemies and ours were standing about, amazed and terrified, for they thought that they could defeat and kill us, as they had done with the followers of the Count and Bohemund, but Almighty God did not allow them to do so. The knights of the True God, armed at all points with the sign of the Cross, charged them fiercely and made a brave attack upon them, and they fled swiftly across the middle of the narrow bridge to their gate.[29]

Just as the first Christian community in Jerusalem lived together with "one heart and mind," so now this new community of knights in the army of the True God were united in their faith and commitment to fight the Turks, who were not simply their enemies but God's too. The author of the *Gesta* was certain that the Crusaders who died in this battle were not just casualties but martyrs. "On that day more than a thousand of our knights or footsoldiers suffered martyrdom," he writes, "and we believe that they went to Heaven and were clad in white robes and received the martyr's palm."[30] The author is aware that he is making a controversial statement. The Franks celebrated "martyrs" like Roland, but this new kind of aggressive martyr was by no means generally accepted by most Christians in the West. Yet when a Norman knight like Roger Barneville died fighting and killing the Turks in an independent attack, he was buried by Adhémar with great pomp and ceremony and was believed to be a martyr by his fellow Crusaders.[31]

There is perhaps no better way of entering the mind of the Crusaders than by looking at the dreams or visions that they produced. It was natural for them to see their dreams as sent by God and we can see how they were ransacking their subconscious to dredge up any shred of comfort that they could. Just as before a battle they would prepare themselves by deliberately making themselves conscious of the presence and protection of God, so too in their sleep or in their visions they were convincing themselves that they had to stay on and fight to the bitter end. This end might be bitter in purely human terms but in the next life the Crusader would be among the most privileged Christians of all. When a notable Crusader died he would often be "seen" by the knights and poor soldiers in battle as well as when they were in repose.[32] These martyred Crusaders would urge them to go forward bravely and tell them that the whole of the heavenly court was on their side: naturally this made them fight with a total belief in the protection of Christ and the saints. One of the best known of these visions was seen by the very pious knight Anselm of Ribemont the day before his own death. In one version of the story he saw the young knight Enguerrand of St. Pol, who had died two months earlier. Enguerrand was glowing with an extraordinary beauty and assured Anselm that "of course those who end their lives in the service of Christ are not dead."[33] He transported the knight to heaven where he showed him his house there, beautiful beyond description, and told Anselm that he himself would be installed in an even more beautiful mansion on the morrow. In another even more telling version of the story Anselm found himself standing on a pile of filth,[34] gazing up at a splendid palace where he could see his former companions, who were so gloriously transfigured that he could scarcely recognize them. One of them, probably Enguerrand, told him that these were the crusading martyrs and that he would join them the next day. This is a useful insight into the mind of a noble but deeply pious knight facing his own death. The image of Anselm straining heavenward from the pile of dung on which he was standing is a perfect emblem of the mental attitude of so many of the Crusaders.

So how did these soldiers of God explain their terrible sufferings? They naturally turned to the Bible, especially the Old Testament. They knew that God's special friends did suffer. Not only had the Israelites themselves suffered from hunger and sickness in the desert but there was also the example of Job. These sufferings had been sent by God himself to chastise his people as a father might chastise his child. Many of the Crusaders saw the unprecedented suffering outside Antioch as another proof that they too were God's special friends, marked by a special destiny. Fulcher of Chartres explained it thus: "It is my belief that, pre-elected by God long before and tested in such a great disaster, they were cleansed of their sins, just as gold is proved three times and is purged by fire seven times."[35] Anselm of Ribemont himself had written before his death that "God, who 'punishes all the sons he loves,' trained us in this way."[36] And Raymund of St. Gilles and Bishop Daimbert of Pisa in a joint letter to Europe said that "for nine months God held us back . . . and humbled us outside Antioch, until all our puffed-up pride had turned back to humility." In this view the Crusaders had got above themselves. They had marched into the East full of Frankish pride and self-assertion. Their victory at Dorylaeum had given them a heady belief that they were a special people. They were not mistaken in this, as events would prove, but first they had to be brought into a more truly Christian frame of mind and God only allowed them to win the city "when such was our degradation that scarcely 100 good horses could be found in the whole army."[37] Raymund and Bishop Daimbert were well aware of the importance of holy poverty. Now that they had suffered absolute degradation, when they were without horses, without money and without the basic means of subsistence, they were stripped of human pride and therefore able to do great things for God.

In the minds of the poor there was a different interpretation of these months of 1097. In many ways the perseverance of the poor pilgrims was quite extraordinary. They suffered more than the knights; they died in greater numbers despite all the almsgiving, and when the army was attacked by the Turks they were in a far more vulnerable position than the knights because they had no defense. The poor had no exalted code of honor which would make desertion difficult. They were used to the art of survival in harsh conditions, and that had to mean compromise. Similarly, what made knights who had been impoverished by the Crusade and reduced to the ranks persevere to the very end? There were many such knights: their horses died, they had to sell their weapons and equipment to buy food and finally resort to begging for bread at the tables of their former colleagues. It would be easy to imagine a knight in this position being filled with a great bitterness against the whole project and its dreams of earthly and heavenly glory. He might well feel like throwing up all his chivalric ideals and making for home. Half the Crusaders were dead and many had understandably deserted, but an enormous number stayed (probably about 50,000).

It seems in fact that through this experience the poor actually gained a new self-confidence during this winter—a confidence that would make them assert themselves against the rich and the powerful and dream of a day when the first should be last and the last first, when the poor would inherit the earth and be honored by the rich. As they watched the rich haughty aristocrats begging for bread, riding clumsy mules as though they were peasants and sharing their own hopeless lot they must have had a new view of the ruling class. Never again would they see them as distant giants who were rendered immune to such ills by the security of wealth and privilege. They began to see the Crusade as a first step in that revolution foretold by Mary in the gospels when she sings that God had reversed the old world order:

> He has routed the proud of heart.
> He has pulled down princes from their thrones and exalted
>   the lowly.
> The hungry he has filled with good things, the rich sent
>   empty away.
>
> (Luke 1:51–53)

The belief that they were the vanguard of this new world led the poor Crusaders to seek a new and more powerful identity for themselves. The Frankish aristocrats were not the only ones with such dreams and visions, for outside Antioch there was the first sign of the poor rising to new power and effectiveness. The initial indication of this self-assertion was that the poor now began to organize themselves into independent bands for their own protection. There was later a rumor that at this point in the Crusade a group of poor orphans formed themselves into a regiment and fought alongside the knights. The most remarkable of these was the band called the Tafurs, which had been founded by a knight who had been reduced to the ranks but became known as King Tafur.[38] It became a terrorist wing of the army which raided the surrounding countryside for food with such extreme savagery that they terrified most of the Crusaders. The Tafurs gave the Crusaders a fearful reputation among the Muslims in the area and it was rumored that they even ate the flesh of their Muslim victims. In the darkest days of the siege this might well have been true. But the Tafurs were not just a menace: Guibert of Nogent is clear that they did the most exhausting work,[39] were tireless in battle and fought with exceptional bravery and ferocity. Pope Urban had not intended to make the poor militant; indeed the Cluniac reform had stressed the image of the poor man as being without a sword. Yet during the famine outside Antioch the poor men learned to assert themselves violently in order to survive.

Gradually the poor came to see themselves as an elite. A popular epic composed just after the Crusade helps us to enter into the visions and dreams of the poor as they struggled to survive outside Antioch.

The *Chanson d'Antioch* shows that, far from seeking holy poverty, the poor were dreaming of a greater share of the goods of this world: they wanted to bring about a fairer distribution of wealth. In the poem the poor of Provence gallop back to the camp and flaunt their booty "to show their companions how their poverty is at an end; others, dressed in two or three silken garments, praise God as the bestower of victory and gifts."[40] God was fighting for the poor to increase their status, just as, to them, he was fighting with the Crusade as a whole to defeat the Muslims. King Tafur cries to his men: "Where are the folk who want property? let them come with me! . . . With God's help I shall win enough to load many a mule."[41] This was not just greed but part of a conviction that by means of the Crusade God was bringing about a new world where a greater justice would prevail.

In the *Chanson* the Tafurs saw themselves as the elite of the Crusaders. At the same time as they were seeking to overthrow the old order, they flaunted their poverty as a badge and as a mark of privilege. King Tafur, in this legendary version of his life, was a Norman knight who voluntarily gave up his wealth and descended to the ranks of the poor people to lead them to glory. Such "voluntary" poor were seen as belonging to the inner circle of Tafurs, for there was plenty of encouragement in the gospels to make the poor believe that they, not the knights, were God's chosen people and that they would take Jerusalem as King Tafur says: "The poorest shall take it: this is a sign to show clearly that the Lord God does not care for presumptuous and faithless men."[42] In the poem the Tafurs force the knights and the richer Crusaders to respect them at last. When the Amir of Antioch complains to the Crusader leaders about the Tafurs' terrorist activities, the leaders admit: "All of us together cannot tame King Tafur."[43] When the barons prove that they are not true Crusaders and show a real reluctance to push on to Jerusalem at one point, it is King Tafur who shames them into accepting his leadership. "We are behaving like false pilgrims. If it rested with me and with the poor alone, the pagans would find us the worst neighbours they ever had."[44] It is King Tafur who crowns Godfrey of Bouillon as King of Jerusalem and Godfrey swears to hold it as a fief from God and King Tafur alone. When the other Crusaders slink off home, it is the poor people who stay on to defend the Holy Land. Fantastic as this sounds, it did contain a seed of truth and the poor did rise to a new power in fact as well as in fiction.

The movement of the poor Crusaders was strengthened by the visions of Peter Bartholomew, a poor servant in the army of Raymund of St. Gilles.[45] On December 30, 1097, there was an earthquake. Some

of the Crusaders even persuaded themselves that this terrifying oc-
currence was a sign of God's protection; they looked into the sky at
the "earthquake lights" and saw a glowing Cross. Peter, however, had
another vision. He was praying in pure terror and it seems that the
trauma of the earthquake tipped him into a hallucinatory state. Events
would show that he was constantly ill—at one point he was losing
his eyesight, which could have been due to starvation, so he was
therefore disposed to visionary experience. As the earth rocked beneath
him, Peter strained desperately to find some sense of hope and safety.
Suddenly he saw a wondrously beautiful young man, whom he later
identified as Jesus himself but who never spoke. This was a common
feature of Christ in the Crusaders' visions. It may indicate an unwill-
ingness to give such a complete divine sanction to their insights and
longings or may simply show that the saints were actually more vivid
figures, at least to the lay Christians, than Christ himself. Alongside
the beautiful young man a less intimidating old man appeared with
sandy hair sprinkled with gray, who revealed that he was St. Andrew.
He told Peter Bartholomew that he had a message for the Count of
St. Gilles and for Bishop Adhémar. He strongly denounced Adhémar
(most unfairly) for failing in his duty as a preacher, and this showed
that Peter did not share the general veneration of the bishop. Count
Raymund, on the other hand, was to be given a special task. In the
ancient Cathedral of St. Peter inside the city of Antioch, St. Andrew
explained, was the holy lance that had pierced Christ's side on Good
Friday. When the city was taken, Raymund and Peter should take
twelve Crusaders and dig for it. Then Peter was suddenly transported
in spirit inside the besieged city and taken to the south chapel of the
cathedral; at this point St. Andrew disappeared into the ground and
reappeared bearing the lance aloft triumphantly. Peter was then returned to the camp outside the walls. This eccentric vision completely
transformed the Crusade and that it should have done so shows how
very much more powerful religion was than political ideas and motivation at this time. The holy lance, it must be remembered, would
be a relic of such extraordinary power that it would in itself be an
omnipotent weapon. Intimately bound up in the holy and powerful
events which saved the world, its discovery would guarantee victory
against the Turks.

But at first Peter was too frightened of the leaders to obey St.
Andrew and he did not deliver his message. St. Andrew had to appear
on no less than four further occasions, and he became more and more
angry at Peter's delay. But Peter still hung back, because he was afraid
that the barons would simply assume that he was trying to get extra

food and would punish him for his blasphemy. Yet the persistence of St. Andrew shows that, however hard he tried to suppress this vision of hope, Peter was still clinging to it tenaciously. At this time he and his master were very busy trying to find provisions for the army; he was not simply sitting back passively and expecting deliverance to descend from heaven. Frequently St. Andrew appeared when Peter was very actively engaged: on one occasion he saw St. Andrew just as he was getting on board a ship that was to take him foraging in Cyprus. In the midst of these attempts to find a human, practical solution, Peter still turned to the vision of the lance. St. Andrew told him plainly that an army which carried the lance into battle would never be defeated: Peter was struggling to convince himself that the Crusade could still be successful as a military and as a holy campaign, however hopeless it seemed at present. He even allowed himself to look forward past the disastrous period at Antioch to the day when the Crusaders would enter the Holy Land. St. Andrew gave Peter a list of rather bizarre instructions for Raymund, when the army should reach the river Jordan in Palestine. Raymund was to cross the river on a raft, rebaptize himself and then preserve the underclothes he was wearing on that sacred occasion forever and put them together with the lance. Yet even though St. Andrew was becoming more irate, Peter still could not bring himself to go to Raymund, but he probably talked to his less exalted companions and the story would have spread quickly. On one occasion, Peter's master claimed to have heard every word that St. Andrew said to Peter, even though he did not see the celestial visitor. His master too was reaching and straining for a vision of hope. But Peter was not yet one of the self-confident poor, who were ready to challenge the rich. This early diffidence would change, but as yet Peter remained fearfully silent.

The Crusaders were making no headway against the city of Antioch, but they could not now abandon the siege and go on to the Holy Land, leaving this powerful enemy city undefeated in their rear. Finally in the summer of 1098 they heard some frightening news. Qawam ad-Daula Kerbuqa, the Turkish Emir of Mosul in Syria, had formed a mighty confederation of the princes in the area against the Franks. His large army had begun its march against the Christians and had made first for Baldwin's newly established Christian principality of Edessa. But by this time Baldwin was so firmly established and the Armenian Christians were still so delighted with their "liberator" that Edessa seemed too powerful, and Kerbuqa felt that the half-starved army at Antioch would be an easier target to begin with. In fact, this confederation was not quite as threatening as it appeared. All the

Muslim princes who had joined Kerbuqa were apprehensive about the power and prestige that he would gain if he managed to defeat the Franks. The dissension in Kerbuqa's army mirrored the dissension in the Seljuk empire at this date; it was this that made it difficult for the Turks to fight the Crusaders effectively. The Crusaders, however, knew nothing of this and when they heard of Kerbuqa's approach some of them (including Stephen of Blois) despaired and deserted.

On June 2, the night that Stephen left, the Christians made the crucial breakthrough. Bohemund had contacted a potential traitor inside the city through his Armenian spies. Captain Firouz was an Armenian Christian who had converted to Islam, but he was becoming dissatisfied with the regime and its religion and had made it clear that, for a price, he would betray the city. That night he sent word to Bohemund that he was ready to do the deed: the Crusaders should bring their ladders to the Tower of the Two Sisters and he would let them into the city. The Crusaders did indeed enter the city that night, crying aloud, *"Deus hoc vult!"* They drove the Turks from the garrison and looted and pillaged the city. The starving Crusaders even ransacked the houses of the Armenian Christians as well as the Muslims, and the streets were filled with dead bodies. Against all the odds, the Crusaders had managed to liberate the venerable Christian city.

Their triumph was brief. On June 4 Kerbuqa's fresh and superbly equipped army arrived outside the walls and began to besiege Antioch. Unless the Byzantines came to relieve the Crusaders, as they had promised they would in a crisis, there seemed no hope that the exhausted Crusaders could survive in the spent city. But the Greeks never came: they had been misinformed and told that Kerbuqa had already conquered the Frankish army. The situation was desperate and on June 10 there was a night of panic. Crusaders began to desert the city and guards had to be posted at the gates to stop them leaving. Yet even in this darkest hour some committed men stopped themselves giving way to fear. There was another outbreak of visions. In the very act of climbing the walls, Crusaders saw saints, angels or dead Crusaders who urged them to stay in the city and to trust in God: he had not forgotten his people and would deliver them from Kerbuqa.[46] During the past two years the people had invested too much of themselves in crusading to abandon it, even in the face of such obvious danger. They could still summon up enough psychic energy to drive away their fear and reassert their conviction that God would intervene as he had intervened throughout their campaign. Though the Turks were at one point attacking the walls that night and seemed to be about to break into the city, Crusaders waited for deliverance.

During the panic and confusion a group of Christians went off to the Church of St. Mary to pray for God's help. After what was probably an intense and exhaustingly emotional prayer session, most of the group fell into an exhausted sleep or trance. One priest stayed awake, or thought he did. Stephen of Valence suddenly saw a beautiful man standing before him.[47] Did Stephen recognize him? asked the man. Stephen noticed that behind the man's head was a cross and he asked if the man were Christ; the figure acknowledged that he was and asked Stephen a series of searching questions about the military organization of the Crusade and reminded him of all the help that he had given to the Crusaders during their two-year struggle. But how they repaid him? Christ asked sternly: with wantonness, fornication[48] and sinfulness. They had ceased to act like a Christian army and had profaned the holy pilgrimage with prostitutes. Why should Christ help them any longer? At this point Mary and St. Peter both rushed to intercede for the Crusaders and Jesus relented. He told Stephen to go to the leaders and to get them to put the Crusade back on the path of righteousness by starting a campaign of liturgical prayer and a moral reform.

It is easy to understand this vision. In a state of heightened emotion in which fear mingled with intense religious fervor, Stephen recalled the extraordinary events of the Crusade that he could only explain by divine intervention and then searched his soul for the reason for God's apparent abandonment. At the end of the vision Stephen was consoled. Christ told him that within five days, provided that there was a moral reform, he would send help. While Bohemund was fighting back the Turkish army outside, inside the Church the priest sought a supernatural answer which he invested with a divine authority. Only thus could he reassure himself at this frightful moment and find the courage to approach and upbraid the leaders.

Meanwhile, outside, Peter Bartholomew was taking part in the fighting, even though he had just recovered from a serious illness. He was almost killed by being crushed between two horses, and at that moment of terror he had his fifth vision of the importunate St. Andrew, who now spoke to Peter so peremptorily that the servant had to swallow his fears and seek an audience with Raymund and Adhémar. Though he seems not to have been totally illiterate, Peter was an uneducated man and would not have been able to come up with the more sophisticated solution of Stephen with its Cluniac concentration on reform and liturgical prayer. Peter sought the solution of the common people, who saw relics as their major contact with the divine and felt that these relics partook of the security and permanence of heaven.

In the chaos of Antioch during that night, neither Stephen's moral reform nor Peter's relic seems irrelevant to the appalling situation of the crusading army. How could either make Kerbuqa go away? Yet even though, in a twentieth-century view, these visionary solutions seem quite impractical, it is important to notice that there was nothing impractical about the visionaries themselves. Stephen not only contemplated the Crusaders' sinfulness, he also reviewed the history of the Crusade and made his Christ inquire about the military command. There was also a point to the moral reform. This was no time for the soldiers to seek a temporary oblivion in sex; they had to preserve their dangerously depleted energy for battle. Peter's visions had all taken place in a highly practical context. The last occurred in the heat of battle and in the very jaws of death itself. Each man had a very sound instinct. Military strategy was not enough at this point and the army had to raise its morale and find a new, shared vision. The other visions of the Crusaders that night which came as they were about to desert the city were important for the visionaries themselves because they made them return to the army, but a new group enthusiasm was desperately required. Searching their souls for reassurance and hope, Stephen and Peter actually saved the army.

The next day both visionaries went to the leaders. Peter met with skepticism, as he had feared. Raymund was deeply impressed, but Adhémar the Cluniac had no time for relics and was probably peeved about the aspersions cast by St. Andrew on his preaching ability. Bohemund shared his doubts: why had St. Andrew chosen a frequenter of taverns as his messenger?[49] He also suspected that Raymund, who also had his eye on Antioch, wanted to use this cock-and-bull story of a relic to get popular support. In this Bohemund was unjust. Raymund believed in Peter to the end of his life and when he got to the river Jordan he and his men faithfully carried out the absurd and meaningless rites that St. Andrew had ordered. Other leaders beside Bohemund were skeptical and these included Tancred, Robert of Normandy and Robert of Flanders. But the common soldiers and the poor were ecstatic—literally. Nobody wanted to spoil the renewed surge of hope and confidence in the city caused solely by the promise of the lance, not even Adhémar.

Adhémar was more disposed to look favorably on Stephen's vision. Stephen was a perfectly respectable priest and his vision was theologically sound. It called for a renewed commitment to the principles of the reform and for an ordered campaign of prayer to relieve pent-up terrors and anxieties.[50] Adhémar made Stephen swear on the gospels that his vision was genuine and then made the leaders swear that they would not desert the city. He decreed that the Crusaders daily sing the anthem *Congregati sunt* from the divine office and there would be a general moral rearmament. When the ordinary Crusaders heard about the vision and the oath they "rejoiced beyond measure."[51]

The following day Peter and twelve other Crusaders from Raymund's army started to dig for the lance at the spot that St. Andrew had pointed out. They dug all day and found nothing and Count Raymund went away dejected. Then suddenly, clad only in his shirt, Peter leaped into the pit and triumphantly produced a piece of iron that could conceivably once have been a lance. The joy and confidence that swept through the army was dramatic and extraordinary. The frightened rabble of only four nights ago had become an army of Christian soldiers who were ready to attack the enemy and were certain of victory. The discovery of the lance was equivalent to the invention of a new deadly weapon to annihilate Kerbuqa. Now the ordinary soldiers and the poor were certain that they could not possibly lose, even though they were weak and exhausted.

Three days before the Battle of Antioch, Adhémar ordered the usual fast and the near-starving men grimly abstained, at the same time as they gave their horses double rations.[52] There can be few examples of a battle fought and perhaps won by such determined mass will power. On June 28 the Crusaders sallied out of the city accompanied by the holy lance itself and a crowd of white-vested priests who were praying aloud. They fell on the Muslims with supreme confidence. During the battle there was a mass hallucination of a whole army of celestial warriors led by St. George, St. Demetrius and St. Mercury, who all lowered their standards to the lance as it passed.[53] Crusaders claimed that anybody who was fighting in the vicinity of the relic was not injured. When the Crusaders actually saw the Muslim army scatter and flee before them, they were in such a state of exultation that they were not surprised. Kerbuqa and the Turks simply did not have a chance because God was fighting on the Crusaders' side. "Why did Kerbuqa flee, he who had such a large army so well provided with horses?" asked Fulcher of Chartres. "Because he had dared to contend against God, the Lord perceiving Kerbuqa's pomp from afar utterly destroyed his power."[54]

The Arab historians are quite clear that Kerbuqa made bad tactical mistakes during the battle and that one by one the other Muslim princes who were with him deserted and fled.[55] The frightening sight of these fanatical, desperate Crusaders must have been the final shock that split the alliance. Though the leaders might not have been ignorant of this, the ordinary soldiers and priests were far more likely to give absolute credence to the idea of the divine intervention. The trauma of Antioch confirmed the new vision of the Crusade that had been evolving ever since the Battle of Dorylaeum. The Crusaders were filled with wonder and astonishment. They knew perfectly well that the odds had been stacked against them throughout the campaign. As Fulcher of Chartres said, "Who could not marvel at the way we, a small people among such kingdoms of our enemies, were able not just to resist them but to survive?"[56] God may not have fed them with manna in the wilderness of Anatolia and Antioch but he had rescued them at Dorylaeum by a miracle: he had punished them for their sins, just as he had punished the Israelites when they disobeyed him during their Exodus from Egypt. Even though their plight in Antioch had looked as dire as the peril of the Israelites at the Red Sea, God had intervened and smashed the enemy just as he had destroyed the Egyptians. The Crusaders must be God's new chosen people; they had taken up the vocation that the Jews had lost. The Franks had indeed found their new Christian mission.

Yet after the success at Antioch the Crusade seemed grounded. At this point more than any other divided leadership crippled the Crusade as Raymund and Bohemund quarreled. They were shattered by their experience and still physically weak. An epidemic of typhus broke out and on August 1 Adhémar died. His death was a grave loss and was a deep shock to the army. Many of the Crusaders had come to see him as their Moses leading them to the Promised Land and, of course, they recalled that Moses himself had died before the Israelites entered Canaan. He was buried with great sadness and pomp—ironically, given his skepticism, in the pit where the holy lance had been discovered. It was finally the poor who took the army in hand and told the leaders what to do.

As the legend of the Tafurs suggested, it was the newfound confidence that the poor had acquired at Antioch that eventually forced their leaders back onto the road to Jerusalem. In late November the Crusaders laid siege to Ma'arret in Syria and on December 12 the city fell. Yet still the leaders sat around quarreling about who should lead the Crusade; the religious impetus seemed lost. But not for the poor, who on January 5, 1099, rebelled and began to tear down the walls of Ma'arret. They had not come to the East to conquer cities and forts, they cried. They had come as pilgrims to Jerusalem. The outcry was so great that on January 13, 1099, Raymund of St. Gilles, barefoot and dressed like a poor man, led his army and a great crowd of pilgrim followers on the road to the south. He was followed the next day by Robert of Normandy and his army.

These two armies tried to take the city of Arqa but found they could make no headway, even when Godfrey of Bouillon and Robert of Flanders joined them. It was here that Peter Bartholomew finally went too far. In March he had a vision of Christ (it closely resembled Stephen's, of which he had clearly been very jealous). Jesus gave to Peter a list of traitors to the cause and demanded their immediate execution; Peter was given the power to excommunicate the judges if he felt they did wrong. For some time the army had been getting very weary of Peter and his endless visions: for many the holy lance had done its work and the cause was now becoming discredited. There was a debate, and nothing so clearly captures the spirit of this Crusade as the spectacle of a council of war passionately discussing the authenticity of a famous relic. To save his own honor Peter offered to undergo the ordeal by fire, the dramatic but standard practice of gauging God's will, and though he walked successfully over burning olive logs holding the lance in his hand, he died twelve days later. He told Raymund of Aguiles that in the flames Christ had comforted him and told him that he would suffer because he had been so slow to obey St. Andrew.[57] The death of Peter finished the lance for most of the Crusaders, but a faithful remnant continued to cherish it. It continued to be led into battle and venerated until Raymund of St. Gilles took it with him to Byzantium and it somehow disappeared. In Constantinople there was already a very well authenticated lance, as Adhémar had pointed out from the first.

On May 13 the siege of Arqa was abandoned and the Crusaders began their march toward Jerusalem. Despite the setback in Arqa the Crusaders had won a formidable reputation for themselves. They were held to be unbeatable and wild stories circulated of their ferocity and apparently miraculous survival. These ironclad giants from the West looked like monsters to the Turks and Arabs, who had heard stories of their cannibalism. The amirs and rulers of the cities granted them free passage and supplies, begging only that they might be spared. The holy journey had ceased to be a nightmare and had become a triumphal procession. There were more visions: St. George and other saints appeared to Crusaders with detailed instructions for finding their relics along the route. As their relic collection increased, the Crusaders felt a new power and mastery, and as they talked over their experience it seemed more and more incredible. Everything now seemed a miracle, even natural phenomena. The light wind that had sprung up when the Crusaders entered Antioch and had muffled the noise they had been making was now seen to have been sent by God;

when they had sallied forth to fight Kerbuqa it was God who had sent the light rainstorm that refreshed them. If a Muslim carrier pigeon were intercepted it showed that even the birds of the air obeyed them.[58] They were now walking in a holy atmosphere where everything seemed divine.

This sense of the divine naturally increased when they arrived in Palestine and the Crusade took on even more the spirit of the pilgrimage. On May 23 they passed Tyre, a place that Jesus himself had visited. The Crusaders truly felt that they were standing on holy ground. The places became even more familiar as they passed through Galilee, Caesarea and what they took to be Emmaus. When they reached Ramleh, the administrative capital of Muslim Palestine, they had a breakthrough. The garrison and the townspeople fled in terror when they saw the fearful Christian army approaching and the Crusaders were able to occupy it without fighting. They had their first foothold in the Holy Land. At Ramleh they found the tomb of their new friend and patron St. George; at once they created a bishopric of Ramleh in his honor and the shrine was solemnly venerated by the whole army.

Finally on June 7, 1099, the Crusaders arrived outside the walls of Jerusalem. Their first sight of the Holy City was marked by a new outburst of extraordinary fervor. After the agonies of the last three years, they had finally reached their goal, and in their highly strung and exalted mood some may have felt that they were gazing at the heavenly Jerusalem described in Revelation. The whole army wept and shouted aloud, gripped by a sudden mass hysteria.[59] But their cries were probably cries of pure rage. Then as now the imposing city in the hills with its powerful walls was dominated by the great mosques of al-Aqsa and Omar. The power and majesty of these buildings—so very much more imposing than almost anything in Western Christendom at this time—must have seemed an affront to God and to the true faith. It could also be that they felt something like the "dread" that Eliezer ben Yehuda would feel eight hundred years later when he saw that the Arabs were so much at home in the land of his fathers. The Crusaders had been told that Muslims occupied the Holy City, but now they could see it with their own eyes. They could hear the call to prayer echoing through the surrounding hills and valleys and it must have seemed a deliberate insult and deeply threatening to their whole enterprise on which they had staked their souls. These Muslims with their mysterious and false religion were polluting the holy ground. They were from Egypt and the Crusaders saw them very differently from the way they had seen the Turks in Asia Minor, not for any ethnic reason, but because in Jerusalem it was obvious that they were the enemies of God.

As usual the Crusaders adopted both a pious and a practical policy. They started to build two siege towers from which to attack the city walls and at the same time consulted a hermit about the best way to take the city. Following his instructions, the whole army processed seven times around the city walls, singing hymns and walking barefoot. They stopped at their holy places outside the city: there was Mount Zion where Jesus had eaten the Last Supper with his disciples, the Garden of Gethsemane where he had prayed in agony afterward and the place on the Mount of Olives whence he had ascended into heaven. At these places, pregnant with divine power, they listened to sermons preached by Peter the Hermit and the other leading prelates. Finally the whole army flung itself on the city walls, convinced in their exaltation that they could conquer it by a miracle of prayer and fasting. The city remained proof against their prayers,[60] however, and as the Crusaders walked back to their camp, listening to the hoots and jeers of the Muslims, who had been watching all this incredulously from the city walls, these loud insults seemed directly aimed against Christ himself. They vowed vengeance.

On July 15, 1099, the Crusaders forced an entry to the city and conquered it. For two days they fell upon the Muslim and Jewish inhabitants of Jerusalem. "They killed all the Saracens and the Turks they found," says the author of the *Gesta*, "they killed everyone whether male or female."[61] The day after the massacre, Crusaders climbed to the roof of al-Aqsa and in cold blood they killed a group of Muslims to whom Tancred had granted sanctuary.[62] The Muslims were no longer respected enemies and a foil for Frankish honor. They had become the enemies of God and were thus doomed to ruthless extermination. They were polluting this Holy City and had to be eliminated like vermin, and from this point in the jargon of crusading the word given to Muslims is "filth." The famous eyewitness account of Raymund of Aguiles shows the Joshuan spirit in which this massacre was accomplished:

Wonderful sights were to be seen. Some of our men (and this was more merciful) cut off the heads of their enemies; others shot them with arrows, so that they fell from the towers; others tortured them longer by casting them into the flames. Piles of heads, hands and feet were to be seen in the streets of the city. It was necessary to pick one's way over the bodies of men and horses. But these were small matters compared to what happened at the Temple of Solomon, a place where religious services are normally chanted. What happened there? If I tell the truth it will exceed your powers of belief. So let it suffice to say this much, at least, that in the Temple and porch of Solomon, men rode in blood up to their knees and bridle reins. Indeed it was a just and splendid judgement of God that this place should be filled with the blood of the unbelievers since it had suffered so long from their blasphemies.[63]

This killing was not just an ordinary battle of conquest; the Crusaders had fallen upon the Muslims of Jerusalem and slain them like the avenging angels of the Apocalypse. It was a judgment of God himself. It was a salvation like the salvation that God had effected at the Red Sea when he slaughtered the whole army of the Egyptians, a violent and ruthless separation of the just and the unjust. The Crusade had indeed become a holy war. The holy journey had ended in a righteous battle against evil in which the soldiers of Christ killed some 40,000 Muslims in two days.[64]

With tears of joy coursing down their cheeks the leaders of the Crusade processed into the Holy Sepulchre. It was a profound psychic encounter with the origin of their faith when they entered the holy atmosphere of the tomb from which Christ had risen from the dead. To celebrate the return of the faith to its most holy and powerful center they sang the office of the Resurrection. Echoing the cadences of the Easter liturgy, which celebrates a new era that has broken upon the world, Raymund of Aguiles wrote:

A new day, new joy, new and perpetual gladness, the consummation of our labour and devotion, drew forth from all new words and new songs. This day, I say, will be famous in all future ages, for it turned our labours and sorrows into joy and exultation; this day, I say, marks the justification of all Christianity, the humiliation of Paganism, the renewal of our faith.[65]

This glorious day happened also to be the feast of the Dispersal of the Apostles, who, according to an old tradition, had left Jerusalem to bring the gospel to the rest of the world. The Crusaders naturally saw this as far more than a coincidence. As Raymund explained: "On this same day the children of the apostles regained the city and fatherland [patria] for God."[66] The new chosen people were thus caught up in the drama of salvation history. The ancient home of the Jews had now become their own fatherland. They had conquered it by divine right in one of those dramatic events in which God had intervened in human history and used his holy people to save the world.

But the Crusaders knew that they had to establish themselves practically in the country and not get carried away by the thrill of victory. First, they needed a king for their Christian kingdom, and a week after the victory the electors, who were probably the higher clergy and some of the nobler knights, offered the crown to Godfrey of Bouillon. Although Godfrey was in some ways a weak and unintelligent man, he had the advantage of embodying the piety and values of most of the Crusaders. It was also moving for the Franks to see the descendant of Charlemagne sitting upon the throne of David and Solomon. But Godfrey refused the title of king: he would not wear a crown of gold, he said, in the place where his Savior had worn a crown of thorns. He would be called the Defender of the Holy Sepulchre and was solemnly invested with this title in the ancient Church of the Nativity in Bethlehem, the birthplace of King David. Godfrey managed to establish the new Frankish state on a secure basis when he defeated an invading Egyptian army at the Battle of Askelon on August 12, while Tancred fought a masterly campaign to subdue Galilee in the north. The great task had been achieved.

Pope Urban had died two weeks after the victory, but he would have been horrified by the massacre in Jerusalem. He had imagined an orderly war of liberation whereby the Western Church would have extended its frontiers and gained the prestige of conquering the Holy City. He would not have praised the fantasies of the Franks about being the chosen people nor would he have approved of the revival of Joshua's violence. It seems that many Christians were initially shocked by news of the massacre, which would never be forgotten by the Muslims of the Near East. When later, wiser Christian rulers tried to secure their kingdom by making overtures to the Muslims, the memory of the cruel bloodbath always stood in the way of true friendship. But in general the news of the conquest of Jerusalem was greeted ecstatically by the Christians of Europe. The new Pope, Paschal II, seems to have been caught up in the general euphoria, and wrote that the Crusaders had fulfilled the ancient biblical prophecies.[67] He spoke joyfully of the discovery of the holy lance and the relic of the True Cross, which the Crusaders had found in Jerusalem, and showed that he was well on the way to endorsing the popular piety of the Crusaders, who had begun to arrive home as conquering heroes.

After the state had been put on a secure military basis, most of the Crusaders returned home, as they had always intended, leaving only a few hundred knights behind. This alone shows that land hunger was not a motive for the majority of the Crusaders. It is unlikely that any of them returned home rich men. Though much booty had been taken in Jerusalem and Askelon, large sums of money and treasure were given by the Crusaders to the churches in the Holy Land or were donated to the new Latin kingdom. In his exhaustive research on the matter, Professor Riley-Smith found only one Crusader who was reputed to have been made rich by the First Crusade. In fact, some of them were worse off.[68] Many of them returned home with damaged health after the traumas of the campaign. Some of them arrived home to face great difficulties that had developed while they were away. Flanders, for example, was in considerable disarray during Count Robert's absence in the East; other Crusaders found that people who had stayed at home had profited by their absence and seized their lands or titles. The most dramatic example of this was, of course, William Rufus' seizure of the throne of England while the rightful heir, Robert of Normandy, was on the Crusade. The chroniclers were not sympathetic to Robert's plight: they wrote that he had been offered the throne of Jerusalem but had refused it out of pusillanimity, and that was why he was punished when he returned home by life imprisonment and by death.[69] Crusading offered spiritual rather than material riches and some of the Crusaders seemed to have come home with deep religious convictions: some actually became monks, others gave donations to churches or built churches at home to commemorate the victory and very many arrived home with relics, the true riches of crusading, which they donated to monasteries and priories, bringing some of the holiness of the East back to the West. Many of the Crusaders seem to have been venerated for the rest of their lives: Robert of Flanders was one of these. He was henceforward known as *Hierosolimitanus*, and other former Crusaders were given similar titles, which suggests that they received a prestige that was similar to that accorded in the Muslim world to those who have made the *hajj* or pilgrimage to Mecca and are called *hajji*.[70]

Indeed, instead of recoiling in horror from the massacre of Jerusalem, people in Europe were gripped by a new passion for crusading. The conquest of the Holy City stirred them as deeply as it had stirred the conquerors themselves, and Jerusalem and the Latin kingdom in the Holy Land became as important to the Christians of the West as the state of Israel is to many Jews in the diaspora today. The euphoria that gripped Europe after the victory of 1099 saw this as just the first in a series of new victories against Islam. As early as September 1099 Raymund of St. Gilles and Bishop Daimbert of Pisa, in their joint letter describing the Crusade, wrote that "the power of the Muslims and the devil has been broken and the kingdom of Christ and the Church now stretches all the way from sea to sea."[71] There was talk of conquering Egypt, Asia, Africa and Ethiopia.[72] There seems also to have been an apocalyptic spirit abroad that saw the conquest of Jerusalem as a prelude to the Last Days.[73] It will be one of the themes of our story that a Holy Land or a Holy City can arouse deep passions and revive great hopes that are inarticulate but absolute and that any attempt to meddle with these feelings can be extremely dangerous for the other side.

For the next fifty years, crusading would be a central preoccupation and a popular pursuit in Europe. Long before there was any form of patriotism for the homeland or any sign of nationalism in the West, hundreds of thousands of people were ready to go to fight for their fatherland in the East. Indeed, immediately after the victory three large armies prepared to set out once more to reinforce the Crusader states and to help the few hundred knights there in their struggle to survive in the Muslim world. It was pointed out to Pope Paschal that many people who had taken the Cross in 1095 had not fulfilled their vows and had ignominiously stayed at home. The Pope at once said that any deserters, like Stephen of Blois and Hugh of Vermandois, as well as anybody who had avoided fulfilling his crusading vow must take the Cross forthwith. But besides these probably reluctant Crusaders, thousands of men and women, who had not thought of going crusading before, entered one of the three armies, inspired by the victory of 1099. This time the emphasis was naturally not on the liberation of the land, because that liberation had been achieved. On these Crusades of 1101 the aspect of the pilgrimage was stressed. It seems that the Crusades of 1101 numbered as many soldiers and pilgrims as the armies of the First Crusade. But this time the Turks of Asia Minor and Syria were ready for them; the shock of their defeat by the Franks at Antioch had pulled them together into a new unity. All three of the armies were massacred. But this did not deter future Crusaders from setting out for the East. Chroniclers put the blame for this disaster on the Crusaders, who, they said, had lacked the high seriousness of the veterans of the First Crusade, which became even more hallowed in consequence.[74] Smaller crusading expeditions were undertaken in Palestine and in Muslim Spain throughout the next twenty years of the new century, establishing crusading firmly in the European imagination.

One of the signs of the reverence with which people looked back to the extraordinary success of the First Crusade was that it inspired more literary effort than any other event at this time. In particular three learned monk-historians, who had not been on the Crusade, wrote accounts which adopted all the popular ideas of the Crusaders and showed that these had quickly been accepted by the establishment. Written within ten years of the conquest of Jerusalem, they show that the Christian Crusade had become a classic holy war. These historians—Guibert of Nogent, Robert the Monk and Baldrick of Bourgeuil—see the Crusade as a full-scale biblical war. For over a hundred years the monks of Europe had been trying to instruct and form the laity, but now the laymen of the Crusade had influenced the monks. In this canonization of holy violence, there is no longer any vagueness about the Muslims. They are a "vile" and "abominable" race, "absolutely alien to God" and meet only for "extermination."[75] After standing out so long against war and hatred, the official Church had accepted the violence of Joshua and canonized it. This "holy journey of our men to Jerusalem" had been an event in salvation history, writes Robert the Monk, making the astonishing claim that there had been no more holy event since the creation of the world and the Crucifixion.[76] The journey to Jerusalem is described by these monks in terms of the Exodus of the Israelites from Egypt: just as the Crusaders had seen themselves as being led along the way step by step by God like the Israelites, so too did he lead and guide the Crusaders, wrote Guibert. The First Crusade, he says, was the greatest event of world history:

If we consider the battles of the gentiles and think of great military enterprises in which kingdoms have been invaded, we will think of no army and absolutely no exploit comparable to ours. We have heard that God was glorified in the Jewish people, but we acknowledge that there is reliable proof that Jesus Christ lives and thrives today among our contemporaries just as he did yesterday among men of old.[77]

We have said not once but many times, and it bears repetition, that such a deed has never been done in this world. If the children of Israel oppose this by referring to the miracles which the Lord performed for them in the past, I will furnish them with an opened Red Sea crowded with gentiles. To them I demonstrate, for the pillar, the cloud of divine fear by day, the light of divine hope by night. To the Crusaders Christ himself, the pillar of rectitude and strength, gave instances of inspiration; he strengthened them, without any earthly hope, only with the food of the word of God, as it were with heavenly manna.[78]

These three learned monk–historians show that the official Church was now ready and eager to revive the holy war of the Old Testament which the Jews themselves had abandoned centuries earlier.

The monks also saw the Crusade as a type of monasticism for the layman. Hitherto the only way to live the Christian life perfectly had been by entering a monastery or by going on a pilgrimage. Now by fighting and killing Muslims the Crusaders had discovered a "new way of gaining salvation," Guibert explained.[79] The Crusaders themselves had come to see their pilgrimage in monastic terms, not simply because of the monastic practices that they had so scrupulously observed under Adhémar's leadership. It was natural. There had always been an inherent tendency to violence within monasticism, but the spiritual writers had stressed an interior quest that had nothing to do with fighting. A monk had been called a "castellan of Christ" and monasticism had been seen as a knighthood of Christ in a holy war against the powers of darkness.[80] The way of the Cross had become a symbol of this monastic holy war and a symbol of the monk's vocation, just as it was for the Crusaders. In contemporary monastic writings it is suggested that the monks are walking on a spiritual journey to a state which they call "the heavenly Jerusalem." This union with God and subjection to his will was the goal of the Christian life, superior to the pilgrimage to the earthly Jerusalem. During the Crusade, however, the new "knights of Christ" began to see their campaign in terms of this spiritual quest also. After the victory at Antioch they had written to the Pope begging him to come out to the East and join them in the last lap of their holy journey, and "open for us the gates of both Jerusalems;"[81] it seems that they believed that their holy pilgrimage was toward both the heavenly and the earthly Jerusalems and that it was not merely an exterior journey and war but also an interior conversion and a spiritual battle which brought them closer to heaven. The Crusade had canonized violence and made it a Christian vocation.

It was not long before the inevitable happened in the Crusader Kingdom of Jerusalem. The precarious states always suffered from a chronic shortage of manpower and desperately needed some committed professional soldiers, who would form a regular army quite independent of the usual feudal bonds. These regular soldiers would be the monks of the military orders. The Church finally gave monks a sword. This did not happen all at once. The Knights Hospitaler of St. John had been founded before the First Crusade. Pious citizens in Amalfi had established a hostel in Jerusalem to care for the poor pilgrims, and a body of knights who bound themselves by monastic vows served the poor there and cared for the sick. This was fully in line with the spirit of Cluny, and now this charitable institution made the humbler acts of charity part of the aristocratic institution of knighthood. The Hospitalers in Jerusalem voluntarily became one with the poor, living lives of "holy poverty" while at the same time remaining part of the noble order of chivalry. Their rule told them, for example, that they should always dress humbly "for our lords the poor, whose servants we acknowledge ourselves to be, go naked and meanly dressed. And shameful it would be if the serf was proud and his lord humble."[82] It is easy to see how, once the conquest of Jerusalem had made crusading a new quasi-monastic movement, this order of knights would be seen to express some of the loftiest ideals of the First Crusade. During the first half of the twelfth century, when Europe was ablaze with crusading enthusiasm, new recruits flocked into the order and so did donations of money. Soon the humble little community was very large and, ironically, very rich.

In 1108 a small group of knights who called themselves the Poor Fellow Soldiers of Jesus Christ presented themselves to the King of Jerusalem. They offered to act as a kind of police force in the Crusader states, protecting the pilgrims, who were unarmed, from marauding Muslims. Because they were given headquarters in the royal palace (the former mosque al-Aqsa which stood on the site of Solomon's Temple) they became known as the Knights of the Temple or the Templars. They too were clearly reformed knights of Cluny, dedicating their lives to protecting the poor and defenseless but, like the Hospitalers, they were bound by monastic vows and a monastic rule. Like the Hospitalers again, they lived lives of holy poverty, adopting a brutal, tough image and completely eschewing the fancy clothes and groomed appearance cultivated increasingly by the secular knights during the early twelfth century. They too quickly became a very large and very rich order with houses in Europe as well as in the Holy Land. They owed allegiance to the Pope alone, so that they had liberated themselves from all secular control according to the principles of Cluny. The Templar dedicated his life to the defense of the holy Kingdom of Jerusalem.

Gradually these two orders took on more and more military duties, though the Hospitalers never abandoned their hostel work. The Templars soon acquired an invaluable knowledge of the topology of the Holy Land. They were also ruthless and efficient soldiers because they bound themselves to obey their superior (who was also their commanding officer). This meant that they were highly disciplined, something that we now see as basic to the military life, but this was not so in the Middle Ages when heroism like that depicted in *The Song of Roland* was the ideal. Knights would not obey their commander; they preferred individual acts of heroism and glory, which could endanger the efficiency and even the survival of the army as a whole. Because of this military strength, the Templars were used more and more by the kings of Jerusalem in their wars against the surrounding Muslim states, until by degrees their old defensive policing duties were laid aside and they became the regular army of the Holy Land. This also happened with the Hospitalers, though their militarization took longer and was even opposed by the popes until as late as the 1170s because it was felt their purpose was charitable work.

In order to establish themselves strongly against their Muslim neighbors, the Christians had to defend their borders in the Middle East. Therefore they either built their own castles or took over and adapted old Muslim castles that had been built at strategic points, and, increasingly, the kings of Jerusalem turned these castles over to the Templars and the Hospitalers because they alone had enough men and enough money to man them efficiently. The monastery had become a real fortress, not just a symbolic one. Here these military monks were doing two things. First, they were rooting Christianity physically and powerfully in the Holy Land. In this respect they can be compared to the *kibbutzim*, for even though the Israeli conquest of the land was a peaceful one, we have seen that it had its aggressive aspects. The military orders' strict poverty was also in line with important ideals of the *kibbutz*. Second, by colonizing the frontiers these new military monks were performing, and simply taking to its logical conclusion, a function that monks had been fulfilling in Europe for years. These monks were pushing aggressively against the frontiers of Islam and were in the front line of the holy war. One day the new chosen people would conquer Islam in Asia and Africa, and these castles were originally seen as springboards for future belligerent action. In the meantime the soldier-monks helped the secular knights who had settled in the Holy Land in their war of expansion during the first half of the twelfth century. They pushed forward the frontiers of the Crusader kingdom over the Jordan on the east bank southward into the Negev as far as Eilat and northward into Lebanon and Syria. It seemed as though nothing could stop the Franks from fulfilling their dream, and the military monks were an essential part of this success and were regarded as a crusading elite.

Few states in the history of the world could have had such an intense and idealistic religious foundation. Yet, in a great irony, the Crusader states rather quickly became more secular in spirit than any state in Europe at this time.[83] Pious, simple Godfrey of Bouillon died at the

end of 1099 in an epidemic and he was succeeded by his brother
Baldwin. Baldwin had spent the last two years in Edessa, establishing
a Western presence there. He and his knights ruled the city but used
the Armenian people as high officials of the government and the civil
service. Baldwin himself married an Armenian princess and adopted
the lifestyle of an oriental ruler. It was a wise policy and helped the
Armenians to adjust to this Latin rule. When Baldwin came to Jerusalem in 1100 he had no scruples about being crowned king. With
his greater taste for luxury, he abandoned holy poverty and lived richly
in a style that the Muslims could understand and appreciate. Egyptian
delegates after the Battle of Askelon had been astonished to find Godfrey sitting on the floor of his tent, bareheaded. Baldwin's autocratic
manner, his strong rule and luxurious court were far more in the
oriental mode than that of feudal Europe. Baldwin and his court began
to adopt Middle Eastern dress, and slowly the Franks of Palestine
learned how to adapt to life in the East, learned to take baths, to build
in the Arab fashion, and learned important lessons of Arab hygiene.
These Western colonists were in the unusual position of having settled
in a country that was far more culturally advanced than their own.
The Crusaders, who had been trying to acquire a new Western identity,
would in the East acquire an oriental one. "Westerners," Fulcher of
Chartres wrote enthusiastically,

> We have become Orientals. The Italian and the Frenchman of yes-
> terday have been transplanted and become men of Galilee and Pal-
> estine. Men from Rheims or Chartres are transformed into Tyrians
> and citizens of Antioch. We have already forgotten the land of our
> birth; who now remembers it? Men no longer speak of it. Here a
> man now owns his house and servants with as much assurance as
> though it were by immemorial right of inheritance in the land.
> Another has taken to wife, not a countrywoman of his own, but a
> Syrian or an Armenian woman, sometimes even a baptised Saracen,
> and then lives with a whole new family. We use various languages
> of the country turn and turn about; the native as well as the colonist
> has become polyglot and trust brings the most widely separated
> races together. . . . The colonist has now become almost a native
> and the immigrant is one with the inhabitants.[84]

Certainly Western pilgrims and Crusaders from Europe were
shocked when they arrived in the Holy Land to discover a new mixed
race of *Pullani* Christians as a result of these marriages between Franks
and Muslims: there are still Palestinians today with blue eyes who
claim descent from the Crusaders. Just as shocking to the visitors or

new immigrants from Europe was the oriental lifestyle of the Franks in Palestine. They seemed effete and alien. Most worryingly, they had, over the years, developed quite a different attitude toward the Muslims. Familiarity and daily contact with Muslims meant that they could not subscribe to the European tendency to imagine the Saracens as inhuman monsters of evil. They also tended to look at the political situation in the Middle East in practical terms and were even ready to make alliances with Muslims if this would further their interests in the area. The Europeans were horrified because they adhered to an absolute policy that would brook no compromise and that saw the conflict wholly in religious terms: it was a fight of good against evil, of God against devils.

But it is still true that Fulcher's view of the new Western "Orientals" was far too rosy. The Kingdom of Jerusalem was still dedicated to warfare when Fulcher wrote his propaganda and was essentially aggressive and belligerent. This was inevitable. The Crusader states were in a state of siege, surrounded by a hostile Muslim world. The Crusaders learned to adapt to the life of the area but for the first fifty years of the existence of their states in the Middle East the Franks fought a ceaseless war of expansion against the Muslims. Their attitude to the Christians of the Middle East was also aggressive; they loathed the Greek Orthodox and the other Eastern sects, seeing them as essentially heretical. Their consequent isolation in the Near East and the fact that their states were essentially military meant that they had little time for any other activities. At a time when Europe was enjoying a period of great creativity and building a new culture, there was no similar cultural achievement in the Crusader states. There were some historians and some good jurists but nobody attained the standards of scholars and artists back home. There was very little sculpture or architecture in the Holy Land and certainly nothing to equal the great Gothic achievements in Europe. The Franks' whole energy had to be concentrated on the war effort. The one great innovation that the Palestinian Franks achieved was their castles, where they learned a great deal from the Arabs. Their building program had to be part of the war machine and the mighty castles along their borders made the crusading kingdoms into fortresses keenly defended by a wall of castles against the Muslim world. These castles made the states safe but they also kept much of the real outside world out. It ensured that the Crusader states remained alien, artificial Western enclaves in the region, despite the small measure of cultural acclimatization on the part of some of the Franks. Israelis often compare their own architecture in, for example, the developments on the hilltops surrounding Jerusalem to the massive Crusader castles. They feel quite a close affinity to the Crusaders, whose situation was in many respects remarkably similar to their own isolated position in the Middle East.

People in the Western world today who think of Islam as "the religion of the sword" would probably expect the Muslims in the surrounding countries to have called a *jihad* against the Crusaders instantly. This is not what happened. The idea of the Muslim holy war had become such a distant, stylized memory to the people of the Middle East by the twelfth century that at first it simply never occurred to them to revive it. Indeed it was quite a long time before they understood that the Crusade itself was in fact a Christian holy war. The great twelfth-century Arab historian Izz ad-Din Ibn al-Athir saw the invasion of Syria in 1097 as part of a new phase of Western expansion to which he attached no particular religious significance. When he describes the sack of Jerusalem, Ibn al-Athir records the facts calmly. He explains that the population of the city was "put to the sword," including a large number of Muslim scholars and ascetics "who had left their homelands to live lives of pious seclusion in the Holy Place."[85] There is no anguished rhetoric about the loss of the Holy Place, no vow to reclaim this Islamic land in the name of Allah, as the theology of *jihad* demanded. The Muslims of the Near East hated these Western invaders, naturally, but in the great heartlands of the Islamic empire there seemed to be a calm indifference about these distant incidents.

One ruler immediately proved an exception to this rule. After the sack of Jerusalem, those Muslims who managed to escape the slaughter began to flee from Palestine into the surrounding Arab countries. A few days after the tragedy of July 15, refugees from Palestine began to pour into Damascus, carrying with them the Koran of Uthman, one of the oldest copies of the holy book. While some of them left out of sheer terror, others believed that exile was an Islamic duty in the event of occupation by nonbelievers. It was dishonorable for Muslims to listen to the insults heaped upon the Prophet by the Franks. As the first refugees stumbled into Damascus, they were greeted kindly by Qadi Abu Sa'ad al-Harawi. He told them that no Muslim should be ashamed to go into exile. The Prophet Mohammad, God's blessing be upon him, had been the first Muslim refugee when he made the *hijra* from Mecca to Medina, and this migration had been the first step in the *jihad* he had undertaken to regain his homeland and free it from idolatry. Similarly, the Qadi explained, the refugees from Palestine must consider themselves *mujahideen*, soldiers in the holy war which they would fight to liberate their homeland and push the Franks into the sea.[86] At once al-Harawi led a crowd of Palestinian refugees to Baghdad, the capital of the Islamic empire, where they staged an angry demonstration. It was the month of Ramadan and al-Harawi and the Palestinians burst into the great Mosque of the Caliph, the successor of Mohammad. Then al-Harawi began to eat ravenously and ostentatiously and was naturally surrounded by a furious crowd of worshipers, who were horrified to see him breaking the fast so blasphemously. Al-Harawi rose calmly to his feet and asked them why they were so upset about his breaking the fast when they seemed quite indifferent to the tragic loss of Jerusalem and the hideous plight of their Muslim brothers who had been forced into exile. Weeping themselves, the refugees "described the sufferings of the Muslims in that Holy City," wrote Ibn al-Athir, "the men killed, the women and children taken prisoner, the homes pillaged."[87] The Muslims of Baghdad wept bitterly in sympathy and the Caliph, who by this time had very little political power, set up a committee to look into the matter. As is the way of such committees, nothing came of it. Al-Harawi was disgusted and led the refugees through the streets shouting: "I see the supporters of the faith are weak!"[88] His call to *jihad* met with complete apathy. Muslims were ready to weep for their brothers but were not prepared to take any practical steps to help them.

There are obvious similarities with the situation in the Arab world today, with one crucial difference. The Arabs and Muslims in the Middle Ages were in a much stronger position than their descendants today and had they united together they could certainly have crushed the isolated, poorly manned Crusader states. But they seemed chronically incapable of doing this. They were either frightened of alienating these monstrous Franks and attracting an offensive against their own city or they were busily engaged in fighting one another. As Ibn al-Athir admits: "It was the discord between the Muslim princes that enabled the Franj to overrun the country."[89] Furthermore, throughout the whole period of the Crusades the Arab and Turkish states of the Middle East seemed to find it impossible to found a secure dynasty. After a ruler died, his achievements were always canceled out by internal strife and his successor had to begin to build an empire all over again. Further, although this may seem surprising to those who see Islam as an essentially martial religion, the Muslims do not seem to have been good or serious soldiers; indeed, in our own day, Arab armies have not been very effective on the battlefield for all their famed violence. At the time of the Crusades, this Muslim instability was fatal: it simply meant more suffering, more humiliation and more refugees who were forced to flee from the apparently invincible Franks as they steadily conquered more and more territory. Similarly, in our own day, Arab disunity has played right into Israel's hands.

The Franks, however, were euphoric with victory and this made them formidable soldiers. Even the tragedy that befell the 1101 Crusades did not dim their confidence. There was still a continuous flow of knights and barons who brought small armies out to help the war effort against Islam. In 1104 the Franks seized Haifa, Jaffa, Acre and seemed all set to take Baghdad itself but, in a rare defeat, they were turned back at Harran. More Palestinians were massacred and refugees crowded into neighboring Muslim cities like Aleppo. In 1109 they took Tripolis, and seized Beirut and Sidon the following year: they now had a fourth state in the Near East, which they called the County of Tripolis.

The Muslims in the area saw no end to these Frankish victories and yet they seemed unable to join forces to prevent them. In 1111 the Qadi of Aleppo led another demonstration to Baghdad to force the Sultan to send help. This time the demonstrators behaved more violently and the Sultan ordered the Amir of Mosul to lead an army against the Franks.[90] But the local Muslim rulers seemed to find this Muslim army as threatening as the Franks themselves. Indeed in 1112 the Amir was assassinated in the Great Mosque of Damascus, on the eve of his offensive against the Christians, and Atabeg Tughitin of Damascus actually made a treaty with King Baldwin of Jerusalem. Muslim leaders seemed to have lost any sense of a united House of Islam; they were prepared to use warlike rhetoric against the Franks to appease the populace but had no intention of enhancing the power of a fellow Muslim ruler by making an alliance with him. As a result of this disunity, the Franks were able to take control of the whole coastline of Palestine and the Lebanon.

But the year 1128 was a turning point. The Sultan of Rum in Asia Minor appointed the Turkish commander Imad ad-Din Zangi as Atabeg of Mosul and Aleppo. Zangi was no paragon: he was often dead drunk and as cruel and ruthless as most men of war at this time. Yet he brought important new qualities to the area. First, he took his responsibilities very seriously and was no wild adventurer. He got the Sultan to give him undisputed authority over the whole of Syria and northern Iraq, which he then proceeded to make good by subduing the local population in a dedicated and remorseless military campaign. Second, Zangi was able to impose a conformity and unity on his army and on the territory he conquered: he made people afraid of him and yet won their respect because he never asked of them anything that he was not prepared to do himself. Third, Zangi was the first serious ruler the area had had for years. Previous leaders had been preoccupied with looting and amassing riches; armies were usually demobilized after a year's fighting so that people could enjoy the spoils of victory, and this meant that nothing permanent was achieved. Zangi never settled in any of the cities he won but slept in his tent on a straw mat for eighteen years in a ceaseless campaign to subdue the area. Finally, Zangi did not rely on force alone. He set up an impressive intelligence system and was thus aware of events in Baghdad, Damascus, Antioch and Jerusalem.

Ibn al-Athir's father was one of his closest friends and had considered that Zangi was "the gift of divine providence to the Muslims."[91] In his committed war effort he actually brought a new peace to the region, which could begin to build itself again. "Before he came," wrote Ibn al-Athir, "the absence of strong rulers to impose justice, and the presence of the Franks close at hand had made the country a wilderness, but he made it flower again."[92] As he conquered one city, one town after another, Zangi brought peace and made the desert bloom.

But one Arab leader stood firm against Zangi. Muin ad-Din Unur, the Amir of Damascus, was determined that his city would not be absorbed into Zangi's empire and he renewed the old alliance with the Christians of Jerusalem in 1140: this treaty would have fateful consequences, as we shall see in the next chapter. For his part, Zangi was absolutely resolved to take Damascus, and in the course of his relentless campaign he besieged the Christian city of Edessa in November 1144. In point of fact, Zangi was not very interested in fighting the Franks but, when Edessa surrendered, he unexpectedly found himself a hero of Islam. In destroying the principality of Edessa and inflicting a major defeat on the Christians, Zangi had achieved what no other Muslim leader had been able to do. His prestige soared and the Palestinian refugees started to talk excitedly about the imminent liberation of their homeland.

Zangi's victory had touched a deep nerve in the Muslim world. The Caliph, doubtless relieved to be off the hook, heaped honorary titles upon him. Zangi became "the pillar of religion" and the "cornerstone of Islam,"[93] even though he had never been a devout man. Everybody assumed that he would immediately press on to liberate Jerusalem, the holy city of al-Quds. But on September 30, 1146, he was assassinated by one of his eunuchs, who was of Frankish origin. After his death he became a legend and this was the first sign of a popular revival of the *jihad* in the Near East. Ibn al-Athir records two stories in the Zangi legend. One says that on the day that Zangi conquered Edessa the Christian King of Sicily had successfully raided the Muslim city of Tripolis in North Africa. When he returned in triumph, he asked a Muslim sage in his court—a man for whom he had great respect—"What use is Mohammad now to his land and his people?" "He was not there [at Tripolis]," replied the old man, "he was at Edessa, which the Muslims have just taken." The court roared with incredulous laughter but the King reproved them: "This man is incapable of speaking anything but the truth."[94] Zangi's secular war had become a *jihad*, with Mohammad fighting alongside the Muslims just as the saints had fought with the Crusaders. The second story shows that the *jihad* was being seen once more as a meritorious act. "Certain honest and goodly men have told me," Ibn al-Athir writes cautiously, "that a holy man saw the dead Zangi in a dream and asked him: 'How has God treated you [i.e., in the afterlife]?' and Zangi replied, 'God has pardoned me, because I conquered Edessa.' "[95] In the history of holy war, one unexpected victory very often leads to an excited belief in a special election so that a secular war can become a war of religion. The dedicated holy war of the Crusaders had inspired a *jihad* in the Muslim world, after centuries in which the practice had been forgotten.

On the night that Zangi died, his second son Mahmoud entered the tent where his father's body lay, removed the signet ring, the symbol of power, from the dead man's finger and placed it on his own.[96] He would continue his father's mission of uniting the Near East but, unlike his father, Mahmoud was a devout young Muslim and would see his military campaign as a holy war. He is usually known by his title Nur ad-Din, which means the Light of the Faith. The succession of Nur ad-Din to power marked the beginning of a new chapter in the relations between the West and the Muslim world. It is also very important that we understand what he meant by a *jihad* and the methods he used to mobilize the Muslims in a holy war against the West, because this will help us to understand the Muslim response to Western aggression in our own day.

Nur ad-Din had, of course, to build his empire from scratch, as even the great Zangi had not been able to found a secure dynasty. He chose to unite the people under him by presenting himself as a truly Muslim leader, living strictly according to the principles of the Koran and the Sharia. The ideal of a legitimate Muslim leader has been of crucial importance in our own day; we shall see this in Chapters 8 and 9. A Muslim leader should never live in luxury: this would be against the nature of Islam, which has a mission to create a just and equal society. Nur ad-Din, therefore, lived frugally and simply; at a time when many oriental rulers lived very opulently indeed, Nur ad-Din's lifestyle was astonishing to his contemporaries and a deliberate challenge to the other Muslim leaders in the area, who were not living up to this Islamic ideal. He lived a devout Muslim life of prayer and study. Where the Christian Crusader was usually uneducated—a man of brawn rather than of brains—in Islam the man of war was expected to be a scholar. Wherever he traveled, Nur ad-Din was accompanied by a crowd of learned imams and Sufis, so that his military campaigns had an obviously religious appearance. Scholars would interpret the political and military situation in the light of Islamic law and the court was famous for its sober scholarship:[97] Nur ad-Din liked nothing more than a tough theological discussion after dinner.

Nur ad-Din's tacit claim to be returning to the fundamental principles of Islam won him the respect of the common people. In particular they were impressed by his devotion to the *jihad* against the Franks, which he claimed was an essential Muslim duty. He looked back not to the theology of *jihad* which had been developed during the eighth century in the Sharia so much as to the Koran. The *jihad*, like any "fundamentalist" movement, was thus a return to basic principles but at the same time it was a new departure to meet the peculiar circumstances of the Near East in the mid-twelfth century. The Koran is clear that, although war is always abhorrent, Muslims sometimes had a duty to fight oppression and persecution, because otherwise all decent values would disappear from the earth (2:252). Mohammad had thus fought the unjust regime of the Qureish in Mecca. Indeed, the passages in the Koran which justify this war also applied with an uncanny accuracy to the present conflict against the Franks:

> Permission to fight is granted to those against whom war is made, because they have been wronged—Allah indeed has power to help them—to those who have been driven out of their homes unjustly only because they said "Our Lord is Allah." . . . If Allah did not repel aggression by means of those who fight against it, there would surely have been demolished cloisters and churches and synagogues and mosques, wherein the name of Allah is oft commemorated. (22:40–42)

Nur ad-Din's *jihad* was not against Christianity as such: the Koran had urged Muslims to respect the People of the Book and the above quotation shows that synagogues and churches as well as mosques were to be respected by Muslims. This *jihad* was a holy war of self-defense. The Koran forbids Muslims to initiate war and strike the first blow (2:191) but goes on to say that "persecution is worse than killing" and oppression must be stopped. For fifty years the Franks had massacred Muslims and driven them from their homes. The Muslims had done nothing to provoke this gratuitous Western aggression and their apathy in the face of this scourge had only made matters worse. A Muslim leader had a clear duty to protect his people from such an enemy and any Amir who did not join Nur ad-Din's *jihad* against the Franks was no true Muslim.

It is obvious that the Muslim ideal of holy war is very different from the Crusade: it is essentially defensive whereas the Crusaders, like the Jewish holy warriors, had made a holy initiative when they attacked the enemies of God and his chosen people. For the first time Muslims had declared war on the people of the West, and in our own day Muslim leaders have argued like Nur ad-Din that it is an Islamic duty to fight against what they see as a new Western aggression. The methods they have used to mobilize the people are almost identical to those used by Nur ad-Din. He began a propaganda campaign, commissioning scholars to write books to develop the theology of the *jihad* and to spread the word to all the important imams in the cities, who would then transmit it to the clergy. In their turn, the clerics would transmit the teaching to the people in the mosques during the sermon that was preached on Friday, the Muslim Sabbath. It is important to notice that the *jihad* depends more on reason and intellect than on the visionary emotion that inspired the First Crusaders, which often saw God intervening to save them with miracles. Muslims do not expect God to suspend the normal course of nature for their sakes but believe that God will only help them if they have made every possible human effort to help themselves. "Verily," says the Koran, "God will not change the state of a people unless they change the state of their own selves." (13:11)

It was, therefore, the Crusaders' brutal behavior in the Near East, not an atavistic love for violence inherent in Islam, which revived the practice of the *jihad* in the Middle Ages. Muslims were actually slow to turn to religion in their struggle with the Franks and Nur ad-Din found that it took a long time for the idea of a holy war to gain total acceptance. We should also note that in his ideology there was no cult of a holy land: nor is the holiness of Jerusalem central to the theology of the *jihad* in the Middle East today. The emphasis is on the liberation of the people rather than on sacred soil. The Crusaders, however, inspired a second movement for the liberation of Palestine among the Jews, the other victims of the Crusaders. The writings of two important Jewish scholars of the twelfth century show that their "religious Zionism" had a great deal in common with the Crusaders' devotion to the Holy Land, and in Chapter 7 we shall see that these religious ideas have gained a new lease of life in Israel today.

Judah Halevi, the eminent poet and physician, had been a young man at the time of the First Crusade. He had been born in Toledo but when the city was conquered by the Christians the position of the Jews deteriorated there and Halevi decided to move to Cordova, in Muslim Spain. Here he lived in peace, but his emigration had made him conscious of an essential rootlessness. He began to argue that Jews could never be truly at home in the diaspora but could only be as God intended them to be in the Promised Land. In his great philosophical work *The Kuzari*, Halevi insisted that the Jews were the only people in the world who had the gift of prophecy but that it was only in the land of Israel that they could fulfill their prophetic destiny. Like the Crusaders, Halevi saw the Holy Land as pregnant with a divine power, which was a tangible force. Only by being physically in contact with the land, by exposing themselves to its spiritual atmosphere, could Jews become prophets and imbibe the holiness that God intended for them:

> The air of your land is the very life of the soul,
> the grains of your dust are flowing myrrh,
> your rivers are honey from the comb.
> It would delight my heart to walk naked and barefoot
> among your desolate ruins where your shrines once stood.[98]

Halevi was profoundly affected by the new crusading pride in Christian Jerusalem and he told the Jews of Spain that this Christian initiative should make them feel ashamed.[99] The powerful, tangible holiness of God was accessible only to the Jews, and the Gentile inhabitants of the land could have no share in it. In his poem "To the Rivals," Halevi scorned the Christians and Muslims who thought that *they* owned Eretz Yisrael: "Why they are nothing but wild asses!"[100] he exclaimed; they would never find the prophecy nor would they encounter the Presence of God. Yet the Jews were doing nothing to recover their homeland. Even though Jews were in no position to organize a military expedition to liberate Israel, it must be a duty for Jews to make the *aliyah* to the holiness of God. In 1140, therefore, Halevi made his pilgrimage to the East and died there the following year. Only a few Jews followed his example, but Halevi's poems and writings were absorbed into the ritual and helped to nurture a sense of Eretz Yisrael as the Jews' real home. Halevi's conception of the Holy Land is not only very similar to the Crusaders' but it is also very close to that of a Zionist like A. B. Gordon.

When Judah Halevi made his *aliyah* to Eretz Yisrael, Maimonides was only about five years old. In 1148 he and his parents were forced to leave Cordova when the Almohads, a fanatical Muslim sect, invaded Spain and tried to get rid of the Jews. Maimonides ended up in Cairo, a scholar, physician and important man of affairs. In Egypt he encountered the holy wars between Muslims and Christians and for a time he was the physician to Saladin's son, when he became sultan. Maimonides' vision of the Holy Land is less poetical than Halevi's, but he certainly shares his sense of Eretz Yisrael as being crucial to the Jewish identity. The Temple Mount is the center of the world, because it took the Jewish people back to their earliest origins, and to the origin of all mankind:

> Now there is a well-known tradition that the place where David and Solomon built the altar in the threshing floor of Arauneh was the same place where Abraham built the altar upon which he bound Isaac. This, too, was the place where Noah built an altar when he came out of the Ark. It was also the place of the altar upon which Cain and Abel offered sacrifices. There it was that Adam offered a sacrifice after he was created. Indeed, Adam was created from that very ground; as the sages have taught: Adam was created from the place where he made atonement.[101]

One day in the future, Maimonides foretold, the Jews would establish an independent state in Eretz Yisrael, governed by the Torah. Only when they ruled from the Temple Mount would a political order fully in tune with God's plan for the world come into being. Such a return of the Jews would thus be a light unto the Gentiles and the beginning of the redemption. Like the Crusaders, Maimonides saw occupation of the Holy Land as essential for the salvation of the world.

The Jewish and the Christian holy wars tended to follow a very similar pattern, and many of the religious Zionists, who see the present conflict as a holy war against Islam, think and behave today in ways that are remarkably similar to the Crusaders. If crusading contributed to the present conflict by producing anti-Semitism in Europe, it also helped to form a religious Zionism that has surfaced again very powerfully and more aggressively today. One of the lessons of the First Crusade is that religion seems to be effective when all else fails. Without their religious faith, the Crusaders would certainly not have survived their traumatic journey nor would they have defeated the Turks. Although the Muslims were much slower to seek this solution, the *jihad* would ultimately prove to be far more effective in getting rid of the Franks than a purely secular war, and in the present conflict both Jews and Muslims have turned to the holy war because they see no other solution. In our own day religion has proved to be a very successful force. But religion also has its grave dangers and can result in failure as well as astounding success. The story of the Second Crusade gives us a clear indication of the different strengths and weaknesses of the Christian (and hence, later, of the Jewish) holy war and the new Muslim *jihad*.

# 1146–1148

## St. Bernard and the Most Religious Crusade

The news of the fall of Edessa horrified the Christians of Western Europe and yet when Pope Eugenius and King Louis VII of France called a new Crusade the response was disappointing: people had heard too much about the horrors of the First Crusade fifty years earlier. But on March 31, 1146, Bernard, Abbot of Clairvaux, addressed a huge assembly of French barons at Vézelay and persuaded them that the fall of Edessa was not a disaster but part of God's plan. He had even "allowed" or "caused"[1] Zangi to conquer Edessa to give Christians a staggering opportunity. He would be with his people on their new Crusade, which was a revelation of divine love and one of the most significant events in salvation history.[2] Bernard was probably the most powerful man in Europe at that time. The King of France was in his thrall and the Pope a member of his religious order. He owed a good deal of his power to his charismatic eloquence. A contemporary wrote that his spiritual and emaciated appearance tended to "persuade his audience before he had opened his mouth."[3] When he had finished his speech in the presence of the King at Vézelay, there was as usual a holy pandemonium. The King knelt down and took the Cross and was followed by such a vast throng of people from all classes of society that the huge stock of ready-made crosses was exhausted and Bernard had to tear his garments to shreds and hand them to the clamorous crowds.

During the next few weeks Bernard toured France preaching the Crusade, and at once barons, knights and poor pilgrims dropped everything and flocked into the King's crusading army. "I opened my mouth; I spoke and at once the Crusaders have multiplied to infinity," Bernard wrote complacently to the Pope. "Villages and towns are deserted. Everywhere you see widows whose husbands are still alive."[4] It seemed as though the whole of France was mobilizing for the holy war in the same way as it had rushed to answer Urban's summons in

1095. Yet there was a great difference. Bernard's rhapsodic and mystical view of the Crusade was very different from Urban's sober Cluniac war of liberation. Bernard had been inspired by the new belief in the Christian holy war, which was now promoted by the establishment, and had taken it to its ultimate conclusion, and his mystical piety would make this the most religious of all the Crusades.

Readers who are not familiar with the story of the Crusades might be puzzled that this expedition of 1146 is generally called "the Second Crusade" by historians. It seems that crusading had never stopped: ever since the conquest of Jerusalem in 1099 there had been a constant stream of expeditions to the Middle East, some of them on quite a large scale. Indeed there are some scholars today who query the long-established historical habit of referring to the "First," "Second" or "Third Crusades." They argue that it makes the picture too neat and disguises the fact that Crusades were going to the Holy Land all the time during the two hundred years that the Franks were able to hold on to their states in the Middle East. Indeed, long after they lost these states, it was not uncommon for kings and barons to take the Cross and vow to march on Jerusalem. But while it is true that the traditional terminology, which speaks of eight Crusades, is in a certain sense misleading, it still expresses an important truth. Certainly there was a constant flow of Crusaders to the East but these were in the main individual expeditions, undertaken by individual lords or knights. But on eight occasions the Popes, the leaders of Christendom, together with the most important secular rulers, declared an international European effort. There were eight of these papal calls to arms; the whole of Europe declared war on Islam eight times during the crusading period. Pope Urban's summons had been the first of these European efforts; the summons of Pope Eugenius, through the golden eloquence of Bernard, was the second time a pope had called for a united European expedition to the East. To understand the special quality of this Second Crusade we have to look at Europe in 1146 in order to see why Bernard was so influential and powerful.

We do not possess the text of Bernard's sermon at Vézelay but we do have some letters that he wrote to prospective Crusaders, so we can form quite an accurate idea of what he might have said. Bernard had many of the ideals of the First Crusaders. Like Urban, he urged the knights to stop killing each other and join forces against Islam. Thus they would save their souls. Great sinners would also benefit from taking part in this campaign, he argued, because they would receive remission of all their sins. Bernard was deeply impressed by the holiness of the land where Christ had lived and died. It had been "embellished by his miracles, consecrated with his blood and enriched by his burial."[5] The fall of Edessa was a territorial disaster, and a cosmic disaster as well because now the holiness of this land was threatened by "evil men."[6] It "really would be an inconsolable sorrow to all succeeding ages, because it would be a loss that could never be recovered."[7] Bernard was convinced that its holiness was only accessible to God's chosen people, who were now the Christians. The Muslims, who might soon be "feasting their eyes"[8] on the holy places, must be annihilated. Already "the earth has been shaken and has trembled"[9] because of the victory of Zangi, and if the Crusaders failed to rise to the urgent necessity of the hour it would be a "boundless shame" and an "eternal disgrace."[10] Bernard's objection to Muslims was not based on any hatred of Islam as a religion, but rather on the fact that they were a threat to the Holy Land and therefore to the whole world.

This view of the Muslims and of the Holy Land is very similar to that of the Crusaders after the First Crusade and since 1100 had been fully endorsed by the Christian establishment. However, Europe was a very different place from the Europe of 1095; there was a greater stability, a new intellectual culture was emerging and, above all, the process of Christianization begun by the reformers of Cluny had now taken effect. This meant that Europeans could now afford to think of themselves as individuals and this was reflected in the new Crusader piety. The first Crusades had been vast collective enterprises, but Bernard specifically preached the Second Crusade as a divine invitation from God to each individual Crusader. As he marched to the Holy Land he was answering a personal call and saving his own soul. God had made himself vulnerable by allowing the Muslim victory in order to make a Crusade necessary and this was a turning point in the history of the world. The new world view of the Crusade makes the history of the world center around the individual Christian soul. The Muslims are simply part of the divine plan, which cannot possibly fail. It takes the myopia of the holy war one stage further. Instead of seeing the Muslims as mere filth, they are now simply tools used and created by God to save his people's souls.

This new piety had sprung from Bernard's religious order—a new order of monks which had been formed by Cluny but which had rebelled against the Cluniac tradition and showed a development in the psychology of Europe. Instead of building up the piety of each monk, Cluny had been dedicated to building up a new Christian society. The great reformer Odilo, Abbot of Cluny, used to be found of saying that if the Emperor Augustus had found Rome brick and left it marble, he had found Europe wood and left it marble.[11] The monk's life was busy and public and his spiritual life was largely communal and liturgical. There was not much time for personal, private meditation. Yet at the end of the eleventh century, when Cluny was most triumphant and when Europe seemed at last to be lifting its head after centuries of oblivion, individual monks within the Cluniac monasteries began to show a new restlessness; they wanted a new individual spirituality. This was rather similar to what had happened in Islam: the first Muslims had been primarily concerned to build a new Islamic society, and, when that had been established, the Sufis had built an Islamic mysticism of love.

In England at about the time of the Norman Conquest a monk of the monastery of Sherborne, who is usually known as Stephen Harding,[12] suddenly threw up the monastic life for reasons that are not clear and for years wandered restlessly throughout Europe in a private quest. Eventually he joined the new monastery at Molesmes in about 1091. Under its remarkable Abbot Robert, Molesmes was engaged in a fierce internal debate. Most of the monks wanted to stick to the traditions of Cluny but, to their dismay, others wanted to cast aside the elaborate Cluniac order and return to the roots of the Benedictine tradition and to the roots of Christianity: they wanted to live a simpler life away from the massive structures and rich monasteries that Cluny had created. To the "traditionalists" these new idealists seemed to threaten that stability which had been Cluny's greatest gift to Europe, to be flirting dangerously with the chaos from which Europe was just recovering. The rebels, who included Robert and Stephen, felt that the complicated rituals of Cluny were far from the spirit of St. Benedict and of the primitive Church and that they wanted to make an exodus into the wilderness and build a new, perfect community. Accordingly in 1098, while the first Crusaders were struggling toward the Holy Land, Robert, Stephen and a few other monks left Molesmes and founded the monastery of Citeaux in Burgundy. It was a new reform movement.

In Citeaux the monks sought solitude and silence; they also wanted to live in a simple building and to return to the poverty of Christ and to a greater purity. In 1110 Stephen Harding became the Abbot of Citeaux and it was during his abbacy that an event occurred which made this obscure little colony the inspiration of Europe. In the year 1112 a troop of forty-eight young knights rode up to the door of the abbey and asked to become "Cistercians." These knights were led by the young Bernard and it was he who was responsible for making the Cistercian order the most powerful institution in twelfth-century Europe. His great piety and ability meant that he was elected abbot of a new daughter house of the order, at Clairvaux, in 1115, when he was only twenty-five years old. From that moment, joining the Cistercians became an irresistible trend in Europe. Bernard went around preaching the new Cistercian reform with his huge charisma; after just one sermon in a village, twenty or thirty young knights or wealthy noblemen would leave their families and follow Bernard and Christ (the two, of course, were identical!) into the Cistercian order. "He is becoming the bane of wives and mothers," a contemporary wrote of Bernard. "Friends feared to see him approach their friends."[13] Bernard had arrived at Citeaux leading forty-seven young companions; a few years later he had founded a new youth movement.

This huge influx naturally meant expansion, particularly since the rule stipulated that no monastery should contain more than twelve monks and an abbot. Besides being the size of the first Christian community of Jesus and his apostles, it was an attempt to build solitude into the very composition of the monastery. These monks wanted to make an exodus from the world and its entanglements and so naturally they went to the uncultivated outskirts of Christendom. On the extreme margins of Europe, therefore, new monasteries were frontier settlements like the *kibbutzim* in Israel later. Because these borderlands were a wilderness, the monasteries in effect became agricultural colonies.[14] To maintain their privacy and independence the monks had to take the land and live off it, and because they could not do it all themselves and still have time for prayer they made an important innovation in the history of Western monasticism. With the monks lived a body of laymen who were called *conversi*.[15] The crusading armies had taken thousands of poor pilgrims with them in the quasi-monastic enterprise of the First Crusade, and now the Cistercians took them into their frontier monasteries. By offering the poor a stake in the monastic enterprise, they were offering them for the first time a cast-iron guarantee of salvation and a chance to live the religious life (the only Christian life) permanently. The Cistercians were thus continuing strongly within the Cluniac tradition at the same time as they were seeking to make an exodus from Cluny and go back to the roots of monasticism. Cluny had set out to "liberate" the Church and the monasteries from secular control; the Cistercians in their fundamentalist monastic movement were making a more radical break with the world and were also continuing the association between monasticism and the poor that Cluny had initiated.

There was one respect in which Citeaux was very different from Cluny. In the older monasteries, most of the monks had been dedicated to the monastic life as young children and had grown up within the walls of these Christian fortresses. The monastic holy war waged against the Devil and the powers of darkness was, therefore, manned largely by an army of conscripts. With our developed notions of freedom and the rights of the individual, this seems an obnoxious idea, but in the less developed society of premodern Europe personal freedom was a luxury that people could not afford. This meant that most monks had never known the chivalric life. Yet when Bernard and his companions rode to the doors of Citeaux, they were young knights who had made an individual decision to embrace the perfect Christian life. This conversion of life was also made by the young men who followed St. Bernard's call, most of whom would have once been knights.[16] As Cistercian monks they would never bear arms again, of course, but this new knightly influx gave the Cistercian order a certain chivalric and military image.[17] There was a military precision in its rule: where St. Benedict had written only broad, general guidelines for his monks, the Cistercian rule legislated for every detail, even for the lifestyle of the monasteries' pigs.[18] There was a military edge to Cistercian piety and to their frontier settlements which were slowly pushing forward the frontiers of Christendom. It is by this time easy to see why St. Bernard, the moving spirit behind this new monastic reform, was able to preach the Crusade so effectively. He was already inspired by many of its ideals and practices.

Yet no fundamentalist movement entirely reproduces the original pattern to which it seeks to return; inevitably it makes innovations to meet the wants of the age. The Cistercians' simplicity was in spiritual terms a new departure. The rule of St. Benedict had been drawn up as Western Europe fell prey to barbarism, and its emphasis was on discipline, stability and defense. By stabilizing his monks physically within the monastery and by subjecting the body and will to a communal discipline, Benedict sought to defend them against the chaos and evil of the rest of barbarian Europe. But by the end of the eleventh century Europe was feeling confident enough to mobilize herself to attack and could abandon this old defensive posture. The First Crusade was the most dramatic of these aggressive projects but there was also a spiritual confidence. The old monasteries had been fortresses, warding off the forces of evil and conserving the old order. In the pioneering monasteries of the Cistercians, the monks were engaged in a spiritual struggle and quest. Resistance had given way to a mystical attack and a contemplative initiative, and the Cistercian was engaged on an inward journey or migration to God himself. In the early Benedictine and Cluniac monasteries, piety had been largely communal; now each monk in the Cistercian settlements was engaged in a personal quest. Hence too Bernard's emphasis on the individual call that God was offering to each Crusader.

But there was a basic ambiguity in Bernard's view of crusading, which sprang from his essentially elitist vision of the Christian life. He believed that ideally everybody should be a monk, because it was only monks who led a truly Christian life.[19] But clearly that was not possible, so God had entrusted the extraordinary privilege of a religious vocation only to the chosen few. Furthermore Bernard was convinced that no monks were closer to the Christian ideal than the Cistercians. Fifty years earlier, Christians had been yearning toward the holiness of the East; in particular they had longed for the holiness of Jerusalem. Now Bernard taught that the Cistercian monasteries were holier than the Holy City itself. Once, an English pilgrim had made a vow to pray at the Holy Sepulchre Church in Jerusalem and on his way there he had decided that he would enter the monastery of Clairvaux instead and become a Cistercian. Bernard wrote that not only had this monk no need to fulfill his pilgrim's vow but that he had already fulfilled it, even though he had not got as far as Jerusalem:

> He has cast his anchor into the very port of salvation. His feet already tread the pavements of the Holy Jerusalem. This Jerusalem which is linked with the heavenly Jerusalem and which is entwined with her in all the deepest feelings of the human heart is Clairvaux.[20]

When Bernard spoke of the "heavenly Jerusalem" he did not mean the city described in Revelation that would descend to earth at the end of time. He used the phrase as a symbol of that union with God that the Cistercian was striving to attain in prayer. It followed that this mystical state was far more "holy" than any earthly city, no matter how deeply associated with Christ. For the Cistercian elite, holiness had become spiritual and removed from the physical world. Naturally a monk who was experiencing God himself in his cloister did not need the second-grade holiness of Jerusalem and the Holy Land. In fact, when Bernard was offered a piece of land near Jerusalem in order to found a monastery, he refused it.[21] His monks did not need a physical contact with the Holy City because they were already in possession of a far more significant holiness and a direct experience of God's love, which was inaccessible to the mere layman.

But for the rank and file the holiness of Jerusalem and Palestine was vital, because it was the closest that they would ever manage to get to God. It was, therefore, important for the layman to go on a pilgrimage there, not only because he would live according to monastic ideals during his pilgrimage, but because the land *was* undoubtedly holy due to its contact with the historical Christ. The layman could not achieve contact with God by means of contemplation, because this esoteric mysticism was only for the Cistercian elite, but he could take part in another secondary but very important Christian task in the Crusade. Crusading was central to Bernard's political vision of Christianity, which needed Christian soldiers. The Cistercians had laid aside their knightly duties for the more important Christian task of prayer; their monasteries were spiritual powerhouses, strengthening and sanctifying Europe, but those knights who had not been fortunate enough to be called to the cloister could fight for God in the world. That was *their* vocation. Europe was beginning to acquire a greater awareness of the power of her mighty neighbors, which seemed to threaten a Christendom that was still vulnerable for all its new confidence. Although neither the Byzantines nor the Muslims had any military designs on Europe, the massive power of these oriental empires made Europeans assume that they were just biding their time before they invaded and conquered their lands. Thus Guibert of Nogent could reproach the Archbishop of Mainz for the Germans' lack of participation in the First Crusade by saying that the Franks alone had defended Europe against the new barbarian invasions of the Turks, even though the Seljuks had neither the desire nor the ability to conquer Christendom.[22] The first Crusaders had had a very vague idea indeed of the Muslim world but now people were beginning to see poor little Christian Europe as an island of the true faith surrounded by hostile infidels. This view naturally affected the idea of crusading. Thus in about 1125 the English historian William of Malmesbury wrote a version of Pope Urban's speech at Clermont:

The world is not evenly divided. Of its three parts, our enemies hold Asia as their hereditary home—a part of the world which our forefathers rightly considered equal to the other two put together. Yet here formerly our Faith put out its branches; here all the Apostles save two met their deaths. But now the Christians of those parts, if there are any left, squeeze a bare subsistence from the soil and pay tribute to their enemies, looking to us with silent longing for the liberty they have lost. Africa, too, the second part of the world, has been held by our enemies by force of arms for two hundred years and more, a danger to Christendom all the greater because it formerly sustained the brightest spirits—men whose works will keep the rust of age from Holy Writ as long as the Latin tongue survives. Thirdly, there is Europe, the remaining region of the world. Of this region we Christians inhabit only a part, for who will give the name of Christians to those barbarians who live in the remote islands and seek their living on the icy ocean as if they were whales? This little portion of the world which is ours is pressed upon by warlike Turks and Saracens: for three hundred years they have held Spain and the Balearic Islands, and they live in hope of devouring the rest.[23]

William's dates are wrong, but this remarkable version of Urban's speech shows a new twelfth-century view of the purpose of the First Crusade. Instead of being a war of liberation, it was a fight for survival. A new paranoia had crept into the Western world view.

Christians had to fight back. Zangi's conquest of Edessa must in this view have looked like the first step toward an Islamic reconquest, just a preliminary to the invasion of Europe. In this natural but distorted view of Islam, the Crusader states were of enormous psychological importance to the people of Europe, who were just waking up from the nightmare of the Dark Ages. We have seen that when they conquered Jerusalem they had at first believed that they would one day settle the Muslim problem once and for all and would ultimately conquer the world, but they had also become more aware in recent years of the power of the Muslim giant. That was what had made Zangi's victory over the Frankish Christians at Edessa so threatening and why Bernard had described this as one of the turning points of history. Bernard, the former knight, was not just lost in mystical ecstasy in Clairvaux. We have seen that, while the rest of his monks led secluded lives, he himself was heavily engaged in the political life of Christendom. He was fully aware of both the strategic and spiritual importance of the Holy Land and had long been convinced that, in order to fulfill its Christian mission in *this* world, Europe had to mobilize herself militarily to defend the faith. That was why he had always been such an enthusiastic supporter of the Templars. Although these soldier-monks were not as exalted as the Cistercians, they were engaged with them in a monastic partnership. In their monasteries in Europe the Cistercians stormed heaven and sought the heavenly Jerusalem in their lives of prayer and contemplation, while the Templars fought for the defense of the earthly Jerusalem. In their pioneering monasteries the Cistercians were pushing forward the frontiers of Europe, while the Templars in their fortresses in the East were pushing aggressively against the frontiers of Islam. Both sets of monks were occupied with the battle for truth, the difference being that the Cistercian elite fought on the spiritual plane and the Templars on the earthly plane. Each needed the other, as body and soul of the same entity. Now the Second Crusade gave the laymen a chance to join in this great monastic enterprise. Bernard had called it a revelation of God's love for the world, and during the Crusade the laymen would experience this love for themselves, not by contemplating God like the Cistercians, but by fighting for him like the Templars.

If the Cistercians were the elite of the monks, in Bernard's view, the Templars were the elite of the knights and of the active Christians, engaged in fighting God's battles for him in the world. He had given them his ardent support for twenty years. In 1126 King Baldwin of Jerusalem had sent two of the Templars to Bernard in Clairvaux and one was Bernard's uncle, André of Montand. The Order of the Temple needed to develop, and Baldwin wanted papal recognition for the Knights Templar, which Bernard made sure they got. Two years later the Council of Troyes made the Templars an official religious order in the Church and approved their rule, which was popularly believed to have been the creation of Bernard himself and was in fact very close to the rule of the Cistercians. Fulk of Anjou and Henry of Champagne, two leading Templars, made a tour of Christendom to drum up support for the Templars and, at a time when crusading was vitally important to the people of Europe, the Templars immediately attracted a vast number of recruits. In 1129 Fulk and Henry returned to the Holy Land, taking with them, wrote a contemporary chronicler, "so large a number of men as never had done since the days of Pope Urban."[24] The order also gained a strong foothold in Europe, and houses of Templars were established in France, Portugal, Scotland and England (the London Temple dates from this time). In their European houses the Templars looked after the interests of the Crusader states at home, and all over Europe these houses of soldier-monks appeared, dedicated to the defense of Jerusalem, uniting the two great Western passions of religion and warfare.

Bernard praised the Templars as ideal Christian soldiers. He saw the sophistication and refinement that were beginning to enter lay life in Europe, and even into knighthood and chivalry, as effeminate and worldly—totally unfitting for a true Christian. In his treatise *In Praise of the New Chivalry* he admires the Templars for maintaining the rough values of his brutal view of Christianity:

> They come and go at a sign from their commander; they wear the clothes that he gives them, seeking neither other garments nor other food. They are wary of all excess in food or clothing, desiring only what is needful. They live all together, without women and children.

No idlers or lookers-on are to be found in their company; when they are not on active service, which happens rarely, or eating their bread or giving thanks to heaven, they busy themselves with mending their clothes and their torn or tattered harness. . . .

They crop their hair short because the Gospels tell them it is a shame for a man to tend his hair. They are never seen combed and rarely washed, their beards are matted, they reek of dust and bear the stains of heat and the harness.[25]

Europe was in a permanent state of war, in Bernard's view, and that meant that a serious Christian had no time for the softer pursuits or for the company of the vile sex of women. He had to be constantly ready for battle and his lifestyle should reflect this harsh and tough reality.

Bernard saw the violent enterprise of the Crusade as a revelation of the divine love and he also saw the Templars as fulfilling the ideals of Christian love, which was both tender and fierce:

These warriors are gentler than lambs and fiercer than lions, wedding the mildness of the monk with the valour of the knight so that it is difficult to know what to call them: men who adorn the Temple of Solomon with shields instead of crowns of gold, with saddles and bridles instead of candelabra . . . who in spite of being many live in one house, according to one rule, with one soul and one heart.[26]

They reproduced, therefore, the values of the first community of Christians who, the Acts of the Apostles said, lived in Jerusalem "with one heart and one soul" (4:32), worshiping daily in the Temple, where the Templars had their headquarters. They had replaced the old peaceful imagery of the Jewish-Christian tradition with shields and weapons, dedicating Christianity to truly martial values in the constant holy war for the true faith. Above all, having dedicated their lives to this war, they were daily and hourly prepared for martyrdom, the highest proof of love:

What in fact is there to fear for the man, whether he is living or dying, for whom to live is Christ and for whom it is a gain to die? He remains in this world faithfully and willingly for Christ; but his greater desire is to be dissolved and to be with Christ; this in fact is better. And so go forward in safety, knights, and with undaunted souls drive off the enemies of the cross of Christ, certain that neither death nor life can separate you from the love of God which is in Christ Jesus, repeating to yourselves in every peril, Whether we live or whether we die, we are the Lord's. How glorious are the victors who return from battle! how blessed are the martyrs who die in battle![27]

St. Paul, whom Bernard quotes extensively here, would have been horrified by the Templars but Bernard was speaking at the end of a long tradition of aggressive martyrdom. In fact for Bernard the ideal Christian death was the death of one who died fighting and killing the enemies of God: "Indeed whether a man dies in bed or in battle, no doubt the death of his saints will be precious in God's sight, but if in battle certainly his death will be that much more precious."[28] The fact that these martyrs went to heaven slaughtering other people bothered Bernard not a whit. He never considered approaching the Muslims as a peaceful missionary and converting them by means of his famous eloquence. The only solution to the "pagan" problem was the holy war. "It would indeed be forbidden to kill pagans if one could oppose in any other way their violence and hatred and oppression of the faithful," he explained to the Templars. "But as it is it is better to massacre them so that their sword is no longer suspended over the heads of the just."[29]

Urban had seen the Crusade as a political, military and territorial affair—a liberation of people and a liberation of a land. The First Crusaders had themselves often been inspired by secular motives as well as by religious ones and their campaign depended on piety and practical common sense. Bernard saw the Crusade as entirely the work of God. The Muslims were not real to him, he and his contemporaries misconceived their intentions as regards Europe and, more dangerously, assumed that they were already in the Christians' pocket because they were simply instruments that God was using for the glorification of the Christian West. If crusading was the revelation of that love of God which "passeth all understanding," Bernard was manifesting a dangerous indifference toward the concrete political and military realities of the campaign he was dispatching to the East. He was teaching his protégés like King Louis to have the Cistercian attitude to life. It would, however, be perilous to bypass reason and practicality on the road to the earthly Jerusalem.

Shortly before the Crusade, Bernard had overthrown reason in the person of the great scholar and churchman Peter Abelard. Abelard was Bernard's rival for the leadership of the young men of Europe. He too had been destined for a military career but, at about the same time as Bernard and his young knights had entered Citeaux, Abelard decided to give up military life and become a scholar. He quickly became a leading scholar and from all over Europe thousands of young men had left home and come to sit at his feet in Paris just as thousands of their contemporaries were entering the Cistercian monasteries. Abelard was a philosopher and a logician. He believed that religion should be an affair of the head as well as an affair of the heart. "A religious man," he taught his young disciples, "must always be able to give a reason concerning the faith that is in him."[30] The young scholars who followed him had inquiring minds and wanted an intelligent quest instead of a scholarship that merely conserved ancient tradition. They supported their master with a passionate devotion. Abelard had become almost a mythical figure in France because of his famous and tragic love affair with Heloise, and after that he had become one of the leading churchmen of his day. Bernard was determined to destroy him, firstly, because he was a rival and, secondly, because he challenged Bernard's mystical view of religion, which saw the truth as an impenetrable mystery that had to be accepted by faith alone. Abelard, he said, referring to St. Paul's famous hymn to charity, was lacking in Christian love: "he sees nothing as an enigma, nothing as in a mirror, but looks on everything face to face."[31]

Bernard wanted to condemn Abelard as a heretic, most unjustly since Abelard had no heretical views—indeed his religious ideas were conventional. Later the Church would come around to his scholastic methods, which were in part the methods of St. Thomas Aquinas. Otto of Freising, a contemporary Cistercian abbot, accused his leader of unreasonable prejudice, suggesting that Bernard was improperly swayed by his hatred of scholars like Abelard and so lent too eager an ear to Abelard's enemies. Bernard summoned Abelard to the Council of Sens, which he packed with his own supporters; when the scholar arrived he found more of Bernard's supporters outside threatening him with violence. Abelard was simply not given a fair hearing and, when Bernard stood up and with his frighteningly persuasive eloquence condemned his teachings, he collapsed. He was by this time a sick man, probably suffering from Parkinson's disease, and he was prey to mental terrors brought on by the traumas of his life. He was condemned and his books destroyed so thoroughly that today we have only a few fragments of them. The Pope himself lit the massive pyre of Abelard's condemned manuscripts and Abelard never recovered from this. He died the following year at Cluny, where the kindly and scholarly Abbot Peter the Venerable had taken him in. The event would have made a great impression on many of the Crusaders who marched out of

Europe with a frightened and unnatural distrust of reason, which Bernard had dramatically taught them by destroying the great Abelard.

Although the Church was at this time officially opposed to the persecution of the Jews and even though there was absolutely nothing anti-Semitic about Bernard's preaching, the laity began to attack the Jewish communities along the Rhine Valley, just as they had done fifty years earlier at the time of the First Crusade. When they heard that the vulnerable Christ was begging Christians to come to his aid and rescue his Holy Land, it must have seemed illogical to many Crusaders not to fight the people who had been responsible for Christ's death. The new wave of pogroms was stirred up by Raoul, another Cistercian. Bernard hurried into the kingdom of Conrad, King of the German peoples, to stop this distortion of the crusading ideal. Raoul, he said, had received no commission, human or divine, to preach in any way. "A monk's vocation is not to preach but to weep," Bernard thundered: he was inspired by the Devil, the father of lies. "Why turn your zeal and ferocity against the Jews?" he asked the Germans; "they are the living images of the passion of the saviour."[32] But not even Bernard's eloquence and charisma could stop the assaults on Jewish communities and individuals. There would be an outbreak of anti-Semitic violence in Europe every time a major Crusade to the Holy Land was preached. Whatever sophisticated ideas might inspire churchmen like Bernard, the element of the vendetta and the blood feud was still strongly present in the crusading ideology of the ordinary lay man and woman, and this meant a holy war against the Jews. The pogroms continued sporadically for some time after the crusading armies had left for the Holy Land: the people who stayed at home felt that harrying Jews was their contribution to the Crusade.

But Bernard's visit to the German Kingdom bore fruit in another way. The First Crusade had been planned as an international project, and indeed many people of many nations had flocked into the armies. But the Crusade had been seen as principally a Frankish achievement. Bernard's Crusade was the second major offensive on the part of Europe in the struggle for the Holy Land—the smaller expeditions to the East which had gone in a steady stream during the last fifty years were private affairs—and Bernard intended this second major Crusade to be truly international. It was essential therefore that Conrad, the King of the Germans and a leading European ruler, should take a German army to the Holy Land and march alongside King Louis. Conrad, however, had no desire whatever to go crusading. He was, after all, an old man in uncertain health, who was in no condition to survive the terrible journey. He felt that he was doing his part in the holy war by fighting the pagan Slavs and Wends of Eastern Europe. He was also fighting the Pope's enemies in Italy and Pope Eugenius certainly did not want to lose Conrad at this point. Neither the Pope nor Conrad had reckoned with Bernard's steely determination when he preached the Crusade in Freiburg, Schaffhausen and Constance.

The Germans responded to Bernard ecstatically, even though they could not understand a word he said. The holy pandemonium was such that people tried to tear Bernard's emaciated body to pieces in their rapture, and several times the frenzy was so extreme that Bernard could not leave his house. There had been famine the previous year and this may have contributed to the outbreak of visionary fervor and miracles of healing. People claimed to be cured of blindness as Bernard's shadow touched them or they threw away their crutches as they listened to his sermons.[33] They began to clamor for the New Jerusalem, rather as the half-starved Franks had done at the Peace of God councils in 1033. All this was most embarrassing for Conrad. On Christmas Day at Speyer, Bernard's crusading sermon failed to move him but two days later, when Bernard yet again addressed the court, he turned his attention to Conrad directly and addressed him as an individual, not as a king. He imagined Christ speaking to Conrad on the Day of Judgment—a Conrad who had refused to go on the Second Crusade: "O man," Christ said, "what have I not done for thee that I ought to have done?"[34] Conrad collapsed, burst into tears and promised to take the Cross. Bernard's eloquent bullying had broken down his resistance, just as it had broken Abelard.

The German triumph gave Bernard a new idea. In March 1147 he arrived in Frankfurt and dispatched a Crusade against the heathen Slavs and Wends. Shortly after this a smaller contingent consisting of English, Flemish and Frisian Crusaders sailed to join the Crusade but they got waylaid in the Iberian peninsulas, where they stayed to help the Christians in the wars of reconquest. They managed to conquer Lisbon and there was a massacre of the Muslim population. St. Bernard's loving Crusade had become a vast three-pronged assault on the Muslims in the East, the Muslims in the Spanish West and the pagans of Eastern Europe. It was a giant international attack on the non-Christian world by the newly mobilized Christendom.

At the end of May 1147 Conrad and his great army left Germany and began the journey through Eastern Europe toward Constantinople. Awed contemporaries spoke of a million men in his army and it seems that there may well have been 20,000 Crusaders. With Conrad went the two vassal kings of Bohemia and Poland and there was a contingent from Lorraine. The German nobles were led by the heir to the throne, Frederick of Swabia. It looked a formidable and impressive army and to an outsider it would have seemed an impressive image of a Christendom united solidly in an implacable hatred of the enemies of God. Yet the army was not so united: there was great trouble between the different ethnic groups and quarrels and rivalries between the German nobles. Conrad was not strong enough in temperament or in body to hold the army together and Frederick was still far too inexperienced to be an effective leader but nevertheless the army managed to journey without much incident through Eastern Europe, and on July 20 the Germans crossed into Byzantine territory, Conrad having first sworn an oath of noninjury to the Byzantine Emperor Manuel.

On June 8 the French army set out. Unlike Conrad, Louis had taken the Cross on his own initiative. He was a very devout young man of twenty-six and had been intended for the cloister until the death of his brother Philip made him the heir to the throne. During a war with one of his vassals he had massacred all the inhabitants of Vitry in Champagne and had been plagued with guilt ever since. Bernard had advised him to make a penitential pilgrimage to Jerusalem, but when Louis heard about the fall of Edessa he resolved to lead a Crusade to Jerusalem instead: killing Muslims in the East would atone for his sin of killing Christians in France. Louis's beautiful young wife Eleanor of Aquitaine also took the Cross. She was one of the biggest landowners in Europe and had brought the whole of southern France more directly under the control of the King of the Franks when she married Louis in 1137. The marriage was not a happy one. Eleanor had involved Louis in the war resulting in the Vitry massacre; she had managed to produce only one daughter—a source of great anxiety to the young couple and to Bernard, their guide. She found the gloomy court of Paris positively barbaric after the south and may have insisted on journeying east with the Crusade. Alternatively Louis may have insisted that she accompany him because he could not trust her at home: fidelity does not seem to have been her strong point and she was far too rich in land—and therefore too powerful—for anybody, even Bernard, to keep her in check.

As one may imagine, Bernard had absolutely no time for Eleanor. She had brought to Paris a refinement and sophistication that seemed to him a deep betrayal of true Christianity. The south had not taken to the Cluniac reform and had remained, though firmly Christian, more thoroughly secular in tone. The court of Poitiers, where Eleanor had grown up, was extremely sophisticated and Eleanor's grandfather, Count William the Troubadour, had filled it with the best poets and scholars of his day. Eleanor was far more intelligent than her husband, who had received only a narrow monastic education; she spoke several languages, wrote poetry and was patron to many courtly poets of the time who adored her and celebrated her in their poetry. When she arrived in Paris she brought poets with her as well as a new fashion for southern clothes and refined southern manners. Eleanor began a little youth movement of her own in Paris; she taught the young people of the court that one did not have to behave like a boor or smell like a Templar to be a brave knight. Instead of despising or rejecting women, southern courtly chivalry worshiped the lady, loving her from afar with no hope of physical possession. For her part the lady educated her knight, inspired him in his knightly duty to the noble ideals of chivalry and refined his manners. Bernard thought this courtly love was obscene and he was probably deeply worried that this woman was polluting the holy Crusade with her presence. She had brought to Paris a cool contempt for fanatical northern religion, and this attitude was beginning to be adopted by the young people. She taught her contemporaries in the court to play games like "Confession," which involved the players in absurd and grotesque penances, and the "Pilgrim Game," where one of the players was the saint in the shrine to whom the others prayed to try to make him laugh by obscene gestures or by tickling him. (The game was finally forbidden in 1240 by the Synod of Worcester.[35]) While most of the Crusaders had been properly schooled in true martial values by Bernard, Eleanor would bring quite a different perspective to the campaign and would throw light on some of its anomalies.

Eleanor used to say of Louis that she thought she had married a man but found she had married a monk instead.[36] In the measured eyewitness account of Louis's chaplain Odo of Deuil we can sense her exasperation with Louis's pious activities when he set out on the Second Crusade on June 8. First he visited a leper colony to perform an act of charity and humility that filled Odo with admiration. Then he went to the monastery of St. Denis where he prostrated himself like a novice before the altar and received the crusading banner from the Pope himself:

> Then when the banner had been taken from above the altar, after he had received the pilgrim's wallet, a blessing from the pope, he withdrew from the crowd to the monks' dormitory. The crowds and king's mother and wife, who nearly perished because of their tears and the heat, could not endure the delay; but to wish to depict the grief and wailing which occurred then is as foolish as it is

impossible. On that day the King and a few of his retinue dined in the refectory with the brothers, and, after receiving the kiss of peace from all, he departed, accompanied by the tears and prayers of all.[37]

There could not be a clearer image of the monastic origin of this Crusade. Louis certainly regarded himself as a pilgrim and as a kind of monk, living the religious life for the duration of the campaign, and this would have some important repercussions.

There had been some talk of King Roger of Sicily providing a fleet to take the Crusaders to the East, but neither the Pope nor Bernard trusted Roger, who later proved to have his eye on Byzantine territory. In any case, Louis and the French wanted to walk in the footsteps of Charlemagne and their ancestors the First Crusaders, so they took the land route. This was their first mistake. The Crusaders who had marched through Eastern Europe in the autumn of 1096 had been careful to prevent any pillaging. Conrad, however, showed no signs of learning this lesson. His army pillaged disgracefully once on Byzantine territory, and on one occasion Frederick of Swabia killed all the Greek monks in a monastery near Adrianople to avenge the deaths of two of the Crusaders. When the Emperor Manuel, not unnaturally, remonstrated with him Conrad simply retorted that after the Crusade he would return and attack Byzantium itself. Once they had crossed the Bosphorus, the Crusaders continued their career of looting and vandalism and, having followed so closely in the dangerous footsteps of Peter the Hermit's Crusaders, most of the German army suffered their fate. On October 25 the Germans arrived at Dorylaeum. The knights dismounted to rest their exhausted horses and the infantry were weary and thirsty. While they were thus off guard, the whole Seljuk army massacred nine tenths of Conrad's army in revenge.

Louis's army kept better order and avoided pillaging, but their journey was difficult. The inhabitants had suffered enough from Crusaders. The food was finished, the local people hostile and the French began to mutter angrily against the Germans. Louis reached Constantinople safely, therefore, but he should have learned from the experience of the First Crusaders that to take the land route was a bad mistake. To wish to follow in the footsteps of Charlemagne and his ancestors was a pious wish but it was also dangerous and impractical. The journey across Asia Minor had almost finished the First Crusade and now it almost finished the Second.

The survivors of Conrad's army with their King joined the French and together the Crusaders began the dangerous journey. The First Crusaders suffered from the heat of summer; the Second Crusaders endured fierce winter storms, and at one point hundreds of German soldiers were swept away by a torrential flood. Otherwise, the Crusaders suffered the same horrors as their predecessors: the Turks had ravaged the countryside, so there was malnutrition and starvation; the poor pilgrims began to die in droves; the horses also died or else were killed for meat; knights were reduced to the ranks; the army was continually harassed by the Turks, who inflicted heavy casualties. At one point, at Kronos, the vanguard were almost wiped out because the leaders did not obey orders. The Second Crusaders were guilty of a culpable impracticality. They had wandered off in a pious dream, hopelessly unprepared. Bernard had failed to anchor his men in the practical realities of campaigning and the result was disorganized disaster, as at Kronos or Dorylaeum. The First Crusaders had managed their similar danger with instinctive practicality and military skill when their vanguard had been attacked by the Turks at Dorylaeum. Odo of Deuil was very well aware of the Crusaders' lack of preparation and throughout his account of the journey he gives practical tips to future Crusaders about what kind of carts to use, for example, or which towns were wealthy enough to provide good provisions: "For never will there fail to be pilgrims to the Holy Sepulchre; and they will, I hope, be the more cautious because of our experiences."[38] Their piety had precluded their common sense and the Second Crusaders would make still more dangerously pious mistakes.

Over a year later, in February 1148, the exhausted army and pilgrims struggled into the Byzantine port at Attalia and camped outside the city. They had to make a decision: should they go the rest of the way by sea, continue with the land route or else divide forces, sending half by sea and half by land? They had realized that they could not go on land any longer and, without any justification, said that their difficulties had been much greater than those experienced by their predecessors. One of the difficulties they claimed was the "treachery" of the Greeks.[39] Manuel, Emperor of Byzantium, like Alexius before him, had little reason to rejoice that a Crusade was coming to the East. The Germans had declared war on him and pillaged his territory and the French had proved difficult and truculent about taking the oath of loyalty. Having these huge Western armies to look after presented grave problems for Manuel—political, military and economic problems not easily solved. Manuel was fighting an endless war against the Turks, but when he heard that the Crusaders were coming he had made a treaty with Mas'ud, the Sultan of Rum. As usual, any treaty with the infidel shocked the Crusaders deeply, but Manuel knew from bitter experience that the presence of the Crusaders was bound to stir up fresh Turkish aggression in which he did not want to get embroiled. He was also being viciously attacked by the navies of King Roger of Sicily. He had, therefore, no reason to welcome the Crusaders or to feel positive about the West, and yet he was a decent man and tried to take care of them as best he could. The Crusaders complained bitterly that he did not feed them sufficiently,[40] yet no state at that time, even an efficient one like Byzantium, could adequately provision such a huge army during the winter. At Attalia, for example, winter stocks were very low and the Turks had ravaged the countryside. The Byzantine governor did what he could but there was not much food available and, instead of appreciating this, the Crusaders simply accused the Greeks of treachery.[41] But the Greek inhabitants of Attalia were also having to go hungry because of this Western army and, when the Turks swept down and started to attack both the Crusaders' camp and the city, the Crusaders blamed the Greeks again for not protecting them adequately. It may well be that the people of Attalia made little effort to protect these unpleasant Westerners whose presence meant that the Turks had attacked their city.

Hostility to Byzantium had long been crucial to the Western identity but during the Second Crusade it reached new heights. Odo's measured and elegant pen drips venom every time he mentions the Greeks: he was convinced that the West should send out another Crusade to attack Constantinople.[42] Odo seems to hate the Greeks more than the Muslims.[43] As the West was apparently gaining in confidence and acquiring a rich and unique culture, it was also growing in intolerance. Not only were Western Christians finding it impossible to live beside people of other religions; they now wanted to destroy their great Christian neighbor, and one day they would succeed.

Eventually, after much agonized discussion, a decision was made which was a crime against the crusading ethos. The army was to proceed by sea from Attalia in ships provided by the Greeks. There was not enough room for everybody, so only the knights, the noblemen and some of the infantry could sail. The rest of the foot soldiers and the huge mass of French and German pilgrims were abandoned with their wives and children outside Attalia. They thus disappeared from history, betrayed by their brothers.[44] All were killed by the Turks or were taken into slavery or else starved to death. To abandon the poor may have been necessary for the survival of the Crusade but it gravely damaged its moral integrity. It would be a long time before crusading could attract the poor again and people looked back nostalgically to the vintage days of the First Crusade when a new, fairer world order had seemed imminent. The decision at Attalia was bitter proof that the gap between rich and poor was greater than ever.

On March 19, 1148, King Louis and his army arrived at the port of St. Simeon. Conrad had been taken ill the previous December and had had to return to Constantinople, where Manuel, with exceptional Christian forbearance, personally nursed the German King who had threatened to attack his empire, and early in March had him and his household taken to Palestine by a Byzantine fleet. In this saga of stupid, blind hatred, it is pleasant to record that Conrad and Manuel became the best of friends. So Louis was the only leader to land in the Christian Principality of Antioch, and as soon as Prince Raymund of Antioch heard of his arrival, he and all his household rode down to welcome him and escort him triumphantly up to the city. The next few days were spent in revelry and feasting and the Franks, stupidly, began to forget some of the perils they had endured and were lured back into an optimistic frame of mind.

After the dreadful journey, Eleanor was delighted with Antioch. She felt far more at home in the sophisticated and luxurious East than she did in Bernard's gloomy Paris, and at Antioch there was the additional delight of a reunion with Prince Raymund, who was her uncle and childhood companion, very close to her in age, and with whom she had years ago enjoyed a rather scandalous relationship before he had left to try his luck in the East. At once the two exiles from Poitiers began to spend a lot of time together and ugly rumors circulated. Louis became pathetically jealous. But Raymund expected far more than a chance for a flirtation from the Crusade. He was watching the steady rise of Nur ad-Din, whose city of Aleppo was only about fifty miles away and a serious threat to his Christian principality. Yet Nur ad-Din was still not invincible and a sudden surprise attack by the mighty French and German Crusaders together with the Antiochene army would almost certainly finish him off once and for all. Raymund suggested to Louis that they make such an attack.

To the utter astonishment of both Eleanor and Raymund, however, Louis flatly refused to do any such thing. He stoutly insisted that he was on a pilgrimage and could not undertake any major offensive until he had prayed at the Holy Sepulchre. This was the spirit of St. Bernard as Louis had, with his limited intelligence, understood it and this type of impractical piety was peculiar to Bernard's most religious Crusade. None of the First Crusaders, even the most pious of them, would have committed this idiocy. Eleanor was furious with her husband. It was the last straw, she said. She had a much clearer grasp of the political reality than her monkish spouse and could not go along with this holy stupidity. If Louis wanted to set sail for the Holy Land, she told him, he would have to go by himself. She and her own personal troops from Aquitaine would stay in Antioch and would attack Nur ad-Din with Raymund. When she got back to Europe she would divorce her inadequate husband and take her great lands elsewhere. Driven out of his mind with jealousy, Louis forcibly abducted her at night, bundled her on board ship and set sail for Acre. Eleanor would remain by Louis's side for the rest of the Crusade but when she sailed away from Antioch she was, at last, pregnant.[45] There would be a silence about the paternity of this new daughter when she was finally born in Europe. By that time Raymund of Antioch had been killed while fighting Nur ad-Din. Eleanor would never forgive Louis.

When the Crusaders finally arrived in the Holy Land, they were royally entertained by the Franks who had grown up in Palestine and who were anxiously awaiting their arrival. Yet it was probably an uneasy meeting. Pilgrims and Crusaders from the West were always shocked to see the Palestinian Franks' luxurious and oriental lifestyle and to discover that they had Muslim friends[46] and that some of the lower orders had married oriental women and produced a race of half-castes. King Louis must have been horrified to learn that the King of Jerusalem actually had a treaty with the Amir of Damascus against Nur ad-Din. To the fervent but simple-minded Crusaders, who had a great deal of faith but no understanding of the political situation in the Near East, this must have seemed a heinous betrayal and must have made a nonsense of their crusading enthusiasm. It may be that the Crusaders shamed the Palestinian Franks into making a fateful decision, which meant that the vast effort of the Second Crusade was entirely wasted.

At the council of war held on July 24, 1148, in Acre, it was decided that the Crusaders and the army of the King of Jerusalem should jointly attack Damascus, the Christians' only ally in the increasingly hostile Muslim world. It is easy enough to understand the Crusaders' ignorant zeal: they would have seen this as a splendid act of faith, which trusted entirely in God and threw human prudence to the winds. Nobody, however, has been able to explain the utter folly of the Palestinian barons for agreeing to this proposal that could only strengthen the young Sultan Nur ad-Din's position: it was inevitable that when Amir Muin ad-Din Unur of Damascus saw that his city was being besieged by his former allies, he would ask his rival Nur ad-Din for help. The decision to attack Damascus is just one example of the danger of seeing politics with the eye of faith, expecting miracles and divine intervention instead of trusting in ordinary political sense.

The siege of Damascus was a fiasco, lasting only a few days. At first the Crusaders made some progress and they conquered some of the orchards outside the city. Then the Palestinian Franks suggested that the Christians move their army under the walls, so that the Muslims from the city did not have cover of trees when they made an attack. The position chosen was so disastrous that the Crusaders accused their Palestinian brethren of being in the pay of Unur, and indeed it may be that by this time the Franks of the Crusader kingdom had realized the lunacy of this campaign. When they saw Nur ad-Din's army arriving to come to the aid of Unur, they might have made a last-ditch attempt to remedy the situation and could even have accepted a bribe from their former ally. At all events, they finally persuaded the Crusaders that they should lift the siege and that the enterprise was hopeless. The army, which had suffered enormous casualties, limped ignominiously back to Jerusalem.

The story of the Second Crusade shows what Bernard's piety and distrust of reason could become in less gifted men: a belligerent irresponsibility. It also shows the danger of a holy-war mentality which believes that ordinary human intelligence and prudence should be cast aside on principle as an act of faith. Such policies are not only irrational, they are also suicidal. Thousands of Crusaders had lost their lives during this expedition and the huge enterprise of the Second Crusade had been entirely wasted. The Kingdom of Jerusalem was gravely endangered by this failure and Nur ad-Din must have felt that the Franks' absurd decision was an answer to his own prayers and a complete vindication of his own holy-war effort. Muslim morale in the area was henceforward much higher and Nur ad-Din would go from strength to strength, slowly building up an empire that would one day almost surround the Christian states.

The failure of his Crusade was a great blow to Bernard's prestige in Europe and people were right to blame him: by removing the Crusade from the realities of life and seeing it as solely the work of God he had encouraged a suicidal policy in the army. It was also a blow for crusading itself. How could a holy war fail if, as Bernard had promised, it was the work of God? Bernard himself was bewildered by the disaster, and the only explanation he could find was that the Christians had been too sinful so that God had withdrawn his help. But the triumph of the "pagans" over the true faith was for Bernard a cosmic disaster that was, literally, the end of the world. It seemed,

he wrote to the Pope, "to point an end almost to existence itself."[47]
The Crusaders themselves blamed the Greeks and that excuse was very
acceptable to Bernard too, but other critics were more forthright. In
Würzburg a monk who had talked to some of the survivors and had
learned how the campaign had been mismanaged, concluded that the
Crusade had not been inspired by God at all but by wicked and stupid
men like Bernard and Pope Eugenius: "Certain pseudo-prophets were
in power," he wrote, "sons of Belial and Heads of Antichrist, who by
their stupid words and empty preaching misled the Christians and
induced all sorts of men to go against the Saracens for the freeing of
Jerusalem."[48] This angry monk was only one of the critics who began
to express doubts about the Second Crusade at that time, but nobody
yet condemned the concept of a holy war as such. They only criticized
aspects of crusading or particular crusading episodes.

Nevertheless there were clear signs that people were seeking a less
bloodthirsty religion and this is most obviously apparent in the cult
of the Virgin Mary that Bernard himself was vigorously promoting.
One of the most famous hymns to the Virgin was supposed to have
been the work of two Crusaders: Adhémar of Le Puy and Bernard
himself. It shows a bleak view of life as a vale of tears and a yearning
for sweetness and consolation which is supplied not by Christ but by
Mary.

> Salve Regina, Mater Misericordiae: Vita, dulcedo et spes nostra
> salve. Ad te clamamus, exsules filii Hevae; ad te suspiramus, ge-
> mentes et flentes in hac lacrimarum valle. Eia ergo, advocata nostra,
> illos tuos misericordes occulos ad nos converte. Et Jesum, benedic-
> tum fructum ventris tui, nobis post hoc exsilium ostende. O clemens,
> O pia, O dulcis Virgo Maria.

> Hail Queen, Mother of mercy; hail our life, our sweetness and our
> hope. It is to you that we cry, exiled children of Eve; it is to you
> that we sigh, groaning and weeping in this vale of tears. Therefore
> do you, our advocate, turn your merciful eyes toward us and after
> our exile show us your son Jesus. O clement, O loving, O sweet
> Virgin Mary.

Even Christians dedicated to the holy war were seeking an alternative
that was more loving than vengeful, and a mediator and advocate who
would be more merciful and compassionate than Jesus, who made
such terrible demands on his followers. Adhémar, who wrote most of
this hymn, had experienced the terror involved in the service of the
crusading Christ during the trauma of the First Crusade.

Other Christians, at the time of the Second Crusade, seemed to reject crusading altogether when they turned to the Virgin Mary. At Chartres the lay people quite spontaneously created a counterpart and an alternative to the Crusade when they decided to build a new church for Mary in their city at the same time as the Crusaders were leaving Europe. There had always been a shrine to the Virgin there, but this lay movement laid some of the first stones of the magnificent cathedral of Chartres which has made the city famous. A building association was formed that organized lay men and women, rich and poor, to quarry the stones themselves and convey them to the site. An awed monk wrote to a monastery in England of the extraordinary scenes he witnessed. Men and women yoked themselves to the huge wagons "like beasts of burden."[49] Nobody could join the building association unless he had reconciled himself with all his enemies, and even though a thousand or more lay people were working together at a time, there was absolute silence, save for the prayers of the priests who accompanied them, "exhorting their hearts to peace." The emphasis in this movement of the Virgin was on peace and reconciliation, not on holy war. At the site of the church the wagons were parked and the people formed "a spiritual camp." Relics were brought in and sick people who were carried into the camp in huge processions were healed. All night long there was singing of hymns and canticles. The similarity to the crusading armies is clear. It seems as though, at a time when their fellows and neighbors were marching thousands of miles to the East, the people who elected to stay at home spontaneously set up a counter-Crusade dedicated to peace and to building up something beautiful at home. They were constructing a holy place in Europe instead of tramping to the Holy City of Jerusalem and were creating rather than destroying and killing. Chartres was not the only example of this constructive building. At the same time other building associations were formed, quite spontaneously and independently, in Normandy, Crusader heartland.[50] All were centered on ancient shrines to the Virgin Mary. Whenever there was a new surge of crusading enthusiasm, there was another building campaign, but these building projects seemed to be trying to separate themselves from the holy war and to be seeking a peaceful alternative, instead of being part of the war effort.

It is often true that the people who are not involved in a holy war tend to be more creative than their territorially minded brethren. We have seen that this is true in Judaism and in 1146 it was also true in Christianity. Indeed Bernard's crusading religion itself seems barren. Not only was his Crusade a disaster but he thwarted creativity at home. As a Cistercian he disapproved of beautiful architecture and would have had no time for Chartres Cathedral; he destroyed Abelard's intellectual movement, and even his mysticism was elitist and exclusive and only for Cistercians. Francis of Assisi would later bring spirituality to the people, and the friars would replace the Cistercians as the leaders of Europe in the thirteenth century.

In the second half of the century other people started to draw away from crusading and its values. Eleanor of Aquitaine, who had always opposed Bernard's holy war, spread the cult of courtly love throughout northern and southern France after she settled in her native Poitiers in 1170. Courtly love became extremely popular among the aristocracy, and it not only challenged the brutal values of crusading Christianity. It also exalted a love that had nothing to do with physical possession, but which idealized the lady who remained remote and distant from her knight. Crusading and courtly love had both been inspired by the love of distant objects—a distant lady and a distant land—but crusading had transformed this love into a lust for physical possession. Courtly love, on the other hand, had more in common with Bernard's view of the heavenly Jerusalem. Eleanor and her daughter Marie of Champagne became the patrons of many troubadour poets and one of their most important protégés was Chrétien of Troyes, who lived only thirty miles from Clairvaux. This proximity to the Cistercians was more than physical because Chrétien's stories show a marked closeness to the mystical ideals of Citeaux. In his stories the journey has changed its character. Like the mystic, the knight is engaged on an individual quest that he undertakes alone, not in the massive Crusader armies. Journeying, seeking and suffering, the knight roams all over the world but his journey has no end in this life. He is in search of love and it is far more important to suffer and even die for this love than to possess the beloved and reach an earthly fulfillment. He confidently expects a union of love that always remains in the future tense, a spiritual promise that inspires his quest for an ideal. Instead of being the prelude to a holy war, in the courtly myth, the journey has became a prelude to love. Instead of leading to an aggressive conquest of a physical land, the new journey of the courtly knight, like the journey of the mystic, has no physical end.

In the world of learning and scholarship, too, Europe was beginning to adopt a less belligerent attitude to the outside world. During the second half of the twelfth century Christian scholars flocked to Spain and Sicily and there discovered a wealth of learning and scholarship among the Arabs and Jews in the former Muslim territories.[51] They began to translate texts from the Arabic and thus discovered the scientific works of Aristotle as well as the philosophical and scientific learning of the Arab world. By translating Arab texts, therefore, these Western scholars were returning to Europe the culture she had lost during the Dark Ages. They found that they had much to learn from Arab scholars like Abu Ali al-Husain ibn Abdulla ibn Sina (d. 1037) and their great contemporary in Muslim Cordova, Abu al-Walid Mohammad ib Ahmen ibn Rushd. These names were shortened and Westernized to become Avicenna and Averroës, who became new sages and guides to the struggling West.

During the period of the Crusades, therefore, some Christians were learning from Arabs and Jews instead of slaughtering them in the name of God, and from this fruitful and positive cooperation a new intellectual life was born in Europe. The Arabs in particular were a light to the Christian West and yet this debt has rarely been fully acknowledged. As soon as the great translation work had been completed, scholars in Europe began to shrug off this complicating and schizophrenic relationship with Islam and became very vague indeed about who these Arabs really were. They were at a deep level unable to identify them with the Arabs and Muslims they were fighting in the Crusades, and "Arabs" tend to get lumped indiscriminately with other "Gentiles" like the Greeks, Assyrians and the Chaldeans. It was rarely acknowledged that the Arabs were not "Gentiles" or "pagans" at all but believed in the God of Abraham. Ludicrous inconsistencies abounded: Thomas Aquinas would praise Avicenna and Averroës but simply dismissed their Islamic religion as pagan error. Others actually refuted "Islam" by quoting Ibn Sina.[52] When Dante imagined the virtuous "pagans" in Limbo in *The Divine Comedy* he duly included Avicenna and Averroës but put them right at the end of a long list of distinguished Greek or Latin scholars whom he preferred to celebrate as his intellectual ancestors.[53] During the Renaissance this classical heritage was firmly established in the consciousness of Europe, and Arabic was dropped from the curriculum and denounced by the new Hellenes as a barbarous tongue. The relationship with Islam and the Arab world was far too complicated for people to cope with in a balanced way. Crusading had made a blind hatred of the Arabs an essential part of the Western identity. Scholars at the time similarly found themselves unable to realize fully that these Greeks whom they were rediscovering so enthusiastically and claiming as their own were actually the ancestors of the hated Byzantines. These peaceful and creative movements at home on one level rejected crusading, at least implicitly, and built up new, exciting structures of thought and art at home. Yet even in the most positive of these attempts to approach the Greek and Arab world there is an unhealthy repression and double-think about people who are at one and the same time guides, heroes and deadly enemies. This is very clear in the scholarship about Islam.

In 1141 Peter the Venerable of Cluny had made a tour of the Benedictine monasteries of Spain and there he met two other visiting monks: Robert of Ketton, an Englishman, and Herman of Dalmatia. Both men were seeking texts on mathematics and astronomy, but Peter persuaded them to cooperate with him on a project of translating major Muslim documents. Robert and Herman worked together with a Spanish Christian, Peter of Toledo, and a Muslim, Mohammad the Saracen, and together they produced a collection of documents that remained very important in the Western understanding of Islam until the sixteenth century. There was a translation of the Koran, a history of the world from a Muslim standpoint, an exposition of Mohammad's teaching, a collection of Muslim legends and an early work of polemic against Islam called *The Apology of al-Kindi*. Subsequently an annotator made some additions to these works, and these were taken by later students to be as authoritative as the texts themselves.[54] This seemed an enormously positive step forward and yet it would produce a tradition of polemic which, far from seeking an understanding of Islam, produced a distorted fantasy and helped to fuel the war effort. Peter the Venerable, a gentle and loving man, wrote a treatise which claims to reach out to the Muslims with love, but the title of his work shows the spirit in which it was conceived: *Summary of the whole heresy of the diabolical sect of the Saracens*.[55] It seemed to be impossible for Christians to see Islam as anything but a failed version of Christianity. The polemic against the Muslims that developed in the Middle Ages and still continues to affect the way Westerners see Islam today perfectly reproduced the polemic of the martyrs of Cordova. The Muslim became the hated shadow-self of the Western Christian, hated therefore with an irrational and neurotic intensity.

The second half of the twelfth century was a time when people were beginning to draw back from crusading and to seek a more peaceful form of religion. Here and there isolated scholars in Europe were questioning the validity of the holy war. Thus the Anglo-Norman Crusader who took part in the Christian conquest of Lisbon in 1147, and who wrote an account of the campaign, reeled back in horror at the thought of further massacres of Muslims like the one he had witnessed. "Stay now your hand, Lord," he pleaded, "it is enough."[56] Isaac, the Abbot of Étoile, was extremely disturbed to hear about a new (unnamed) military order, which "despoils licitly and murders religiously." Isaac calls this order a *monstrum novum* (a modern abomination) and finds it impossible to square the cruelty of the order with

"Christ's clemency, patience, or manner of teaching."[57] Walter Map (d. 1209), Eleanor of Aquitaine's secretary, also found the military orders worrying. It was "with the word of the Lord, not with the edge of the sword" that "the Apostles conquered Damascus, Alexandria and a great part of the world."[58] None of these writers condemned crusading entirely, but they do show that here and there people were beginning to see a deep contradiction between the Crusades and the teaching of Christ. Most people repressed this perception very thoroughly and Crusades continued to set out for the Holy Land, but it is significant that when the scholars of the period turn to the study of Islam they continue to see it as the religion of the sword, a view that is still accepted as a self-evident truth by large numbers of people in the Western world.

Islam, we have seen, is no more violent than either Judaism or Christianity and indeed set a pattern of peaceful coexistence and conquest early in its history. What the Western scholars of the twelfth century were doing was creating a fantasy that had very little to do with Islam, but which had a great deal to do with the problem of Christianity's violence. When Robert of Ketton translates the words of Sura 88 in the Koran, "For thou art to be a teacher not a coercer," the Annotator leaps in with an astonishing attack on Mohammad:

> Why then dost thou teach that men are to be converted to thy religion by the sword? If thou art not a coercer but a teacher, why dost thou subject men by power, like animals and brute beasts, and not by reasoning like men? In fact, like the liar you are, you everywhere contradict yourself.[59]

The Annotator is commenting on words that state unequivocally that Islam is *not* a religion of the sword; he also had before him in the Koran Mohammad's positive teaching about the People of the Book and his admonitions to his followers to exercise restraint in their *jihad* against Mecca, which was to be a defensive and not an aggressive war. Yet although the Western scholar has evidence in front of him that contradicts his thesis, what he "sees" is the violence of Islam. He cannot be convinced by the Koran: because Mohammad is a "liar," you cannot trust a word he says and so the evidence of the Koran is worthless. Islam *has* to be a violent religion because Europe would have it so. Peter the Venerable, a kindly, tolerant man who accused St. Bernard of a heartless intolerance when he took Abelard into Cluny after the Council of Sens, insists at the opening of his thesis that he wants to reach out toward the Muslims in love: "I approach you, not as men often do, with arms," he writes to the Muslim he imagines reading his book, "but with words; not with force but with reason, not in hatred but in love. . . . I love you, loving you I write to you, writing to you I invite you to salvation.[60] It is a positive approach, just as the translation work that he initiated in Spain was positive. Yet Peter will also ignore what is on the page in front of him and instead understand what he "knows" at some deep but obscure level to be "true" about Islam. Thus, when he read Ketton's translation of the Koran, he had before him plenty of texts which show that Mohammad urged Muslims to speak courteously with the People of the Book and to stress their common ground: "Our God and your God is one" (29:46). Yet Peter seems convinced that, alone of all religions in the world, the Koran refuses to discuss religion—unlike the Persians, the Greeks and the Romans who, in Peter's view, all sought the truth in peace. There was no substance in this belief. Muslims punished Christians who insulted Islam and the Prophet, but were perfectly ready to listen to a person of another religion expounding their religious views. Instead of reading the Koran as a whole, Peter will find an isolated verse in the Koran, take it quite out of context and then enlarge rhetorically on the meaning he extracts from this distorted text:

> For what is this? *If anyone wish to dispute with thee, say that thou hast turned thy face and the faces of thy followers to God.* O Mohammad . . . if you make no other reply, except about turning your face and the faces of your followers to God, shall I believe what you say to be true? Shall I believe you to be a true prophet of God? Shall I believe the religion which you delivered to your people to have been delivered to you by God? I shall indeed be more than a donkey if I agree; I shall be more than cattle if I consent.[61]

Words that refer to purely internal Muslim affairs have been taken as a general statement of exclusion of any other point of view. Instead, Peter claims, Islam imposes itself by the sword alone and with horrible violence. "Words fail . . . at such bestial cruelty."[62] Even a fair-minded man like Peter was impelled to lay aside reason and objectivity when he came to view Islam and still needed to see it as a violent and intolerant faith.

Neither the Annotator nor Peter the Venerable considers the Crusades. The Annotator does not recall Bernard's remark that the pagan problem can only be solved by the sword. Peter the Venerable could condemn the use of force and insist that he would approach Muslims only in a spirit of love, and yet when Louis VII left for the Crusade he wrote to him saying that he hoped he killed as many Muslims as Moses (sic) and Joshua killed Amorites and Canaanites. He wrote also to the Grand Master of the Temple, expressing his lifelong admiration of the order in its fight against the Saracens. It was a paradoxical and neurotic complex.

Just as it was impossible for Christians to see Islam as anything but a failed form of their own religion, so too it seemed impossible for them to see Islam as anything other than a violent religion, even though evidence to the contrary was staring them in the face. The Muslim had early established himself as the Christian enemy, and as such a part of the emerging identity of Western Christendom. He was, therefore, part of the Christian soul and was made to carry the burden of Western anxiety about Christian violence. Books and television programs today that sport titles like *Sword of Islam* or *Militant Islam* are still reverting to that old stereotype, and the obstinacy with which people still cling to the idea of Islam as "the religion of the sword" shows that at some level people *need* to believe it. Certainly in Israel today hawks like Raphael Eytan will justify taking a hard line with all Palestinians on the grounds that the religion of Islam teaches Muslims to believe that all men of all other faiths are their enemies and have to be destroyed with violence.[63] To make peace with them is, therefore, impossible and this means that Jewish violence is justified and necessary.

At the same time as some medievals in the West were worrying about Christian violence, many others were worrying about sex. Celibacy and chastity had been part of the Cluniac program for the Christianization of Europe. During the twelfth century the popes were still fighting a battle against married clergy and in 1215 would finally succeed in imposing celibacy. At the same time penitentials and pious sermons presented sex as an expression of Original Sin and as incompatible with holiness. Bernard himself illustrates the sexual neurosis of the period. He was a dedicated misogynist in a long tradition of Christian misogyny and was so unable to cope with his sexuality that, when his own sister came to visit him wearing a new dress, Bernard flew into a violent rage and called her a filthy whore and a clod of dung. Even Abelard and Heloise, the two great lovers of the period, did not glory in their passion like Romeo and Juliet but were both convinced that their love was deeply sinful, that marriage was a dishonorable state and that they both richly deserved the tragedy they suffered.[64] Islam does not denigrate sexual pleasure, but considers it a great gift of God, and teaches that the married state is more natural and a higher state than celibacy. Indeed, the fleshly strain that we find in the poetry of some of the troubadours was probably influenced by Arab love poetry and Muslim mystical poetry,[65] which describe both the love of men and women and the love of God in frankly erotic terms. But the Christian scholars of the period could only condemn this appreciation of sexuality and therefore they attacked "Islam" as a religion that had been deliberately set up to encourage promiscuity and lust. One biography of Mohammad by a Pisan author has Mohammad say to his followers: "You have established me as king that I may furnish you with an easier religion, by which you may both serve God and freely enjoy the delights of the world."[66] There is an ill-concealed envy in much of this. Biographies of Mohammad by Christians describe the Prophet's sex life in a manner that reveals far more about their own sexual problems than about the facts of the Prophet's life. The Koran was said, quite incorrectly, to condone homosexuality and to encourage unnatural forms of intercourse. One scholar claimed that the foulness of lust among Muslims was inexpressible; they were deep in this filth from the soles of the feet to the crown of the head.[67] Soon the Church would accuse any out-group in Christendom of excessive and unnatural sexual practices and twelfth-century Christians stigmatized the "heresy" of Islam by cursing what they considered its sexual laxity. Today we continue in this tradition: at a time when many people in the West are liberating themselves from the sexual repressions of their Christian past, Islam is constantly denigrated as a sexually repressive religion. We have completely reversed the old stereotype and not many people seem interested in the truth of the matter or wish to find out about Islam itself. They simply want to bolster their own needs against their long-established counterimage: "Islam." I will discuss this in Chapter 8.

By the time of Thomas Aquinas Islam was considered a Christian heresy that encouraged sex and violence. The Muslim had acquired a new identity in the West that was entirely a Western creation and did not spring from any real contact with Muslims. In the Crusader states, writers did not produce these fantasies because they were surrounded by real Muslims who would have made such distortion impossible. At the same time as scholars in Europe were producing this image of Islam, the Devil was becoming a new force in the Christian imagination and gaining a power he never had in the Bible. He was becoming a monster of enormous power who was also a distorted human being. Often he had animal characteristics or monstrous genitals, aspects of humanity that the Church was teaching Christians to reject. One could say that one of the great problems of ethical monotheism as expressed by Christianity is that it encourages an unhealthy projection. Because it is axiomatic that there is no evil in God, this makes it difficult for Christians to accept what is either evil or what they are told is evil in themselves. They tend to reject this "evil" and, once they have rejected it, it becomes inhuman and monstrous with threatening power. The Devil is the greatest of these projections and is unique in its horror to Christianity. The monstrous Muslim is clearly a similar projection: Christians could not accept their holy violence or their repressed sexuality, so they projected all this onto the enemies they were fighting in the Holy Land, who were already seen as the inhuman enemies of God.

There were also new fantasies about the Jews, the other victims of the Crusaders. Although the official Church prohibited the persecution of Jews, Churchmen had ambivalent attitudes which affected the people. Gregory VII pointed out that in their own Bible they had constantly sinned and God had to punish them. It also seemed inconceivable that the Jews who had witnessed Jesus' miracles and teaching could reject him, and this made people begin to see them as extraordinary beings—almost inhuman. This sense of the Jews' otherness was compounded by their use of foreign practices like circumcision, Sabbath worship and special dietary laws which set them apart from their Christian neighbors in the diaspora. And, as with many such out-groups, myths and legends developed about the Jewish people: Jews were said to have secret tails, for example, or a peculiar smell. These fears and fantasies fueled the wave of persecution that broke out each time a Crusade was preached.

In 1144, however, a new horror crept into the mythology about the people of Israel. Just before Easter and Passover a small boy called William disappeared from his home in Norwich, England, and his body was later found abandoned in the forest nearby, with many lacerations. His mother and a local priest accused the Jewish community of the murder and this was confirmed by some Christian servants who worked in a Jewish household. They claimed to have watched William's murder through a chink in the door and seen their Jewish masters crucify William and pierce his side. The local sheriff refused to believe these tales and hustled the Jews to safety in Norwich castle. Two years later, however, at the time of the Second Crusade a bishop was appointed to Norwich who approved of the cult of "Saint" William, which had flourished because of the manner of his death. There was a new anti-Semitic outbreak in the city and one Jew was killed. William's tomb now became an official cult center with pilgrims and a profusion of miracles, and this naturally led to a new hostility against his so-called murderers. At about this time another element crept into the myth. It was pointed out that the day the murder was discovered was March 22, in that year the second day of Passover.

It was well known that during this season Jews ate special unleavened bread and there was also a legend that from the moment that the Jews had sent Jesus to his death with the cry "His blood be upon us and upon our children" they had been subject to a special curse. Jews had suffered from hemorrhoids and the only remedy that could save them was, their sages said, "the blood of Christ." The sages had meant that the Jews should be converted to Christianity but the Jews had misunderstood them, with their usual perversity, and decided that they had to murder a Christ substitute each year and mix his blood with their special Passover bread. In 1146 one Theodore of Cambridge, a convert from Judaism, came forward with a tale that linked William's death with this Jewish practice. Every year, he said, a Jewish council in Toledo appointed one of the Jewish communities in the diaspora to perform this murder and acquire the necessary blood and in 1144 the lot had fallen to Norwich.[68] Two anti-Semitic legends thus became associated with William's shrine in Norwich: ritual murder and the blood libel. Stories like this circulated fast within England and Europe and every time a child disappeared in suspicious circumstances the Jews would be blamed.

What was clearly happening was that, in a rather different way from the Muslims, the Jews were being made the alien and the enemy of Christians. New fantasies would be produced about both these crusading victims as the xenophobia of Europe increased and the Jews would suffer especially from the new craze for persecuting heretics in Europe, which will be discussed in Chapter 10. The Jews were becoming inhuman and monstrous beings and, like the Muslims, were acquiring a demonic identity in the imagination of the Christian West.[69]

While Europe was building a new cultural tradition, she was increasingly haunted by inner demons which were the product of the Crusade. Meanwhile, in the Near East, Nur ad-Din was building his new empire shrewdly and rationally, content to bide his time. Even though Damascus had been forced to ask for his help against the Second Crusaders, for example, the city did not submit fully to Nur ad-Din until 1154. This submission was not gained by unrealistic violence but by means of peaceful propaganda: continually Nur ad-Din appealed to the people in the city, pointing out that *he* was their only protector against the Franks and that, by refusing to join his *jihad*, Damascus was becoming isolated from the rest of the Muslims in the area.[70] When Nur ad-Din was finally led in triumph into the city it was by popular acclaim.[71]

But at this time another *jihad* was being waged whose methods are very familiar to us today and which, at first sight, seems more irrational and closer in spirit to the emotional extremity of the Crusaders. This *jihad* had been launched by a sect from Iran, who were known by their enemies as Hashishin because they allegedly used marijuana to achieve exotic mystical states. They occupied mountain fortresses in what is now Syria and Lebanon until they had achieved what amounted to a mini-state in the mountainous region between Muslim Hama and Christian Latakia. The Hashishin were not interested in fighting the Christians; their *jihad* was aimed at Sunni Muslims and its deadly effectiveness was very useful to the Crusaders in their own struggle against the Sunnis in the area. The Hashishin were Shiites; that is, they differed from the Sunni majority in refusing to accept the Baghdad caliphate as legitimate: they believed that the leader of the Muslim world should be a direct descendant of Ali, the Prophet Mohammad's ward and son-in-law. Their *jihad* was an attempt to secure the victory of Shiism, which they believed would inaugurate a golden age under a Muslim Messianic figure known as the Hidden Imam. When they joined the esoteric sect, each of the Hashishin made a *hijra* to their seemingly inaccessible mountain fortresses, withdrawing from the world. There they practiced a form of mysticism, which introduced the initiate to secret knowledge of what they claimed was true Islam. But their *hijra* was only a prelude to their *jihad* of terrorism. Individual members undertook the murder of prominent members of the Sunni establishment in missions that were suicidally dangerous and which made the murderer a holy martyr for Islam. The Hashishin gave us our word "assassin."[72]

Though the Assassins may seem like mindless fanatics, they were, like their counterparts today, almost inhumanly rational in their *jihad*. Their suicide missions were conducted coldly and with full deliberation. Discipline was the keynote of their organization together with an absolute loyalty and obedience to their sheikh, whom the Christians called "the Old Man of the Mountain." Interestingly, the first response of the West to these Muslim terrorists was admiring and even reverent. They were even absorbed into the courtly love myth: troubadours sang of their exemplary courage, fidelity and devotion and promised to serve their ladies as selflessly as the Assassins served the Old Man of the Mountain.[73] The crusading West could easily understand this love that expressed itself in violence and was far more sympathetic to the Assassins than most other Muslims.

In 1157 Nur ad-Din became seriously ill and did not recover for nearly two years. This gave him time to reflect on his future policy and he decided that it was now time to begin the *jihad* against the

Franks in earnest. His emirs urged him to start by attacking Antioch but Nur ad-Din refused, pointing out that by rights Antioch belonged to the Byzantine Christians, not the Muslims. Cautious as ever, Nur ad-Din knew that the time was not yet ripe to make an attack on Jerusalem: Manuel had recently been able to extend his military power further into Anatolia, and this resurgence of Byzantium in the north made Nur ad-Din seek a new theater of war. He did not have to wait long. In 1162 King Amalric of Jerusalem invaded the Shiite state of Egypt, suddenly aware of the strategic value of such a conquest. Nur ad-Din, therefore, sent his commander Shirkuh to Egypt to support the Shiite Caliph there against this new Frankish offensive and in Egypt a new hero of the *jihad* was born.

# 1168–1192

## A Religious *Jihad* and a Secular Crusade

In December 1168 the young Caliph of Egypt sent a desperate message to Nur ad-Din, pleading for more military help against King Amalric, for the struggle against the Christians had entered a new phase. Amalric had recently seized Bilbays and massacred all its inhabitants, and to save Cairo from the Christians its citizens had burned down the old city in a fire which raged for fifty-four days. At once Nur ad-Din sent for his brilliant Kurdish commander Shirkuh, who had fought an extraordinary series of campaigns in Egypt during the last six years. A one-eyed, obese, tough old warrior who was worshiped by his troops, Shirkuh jumped at the chance to finish the Egyptian problem once and for all. He turned to his nephew and cried: "Yusuf, pack your things! we're going!"[1] Yusuf could scarcely have been more different from his uncle. He was a slightly built young man of thirty-one, with handsome melancholy features that would suddenly break into a dazzling smile. He had delicate health and a sensitive temperament that moved him easily and frequently to tears. Yusuf had fought in Egypt with Shirkuh two years earlier and had horrible memories of the campaign, so he was terrified when he heard his uncle's order: "I felt as if my heart had been pierced by a dagger, and I answered, 'In God's name, even if I were granted the entire kingdom of Egypt, I would not go.' "[2] But Shirkuh insisted that his presence was vital and Nur ad-Din peremptorily ordered the young man to prepare for his immediate departure. Yusuf set off, he recalled later, "like a man being led to his death."[3] Yet this reluctant young emir would become one of the most remarkable and dedicated heroes of the *jihad*. More usually known by his title Salah ad-Din (the Righteousness of the Faith), he was revered by both East and West and was the only Muslim hero to be given a Western version of his name by his admirers in Europe. What transformed Saladin into a courageous and passionate soldier of Allah?

In the event there was no fighting, for Amalric had withdrawn his troops, who had been horrified by the dedicated hatred of the Cairenes. Shirkuh was hailed as the liberator of Egypt. The Shiite state had been very powerful and a great threat to the Crusaders when they first arrived in Palestine seventy years earlier but it was now in decline and the Egyptians welcomed the chance of a strong leadership which would bring order to their country. The Caliph possessed very little real political power and Egypt was ruled by a vizier but none of the recent viziers had been able to establish a strong government. Just ten days after his arrival Shirkuh became the new vizier and Egypt became part of Nur ad-Din's empire. This drastically altered the balance of power in the Near East and the Christians of Byzantium as well as the Franks in the Crusader states were appalled by this new Muslim unity. But two months later Shirkuh died of a massive bout of overeating and a new vizier had to be elected.

There were many doughty emirs in the army who had a claim to the title but nobody wanted a strong vizier at this delicate moment in Egypt's history. Some of the Egyptians were having second thoughts about joining Nur ad-Din's Sunni empire and wanted a vizier who would be amenable to some control. Nur ad-Din himself wanted a vizier who would not make Egypt a base for his own personal power and who was not too strong a character, therefore. There was one obvious candidate. Ibn al-Athir writes that Yusuf was named as vizier "because he was the youngest, and seemingly the most inexperienced and weakest of the emirs in the army."[4]

But this reasoning was dangerous. We have seen how a sudden unexpected reversal of fortune can make a whole people feel that it has a divine destiny and the same is undoubtedly also true of individuals. Saladin suddenly found himself with the title *al-Malik al-Nasir* (the Victorious King). He was dressed in the white and gold turban of the vizier and a scarlet-lined tunic; a jewel-encrusted sword was placed in his hand and he was mounted on a splendid chestnut horse with a jeweled bridle. He was now living in the vizier's palace. A sensitive man, Saladin found this astonishing and even shocking: he, who had not wanted to come to Egypt at all, was now its honored vizier. He could only explain it as the will of God: he must have a divine calling. From the moment he was elected vizier, Saladin was a transformed man. He had a religious conversion and started to live a very devout life. As befits a Muslim ruler, he lived frugally in the midst of the luxurious trappings of his office: at the end of his life he left only forty-seven drachmas, even though he was the most powerful man in the Middle East.[5] He gave away whole provinces to anybody who asked him and distributed massive sums to the poor: his long-suffering treasurers used to keep a reserve hidden from him for emergencies. He also began a serious course of study with leading Muslim scholars and got one of them to write a catechism of the faith for his personal use, which he studied with delight. His friend and biographer Baha ad-Din says that he became a confident theologian and loved a lively debate.[6] But his faith was also distinguished by strong feeling. Whenever he was free from affairs of state, he would read the *hadith* (traditions about the life of Mohammad). He and Baha ad-Din always made the morning prayer together and Saladin would often weep with emotion. Tears would flow again when Saladin heard a particularly moving recitation of the Koran.[7] As soon as he became vizier, therefore, he had a new religious identity, centered on the beliefs, the principles and the passions of Islam.

But Saladin was convinced that God had chosen him for a specific task. Years later he said: "When God gave me the land of Egypt, I was sure that he meant Palestine for me too."[8] He had been appointed to lead the *jihad* against the Franks. It is not surprising that when he turned to religion he immediately dedicated himself to the *jihad*. He had grown up in Nur ad-Din's court and there the *jihad* was seen as essential to the integrity of Islam. What was astonishing was the depth of his commitment and the extent to which the timid young man who had begged not to accompany the army had been changed by his conversion. Baha ad-Din writes that he seemed obsessed with the *jihad*:

> The Holy War and the suffering involved in it weighed heavily on his heart and his whole being in every limb; he spoke of nothing else, thought only about equipment for the fight, was interested only in those who had taken up arms, had little sympathy with anyone who spoke of anything else or encouraged any other activity. For the love of the Holy War and on God's path he left his family and his sons, his homeland, his house and all his estates, and chose out of all the world to live in the shade of his tent, where the winds blew on him from every side.[9]

It seems that his old fears had completely gone: he never left the front line, even when he was ill—which often happened as his health was never robust. During a campaign he made it an inflexible rule to make at least one circuit of the enemy camp every day and "in the thick of battle he would move through the ranks, accompanied only by a page with a war horse led on a bridle."[10] In this way he created a sense of unity and common purpose in the army. His religious conversion had obviously unlocked the complex of his former terrors and touched reserves of strength that nobody, least of all himself, had known that he possessed. He was now a powerful and formidable man.

This confidence and sense of purpose manifested itself very quickly. In the first few months of his rule he put down a revolt in the Egyptian army and smartly repelled a joint Christian attack by Amalric and the Emperor Manuel. Then he obeyed Nur ad-Din's orders and replaced Shiite Islam with the Sunni tradition in Egypt. This was potentially very risky, as the Egyptians could have been incited to revolt when their faith was changed. Saladin himself was not wholly convinced that such a drastic step was really necessary, for the difference between Sunnis and Shiites is only political and not theological and in no way resembles the differences between Catholics and Protestants in Christianity, for example. Saladin had become very fond indeed of the young Shiite Caliph of Egypt, who was a delicate man like himself and was actually on his deathbed.[11] But events were taken out of his hands when a Sunni visitor from Mosul climbed into the pulpit of a mosque in Cairo one Friday in September 1171 and prayed in the name of the Caliph of Baghdad, whom the Shiites considered a usurper. In fact, there was no response to this potential act of provocation. The caliphate—a political institution only—had long been moribund and the Egyptians were enjoying the new security that Saladin's strong rule had been able to establish in Egypt. They were ready to accept the Sunni faith, if that was part of the package. Saladin discovered that this had actually brought him more power: once there was no longer a Caliph, the Vizier was sole head of state, in name as well as in fact. If Nur ad-Din had hoped that imposing Sunni Islam on Egypt would bring this province more firmly under his personal control, he was mistaken.

For Saladin's enthusiasm for the *jihad* brought him into direct conflict with his master. He believed that God had called *him*, not Nur ad-Din, to liberate Palestine and this seems to have caused Saladin a great deal of perplexity. If he fought under Nur ad-Din's banner this would be to surrender what he firmly believed to be his divine mission, because he, Saladin, was supposed to lead the *jihad*. The difficulty of his position appeared dramatically on two separate occasions in 1171 and 1173, when the sequence of events followed exactly the same course. Both times Saladin led an army east of the Jordan and besieged the Christian castle of Shawbak; on both occasions Nur ad-Din promptly set out from Syria to join him in this holy war effort and, at once, Saladin abandoned the siege and returned home to Egypt. He seemed very anxious indeed to avoid a confrontation with his

Sultan and he may well have feared that his newfound confidence would evaporate when he came face to face with Nur ad-Din and insisted on leading the *jihad*. By no stretch of the imagination could Nur ad-Din be reckoned one of the unworthy leaders, whom Muslims could reject on religious grounds. He was widely revered as a saint: throughout Syria, Muslims now offered prayers in his name and saw him as the savior of Islam. How could Saladin have justified his position to such a pious and committed Muslim?

Nur ad-Din himself was becoming deeply suspicious of this new Yusuf. Each time Saladin retreated from Shawbak, Nur ad-Din sent an angry missive to the young Vizier, demanding a show of obedience and loyalty. In 1174 he clearly decided that matters had gone too far and prepared an army to march to Egypt to bring its contumacious Vizier to heel and Saladin was certain that he was finished. Then it seemed that providence intervened dramatically in his life once more; on May 15, 1174, in the midst of his preparations, Nur ad-Din suddenly died of a heart attack at the age of sixty. Not surprisingly, Saladin saw this as God's confirmation of his divine mission.

The death of his master seemed to release yet another level of aggression and confidence in Saladin, which he badly needed if he was successfully to become the Sultan of Nur ad-Din's empire. Naturally there was opposition to this ambitious young man, who had seemed to be the avowed enemy of a saint. Nur ad-Din had inspired great loyalty and had a devoted following; one of his admirers was the historian Ibn al-Athir, who never wholly forgave Saladin for his behavior to his hero. In Syria, most of the emirs supported the leadership of al-Salih, Nur ad-Din's son, who was only eleven years old, and were absolutely incensed when Saladin claimed that he should be al-Salih's regent. Saladin began a long, patient campaign to win the support of the people, just as Nur ad-Din had done before him. He used the same methods and gradually, paradoxical as it may seem, he was seen as the most worthy successor of a sultan who had considered him a traitor. Saladin's greatest strength was that his new religious fervor enabled him to present himself to the common people as a devout Muslim ruler, who practiced and in some respects even surpassed the virtues of the saintly scholar and warrior Nur ad-Din. He was not only scrupulous about living frugally and giving alms generously, but he was a shining example of the accessibility that a Muslim ruler should have vis-à-vis the people. Devoted and generous as Nur ad-Din undoubtedly was, he had also been a rather formal, distant man, who tended to inspire a certain awe. Tradition says clearly that a Muslim leader must not separate himself from his people—and in our own day heads of state in the Middle East have made themselves vulnerable to revolutionary violence because they have failed to observe this important Islamic virtue. Saladin, however, astonished his contemporaries by his informality and friendly identification with the common people and his soldiers. He always ate with his soldiers and retired from them only to pray. He never demanded special treatment: he even let himself be ordered about on occasion by a troublesome servant who wanted him to sign some papers when he was exhausted. Baha ad-Din seems put in a constant state of shock by Saladin's casual manners and cheerful affability: one must remember that in general the oriental style of rule tended to be despotic at this time. When Saladin simply smiled at Baha ad-Din when his mule kicked him in the thigh or splashed him with mud, instead of threatening dire displeasure and punishment,[12] nobody could quite believe it.

It was, therefore, as a warm and affectionate human being that Saladin appealed to the people and this proved a very powerful weapon indeed against those emirs who supported the leadership of Nur ad-Din's son, who did not have this Islamic charisma. Saladin's court was revolutionary in its informality at the same time as it was a challenging return to fundamental Islamic principles. Saladin's compassion was a byword, even among his enemies the Franks. He was constantly moved to tears at the sight of suffering and on one occasion he wept bitterly when a Frankish woman came into his presence in great distress because her daughter had been taken by the Muslim soldiers during a raid. The woman said she had heard of the famous kindness of the King of the Muslims and Saladin at once ordered a search for the child, who was promptly returned to her mother.[13]

But it was his devotion to the holy war of self-defense against the Franks that did more than anything else to convince the people that Saladin was a worthy successor to the great Nur ad-Din. Saladin made very successful use of propaganda, in which the *jihad* was presented as essential to Muslim integrity, with all the zeal of Nur ad-Din. He mounted an education campaign in the army: for the first time in the history of Islam the *hadith* were read to the troops when they were drawn up for battle, and more reading and discussion of the Scriptures took place while the army was mounted in the saddle and advancing toward the enemy.[14] None of the other emirs showed such devotion to the *jihad* that had been so central to the message of Nur ad-Din. It was thus that, slowly and patiently, Saladin became head of the largest empire that the Muslim world had seen for centuries. The city of Damascus had opened its gates to him voluntarily very soon after Nur ad-Din's sudden death and Saladin followed this up by conquering the cities of Homs and Hama in Syria. He still had a long struggle ahead of him against Aleppo and Mosul, which remained loyal to al-Salih, and in 1176 he narrowly escaped being killed by the Assassins. But eventually, when al-Salih died in 1181, Saladin entered Aleppo in triumph as its ruler and for the first time in their history the Crusader states found themselves surrounded by a large and united Muslim empire that was dedicated to their destruction. How would they react?

The Christians' position was very serious indeed, once they were encircled by this new Muslim giant. They were entirely isolated in the Middle East, in much the same way as Israel is today. Their belligerent religion had not only antagonized the Muslim world and revived the practice of the *jihad* but had also alienated the Greek and oriental Christians, whom some of the Franks hated even more than they hated the Muslims. They clamorously condemned the Greek Orthodox, the Jacobite, Coptic and Armenian Christians as heretics and in doing so they very effectively alienated natural allies in the area, who would have been invaluable sources of support in the present crisis. Like Israel today, the Crusader states were entirely dependent upon support from the West but when they begged the popes and kings of Christendom to send a new Crusade to help them against Saladin, nobody came. The fiasco of the Second Crusade had made people wary of the dangers of crusading and it would take a catastrophe to inspire Europe to make a third great international assault against the Muslim world.

As if their situation were not perilous enough, the Frankish Christians were bitterly divided among themselves and, again like Israel today, they had split into two main camps, which we could call the doves and the hawks. The doves were usually men who had been born in the Middle East and who were more oriental than European in outlook. These barons believed that it was essential to keep the peace and not provoke Saladin: the Kingdom would not survive a full war against his powerful empire and it was vital, therefore, to maintain good relations until a Crusade arrived from the West. They were used to Muslims and could not regard them as the monsters that haunted the Crusaders' imagination. The hawks, however, were usually new immigrants, who had been inspired to emigrate by the intolerant crusading fanaticism of Europe. They were appalled by the friendly relations that sometimes existed between Christians and Muslims in the Holy Land and were convinced that any peace treaties with the infidel were deeply dishonorable. Christians should not resort to dovish tactics that relied on human prudence: they should trust in the Lord, who would never allow his people to lose the land that he had miraculously enabled them to win.

The hawks tended to cluster around the royal family. To add to the Franks' troubles, the new King of Jerusalem, who had succeeded his father Amalric in 1174, was a leper. Baldwin IV was a young man of immense courage and determination but he was dying: his illness meant that he was often unable to rule and had to surrender power to a regent. Nor could he control his barons, who wanted more power for themselves in the same way as barons in Europe were beginning to struggle against their kings. The King and his family, therefore, needed loyal friends and tended to woo newcomers to the Holy Land with gifts and promises of power. The chief of these hawks was the notorious Reynauld of Chatillon, who had arrived in the East shortly after the fall of Edessa in 1147, greedy for gold and Muslim blood. He had married the widow of Raymund of Antioch, Eleanor's friend, and taken control of the principality, and for ten years he pursued a career of brutal cruelty which naturally stirred up local hostility to the Franks. In 1156, for example, during a quarrel with Emperor Manuel of Byzantium, he had tortured the Patriarch of Antioch, coated his wounds with honey and exposed his body to the glaring sun so that it was ravaged by insects. The Patriarch capitulated and gave him enough money from Church funds to mount a devastating attack on the Byzantine island of Cyprus, which he pillaged so savagely that it has never fully recovered from the assault. He massacred thousands of men, women and children and finally gathered all the Greek monks together, cut off their noses and sent them back to Constantinople. Reynauld would have had no compunction about wounding his fellow Christians in this way: a typical Crusader, he saw the Greek Orthodox as heretics and therefore worthy of such punishment. Reynauld also looted Muslim territory and his frequent raids of brutal plunder and vandalism must have helped Nur ad-Din's propaganda for the *jihad*. It was during one such raid in 1157 that he was captured by the Muslims in country north of Aleppo and he remained a prisoner until al-Salih released him in 1175. Not surprisingly, he returned to the Crusader states seething with hatred of Muslims and at once put himself on the front line of the holy war against Islam by marrying the heiress of Moab, Krak and Shawbak, east of the Jordan, which, we have seen, had been besieged twice by Saladin in the last four years.

Another leading hawk was Gerard of Ridfort, who had come east in 1173. He had first taken service under the dovish leader Count Raymund of Tripolis, and Raymund had promised him the hand of the next available heiress. But the following year, when a suitable heiress did become available, Raymund broke his promise and gave her to a wealthy Pisan merchant, who somewhat ingallantly put her on the scales and offered Raymund her weight in gold. (Apparently the lady weighed about 140 pounds). Gerard never forgave Raymund: he left Tripolis in a huff and joined the Templars, rose swiftly through the ranks and became Grand Master in 1179—a crucial position in the Kingdom. He continued to hate all doves like Raymund and was full of the same aggressive chauvinism as Reynauld, as his subsequent behavior showed clearly.

In 1180 two new hawks joined the royal circle. First was the new immigrant Guy of Lusignan. He was a handsome but ineffectual man yet he became very important in the Kingdom of Jerusalem when he married the Princess Sibylla. The marriage in itself had caused a scandal because, in order to get Guy, Sibylla had jilted the very important dovish baron Baldwin of Ibelin. The insult to this venerable baronial family had been serious enough but it was even more scandalous that this foolish young man was a possible heir to the throne: the only other person in line was the child Baldwin, Sibylla's son by a previous marriage. That same year there was another scandal when Agnes, the Queen Mother, secured the appointment of Heraclius, Archbishop of Caesarea, to the patriarchate of Jerusalem. His good looks seem to have been his only qualification for the post. He too was an archdove and had been elected over the head of the historian William, Archbishop of Tyre, who was a much more serious candidate. William, who was a committed dove, ended his *Deeds Done Beyond the Sea*, a long history of the Crusader states, shortly afterward, sickened by the state of the country and too disgusted to continue his work:

> Up to the present time, in the preceding books, we have described to the best of our ability the remarkable deeds of the brave men who for eighty years and more have held the ruling power in our part of the Orient, and particularly at Jerusalem. Now, in utter detestation of the present, amazed at the material which is presented before our eyes . . . we lack the courage to continue. In the acts of our princes there is nothing which seems to a wise man worthy of being committed to the treasure house of the memory, nothing which can contribute refreshment to the reader or confer honour on the writer. Truly we can lament with the prophet [Jeremiah] that there has perished from our midst "law from the priest, counsel from the wise and the word from the prophet."[15]

Jeremiah had predicted that the sins of Israel would cause the chosen people to lose their land and his prophecy had come true when the Jews were deported to Babylon in 589 B.C.E. It seemed as though the

Crusaders, God's new chosen people, were now facing the loss of their Kingdom, entirely through their own stupidity and intolerance.

During the first years of the Leper King's reign, Raymund of Tripolis, the leader of the doves, had been the regent and he had worked hard to keep the peace. Raymund looked more like an Oriental than a Westerner, with his dark, tanned skin and hooked nose. He spoke fluent Arabic, read Arabic and Islamic texts and naturally saw the Muslims as normal human beings, not as monstrous enemies of God. He wanted the country to survive and was not willing to risk national security by making the Kingdom of Jerusalem the aggressive vanguard of Christendom. Saladin was not yet strong enough to launch a full-scale attack on the Kingdom but, with a wary eye to the future, Raymund pursued a policy of appeasement. In 1177, however, the Leper King Baldwin took up his kingship and Saladin took advantage of the transition to make a surprise attack on the Kingdom. It was an uncharacteristically rash decision; Saladin was soundly defeated but Muslim enthusiasts continued to infiltrate the Christian states and ravaged the countryside. The attack was a frightening demonstration of the new Christian vulnerability in the Middle East: any moment of internal weakness would be an invitation to the Muslims to attack. King Baldwin asked Saladin for a truce and Saladin was glad to agree: the harvest had been bad that year and he was not yet ready for a full-scale war.

But even if it had not been convenient, Saladin would have had to make peace, and here we see an essential difference between the Christian extremists in a Crusade and an extremist in the Islamic *jihad*. The Koran says that war is so obnoxious that, provided the conditions are not harmful to Islam, Muslims must cooperate if the enemy proposes a truce or asks for talks, even though a truce should not exceed ten years (8:62–63). However keen Saladin was to expel the Franks from Palestine, he could not present himself to his own people as a pious Muslim and refuse to sign an acceptable truce without damaging his Muslim integrity. Saladin was always very scrupulous about this and never broke a truce in his life.

A Christian hawk like Reynauld of Chatillon, however, felt that a truce was quite incompatible with his religious integrity. From his castles on the east bank of the Jordan, Reynauld could watch the rich Muslim caravans marching along the trade routes to the infidel city of Mecca and the sight was an intolerable temptation. In the summer of 1181 he attacked one of these caravans, which was accompanied by a band of pilgrims who were making the *hajj*. This flagrant and deliberate breach of the truce released Saladin from his obligations but, even more shockingly, Reynauld followed this assault by setting out to attack Medina. Saladin's nephew Faruk-Shah quickly intercepted Reynauld and drove him back to Moab but the whole incident had been deliberately provocative. By threatening Medina, the site of the Prophet's grave, and violating the sanctity of the *hajj* Reynauld had made an unequivocal assault on the integrity of Islam. He would repeat this sacrilegious attack on two more occasions. In Reynauld, we can see the danger of religious extremists in the state of Israel today, who also think that a peace treaty with the Arabs is sinful and who are fighting a holy war against Islam. I shall discuss their views in the next chapter.

Reynauld refused to climb down and apologize: even the Leper King could not make him return the booty he had seized. When Saladin retaliated by capturing a Christian pilgrim ship and taking 150 pilgrims as hostages, Reynauld still refused to return the booty. No one knows what happened to the hostages; they probably became slaves. Reynauld's aggressive bravado had damaged the whole country because, released from the obligations of the truce, Muslims began to make raids in Christian territory. Villages and crops were devastated in Galilee, Beirut was besieged and the Muslims conquered the Christian fortress of Habis Jaldack in the Transjordan. More importantly, Saladin's prestige increased in the Muslim world, for Reynauld had shown the Muslims that the Christians were indeed dangerous enemies to Muslims and to Islam. There were more converts to the ideal of the *jihad*.

As the Muslims became more united, the Christians in the Kingdom of Jerusalem came to the brink of civil war. King Baldwin had been persuaded by his hawkish advisers that Raymund had been plotting against the government. When Raymund, who had recently married the heiress of Tiberias in Galilee, set out to take possession of his new territory, Baldwin would not let him enter the Kingdom and it was only after furious protests by the barons that the King was persuaded of Raymund's innocence. The incident showed how the sick young King was being pushed in the direction of war by his advisers. The same advisers had urged him to support Reynauld the previous year. Later in 1181 the King became so ill that it was clear he was no longer capable of rule, and this time the King appointed the weak and ignorant Guy of Lusignan as regent. Guy, who seemed not to have a single independent idea in his head, had none of the decisive qualities that were necessary in this perilous situation.

These internal quarrels were extremely dangerous, happening, as they did, when Saladin was completing the building of his united empire. Common prudence should have suggested not only that this civil strife should be patched up as quickly as possible but also that the Franks should keep a low profile in the area until they had got their own house in order. Such reasoning was, of course, anathema to the hawks, who believed that Christians should throw caution to the winds as a sign of their faith in God, and it was in that disastrous year 1181 that Reynauld made his most provocative assault on Islam—an assault that was different in kind from anything attempted by a Crusader before. The consequences for the Kingdom were disastrous. Reynauld's plan was not only to mount an attack on the holy city of Medina but to attack Mecca itself, the holiest city in the Muslim world. He would drag the Prophet, "the accursed camel driver," from his grave and then press on to Mecca and raze the Ka'aba to the ground. There was a remarkable flair and simplicity in this plot: Reynauld built a fleet of collapsible ships, tested them on the Dead Sea, dismantled them again and conveyed them 130 miles through the Negev to the port of Eilat on the Gulf of Aqaba. Then Reynauld's Christian pirates sailed into the Red Sea, looting and pillaging the ports of Arabia, until they reached the port of Rabiqh, near Mecca. There was terror in the holy city: it was centuries since anybody had threatened to violate its holiness and Reynauld, or Brinz Arnat as he was known, became the enemy of the whole Muslim world, just as he would have wished.

Fortunately Saladin's brother Saif ad-Din al-Adil rushed from Egypt to the rescue, defeated the Christian navy and carried the prisoners into Medina, lashed to the backs of camels. The pirates were executed but Reynauld, who had already returned to Moab, escaped this fate and would live to do even more damage to peace in the Middle East. When Saladin heard of the attack he vowed to kill Reynauld with his own hands. Not surprisingly, this deliberate provocation greatly enhanced Saladin's position. His *jihad* was now seen as essential, for the Christians had shown themselves in their true colors. No Muslim could ignore a projected attack on Mecca; they might not be willing to fight themselves, but all would have to give at least notional support to the holy war of self-defense against the Franks. In 1183, as we have seen, Saladin became lord of Aleppo and the most powerful ruler in the Middle East: he could now afford to begin the liberation of Palestine. In September 1183 his army crossed the Jordan and invaded Galilee. Guy instantly mobilized the Kingdom and the army camped opposite Saladin at the Pools of Goliath. Hawks like Reynauld urged Guy to attack but Baldwin of Ibelin and his brother Balian told him to sit tight; it would be fatal to attack Saladin's numerically superior army, but the Sultan would not be able to keep his army together in hostile territory for long: the troops would have to go home for the harvest. They were proved right. Saladin tried to lure the Christians into battle but they sat still and eventually Saladin was forced to retire.

Yet this victory did Guy no good at all: he had not only quarreled with the hawks and been despised by the common soldiers because of his passive stance before Islam, but the King dismissed him from the regency and reinstated Raymund. The doves seemed ascendant once more and Baldwin made a will that would make Raymund regent after his imminent death: if his little nephew Baldwin V should die before reaching the age of ten, the succession must be decided by the Pope, the Holy Roman Emperor and the Kings of France and England. Baldwin also made a valiant attempt to unite the royal and baronial parties. In 1180 it had been agreed to marry the King's half sister Isabella, who was also the stepdaughter of Balian of Ibelin, to the young Humphrey of Toron, the stepson of Reynauld of Chatillon. Isabella was now eleven years old and ready for the marriage. The wedding would be a powerful symbol of the unity of the doves and the hawks.

In fact the wedding of Humphrey and Isabella was devastated by the *jihad*. Reynauld had insisted that it should take place in his castle at Kerak in Transjordan. During the celebrations the wedding guests heard that Saladin was approaching with his army. Reynauld's castles were old targets for Saladin, who set up eight catapults and began to bombard the walls with huge rocks. The story of the wedding of Kerak shows how very different things could have been between Christians and Muslims, for both sides responded to the situation with a courtly flair and imagination. Even though the rocks were making the mighty walls of the castle shudder, the celebrations gamely continued and the Franks courteously sent out some of the special wedding food for Saladin. They explained that a wedding was in progress, and Saladin gave orders to his men not to attack the wing of the castle where the young couple was spending the night. Eventually Saladin could make no headway against the powerfully fortified castle and had to retire. Baldwin IV, who had been too ill to attend the celebrations, had hurried to defend the castle with his troops and was carried into it on a litter in triumph. The grand gesture of Kerak had come to have a different meaning from that which had been intended. It did not unite the wedding guests, who left the castle as bitterly divided as ever. The wedding had shown the vulnerability of the Christian state: now that the Muslims were determined to destroy the Kingdom of Jerusalem, the Franks would always have to be ready for battle.

They could never relax completely in joyous celebrations, because the enemy was always at the gate. The incident also showed that Muslims and Christians actually shared many of the same courtly values and on this level could respond to one another very well. Sadly, what drove them apart was their religion.

In March 1185 Baldwin IV finally died of his leprosy and his will came into effect. The little Baldwin V, who was only seven years old, succeeded to the throne and Raymund became the regent. At a council of war he asked the barons what should be done. The country was in no state for war and the barons agreed that Raymund should ask Saladin for a truce. A truce was agreed for four years and the Crusader state tried to build up trade again and, above all, to persuade the West to send a Crusade to help them. But the peace did not last long. In August 1186 Baldwin V died at Acre; Raymund was present at his death together with Joscelin the Seneschal and afterward Joscelin advised Raymund to return to Tiberias and call an assembly of the barons to discuss the implementation of Baldwin IV's will, which had made provision for the succession. He himself would convey the little corpse to Jerusalem for burial.

Yet Joscelin proved to be privy to a palace plot, for while Raymund was at Tiberias there was a coup. In the Holy Sepulchre, the Patriarch Heraclius crowned Guy and Sibylla King and Queen of Jerusalem: Gerard of Ridfort witnessed the ceremony. At first the barons tried to stage a countercoup by presenting Humphrey of Toron and Isabella as claimants to the throne, but at the last moment Humphrey broke down and rushed to Guy to beg for forgiveness. The barons realized that all was lost and they all submitted, except for Baldwin of Ibelin, who left the country in disgust, and Raymund of Tripolis, who withdrew to his lands in Galilee.

At this point Reynauld of Chatillon broke the truce again. For the last three years he had been kept in check by Raymund but now that Guy was king his energies were unleashed once more. Only a few weeks after the coup he attacked another caravan of merchants and pilgrims on their way to Mecca, massacred all the armed men and herded the rest into captivity in his castle. One of the captives was Saladin's sister. When one of the prisoners actually dared to remind Reynauld of the truce, he scornfully replied: "Let your Mohammad come and rescue you!"[16] The same pattern of events repeated itself. Saladin said that if Reynauld restored the booty and freed the prisoners he would honor the truce. Naturally Reynauld refused and Saladin swore that he would slay him with his own hands.

Saladin now called a full *jihad* against the Franks, the enemy of

Islam. Thousands of cavalry and infantry began to stream toward Damascus from all over his empire. Damascus was crammed with soldiers and waving banners, and surrounded by a mass of camel-skin tents in which the soldiers sheltered themselves from the sun. For the first time for centuries, Islam was mobilized in an effective full-scale holy war. Yet still the Christians did not seem to appreciate their peril and continued to quarrel about their own concerns. Raymund saw the end of the kingdom approaching irrevocably, and to salvage something from the wreck he made a private treaty with Saladin, who in return promised not to attack Tripolis and Galilee. This was treasonous and it gravely damaged the Christian resistance, because Guy was now deprived of all Raymund's troops. The hawks acted with their usual belligerence and set out with Guy to attack Raymund at Tiberias. Balian of Ibelin had to come forward and explain to Guy the obvious fact that if he attacked Raymund with his depleted troops Saladin would attack them with his massive army because Raymund was his ally. The whole army would be destroyed. Guy tended to agree with the last person to speak to him strongly and he called off the attack.

Encouraged by this success, Balian decided to try to arrange a peace between Raymund and Guy, so that the Christians could meet Saladin with a fully united front. He went to Guy and explained to him how isolated he was. Antioch had made a truce with Saladin, to dissociate itself from the dangerous folly of the Kingdom of Jerusalem. Guy had lost his best knight in Baldwin of Ibelin. If he lost Raymund too, he was finished. Guy agreed to try to make peace and on April 29, 1187, a peace delegation, led by the Grand Masters of the Temple and the Hospital, set out for Tiberias, planning to meet Balian later in the castle of La Feve in the Plain of Esdraelon in Galilee.

On April 30 Saladin's son al-Afdal approached Raymund with a request: could the Muslims send a reconnaissance party through Galilee? Raymund could not refuse this embarrassing request from his new ally and gave permission for the Muslims to enter his territory, provided that they did no harm to any town or village and went back to their own territory before nightfall. Al-Afdal readily agreed and Raymund issued orders that all the people of Galilee should remain in their homes the next day. On May 1 he watched an army of 7000 Muslims ride past his castle in Tiberias into Galilee. That evening he watched them ride back as agreed, leaving the country before nightfall. However, on the spear of each of the vanguard was the head of a Templar knight.

Raymund's orders had reached La Feve on the evening of April 30 and there was Guy's delegation, waiting for Balian of Ibelin, who had not yet arrived. When Gerard of Ridfort heard that the traitor Raymund had ordered him to hide from the Muslims, it was more than his hawkish heart could stand. He sent out orders to all the Templars in the area to join him at La Feve. James Mailly, the Marshal of the Temple, duly turned up with ninety knights, and the following morning forty secular knights joined them from Nazareth. The little band of Christians rode out to find the Muslims but, when they saw the large host watering their horses at the springs of Cresson near Nazareth, James Mailly and the Master of the Hospital quite sensibly wanted to turn back. Gerard was disgusted. He taunted the Master of the Hospital with cowardice and sneered at James: "You love your blond head too much to want to lose it."[17] Templars had vowed absolute obedience to their Master, and James replied: "I shall die in battle like a brave man. It is you who will flee as a traitor."[18] In the spirit of Roland at Roncesvalles, Gerard led the company in a suicidal charge against the Muslim army: it was a massacre. All but three of the Templars and knights were slain, and among the three survivors was Gerard of Ridfort.

The disaster of Cresson shook the whole Kingdom. Inevitably there was an outcry against Raymund of Tripolis, who was accused of conversion to Islam. Raymund himself was shaken by the disaster, so he agreed to break his treaty with Saladin and put his troops at the disposal of the King, and the Franks began to mobilize their forces to meet the Muslim threat. The entire army of the Kingdom of Jerusalem gathered at Acre and then marched from Acre to Sephoria; but, says Ibn al-Athir, "they were reluctant and demoralized." The Muslims themselves were not entirely convinced that a pitched battle was a good idea. Some of the emirs advised Saladin to weaken the enemy by repeated skirmishes instead; others said that the Muslims were beginning to get impatient: when was this famous *jihad* going to be fought? Saladin himself concluded that the Muslims could not let this opportunity pass without "striking a tremendous blow for the *jihad*."[19] The battle must be fought before the autumn, which was the end of the fighting season, for the troops had to return home for the harvest. But would the Franks, who could be very cautious warriors, as he had discovered in 1183, be lured into battle?

He decided to lay a trap for them and prayed that the Franks would walk into it. On July 1 he took his army over the Jordan into Galilee, camped half of it near the lake and with the other half he attacked Tiberias, which fell to the Muslims after an hour of fighting. Raymund and his sons were at Sephoria with the army but the civilians of the city took refuge with the Countess in the garrison and she sent word to her husband to tell him what had happened.

Twenty miles away in Sephoria, the Franks engaged in a fierce argument about what should be done, and the doves and the hawks both tried to persuade Guy, who was dithering as usual, to follow their policies. Raymund was for staying put. He understood Saladin's plan and though Tiberias was his own city he was prepared to let it go for the time being. He knew that nothing dreadful would happen to his wife and the citizens of Tiberias. They would simply be taken to Damascus and could easily be ransomed later. If the Christians just stayed put, Saladin would have to go back home again, as he had in 1183, and then the Christians would easily reconquer Tiberias. At present it was better to lose one city than to risk the whole army and lose the whole Kingdom.[20] This was a disgusting policy to hawks like Reynauld of Chatillon. He accused Raymund of being a Muslim-lover, waved aside his arguments about the immense size of Saladin's army ("a large load of fuel will be good for the fires of hell!"[21]) and urged the King to cast aside these timid, prudent policies and fling his army bravely against the enemy of God.

Guy himself was in a dilemma. He had suffered gravely when he followed Raymund's advice in 1183 and he was bound, as a feudal monarch, to go to help his vassals in Tiberias. But after the shock of the Cresson massacre, he was less inclined to listen to Reynauld's suicidal belligerence, and at the end of the council of war he decided to side with Raymund. Unfortunately he obeyed the last speaker to address him sternly, as was his wont. Late at night Gerard of Ridfort, the "hero" of Cresson, went secretly to his tent and chided him severely for listening to the traitor Raymund.

This is the first task which has fallen to you since you were crowned. And know well that rather than see that, the Templars would put on their white mantles and sell and pawn them lest the humiliation the Saracens have caused me and all of them together be not avenged. Go have it announced throughout the army that all should arm and every man go to his company and follow the standard of the Holy Cross.[22]

As usual Guy did what he was told; the army assembled itself and started to march toward Tiberias. Saladin could not believe his luck as he watched the Franks fall neatly into his trap. An extreme religious chauvinism that ignored normal reasoning and military and political good sense had pushed the whole Christian army into a battle that it was most unlikely to win. The fanaticism of a disaffected minority had prevailed over the more peaceful and sensibly secular policies of the barons, and the Kingdom of Jerusalem had been put at the mercy of an enemy that was determined to annihilate it.

The army trekked across the hills of Galilee in the blazing summer heat, burdened by its armor and equipment. A journey that should have taken only a few hours lasted all day. Saladin sent snipers to follow the rear guard and pick off any stragglers. He had cut off the normal water supplies and many wells and springs had been dried up, so the soldiers were half crazed with thirst. Eventually they arrived at the Sea of Galilee in an exhausted state to discover that Saladin's camp had cut them off from the water. Some of the barons urged the king to fight their way through to the lake, but Guy was moved by the plight of his soldiers and the pleas of the Templars to pitch camp for the night. They camped on slopes near the hill called the Horns of Hittin, where Jesus was traditionally supposed to have preached his pacifist religion in the Sermon on the Mount. The barons thought that there was a well at the site of the camp, but on arrival they found that it was dry. Raymund of Tripolis, cried aloud, "Ah, Lord God, the war is over; we are dead men; the kingdom is finished."[23]

The misery of the Christians, most of whom were becoming dangerously dehydrated, was increased by the Muslims, who burned large fires which sent acrid smoke in their direction. Even worse were the sounds of jubilation from Saladin's camp. There the fresh, rested Muslims suddenly saw victory in their grasp in a reversal that they had not expected and, as one would expect, there was a new burst of religious fervor. July 3 that year was the night of 26/27 Ramadan, the holiest night of the Muslim year, for it was the night that Mohammad had received the first words of the Koran from God. As the Koran says, this night of Qadr (destiny) is better "than a thousand months":

On that night the angels and the Spirit by their Lord's leave come
     down with his decrees.
That night is peace, till break of dawn. (97:5)

As they waited for the dawn, the men of Saladin's army waited for a divine judgment. Saladin's secretary and chancellor Imad ad-Din al-Isfahani saw the night of Qadr that year as the separation of Good and Evil:

Night separated the two sides and the cavalry barred both roads.
Islam passed the night face to face with unbelief, monotheism at

war with Trinitarianism, the way of righteousness looking down upon error, faith opposing polytheism. Meanwhile the several circles of Hell prepared themselves and the several ranks of Heaven congratulated themselves. Malik [the Guardian of Hell] waited and Ridwan [the Guardian of Paradise] rejoiced.[24]

The approaching victory had increased the conviction of the righteousness of the *jihad*, as is always the case in a holy war. Spontaneously the Muslims interpreted the coincidence of the date as a providential decree, just as the Christians had seen a divine significance in the date of their conquest of Jerusalem in 1099. This *jihad* was no ordinary war of conquest for Saladin's soldiers of Allah; it was a cosmic battle and an act of salvation history.

But Saladin continued to plan practically and carefully; he had no intention of abandoning wise policy for holy enthusiasm, and while his men were chanting hymns and praises, he deployed them around the Christian camp until it was completely encircled. As the chronicler says, not a cat could have slipped through the net. After the dawn had ended the peace of the night of Qadr, the Muslim assault began. The Christian infantry could only think of water and they rushed down the hill toward the Sea of Galilee that was glinting invitingly. They were driven back up the hill and either slaughtered or taken prisoner; hundreds of men lay on the hillside, wounded and with swollen, blackened mouths. The cavalry, however, fought bravely. Raymund of Tripolis led a charge that succeeded in breaking the Muslim line, but then the Muslims simply closed behind them and they could not rejoin their companions. Raymund escaped from the battle but died of rage and grief soon afterward. Balian of Ibelin also fought his way out and was one of the last Christians to escape. The cavalry continued to charge against the enemy and eventually Saladin and his son al-Afdal watched the royal tent overturned on the Horns of Hittin where the King had retreated. At that moment Saladin knew that his dream had become an established fact. "My father dismounted and bowed to the ground," al-Afdal recalls, "giving thanks to God with tears of joy."[25] The Christian army had been soundly defeated and the Kingdom of Jerusalem was lost.

After the battle Saladin had two important prisoners of war brought to his tent: King Guy and Reynauld of Chatillon. Both men were half dead with exhaustion and made desperate with thirst. Saladin handed a goblet of water iced with the snows of Mount Hermon to Guy, who drank and passed the goblet to Reynauld. It is a custom in the Arab world that a host may not kill a man to whom he has given food or drink and when Saladin saw Reynauld drinking he pointed out that he had not given *him* permission to drink. "I am not therefore obliged to show him mercy," he said with a terrible smile.[26] He then took his sword and cut off Reynauld's head and dragged the corpse to the feet of the terrified Guy. Yet to Guy Saladin mildly remarked that one king did not kill another and he explained kindly that Reynauld had only been executed because of his great crimes and treachery. Guy was taken to Damascus for a time and then allowed to go free. This famous story perfectly illustrates Saladin's attitude, which is a new one in the holy war. He did not want to massacre all the Christians indiscriminately, on the Joshuan model. To individual Christians like Guy he could be kind, almost to a fault. To release the king of a people you have just conquered is not a very wise policy and Saladin would pay dearly for this kind of clemency. Reynauld, however, who had planned to attack Mecca, could expect no mercy. A few days later Saladin had all the prisoners of war who belonged to the military orders brought into his presence and massacred in cold blood. The Sufis in his army begged for the honor of killing one prisoner each and Saladin watched the executions smiling with joy. He rightly judged that, of all the Christians in the Holy Land, they were the ones most dedicated to the war against Islam. Imad ad-Din, who was present at the massacre, wrote in his history of Saladin: "On that day I saw how he killed unbelief to give life to Islam and destroyed polytheism to build monotheism."[27] The massacre was a religious act of salvation.

Yet the Koran states clearly that prisoners of war must not be ill treated in any way and that, once the fighting is over, prisoners should either be ransomed or released as a favor, as Saladin released Guy (47:5). Prisoners whose ransoms remained unpaid were to be distributed among those who had taken part in the fighting and were to be allowed to earn enough money to pay the ransom themselves; their captors were admonished to help them out of their own pockets (24:34), for the ransoming of captives was considered to be a highly commendable act (2:178). The *hadith* lay down even more stringent requirements. Mohammad directs Muslims to treat their prisoners as full members of their own family: "You must feed them as you feed yourselves, and clothe them as you clothe yourselves, and if you should set them a hard task, you must help them in it yourselves.[28] Ill-treatment became the prisoner's ransom and if a captive were cruelly treated he must be allowed to go free. In general the Muslims seem to have observed these practices but Saladin's massacre seems a flagrant breach of this humane code and marks a new level of intransigence in the *jihad*. The Koran does say that punishment can "be proportionate to the wrong that has been done you" and it may be that the massacre was seen as a retaliation for all the savage massacres that the Christians had inflicted upon the Muslims, but the Koran immediately goes on to recommend forgiveness: "It shall be best for you to endure your wrongs in patience" (16:127). However, the Koran is also very emphatic about the importance of steadfastness and determination in war. One way of limiting the horrors of war was to bring the fighting to a speedy conclusion and to that end Muslims must take firm measures to ensure that hostilities cease as soon as possible. To release or to allow to be ransomed people who had so recently shown themselves to be dedicated enemies of Islam, like Reynauld and the Templars, would mean that there would simply be more Christian atrocities and more fighting. Saladin seems to have been torn between his natural compassion and his determination to rid Palestine of the Christian menace and, as we shall see, this led him into trouble.

Because the whole Christian army had been destroyed at Hittin, there could be no major opposition to Saladin's occupation of the rest of the Kingdom of Jerusalem. Knights who escaped from the battle and civilians who fled from the occupying Muslim army began to congregate in Tyre, where they established themselves under the leadership of one Conrad of Montferrat, who had only been in the Holy Land by the merest chance. A resident of Constantinople, he had been involved in a murder there and hurriedly escaped as a "pilgrim" to Jerusalem. As his ship approached Acre he noticed that the town seemed to be deserted and naturally he thought that this was odd. When he heard about the Christian defeat he immediately set off to Tyre to organize the Christian resistance there and it was due to his prompt action that the Franks managed to keep this last foothold in the Holy Land. Other committed knights did not merely seek a refuge in Tyre but went straight off to Jerusalem to try to save the Holy City from the infidel. Ibn al-Athir tells us that many survivors of Hittin concentrated there, together with the civilians in the area and the inhabitants of Askelon. There was "a great concourse of people there, each one of whom would choose death rather than see the Muslims in power in their city."[29] Jerusalem was crucial to the Christian holy war and must be defended to the bitter end.

It had also become important to the Muslims and here again Saladin pushed the Muslim *jihad* into a new direction. In the Jewish and the Christian holy wars the idea of a holy land is crucial but this is not the case with the *jihad*. Indeed many Muslims right up to the present day would consider the veneration of a "holy land" to be idolatry, because it is raising a mere physical reality to an unacceptably high

status. Certainly Muslims regard Mecca as a holy city but their pilgrimage there is an affirmation of faith, not contact with a land which
is intrinsically or physically holy. Mecca is sacred because of its associations with the roots of the religion, and when the Caliph Omar
conquered Jerusalem in 637 Jerusalem became the third most holy
city in Islam and a place of pilgrimage for Muslims because it had
associations with Mohammad and some of the earlier prophets. Saladin
had originally been inspired to fight the Franks because they were the
enemies and oppressors of the Muslim people, rather than by a passionate devotion to Jerusalem.

But Jerusalem has important associations for Muslims. When Saladin and his army arrived outside the city walls and camped on the
Mount of Olives opposite the city, the Sultan at once asked to be
taken to a spot where he could see the Dome of the Rock and al-
Aqsa, the old Muslim shrines that dominate the city. He was aware
that the conquest of *this* city was quite different from his conquest of
the other cities of Palestine and he gave a rousing sermon to his army,
reminding them of the importance of Jerusalem in the Islamic revelation. The very first Muslims had prayed facing Jerusalem, he told
them; the Prophet Mohammad had made his Night Journey there in
the years before the *hijra* to Medina: he had alighted on the ancient
Rock and thence ascended to heaven and spoken with Moses and
Jesus, linking Islam with the two older religions. Jerusalem was also
associated with the ancient Jewish prophets of God's revelation, and
with David, Solomon and Mary, the mother of Jesus. At the end of
his sermon, Imad ad-Din tells us, Saladin vowed to restore Jerusalem
to Islam and "took an oath not to depart until he had honoured his
word and raised his standard on the highest point and had visited
with his own feet the place where the Prophet had set foot."[30] After
Saladin had finished speaking, his soldiers looked at the holy city of
al-Quds with new eyes and found a new motive for fighting the Franks,
who had profaned the Dome of the Rock with a cross. When the
Franks had conquered Jerusalem eighty years earlier, there had been
no great outcry about its loss in the Islamic world and indeed most
Muslims seemed to have been even more indifferent to its fate than
they were about the massacres and the plight of the refugees. But,
right up to the present day, actually confronting Jerusalem stirs up
very deep feelings in people of all three religions. In the summer of
1187 Christians and Muslims prepared to do battle once more for the
Holy City.

The Christians were desperately afraid and for good reason. However many thousands of people had congregated in Jerusalem, they

could not oppose Saladin's powerful army effectively, because they had no knight there who was experienced enough to lead the battle and most of them were civilians. Would Saladin deal with them as they had dealt with the Muslims in 1099? Then, as if in answer to their prayers, the distinguished baron Balian of Ibelin arrived. He had no intention of taking part in the fight for Jerusalem. After Hittin he had had enough of war and had simply come back to collect his wife, who had been in Jerusalem at the time of the Battle of Hittin, and take her back to Tyre. He explained this to Saladin and courteously asked Saladin's permission to enter the city; the Sultan granted his request on condition that he stayed there only one night.[31] Balian swore to observe this condition and entered the city. Once inside, however, the people begged him to stay and lead them in their final desperate struggle. Balian felt deeply torn. He had a duty to protect his people and also a religious duty to defend Jerusalem, but he had given his word to Saladin that he would not stay in the city. To resolve his dilemma he took a course of action that gives us another clear example of the mutual respect and consideration that could have existed between the Muslims and the Christians, if only religious idealism had not come between them. He went to Saladin to explain his position and Saladin gave serious thought to the problem. Eventually he concluded that, since Balian felt that he had a religious duty to stay, he would release him from his oath. Both men believed in the same code of honor; both respected the sanctity of an oath.[32] Balian did not think that religion absolved him from an oath with an infidel, as Reynauld had, and Saladin was able to enter sympathetically into Balian's position, even if this worked out to his disadvantage.

Saladin had made the Christians an offer. If they handed the city to him unconditionally there would be no bloodshed. The Christians, predictably, refused this offer and the fighting began.[33] It was soon clear to them that they had absolutely no chance at all and would have to sue for peace, but now Saladin took a hard line. They had refused his offer of a peaceful solution so now, he swore, "We shall deal with you, just as you dealt with the population when you took it . . . with murder and enslavement and other such savageries."[34] The whirligig of time had brought its revenge to the Christians and added a new twist of horror to the vicious cycle of the holy war. The Christians sat and waited for death, but then Balian came up with a solution. He went to Saladin again and made a desperate threat. There were a large number of people in the city, he said, but at the moment they were only fighting halfheartedly because they were still hoping that Saladin would spare them with his usual celebrated clemency. But if they saw that death was certain they would take truly desperate measures:

> If we see that death is inevitable, then, by God, we shall kill our children and our wives, burn our possessions, so as not to leave you with a *dinar* or a *drachma* or a single man or woman to enslave. When this is done, we shall pull down the Sanctuary of the Rock and the Mosque of al-Aqsa and the other sacred places, slaughtering the Muslim prisoners we hold—5,000 of them—and killing every horse and animal we possess. Then we shall come out to fight you like men fighting for their lives, when each man, before he falls dead, kills his equal.[35]

Saladin consulted with the imams and jurists in his army. Was it lawful for him to break the oath that he had sworn to take the city with bloodshed, if he could thereby spare the holy mosques? They decided that it was and Saladin prepared to occupy the city peacefully, but his financial advisers insisted that he take the Christians prisoner and demand adequate ransoms.[36]

On October 2, 1187, Saladin and his army entered Jerusalem as conquerors and for the next eight hundred years Jerusalem would remain a Muslim city. In the next chapter we shall see that its conquest by the Jewish state in 1967 initiated a fresh round of holy wars in the Middle East. By another holy coincidence that was fervently noted by the Arab chroniclers, Saladin's victory occurred that year on the day when Muslims commemorated Mohammad's Night Journey. Saladin kept his word, and conquered the city according to the highest Koranic ideals. He did not take revenge for the 1099 massacre and now that hostilities had ceased he ended the killing (2:193, 194). Not a single Christian was killed and there was no plunder. The ransoms were deliberately very low, but still there were thousands of poor people who could not even afford them and who were therefore taken prisoner by the Muslims. There were so many prisoners that it was said that a Frankish slave could be purchased for a sandal in Damascus. But large numbers escaped this fate because Saladin was moved to tears by the plight of families who were rent asunder and he released many of them freely, to the despair of his long-suffering treasurers. His brother al-Adil was so distressed by the plight of the prisoners that he asked Saladin for a thousand of them for his own use and then released them on the spot.[37] All the Muslim leaders were scandalized to see the rich Christians escaping with their wealth, which could have been used to ransom *all* the prisoners. When Imad ad-Din saw the Patriarch Heraclius leaving the city with chariots crammed with treasure, he urged

Saladin to confiscate it. But Saladin refused. The Koran said that oaths and treaties must be kept to the letter and it was essential that the Muslims should observe the legalities. "Christians everywhere will remember the kindness we have done them," he said.[38] Heraclius paid his ten-dinar ransom like everybody else and was even provided with a special escort to keep his treasure safe during the journey to Tyre. Saladin was right that the Christian world was impressed with his clemency. Even though it was Saladin who deprived Christianity of Jerusalem, he has been venerated in the West. Legends grew up that he had received Christian baptism and had been dubbed a Christian knight. People must have been subliminally aware that Saladin had behaved in a far more "Christian" way than the Franks.

But his mercy earned him the disapproval of his own people. All the Christians that he released swelled the resistance at Tyre, and Saladin would find it impossible to dislodge them. Ibn al-Athir is critical:

> Every time he seized a Frankish city or stronghold such as Acre, Ascalon, or Jerusalem, Salah ad-Din allowed the enemy soldiers and knights to seek refuge in Tyre, a city that had thus become impregnable. The Franks of the littoral sent messages to the others overseas [in Europe] and the latter promised to come to their rescue. Ought we not to say that in a sense it was Salah ad-Din himself who organised the defence of Tyre against his own army?[39]

In fact Saladin's clemency contravened the ruling of the Koran because, instead of ensuring that the conflict with the Christians was ended once and for all, he had unwittingly prolonged it. There would be more Crusades to the Holy Land for the recovery of Jerusalem, more bloodshed and massacre, and it would be another hundred years before the Muslims finally evicted the Western Christians from the East. At the start of his career Saladin had been a reluctant soldier and, despite the zeal for the *jihad* that he later developed, his emotional and sympathetic nature finally made it impossible for him to be a really ruthless soldier in the holy war. Yet in this long chronicle of bloodshed and horror this failing must surely make Saladin one of the most attractive characters in the history of the holy war.

Once he was inside Jerusalem, Saladin set about purifying the holy places from their long pollution. Al-Aqsa had been the headquarters of the Templars, and they had built living quarters around and against the mosque and had taken up some of the sacred mosque itself with storerooms and latrines. On the Dome of the Rock there was a giant golden cross and as soon as the Muslims entered the city some of them had climbed up the cupola and taken it down—an event that caused an immense commotion. "When they reached the top a great cry went up from the city and from outside the walls," says Ibn al-Athir, "the Muslims crying the *Allah akhbah* in their joy, the Franks groaning in consternation and grief. So loud and piercing was their cry that the earth shook."[40] Inside the mosque, the great rock on which Abraham had bound Isaac and upon which Mohammad had alighted after his Night Journey had been hidden by the Franks with a marble covering and the mosque was full of statues and images, which the Muslims consider idolatrous. All these signs of Christian occupation had to be erased and the mosques returned to their former state. Workers purified the mosques, sprinkled them with rose water and on Friday, October 9, the Muslims celebrated their Friday prayer in al-Aqsa so that "Islam was restored there in full freshness and beauty."[41]

Another innovation made by Saladin to the old *jihad* concerned the Franks' expulsion from the Holy City. Hitherto Christians, as one of the People of the Book, had always been allowed to worship freely in Muslim cities. Now Saladin excluded the Franks. Again, this was not a war against Christianity *per se*. The Greek and Eastern Christians, who had not persecuted and oppressed the Muslims, were permitted to remain in the Holy City and in the Holy Sepulchre but the churches built by the Christian Crusaders were turned into mosques and madrassas. In this respect, Saladin had taken a leaf out of the Christians' book. When the First Crusaders conquered the Holy Land, no Jews or Muslims had been allowed inside Jerusalem: mosques and synagogues had either been destroyed or profaned or converted into churches. Now, after Saladin's victory, the Franks were no longer considered People of the Book: notices were fixed above the doors of former churches stating that Saladin had conquered the building from the polytheists.[42] But this new exclusiveness did not apply to the Jews, the other People of the Book. Saladin invited them back to their Holy City, to live there side by side with the Muslims. Throughout the Jewish world Saladin was hailed as the new Cyrus and there was a new enthusiasm for *aliyah*: huge bands of Jews emigrated from the diaspora to Palestine, convinced that the messianic age was at hand.[43] Jews like Judah Halevi had been urging the Jews to return to the Holy Land for years but now that the ban on Jerusalem had been lifted the idea of a return to the Promised Land took root and there was a new wave of Jewish settlement in the country. In the light of recent history, it is surely an irony that this early religious Zionism should have been inspired by an Islamic conquest of Jerusalem.

After the conquest of Jerusalem, Baha ad-Din tells us a story that shows the new Muslim view of the Frankish Christians. He and Saladin were riding along the coast of Palestine and were looking at the wild, wintry waves. The sea horrified Baha ad-Din, who had scarcely seen it before. He had just decided that anybody who went to sea voluntarily must be mad, when Saladin astonished him by saying: "I think that when God grants me victory over the rest of Palestine I shall divide my territories, make a will stating my wishes and then set sail on this sea to their far-off lands and pursue the Franks there, so as to free the earth of anyone who does not believe in God."[44] Saladin could no longer believe that the Franks worshiped the same God as he, any more than Westerners at this time could imagine that the Muslims believed in the same God as themselves. East and West had entered a new phase of mutual antagonism: neither could see the other accurately.

It is hardly surprising that the Franks of the West should have come into Saladin's mind when he looked at the Mediterranean, because after his conquest of Jerusalem the Muslims were anxiously awaiting a new Crusade to sail to the defense of the Christians. Immediately after the Battle of Hittin, King William of Sicily had set sail to consolidate Christian resistance at Tyre. Then, in 1189, Guy of Lusignan, who had been released from captivity, sailed from Tyre to Acre and, in a quite uncharacteristic display of daring and decisiveness, had managed to besiege the Muslim garrison in the city against great odds. More Crusaders sailed at once from Denmark and Frisia to help the siege at Acre and preachers sailed from Palestine to recruit more help from Europe. Ibn al-Athir gives us an interesting insight into the Christian propaganda with its distorted imagery of Muslims and Islam:

> To incite the people to vengeance, they carried with them a painting of the Messiah, peace be upon him, bloodied by an Arab who was striking him. They would say, "Look, here is the Messiah and here is Mohammad, the Prophet of the Muslims, beating him to death!" The Franks were moved and gathered together, women included; those who could not come along would pay the expenses of those who went to fight in their place. . . . The religious and psychological motivation of the Franks was so strong that they were prepared to surmount all difficulties to achieve their ends.[45]

These propaganda devices ring true: they are the sort of distortions people use to recruit soldiers for a long and difficult war. The Muslims were able to respect the religious zeal of the Crusaders: Saladin told his troops that they must match the piety of the Christians: "All they have done, and all their generosity, has been done purely out of zeal for him they worship,"[46] he said, pointing out sadly that there was no such devotion in the Islamic empire: nobody in Baghdad or Iran had answered his call for help in the *jihad*.

Yet the Crusaders who were beginning to assemble their armies in response to Pope Gregory VIII's call for a Third Crusade were not as fervent as Saladin thought. Undoubtedly the loss of Jerusalem was shocking: it would be similar to the distress Jews would feel today if they lost the Holy City. The Muslim victory was very threatening indeed: *why* had God allowed the Saracens to triumph? The people clamored for a major Crusade to recover Jerusalem and, when they saw the most powerful monarchs in Christendom taking the Cross in response to this popular appeal, there was a huge surge of hope: surely this massive Christian offensive could not fail. All eyes turned toward Acre.

But it was not until 1191, nearly four years after the disaster at Hittin, that the main crusading armies reached Acre. Even though the situation in the Holy Land was grim and desperate and the Christian toehold in the Holy Land was very precarious, the crusading leaders took their time. When Bernard preached the Second Crusade in 1146 it had only been a matter of months before Conrad and Louis set off to the East. In 1187, however, the Crusaders were far too concerned with business at home to hasten to the Middle East. Three of the leaders were actually at war with one another: King Philip Augustus of France and King Henry II of England were constantly invading each other's territory in France and Prince Richard fought first with his father Henry and then switched sides and joined Philip. On July 6, 1189, Henry died: it is doubtful that he ever intended to fulfill his vow, but Richard, who succeeded him on the throne of England, was eager to go crusading. This was not out of religious fervor: Richard was a soldier and the Crusade was an exciting and glamorous military challenge. Philip Augustus was far less enthusiastic but knew that it would be impolitic to alienate public opinion by any further delay. He and Richard made a formal peace treaty and agreed to leave for Acre later that year.

On September 3, shortly before his departure, Richard was crowned in Westminster Abbey. The kingship of England meant little to him: he was more French than English in spirit and was very much the son of his mother, Eleanor of Aquitaine (who had divorced Louis VII and married Henry after her return from the Second Crusade). The coronation of the first King of England to take the Cross unleashed a powerful excitement in England, however, and at once the darker passions of crusading emerged. A deputation of Jews who were attending the coronation was attacked by the crowd: as always, crusading fervor meant an outbreak of popular anti-Semitism. The mob then went on to attack the Jewish community in London. As one of the chroniclers puts it: "Many of those who were hastening to go to Jerusalem determined first to rise against the Jews." It seemed that Jews and Muslims were now fused in an unholy alliance in the Western consciousness: when you set out to attack one of these enemies of God, it was now a reflex to attack the other.

Richard was no anti-Semite nor did he have any hatred of Muslims *per se*: he saw Saladin and his army as ordinary military foes. Indeed Richard had always favored the Jews, who had helped to finance his expensive wars. He quelled the riots in London and allowed one Jew, who had saved his life by submitting to baptism, to adjure his baptismal vows. But he could not control this crusading anti-Semitism. As Easter and Passover approached the following year and as more Crusaders left home to join Richard's army, all the buried fear and hatred of the Jews exploded: the Jews had slain Christ; they murdered children and baked their special Passover bread with their blood. Pogroms erupted all over the country. The most serious of these took place at York, where the Jewish community was massacred, and at Norwich, which had a tradition of anti-Semitism. As the chronicler records: "All the Jews who were found in their own houses in Norwich were slaughtered; some had taken refuge in the castle."[47]

Meanwhile, a very spectacular crusading army had left Europe. On March 27, 1188, the Holy Roman Emperor Frederick Barbarossa took the Cross but a whole year elapsed before he fulfilled his vow. Finally he set out in early May 1189, taking the dangerous land route to the Holy Land. It was the largest force ever to leave Europe: awed contemporaries estimated that there were 50,000 cavalry and 100,000 foot soldiers. Frederick was the first emperor of the West to take the Cross and inevitably, when they saw his vast army marching east, people recalled the dream of the Last Emperor of ancient prophecy who would conquer the East and force the return of Christ and the Last Days upon the world. An eruption of apocalyptic hopes seized many of the soldiers in Frederick's army, which was exactly what the aging Emperor intended. His lifework had been to revive the Holy Roman Empire of Charlemagne and to establish himself and his descendants as emperors of Europe. He had already acquired an aura of glamour and prestige. One of his methods had been to appropriate Charlemagne, the Frank, as the ancestor of the German people. Frederick had got Charlemagne canonized in Germany and had commissioned a monk at Aachen to write a new version of *The Legends of*

*Charlemagne*, which made much of Charlemagne's legendary pilgrimage to Jerusalem and his so-called "holy wars" against the Muslims of Spain. Doubtless Frederick's choice of the land route was prompted by the image of himself walking in Charlemagne's footsteps to the Holy Land. Frederick knew that the Emperor Alexander the Great had ruled the known world after his victory in the East and he hoped that a victory over Saladin would bring him a similar glory and power. Naturally Saladin watched the slow approach of this mighty German army with dread.

Then a totally unexpected event occurred which seemed like a new "salvation" for the Muslims. The land route had proved as dangerous as ever and many of the Crusaders died. On June 10, 1190, the army arrived at the river of Calycadnus in the plain of Seleucia. Fully clad in his armor, Barbarossa leaped into the raging river, either to cool himself or in a display of crusading bravado, but the shock proved too great and he probably suffered a heart attack, drowning instantly. It was the end of the Crusade. Without their Emperor, the Germans lost the special appeal of their imperial expedition. Thousands deserted and only a tiny remnant limped into Antioch. To Saladin, this dramatic event seemed to have been arranged by God and his conviction of righteousness soared. The death of the Emperor was a great blow to the West. But if their apocalyptic dreams were over, there was still hope for the Third Crusade and people eagerly watched the progress of Richard's and Philip's armies, which had set out from Vézelay in July 1190.

This progress was slow. As agreed, both kings and their armies met in Sicily as they intended to sail to Acre rather than risk the disastrous land route. Once in Sicily, however, they spent so much time sorting out their own private feuds and quarrels that winter had set in and it was decided to wait for more clement weather. It was not until the spring of 1191 that the two armies finally set sail for Acre, where the Christians were in desperate straits. Philip arrived first and promptly began to reorganize the siege but Richard still delayed, capturing Cyprus and a Muslim supply ship as part of a personal adventure. Yet his arrival on June 6 was decisive to the exhausted Christian army. Richard was a far more charismatic figure than the colder, less attractive Philip: he was handsome, glamorous, a poet and troubadour and a first-class soldier. When he finally arrived with twenty-five ships bearing arms, men and equipment, there were huge demonstrations of excitement and hopes were high: the Franks lit great fires in celebration. "As for the Muslims," wrote Baha ad-Din, "their hearts were filled with apprehension." They knew that he was a formidable enemy:

"His kingdom and standing were inferior to those of the French king, but his wealth, reputation and valour were greater."[48] There was panic in the Muslim camp but Saladin urged his men to rededicate themselves to the *jihad* and to trust in God's undoubted support.[49]

The siege of Acre had been the most protracted and desperate of the whole crusading movement. Inside the city the Muslim garrison and civilians had suffered a siege of two years. Around the city walls camped the Christians and encircling them was Saladin's army, unable to reach the Muslims inside the city. There were sickness and bitter political strife and rivalry inside the Christian camp and this was only exacerbated by the rivalry and potential enmity between Richard and Philip. But Richard saved the day: while Saladin was ordering special readings of the *hadith*, his tactics were far more pragmatic. There were no rousing sermons, no fasts. Instead Richard offered gold pieces to any man in the army who could take a stone from the city walls, which the Crusaders were trying to break down. This would have been unthinkable in any previous Crusade, but it worked. The holy war had changed sides, as it were, for now it was the Muslims who were religious and the Christians who were secular in their motivation, but their holy zeal could not save the Muslim garrison, who were finally forced to surrender to this new Christian onslaught. When Saladin saw the Christian banners being unfurled from the city walls on July 12, he wept like a child.

Negotiations began. This simple statement marks a turning point in crusading: no other Crusaders from the West would have considered making terms with the infidel but Richard and Philip were pragmatists and saw nothing amiss in diplomacy, which was a normal part of the war game. As for the Palestinian Franks, the disaster of Hittin had shown them the danger of unrealistic religious chauvinism. In meetings with the Muslim army it was agreed that Acre would be surrendered to the Christians, together with 15,000 Christian prisoners of war. Saladin must return the True Cross, which had disappeared after the Battle of Hittin. Once the terms had been agreed, Philip decided that he had done his duty and went home and Richard, now the sole leader of the Crusade, planned a new campaign against the Muslims.

Even though his men were thoroughly enjoying a vacation in Acre, Richard was eager to press on. He found himself financially burdened by the large numbers of prisoners of war and on August 20 he had 2700 Muslims, including women and children, brought outside the city walls and killed in cold blood and in full view of Saladin's army. When Saladin had had too many prisoners, he had released thousands of them but this had backfired and led to an effective Christian resistance in Tyre and Acre. When Richard had too many prisoners he killed them, but this ruthless pragmatism also proved to be a mistake: Muslim morale was at a very low ebb, but when Saladin's army saw that the Franks were as ready as ever to commit atrocities they dedicated themselves to the *jihad* with new determination, realizing that there could be no peace for them until they had expelled the Christians from Palestine.

Hostilities resumed. The Crusaders were not used to the heat and many suffered severe sunstroke, fainted, fell from their horses and were killed where they lay. Nevertheless Richard was able to press on down the coast as far as Caesarea, where he asked for new talks but, as he demanded—quite unrealistically—nothing less than the return of the whole of the Holy Land, including Jerusalem, the peace negotiations broke up. Richard's army continued to thrive: he defeated Saladin at Arsuf, and the Muslims began to look askance at their leader, who seemed to have lost his old touch. Then the Christians managed to reconquer Jaffa and, once again, Richard asked for a truce. Both sides needed a rest and Richard realized that, despite his recent success, the Crusaders were in no position to recover the whole country: even if they achieved this, the Palestinian Franks would never be able to hold the Holy Land against the Muslims once the Crusaders had gone home. He wanted to recoup some of the Christian losses by diplomacy but al-Adil, who was in charge of the negotiations, shrewdly understood the Christian position and urged Saladin not to give in too easily. Richard and Saladin never met: even though Richard was fascinated by the great Sultan, Saladin said that it was not fitting for two kings to meet while they were at war. So Richard dealt with al-Adil and soon became very fond of him, calling him "my brother and my friend."[50] For his part, al-Adil did not share Saladin's extreme view of the conflict and was perfectly prepared to make friends with Christians, provided, of course, that they did not pose a serious political threat. He and Richard were both secularly minded pragmatists and in Chapter 10 we shall see that, for the rest of his life, al-Adil was ready to accept a peaceful coexistence in Palestine whereby Christians and Muslims lived side by side in harmony and to the material profit of each.

But in spite of all this good will, which made this Crusade different from any other, there was deadlock when the question of Jerusalem came up. Richard insisted that the Holy City belonged to the Christians: "Jerusalem is for us an object of worship that we could not give up," he wrote to Saladin, "even if there were only one of us left." The same applied to the rest of the Holy Land: "It *must* be consigned to us."[51] Even the realistic Richard could not be rational about the "holiness" of Jerusalem but spoke with the inarticulate urgency that has so often, right up to the present day, made it impossible for people to be objective about the Holy City. Richard was emotionally convinced that the Christians "must" possess the Holy Land at a very deep level, too deep to explain; because Jerusalem was central to his Western identity, the Christian right to the city seemed self-evident. Saladin, whose *jihad* had always been more rational, had no difficulty in putting his case forward logically and politically:

> Jerusalem is ours as much as yours: indeed it is even more sacred to us than it is to you for it is the place from which our Prophet accomplished his nocturnal journey and the place where our community will gather on the day of Judgement. Do not imagine that we can renounce it or vacillate on this point. The land was originally ours, whereas you have only just arrived and have taken it over because of the weakness of the Muslims living there at that time.[52]

Richard's next move was an extraordinary proposal that shocked both sides. He suggested that his sister Joanna should marry al-Adil and that the couple should rule the Holy Land between them, as Muslim King and Christian Queen.[53] This, of course, would be exactly what Richard would have suggested in a similar situation in Europe: it is a very clear demonstration of the fact that Richard saw the Muslims as normal human beings, with whom one could make perfectly reasonable arrangements by means of diplomacy and marriage alliances. He never saw them as the monstrous enemies of God. But, as one might expect, this proposal was far too radical and, indeed, the solution of sharing the Holy Land is still rejected passionately by many of its inhabitants today. Al-Adil was visibly intrigued and tempted by the proposal, but Saladin merely dismissed it, assuming that Richard must be joking. For her part, Joanna refused point-blank to marry an infidel and horrified churchmen pointed out to Richard that such a marriage would be invalid. Nothing daunted Richard, and he asked al-Adil whether he would be willing to become a Christian to get around this and al-Adil declined very politely but invited Richard to dinner at Lydda on November 8.[54] The banquet was a great success and Christians and Muslims exchanged gifts and parted with warm avowals of eternal friendship. It was meetings like this which showed the futility of the religious strife, for, as was always the case, in secular ways Muslims and Christians at this time had a great deal in common. Richard fully realized that the conflict was wasteful and pointless. He had written to Saladin: "the Muslims and the Franks are bleeding to death, the country is utterly ruined and goods and lands have been sacrificed on both sides. The time has come to stop this."[55] Saladin agreed. He was anxious for peace for his own reasons but the terms of peace had to reflect the realities of the situation. He was certainly not going to accede to Richard's demands for the return of Jerusalem to the Christians nor could he countenance the idea of the marriage between Joanna and al-Adil, which seemed a frivolous suggestion. Saladin had great respect for Richard as a soldier but he found him essentially lacking in the seriousness that he, Saladin, expected of a great knight.

At the end of the year the talks had reached deadlock again, so the fighting resumed, but still both sides were in constant touch and ready to talk. Richard managed to conquer more towns along the coast as far as Askelon, but Saladin was always able to take back one city whenever Richard had won another. It was a military stalemate. Twice the Crusaders advanced as far inland as Beit Nuba, which is only twelve miles from Jerusalem, and on both occasions the common soldiers became inspired for the first time by the old crusading passions. The mere proximity of the Holy City had, as usual, touched some vital nerve and they longed to go forward and conquer. Inside Jerusalem, the Muslims were certain that the Christians would advance and knew that in that case they would be in for a hard siege and perhaps even a defeat. They also knew that the Crusaders would not behave like Saladin and that there would be another massacre, perhaps even more violent than the massacre of 1099, as the Christians avenged Hittin. Although the emirs blustered and protested their loyalty, there was panic in the city and the leaders feared a massive desertion.

Saladin's reaction to this crisis gives us a telling view of the essentially practical nature of the Islamic *jihad*. He was deeply depressed by the events of the Third Crusade, for which he had to blame himself in large measure, and the first time Richard's troops reached Beit Nuba it seemed to him that all was lost. The enthusiasm for *jihad* was still very new in the Muslim world and had not taken deep root; he was very much afraid that his emirs would desert and all night long he and Baha ad-Din sat up, turning over all the possible courses of action and discussing first this solution and then that. They felt increasingly desolate: "It was winter," wrote Baha ad-Din, "and we were alone but for God."[56] Yet they could find no solution to their frightening predicament and Saladin seemed overwhelmed with despair. Eventually they went to bed, but scarcely had their heads touched the pillow when the muezzin called the faithful to the dawn prayer. Baha ad-Din went back to the Sultan's room to make his prayers with him as usual and found Saladin washing himself. Both men looked at each other blearily and admitted that they had not slept a wink. But that morning Baha ad-Din had an idea—an idea that would have occurred to a Crusader long ago. Why did they not pray about this? he asked. They had done everything they possibly could, exhausted all their human resources, and there was nothing more they could do. Surely they should put the matter in God's hands. Ninety years earlier, when the First Crusaders had found themselves facing almost certain disaster in Antioch, they had turned instinctively to prayer and had saved themselves by finding a visionary solution. But Baha ad-Din clearly felt that prayer for divine aid was a rather controversial idea, for he seemed to need to argue it out:

> on this subject there is an authentic *hadith* of the Prophet, saying: "My God, all my earthly power to bring victory to your Faith has come to nothing: my only resource is to turn to You and to rely on Your help and trust in Your goodness. You are my sufficiency, You are the best preserver!" God is too generous to let your prayers go to waste.[57]

It seemed a novel suggestion to Saladin too: "How shall we do it?" he asked, a question that would have seemed patently unnecessary to a Crusader. Baha ad-Din did not suggest an outpouring of personal prayer or a mystical flight but a very formal and official petition. He advised Saladin to give alms privately and perform two *raka'at* (ritual prostrations) at the Friday prayers that afternoon at al-Aqsa. Saladin followed his secretary's advice. He performed two *raka'at* on the very spot whence the Prophet ascended to heaven during the Night Journey. "I saw him prostrate," Baha ad-Din recorded, "with tears running down his white beard and on to his prayer-mat, but I could not hear what he said."[58] The story shows us that, unlike the Jews and Christians in their holy war, Muslims do not expect God to intervene to save them. Theirs is a more self-reliant faith and they feel that God expects them to fight as though everything depended upon them. God will not help them unless they have made every effort to save themselves first.

On the very same day the captain of the advance guard brought Saladin some marvelous news. The Franks had left Beit Nuba and were marching back to the coast. The danger was over. But where a Christian would have seen that as entirely due to God and an answer to prayer, Baha ad-Din gives a very accurate account of Richard's own very practical reasons for withdrawing and not attacking the city. The Templars and Hospitalers had persuaded him that conquering the Holy City would be useless and ultimately even dangerous for the

Christians who lived in Palestine. After the Crusaders had gone home, Saladin would certainly reconquer al-Quds and might follow that by a new offensive against the Franks in their coastal cities. Further, the winter rains were very heavy and the hills around Jerusalem almost impassable. Previous Crusaders would have scorned such prudence and caution and Richard's men, inspired for the first time by religious zeal, clamored for him to go forward. Richard, the secular pragmatist, would not dream of leaving it all in God's hands and went back to Jaffa, persuaded by these eminently sensible suggestions. His secular crusading was in fact very close in spirit to Saladin's Islamic *jihad*, which turned to God only as a last resort. On the second occasion that Richard's army reached Beit Nuba he managed to capture a large Muslim convoy carrying food and equipment to Jerusalem, taking rich booty and thousands of horses and camels. Yet still Richard would not capitalize on his victory for the same pragmatic reasons. One day, while he was riding in the hills that surround Jerusalem, he suddenly came within sight of the Holy City. Instantly he covered his face with his shield and turned away: he would not look at the city, he cried, that God had not allowed him to conquer.[59] This was a knightly gesture, but in reality Richard had no intention of jeopardizing the security of the Christians in Palestine by pressing on to Jerusalem.

By August he was desperate for a settlement. There was absolute military deadlock between the two sides; his troops, having been twice balked of the chance of conquering Jerusalem, were furious and almost mutinous; he had bad news from home, where Philip Augustus—his former fellow Crusader—had invaded his lands in France. Finally Richard himself became ill. Saladin graciously sent him his own doctor and sent gifts of fruit and snow to make cooling drinks, but he remained adamant and would make no further concessions. Eventually, on September 2, Richard capitulated and a treaty was signed for five years, which showed that both sides had had to compromise. Saladin had to accept that he was not going to be able to throw all the Franks into the sea and then pursue them into Europe. Instead, there would be a thin coastal kingdom stretching from Jaffa to Beirut which would have its capital at Acre, though its king would still wistfully call himself King of Jerusalem. Richard had to accept that he was not going to reconquer the Holy City but he had won the right for Christian pilgrims to pray there. Muslims and Christians had to recognize each other's existence in Palestine and in the Holy City.

The story of the fall of Jerusalem and the Third Crusade seems to suggest that where practical realism prevailed there was a possibility of peaceful coexistence and mutual respect. It was their religions that drove the Christians and Muslims apart. Otherwise they shared the same courtly values. Saladin and Richard both respected each other as knights. At one moment during a battle at Jaffa, when the Crusaders' cavalry seemed exhausted, Richard himself led the spearmen in a charge against the Muslims, and Saladin was almost beside himself with furious admiration. When he saw Richard's horse fall under him, the Sultan at once sent his groom into the fray with two fresh horses for the brave King of England.[60] It is another example of the secular grace with which Muslim and Christian could respond to one another in gestures that both perfectly understood. In Europe there were many similar legends about the two great knights Richard and Saladin. In one of these, Richard entered Jerusalem incognito and dined with Saladin: they had a very amicable meal and in the course of conversation Richard asked the Sultan what he thought of the King of England. Saladin replied that Richard excelled in the chivalric virtue of bravery, but that he was sometimes inclined to spoil this by being too rash in battle. For his part, he, Saladin, preferred to cultivate the chivalric virtues of moderation, even in battle.[61] The story shows that in Europe Richard and Saladin were both seen as exemplars of the chivalric ideal. It is a criticism of Richard and praise of the Sultan who conquered Jerusalem but who was still seen as a true knight with qualities that Richard lacked. Instead of seeing the Muslim and the Christian as polar opposites, the legend shows them as two halves of the ideal.

The legend of Richard in Europe is revealing in another way. He must surely be one of the most famous of the English kings and yet after his coronation he spent only a few months in the country, which he bled dry to pay for his campaigns in France and in the Holy Land. Yet during his absence on the Crusade he became known as the Lionheart and is reputed to have been a great King of England simply because he led an army to the Holy Land. It shows that crusading was deeply important as a value in Europe, for all that it seemed to be becoming a rather secular pursuit. Perhaps one of the most famous legends about Richard concerns his favorite troubadour Blondel of Nesle. On his way home from Palestine, Richard was taken prisoner in Austria and Blondel wandered throughout Europe, searching for him. One day he sat beneath the walls of the castle where Richard was a prisoner and sang a song that he and the King had composed together. Halfway through he paused, and Richard, who had been listening in his cell, took the song up and Blondel could go to England and tell the people where Richard was. The story shows a yearning devotion to the Crusader King, who seems bathed in a highly idealized and romantic light, even though he was really a ruthless and even cruel pragmatist. For those who stayed at home, crusading was becoming a distant and glamorous affair, very different from the bloody reality. Yet there was another legend too that shows a buried worry about this new kind of Crusader who sailed home without bothering to go and pray at the Holy Sepulchre: he is reputed to have eaten Muslim flesh with relish—he had been sick unto death at the siege of Acre and developed a craving for pork. Because there was none available in this Muslim country, the desperate cook served up Saracen flesh instead and Richard not only found it quite delicious but was instantly cured. He rose from his bed immediately and went out to massacre a few thousand Muslims. When he found out what he had eaten, he simply roared with laughter. During the First Crusade, the Tafurs had been said to eat Muslim flesh, but they had not enjoyed it like Richard, who seems to break this taboo quite easily and feel no disgust. This story was very popular in France during the reign of Richard's enemy Philip Augustus, but it may reflect a repressed view of crusading as a monstrous activity, especially when one bears in mind the sympathetic legends that were developing about Saladin.[62]

The story of Richard's Crusade shows a certain cooling of the religious atmosphere among the Franks; similarly, after the death of Saladin in 1193 al-Adil eventually ruled in a more secular spirit than his brother. The practice of the holy war had no strong roots among the Muslim people of the Middle East; once the Christian threat had declined, the enthusiasm for *jihad* died a swift, natural death. In Europe, however, the practice of the holy war was now central to the developing Western mentality. Europeans continued to declare war against the Muslims in the Near East and large, ever more efficiently equipped forces of Western Christians arrived to fight for the recovery of Jerusalem in a war to promote the interests of God's people against the evil infidel. These Crusades were often very embarrassing to the Franks in the area; Muslims and Christians had both discovered that they could coexist to their mutual enrichment and the Franks were reluctant to jeopardize their precarious position in Palestine by a renewal of the holy war. Had the people of Europe abandoned crusading as the Muslims abandoned the *jihad*, the Franks might have kept their states for longer than they did.

In 1987 the anniversary of the eighth centenary of the Battle of Hittin passed quite unnoticed in Europe. Today crusading enthusiasm takes other forms, as we shall discuss in Part III of this book. But in Israel the anniversary of Hittin was commemorated with deep interest by both Arabs and Jews. It is easy to see why the victory of Hittin should be an exciting idea to the Palestinians. Ever since the days of the Balfour Declaration their poets had been calling for a new Saladin to lead his people to victory: Saladin, the Kurd, had become an Arab hero. After Hittin, Saladin had built an inn and a mosque near Jericho, dedicated to the Prophet Moses, for the use of the Muslim pilgrims who were now able to visit their holy places in al-Quds. It had long been a custom in Palestine to process each year from this Nabi Musa complex in the Judean desert to Jerusalem, in memory of the Muslim return to their holy city in 1187. Not surprisingly, this annual event had become an aggressive event in the Palestinian year since the creation of the state of Israel. It was a strong reminder of the crusading period, when the Muslim people had successfully repelled the invaders from the West, as the Arab historians increasingly reminded their people. On July 3, 1987, there was a special rally on the mountain of Hittin itself and meetings of Palestinians throughout the country discussed the importance of this event in the history of the region.

The Israelis naturally took a more somber view of the anniversary but they certainly did not ignore it. There were several programs on the Crusades that week on Israeli television and on July 3 itself Joshua Prawer, the distinguished Israeli historian of the Crusades, gave a lecture on the significance of crusading on the 9 P.M. television news. Nobody was resorting to simplistic ideas of history repeating itself or of a deterministic force in the historical process to suggest that *any* Western state in the region would inevitably be ejected. But the fall of the Kingdom of Jerusalem struck a chord of recognition: people could see some worrying resemblances between the position of the Christians on the eve of Hittin and their own. Thus people pointed to the deep divisions in Israeli society. Gloomy commentators quite often speak of the possibility of a civil war in Israel, particularly dwelling on the conflict between religious and secular Israelis, who have very different ideas of what the state should be and do. In 1987 Israelis were uncomfortably aware that they had a radical religious minority on the far right that was pursuing belligerent policies that many felt to be dangerous: in 1984 members of the Jewish underground had actually plotted to blow up the Dome of the Rock and al-Aqsa, an act which would have roused the united hostility of the whole Arab world. This seemed remarkably close to the spirit of Reynauld of Chatillon's attempt to attack the holy cities of Mecca and Medina. Could the religious far right push Israel into a new war with the Arabs or cause a civil war within the country as Reynauld and his followers had done? These were disturbing questions.

Further, the Christians had lost their kingdom in one day, in one battle. Israelis are deeply aware that, while the Arabs can afford to lose war after war, they cannot lose a single one. The trauma of Hittin haunts many Israelis, not surprisingly because Israel, like the Christian states, is surrounded by a hostile Muslim world which refuses her right to exist. Like the Crusaders, Israel had profited from the disunity in the Arab world. But there is always the possibility that the Arab states will one day find a new charismatic Saladin—possibly a radical Muslim leader—to unite them in a joint and successful war against the state of Israel.

In the next two chapters we shall consider the revival of the idea of a holy war and the rise of religious extremism on both sides of the Arab-Israeli conflict and assess its danger: could religion be as perilous or (depending on your point of view) as profitable in the region as it was during the Middle Ages? It is an appropriate point at which to move into the modern period. After the Third Crusade there was a religious détente in the Middle East on both sides of the conflict. Passion for the holy war was really only a European enthusiasm henceforth, and in Part III we shall examine this new phase of Western crusading which has lasted to the present day. This is the time to look at the revival of religion in the Middle East. The Arab-Israeli problem began as a deliberately secular conflict on both sides, but on both sides religion is becoming more and more important and this could have fateful consequences. Israel in particular is vulnerable to internal division and to the religious revival in the Muslim world, just as the Christians were in the Middle Ages. Further, the nightmare of a concerted Arab attack led by a charismatic leader is no chimera: Israelis have already experienced this horror. In 1967 on the eve of the Six Day War it seemed that the unthinkable was about to happen and that Israel would fall before the invading Arab armies who were led by the Arab hero of Suez: Gamal Abdel Nasser.

# 1967

# Zionism Becomes a Holy War

In 1967 the state of Israel seemed to be surrounded by a powerful circle of enemies who were dedicated to her destruction. In 1966 there had been a left-wing coup in Syria, which made that country a close ally of the Soviet Union. The new regime was deeply sympathetic toward the Palestinian *fedayeen* movements, particularly those with socialist ideologies like the PFLP and the PDFLP. It encouraged them to make a new series of terrorist raids in Israeli territory from Syria. Hafez al-Assad, the new Defense Minister, taunted Nasser for his cowardice in avoiding a confrontation with Israel: Syria seemed to offer a challenging claim to be the leader of the Arab nation. On May 13, 1967, the Soviets informed Syria that Israel was about to invade its territory. Soviet intelligence may have been misinformed here: there was no plan for such an invasion, though there was talk of further retaliation against Syria to stop the new surge of *fedayeen* activity. Nasser could hang back no longer and on May 17 he began a series of provocative acts which allied him with Syria in a state of war against Israel. First, he moved 100,000 Egyptian troops into the Sinai Peninsula, which had been a demilitarized zone since the Suez war. The following day he ordered UN forces to leave the area and the UN complied. On May 22 he closed the Gulf of Aqaba to Israeli shipping and on May 23 Israel declared this to be an aggressive action against her sovereignty, with the full support of the United States. On May 30, King Hussein of Jordan signed a military agreement with Egypt and Iraqi troops began to gather in Jordan. A new Arab alliance, based entirely on enmity to the state of Israel, had been achieved and the Jewish state was now even more tightly encircled than the Crusaders had been by Saladin and his supporters.

Nasser's initial reluctance seemed to have been swept aside by the force of his own rhetoric: Egypt was now prepared to defend Syria, to restore the Palestinians' rights and to avenge the honor of the Arab nation. The Arabs were despised by Britain, America and Israel, who were prepared once again to harry the Arab people. Only the Soviet Union was their friend. But Egypt was now prepared:

> Every one of us is ready to die and not give away a grain of his country's sand. This for us is the greatest honour. It is the greatest honour for us to defend our country. We are not scared by the imperialist, Zionist or reactionary campaigns. We are independent and we know the taste of freedom. We have built a strong national army and achieved our aims. We are building our country. There is currently a propaganda campaign, a psychological campaign, and a campaign of doubt against us. We leave all this behind us and follow the course of duty and victory.[1]

During the past twenty years the Israelis had become horribly familiar with the rhetoric of Arab leaders like Nasser, who had persistently vowed to annihilate the Jewish state, exterminate its Jewish population and drive all the Jews into the sea. Now that they were finally confronting a united Arab world, they assumed, naturally enough, that the Arabs would carry out their vow. The terrifying period before the June War of 1967 has become known as the *Hamtana*, the waiting period. The Jews were waiting to be annihilated. The Holocaust was ever present as a terrible possibility and the new Arab anti-Semites now seemed confident that they could defeat the Israeli army. In contrast to Nasser, the Israeli Prime Minister Levi Eshkol mumbled confusedly in his speech to the nation and young Jewish soldiers broke their radios and wept with terror and shame. Eshkol seemed typical of the old Jew, whom Zionism had sought to replace. But there was a hidden strength beneath the unpromising exterior and Israeli leaders like Moshe Dayan and Yitzhak Rabin were quietly confident of the ability of the Israeli Defense Forces to repel the Arab attack.

On June 5 the Israelis felt justified in launching a preemptive strike against Nasser and that morning they destroyed almost the whole of the Egyptian air force on the ground. Eshkol and Dayan assured the nation that this was to be a war of defense, not a war of aggrandizement. The Israelis had no designs on "one foot of Arab territory," Eshkol promised.[2] The extraordinary events of the next six days, however, changed all that. Jordan and Syria had been misinformed about the confrontation with Egypt and had no idea of the full strength of Israel's victory, which had knocked Egypt out of the war before it started. Accordingly, Jordan and Syria entered the war and Israel felt justified in attacking Jordanian and Syrian territory. On June 7 she conquered the Old City of Jerusalem and during the next two days she followed up this important victory by taking the area now known as the West Bank from Jordan and the Golan Heights from Syria as well as Sinai and the Gaza Strip from Egypt. In six fateful days Israel had not only repelled her enemies and proved their might to be ineffective but she had conquered extensive territory.

We have seen that an unexpected victory or a dramatic reversal of fortune has often made people feel that they have a special divine destiny. The Six Day War made a powerful and deep impression upon the Jewish people, who felt that they had been providentially snatched from destruction and given the victory as dramatically as when God had saved the ancient Israelites at the Red Sea. Indeed the philosopher Martin Buber made that very comparison between the Exodus from Egypt and the June victory.[3] Yitzhak Rabin, who had liberated the Old City of Jerusalem, which had been closed to Israelis since 1948, described it as a moment of religious revelation: it "revealed as though by a flash of lightning truths that were deeply hidden."[4] "It was a truly religious moment," says the Israeli scholar Harold Fisch, "the experience of a miracle. It had a special metaphysical character."[5] The victory also had a profound effect upon the Jews of the diaspora, just as the Crusaders' conquest of Jerusalem had stirred the Christians of Europe. "God has had a dream," wrote the American Zionist scholar Abraham Heschel, "and the task of Israel is to interpret that dream." He saw the victory as yet another example of God's continuous love affair with his people, of which the creation of the state of Israel and its preservation and enlargement were just the latest examples. "In the upbuilding of the land we are aware of responding to the Biblical Covenant, to an imperative that kept on speaking to us throughout the ages, and which never became obsolete or stale."[6] Just as the Crusaders had seen their victory as an act of salvation history that had vital consequences for the whole world, some Zionists began to feel that they had a religious mission and were acting out the divine plan. In this exalted mood, there was no question in the minds of many Israelis that they had a right to keep the territories they had conquered from the Arabs, even though in November 1967 the United Nations in Resolution 242 ordered Israel to return to her borders before the outbreak of hostilities.

The Labor government of Levi Eshkol, which was later led by Golda Meir and then by Yitzhak Rabin, applied the old Zionist flexibility to the new situation. At first the Laborites were clear that they were establishing an occupation in Gaza, the West Bank, Sinai and the Golan Heights; even though this had been the result of a war into which they had been impelled by the Arabs, they would make this the most beneficent occupation in history. Then they decided that they would hold on to the territories until a final peace was achieved with the Arab world, when they would exchange territory for peace. Finally, they began to see the territories as essential to Israel's security. At last Israel had defensible borders and the occupied territories would be settled by military settlements to ensure that there would be no more harrying of Jews by *fedayeen* or aggressive Arab states.

In this the Labor government was officially committed to putting a brake on the fierce enthusiasm and heady visions of many Israeli people after the Six Day War. But not everybody was exultant. War, even a just and victorious war, can produce extreme and contradictory reactions in a nation. The violence, the loss of life, even conquest itself can prove to be problematic and to induce a profound depression. Israel's six-day victory was no exception. Many of the young people, who had been brought up on the *kibbutzim* and were imbued with the moral visions of Labor Zionism, were utterly dismayed by the experience of war. Many of them had wept when they were reunited with the Wailing Wall in the Old City of Jerusalem: tough young commandos had leaned against its stones and wept in much the same way as the Crusaders had wept when they entered the Holy Sepulchre in 1099. But others were surprised to find that they felt nothing at all. One young soldier recalled that when he heard about the Jerusalem victory he simply felt numb and another said that even as they crossed into Jordanian territory as victors, cheered on by enthusiastic crowds, he felt dazed, unhappy and in a dream.[7] There was also widespread dismay among these young *kibbutzniks* when they encountered the Arabs in the new territories.

Shortly after the Six Day War, some leftist intellectuals from the *kibbutzim* felt that they had a duty to record this obscure and urgent distress that the war had aroused in their young. They recorded their findings in a book called *The Seventh Day*,[8] which has become a *cause célèbre* in Israel. In Chapter 3 we noted that the Zionist ideology did not infallibly give to Sabras an absolute conviction of their right to the land; further, that the moral ideals of Labor Zionism had filled many younger Zionists on the left with a sense of guilt toward the Palestinians. In *The Seventh Day*, the editors showed that many of the young soldiers, who had either been very young or had not been born in 1948, had no answer when they were asked why they had more right to the land than the Arabs: they just shook their heads blankly. Some were shocked to discover that the Palestinians in the refugee camps in the occupied territories, who had fled there in 1948, were still yearning to return to *Falastin*. They were horrified and filled with inarticulate distress when they heard that the Palestinians regarded Israel as *their* country and actually heard them talking about their "homes" in cities like Beersheba or Haifa, which were now completely Jewish. "It made my blood boil," one of them said. "I remember I couldn't grasp it. After all, nineteen years had passed. . . . How dare you say that you are from Beersheba . . . that you come from Rehevoth."[9] The *kibbutzniks* did not produce *The Seventh Day* in order to make trouble. They regarded this distress among many of their young people as a crisis for the country. They felt they had a duty to make their fellow countrymen aware of a very real problem. The eminent Israeli scholar Eliezer Schweid has agreed that this deep lack of conviction is a problem for the Jewish state and that it must be dealt with.[10] During the 1970s nearly half a million Israelis left the country, mainly for the United States. Israel simply cannot afford to lose citizens in this way. People like Schweid and the editors of *The Seventh Day* are convinced that they had a responsibility to face up to this problem, rather than to push it under the carpet. Neither they nor the young soldiers interviewed had any desire to destroy the Jewish state; nor did they wish it to disappear. But they found it very difficult, even agonizing, to confront the moral problems raised by their country, for which they had fought so bravely and efficiently.

Some of *The Seventh Day* interviewees found themselves actually identifying with the Palestinians. During the Six Day War some 400,000 Palestinians fled the Israeli occupying forces and took refuge in the diaspora. Not surprisingly, many of the idealistic young soldiers were worried that Israel was causing such suffering, even though the war had not been of her choosing. One soldier remembered "a terrible feeling" when he met the Palestinians in the occupied territories as a conqueror:

> Kids, three or four years old, already knew how to raise their arms. For me this was awful. Kids the age of my son walk with their arms above their heads. I remember that old men and women came to implore. It was an awful feeling, awful. It's a horrible feeling to have to explain to these women that nobody intends to kill their husbands. Horrible, and I can't free myself from it.[11]

Amos Elon points out that the soldier was probably subconsciously recalling the famous photograph of the terrified Jewish child holding his hands above his head in Nazi-occupied Poland, a photograph with which every Israeli is familiar. Other soldiers made the same connection. As one of them said:

"If I had a clear association with the . . . holocaust, it was in a certain moment, when I was going up the Jericho–Jerusalem road and the refugees were streaming down. . . . I felt directly identified with them. When I saw those children carried in their parents' arms, I almost saw myself carried by my father . . . my identification was precisely with the other side, with our enemies." Still another soldier bitterly admitted that when he entered an Arab refugee camp in order to put down a disorder, he felt "like a Gestapo man . . . I thought of home, I thought my parents were being led away."[12]

Zionism had encouraged the Jews to care about poverty and oppression; it had taught the Sabras to hate tyranny and persecution. When Israel entered the territories in 1967 she did so as part of an unavoidable war. Not one of these soldiers had questioned the justice of the Israeli cause. But when they saw the suffering that war involved they recoiled in dismay. They are not the first young soldiers to make such a recoil, however legitimate the war may have been. For twenty years, writers who had been strongly committed to Zionism had tried to make their people see the conflict from the Arabs' point of view and, in their own way, the *kibbutznik* soldiers in *The Seventh Day* had instinctively identified with the Arabs. They were wrong in thinking that the Israelis were neo-Nazis, of course, but they had been impelled by that compassionate strain in the Zionist ideology which encouraged this kind of sympathy and empathy with the unfortunate.

It is well known that the survivors of a catastrophe are often assailed by deep guilt: why have they survived when so many other, worthier people perished? Those who survived the Holocaust are often given to this kind of guilt and, if it is kept within positive and moderate bounds, guilt can be productive. The leading poet Yehuda Amichai had fled Nazi Germany with his parents when he was twelve years old and had come to Israel as a refugee. After the Six Day War he wrote this short poem: "On the Day of Atonement."

On the Day of Atonement in 1967
I put on my dark holiday suit, and went to the Old City in
    Jerusalem.
I stood for some time,
before the alcove of an Arab's shop,
not far from the Damascus Gate,
a shop of buttons and zippers and spools of thread in all
    colours,
and snaps and buckles.
A glorious light and a great many colours

like a Holy Ark with its doors ajar.
I told him in my heart that my father, too,
had a shop of threads and buttons.
I explained to him in my heart all about the tens of years
and the reasons and the circumstances
because of which I am now here
and my father's shop is in ashes there,
and he is buried here.

By the time I had finished,
it was the hour of "the Locking of the Gates."
He too pulled down the shutter and locked the gate,
and I went home with all the worshippers.[13]

The prophets and sages of Judaism had taught Jews to examine their actions and exercise compassion and imaginative sympathy for others. We have seen that this Jewish tradition was inherent in the high ideals of Zionism in its early days and writers like Amichai feel that they have a mission to keep this moral sense intact.

That the Israelis were open to this approach is evident in the fact that Amos Oz's novel *My Michael*, with its bleak and desolate view of Israel and its sympathy for the Arabs, became a cult book after the Six Day War. At a time when they could have been feeling triumphantly righteous, many Israelis felt something like desolation. In 1967, Oz published an article in the newspaper *Davar*, reflecting on the victory in terms of the Laborite ideal. We have seen that the government was preserving these ideals itself by admitting, first, that they were occupiers and insisting that this Israeli occupation had to be beneficent—the best in history, just as the Founding Fathers had insisted that the new Israel would be a light to the *goyim*. The only justification for the occupation was the notion "territories for peace." Oz commented:

For a month, for a year, or for a whole generation we will have to sit as occupiers in places that touch our hearts with their history. And we must remember: as occupiers, because there is no alternative. And as a pressure tactic to hasten peace. Not as saviours or liberators. Only in the twilight of myths can one speak of the liberation of a land struggling under a foreign yoke. Land is not enslaved and there is no such thing as a liberation of lands. There are enslaved people, and the word "liberation" applies only to human beings. We have not liberated Hebron and Ramallah and El Arish, nor have we redeemed their inhabitants. We have conquered them and we are going to rule over them only until our peace is secured.[14]

Religion does not have to be a dangerous element in politics. It can encourage morality and decency in public relations and foster a concern for others. There is a Talmudic story of the great Rabbi Hillel, who was at the height of his powers shortly before the birth of Christ, which shows the centrality of this principle of putting yourself in somebody else's position in Jewish thought. It is said that a Gentile had come to the rabbi and promised to convert to Judaism, provided that Hillel could recite the whole of the Torah to him while he stood on one leg. Hillel replied: "Do not do unto others as you would not have done unto you. That is the whole of the Torah: go and learn it."[15] Such a religious tradition inculcates a habit of concern for other human beings and forces people to make connections that can be painful but which can also lead to peace and compromise. People like Oz felt that the Israelis had a duty as victors to try to understand the Arabs' point of view in a way that was more positive than the confused guilt that plagued the young soldiers of *The Seventh Day*.

Ben-Gurion had no interest in the occupied territories. He did not see Jerusalem as a Holy City and its recovery as a metaphysical event. He referred to the Israeli conquest there as the acquisition of so much real estate. He also felt that the territories must eventually be returned because Israel already had plenty of land for its needs. If anybody wanted new lands to conquer, they should come and join him in the Negev (he was living there on the *kibbutz* Sde Boker) and return to the old pioneering ideals of the conquest of the land by labor, not by arms. He was in no mood for triumph or righteousness. The Zionist project was by no means finished. There was a lot of hard toil to endure yet. He returned to the old language of religious Judaism, as Zionists had always done. But he did not see the dramatic salvation of the Red Sea and the return of the Jews. At the very end of his life, in 1969, he said: "This is not a nation, not yet."

> It is an exiled people still in the desert longing for the flesh pots of Egypt. It cannot be considered a nation until the Negev and Galilee are settled, until millions of Jews emigrate to Israel and until moral standards necessary to the ethical practice of politics and the high values of Zionism are sustained. This is neither a mob nor a nation. It is a people still chained to their Exilic past—redeemed but not fulfilled.[16]

He was addressing a new spirit abroad in Israel that he disliked intensely. It is true that the Labor government was trying to apply the old Zionist ideals to the new political situation, but a rhetoric had developed and was used by the Laborite leaders themselves that did indeed speak of redemption and fulfillment, and which could, if not properly moderated by some degree of ethical realism, lead to a loss of the moral standards that Ben-Gurion had always considered to be essential to the Zionist enterprise.

Zionists, we know, instinctively used religious words to explain their movement and after 1967 the word "holy" came into Zionism for the first time. This was essentially different from that sense of love of Eretz Yisrael which had made it sacred in secular ways to the early settlers. It was referring to the "holiness" that is essential to the biblical tradition and which is an absolute value. When Prime Minister Levi Eshkol entered the Old City for the first time, he said: "I see myself as a representative of an entire nation, and of many past generations whose souls yearn for Jerusalem and its holiness." This might seem innocuous, but it was the holiness of Jerusalem that had inspired the rebels against Rome in a revolution that ultimately lost Israel its land and which, however heroic it had been, had also been opposed by the majority of the Jewish people. It was this kind of absolutism that Ben-Gurion condemned because he, together with many other Laborites, felt that it was a violation of the cautious gradualism and pragmatism that had made the Jewish state a political reality in 1948, against all the odds. Once people started to think of the secular land of Israel as a holy land there was a danger of unrealistic absolutism. Moshe Dayan demonstrated this when he said: "We have returned to all that is holy in our land," when he himself entered the Old City for the first time. "We have returned to it never to be parted from it again."[17]

Dayan was making a claim that his government was not yet ready to endorse. He made it again a few months later, on August 3, when he presided over a ceremony on the Mount of Olives, which had always been a favorite spot for Jews to be buried because the Messiah would arrive there and the Jews buried there would be the first to greet him when they rose from the dead. Despite the secular policies of Labor Zionism, the government had decided to reinter on the Mount of Olives the bodies of the soldiers who had died in the 1948 war. They had fought for the Jewish homeland and had been a secular Messiah for the Jewish people. Dayan spoke of the sacred dreams of the Zionists and of the return of the Jewish people to the West Bank, which had such hallowed associations:

Our brothers, who fought in the war of Independence: we have not abandoned your dream, nor forgotten the lesson you taught us. . . . We have returned to the Mount, to the cradle of the nation's history, to the land of our forefathers, to the land of the Judges, and to the fortress of David's dynasty. We have returned to Hebron, Shechem, Bethlehem and Anatoth, to Jericho and the ford over the Jordan. Our brothers, we bear your lessons with us . . . we know that to give life to Jerusalem we must station the soldiers and armour of the Israeli Defence Forces on the Shechem mountains and on the bridges over the Jordan.[18]

This was in direct opposition to official government policy. The West Bank was "holy" in the way that the old state of Israel in Galilee and on the coastal plain was not. It was biblical country, the country of Abraham, Joshua and King David. At Hebron was the great tomb of the patriarchs Abraham, Isaac and Jacob, venerated by Muslims and Christians as well as by Jews. At Shechem (the Arab town of Nablus) Joshua had made a covenant between the tribes of Israel and God, after he had conquered the country. Bethlehem had been the birthplace of King David, a mighty slayer of the enemies of God. At Bethlehem too was the tomb of Rachel, the wife of Jacob, who was said to have risen and wept as she watched the children of Israel passing her tomb on their way to exile in Babylon in 589 B.C.E. Decades earlier, Zionists had committed themselves to a return to the land of Israel, because that land had been deeply embedded in the Jewish identity. Zionists had fiercely opposed the idea of seeking a homeland in neutral territory like Uganda for precisely this reason. The conquests of 1967 had returned the people of Israel to the land that had been the birthplace of much of this strong Jewish identity, and the same spirit that had led the early Zionists to reject any other land, against all reason, seemed just as clear to Dayan in 1967. He presented Jerusalem as so quint-essentially Jewish that the city would in some way perish if the Israelis withdrew their forces from the "Shechem mountains" and the Jordan bridges. It was also true that on the "holy" West Bank the Israelis had made a reunion with a Judaism that saw the integrity of their people as essentially tied to the physical possession of the Holy Land and to ruthless, absolute rejection of the claims of the *goyim*.

As early as August 1967, therefore, there were signs of a new, absolutist Zionist policy that was, as yet, in contradiction to official Israeli policy. In that same month the Arabs showed a similar abso-lutism. At the Khartoum Conference, which began on August 19, the Arab states issued their three famous "noes": no to peace with Israel, no recognition of the state of Israel and no negotiations with Israel concerning any Palestinian territory. The Arabs committed themselves to the old absolutism that had helped them to lose Palestine in the first place. The humiliation that the 1948 defeat had brought to the

Arabs was dramatically increased by their abject humiliation in 1967.
Such a crushing defeat can lead to extreme and negative solutions. In
Europe, after the First World War, the German defeat led to a despair
and collapse of morale that made the rise of Adolf Hitler possible. At
the Khartoum Conference a similiar collapse of confidence led to the
adoption of that absolute negativism that could produce no realistic
solution to the problems facing the Middle East.

Naturally, this Arab negativism fanned the flames of Israeli extremism. But events immediately succeeding the Six Day War showed
that Israelis did not turn to absolute policies simply in reaction to the
outright Arab refusal to consider any peaceful coexistence with Israel.
Labor Zionism had imbued some Israelis with moral worries after the
Six Day War, but in other Israelis it seemed that it had created a
hunger that it had not, in recent years, been able to nurture. Pioneering, in the early days, had been exciting and rather aggressive. In the
days that had passed since the establishment of Israel, it had become
a bit tame. Zionism had created a need, in some Israelis, to conquer
new lands by means of settlement. Thus, once they had admitted that
they were going to hold on to the occupied territories despite the UN
disapproval, the Labor government established settlements in the old
style along the valley of the river Jordan to ensure the security of the
state of Israel. These were new *kibbutzim* and were at one and the
same time agricultural and military settlements. Israel had responded
to the challenge of the occupation in an idiosyncratic way dictated by
a strong colonizing Zionist tradition. In Sinai, Haim Bar Lev established a system of military outposts against Egypt which he believed
to be impregnable. The ideological justification for these new military
colonizing adventures was defense. Israel was not thereby officially
conquering new territory; it was simply making the Jewish people safe
from Arab aggression. Yet it would be a mistake to see the mood of
Israel after the Six Day War as inherently fearful and terrorized by
Arab might. On the contrary, a confidence in Israel's military power
set in which proved to be illusory. Because Israel was now much better
positioned to repel the violence of the *fedayeen* against her own official
territories and because of the crushing defeat she had inflicted on the
Arabs, Israelis began to expect that the Allon line of settlements in
the West Bank and the Bar Lev line would secure her against any Arab
aggression, and this mood of heady confidence was shown to be misplaced when the Egyptian and Syrian armies easily broke through the
lines of Israeli defense in their surprise attack in the October War of
1973.

Some Israelis, then, were troubled after the 1967 war; others had a heady new confidence. The newly confident strain showed itself immediately after the war in projects that expressed the old pioneering hunger of Zionism without official sanction. Individual Israelis started to take a pioneering intiative, in the same spirit as the early Zionist settlers in Palestine. They would not wait for the territories to become Jewish officially but would do it themselves. Immediately after the war a group of writers, intellectuals and politicians formed the Movement for the Land of Israel, which gave financial and moral support to any Israelis who wanted to found *kibbutzim* in the new territories. Just days after the cease-fire, Kibbutz Merom Hagolam, the first of these settlements, was established on the Golan Heights near Quneitra, very close to the new border and only fifty kilometers from Damascus.[19] These settlers, without waiting for government endorsement, claimed that they were returning Israel to the spirit of early Zionism. They would lovingly cultivate the land of Israel that had been won so dramatically and would press aggressively against the frontiers of the Arab world. They were not at all distant from the ideology that had prompted the crusading military orders in the establishment of their border settlements. These new settlers were dreaming of a "Greater Land" of Israel. It was a secular movement and was not returning to the biblical definition of the land that God had promised to the Jews as much as to the spirit of Jabotinsky, who had demanded a state for the Jews on both sides of the Jordan, and to the spirit of Lehi, the so-called Stern Gang, which had envisaged a huge Jewish state that took in large areas of what is now Egypt, Jordan, Iraq, Syria and Lebanon.

The possibility of a Greater Land of Israel had created a new right-wing movement in the country. For nineteen years Begin and his Herut Party had been in the wilderness but these new settlers were returning to the ideals of Jabotinsky, Begin's hero, and were combining this vision with the pioneering vision of the Second Aliyah. But it also adopted a new policy, which turned the earlier movement on its head. The old Zionism, whether it was the Zionism of Ben-Gurion or of Jabotinsky, had always maintained that the Jews had a choice: they could either wait in the diaspora for the Messiah or they could save themselves. Now the new right proclaimed that they had no choice and made the phrase *en brerah* (no alternative) a rallying cry and slogan.[20] They insisted that Zionism had not been an active movement so much as a purely reactionary one. Throughout, the Jews had been coerced by their enemies so that they had no choice but to act as they did. Hitler, the British, the Palestinians and finally Nasser had attacked the Jews, forcing the Zionists to adopt one policy after another in order to survive. Thus the veteran *kibbutznik* Yitzhak Tabenkin rewrote Zionist history after 1967:

> We were coerced by history, left with no option. From scattered colonies to National Home, to a State in part of the Land and from that to the liberation of the Land of Israel as a whole. A process we did not initiate. At each stage we had no option (*en brerah*) but to respond to a demand made on us. We are manifestly coerced by the logic of tragedy and redemption.[21]

Tabenkin uses words like "redemption" and "liberation," which were condemned by Amos Oz, who was closer to official policy than Tabenkin at this point, to explain the new Israeli urge to expansion. But it denied values that earlier Zionism had deemed essential to make Jews take full human responsibility for their own fate. This post-1967 ideology showed that, because Israelis were coerced by the logic of tragedy, they were in the grip of fate and need take no responsibility for their actions. They certainly need not obey the United Nations Resolution 242: "There is no alternative of [sic] going back to the old boundaries," said a Greater Land spokesman after the war; "we are condemned to be strong."[22] This spirit also turned its back on an essential tradition of the Jewish religion which stressed personal accountability and moral responsibility. It had reverted to a more primitive view, which saw man as a helpless being who was quite unable to control his fate.

From 1967 these belligerent voices were heard loud and clear in Israel. But they were opposed both within Israel and also in the diaspora. Diaspora Jews created a movement which was eloquently called *Brerah*. They insisted that the Jews *did* have a choice. They were no less fervent Zionists than the Greater Land Movement but they were inspired by Zionist veterans like Nahum Goldman, who felt that Israel was in danger of overreaching itself: a terrible nemesis awaited all those who ignored realities in unrealistic and absolute dreams. *Brerah* felt that these expansionist visions would increase Arab resentment and corrode Israeli morality. Israel had had a difficult history and had definite problems that it was dangerous to ignore. In 1967 the issues had been clear. Israel had had to attack. Yitzhak Rabin had been correct in his speech at the Hebrew University just after the war when he spoke of "The Right of Israel." He spoke of the Israeli soldiers' "burning faith in their righteousness" and claimed that they were "carried forward by spiritual values, by deep spiritual resources, far more than by their weapons." He had concluded that, for this spiritual strength, Israelis had "no rational explanations, except in terms of a deep consciousness of the moral justice of their fight." But, *Brerah* asked, if Israelis were going to pursue policies that were in their own way as absolutist and as negative as those that the Arabs had adopted once again at Khartoum, what became of this Israeli moral superiority? Israel was in danger of sinking to the level of the kind of unrealistic values that she had always professed to despise. *Brerah* was true to the spirit of the old Zionism, which had been remarkably positive in responding to challenges when the Arabs maintained a destructive, negative stance. But the new *en brerah* thinking was negative and in danger of ignoring the political rights of the Arabs in the occupied territories. The Laborites had insisted that the occupation must be beneficent. But the *en brerah* idealists were showing a tendency that could ignore the rights of the conquered Palestinians in an absolutist pursuit of Israel's own destiny. It could maintain that the Israelis had "no choice" about the fate of these Palestinians in the territories, whereas the Israeli government was officially committed to the idea that Israel *did* have a choice and would exercise this choice with compassion and for peace. *Brerah* flourished for a while but soon fizzled out, due to the new intransigence that was slowly seeping into Israel, even during those ten years after the June War when Labor continued to form the government.

This became dramatically apparent in 1971. Nasser had died and his successor, President Anwar Sadat, made a startling offer on February 4, 1971. It was an entirely new departure for an Arab ruler and should have been, at least, noted with interest. Sadat said that if Israel withdrew her forces in the Sinai Peninsula to the passes he would open the Suez Canal to Israel, withdraw Egyptian troops from the east bank of the canal and enter into negotiations with Israel with a view to signing a peace treaty with her. For decades the Israelis had been treated to pure rejection and violence from the Arabs. They had constantly bemoaned their isolation and lack of friends in the region. At the time of writing, many Israelis look back with nostalgia to Sadat and sigh that if other Arab leaders had been like him history would have been very different. But in 1971 they totally ignored his offer.[23] To dismiss it with contempt as patently insincere would have been an understandable response, given the long tradition of Arab hatred of Israel. But Israel did not even give Sadat's offer the courtesy of this negative consideration. Golda Meir made no response at all, one way or the other. Six months later Defense Minister Moshe Dayan showed a similar willingness to ignore this Arab peace initiative. What had happened to Labor's commitment to the principle of territories for peace? Ignoring Sadat, he declared that because of entrenched Arab enmity he was "forced" to establish a settlement at Yamit, in Gaza, to be manned by members of Herut, Menachem Begin's party. "If the Arabs refuse to make peace, we cannot stand still," he said, invoking the spirit of *en brerah*. "If we are denied their co-operation, let us act on our own."[24] Two years later, in April 1973, at a ceremony on Masada, Dayan made a provocative speech which could not even claim to make the third of Labor's justifications for keeping the territories (Israel's defense and security) his priority. The speech described an expansionist vision, calling for a Greater Israel "with broad frontiers, strong and solid, with the authority of the Israeli government extending from the Jordan to the Suez Canal."[25]

Only a few months later, on October 6, Sadat's forces made their astonishingly successful invasion of the Sinai on the feast of Yom Kippur, the Day of Atonement. The Egyptians smashed through the apparently impregnable Bar Lev line in a surprise attack, while the Syrian troops invaded the Golan Heights, also taking Israel entirely by surprise. The complacency which had tended to prevail since 1967 was shattered. Israelis could no longer claim that the Arabs were useless on the battlefield: this assault showed a considerable advance in military skill. Israel felt acutely that she had been caught napping; although the IDF managed to push the Arabs back, they had a frightening demonstration of their isolation in the Middle East. One of the reasons Sadat gave for the October War was the establishment of the Yamit settlement and Israel's threat to establish a state extending into Arab territory to the Suez Canal. I shall discuss Sadat and his peace initiatives in the following chapter. Here it is sufficient to say that the Yom Kippur War restored a great deal of confidence to the Arabs. They no longer felt so humiliated; once he had established his military efficiency, Sadat was in a position to make another peace offer, this time from a position of greater strength.

The two wars of 1967 and 1973 did not merely promote a new form of secular Zionism; they also fueled an aggressive religious movement. At first these religious Jews, who would ultimately constitute the new far right, would represent only a small minority but they would gradually become a real threat to Israel. At the time of writing, they have become one of the government's greatest problems and are seen to endanger the possibility of peace in rather the same way as did Reynauld of Chatillon, whose followers were similarly a belligerent religious minority in the Kingdom of Jerusalem but who yet brought the Christians into a fatal confrontation with Saladin.

It will be recalled that, from the time of the Second Aliyah, religious Jews had been settling alongside the Labor Zionists in Eretz Yisrael.

The Mizrachi, who sought to establish a "spiritual center" for the Jews, did not want a secular state; they wanted a religious state based on the Torah. They believed that ultimately the secular Zionists would return to religion and that, once that conversion had taken place, the Messiah would come and establish the Kingdom of God. The secular Zionists regarded these Mizrachi settlements with tolerance but did not take them seriously. A crucial figure in this religious Zionism was Rabbi Abraham Yitzhak Kook, the leader of Mizrachi. He did not feel at all antagonistic to either the secular settlements or their aims. He thought that they were fulfilling God's plan without realizing it. Kook was always quick to praise the achievements of the early *kibbutzim* and their pioneering effort, seeing them as complementary to his religious plans for the Judaizing of Palestine. "We lay *tefillin*," he was fond of saying, "and the pioneers lay bricks."[26] The religious settlers lived according to Torah and the pioneers, whether they understood this or not, were fulfilling a priestly task.[27] All Jewish activity, he claimed, be it secular or religious, should at this crucial time be seen as "the light of the Messiah."[28] The settlers of the Second Aliyah had believed that they would help to save the world by helping to inaugurate the socialist millennium; at the same time, ignored by them, Mizrachi, under the leadership of Rabbi Kook, were awaiting the imminent Messianic redemption foretold by the prophets, which would bring about a new era of prosperity and peace for the whole world. "All civilisations will be revived by the renaissance of our spirit," Kook wrote. "All quarrels will be resolved and our revival will cause all life to be luminous with the joy of fresh birth."[29] Kook's view of Eretz Yisrael was close to that of Judah Halevi, the twelfth-century religious Zionist. By immersing themselves in "the land's towering holiness" the Jews would save themselves. In exile Judaism had become weak because it had no Temple. Without Temple worship on Mount Moriah in Jerusalem, the Torah could not be observed in its entirety, so it was not possible to live a fully Jewish life. The Torah reflected the conditions of daily life in Palestine and the very different conditions—climatic, social, economic—that prevailed in the diaspora also meant that diaspora Jews were living a life that was alien to the spirit of the Bible in many ways. Further, in the diaspora, Kook said, Jews were inevitably infected by the corrupt, secular values of the Gentiles:

> The air of the gentile lands holds the Jews back. The impure soil that is everywhere outside the land of Israel is thus suffused with the stench of idolatry and the Jews there are worshippers of idols

in purity. The only way in which we may escape the disgrace of idolatry is for the Jewish people to gather in the land of Israel.[30]

It should not be a surprise to see how close this religious Zionism was to the spirit not only of Judah Halevi but also to a secular Zionist like A. B. Gordon, who was practicing the religion of Labor (*avodah*) in Kibbutz Degania at the same time as the Mizrachi were making their Torah settlements. Gordon also saw Eretz Yisrael as imbued with a power that was unique: only there could a Jew be truly himself. Only in Eretz Yisrael could a Jew liberate himself from the shame of the diaspora. It will be remembered that before his conversion to Labor Zionism Gordon had been an Orthodox Jew. Labor Zionism had been a translation of old religious passions into a secular idiom. Like the Laborites, Mizrachi settlers were gripped by a belief in an approaching millennium and were committed to redeeming the land and redeeming the Jewish people by means of *avodah*. The difference was that, for a secular Zionist like Gordon, *avodah* meant labor, work, but for Rabbi Kook *avodah* meant worship, religious observance; it meant keeping the 613 commandments of the Torah in the land of the Bible and working for the restoration of the Temple.[31]

For the first twenty years of the history of the state of Israel, the religious Zionists were content to keep a low profile and the seculars scarcely seemed aware of their existence. But by 1967 the religious had become very worried indeed and felt it was time to take drastic action and to break cover. They had believed that the powerful experience of actually living in the land of their forefathers would impel Jews back to the Torah. But in the view of the religious Zionists, instead of encouraging Jews to return to the Bible the state of Israel was becoming more materialistic and more polluted with secular idolatry than some of the diaspora countries. Israelis were worshiping false gods like money, pleasure or even man-made ideologies like secular nationalism in place of Yahweh. They were therefore polluting the sacred soil of Israel. During the *Hamtana* period, while the Israelis waited for the outbreak of the Six Day War, convinced that they were about to be exterminated, the religious Zionists in their settlements and yeshivas had their own interpretation of the forthcoming catastrophe. Three weeks before the outbreak of war, Rabbi Kook's son, Rabbi Zvi Yehuda Kook, gave his annual address on the anniversary of the creation of the state of Israel at the important Merkaz Harav yeshiva in North Jerusalem. Usually the rabbi praised the labors of the state but this year his message was very different. "We have sinned!" he cried and the audience began to weep.[32] The nation had been guilty of grave infidelity. How, the rabbi asked, could a truly Jewish state allow the Temple Mount to remain in the hands of the *goyim* of Jordan? How could the chosen people be content to settle in the Negev and in the coastal plain, when the true Holy Land was in enemy territory? What kind of Jewish state allowed the holy cities of Hebron, Shechem and Jericho to remain unliberated? When the IDF actually did liberate these "holy" cities a few weeks later, Rabbi Kook was hailed by his followers as a true prophet of Israel. Like some of the seculars, they naturally saw the extraordinary victory as an act of God; for them it also heralded the approaching Messianic redemption.[33] After the war, therefore, the religious Zionists were no longer willing to take a back seat in the state of Israel. They felt that God had done his part and now they had to ensure that the government completed his work. They would have agreed entirely with the view of Abraham Heschel, whom I quoted earlier: "God has had a dream and it is the task of Israel to interpret that dream." They came vociferously out in the open, determined to interpret God's will into concrete facts.

The emergence of this passionate religious Zionism, which they had ignored for so long, was a terrible shock to many of the Laborites. Amos Oz recorded an early meeting between left-wing intellectuals and *kibbutzniks* and the religious Zionists at the Merkaz Harav yeshiva. The *kibbutzniks* were dismayed by the shrill nationalism that seemed to have gripped many of their fellow countrymen, who were determined to stay in the newly occupied territories whatever the cost. Like Ben-Gurion, the leftists wanted to rid Labor Zionism of a righteous triumphalism which they felt to be alien. They had, therefore, gone to the Merkaz Harav yeshiva to seek the advice of the scholars and students there, hoping to tap the rich, compassionate element in the Jewish religious tradition. They fully expected to explore the wisdom of the prophets and sages with the rabbis in order to remind their fellow countrymen of these ancient Jewish values. Instead they had the shock of their lives. For the first time they heard the unfamiliar rhetoric of the Jewish "holy war." They heard, Oz recalls, an enthusiasm that was alien to them: "ecstasy over the Wailing Wall and Biblical sites in the West Bank, the talk of victory and miracles, Redemption and the Coming of the Messiah."[34] The Christian Crusaders would have understood this kind of language and ideology very well, for it had translated many of these apocalyptic ideas and the passion for holy places into Christianity. In the twelfth century Judah Halevi had sensed this affinity. But for Oz and his fellow Laborites this religious Zionism seemed heartless, fundamentalist and a contradiction of values that were essential to Judaism. The rabbinical students seemed

> crude, smug and arrogant, power-drunk, bursting with messianic rhetoric, ethnocentric, "redemptionist," apocalyptic—quite simply, inhuman. And un-Jewish. The Arab human beings under our dominion might never have been. It was not an affair of, as it were, human distress, but of signs and oracles, of tidings of "the end of days" and of the beginning of Redemption.[35]

Even though these rabbis must at this point have seemed a very small minority and could have been dismissed by a contemptuous observer as "the lunatic fringe," not to be taken seriously, Laborites like Oz instinctively saw them as a danger.

But the rabbis were not content with words and rhetoric. They wanted action, which once again took an essentially Zionist form. Immediately after the victory of 1967 Rabbi Moshe Levinger, a graduate of Merkaz Harav and a disciple of Rabbi Kook, became a pioneer in the holy land of the West Bank. He went straight Hebron and squatted for six months in the Park Hotel. Then he transferred himself and his followers to a nearby former Jordanian army camp, which was now empty. He refused to leave until the government gave him permission to build a settlement and sent soldiers to guard the settlers from the Arabs of Hebron, who naturally saw this as a provocative act. Together with Rabbi Eliezer Waldman, another graduate of Merkaz Harav, he built the settlement of Kiryat Arba, the ancient biblical name for Hebron. But this was not all: with tireless energy, Levinger went on to build one new colony after another on the West Bank and very quickly the religious settlers had established the Etzion Bloc of religious colonies between Jerusalem and Hebron. Despite UN Resolution 242, these rabbis were making Jewish presence an established fact in the heavily populated West Bank area. They had no intention of trading this territory for peace; nor did they see it primarily as a question of Israel's military security. They were redeeming the Holy Land from the *goyim* by living full Jewish lives in accordance with the Torah. They also saw themselves as fulfilling the ancient prophecies that foretold the Jews' return to their land immediately before the coming of the Messiah. The early Zionists had not sat back passively to wait for an official, political solution to the Jewish problem: they had acted in order to make Jewish presence in Palestine an established fact. Now the rabbis were continuing this tradition, but in religious terms. They were not going to sit back and wait for the prophecies to be fulfilled. They would fulfill the prophecies themselves by returning to the land of the Bible in order to hasten the coming of the Messiah.[36] The rabbis were quite aware that the government was embarrassed by their venture: Israel was not supposed to be colonizing these occupied territories. Unlike the Allon settlements, which the government had established on the West Bank, these could not be justified as an essential security measure and a military necessity. Nor were these religious settlements like those of the Greater Land Movement, which were all in relatively uninhabited territory. This new colonizing venture meant creating colonies in densely populated cities like Hebron and involved the confiscation of land from the Arabs.

In their settlements the rabbis studied Torah. The important yeshiva Bar-Etzion was founded by Rabbi Haim Drukman in the Etzion Bloc. Unlike other Orthodox yeshivas, whose students are not obliged to do military service, much to the chagrin of many secular Zionists, the Bar-Etzion students were intensely patriotic and saw national service as an important religious duty. This was quite a different form of religious orthodoxy and the Labor government were not at all certain how to deal with it. They were reluctant to give the rabbis land and permission to settle, because such a colonizing project was illegal and against their own official policy. But the rabbis were always able to play one political leader off against another, so that they invariably got what they wanted. These settlements touched something very deep in the Zionist pioneering identity of some Laborites, just as the Greater Land Movement did. A Laborite like Shimon Peres was very supportive of the religious settlers.[37] In these early days some Laborites thought that settlement in the West Bank might actually help Arab-Jewish relations: by living side by side with these settlers, people hoped that the Arabs might come to tolerate the Jews. Thus Moshe Arens pointed to the relatively calm atmosphere in towns like Haifa and Acre, which had a mixed Arab-Jewish population as compared with other places like Petah Tikvah or Nazareth where Jews and Arab lived separately and had more extreme ideas about one another. The Laborite Israel Galili thought that by sharing the harsher conditions that prevailed in Arab areas the religious settlers were living a new form of socialist Zionism.[38] Indeed, it seemed to many Israelis that the rabbis had snatched the pioneering torch from the hands of Labor, and the rabbis encouraged this by proclaiming that *they* were the true heirs of the early Zionist movement: the Labor leaders had got soft and their policies smacked of weakness and compromise. God had given an extraordinary opportunity to Israel and had dramatically increased her territory overnight but the Labor government had refused to make the most of it.

In fact it became apparent that the Laborite leaders were looking at these religious colonies with rather rosy vision. They were not likely to improve Arab-Jewish relations because they depended upon confiscation of Arab land, which naturally caused resentment. Similarly, because these settlements were guarded by the IDF they were at once associated with the military aspects of the unpopular occupation in the eyes of the Arabs and resentment was increased by the different laws that applied to Jews and Arabs. The Arabs were subject to the laws of the military occupation and these were often harsh, whereas the Jewish settlers were subject only to the laws of the state of Israel and were exempt from curfews, policing and military supervision.[39] Relations between Arabs and Jews were also being ruined because of the provocative behavior of many of the settlers, who had no interest in appeasing the *goyim* and who flaunted their Jewish religion and their determination to stay and wrest the land from the Arabs. When this led to Arab violence, the settlers would take the law into their own hands and retaliate in kind. They insisted that the Arabs respected this: they could understand it much better than what the settlers saw as the mealymouthed sympathy of Laborites like Oz.[40]

But despite the problems that were obviously beginning to arise, the Labor government could not quite abandon the rabbis and their settlements. They gave them government grants and encouragement. Thus this very small religious minority was able to attract powerful support. Not only did the rabbis appeal to some leftists, their aggressive territorial attitudes also appealed to the young secular Israelis in the Greater Land Movement. Some of these joined the religious colonies, as did tough young soldiers in crack army units. They might not share the religious ideals of the rabbis but they respected their courage and the clarity of their position. They seemed to be in tune with the uncompromising spirit of a leader like Moshe Dayan. The years that succeeded the Six Day War were years of confidence in Israel. True, Israelis were being appallingly harassed by international Arab terrorism, such as the tragic incident at the Munich Olympic Games in 1972, but at home Israelis felt secure. The *fedayeen* in Arafat's new PLO were inflicting heavy casualties on the army on the Sinai border but the IDF was confident that they could repel that threat. The new territories had created a security area around Israel which made it harder for *fedayeen* to make their raids, and the Black September incident showed that the PLO had appalling difficulties in the

Arab world. As for the Arab states, Israelis believed that they had learned their lesson in 1967. It was this confidence that led Dayan, a supporter of the settlement movement, to make his provocative statement on Masada in 1973 shortly before the Yom Kippur War. Despite the cautious policies of the Labor government, Israel seemed set for expansion.

The October War was a salutary shock to this false confidence. Israel felt her isolation in the area keenly and realized that she could not afford to relax her vigilance. The Arabs seemed intent on destroying Israel and this time they had made a much better showing on the battlefield. The Arabs could afford to lose war after war, but Israel could not afford to lose a single war. The Crusaders had discovered the same thing at the Battle of Hittin, when they had lost their kingdom in a single day. A harder attitude set in. The country was still committed to a Labor government and in 1974 Yitzhak Rabin became Prime Minister. Rabin, like Dayan, could have been seen as a stirring example of the old Labor Zionism. He had been raised on a *kibbutz* and had been intended for farming but instead he joined the Palmach and had a brilliant military career. Like Dayan, he had been a hero of the Six Day War. But he was not a popular Prime Minister, for he seemed grim and uncharismatic. He believed that the Israelis should exchange the territories for peace: they should give back heavily populated areas on the West Bank and the Gaza Strip to Jordan and Egypt, thus ridding themselves of the recalcitrant Arab population. But Israel should retain certain strategic zones in the territories for her own defense.

This was anathema to the pioneering rabbis. It seemed that the Labor government was determined to resist God's plan for his people and that further punishments would follow it there was further loss of faith. As Rabbi Waldman explained:

> In 1967 God gave us a unique opportunity. But the Israelis did not seize it. They did not colonize the newly-conquered land. They left all the options open. It's as if they had refused the offer of the Almighty while at the same time thanking him. Therefore God inflicted upon Israel the sufferings of the Yom Kippur war.[41]

On the day after Rabin became Prime Minister, Rabbi Levinger founded the Gush Emunim, the Bloc of the Faithful. Hitherto the pioneering rabbis had worked within the confines of the National Religious Party, but they had increasingly found that the NRP was too limited to satisfy their needs: it was concerned with ensuring that the secular government remained true to important Jewish laws like the dietary proscriptions and Sabbath observance. They were concerned with banning public transport on Saturday and ensuring that El Al, the Israeli airline, did not fly on the Sabbath. They were anxious to make restaurants kosher, to forbid pig farming and to ensure that the marital laws of Israel remained true to the Torah. The radical rabbis of Merkaz Harav found the NRP lacking in political perspective and by founding Gush Emunim they were declaring independence. This was the first party of the newly emerging far right.

Gush Emunim is not a political party seeking seats in the Knesset. It is a pressure group dedicated to making the nation understand the importance of retaining the Holy Land of the West Bank. Amana, its colonizing branch, is dedicated to planning new settlements on the West Bank and to urging diaspora Jews to make *aliyah* in order to man them. They were helped by the new religious mood in Israel after the Yom Kippur War. This shock had led many Israelis and diaspora Jews to return to their religion and to Torah observance. Some of these found the ideology of the rabbis inspiring and exciting and they did join Amana. We have seen that nearly half a million Israelis left the country during the 1970s. This was serious for Israel, which needed more people to make *aliyah* and could not afford to lose citizens. During the 1970s only about 384,000 people made *aliyah*. This trend has continued during the 1980s. More Israelis continue to leave, and the number of new settlers fell to 185,000. Even the Russian Jews prefer in the main to go to the United States when they leave the Soviet Union.[42] Rabbi Levinger is not alone in his concern to encourage Jewish immigration. He and his colleagues have toured America, to encourage the Jews to return to Israel. They have not proved to be as successful as they had hoped. Levinger's aim is to increase the number of Jewish settlers on the West Bank to a million. At present it has been estimated that there are only about 30,000 Jewish settlers in the occupied territories. Only about two percent of the population of Israel follows this form of Judaism. Some Israelis have been willing to move into the occupied territories because housing is cheaper there: of the 150 settlements in the territories at the time of writing, only about 30 are affiliated to Amana.[43] The rest have been installed by the government. Gush Emunim is a small minority movement but, even though it is, numerically, no great threat, events have proved that it is a danger to the country, as we shall see.

In many of these settlements Amana settlers live a communal life. They have established themselves at places of religious interest and importance. Thus there are settlements at Tekoa, the home of the prophet Amos, at Ofra, near Shechem, and at Shiloh, the site of the ancient sanctuary of Yahweh. That these are populated areas and that the Arabs find this organized Jewish presence threatening and provocative does not worry members of the Gush, because the rights and interests of the *goyim* must take second place to God's plan for his chosen people and for the whole world. If anybody asks Rabbi Levinger whether he is concerned that his movement is endangering the peace process, he replies:

> No. The advance of the Jewish people, the fulfilment of the Redemption of the Jewish people and Eretz Yisrael—these are more important than any hypothetical peace. It is through all this that the world can be saved.[44]

He is convinced that his settlements are the first signs of the coming of the Messiah and the Kingdom of God and so he pursues his course oblivious to its mundane political consequences. A religious movement on the far right despises a Zionist who tries to see things from the Arabs' point of view. As Yisrael Harel, chairman of the Council of Jewish Settlements, has said, there must be a return to "absolute truth," which admits of no valid "other sides."[45] The Arabs are merely a trial, whereby God is testing his people. The members of Gush, like the other members of the new far right, are implacably opposed to any peace process. Harriet, an American Jew who made *aliyah* to join the Tekoa community, told Amos Oz:

> "In the Six Day War, and the Yom Kippur War, too, we should never have stopped. We should have gone on, brought them to total surrender! Smashed their capital cities! Who cares what the goyim were yelling?" After some thought, she adds, "But that wouldn't have brought peace, either. Maybe it would have given us some quiet, but not peace. Because this is a religious war! A holy war! For them *and* for us! A war against all of Islam. And against all the goyim."

If the Israeli leaders are cowardly enough to sign a peace treaty with the Arabs that would hand back the West Bank, she added, then the Gush should act independently to provoke a new war and preserve the integrity of Judaism.[46]

This kind of talk in a highly sensitive area is dangerous and it fills Israelis who *are* concerned with the peace process with dismay. When people become familiar with inflammatory rhetoric they get used to extreme and unrealistic positions. Israelis on the left who are still clinging to the old high-minded idealism insist that it is dangerous to get into the habit of thinking that the Arabs don't matter. Of all people, the Jews cannot afford to ignore the identity and rights of others.

Nevertheless, if the Gush Emunim have never been a threat in numerical terms, it must be remembered that they enjoyed the support of a large number of Israelis on left and right, as we have seen. Many of these would never consider actually joining Amana and moving to the West Bank: Shimon Peres remained at a distance and other sympathizers had even less connection with the Gush and found some of their ideas bizarre. But they liked them for insisting on the Jewish right to stay in the territories. Many people admired their absolute certainty. Their hard-line position had been conveyed into mainstream thought and it represented a definite swing to the right during the 1970s. This became clear in the 1977 elections, when Labor lost its majority for the first time and Menachem Begin, the old Irgun extremist, who had been in the wilderness since 1948, became Prime Minister.

Begin headed the new Likud Party, which had amalgamated Herut and the Liberals. Likud dropped the old "land for peace" ideal of the Laborites. It will be recalled that Begin was a passionate admirer of Vladimir Jabotinsky, and one of the first things he did on taking office was to arrange to have the remains of his hero brought to Israel from the diaspora. Jabotinsky had pressed for a land on both sides of the Jordan and Begin's Likud followed him in pressing for the old biblical definition of the borders of the Jewish state:

> That very day, the Lord made a covenant with Abram and he said: "To your descendants I give this land from the River of Egypt to the great River: the River Euphrates, the territory of the Kenites, the Kenizzites, Kadmonites, Hittites, Perizzites, Rephaim, Amorites, Canaanites, Girgashites, Hivites and Jebusites" (Genesis 15:18–21).

Begin had gone to the polls committed to extending the territory of the Jewish state and to promoting the ideal of the Greater Land of Israel on both sides of the Jordan. Begin was also a survivor of the Holocaust but, unlike many other survivors, he had no guilt about his survival. He had arrived in Eretz Yisrael in the early 1940s committed to revenge. He had quickly developed a strong hatred and contempt of the Arabs and felt no compulsion to see things from their point of view.

Neither did his main supporters, the oriental Jews who had been forced to flee the Arab countries in 1948. These Sephardic Jews had come to hate the Labor Party: they claimed that when they arrived in Eretz Yisrael the Labor Zionists had seen them as "Arabs" and made them into second-class citizens; that they had been given inferior housing and education; that their traditions had been scorned and that the Laborites had tried to make them drop their old oriental culture to become good Zionists. It is certainly true that the Laborites had made grave mistakes in their treatment of the Sephardim and their resentment had shocked Golda Meir's government when the oriental Jews rioted violently in 1972. The hatred and resentment of Sephardim for Ashkenazim in Israel is still painful and obvious at the time of writing. Like Begin, the Sephardim had no guilt about the Arabs: they had experienced the full brunt of the new Arab anti-Semitism which had developed after the creation of the state of Israel and the Arabs' humiliating defeat in 1948. They had lived for centuries in the Arab world and bitterly resented having to leave their homes. When they got to Israel, they had no compunction about taking the place of the Palestinians who had fled. Similarly, they found Begin's Likud ideology a relief. Zionism was a complex movement born out of European preoccupations. The Sephardim had found it an alien, puzzling ideology, but Begin's appeal to biblical values made sense to these oriental Jews, who were often still deeply religious. They were also delighted to get rid of the Labor government and hailed Begin as their champion and hero.[47]

"We were granted the right to exist by the God of our fathers," Begin insisted, "at the glimmer of the dawn of human civilization nearly 4,000 years ago. For that right, which has been sanctified in Jewish blood from generation to generation, we have paid a price unexampled in the annals of the nations."[48] This was music to the ears of the Sephardim and naturally Begin's own strong religious commitment was welcome to the religious right. Because Begin was committed to establishing the largest state of Israel that he possibly could, he enthusiastically established government settlements in the territories. But precisely because he was committed to a maximalist position as regards land, he was able to trade territory for security more blatantly than any Labor Prime Minister had dared to do.[49] In the next chapter I shall discuss in more detail the Camp David agreement that Begin signed with President Anwar Sadat of Egypt in 1979. This meant that Israel lost the Sinai but, in return for recognition of the state of Israel and security on her southern frontier, Begin was ready to give up land that was neither included within the borders of the Promised Land in the Bible, nor part of Jabotinsky's vision of Greater Israel. But Begin was still committed to expansion: on the day that he announced the Camp David agreement he also announced the establishment of twenty new government settlements in the West Bank. Further, despite the peace treaty, Begin was filled with no friendly feelings toward the *goyim*, be they Arab or American. His experience of anti-Semitism had left an indelible impression upon him and he always viewed Jews' relations with Gentiles in the light of this absolute hostility. In fact he called Camp David itself in the Maryland hills "a concentration camp de luxe."[50]

Begin's treaty with Egypt led to the formation of two new movements in Israel. The first was founded when the negotiations between Egypt and Israel had stalled and young leftists created the Shalom Akshav or Peace Now movement. This was not a political party but a pressure group, whose name describes its objective clearly: peace is a priority. Somebody has to be ready to halt the escalation of violence, which will inevitably get out of control if it is not brought to an end. For decades Arabs and Jews had been caught in a spiral of violence, of strike and counterstrike, attack and retaliation. One side had to be prepared to call a halt and seek compromise. Peace Now gained a large following: after the Sabra and Shatilla massacres in Lebanon they were able to mount a demonstration of 400,000 people in Tel Aviv in 1982. But they had one defect: Arabs were not allowed to be members. This was rectified by Uri Avnery when he founded the Progressive List for Peace, which is a political party seeking votes in the Knesset and which has both Arabs and Jews as members. In the 1984 elections the PLP gained two seats in the Knesset, 1.8 percent of the vote.

The new right, however, had a very different reaction to Camp David. In protest against this peace treaty with the Arabs, a group of well-known Israelis, religious and secular, formed the Tehiya or Renaissance Party. The ideal of *tehiya* had been very important in the ideology of the Lehi (the Stern Gang) and Tehiya follows closely in the footsteps of this earlier extremist group. The leaders of Tehiya enunciated three important principles. First, war is unfortunately a fact of life in Israel and if the country is to survive Israelis must stop regarding war as a dirty word. Second, Israel must never withdraw from any of her territories, because once one concession is made to the Arabs it would be seen as legitimizing other Arab claims: to withdraw from the West Bank would lead to the demand to withdraw from Galilee, which is just as "Arab." Third, the Camp David accords must be rejected: there must be nothing in Israeli policy to feed Arab hopes, no "keeping the options open." Annexation of the occupied territories must be made irreversible by settlement and colonization.[51]

The leaders of Tehiya had no guilt about the Arabs and adopted attitudes of notable hostility. Geula Cohen, for example, a mystical believer in Judaism but not an observer of the Torah, was a member of the Irgun and had published her autobiography, *Woman of Violence, Memoirs of a Young Terrorist, 1943–1948*. Raphael Eytan would be chief of staff in the IDF during the Lebanon war and would be censured for his role in the Sabra and Shatilla massacres. Rabbi Eliezer Waldman has maintained that the kidnapping of three Israeli officers in Beirut was God's punishment of the Israeli government for punishing acts of Jewish terrorism against Arabs.[52] The eminent physicist Professor Yuval Neeman, the founding father of the party, who comes from a Labor background, would be prepared to grant Arabs Israeli citizenship, provided that they offered absolutely no threat to the security of Greater Israel.

When Neeman announced the formation of the party in 1979, he confidently expected to win twenty seats in the 1981 elections. This was most unrealistic: it would have been an unparalleled feat for an Israeli political party to achieve such success in the first two years of its existence. In the event, Tehiya gained only three seats in 1981 (2.6 percent of the vote). But Tehiya remains the largest and most important party on the far right. At each election support for the party has steadily grown, another indication of the hardening of Israeli public opinion.

The early 1980s were overshadowed by the Lebanon war. It was undertaken ostensibly in order to make Galilee safe from the raids of the Palestinian *fedayeen* in Lebanon but the Israeli army did not withdraw once it had achieved its objective of expelling the PLO from the country. It seemed part of Israel's policy of expansion and became most unpopular both at home and abroad. The Sabra and Shatilla massacres damaged Israel's reputation internationally, the long war ruined the economy and the loss of Israeli lives in what some considered an unjust war alienated many Israelis. More Israelis joined the peace movements. There was also a new movement in the army. Israeli law makes no provision for conscientious objection to military service, because the Israeli people have never wanted it. Until the Lebanon war, Israelis had been proud of their army and had seen its activities and wars as entirely necessary. But during the Lebanon war a group of officers formed a movement called Yesh Gvul (There Is a Limit): there were some things that no Israeli soldier should be required to do. In 1984 members of Yesh Gvul encouraged reservists in the IDF to refuse to serve in the occupied territories: many felt that the duties they were asked to perform in Gaza and the West Bank were inhumane and deprived the Palestinians of basic human rights. Since that time a steadily increasing number of Israelis have been ready to go to prison rather than to serve in the territories, and as some of these are very distinguished veterans this has been a great crisis for both the army and the government. The movement was supported by the controversial Professor Yeshayahu Liebowitz, who is also an Orthodox Jew. He shows that religion does not need to impel an Israeli to violence and extremity: he advocates a separation of religion from politics in Israel, condemns the current aggressive nationalism as idolatry and accepts the idea of a Palestinian state. He insists that in order to maintain its moral integrity Israel must hand back the territories and condemns the behavior of Israel there as fascism.[53]

Other Israelis were also insistent that Israel must withdraw from the occupied territories, simply in order to ensure her survival. Notable among these was Professor Y. Harkabi, the former head of military intelligence whose book, *The Fateful Decision* (1988), points to a worrying demographic argument. If Israel holds on to the territories, she will include 2.2 million Palestinians in her enlarged state. These Palestinians will have to be enfranchised if Israel is going to retain her commitment to democracy. In fifteen years, Harkabi argues, the Palestinians, whose birth rate is higher, will have become a majority. They will be able to exercise their democratic right to reform the Law of Return, which promises instant citizenship to any Jew who makes *aliyah*. Once they are a majority in the country, the Palestinians will be able to ensure that Palestinians are also allowed to return to their country and become citizens. The Jews are not making *aliyah* but the Palestinians will certainly come to Israel. In effect, Israel will cease to be a Zionist state. When Harkabi published his book in 1988 he was convinced that Israelis would see the force of that argument. When the book made very little impact and no impression on Israeli policy, Harkabi was given to saying that Israel had committed herself to a certain death.

But other Israelis condemned this peaceful trend in Israel. On June 2, 1980, car-bomb explosions injured the two Arab mayors of Nablus and Ramallah: one lost a foot and the other both legs and it was considered certain that the culprits were members of the Jewish underground. Rabbi Eliezer Waldman of Tehiya was one of the suspects but he was released owing to lack of evidence. Tehiya does not condemn terrorism: its members may not commit terrorist acts precisely *as* members of their party because this would mean that the government could outlaw Tehiya as a terrorist group. But it approves of those of its members who commit terrorist acts as private individuals.[54]

In 1984, as I have already mentioned, members of the Jewish underground were discovered to have plotted to blow up the Dome of the Rock and al-Aqsa. Rabbis of the right did not condemn this attempt: the Messiah could not come until the shrines on the Temple Mount had gone. This aggressive act was also pleasing to members of Gush Emunim. It showed that the Jews were ready to cast worldly prudence aside and court the enmity of the united Arab world as well as damaging Israel's international support. Only when the chosen people were prepared to throw caution to the winds would God step in and save his people.

Crusaders had also believed in extreme policies that defied human common sense. They had also pursued aggressive and deliberately provocative religious policies and in doing so they were largely responsible for the fall of the Kingdom of Jerusalem. But it could be argued that the far right is still only a small minority in Israel. In the 1984 elections they secured only six seats out of a total of 120. The peace parties PLP and Civil Rights achieved five seats. It is possible to argue that the two extremes of right and left are pretty evenly balanced. But the danger is more insidious than that. This became clear when the late Rabbi Meir Kahane managed to win a seat in the 1984 election even though his party Kach was denounced by all political parties without exception, even those of the far right. The Gush Emunim, Tehiya and Morasha (a far right party led by Rabbi Haim Drukman, which is also committed to colonizing the territories) all found Kahane and Kach a deep embarrassment. To understand the significance of Kahane's election, we need first to examine his ideology and then to look at the way one of the most obnoxious of these policies has spread beyond the confines of Kach. The real danger of the far right is that their ideas become acceptable to people who would not necessarily accept all their policies but who might be prepared to include one or two of these in a less threatening package.

Meir Kahane arrived in Israel in 1974 after a long history of religious zeal which had often expressed itself in violence. In America he had been an FBI agent and had penetrated a conservative and allegedly anti-Semitic organization. He then founded the Jewish Defense League in New York, which mounted a terrorist campaign against young blacks who attacked Jews in the streets and also against the Soviet Union, because of its anti-Semitic policies. Then he made *aliyah* and founded Kach (Thus It Is!). Kahane was clear that, like the leaders of Tehiya, he approved of terrorism against the enemies of Jews, though he could not allow Kach's association with terrorism to become manifest.[55] But it is widely believed that TNT (Terror Against Terror), a movement in the Jewish underground, is the military arm of Kach. Kahane insisted on a solution to the problems of Israel that shocks some Israelis and intrigues others because of its ruthless simplicity: every single Palestinian in the country must be forcibly deported. This is a blatantly racist solution and Jews have suffered far too much from such racism to encourage it among themselves. But Kahane was adamant that there is no other solution and it is difficult for Israelis to counter his arguments.[56]

Kahane pointed to the demographic problem, described by Professor Y. Harkabi, which is Israel's nightmare. If Palestinians are allowed to remain in the country and in the territories they will attain a majority and destroy the Jewish state. Kahane suggested that Arabs should be offered financial inducements to leave, but if that failed, then Israel would have to use force: "I am not about to ask them to leave," he said, "I want to make them leave . . . I want to scare them."[57] Kahane had no interest in the peace process: when he would arrive in an Arab town like Umm al-Fahm he had no intention of trying to win Arabs over. He was telling them to leave. When there were riots against Arabs in Afula, Kahane visited the town and praised the townsfolk: they were not rabble-rousers, he cried, they were "good, loyal Jews."[58] Whenever he turned up to speak, members of the left also turned up to demonstrate their disapproval. At Afula, people from the nearby *kibbutzim* blew whistles so that he could not be heard. At other rallies, leftists have handed out pamphlets to the Arabs, apologizing to them. But it is also true that whenever he spoke hundreds of young people turned up and cheered him enthusiastically. This, more than anything else, worried, and continues to worry, many Israelis.

As long as Kahane remained an outsider, he was no real threat. But when he was actually elected to the Knesset in 1984 and the result revealed that Kach had 1.2 percent of the vote, people became alarmed. There was widespread disgust and dismay. The result of the 1984 election showed that the Likud had lost its clear majority: the Lebanon war had been very damaging to its interests. Labor secured 44 percent of the votes and Likud 41 percent. There was to be a coalition government between Labor and Likud. But Kahane's election, as well as the increase in the number of seats of the far right parties, revealed a sinister trend that made Likud the center party. President Haim Herzog refused to receive Kahane; the left called him a Jewish Hitler and Yitzhak Shamir, the new leader of Likud, declared him "negative, detrimental and dangerous."[59] It was considered shameful that he should be a member of the Jewish parliament, that he should propose laws similar to the Nuremberg laws in the Knesset.[60] For decades

Israelis had got used to the Arabs calling Israel a racist state but now a member of the Knesset was saying the same thing loudly and publicly: his argument was that the Law of Return was a racist law, which excludes Arabs because they do not have the right genetic inheritance. The only possible justification for the exclusion of the Arabs was a religious imperative. God had told Moses that the *goyim* must not live in the Promised Land: "God wants us to live in a country of our own, isolated, so that we live separately and have the least possible contact with what is foreign, and so that we create as far as possible a pure Jewish culture based on the Torah."[61]

Kach is the most blatantly reductive, monistic and crusading party in the far right. Instead of seeing Judaism as a rich, complex tradition that evolved a whole civilization over the centuries, Kahane saw the integrity of Judaism as reduced to one message:

> There are not several messages in Judaism. There is only one. And this message is to do what God wants. Sometimes God wants us to go to war, sometimes he wants us to live in peace. . . . But there is only one message: God wanted us to come to this country and to create a Jewish State.[62]

Kahane had no time for Western humanism and he saw democracy as against the Torah. He wanted a Torah state. Kahane also believed that the Messiah will come very soon. If the Jews deserve him and establish themselves in Israel, he will come in glory, but if the Jews fail in this he will arrive in a terrible anti-Semitic catastrophe.[63] Kahane was not upset by the thought that his policies may lead to a renewal of anti-Semitism. He thought that would be a good thing because persecution would mean that the Jews would have to leave the diaspora and come to Israel.[64]

By 1987, however, it looked as though Kahane had overreached himself. His racist diatribes had produced disgust and everyone seemed weary of him. But in July that year the well-known general Rahavam Ze'evi advocated the policy of the "transfer" of large numbers of Palestinians from the occupied territories to Jordan. Ze'evi expressed the plan more elegantly and euphemistically than Kahane: the word "transfer" seemed more acceptable than the word "deportation." The plan was roundly condemned by both Peres and Shamir but Rabin pointed out that, if Israel was going to stay in the territories, transfer was the only viable way of preserving the Zionist state. Ze'evi's transfer plan Rabin argued, proved the bankruptcy of the Greater Land Movement.[65]

But Ze'evi won supporters. Not surprisingly, he found support among the far right. Both Tehiya and Morasha considered the plan feasible, though Tehiya preferred the use of the term "agreed removal" to transfer. Indeed Raphael Eytan shortly afterward founded his own Tzomet Party, based on the transfer plan. More alarming was the support given by Defense Minister Michael Dekel, who declared in his official capacity that "the Western states are politically and morally duty bound to see the transfer of the Arab population from Judaea and Samaria (the West Bank) to their own state, the Hashemite Kingdom of Jordan."[66] But most worrying of all was the support Ze'evi received from the general public. Nearly half the Jewish respondents to opinion polls that month favored the idea in theory, if not in practice. Kahane had made the idea of the transfer or deportation acceptable. The pollsters were particularly worried by the unashamedly racist and fascist views expressed by young people. Surveys have shown that future voters hold anti-democratic views: they would be quite prepared to deny the Arabs free speech and to forbid them the freedom to form political organizations.[67]

On October 18, 1988, Kahane was forbidden by the Israeli Supreme Court to stand for the 1988 elections, on the grounds that his policies were antidemocratic and an incitement to racism. Kahane was unrepentant. After the Supreme Court decision he still insisted that he wanted the Arabs out. But he also contended that the greatest victory of Kach was that it had made the concept and policy of transfer legitimate. Israelis who would balk at many of Kahane's policies, like his plans for a Torah state or his rejection of democracy, have taken to the idea of transfer. One pollster, Dr. Eliezer Katz, found that 19 percent of Israelis believed that transfer would "allow the Jewish and democratic nature of Israeli society to be maintained." Until 1987 the whole idea of transfer was unmentionable, a taboo. But, Dr. Katz argues, it had now gained legitimacy, become a focus of public discussion and swept through the right.[68] Transfer or deportation is a crusading solution, as we have seen. Many Israelis have felt sympathy with the plight of the Palestinians and have been distressed by the Palestinian exodus of 1948. Others might subconsciously have devoutly wished for the Arab problem to disappear but until very recently the idea of a planned deportation was considered too dangerous even to imagine. Jews had suffered too much themselves from expulsion and from fantasies of elimination. But Kahane made the idea in some sense acceptable. In the 1988 elections the two transfer parties, Raphael Eytan's Tzomet and Rahavam Ze'evi's Moledet, each gained two seats. Kahane had gone but transfer was in, with 3.6 percent of the votes.

The legitimation of transfer shows the real dangers of the far right policy. Most Israelis would never vote for their parties because they would find the message in toto too radical or unrealistic. But they may well accept one or two ideas, even if they choose the most unacceptable of all. Further, the vociferous publicity that Kahane aroused made people familiar with his truly horrible ideas, and familiarity with ideas can also lead to a familiarity with the realities that lie behind them. What is very worrying is the radicalization of the young. As they watch a parliament hamstrung by the failure of any one party to achieve a clear majority, they seem to be turning to the clarity of the far right position and some seem to be indulging the fascist dream of a "strong man" who will overturn the present system and "make order in this chaos."[69] It may also be the case that the far right are making young people in particular accustomed to the obnoxious idea that terrorism against Arabs is a legitimate activity.

In the account of the fall of Jerusalem we noticed that a radical minority could endanger the security of the whole state. The settlers in the occupied territories are very different in their methods from Reynauld of Chatillon in some respects, but it is also the case that more moderate Israelis consider them a menace and a threat to Israeli security. They are also guilty of making the already intractable conflict between the Arabs and Jews more extreme: their provocative actions have caused an extreme reaction on both sides of the conflict. It is a polarization that Israel cannot afford. The danger posed by the Jewish settlers has become particularly clear during the Palestinian uprising.

The settlers had long got used to dealing summarily with Arabs in the territories. If Arabs threw stones at the cars of settlers, the settlers themselves would take the law into their own hands and smash car windows in Ramallah or Nablus. Sometimes there was violence and bloodshed. The behavior of the settlers is considered one of the causes of the uprising. Thus the leftist writer Amnon Rubinstein has argued that Israel also has an occupation of sorts in South Lebanon but there has been no uprising because there are no Gush Emunim settlements there.[70] Israel presents herself as the opponent of terrorism in the region: it is very embarrassing for the government when their own citizens take the law violently into their own hands and avenge blood with blood. It is descending to the same level as the Arab terrorists. During the uprising the settlers' behavior seemed to be uncontrollable. Thus in November 1987, in the very early days of the *intifada*, a group of schoolgirls from Gaza threw stones at the passing car of some settlers and the occupants promptly opened fire. One seventeen-year-old girl was killed and others were severely wounded.[71] Incidents like this naturally filled the Palestinians with greater determination and the army found that they also had to bear the brunt of the Arab hostility aroused by the settlers.

On April 6, 1988, the evening papers described a tragic incident on the West Bank. A group of teenagers from the Gush Emunim settlement of Elon Moreh had gone for a hike. They had been attacked by the Arabs of the nearby village of Beita, who had pelted them cruelly with stones and one sixteen-year-old girl, Tirza Porat, was stoned to death. In the early stages there was outrage and horror among the Israelis. It revived the old Jewish nightmare of a young girl set upon by "pogromists and murderers."[72] The Israeli Arabs waited fearfully for reprisals. But even in the very early accounts of the incident Israelis and Arabs noted some strange discrepancies in the story. It appeared that two Palestinian youths had also been killed and that was puzzling, given that the young Jewish teenagers had been out on a nature ramble and were, presumably, unarmed. Further, it seemed that the Arabs of Beita had sent for the Red Cross ambulance and that some had hidden the other children in their houses.

Despite these puzzles, a lynch-mob fury swept through Israel. At Tirza's funeral, which was attended by Prime Minister Yitzhak Shamir, the crowds shouted: "Wipe Beita off the map!" The army had already moved into Beita and destroyed seventeen homes but the Israelis were clamoring for further vengeance.

The army's investigation, however, produced quite a different story. It appeared that the children had been accompanied by an adult, Romain Aldubi, who was carrying an M16 machine gun. Aldubi was known as one of the most lawless settlers in the area: his violent activities had caused the army to forbid him to enter Nablus, for example. Elon Moreh was a particularly militant settlement and the army had told the settlers that it was dangerous for them to walk around the area unaccompanied. Despite this, the army had not been informed about the hike. It appeared that the hike itself had not exactly been a peaceful ramble of nature lovers. One of the teenagers had artlessly told the TV reporters that they had decided to walk to Beita in order "to show the Arabs who was master."[73] It was their way of proclaiming that they had the right to walk wherever they chose on the West Bank and that neither the Arabs nor the army were going to limit their activities. The forensic evidence, moreover, revealed that Tirza had not died of stoning but from the bullet of an M16, like the one carried by Aldubi. The army made a careful inquiry and insisted on publishing its findings, despite the near hysterical protests of the right. The army discovered that the confrontation had been largely sparked by Aldubi, who had opened fire on very trivial provocation and killed a Palestinian youth. He then seemed to have gone berserk and started shooting in all directions, killing Tirza and the other Palestinian boy and injuring others. The villagers sheltered the children in their homes and called the ambulance, while some of the Arabs managed to wrest the gun away from Aldubi. The military authorities were deeply embarrassed about their overhasty response and offered the people of Beita compensation for their lost homes.

The revelation of this far less inflammatory version of the tragedy stopped the wave of blood lust that had seemed in danger of sweeping through Israel. But the right clung to the original story and it was bizarre and somehow very disturbing to see a girl from Elon Moreh appearing on the television news immediately after a spokesman for the army had explained yet again what really seemed to have happened. The girl from Elon Moreh read a poem in memory of Tirza: it called upon the Jewish people to build a new settlement in her honor on the site of the village of Beita, the home of her murderers. There seemed to be no connection between the two versions, which were left schizophrenically side by side. The politicians of the left denounced the settlers in the territories for continuing to spread inflammatory tales of Beita; the last thing that Israel needed was riots against the Arabs in Israel itself. The radical Jewish peace group End the Occupation Committee picketed Mr. Shamir's residence and when they were attacked by Kahane's followers they fought back. The tragedy of Beita had shown how very dangerous the settlers' provocative presence could be in the territories. It meant unnecessary loss of life in which Jews as well as Arabs suffered; it led to an escalation of an already nigh impossible situation and it led to divisions among the Israelis themselves.

The following week, in an article in *Ha'aretz* on April 14, Amnon Rubinstein pointed out the problem of the grave security burden which the settlements are imposing on the Israeli army:

> The army's limited forces are obliged to act as a police force and an escort to a handful of extremist settlers instead of doing their real job, which is to prepare for war, fight terrorism and guard our borders. Moreover the real security burden is far heavier. Gush Emunim's policy will inevitably light a fire which can only end with an apocalypse of some sort, with another war, a civil war or an attempt to forcefully expel all Arabs from the country. It is irrelevant whether this is the group's conscious or merely subconscious aim.

Rubinstein is quite sure that the settlers did not originally envisage any such terrible outcome: he recalled the early idealism of the settlement movement and the hopes that people like Moshe Arens and Israel Galili had placed in it. But since the beginning of the *intifada* the settlers had become an intolerable burden and the source of terrible danger. If Rubinstein is right, the settlers could prove to be dangerous, just as Reynauld of Chatillon was dangerous to the Kingdom of Jerusalem. Impractical and overzealous extremists can very easily ignite an already inflammable situation.

The frustrations aroused in the Israelis, among both the army and the civilians, about Israel's inability to end the *intifada*, is creating a serious problem. Again, it seems that the young are turning toward the right. Veteran soldiers of long standing come home from their reserve duty in the territories and say: "Never again!" Some go to prison rather than return. This is causing a collapse of morale in the army, which is becoming critical. But the young, inexperienced soldiers are both frustrated and sickened and tend to turn to a hard-line solution.[74] Often they convert their families to this position. The frustration in the country can easily turn to lynching and mob violence. The Beita incident might have sparked off some horrible violence had not the army, to its great credit, quenched it by insisting on publishing the true version of the events. The danger is that violence breeds violence in a seemingly endless cycle. Thus on July 6, 1989, a Palestinian driver crashed the bus he was driving, killing fourteen Israeli passengers. According to police and Arab sources, Abdul Hadi Salman Rassem, the driver, had acted to avenge the alleged beating and imprisonment of his brothers during the *intifada* by Israeli soldiers. Violence to Palestinians had led to horrific violence against Jews.

The tragedy sparked a series of riots which shocked the Israeli government. Throughout the country Jews took to the streets shouting: "Death to the Arabs!" It was the most violent backlash since the beginning of the *intifada*. The Jewish crowds stoned Palestinian cars, wounded Arabs and killed at least one Palestinian. Jamal Nasser, from Gaza, was hit on the head with a stone while he was driving through the Negev Desert. He was killed, the car overturned and his four passengers were injured. Most ominously, the home of Dedi Zucker, MK, an outspoken critic of army excesses in the territories, was attacked by the rioters. Zucker was dismayed:

The real damage is for the democratic structure of this society, because it's the first time that the house of a member of the Knesset was attacked so bitterly, so strongly. I'm afraid the real damage is the fact that once they have started it they do not differentiate between an Arab and a Jew, and a member of the Knesset.[75]

The newspaper *Ma'ariv* spoke of "the terrible deterioration of Israeli society" and the Jerusalem *Post* wrote sadly that "Jews, the victims of racist prejudice throughout the ages, are now committing the worst kind of racism themselves and are meting out collective punishment."[76] Zionism had originally encouraged a high moral standard in the Jewish people but the violence of a long struggle had wrought grave damage to Israeli society. In escalating the violence in the territories, in fighting other Israelis who want peace and in getting the young accustomed to the rhetoric of hatred and violence, the far right groups must bear some responsibility for the dangerous situation that exists in Israel at the time of writing.

The *intifada* has not only inspired extremism; it has also inspired in many Israelis a new desire for peace. Since the uprising began, some forty-six new peace groups have emerged. Some observers say that this is a healthy sign; others are concerned that these many groups are splitting the opposition to the right into too many factions and would favor a more united stand.[77] There have been some impressive demonstrations. On the day after the fortieth anniversary of the state of Israel on Independence Day, 1988, there was a large demonstration of about twenty of these groups, reminding the nation that, despite the celebrations, there were urgent realities that had to be addressed. On July 4 that year a rally was held by military groups to mark the twenty-first anniversary of the occupation of the West Bank and Gaza. It was attended by about 10,000 Israelis. The rally was preceded by a procession through Tel Aviv with banners calling for an end to the occupation and for "Israel-Palestine peace." The marchers also used the old rallying cry that had been used during the Lebanon war: "Bring the soldiers home!" this time, of course, referring to the army's involvement in the territories.

There are clearly people in Israel who want peace. They know that somebody has to compromise in order to call a halt to the endless cycle of violence that could so easily get out of control, as the events in July 1989 show so clearly. The presence of extremist groups at such a time of tension must be dangerous. People who call for racist solutions and advocate terrorism against Arabs constitute only a small minority of the Israeli population. But their presence is disedifying: it pulls down the general moral tone of the society and accustoms people to unacceptable solutions. When a member of Gush Emunim is tried by an Israeli court for killing an Arab, is let out on bail and is greeted as a hero by his far right supporters, this fills many Israelis—members of Likud as well as Laborites—with dismay and despair. They feel that the situation is getting out of control and that the ethical values which were so important to early Zionism are being lost. At a time when the government finds it hard to gain an effective majority and seems locked in internal disputes of a complex nature, the utter simplicity and certainty of the extremists is attractive to the young of Israel, who seem at the time of writing to be turning to undemocratic ideals, doubtless under the influence of people like Kahane.

On November 14, 1988, Israel held its elections. On November 15, as we have seen, Yasir Arafat declared Palestinian independence and recognized the existence of a Jewish state. On July 31 that year King Hussein of Jordan had relinquished any claim to the West Bank, thus obviating those peace plans that had hoped to circumvent negotiations with the PLO, like that proposed by American Secretary of State George Shultz and the peace plan of Shimon Peres; both depended on some sort of Jordanian solution to the problem of the West Bank.[78] There was now only the PLO to talk to and in Algiers on November 15 Arafat removed the last obstacle to negotiations by recognizing the right of Israel to exist. Arafat began to receive recognition for his proposed state of Palestine and was congratulated on his initiative. The former terrorist, as Israelis noticed with anguish, was becoming a hero of peace while Israel was seen desperately trying to come to terms with the unpromising election results.

The most dramatic feature of these elections was the rise of the religious parties, which gained a record number of sixteen seats in the Knesset. These parties tend to adopt hawkish policies toward the Arabs and to see the Arab-Israeli conflict as a religious holy war. Thus the National Religious Party, which gained five seats, had originally been dovish on territorial issues but today maintains close links with its offspring Gush Emunim. The ultra-Orthodox party Degel Hatorah, which gained two seats, is inspired by a Messianic mysticism; Shas, the Sephardic religious party, which won six seats, sees the passing of further religious legislation within Israel as its priority but had recently issued a series of rulings denying Gentile rights in Israel. One of the most disturbing results was the five seats gained by the Agudat Yisrael, backed by the Hasidic rabbis of Gur and Lubavitcher. This party seems not primarily interested in the problem of the Arabs; its main ambition is to pass a law which would accept as Jewish only those converts who have undergone the lengthy process of conversion to Orthodoxy. Its electoral success was insulting to those Reform and Conservative Jews whose converts would, in the view of Agudat Yisrael, no longer be considered true Jews. As Israel is so dependent upon support in America, most of whose Jews belong to Conservatives or to Reform Judaism, this was very distressing to the Jews of America as well as a blatant discounting of an essential fact about Israel, which would not survive for one day without the United States.

Israel, which was founded by defiantly secular idealists, seems to be swinging toward religion. This, we have seen, can be highly dangerous. At the time of the Crusades, Christians and Muslims could relate to one another positively when they were not inspired by a bellicose religiosity to see the other as the enemy of God and the conflict between them on a cosmic plane. A certain type of religiosity can encourage people to view the enemy in a special category, depriving him of the considerations that we would apply to a normal human being; it can lose touch with the concrete realities on the ground because it is too busy gazing heavenward and, finally, it can admit of no compromise. We have seen that the far right groups are either highly religious or, in the case of Tehiya, an alliance of extreme religious people with fanatic seculars. Their policies are absolutely uncompromising and do not apply to the Arab-Israeli conflict the ordinary ethical and moral values that would pertain elsewhere. In the 1988 elections the far right achieved seven votes and within the far right there was a swing toward the notion of transfer: Tehiya got three votes and the two transfer parties, Tzomet and Moledet, as we have seen, got two each. The results show that almost one fifth of the members of the Knesset have extreme policies that will admit of no compromise and most of these are deeply religious people.

In these elections there was another hung parliament: Likud, with forty MKs, beat Labor by one seat. Prime Minister Yitzhak Shamir is not a religious man but he is a former member of Lehi, whose ideology is not dead but has recently seen a "renaissance" in Tehiya, which follows in its footsteps. Old Lehi members like Shamir have not abandoned their party: they still meet and talk. Lehi, we have seen, was a secular party but advocated an Israel with the boundaries promised by God in the Bible. One of its most extraordinary principles was the commitment to rebuilding the Temple. We do not know exactly what Mr. Shamir thinks of these matters today but recently he met with the leader of a sect which is dedicated to the rebuilding of the Temple (which, of course, would mean that the great Muslim mosques would have to be demolished). The sect had even designed the robes that would be worn by the High Priest. Mr. Shamir is said to have given this group support and encouragement, and this in itself does not bode well for peace. Immediately after the elections, Shamir promised the country that he would never negotiate with the PLO and considered forming a government with the religious parties. At a time when Arafat, secular leader of a secular movement, was being congratulated by governments on his peace initiative, Israelis were watching their own leader courting hawkish religious extremists. Eventually, however, Likud revived the coalition with Labor.

But the swing toward religion in Israel was even more marked in the 1990 elections. The religious parties gained only a few more seats (Agudat Israel: 8; Shas: 6; National Religious Party: 4; Degel Hatorah: 2), but this time they really did control the formation of the new government. For three months the world watched Peres and Shamir running after the rabbis in a desperate attempt to gain a tiny majority. It was a telling and chilling demonstration of the growth of religious extremism in Zionism, which had once been a defiantly secular movement. In June 1990 Shamir finally managed to pull together a right-wing coalition that was heavily supported by the far right and by the religious parties. Commentators gloomily agreed that the prospects for a Middle East peace had never looked so bleak. Washington had broken off talks with the PLO, because Arafat had refused to condemn a failed attack on Israel by Palestinian extremists in late May 1990. But the United States still continued to support Shamir's government, even though it seemed an enemy to ideals of liberty and democracy that had once thrilled American hearts. Ministerial posts had been given to representatives of Tzomet and Tehiya: in his new cabinet Shamir, a former terrorist and avowed enemy of the peace process, looked like a moderate. Moledet, the "transfer" party, was crucial to Shamir's coalition and, even though it had no seats in the cabinet, the party pledged continuing support for the new government. Shamir's new allies considered that democracy was at best a questionable concept; they were not committed to peace but to territorial expansion and racial supremacy. With their support, Shamir set his face against any compromise for peace, even though this meant defying the United States. On June 27, 1990, he sent a twelve-page overnight telegram to President Bush, spelling out a brutal and categorical "no" to the proposals made by Secretary of State James Baker for talks between Israel and the Palestinians.

There are still people in Israel who are committed to a peaceful solution; they argue that Israel must negotiate with the PLO and watch the new wave of intransigence and hatred in their country with real anguish. There is a growing appreciation in Israel of the dangers of a certain type of religion. In 1988 the Israeli Institute of Military

Studies carried out a survey to discover the reasons why Israeli youths were prepared to serve in the army. The researchers found that young secular Israelis saw military service as a way of serving the state, but that hatred of the Arabs was the prime motive for young religious Israelis. The researchers also discovered that hatred of Arabs was twice as strong in the Jewish religious schools as in the secular schools: in the religious schools, 51 percent of the boys and 68 percent of the girls said that they hated all Arabs, while in the secular schools only 32 percent of the boys and 28 percent of the girls made the same declaration of hatred. In the religious vocational schools the percentage was far higher: 71 percent of the boys and 78 percent of the girls were Arab-haters.

This does not bode well for the future. But intransigence is also on the increase among the adult Israeli Jewish population. In a symposium held at the University of Haifa in June 1990, Sammy Smooha, professor of sociology at Haifa and world authority on the analysis of Israel's Jewish and Palestinian societies, revealed that religious chauvenism was rising. Even in 1988, 59 percent of the adult Israelis questioned in his survey supported the project of "transfer"; 58 percent would deny all Arabs the right to vote in parliamentary elections in Israel; 74 percent were for active discrimination against the Arab population in all walks of life. In an article that published the results of all these surveys in June 1990 in a Western periodical, Israel Shahak argued that Western commentators must become more familiar with these disturbing trends. These painfully honest and commendably self-critical Israeli surveys have been much discussed in the Hebrew press but tend to be ignored outside Israel. As a result, the West has often misunderstood Israeli politics and has seen the success of the Right as the result of the political manipulation of individuals rather than as a consequence of deeper and more worrying tendencies. Shahak also argued that Western commentators were quite right to condemn the new wave of anti-Semitism, which disturbingly surfaced in Europe during the late 1980s, but added that they must realize that hatred of Arabs was far more widespread among Israelis than was hatred of Jews among latter-day Europeans.[79]

There is a further irony. Shamir's extreme government was able to come to power after the extraordinary migration to democracy in Eastern Europe in 1989 and at a time when the Soviet Union was also making painful steps toward the democratic ideal. Soviet Jews were at last to be allowed to emigrate to Eretz Yisrael. The Western world naturally applauded these movements, yet Israel, its chief ally in the Middle East, seemed, under Shamir, to be retreating from democracy. There were signs that Israel sought to use the prospect of the forthcoming immigration from the Soviet Union as a justification for further territorial expansion. In response to concern expressed by President Bush, Shamir replied in June 1990 that while the Israeli government would not settle Soviet immigrants on the West Bank, it would not deter any new immigrant from making a settlement in the occupied territories. A peace move from its old anti-Semitic foe had, in the climate of religious and political intransigence, been translated into a new act of war against the Palestinian population.

Religion should be a force for mutual respect and compassion, but it can also become a catalyst of hatred. This danger seems to be as great a threat in the Middle East today as it was at the time of the Battle of Hittin. In Chapter 3 we saw that Palestinians feared that their own cause might succumb to religious extremism and that Issam Satawi, who became a martyr for the peace process, was convinced that some solution must be found before religious radicals replaced secular leaders on both sides of the conflict. It seems that it may now be too late for Israeli leaders to seek a secular *modus vivendi* with the Arab world, unless the moderates in the country are able to attract more support from their Western allies. But there has also been a religious revival of an intransigent nature in the Islamic countries of the Middle East. In the next chapter we shall see how this contributed to the tragedy of President Anwar Sadat of Egypt.

# 1981

## The Death of President Anwar Sadat: Holy War and Peace

On October 6, 1981, President Anwar Sadat was officiating at the victory parade celebrating the October War against Israel in 1973. Suddenly one of the trucks in the parade pulled out of line just in front of the presidential stand and when Sadat saw First Lieutenant Khaled Islambouli jump out and run toward him, he assumed that the young man was going to salute him and stood up to receive the tribute. Then a second officer threw a hand grenade and there was a burst of machine-gun fire as the four assassins mounted a formidably efficient attack. Khaled shot round after round into the body of Sadat, even after he had himself been wounded in the stomach, crying: "Give me that dog, that infidel!" After fifty seconds the security officers managed to stop the attack, but not before seven other people besides Sadat had been killed and twenty-eight others wounded.[1] The assassination of Sadat shocked the world in much the same way as the assassinations of President Kennedy or Martin Luther King. Sadat was the first Muslim leader in the Western world since Saladin to gain the respect and admiration of the West, but where Saladin had been a hero of the holy war, Sadat was a hero of peace. His historic journey to Jerusalem in November 1977 had become a twentieth-century legend of peace in an increasingly violent world, but the young men who shot Sadat did not see him as a hero and neither did millions of his own people. The date of his death is significant: it was the anniversary of his October War that had given back to the Arabs the self-respect they had lost in 1967. In the Islamic calendar, Sadat died on the feast of the Eid el-Adha, which commemorates Abraham's sacrifice, and he had made his journey of peace in 1977 on the eve of the very same feast. His assassins shot Sadat because he was an infidel ruler who had abandoned the sacred duty of the *jihad* and made a shameful peace with the enemies of God.

The comparison with Saladin is fruitful. Until the twentieth century

Saladin had actually been more widely revered in the West than he was in the East, even though he had been the sworn enemy of Western Christendom. Sadat had been a friend to the West and had signed a treaty with the vanguard of the West in the Middle East, but when he died his own people did not mourn him. When Nasser died in 1970 thousands of people had poured onto the streets of Cairo, weeping and tearing their garments for the Arab hero who had staunchly defied Israel and the West. On the night of Sadat's death, the streets of Cairo were eerily silent, even though he was already being mourned and eulogized on news programs in Europe and America.[2] At his funeral on October 10 Western leaders flocked to pay tribute to a great man. At their head were three former Presidents of the United States, Secretary of State Alexander Haig and Defense Minister Caspar Weinberger. Prime Minister Begin of Israel was there, with his Interior Minister Yosef Burg and his Defense Minister Ariel Sharon, the dedicated hawk and Arab-hater. There were chancellors, prime ministers and presidents from Europe, and Prince Charles represented Britain. But there were no dense crowds of Egyptian mourners and no other Arab leaders at the funeral: after Sadat signed the Camp David treaty, Egypt had been expelled from the Arab League. It seemed that his death could not simply be ascribed to a few unbalanced fanatics but that at some level it had been endorsed by the whole Arab world. Why was this man of peace so deeply hated by his own people? The story of Sadat shows that, despite Camp David, there was no real will to peace on either side of the conflict and it also shows how deeply religion has inflamed the originally secular conflict in the Middle East. When Saladin and Richard signed their treaty in 1192, it marked the beginning of a détente in the holy war, but religious extremism on both sides of the conflict has made peace seem dangerous and impossible. Sadat's tragedy shows that a man who has presented himself as a religious president cannot safely become a president of peace.

When Sadat came to power in 1970 the Egyptians did not hate him but they did not really take him very seriously. He lacked Nasser's strength and stability, perhaps because of his traumatic childhood. His father had married a black woman and had five children by her, of whom Mohammad Anwar was the second. But later, when he moved his family from the village of Mit Abu el-Qom to a four-room flat in Cairo, he married a white Egyptian girl and had fifteen children by her. Sadat's mother was reduced to the level of a slave and moved into a room with her five dark-skinned children, who frequently saw her beaten and humiliated. Throughout his life Sadat was obsessed by his dark skin and always had a desperate need to be liked and accepted.[3]

In addition to these misfortunes, he seems to have failed to get into one of the better schools, as his elder brother Taalat had done, and so he clearly lacked Nasser's intelligence.[4] His basic insecurity made him enjoy belonging to a close group and this got him involved in some dubious and rather foolish cloak-and-dagger conspiracies before he joined Nasser's group of Free Officers, which successfully staged the revolution of 1952.[5] Some of the members of this group were opposed to Nasser's recruiting Sadat,[6] because they felt he was a light-weight, but Nasser seems to have been genuinely fond of him, though he was aware of his shortcomings. People do seem to have liked Sadat, and his eagerness to please was one of his endearing characteristics. The Free Officers probably felt that their reservations about Sadat were justified, however, on the night of the coup in 1952. Sadat had been ordered to come to Cairo from Gaza, where he was stationed, and to await instructions, but instead he took his wife Jihan to the cinema and when he got back to their apartment he found a stiff note from Nasser to say that the coup had taken place and where was he?[7] During Nasser's rule Sadat was the Speaker in the Egyptian parliament for ten years, largely because of his histrionic talents. He always had a love of the theatrical and one of his earliest ambitions had been to become an actor. Nasser gave him the job of Speaker because he said that Sadat had a good voice and could orate with as much rhetoric as the Syrians.[8] In 1969 Sadat became Vice-President because Nasser felt that it was his "turn"—all his colleagues had had a chance at the post and everybody enjoyed seeing Sadat's obvious delight in the job.[9] Nobody thought to remove him from office, because the last year of Nasser's life was a very hectic and indeed tragic year in the Arab world. In any case Sadat was associated in people's minds with Nasser. In the last years of his life, when Nasser was constantly depressed by the catastrophe of the Six Day War and was in failing health, he liked to spend his evenings with Sadat, who was an old and undemanding friend. Sadat himself always seemed devoted to Nasser and used to call him *mu'allan* (teacher).[10] When Nasser died unexpectedly in 1970 Vice-President Sadat automatically took over until the election of a new President, and many people assumed that he was just a caretaker. In rather the same way, nobody had thought much of Saladin when he became vizier of Egypt.

But, like Saladin, Sadat managed to gain the political support of the Egyptian people and become a strong leader. He won the presidential election of October 1970 by presenting himself to the electorate as the successor of Nasser, as Saladin had presented himself as the successor of Nur ad-Din. Like Saladin, Sadat had to put down a revolution in the army after coming to power and was thus able to demonstrate that he truly was the master of Egypt.[11] Now he had to justify his power by means of his achievements. In Western democracies a leader derives his legitimacy from the institution itself and from the state, but in a Third World country a leader derives his legitimacy from what he manages to achieve. Once Sadat had secured himself in power, he had to produce achievements equal to Nasser's, but this was difficult. Nasser had been revered all over the Arab world and was almost a legend. What could Sadat do that would not seem an anticlimax?

Despite Sadat's apparent love of Nasser during his life, he seems to have harbored a deep resentment of his leader and after Nasser's death this surfaced quite violently. The successor of Nasser began to tell his people that Nasser had made terrible mistakes and that he, Sadat, was the savior of Egypt. This was naturally very confusing to the people, who had been told that everything was wonderful during Nasser's rule.[12] Sadat began to reverse Nasser's policies. Nasser had sought to make the Arab people proud and independent and had rejected the Western imperialists as the Arabs' enemies. Now Sadat sought to make Egypt a client of America in rather the same way as Israel and Iran were: he was fond of calling Shah Mohammad Reza Pahlavi "my friend the Shah."[13] In 1972 he expelled the 1500 Russian advisers that Nasser had installed in the country, clearly hoping to endear himself to the United States, and at first this seemed to give the Egyptians a new power and independence. His high-handed treatment of the Soviets made them respect and fear Sadat: in 1973 they gave him far more arms than they had given Nasser in 1967. In the early years of Sadat's rule he began to show the Egyptian people that he had a power and strength that they had not seen in him before.

Sadat knew that he must find a popular power base to rival the popular support that his Nasserite or Marxist rivals enjoyed, so he turned to religion. Saladin had taken an Islamic identity as soon as he came to power, and Sadat also presented himself to his people as the Pious President. He liked to be photographed praying in the mosques, wearing traditional Muslim dress with the ash mark on his forehead, proving that he was a good Muslim who bowed to the ground in prayer five times a day. There is no reason to doubt the sincerity of Sadat's piety, but it is also true that his new religious identity seemed certain to be popular among the people because there had been a religious revival in Egypt after the Six Day War in 1967, when many people had turned to religion in order to make sense of the catastrophic defeat. We have seen that there was a rather similar religious revival in Israel and in the Jewish diaspora after the near disaster of the 1973 October War. After 1967 people in Egypt seemed to think that the Jews must have won because they had proved to have been truer to their religion than the Muslim Arabs, who had turned to alien ideologies like socialism. We have seen that in fact, before the Six Day War, Israel was still largely secular in spirit but it seemed to the Egyptians that the Zionist devotion to the land of Israel must be religiously inspired. They sought to return to the religious traditions of Egypt that seemed more powerful and natural than the imported Western ideologies. Many young Coptic Christians became monks and Muslims joined Sufi orders. Between April and July 1968 many thousands of Copts and Muslims claimed to have seen Mary, the mother of Jesus, at Zeitoum in northern Cairo. Mary, who is revered in Islam as well as in Christianity, was believed to have come to comfort the people of Egypt for the loss of the Holy City, Jerusalem. Many felt that the apparitions were a sign that God had relented toward Egypt and would lead the Arabs to victory.[14] The struggle with Israel was becoming a religious struggle at a deep, popular level and the people spontaneously sought a visionary comfort in their distress, rather like the First Crusaders. So when Sadat presented himself to his people as the Pious President this was seen as a hopeful sign but ultimately religion proved fatal to him.

Sadat gave Egypt a more distinctive Islamic identity than it had had under Nasser. New mosques were built and the rich were encouraged by tax cuts to contribute to this holy building project. Islamic laws were reintroduced: it became a capital offense to apostasize from Islam and there was talk of punishing thieves by cutting off their hands. The sale of alcohol was forbidden on the streets and confined to bars and clubs. An Islamic radio station presented recitations of the Koran and Koranic sermons all day long but even secular programs were interrupted by the muezzin summoning the faithful to prayer. But, by encouraging Islam, Sadat was unleashing a very powerful force that he would be unable to control. He had wanted to tether the religion to his own regime but in fact renewed contact with Islam encouraged a new revolutionary radicalism in Egypt. The Egyptians, of course, were not the only people to discover the power of Islam at this time. During the 1970s there was a vigorous Islamic movement in Iran that should have been a warning to Sadat. He was a great friend of the Shah of Iran; he saw Iran, which was at that time a progressive, modernizing country, as a model for his Egypt. But in 1979, the same year as the Camp David treaty between Egypt and

Israel, an Islamic revolution overthrew the Shah's powerful regime and the exiled Shah Mohammad Reza Pahlavi took refuge in Egypt.

Nasser had understood the Islamic danger very well. In 1954 a fundamentalist group known as the Muslim Brotherhood had made an attempt against his life: Nasser had outlawed the Brotherhood and jailed the brethren. He was a sincere Muslim but wanted to keep religion and politics separate, on the Western model. This was abhorrent to the Muslim Brothers as it would be to all radical Muslims. Sadat certainly wanted a secular, not an Islamic Sharia, state but he wanted also to make religion an asset to his regime and to court religious groups. He thought that his encouragement would make these Muslim societies support his regime. In 1971 he began to release the Muslim Brothers whom Nasser had jailed. It was meant to demonstrate that he was a much better friend to Islam than Nasser had been. The Brotherhood was not allowed to exist as an official body but it was permitted to publish its own magazine, *al-Dawa* (*The Call*). Unfortunately for Sadat, it issued a call to radical revolutionary ideas that found many willing ears in Egypt.

The revolutionary strain had been present in Islam since the very beginning and it was not surprising that the Shiites of Iran and some of the Sunni Muslims of Egypt should apply this to their own predicament. The Prophet Mohammad himself was a revolutionary of sorts, fighting the corrupt regime of the Qureish in Mecca: his aim had been to build a society that would surrender to God's will and implement a new form of social justice. Religion and politics had been inseparable in his vision. His immediate successors continued this tradition and the revolutionary element in Islam continued even after Islam became a world power. The first four caliphs after Mohammad developed an ideal of the true Muslim leader that has been very important in Muslim history and it would prove fatal to both the Shah and to Sadat. We must, therefore, examine it in some detail.

After the death of the Prophet in 632, the people elected his friend Abu Bakr as his first caliph or successor. But there was a group of Muslims who believed that Mohammad would have wanted his son-in-law and ward Ali ibn Talib to be the leader (Imam) of the Islamic community. Ali accepted the caliphate of Abu Bakr, but Ali's followers, who called themselves the *Shi-ah-i Ali* (the partisans of Ali), did not and they regarded the caliphs as unlawful rulers. This was the beginning of the Sunni-Shia conflict. It must be stressed that it was and remains purely political. It is wrong to compare it to the Protestant-Catholic division in Christianity, which is a theological dispute. Shiites and Sunnis have no theological quarrel: both accept the same Muslim creed and adhere to the moral teachings of Islam, though both traditions have developed their own particular emphases and pieties.

Abu Bakr was succeeded by the Caliphs Omar and Uthman. Finally Ali became the Fourth Caliph but the Shiites called him the First Imam. The first four caliphs were deeply pious men, even though they were not all politically astute. They became known as the Rightly Guided Caliphs (*rashidun*), setting a standard which later caliphs and sultans could not match. Abu Bakr had shown the qualities of a true Muslim ruler at his accession to power when he told the people that if they noted any un-Islamic traits in him they must correct him without fear: the Caliph must be controlled by both Islam and the *umma* (the community). Ali was especially insistent on the qualities of a good Muslim ruler and his sayings were much beloved by the revolutionaries of Iran. He taught that the "common people of the *umma* are the pillars of the religion, the power of the Muslims and the defence against enemies." The Muslim ruler must not seclude himself from the people, must not live in splendor, must not be a dictator. He must rule by consultation. He must not create an elitist society and must take special responsibility for the poor, ensuring that wealth was fairly distributed. The ruler, Ali taught, must be merciful and compassionate, like Allah himself, and minister to a just society.[15]

The caliphs who succeeded the *rashidun* did not measure up to this ideal and henceforth Muslims called unworthy rulers *munafiqeen* (hypocrites).[16] A *munafiq* put his personal political aims and his dynastic interests before his Islamic duties and so he was a Muslim only in name. Both the Shah and Sadat were regarded as *munafiqeen* by their radical Muslim subjects. Indeed, one could say that the Muslim world has had its share of despotic rulers living in the lap of luxury but this does not mean that Muslims have forgotten the ideal. There is a similar anomaly in Christianity: few of its rulers, however pious, have lived up to the principles of Jesus, who was even more radical in this respect than either Mohammad or the Rightly Guided Caliphs. He taught that wealth must be abandoned and that no one should be called "lord" in the Christian community.[17] But the failure of Christian rulers to live up to this ideal does not mean that the radical message of Jesus was forgotten. Throughout Christian history there have been Christians who fought the establishment in the name of Christ. Indeed, many Crusaders were inspired by this egalitarian ideal. Similarly in Islam, after Ali was killed in 661 and the Umayyads seized the caliphate, the ideal persisted, even though the Umayyads were regarded as *munafiqeen*. The caliphs soon lost the support of the masses and ceased to be a real power in Islam. In times of trouble Sunni Muslims looked to other rulers, who enshrined the Islamic ideal more accurately. We have seen that, at the time of the Crusades, Nur ad-Din and Saladin were able to build empires by presenting themselves to the people as true Muslim rulers. Their qualities of piety, accessibility, austerity and concern for the people gave them a legitimacy that their rivals in the Near East could not command.

In the Shia tradition especially, revolution has been an important ideal. The Shiites remained true to the descendants of Ali and considered them to be the only legitimate ruler of the Muslim people until the line finally expired in the tenth century.[18] When the eleven successors of Ali assumed the title of Imam, this was essentially a revolutionary act against the caliphate and indeed many of the Imams were murdered by the caliphs.[19] They were ready to die for the Muslim values they represented. The courage and piety of the revolutionary Imams was most perfectly manifest in the Third Imam, Husain, the grandson of the Prophet Mohammad. He was hounded by the Ummayad Caliph Yazid, who even tried to have him assassinated in Mecca, a sacrilege which shocked the whole Muslim world. In 680 the people of Kufa in modern Iraq offered Husain sanctuary and he set off with a small band of followers to build an alternative Islamic society there, according to the principles of his grandfather Mohammad. But he was surrounded by Yazid's army on the plain of Karbala, seventy kilometers from Kufa. His followers refused to leave their Imam, even though they had no chance of surviving the encounter with Yazid. They believed it was their duty as devout Muslims to fight this tyranny unto death and accordingly they and Husain were slaughtered.

Shiites and Sunnis all look back in horror at the immoral murder of the grandson of the Prophet and Husain has been a hero and a saint in both traditions. We will see that Husain was a great inspiration to the Iranians during the Islamic revolution. The duty of fighting tyranny and oppression would also inspire many Sunni extremists to oppose Sadat's regime and some of these were ready to die as martyrs. The word "martyr" in Arabic is *shaheed*, which, like the Greek word *martyrion* means "witness." These modern Muslim martyrs felt that they were bearing witness to important Islamic principles.

This is clearly a noble tradition but it remains true that we in the West feel very uneasy about Islamic radicalism. Quite understandably, we fail to see how the Ayatollah Khomeini resembled the ideal Islamic leader. We see Muslim extremism as irrational and as opposed to progress. We find it cruel, violent and ruthless. Some of our objections are valid but we should perhaps try to understand the positive power of some of these Islamic ideals. It is difficult for us to see this militant Islam as a positive force but there is no doubt that it has given a new confidence to many thousands of people in the Middle East. Only by looking at the original ideals can we see how the Ayatollah was a great aberration. Radical Muslims claim that we in the Western world have damaged and exploited them; it is hard for us to appreciate this but we should try to make an imaginative effort to understand what radical Islam was *trying* to do, in order to break the vicious cycle of hostility and incomprehension that damages us all.

The rise and progress of the Islamic revolution was a crucial element in Middle Eastern politics during Sadat's presidency so we shall examine it briefly before returning to Sadat's story. The Iranian holy war provided an ironic and tragically prophetic counterpoint to Sadat's peace initiative and courting of the West. It was a warning. In the West we tend to be suspicious of religious people who get involved with politics. We see Iran as an unholy example of the danger of such an alliance but it is also true that Christians who have piously said their prayers and given tacit support to oppressive governments or who have encouraged poor people to accept their lot in the hope of a heavenly reward are also guilty of betraying essential Christian principles. In England today some Christians claim that the Church of England must separate itself from Margaret Thatcher's government, which they see as unjust and unchristian. In Islam, religion and politics had been inseparable since the time of the Prophet, because of this Islamic emphasis on social justice. For centuries people have looked to the clerics, therefore, for political guidance and support against a corrupt regime. In Shiite Iran, for example, the Muslim clergy had established a tradition whereby they had become the guardians of the people against the oppressive government of the shahs. Many of the mullahs lived and taught in the ancient city of Qum, about fifty kilometers from Teheran. By the beginning of this century, Qum had a position which was unique in the Muslim world; it was the unofficial religious capital of Iran, a capital of the "Alternative Iran" which protected the people against the shahs.[20] It is against this long clerical tradition that we should see the Islamic revolution that toppled the regime of the Pahlavi dynasty in 1979.

It is, of course, ironic that the Muslim ruler who should have succeeded the Shah that year was the Ayatollah Ruhollah Khomeini, whose Islamic regime seems to have been even more cruel than that of his predecessor. It was George Orwell, in *Animal Farm*, who pointed out that a revolution always seems to come full circle to create a new form of tyranny, equal to or even surpassing the one it replaced.

It is a sad fact of human nature that when we struggle heroically to create a better world, we keep repeating the old mistakes. The French Revolution of 1789 thrilled many young idealists in Europe with its dream of liberty, equality and fraternity, its heroic feats and astonishing success, against all the odds. Then these same idealists were revolted by the reign of terror led by Robespierre. The Russian Revolution against the tyranny of the tsars led to the bloody purges and produced Stalin. It seems that revolutions are often regarded with horror by their contemporaries and create truly appalling leaders: Khomeini and his regime in this respect are simply conforming to type. At the time of writing, there are signs that Khomeini's successor Hojatolislam Hashemi Rafsanjani intends to inaugurate a more moderate regime, and it may well be that this will prove to be the point when the revolution becomes, to some degree, normalized.

The regime of Shah Mohammad Reza Pahlavi, which had been backed first by Great Britain and then by the United States, had seemed to be one of the most powerful and progressive in the Middle East. It had also seemed impregnable. There had been various attempts to bring it down, including the nationalist revolution of Mohammad Mossadeq in 1953, when the CIA had stepped in smartly, quelled the revolution in an organized countercoup and put the young Shah back on the throne. It was, therefore, very disturbing when the whole of Iran, fueled, as it seemed, solely by Islamic ideology,[21] rose as one and managed incredibly to overcome the Shah's army, forcing the Shah himself to flee on January 16, 1979. During the previous year, while the long peace discussions between Israel and Egypt were taking place at Camp David, people in the West had watched the rise of an extraordinary Islamic holy war in Iran. Thousands of virtually unarmed Iranians had poured onto the streets, challenging the Shah's soldiers to shoot them; hundreds of them were killed. Massive crowds of workers as well as people from the professional and middle classes defied the curfew and charged the forces of SAVAK, the Shah's secret service; they were fired by the Islamic war cry "*Allahu Akhbah* [God is great]!" which echoed from loudspeakers on the rooftops. Hundreds of Iranian civilians had donned the white robes of the martyr, ready to die in this new *jihad* for Islam. Iranian women threw aside their Western clothes and shrouded themselves in the all-concealing chadar as a revolutionary act; they too rushed out onto the streets with crude weapons and machine guns, crying, "Allah! Koran! Khomeini!" Religious processions in honor of the Imam and martyr Husain paraded through the streets and the participants clenched their raised fists and shouted, "Down with the Shah!" in such vast numbers that the army did not dare to shoot. To most Western people it seemed that Iran had been gripped by a mass religious insanity. There was general ignorance about the nature of Islam, which seemed a primitive and destructive force that hurled individuals toward suicide and a whole people to a fanatical, backward-looking regime.

It was particularly shocking because this revolution seemed to be directed not only against the Shah, whose regime had, everybody acknowledged, been corrupt, tyrannical and cruel. It also seemed to be a *jihad* against "us" in the West. It was particularly disturbing for Americans to see the United States depicted as "the Great Satan." It seemed that the Iranians had rejected the gift of progress and were deliberately returning Iran to the Dark Ages. This was a Western exaggeration: the revolution is not opposed to progress as such but Iranian hatred of the West makes it very difficult for *us* to look at the revolution objectively. Hatred of the West continued after the revolution and reached a horrifying climax under Khomeini. Rafsanjani has shown signs of seeking to normalize relations with the outside world but this will take time. Whatever the West thought of Khomeini, the people of Iran remained devoted to him. The grief and dismay of the crowds at his funeral showed that they would not easily abandon the principles of their beloved Imam, and certainly no one wants to renege on the revolution itself. It is difficult for us in the West to believe that the Iranians prefer an Islamic state to a secular state dedicated to development and Western democracy. But it appears that this is the case.

Part of our problem has been our lack of understanding of Islam. This made it impossible for us to interpret the symbols of the revolution. Too often the media concentrated on the more negative aspects so that we were continually shown massed, chanting crowds who seemed merely brainwashed. After the revolution the hostage crisis understandably dominated any discussion of Iran, especially in the United States. But there were commentators who did understand what was happening. Thus the French Marxist scholar Maxime Rodinson, an expert on Islam and the Middle East, was adamant that this was not a fanatical coup but a revolution with a coherent ideology that must be taken seriously. There were complex issues involved, he argued, that must balance the hostage crisis if we were to see the situation as it was. More was involved than hatred of the West and, like any revolution, this had positive elements.[22] The Marxist revolution of 1917 had been inspired by nineteenth-century ideology. This ideology had also inspired the Chinese revolution of 1949. The Islamic revolution of Iran was not a fundamentalist return to primitive barbarism, even though it made use of old Islamic principles. It was the first real twentieth-century revolution, applying the revolutionary principles inherent in Islam to a contemporary situation in a quite distinctive way. It will be a long time before most people in either Britain or America are able to let old wounds heal and appreciate this point of view.

In Europe, where memories of Hitler are still fresh, people tended to assume that Khomeini exerted the same hypnotic effect on the chanting Iranian crowds as Hitler had manifested during the Nuremberg rallies. But this does not seem to be the case. The principles of the revolution had been explained to the people by the mullahs in the mosques and they addressed traditions and emotions that were deeply embedded in their Muslim identity. Previous attempts to overthrow the Shah had failed because they had depended on foreign ideologies like socialism or nationalism and these were alien to the vast majority of the people. Thus Mossadeq, for example, had never been able to get the grass-roots support of the masses. But when the duty of revolution against the hated Shah was explained to the people in Islamic terms, they not only understood but were able to develop and apply its principles spontaneously, without being directed or orchestrated from above. When various working-class revolutionaries were asked during the 1978 revolution who gave them instructions, they answered: "No one in particular. Everyone agrees. There is really no organisation. . . . But by firing on us, the army has forced us to organise ourselves and even to arm ourselves. We listen to Khomeini."[23] But Khomeini was at this point thousands of miles away in Paris: the people listened to him on tapes, they listened to the sermons of the mullahs and applied the principles of the Islamic revolution themselves, able to do so because they could relate to them at a profound level.

Fundamental to the revolution was the desire to find themselves again and to throw off the alien Western lifestyle and values that had crept into the country during the long years of British and American domination. Again, this is difficult for us to understand. We had genuinely thought that we were helping the people of Iran, at the same time as we were ourselves benefiting from her resources, by bringing progress and enlightened values to the country. But, as I said earlier, we must try to understand that for the people in the Third World the "culture shock" experienced has been a very real trauma. The mullahs of Iran had long been worried by the Shahs' courting of Western imperial powers, and indeed secular Iranian writers had discussed the disturbing effects of a trend which they called "West-toxication." They described Westernized Iranians as particles of dust suspended in the air, in touch with neither heaven nor earth. The mullahs in particular saw that ideologies like socialism or nationalism, which might work very well for Western people, were doomed to disappoint Iranians because they touched nothing fundamental in their cultural experience: they were "idols," false gods who promised more than they could fulfill. Indeed, many of those middle- and upper-class Iranians, who had been educated in the West, returned home strangely dissatisfied. They found it difficult to articulate this feeling of inchoate distress but they felt rootless and lost, at home in neither East nor West. In their poetry and writings the frequency of themes like loneliness, nothingness, walls, fatigue and darkness show this malaise. They felt that they had lost their identity.[24] Once they had lost that sense of excitement at the novel Western way of life, many younger Iranians felt caught between two worlds and in need of a clear identity. Therefore, they as well as the working-class people, responded to Khomeini when he said: "We have completely forgotten our own identity and have replaced it with a Western identity." Muslims had "sold themselves and do not know themselves, becoming enslaved to alien ideals."[25] By returning to Islam, which had formed and shaped Iranian culture for thirteen hundred years, the Iranians would find themselves again.

We have seen that the search for a new and positive identity has been crucial in the ideology of the holy wars we have considered. It is part of the monotheistic tradition shared by all three religions of Judaism, Christianity and Islam. We shall see that it was also central in the ideology of the Sunni extremists in Egypt at the time of Sadat. So was the concern for social justice and equality. Iranians who were left cold by Marxist analyses of the situation in their country under the Shah could understand exactly why he was a bad ruler when the principles of Abu Bakr or the Imam Ali were applied to the Shah's regime. They had been unmoved by a nationalist explanation of why they should throw off the shackles of the United States and take control of their own destinies. But the call to action was deeply embedded in the Islamic tradition. When Khomeini said that "Faith consists of this form of belief that impels men to action,"[26] they could understand exactly what he meant. Islam had always championed the cause of the poor and had encouraged them to stand up for their own rights. Neither the United States nor the Soviet Union had been a real friend to the poor, Khomeini argued. There was no reason why there should be abject poverty in Iran, which was an oil-rich country, but the imperial powers had simply exploited this resource so that the people had never benefited from it themselves. Now they had a duty, as good

Muslims, to fight oppression and to "seize their own rights." The people had enormous power and if they united together and formed a solid revolutionary front there would be nothing that the great powers could do to stop them. Filled with the apocalyptic vision that we have seen inspiring other holy war ideologies, Khomeini argued that the poor must take their destiny into their own hands and initiate change by declaring war against the *mostakberin*, the ruling classes. Muslims must lead the way and be a vanguard for all the poor people of the world who had been damaged by the imperialism of the superpowers. The Islamic revolutionary *jihad* would bring about a new world order.[27]

The way this was achieved seemed very bizarre to us in the West; similarly the way that extremist Sunni Muslims behaved in Egypt at the time of Sadat also seemed very peculiar. This was, of course, because we did not understand the Islamic principles behind many of these revolutionary themes. Thus the processions in honor of Husain, the donning of the white robes of the martyr and slogans like "There were no bystanders at Karbala" seemed incomprehensible. Western commentators often described the "lust for martyrdom" that seemed to have gripped Iran and blamed Shiism for this unhealthy, masochistic urge. But the Husain story was not extolling martyrdom for its own sake: it was a powerful expression of a revolutionary struggle against tyranny. In the days that led up to the revolution, the people had begun to plumb the depths of the story of Husain at Karbala and to see it in a revolutionary light. The people had got used to seeing Husain as a patron saint, a distributor of benefits.[28] When they celebrated his death during the month of *ashura* in the traditional passion plays and processions they had usually sympathized with him and empathized with his sufferings. The passion plays had over the years come to be a form of folk mysticism; without these popular celebrations it is unlikely that Shiism would have survived among the people of Iran. The climax of the cycle of passion plays comes not when Husain actually dies but when he puts on the white shroud as a sign that he is ready to die as a martyr in the battle against Yazid. The people, who have throughout been empathizing with the story, at this point weep and groan. They seem during these plays to have broken through a barrier in rather the same way as a mystic does when he achieves an alternative state of consciousness.[29] During the *ashura* celebrations of 1978, which coincided with the climax of the revolution, it became clear that the people were seeing Husain in a very different way. Instead of the patron saint and the pitiable but noble martyr, the people saw him as an intrepid revolutionary who fought

to the death against tyranny. Now when he put on the white shroud
in the plays, the audience responded by doing the same, declaring that
they were ready to die in the struggle against the Shah. The emotional
character of the plays gave this decision a resounding depth and its
mystical element enabled people to break through their natural barrier
of fear and selfishness and face the possibility of death at the hands
of the Shah's army. A few days before the 1978 *ashura*, a woman
explained this fundamental change in the religious attitude among the
ordinary Muslim of Iran:

> This ashura there'll be mourning but with a big difference. There'll
> be mourning with victory. Now we are more aware of the teachings
> of Husain. Now everybody knows *why* Husain went to fight Yazid.
> Before they didn't know. Three nights ago I went to a *rauzeh* [a
> formal recitation of the Kanbala story] and the *rauzekhan* [reciter]
> called Husain *rahbar-e enqelab* [leader of revolution]—and he wasn't
> an educated *rauzekhan*, just a simple one. He'd never called Husain
> that before. Before they pitied Husain rather than admiring his
> courage. Now people are more aware of the whole meaning of
> religion.[30]

To outsiders, this Husain cult seemed fanatical and strange. We are
used to more abstract and intellectual revolutionary ideologies. But
the Husain imagery touched a very deep chord in the thousands of
simple Iranians who braved the guns of the soldiers. Even though the
emphasis on Husain as revolutionary was new, it was not an aberration. It was rather a return to the original spirit of Karbala and was
in line with a strong Islamic tradition that provided a very powerful
impetus to action. Often outsiders misinterpreted this Islamic imagery.
We in the West were particularly horrified to hear America called "the
Great Satan." Not surprisingly, we thought of the Christian Satan, a
figure of monstrous evil. But actually in Islam, as in Judaism, Satan
is not a terrifying and omnipotent monster; he is the tempter, who
tries to lure Adam away from true belief. In rather the same way
America was seen to have encouraged the Shah to try and tempt the
Iranians away from Islam into secular, Western modes of thought. In
popular Shiism, Shaitan is a poor trivial creature who asks Allah for
gifts that man has and is easily fobbed off with frivolous, secular
trumpery. It was a triviality that was similar to the casinos, bars and
boutiques of the Shah's Westernized Teheran.[31] In other words, when
they called America "the Great Satan," Iranians were not saying that
America was monstrously evil but, using the Islamic figure of Satan,
they were saying something less threatening and more precise. Indeed

the depictions of America as the Great Satan showed a politician like Carter or Reagan as an outsize rabbit dressed in an Uncle Sam costume. It was funny rather than terrifying. Later, of course, under Khomeini, the hatred of the United States became exaggerated and frightening but it would be wrong to think that this fanatical loathing was inherent in the ideology of the revolution. As we have seen, Rafsanjani has a more balanced view of the West and also of the Soviet Union.

Indeed, the Iranian revolutionary ideology could be exciting and rather beautiful in the early days. Thus the teaching of the layman Dr. Ali Shariati was particularly inspiring to the Western-educated middle and upper classes. He also taught that the Iranian people had lost their true nature and had to return to their Islamic roots to be healed. Islam was a religion of the people; it was a revolutionary active faith. A return to Islam, he taught, did not have to mean a return to the world of the seventh century. Iranians should follow the example of the Prophet himself, who had grafted the new monotheistic faith onto ancient Arabian paganism, so that Islam grew creatively from the past. Shariati was helping his people to rediscover themselves in a creative encounter with their past. Only by putting down strong roots in the past could a person grow healthily and face the future with confidence. Iranians did not need to turn to foreign ideologies: in Islam they had the most dynamic ideology in the world. Shariati pointed out that the very word *umma* (community) came from the Arabic root: to go, to move. He discussed the important Muslim principle of *ijtihad* (independent reasoning), which the clerics had narrowed to the interpretation of the Koran and the Sharia. Shariati argued that *ijtihad* should encourage every single Muslim constantly to correct and change his ideas: it was a call to perpetual revolution and, if followed sensibly, would not allow Muslim society to stagnate and get trapped in stale, outworn habits. Finally, he used the Muslim notion of *hijra*, which we have seen was a very important ideal in Islam. The notion of a migration has been crucial in our story and vital in the holy war ideology of all three religions. Shariati taught that *hijra* could be a physical *hijra* like Mohammad's migration to Medina or it could be an internal *hijra* that committed each Muslim to an endless "choice, struggle, a constant becoming." Man was committed to a migration within himself, "from clay to God; he is a migrant within his own soul," a "being in the process of becoming," committed to endless quest." We shall find that the *hijra* ideal was also very important in the ideology of the Sunni extremists in Egypt.[32]

Shariati was against the clerical domination of Iranian Shiism, yet before the revolution his picture was carried through the streets along-side Khomeini's. In 1973 he was captured by SAVAK, tortured and deported. He died in 1977 in his apartment outside London at the age of forty-four. At the time people believed that he had been mur-dered by SAVAK agents, though the latest view is that he probably died from the injuries he had sustained in prison. Either way, SAVAK killed him and this is ironic: it is not at all clear that Shariati would have either approved of the Khomeini regime or that he would have survived in it.

The ten years of Khomeini's rule were indeed disastrous for Iran. Its cruelty and violence exceeded that of the Shah and it is impossible to see him as the model Islamic ruler as propounded by the four Rightly Guided Caliphs. Naturally, this has called the legitimacy of the whole revolution into question. But to dismiss the Islamic revo-lution as wholly negative and atavistic would be unbalanced. It may well be that a more moderate era is beginning, just as the French Revolution saved itself from the excesses of Robespierre and returned to the original spirit of liberty, equality and fraternity. We shall have to await developments. In any case, it will take the Americans and the British a very long time to recover from the hatred and cruelty they have experienced at the hands of Khomeini, just as it will take the Iranians a very long time to recover from the injuries they feel that they have sustained at the hands of the West. On both sides we must learn to beware of the tendency to demonize and struggle to attain an objectivity that will ultimately heal the old wounds. But at the time of writing this may be impossible, particularly for the people of the United States.

The important thing for us to bear in mind is that the Iranian Revolution formed the backdrop to the Camp David discussions. The *jihad* in Iran accompanied the slow progress toward a peace settlement. Not only that, it transpired that there was a similar Islamic enthusiasm at work in Egypt and that this proved fatal to Sadat himself. His peace treaty was not the main motive for his murder but it was one of the three motives listed by Khaled Islambouli at his trial. The Iranian *jihad* was not primarily concerned with Israel but in Egypt the theme of the Holy Land became entwined inextricably with the new surge of Islamic radicalism. Thus it is more a part of our story than the Iranian Revolution. The radical Islamic groups that sprang up in Egypt during Sadat's period as President often seem as bizarre in their practices as did certain aspects of the Iranian Revolution but they were inspired by many of the same ideals and passions. This was not due to slavish imitation but because Islam, be it Sunni or Shiite, fosters a particular revolutionary mentality. Sadat had not realized that when he presented himself to the Egyptians as the Pious President he was actually inviting a comparison of his regime and rule with the principles adumbrated by the Four Righteous Caliphs. He had hoped to promote an establishment Islam that would support his regime; instead his encouragement of Islamic groups led to the development of various movements that rejected and, finally, killed him. Further, the development of this powerful religious extremism made it not only difficult but also extremely dangerous for any future Arab leader to consider signing a peace treaty with Israel.

We have seen that in 1971 Sadat had offered to begin peace negotiations with Israel but that this initiative was scorned. He then began his period in office with a preparation for war. He rightly judged that if he wanted the Americans to take him seriously and see Egypt as a valuable asset, he must show that they were a formidable force on the battlefield. In any serious peace negotiations an Arab leader could only get good terms for his country if he argued from a position of strength. After the disaster of the Six Day War, Egypt's position was one of abject weakness. Accordingly the troops were intensively trained for a new offensive against Israel, which began on October 6, 1973. This time the Egyptians made no dramatic warnings, as Nasser had done, and the combined Syrian-Egyptian assault on the fast of Yom Kippur was a terrible shock to Israel. Sadat, probably astute, realized that the Arabs were still not strong enough to beat Israel but this time their performance was astonishingly improved. Egyptians sailed through the formidable Bar Lev line, which Israel had considered impregnable, as easily as they had done during their rehearsals and it was days before Israel was able to repel the attack. The new religious spirit in Egypt had affected the October War: the code name for the operation was Badr, after the Prophet's first victory against Mecca, and the battle cry was *"Allahu Akhbah!"* Just as the Israelis call this the Yom Kippur War, the Arabs call it the War of Ramadan. The Egyptians naturally saw their relative success as God's endorsement of their cause, in the time-honored manner of the holy war. They turned more fervently to Islam than ever before because it had proved to be such a powerful weapon.

Now Sadat could begin to consider the peace option once more. He had avenged Arab honor, which had been so disastrously impaired in 1967, and there was no longer the same need for the Egyptians to feel defensive and instinctively hostile and negative to the thought of peace. The achievement of the October War also enhanced Sadat's prestige in his own country. He could now point out that whereas

Nasser had disgraced the Arabs in 1973 he, Sadat, had made it possible for the Arab nations to hold their heads high once more. But Sadat wanted to go one stage further. He wanted to be able to say that whereas Nasser had lost the Sinai Peninsula in 1967 he had recovered it for Egypt. Now that he had vindicated the honor of the Arab nation on the battlefield and proved that Egypt was a force to be reckoned with, he indicated to Henry Kissinger during the negotiations after the war that he was seriously thinking of renewing the peace offer he had made in 1971, which Prime Minister Golda Meir and Defense Minister Moshe Dayan had so contemptuously rejected.[33]

In 1973 the Arabs seemed set for a new, victorious phase in their history and it really looked as though they might be about to recover from the centuries of colonial humiliation. They had distinguished themselves on the battlefield and discovered a new weapon in their oil, which many religious Arabs saw as Allah's gift to his chosen people. When OPEC announced its embargo to force the world to take the plight of the Palestinian Arabs seriously, the whole world suddenly seemed to be at their mercy: the superpowers were rendered helpless, if enraged, and Western Europe was distraught. Old buried hatred of the Arab world, which had been firmly embedded in the Western consciousness since the Crusades, surfaced again, and it looked as though the Arabs still wanted to take over the world. In fact, the Arabs were no more eager to do this in 1973 than they had ever been. They simply wanted to take their destiny into their own hands, right the wrongs that they felt had been done to their people and force the world to respect them again. None of these hopes materialized, however, and for this failure Sadat and his peace policy must bear a good deal of responsibility.

After the war Sadat told his people that they were at the beginning of a new, exciting era and he initiated an economic policy that he promised would bring wealth and success to Egypt. But Sadat was no economist. As the Americans would discover later, he had no interest in or understanding of the subject, so it was not really surprising that his new policy turned out to be a disaster. He called it *infitah* or Opening and it is one of the ironies of Sadat's tragedy that his plans for peace and reconstruction often fell into the pattern and idiom of the holy war, like an accidental but uncannily accurate parody. *Infitah* comes from the same Arabic roots as *al-Fatah*, the name given to Mohammad's conquest of Mecca. *Al-Fatah* had been the long climax of Mohammad's struggle to achieve an independent and essentially Islamic identity, but *infitah* meant a new foreign invasion. *Infitah* opened Egypt up: foreign currency, foreign investment and foreign imports were encouraged and great tax benefits lured many Western investors. Unfortunately this also meant that Egyptian businesses and goods went to the wall, and Egypt seemed to be acquiring a new subservience to the West and a new Western appearance. It was here that Sadat's image as the Pious President began to tarnish: many Muslims started to see him as a *munafiq* who had sold the honor and independence of his people as no true Muslim should.

A Muslim ruler must create a just and equal society, but in Sadat's Egypt there was an unacceptable amount of corruption and a new gap between rich and poor. The only people to benefit from *infitah* were the foreigners and the Egyptian millionaires, not the smaller Egyptian businessmen. Only 4 percent of the young Egyptians would find well-paid employment and a successful future in this new Egypt. The rest faced a harsh alternative. If they stayed in Egypt they faced unemployment or miserably paid state employment and permanent homelessness, because even the smallest apartment was extremely expensive. It became impossible for Egyptians to marry and start a family until they had acquired some capital, and people began to feel hopeless and despairing. The only way to improve their lot was emigration. In the developing and wealthy Gulf states, young Egyptian intellectuals and skilled laborers were able to earn a great deal of money, and thousands of Egyptians left their country for long periods, sent money home from the Gulf and saved for their own future. In exile, they joined the Palestinian refugees, who were also doing well in the Gulf, and with them formed a new elite in the Arab world that was often resented and feared. Thousands of peasants also left Egypt to work in other Arab countries, where they could find just enough money to build a house or buy a tractor when they returned home. Sadat was forcing many of his fellow countrymen to make a *hijra* from their homeland because he had made it impossible for them to live there.

Clearly a policy like *infitah* did not look well, coming as it did from the Pious President. Sadat's own lifestyle also belied his claim, because he was living in grossly un-Islamic splendor: he had 120 rest homes, many of which had been refurbished at a cost of millions of Egyptian pounds; he started to wear clothes of expensive Western designers; and he was increasingly seen hobnobbing with capitalists like David Rockefeller. His wife Jihan dressed like a Western woman and adopted Western manners, which shocked many Egyptians. She went down very well indeed in the West, and when state visitors arrived she would often kiss them on the cheek, which seemed frankly scandalous to the newly pious Egyptians. A true Muslim ruler should never become isolated from his people, but Sadat led a very secluded, luxurious life.

He developed a strange restlessness and was constantly on the move from one of his rest houses to another, traveling by helicopter and accompanied by only a few cronies and his family. If problems arose he would often take off alone to ponder in private, as though a solution would drop directly from heaven instead of arriving during a consultation with his colleagues. Sadat's isolation was not only un-Islamic but dangerous for any ruler. Mohammad Heikal points out that from a helicopter Egypt looks a particularly peaceful land, but Sadat did not have his feet sufficiently on the ground to see the real dangers he faced in his own country.[34]

In their distress many young Egyptians naturally turned to religion, and this continued the religious revival which had begun in 1967 and which might otherwise have died a natural death. They flocked into Islamic groups which the Pious President encouraged and protected. This was especially true in the universities, where the Islamic student associations (the *jama'at islamiyya*) began to control the campus after the October War, and Sadat encouraged this because they were proving to be powerful opponents of the Nasserite and Marxist unions. In 1975 he issued new decrees which enabled them to take over the student unions completely and by 1976 they had become the leaders of the students.[35] The campus took on an Islamic appearance. Young men grew beards and wore the gallabiyah, and women shrouded themselves in the chador. They insisted on the segregation of the sexes, on separate classes and buses for men and women, and began to hold huge prayer gatherings. All this seemed perverse to most people in the West. It looked as though these students, who were often among the most intelligent, were throwing off the freedoms and humanism of the enlightened West and turning back to an outdated, puritanical religion which subordinated women to men and condemned sex as impure, shrouding the bodies of these young men and women from view. Something similar has also happened among the religious Jews in Israel. In recent years there has been a far greater emphasis on the separation of Jewish men and women there. A few years ago practicing Orthodox Jews of the religious parties would very often organize an outing which would include mixed bathing, but now this would be unthinkable. Similarly more women are keeping their heads covered with a scarf and refusing to wear short sleeves than was common among religious Jewish women not long ago.[36] We in the West tend to find this very disturbing, so it is important to see what it means, even though this will entail a digression from our story.

People who come from the Christian tradition assume that the segregation of the sexes and the assumption of concealing dress in both Judaism and Islam springs from a hatred of sex, because Christianity has been very negative about human sexuality throughout its history, as I have shown at length elsewhere.[37] Despite the official teaching that sex and marriage were part of God's plan, a neurotic hatred of sex grew up that was quite distinct from the doctrine and which meant that marriage was regarded as a distinctly inferior Christian vocation and that sex was a disgusting, unholy activity. The hatred of sex survived the Reformation and Luther brought it firmly into the Protestant tradition. This distrust and fear of sex is unique among the major religions of the world and there is nothing like it in either Judaism or Islam. Judaism has always stressed the holiness of married, family life, which is why it punishes adultery so severely. Perhaps the Jewish attitude to sexuality can be best understood by considering briefly the commandments that forbid a man and wife to have intercourse while the woman is menstruating and for seven days afterward, when she takes a ritual bath. This "purification," as the Hebrew word is translated in English, suggests that the woman is dirty or "unclean," but in fact this is not so. There is a strong rabbinical tradition that says that the period of abstinence is required in order that the couple will enjoy sex more afterward and that the man does not take his wife for granted as a sex object: "Because a man may become overly familiar with his wife, and thus repelled by her, the Torah said that she should be a *niddah* [sexually unavailable] for seven days [after menses] so that she will be as beloved to him [afterward] as on the day of her marriage" (Niddah 3lb).[38] Before going to the synagogue on Yom Kippur or one of the major festivals, a man is told to take a ritual bath, *not* because he is unclean, but in order to be more holy for the holy time during the service. Similarly menstrual blood is not dirty or a defilement, but after a period of separation a woman "purifies" herself to make herself more holy for what happens next: sexual relations with her husband. The idea that sex could be holy in this way is quite foreign to the Christian world view.[39]

It is also true, as I have said earlier, that Islam has a very positive attitude to sexuality. The Prophet himself seems to have been a highly sexed and passionate man, who saw no value at all in celibacy and is said to have decreed that there was to be no "monkery" in Islam.[40] Yet in the West we tend today to think that Islam is a sexually repressive religion, because "we" are trying to free ourselves from the repressions of Christianity. The barbaric practice by *some* Muslims of clitoridectomy encourages this belief.[41] In the last century this disfiguring operation was performed on English Christian girls, with the approval of society, but it was performed for quite different reasons.[42] A Muslim may insist that his daughter have the operation because he owns her and is afraid that her normal sexual urge might lead her to wander off with other men before she is given to a husband. It comes from a primitive impulse that seems to be common in many societies. It made some of the Crusaders lock their wives into extremely painful and dangerous chastity belts while they were in the Holy Land. In Victorian London, however, the girl usually had the operation because she had been found masturbating and enjoying her sexuality, which would have horrified her parents because they were terrified of sex.[43] The practice has not been upheld by a majority of either Muslims or Christians and it must be condemned for whatever reason it is performed. But the difference is important. Clitoridectomy was originally an African, not an Islamic custom: it is certainly not laid down in the Koran, any more than it is in the Gospels. On the contrary, Mohammad is said to have told Muslim men that they have a positive duty to satisfy their wives sexually; some of the rabbis told the Jews the same.[44] This is quite contrary to the spirit of the Fathers of the Church, who told Christians that if a man enjoyed sleeping with his wife too much he was committing fornication.[45]

The second thing that distresses Western people is that, at a time when the progressive West was promoting the ideal of the equality of the sexes, some Jews and Muslims today seem to be retreating to the old inequalities. It must be said that no religion in the world as far as I know has in practice been very good news for the position of women. Religions have until recently been male affairs like most other institutions. But people from the Christian tradition rather enjoy saying that Judaism and Islam are particularly repressive of their women. Again, this needs qualification. Judaism is a religion that proclaims the holiness of things by separating them. The Torah separates Sabbath from the rest of the week, milk from meat, and Jews from Gentiles. The "holiness" of the land of Israel should probably be considered in this context; it is partly for this reason that the *goyim* are forbidden in the Torah to live there. The Torah also separates men from women; in Orthodox synagogues men and women sit separately and men and women have different religious duties. As one would expect, the women's duty centers on the home and the husband's on prayer and study. The Bible and the Halakah teach that women are blessed by God, but each morning in the synagogue a Jew must thank God for not making him a Gentile, a slave or a woman. Jewish feminists, who want to preserve the ancient traditions, will argue that the Torah is not wrong to encourage a separation of the roles of men and women because this way it preserves and celebrates the holiness or identity of the sexes as different and distinct. But they still argue that Halakah must be developed so that women are no longer forced to take an inferior position in the community.[46]

In the West people are particularly wedded to the idea that Muslims oppress their women by divine command. But in fact Mohammad's first converts were women, who found the religion liberating.[47] The Koran gives women divorce rights and inheritance rights, which are not the same as those of men, but which women in the enlightened West would not receive for over a thousand years. In the early Muslim community Mohammad's wives were very powerful people, and after his death were consulted about religious matters, particularly Aisha, his favorite wife. There is nothing about the veiling or separation of women in the Koran; this practice did not creep into Islam until the third or fourth generation after the Prophet and it has been suggested that it came from Christian Byzantium, which had always treated its women in this way.[48] Certainly a Muslim feels he "owns" his wife, but many Western men would feel the same. The Koran and the *hadith* both tell men to love their wives tenderly and live with them happily (see, for example, Koran 30:22).

The return to traditional values in Judaism and in Islam today in the Middle East has been for different reasons. In Israel it has been inspired by the desire to establish a strictly religious identity and is just part of a general return to minute observance of the Torah. Religious women who now cover their heads will also forbid their children to watch television, because of the prohibition of images in Judaism. In Sadat's Egypt, however, the young people of the *jama'at islamiyya* who returned to Islamic dress and the segregation of the sexes had a rather different reason. The Muslim student unions were encouraging their members to improve their lot by their own practical efforts instead of waiting for the government to help them, as the Koran enjoined. Egyptian universities are not like their counterparts in Europe and America. They can be heartless, mechanical factories. In Arabic they are called "universities of large numbers" and there is indeed vast overcrowding.[49] Students attending the compulsory lectures would often have to sit two or three to a seat. Only a few lucky people in the front rows would be able to follow a demonstration on a blackboard and if the loudspeakers broke down almost nobody could hear a word that was said. Because success in the examination meant regurgitating these lectures accurately, lecture manuals had to be bought at some cost and learned by heart. There was little intellectual freedom. The students who achieved the best grades when they graduated from high school were automatically placed in one of the "elite" subjects like engineering, medicine or pharmacology. If a bright student wanted to study literature or law, which were not elite subjects, he would have to accept the fact that he would be studying with inferior teachers or classmates and that his chance of success after university was even more remote than it was already. This was a relic of the Nasser period; it was modeled on the Soviet system and was designed to produce a nation of technicians, not scholars. In addition to these other difficulties for the students, there was great overcrowding in the dormitories, which made studying impossible in the evenings, and the students would be transported from these inhumanely huge student blocks on hideously overcrowded buses.

The success of the *jama'at islamiyya* was that its members addressed these problems effectively and practically, as good Muslims should. They used to hold revision sessions in the mosques before examinations, where students could study in peace and quiet, and they issued cheap versions of the lecture manuals. Above all they tackled a particularly distressing aspect of the overcrowding. Because young Egyptians could not afford to marry until very late and because the sexual revolution that happened in the West during the 1960s did not spread to Third World countries, one of the great problems of Sadat's Egypt was sexual frustration among the young. For young men and women to sit crammed together on the same seat during lectures or jammed together on buses was clearly intolerable for both. Women found themselves harassed by desperate young men, who found that they could not stand this tantalizing promiscuity. In these extremely difficult circumstances, the message of the Islamic segregation of the sexes was music in the ears of many of these strained young people. Women would find themselves freed from unwelcome attentions in the chador and it seemed to make good sense for men and women to live and study apart.[50]

But, given that Islam values sex so highly, why did these young people not use contraception? Why did the women not go on the pill? Some certainly did, but the members of the *jama'at islamiyya* felt that this was an unacceptable solution. Contraception and the permissive society were Western products and therefore unacceptable for most of the young people, who, with good reason, felt that the West was not their friend. But it was not simply a negative rejection. These Egyptians wanted to keep to their *own* family and social traditions, which would be undermined by this Western way of life. Muslims in the Middle East were not as enamored as Westerners were of this Western "freedom." The way sex was used to sell products and was trivialized and commercialized seemed to denigrate an important

value. Iranians also had rejected the triviality of the Great Satan and
had expressed their separation from it by reverting to their own traditional dress. In the case of women, Egyptians felt that Western
clothes were not always liberating. They can reduce a woman's dignity
by making her a mere sex object and it is undeniably true that, while
we are rightly proud of the freedom and respect that we have *begun*
to give to women in Western countries, this liberation has not halted
that Western habit of enslaving and exploiting women through a
heartless advertisement and sex industry that pays very little attention
to human dignity. Many Western feminists would agree with this.

Clothes are, of course, extremely important in expressing one's identity and it is interesting that in Israel, Egypt and Iran the assumption
of a different costume has naturally symbolized the assertion of a new
self. Similarly the relations between men and women could be said to
express most clearly the values of a society, so that it is natural when
one society feels threatened by another that one of the first signs of
a desire to resist this foreign coercion should center on issues of sexual
morality and the position of women. Yet the extreme measures to
which Muslim men and women have been willing to go to express
their distance from the Western point of view is very disturbing to
us. This entire rejection of our way of life seems unbalanced because
our way of handling the relations between men and women is very
crucial to *our* sense of self. No society has as yet found a really sat-
isfactory solution to these problems. In Western countries we have
tended to swing from a period of sexual freedom to an extreme sexual
repression. This phenomenon, which is unique to Western society,
shows that we tend to be particularly sensitive on this issue and to
have ambiguous views. This may make us more stridently convinced
that our current way is the "only" way of managing these matters.
We should not condemn Muslim people for choosing to go their own
way, rather than to follow us in our confusion.

But the return to Islam did not end there. Resuming traditional
dress touched a deep chord in the Islamic identity of these students.
Sadat may have praised and encouraged these Muslim groups and
thought that he was establishing a popular power base for his regime,
but he was actually creating a Frankensteinian monster that would
devour him: Khaled Islambouli, his assassin, was a member of the
*jama'at islamiyya* when he was at university. One began by opting not
to sit next to a woman and found that one was beginning to make a
radical break from the regime. During Islamic festivals the *jama'at
islamiyya* would hold "camps," like the similar camps held by their
rivals, the Nasserites and the Marxists.[51] Here they did not simply

spend their time studying the Koran; there was also a great deal of
sport and practice in self-defense. The camps were trying to recreate
a perfect Muslim society lived according to the spirit and values of
the *rashidun*, the Righteous Caliphs. It was a retreat from the un-
Islamic world of Sadat's Egypt and an experiment in the Islamic utopia,
the creation of a perfect alternative world. Naturally this involved
discussion of the regime in Egypt, which seemed to have no concern
whatever for the fate of these young people. There would be lectures
criticizing the regime and condemning it as *jahiliyya*, the term used
to describe the barbarous pre-Islamic period in Arabia, before Mohammad gave the Arabs power and a new identity. Egyptians had
been told for years that their identity was anti-Western and now the
Pious President seemed to be inviting the West to invade the country
and drive out the Egyptians themselves. By returning to their own
Islamic, un-Western roots, the students were beginning to recover a
sense of self-respect and a new source of personal power.

However radical the *jama'at islamiyya* was naturally and inevitably
becoming, there were other young Muslims who sought an even more
radical answer; a new Muslim underground was being formed, and it
sought a more extreme solution than the Muslim Brotherhood, which
now cooperated with the regime. Many Muslims had been profoundly
influenced by the writings of Sayyid Qutb, a Muslim Brother who
had in his turn been influenced by the Pakistani Brother Abu el A'ala
Mawdudi, who was also being eagerly read by young radicals in Iran.
Qutb had been imprisoned by Nasser in 1954 and had read Mawdudi's
book, *The Four Expressions*, while in prison. It had a great effect on
him. Mawdudi told Muslims that they must refuse to compromise
with the corrupt regimes which oppressed Muslims throughout the
Islamic world and which violated essential Koranic principles. Muslims
must be ruled by God alone and must reject the idols of false ideology
and values placed before them by the *munafiqeen*.[52] Sayyid Qutb himself wrote several books which developed Mawdudi's ideas. He returned to the old paradigm of the *hijra-jihad*. In *The Shadow of the
Koran* and *Signposts on the Road* he taught that there were two necessary
stages in the struggle for a truly Islamic society. First was the period
of weakness (*istidhaf*) when devout Muslims were in no position to
fight the regime effectively. Instead they should withdraw from the
corrupt society as Mohammad had withdrawn from his period of
weakness in Mecca and made the *hijra* to Medina where he gained a
new power. Once Muslims were truly separate from the un-Islamic
world, they should build an alternative Islamic society where they

would recover the strength necessary to end the period of *istidhaf* and wage a *jihad* against the infidels.[53]

The Egyptians who became disciples of Qutb were divided about how to interpret his teachings. Some formed the *jama'at al-uzla al-shu'uriayya* (Spiritual Detachment Group). They secretly pronounced a decree of excommunication (*takfir*) on the corrupt society, but because they were still in the period of weakness they would conceal their views and pray before an imam whom they actually condemned as an infidel because he supported the government. Thus concealed and spiritually separated from society, they would wait for the period of power when they could fight a *jihad* against the infidels with a good chance of success.[54] Others felt that this was not a sufficiently radical solution and followed Sheikh Ali Abduh Ismail into the small Society of Muslims, but the group disintegrated in 1969 when Sheikh Ali defected and the sect was left with only one member.[55] Shukri Mustafa was a young, poorly educated Muslim from Middle Egypt, whose inhabitants are usually considered simple rustics by their fellow countrymen. He had been imprisoned by Nasser in 1965 but released in 1971 as part of Sadat's new approach to Islam. This did not endear the regime to Shukri, however, and he was soon preaching with such success in the hamlets and villages that by 1972 the police were already watching him carefully. They called the group the *Takfir w'al hijra* (excommunication and *hijra*) because Shukri declared that Sadat's regime was an infidel regime and he condemned any Muslim who supported it. He urged his followers to withdraw from Sadat's Egypt and openly form an alternative Islamic society. For a time the members of his group lived in the desert, but later most lived a communal life in apartments in the poorest areas of the cities, which necessarily associated the Society of Muslims with the poor and outcast people of Egypt.[56]

Shukri preached a fundamental return to the Koran and denied that the later Islamic tradition had any value: imams who had written learnedly about the Koran had idolatrously elevated their purely human learning and made it an idol. Many imams had actually supported the infidel and hypocritical regimes of the *munafiqeen*. As examples he cited Sheikh Mahmud Shaltut of the al-Azhar Madrassa, who had in Nasser's time issued a *fatwa* which declared banking interest to be legal, even though many Muslims condemned it as usury, or Sheikh Su'ad Jala, who had recently declared that Muslims were allowed to drink beer. Shukri taught that no Muslim who was serious about his religion could continue to live in this regime; the state of Egypt, he said, was as dangerous an enemy to the Muslim people as the state of Israel and none of his followers should contaminate themselves by joining the Egyptian army or taking any state employment. All contact with the state was strictly forbidden. Many young Egyptians who were confused by the volte-face of Sadat's new Western Egypt and who found their lives miserable and hopeless took comfort from this absolute denial of the state and this return to old Islamic values. Shukri taught that the Muslims were too weak to stage a *jihad* against the regime and that when they were confronted with as powerful an enemy as the state of Egypt they should flee, as Mohammad had very wisely fled from Mecca when he had been persecuted there. In seclusion they would find new strength to fight the unbelievers.

The young people who followed Shukri and made the *hijra* into the communes were desperate with misery, and in the new Islamic world that they tried to create they found their lives entirely changed. They had accommodation they could afford, they were able to marry young and the diplomas and certificates they had painfully acquired in the universities were condemned as worthless rubbish. There were many educated people in the movement, even though Shukri condemned education as worthless.[57] This was not a purely negative position but a confused comment on the economy. Most state employees with education carried far less than an unskilled worker and could only keep their families at subsistence rate; an illiterate country girl who became a lady's maid could earn more than an assistant professor. In these circumstances, Shukri argued, it was indeed pointless for Egyptians to learn to read. There was a similar clumsy extremism in his solution to the marriage problem, which shocked many of his opponents. Shukri reintroduced the old village habit of arranged early marriages. Members of his group were married very young and the match was arranged by Shukri himself. Several young couples shared a room in curtained-off cubicles. The group supported itself by manual labor and by growing vegetables, but this was not enough, so Shukri sent his young men to the Gulf in turn in a new *hijra*. There they joined the thousands of their countrymen who had been forced to emigrate and sent money home to the community. On their return they were entitled to a wife.[58] Shukri's policies seemed eccentric and bizarre but he was implicitly pointing to serious abuses in society. The movement was a passionate rebellion of the poor and oppressed, which presented an alternative Egypt on the margins of the great cities. Shukri's communities were actually creating a distorted mirror image of Sadat's Egypt, where people could marry young instead of suffering frustration, could reject the new secular values and materialism the regime was encouraging and return to Islam, and the men who made the *hijra* to the Gulf called attention to the fact that life was impossible for most people in Egypt.

The *hijra* of Shukri and his many disciples was itself an aggressive act because it was making a powerful statement about the miseries of many Egyptians who found their lives intolerable. But the *hijra* ultimately led to a more direct *jihad*, even though Shukri insisted that his followers should flee from a confrontation with the enemies of Islam. The first indication of this new *jihad* against the state was an unsuccessful dress rehearsal for Khaled Islambouli's operation in 1981 and it was carried out not by Shukri but by one of his rivals. In 1974 Saleh Sarrieh, a young PhD student who belonged to a group called the Islamic Liberation Party, led a band of followers to the Military Technical College, where they collected arms and volunteers. Then they marched on to the government headquarters. Their aim was to assassinate Sadat and to establish an Islamic state, but the movement was hopelessly small and was very easily crushed.[59] It demonstrated that Muslims were indeed too weak to undertake effective action against Sadat and that Shukri and his followers had been quite correct when they confined themselves to the *hijra* and to creating an Islamic world of their own where the values of modern Egypt no longer applied. But Sarrieh's coup also proved fatal to Shukri. One of the members of his party who was imprisoned after the attempt decided to become a member of the Society of Muslims but challenged Shukri's leadership. Another member who was released tried to lure some of Shukri's followers into a rival group of his own. There was a period of crisis in the community and Shukri decided to take action against the "apostates," as he called them, by attacking their homes on December 18 and 22, 1976.[60] This was a fatal decision, because Shukri had now made himself vulnerable to the law by attempting to kill Egyptian citizens. The police stepped in and arrested fourteen of Shukri's followers and a warrant was issued for Shukri's arrest. Until this point the Society of Muslims had formulated no very clear tactics about how to deal with the state but now they saw their movement condemned on the front page of the official Cairo newspaper *al-Ahram* as "a group of fanatical criminals."[61]

During the first six months of 1977 Shukri tried to counter this attack peacefully and to give his group a more positive image. He tried, without success, to publish a book called *The Caliphate*, to issue communiqués which explained the true nature of his group, and to deliver statements on radio and television. None of these measures worked and Shukri felt his leadership in danger. In July members of the movement kidnapped Sheikh Mohammad el-Dhahabi, a former minister of the religious endowment, and published a list of demands: they wanted the lies that had been published against them retracted, they demanded that their fourteen "martyrs" be released and that a "committee of experts" be set up to examine major government institutions, something that was quite impossible in Sadat's Egypt. The Egyptian government refused to negotiate with these terrorists and when the sheikh's body was discovered on July 7 there was a public outcry. This type of religious extremism was quite new to Egypt. What kind of Muslims would murder one of their coreligionists? Shukri and a large number of his disciples were arrested and Sadat convened a special military tribunal to try the case.[62]

At the same time that Sadat was releasing the Muslim Brothers imprisoned by Nasser, he found himself filling up the jails with new Muslim prisoners who declared themselves hostile to the regime of the Pious President. It was a delicate and uncomfortable position and as the tribunal hearings proceeded he found that the establishment had declared war against Islam. Abdul Halim Mahmoud, the sheikh of the al-Azhar mosque in Cairo, rejected Shukri's ideas but explained that, because Egypt had long been governed by people whose political philosophy was not rooted in the religious tradition of the country, many of the young people were muddled and disoriented. It was this that caused Shukri and his companions to see Sadat's Egypt as *jahiliyya*. The military prosecutor took quite a different line. On October 11 the military prosecutor explained the phenomenon as being due to the spiritual vacuum in the country. The ulema of Egypt had failed in their duty to instruct the youth in their religion and the root of the problem lay in al-Azhar's failings, not the government's. Naturally the ulema were furious and issued an angry reply; a new rift opened between the government and the religious establishment at a most important time.[63] Shukri was hanged with four other companions shortly after the conclusion of the trial in November 1977 and it is deeply significant that at that time the newspapers presented two main stories and pictures to their readers. One was of young, desperate bearded Muslim extremists who were being presented as the enemies of the state; the other was Sadat's historic journey to Jerusalem on November 8, 1977. The Pious President was about to become the President of Peace.

Early in 1977 there had been another eruption which showed alarmingly how desperate the Egyptian people were becoming and this was causally linked to Sadat's decision to go to Jerusalem on a mission of peace. Paul M. Dickie, the American director of the International

Monetary Fund in Egypt, had recently recommended drastic measures to rescue the economy, which included the devaluation of the Egyptian pound and a great reduction in the subsidies that the government paid every year on staple food and clothes.[64] Most of the impoverished Egyptians depended on these subsidies for their livelihood and the members of parliament were horrified at the possible consequences of putting a fresh financial burden on the people. They also pointed out that there were wider political implications: if Egypt allowed her economic policy to be dictated by the United States she would inevitably isolate herself from the rest of the Arab world and lose the leadership which Nasser had established. Sadat, who remained frighteningly impervious to the plight of his own people, and who never fully appreciated Egypt's uniquely important strategic position in the Middle East and North Africa, turned a deaf ear to these protests. On January 17 the government announced that there would be a substantial rise in the price of twenty-five essential goods and on January 18 the people went onto the streets; the police could not control them and 160 people were killed. Sadat himself was in Aswan that day and astonishingly did not hear about the riots until four o'clock in the afternoon[65] (a telling indication of his isolation from the people) when the crowd charged against the rest house in Aswan. Sadat had to escape by helicopter, and a plane stood by, ready to take the Sadats to Teheran. The next day, however, the army was brought in to quell the riots and Sadat restored the food subsidies. Clearly his credit was running low and he realized that he would have to regain the support of the people by doing something really dramatic, which would lead their minds to higher things. The answer was the peace process.

During President Jimmy Carter's first year in office there was renewed effort in Washington to bring peace to the Middle East, but the Arabs were naturally suspicious of the interference of a great power friendly to Israel, and Israel had recently demonstrated that she was ready to make no concessions over the territories. In 1977 Menachem Begin had been elected Prime Minister and had dedicated himself to the establishment of Greater Israel on both sides of the Jordan. The prognosis for peace was not good, but Carter manfully persevered and began a preliminary round of discussions with individual Arab and Israeli leaders. He favored the "comprehensivist" approach, which sought an overall agreement between Israel, the Palestinians and the Arab states, and did not want a series of separate peace treaties between individual states and Israel, which would almost certainly ignore the Palestinian problem.[66] Carter was distressed to find that Begin was most reluctant to take part in a conference that would put pressure

on Israel to evacuate the territories as an essential part of the peace
process, and he found Sadat's eagerness for peace attractive and impressive. It was very worrying indeed to many Israelis when the U. S.
State Department issued a peremptory public statement, which
showed none of the usual deference to the Israeli position:

> The status of the Palestinians must be settled in a comprehensive
> Arab-Israeli agreement. This issue cannot be ignored if the others
> are to be solved. Moreover, to be lasting, a peace agreement must
> be positively supported by all of the parties to the conflict, including
> the Palestinians. This means that the Palestinians must be involved
> in the peace-making process. Their representatives will have to be
> at Geneva for the Palestinian question to be solved.[67]

Israel's bogey of a Palestinian state seemed to be coming perilously
near.

Sadat rescued Israel. He had his own misgivings about a Geneva
conference, which would be far too helpful to his rival President Assad
of Syria. First, it would naturally involve the participation of the
Russians, his protectors, and Sadat had tried to limit the role of the
Soviets in the Middle East. A renewed Russian influence in the area
was not in the interests of the United States, and Israel was able to
make great capital out of this in her opposition to Geneva. Secondly,
since Assad had intervened in the civil war in Lebanon and acquired
power there, he had also made himself master of the PLO, who had
their headquarters in Beirut and a power base in the south. Assad had
probably refused to allow Arafat to speak to the Americans during
the preliminary talks. He was noisily loyal to the Palestinian cause and
would make certain that before the conference access to the PLO
would have to come through Assad himself, which would greatly
enhance his prestige. It looked as though Assad would emerge as the
Arab leader of the conference and Sadat sought to pre-empt this.[68]
He resolved his dilemma by reverting to the classic principle of a holy
war: he would not wait for the Americans and Russians to bring peace
to the Middle East but would do it himself. His peace policy would
come to be called the "initiative," but this initiative was supposed to
be a prelude not to a holy war, as was the way of such initiatives, but
to a full and lasting peace.

On November 9, 1977, Sadat addressed the members of the Egyptian parliament and promised them that he was ready to go "to the
ends of the earth for peace. Israel will be astonished to hear me say
now, before you, that I am prepared to go to their own house, to the

Knesset itself, to talk to them."[69] The delegates and Arafat, who happened to be present, all assumed that this was Sadatian rhetoric and applauded loudly.[70] Others thought that, because Israel would certainly refuse, Sadat was unmasking "the true face of Israel, who presents herself as a lover of peace,"[71] as a broadcaster put it. It is true that at first Begin's response to the offer was grudging but on November 15 he seemed to grasp its historic importance and invited the President of Egypt to come to Jerusalem the following week. Sadat accepted, despite the bitter opposition to his plan among the Arab leaders. As Pious President, he might have claimed that he was bound by the Koran to respond to any overture for peace (Koran 8:62).

When Sadat equated Israel with "the ends of the earth" he had pointed to the immense psychological distance that had developed between Israel and the Arab states since 1948. Ezer Weizmann, the Israeli Defense Minister at the time, has written that in the twentieth century there have been two great journeys: the journey of the first men to the moon and President Sadat's journey to Jerusalem.[72] In emotional terms it was one of the longest and bravest journeys that have been described in this book, but this time it was seen as a prelude to peace, not war. When Sadat landed at Ben-Gurion Airport, just after the end of the Jewish Sabbath, he made an almost magical impression: tall, beautifully dressed and with a powerful presence, he seemed a dignified ambassador from a distant world, who was breaking down the wall of hostility and arriving as a vanguard of peace. Glued to their television sets, Israelis and Egyptians watched their leaders talk together with apparent cordiality. It seemed that an unimaginable event had come to pass: the monsters had become human beings, who could converse together and perhaps live together in peace.

The theme of the peaceful pilgrimage continued the following day. By one of the holy coincidences that recur in the story of holy war, it happened to be the Eid al-Adha (which commemorates Abraham's offering of Isaac) and Sadat went first to the Temple Mount, the site of Abraham's sacrifice, and prayed in al-Aqsa. Then he visited places sacred to Christians and Jews: the Holy Sepulchre and Yad Vashem, the Holocaust memorial. He began his speech in the Knesset that afternoon with a reference to the importance of the Holy Land to all three religions: "We all love this land, the land of God, we all, Muslims, Christians and Jews, all worship God."[73] This set the deeply religious tone of his appeal for peace. Constantly Sadat called for religious coexistence: the presence of the Christian and Muslim shrines in Jerusalem showed that "politically, spiritually and intellectually"[74] Christians and Muslims look to Jerusalem with reverence and see the "city of peace" as centrally important. He insisted that it was time to abandon the intolerance of the Crusades and to return to the spirit of Caliph Omar and Saladin,[75] who had encouraged peaceful coexistence in the Holy City.

The theme of coexistence was central to the speech and this meant that, as Sadat saw it, the Arabs were now prepared to live alongside the Jewish state. Many Knesset members wept when they heard Sadat's extraordinary words: "You want to live with us, part of our world. In all sincerity I tell you we welcome you among us with full security and safety. This in itself is a tremendous turning point, one of the landmarks of a decisive historical change."[76] Politically, his speech was pure comprehensivism. He insisted that he had not come to conclude a separate treaty between Egypt and Israel but to settle the problem of the Arabs and Jews. The Israelis must evacuate the occupied territories and there could be no peace without a just settlement for the Palestinians, who were the crux of this problem.[77] Even the United States, Israel's first ally, had decided to face up to the Palestinian question:

> "If you have found the moral and legal justification to set up a national home on a land that did not all belong to you, it is incumbent upon you to show understanding of the insistence of the people of Palestine for establishment once again of a state on their land. When some extremists ask the Palestinians to give up this sublime objective, this in fact means asking them to renounce their identity and every hope for the future."[78]

This would not be welcome to the ears of his Jewish listeners, and yet Sadat asked them to recall, on this feast of al-Adha, their common ancestor Abraham, who was prepared for sacrifice, even the sacrifice of his own son. It was a characteristically religious appeal but, given the increasingly religious nature of the Arab-Israeli conflict, a powerful one. Abraham had given his descendants an example of the sacrifice that the Arabs were asking the Jews to make—a sacrifice of lands and ideals that were precious to them and central to their identity: "Abraham went, with dedicated sentiments, not out of weakness but through a giant spiritual force and a free will to sacrifice his very own son, prompted by a firm and unshakeable belief in ideals that lend life a profound significance."[79] Begin had no intention of making any such sacrifice, but in his reply to Sadat he was content himself to point to a connection between Arabs and Jews, which concentrated upon Sadat's journey:

"The flight time between Cairo and Jerusalem is short, but the distance between Cairo and Jerusalem was until last night almost endless. President Sadat crossed this distance courageously. We, the Jews, know how to appreciate such courage, and we know how to appreciate it in our guest, because it is with courage that we are here and this is how we continue to exist, and we shall continue to exist."[80]

There was a defiance in the last words that Sadat would probably have understood very well. Yet on November 20, 1977, Sadat was the star: by his dramatic journey he had attracted the attention and sympathy of the world away from Israel toward the Arabs.

Yet the Arabs were not appreciative of this and events would very shortly prove that they were right to distrust the initiative. At first, however, their rejection was muted. When President Assad of Syria formed the Front of Steadfastness against Egypt, only three countries and the PLO responded. Yet none of the Arab leaders went to the conference Sadat summoned in Egypt on December 14. Sadat really thought that his initiative could achieve a comprehensive peace, but when the American and Israeli delegates met at the Mena House Hotel, the empty seats of the Arab delegates showed the world that only Egypt was interested in making peace with Israel. It soon became apparent that, though Sadat may have been the first to take the initiative, he would not be able to retain it. Flags of all the invited delegations were in position all around the conference table; Eliahu Ben-Elissar, the head of the Israeli delegation, insisted that the Palestinian flag be taken down, and Sadat was forced to obey. Despite his insistence in Jerusalem that the Palestinians were the crux of the matter, the Israelis were saying no to direct negotiations with the PLO and no to an independent Palestinian state. Ben-Elissar then insisted that the Palestinian flag be taken down *outside* the hotel and Sadat was forced to order that *all* the flags be lowered so that his ditching of the Palestinians should not be so dramatically apparent to the outside world.[81]

Sadat's next meeting with Prime Minister Begin on December 25 showed even more strikingly that the Israelis had managed to take control of the peace initiative. Begin began by taking from his briefcase documents that purported to prove that, when a country had been provoked to attack, it was lawful for the attacked country to keep territory gained during the war. Nasser had attacked Israel and threatened to throw the Jews into the sea, and, Begin concluded: "So, Mr. President, you agree that this makes us legally justified in keeping the territory we conquered."[82] He was prepared, however, to consider returning the Sinai, as long as the Israeli settlements remained, under armed guard. Sadat decided to bring this humiliating open session to a close, but it was now quite apparent that he had been maneuvered into making a separate peace with Israel, and that nothing was to be done about the West Bank, or "Judaea and Samaria" as Begin provocatively called them in the open session. Then came a press conference at which Begin made Sadat read out the conclusions of the meeting. Never again would Israel and Egypt make war, and as for the West Bank: "The position of Egypt is that in the West Bank and Gaza a Palestinian state should be established. The position of Israel is that Palestinian Arabs in Judaea and Samaria (namely the West Bank of the Jordan) and the Gaza Strip should enjoy self-rule."[83] Mohammad Heikal recalled the devastating effect that this had upon most Egyptians. To see their President, flanked by Begin and Dayan, talking about "Judaea and Samaria" was profoundly disturbing and showed an Egyptian weakness and willingness to compromise on essential principles that were entirely new.[84]

What Begin meant by "self-rule" for the Palestinians was shortly revealed in what became known as the Begin Plan. In Gaza and the West Bank, Arabs should be given "autonomy"; this was not autonomy in the usual sense of the word, but a political dependence and subservience. Israel would keep sovereignty of the region and asked that "for the sake of agreement and peace" the problem of these territories be shelved for the present. In the meantime the Palestinians would be able freely to elect their own "administrative council," but security and public order would stay in Israeli hands. In other words, the army and the police would remain in the West Bank. Next, the "Palestinians" should choose either Israeli or Jordanian nationality.[85] What "autonomy" meant in effect was that there would be no "Palestinians" left on the West Bank or in the Gaza Strip. It also meant that, to make good Israel's claim to these territories, more settlements would be established there. On the subject of Sinai, Begin remained suggestively silent.[86]

On January 4 Carter and Sadat had met at Aswan and jointly declared that there could be no peace in the region unless the Palestinians were given self-determination, and on January 18 Sadat withdrew his delegates from the peace talks. It seemed that on the subject of the Palestinians he was too far in spirit from the Begin Plan to continue negotiations. But in fact Sadat was moved to withdraw by quite a different problem. He had got wind of the secret Israeli decision to "bolster" the Israeli presence in the Sinai by establishing six more settlements there. Sadat had already shown that he was prepared to lower the flags of Palestinian independence and go for a separate deal, but on the subject of the Sinai he remained immovable. He would let the West Bank go and leave the Palestinians out of the discussions, but if there was to be peace the Sinai had to be returned whole and entire to Egypt. As he said to Ezer Weizmann: "I am ready to conclude a contractual peace treaty, with ambassadors, with freedom of navigation, everything. But you are getting out of Sinai! That includes all the settlements! They've got to go!"

At this point the peace process slumped. The Arabs were unanimously agreed that the initiative simply meant another defeat at the hands of Israel, who had no intention of discussing the Palestinian problem seriously and no intention of returning any territory. Many Israelis simply did not want peace if that meant handing over any land. Seculars saw the territories as necessary to the security of the state, but most people felt with the religious right that the West Bank and Gaza "belonged" to the Jews and were essential to the Jewish identity. Ezer Weizmann noticed in the eyes of many of his fellow countrymen "a strange glint of satisfaction" that the peace process had failed.[87] But other Israelis were ashamed that their country was lagging behind on the road to peace and it was during this period that the Peace Now movement was founded.

Yet America was determined to push the peace process through somehow, although only one leader in the whole of the Middle East felt that peace was either possible or desirable. When Sadat made his visit to America in 1978 he got a hero's welcome, but Begin, who followed him, got a very chilly reception. Israel seemed grudging and ungenerous beside Sadat, and Carter found it hard that Begin, whom he respected as a religious and sincere man, should be so unwilling to make peace. A period of tension between Israel and the United States is always uncomfortable for both parties; and it was clear that a compromise must be found. Finally Moshe Dayan and Cyrus Vance discovered a way to break the deadlock. Instead of going all out for a comprehensive solution that seemed impossible to achieve at this point, there should be a separate peace treaty between Israel and Egypt which could be negotiated now, and later further negotiations would settle the problem of the West Bank and the question of the Palestinian inhabitants. In the meantime the Begin Plan should be accepted as a *framework* of principles that would govern the interim, transitional period before the full peace was signed. Sadat was by this time ready for a separate peace and this was also less threatening to Israel, because it shelved the problem of the West Bank in a way favorable to the Jewish state.[88]

From September 5 to 18, 1978, Begin, Carter and Sadat and their officials conferred at Camp David in the Maryland hills and finally, after a great deal of tension, Begin and Sadat signed the Camp David accords. These would be ratified by the full treaty the following year. They stated that there would now be peace between Israel and Egypt and that Egypt would take back the Sinai. Israel would withdraw her troops and evacuate the settlements in stages and would be allowed free passage through the Straits of Tiran and the Suez Canal. Besides the peace treaty between Israel and Egypt, there was a "Framework for Peace," which looked forward to future hypothetical negotiations between Israel, Egypt, Jordan and the "representatives of the Palestinian people," who were clearly not going to be members of the PLO. These discussions would decide the fate of Gaza and the West Bank and the fate of the "inhabitants" of the country, who would in the meantime choose between Israeli or Jordanian citizenship. The Framework foresaw a transitional period of five years, when the territories would be governed according to the principles of the Begin Plan, with the inhabitants of the land enjoying "administrative autonomy." The land itself would still belong to Israel.[89]

To Begin's credit, he had always made his position perfectly clear. He had no intention of giving up the holy lands of the Jews, and when he announced on the day that the treaty was signed that the government was going to establish twenty new settlements on the West Bank, nobody could accuse him of being inconsistent.[90] He knew very well that none of the Arab states would accept the Framework for Peace, that there would be no future negotiations with Egypt, Jordan and Palestinians and that things would continue as they were for a long time to come. In the meantime, settlements would establish the fact of Israeli occupation and make it very difficult to turn the territories back to the Arabs at any future date. When all the other Arab states, including Jordan, joined Syria's Front of Steadfastness after the signing of the treaty, he must have been delighted. Yet we know that other Israelis saw this hard line as a betrayal of the Jewish people. After Camp David, the far right Tehiya Party was founded and members of the Gush Emunim would never forgive Begin for forcibly evacuating the Jewish settlers in the Sinai. They had seen the settlements there as the front line of the chosen people in the holy war against Islam. The peace treaty with the *goyim* was a sinful treaty with the enemies of God.

Had Sadat simply gone for a separate peace treaty, he might have suffered less from his Arab brothers, who denounced the Framework for Peace as a betrayal of the Arab people. It had sold out the Palestinians, betrayed the PLO, who all the Arabs had decided were the only valid representatives of the Palestinian people, and had betrayed essential principles of Arab unity by colluding with the United States and Israel, the enemies of the Arab people. They pointed out that Israel was daily saying that the Jews would never withdraw from the West Bank and Gaza and that the Framework for Peace was, therefore, a farce. Camp David had given Israel the chance to build more settlements and continue the draconian occupation of the West Bank and Gaza. As President Assad said:

> To us, peace means that Arab flags should fly over the liberated territories. Under the Camp David accords, peace means that the Israeli flag should be hoisted in an official ceremony in Cairo, while Israel is still occupying Egyptian, Syrian and Palestinian territory and is still adamantly denying Palestinian rights.[91]

On March 31, 1979, the Arab summit issued a communiqué which threw Egypt out of the Arab League, severed all diplomatic relations between Egypt and the other Arab countries and transferred the headquarters of the League from Cairo to Tunis. Egypt was now quite isolated from the rest of the Arab world. Instead of being its leader, she had become a pariah. Arab unity had been gravely damaged and the position of the Arab people consequently weakened.[92]

The Egyptians themselves became increasingly unhappy about Camp David. Many people were as distressed as their Arab brethren about the implications of the Framework for Peace. When Sadat tried to encourage Egyptians to visit Israel as tourists to help the process of "normalization," the Egyptians voted with their feet and refused to visit a country which was mistreating their fellow Arabs. They were also distressed by their isolation from the rest of the Arab world.[93] Egypt was now forced away from her Arab identity and the isolation of the country meant that she was inevitably thrown under the shadow of the West. This was very disturbing to a people who had seen their Arab identity as essentially anti-Western and they resented the increased Westernization of their country after Camp David. They were disturbed by the procession of Western superstars through Egypt. When Frank Sinatra gave a concert at the foot of the Pyramids, many felt that this cheapened Egypt, which seemed to be abandoning its ancient dignity and becoming the playground of the West.[94] When Elizabeth Taylor visited Cairo in 1979, people were disgusted that

Sadat greeted her as the Queen of Egypt because she had once played Cleopatra, and the army officers who were guarding her hotel and escorting her around the country felt degraded. "My God," one of them said. "What are we doing here, guarding an actress?"[95] Sadat himself seemed to have become a Western superstar, jet-setting with wealthy capitalists and playboys. The adulation he received in the West started to go to his head: he became overconcerned with his own personality cult, treated the nation to long, rambling talks about his life, spent as much time discussing the filming of his autobiography with a director as he spent on affairs of state and had himself constantly, obsessively photographed.[96] Opposition to Sadat and disillusion with Camp David grew in Egypt, but none of his opponents watched the Pious President of Peace more critically than the religious.

The Muslim Brotherhood had not opposed the regime but had tried to enter the centers of power themselves and effect a reform from within. Thus their magazine *al-Dawa* had not criticized Sadat or his policies. But the Camp David accords broke this tradition abruptly. On September 20, 1978, an article bitterly attacked the Framework for Peace for the same political reason as the other Arab leaders, but the prime cause of the Brothers' disapproval was that such a treaty was a violation of the Sharia. Israel was now part of the House of War and no regime that claimed to be Muslim could make such a peace. "If the Muslims renounce the effort to recover any part of their alienated land when it is possible for them to do so, they are all in a state of sin," the author declared absolutely. "History will judge the present generation harshly, rulers and ruled alike, for having preferred material well-being to honour and religion."[97] Camp David was incompatible with Islam and the *jihad* was essential to true Muslim integrity. *Al-Dawa*'s cover for May 1981 depicted the Dome of the Rock, chained with a padlock stamped with the Star of David. A hand clutching a hatchet was about to smash the lock.[98] The Egyptian state might have signed a peace treaty with the Jews, but for Muslims the old problem remained: the third most holy shrine in Islam was under the control of the enemies of God. Sadat could be a Pious President in 1973 when he was fighting a *jihad* against Israel, but not when he wanted to make peace. The Koran did *not* countenance a peace that harmed Islam and continued the oppression of the Muslims of Palestine.

In 1979–80 *al-Dawa* published a series of articles on the children's page entitled "The Four Horsemen of the Apocalypse" which identified the four enemies of the Muslims and suggested, by implication, that the Muslim lands faced an apocalyptic situation and that the Last

Judgment was approaching. This feeling is shared by most Muslim extremists and naturally this gives a new edge to the *jihad* effort today, as it has done throughout the history of the holy war. The first of these four horsemen was the Crusader (the Christian or the Western imperialist—the two, for obvious reasons, are one). Not all Christians are Crusaders, the author points out, but many of them invade the lands of Islam and poison the minds of Muslims with alien ideas. Some of them assume a pious disguise and come as missionaries, evangelists or ecumenists; the orientalists spread doubt and confusion and discredit the name of the Prophet and of Islam with lying tales; and above all the imperialists seek to subjugate and persecute the Muslim people.[99] The second horseman is the Jew and he is quite different from the Crusader because all Jews are essentially evil. The author asks his readers if they have ever wondered why God cursed the Jews, when he had once preferred them to all other peoples. Quoting heavily from the Koran, the author answers his question:

> His preference was met with ingratitude and denial of divine power. *The Jews say: "God's hand is chained." May their own hands be chained! May they be cursed for what they say* (5:64). It may happen that a man lies or falls into error, but for a people to build their society on lies, that is the specialty of the children of Israel alone! *The Jews who listen to the lies of theirs and pay no heed to you* (5:41). *They listen to falsehoods and practise what is unlawful* (5:42). Such are the Jews, my brother, your enemies and the enemies of God.[100]

Instead of making peace with the Jews, Muslims should "annihilate their existence." In the new, religious Egypt the Muslim fantasies about Jews that had surfaced in the very early days of the conflict were being revived. This Islamic anti-Semitism was a distortion of Islam itself as much as it was a distorted picture of the Jewish people, and by quoting the Koran out of context, Mohammad's early vision of coexistence with the People of the Book had been lost. In this view, Muslim integrity depends on a pious extermination of the enemies of God just as it depends upon a fight for the holy city of al-Quds. This hatred of the Jews also surfaces in the portrait of the last two horsemen of the apocalypse: the Marxist and the Secularist. The author points out that Karl Marx was a Jew and that Marxism is therefore part of the Jewish conspiracy to take over the world. The first Secularist was Kemal Ataturk and the author argues that he was a secret Jew who overthrew the Ottoman sultans to punish them for not giving Palestine to the Zionists.[101] A President who had not only made peace with the diabolical Jews but who was also courting the Crusaders could not be a true Muslim. In the Crusader Kingdom during the 1180s religious extremists had found peace treaties with the enemies of God intolerable and had insisted on war, and in Sadat's Egypt as in Begin's Israel new religious extremists adamantly rejected the possibility of peaceful co-existence, which they saw as a fundamental threat to their religious integrity.

Sadat had preached peace in the Knesset by evoking the old Islamic ideal of coexistence but the Egyptian Muslims saw the President of Peace as the enemy of Islam and Sadat perversely went out of his way to reinforce this impression. The peace process was from start to finish accompanied by a new offensive against Egyptian Muslims. His journey to Jerusalem had coincided with the execution of Shukri and the attack on the ulema. When he got back from Camp David in 1978 he started to curtail the power of the *jama'at islamiyya*, denouncing its members and suppressing their achievements such as the cheap lecture manuals. The students simply hardened their opposition to the regime. In 1979, at the end of Ramadan, they staged a formidable demonstration which showed the government that they were still very much alive and the neo-Muslim Brother Yusuf al-Quwardi made a passionate plea for an Islamic identity for Egypt:

> Egypt is Muslim, not pharaonic; it is the land of Amr Ibn al-As [the Arab commander who conquered Egypt in 640] and not of Ramses ... the youth of the *jama'at islamiyya* are the true representatives of Egypt and not the Avenue of the Pyramids, the theatre performances, and the films. ... Egypt is not naked women, but veiled women who adhere to the prescriptions of divine law. ... Egypt is young men who let their beards grow ... it is the land of al-Azhar![102]

The students did not want the West and they made sure that it would not penetrate the campus, which from 1979 to 1981 became an Islamic oasis in the desert of Sadatian Egypt, as Shukri's communities had tried to be. Films, theater and art of Western origin or which presented the Jews sympathetically were forbidden; couples who violated Islamic law were physically attacked. The *jama'at islamiyya* fought against the West defensively by withdrawing from the world in a *hijra* and fighting against the alien values that besieged them. In 1980 this *jihad* became a more direct offensive against Sadat.[103] On the feast of al-Fitah which ends Ramadan, the students held a huge prayer rally outside the President's house, exhorting him to rule as a good Muslim. On the Eid al-Adha they were forbidden to hold a camp on the Cairo campus, so they left the university, marched over the Nile and occupied the Saladin mosque for twenty-four hours. In the mosque built by the truly devout Muslim hero of the holy war, they denounced Camp David and condemned Sadat as a Tartar because, like the Mongols who had converted to Islam in the thirteenth century, he was a Muslim only in name.

The Islamic opposition was not confined to the students but was spreading to the common people.[104] As in Iran, the mosques played a crucial role and did what the newspapers had been able to do in times of greater freedom. Certain sheikhs like Sheikh Mahalawi, Sheikh Eid and Sheikh Kishk became noted, popular critics of the regime and in their Friday sermons they regularly preached to huge audiences on forbidden topics like the Shah, corruption, Camp David and the iniquities of the Jewish people. Cassettes of their sermons sold like hotcakes and were suddenly ubiquitous: they would blare from tape recorders all over Egypt, in the fruit juice stores, in restaurants and in garages. Egyptians drank in these fiery denunciations of the regime as eagerly as the Iranians had imbibed the message of Ayatollah Khomeini. The cassette recorder had become a powerful weapon in the holy war. As they listened obsessively to these militant sheikhs, Egyptians were learning to see Sadat, the Jews and the Western Crusaders as essential enemies.

In his book *The Hidden Pillar*, which was privately circulated, Abed al-Salem Faraj takes this new belligerent Islam to its logical conclusion in a way that is quite new.[105] He argues that the *jihad* was one of the "pillars" of Islam and was central to it. This was an extraordinary innovation that, in those days of heightened tension, many Egyptians were prepared to accept. A Muslim's first duty was the war against the Jews for the recovery of al-Quds, but first Muslims must fight a *jihad* against their Tartar rulers, who were all "apostates from Islam, nourished at the table of colonialism, be it Crusader, communist or Zionist."[106] Once they had Islamized their countries, Muslims could fulfill their sacred duty of fighting a *jihad* against the rest of the world. Where the Islamic students' union and Shukri's followers had begun by tackling their own acute problems and had become enemies of the regime at a later, secondary stage, Faraj's starting point was not *hijra* but *jihad*. He thus limited Islam to one aggressive doctrine and excluded many other more complex traditions, in the same way as Crusaders and religious Zionists had produced caricatures of their religion. Faraj's militancy was closer to the postrevolutionary militancy of Khomeini in its focus on the *jihad*. Saladin certainly saw the *jihad* against the Franks as central to the Islamic identity but he was quite prepared eventually to sign a peace treaty with Richard. His *jihad* had been inspired by the aggression of the Franks, but Faraj's book was a reaction against the new peace. Before 1977 the "Tartars" had at least been committed to the struggle against Zionism, he explained, but now that Sadat had betrayed Islam the people must take the initiative and make war themselves.

The members of the Jihad Group to which Khaled Islambouli belonged had Faraj as their spiritual guide and dedicated themselves to the *jihad*. The organization of the movement was both compact and loose. Members belonged to cells and each cell was called an *anqud*, a bunch of grapes.[107] If one *anqud* were plucked from the vine, the others could continue to thrive. Secrecy was now essential, for belonging to any controversial organization was extremely perilous. Sadat had become obsessed with the need to uproot all the opposition that was building up against him in Egypt, and in 1978, during the peace process, he declared war against thousands of his own people by issuing what he called the Law of Shame. Any deviation in thought, word or deed from the establishment line was punished with loss of civil rights, withdrawal of passports and sequestration of property. Citizens were forbidden to criticize Islam, the state or its policies. (In Sadat's eyes "Islam," of course, meant something very different from the way extremists saw religion.) Egyptians were also forbidden to join organizations, take part in broadcasts or issue publications that threatened "national unity or social peace." Private criticism of the regime was also forbidden and anybody who gave "a bad example to the young" in word or deed was subject to the Law of Shame. This was naturally as repugnant to the Islamists as Camp David and increased the determination of men like Khaled Islambouli to rid Egypt of the tyrant.[108]

In the last months of his life Sadat's iron-fist policy tightened its grip. On September 5, 1981, he arrested 1536 of his opponents: cabinet ministers, politicians, journalists, judges, intellectuals, sheikhs and members of Islamic groups were rounded up and thrown into prison without trial. Sadat seemed to be out of control. At a press conference he announced that his security forces were still rounding up the last of his enemies. When an American journalist asked him if he had cleared his action with President Reagan during his visit to the United States the week before, Sadat completely lost his temper: "If this was not a free country," he said, "I would have you shot."[109] Realizing that he had made a dreadful impression, he tried again on September 15 in a televised fireside chat to the nation which lasted four and a half hours and which became an incoherent rant. During the last hour he attacked his Islamic opponents in a way that gave grave offense. He sneered at the girls in their "black tents" and the bearded young men;[110] he attacked Sheikh Mahalawi viciously and concluded: "Now this lousy Sheikh finds himself thrown into a prison-cell, like a dog."[111] One of the Islamists in prison was Mohammad Islambouli, the brother of Sadat's assassin.

On September 23 First Lieutenant Khaled Islambouli was told by his commanding officer that he had been chosen to take part in the victory parade commemorating the October War of 1973. At first he protested: it was the Eid al-Adha and he had been going to spend the day with his family. After some more argument the officer repeated his order and Khaled said: "Very well; I accept. Let God's will be done."[112] He had taken up the duty of the *jihad*. First he went to consult Faraj, who issued a *fatwa* ordering the assassination. Next he consulted Colonel Zumr, the military head of his *anqud*, but the colonel opposed the plan: killing the President was not enough. The *jihad* group was dedicated to overthrowing the whole regime and would be unable to do that before 1984 at the earliest. The *fatwa* took precedence over Zumr's judgment, however, and Khaled and Faraj went ahead with their plans. Faraj produced three companions for him and on the day of the parade Khaled managed to send the officers who were supposed to be in the procession with him on leave, replace them with his fellow conspirators, hide the grenades under the seat of the truck and carry the guns through the inspection points into the procession without removing the strikers. The four young men then rode forward to kill the President of Peace and achieve the crown of martyrdom.[113]

At his trial Khaled gave three reasons for murdering Sadat. The first was the suffering of Muslims under Sadat's regime of oppression and tyranny; second was the Camp David agreement with Israel; third, the imprisonment of the Muslim clergy and faithful on September 5. When he was asked if he had considered the effect his action would have on his parents, he replied, "I thought only of God."[114] Khaled, Faraj and the other three assassins were executed and eighteen other members of his *anqud* were sentenced to seventeen years' hard labor. The religious passion for the *jihad* is still not dead, however: during the summer of 1987 three leading members of the government were assassinated by members of *jihad* groups like Khaled's. There are frequent violent Islamic rallies at which the demonstrators burn the Israeli flag and call for a resumption of the *jihad*.[115]

When Anwar Sadat signed the Camp David treaty he was signing his own death warrant. He must have been aware of the risk he was taking. On July 20, 1951, King Abdullah of Jordan was murdered on the steps of the al-Aqsa mosque in Jerusalem by Palestinian nationalists and supporters of Hajji Amin. As a boy, the present King Hussein saw his grandfather die, and he has always shown a very healthy respect for the delicacies of the peace process between Israel and the Arab countries. But Sadat's death was different from King Abdullah's because it was inspired not solely by Arab nationalism but by religion, and the death of the Pious President has now set a precedent that no future Arab leader can ignore. In all Arab countries there are cells dedicated to the *jihad*, and their members will permit no peace with the enemies of God. Sadat's death shows how thoroughly the old secular struggle has become a religious conflict and it also shows that the holy war mentality is stronger in the 1980s than it was in 1192, when Richard the Lionheart and Saladin could make peace with each other and still be honored by their contemporaries.

On both sides of the conflict, the radical religious movements are remarkably similar. The Israeli right focuses on the ideal of the Holy Land, while the new *jihad* concentrates on the Islamic ideal of a just society, but both Jewish and Muslim enthusiasts want to replace their secular governments by a religious polity, governed by the Torah or the Sharia; both believe in an imminent apocalypse; both are anxious to shake off Western patronage in order to return to the rule of God; both regard the destruction of the enemy as a prime religious duty and are ready to throw caution to the winds to achieve their aims. There are obvious similarities with the extremism of the Crusaders in the Middle Ages, but even the most zealous Crusaders were content to live under a relatively secular style of government in the Holy Land.

The new religious enthusiasts in the Middle East give the political struggle an absolute quality that will admit of no compromise. It now seems that the spirit of the holy war is so deeply ingrained in the area that even a peace initiative can be a prelude to a new holy war. Sadat's peaceful pilgrimage to Jerusalem led inexorably to the formation of the New Jihad Group and to the *jihad* of Faraj and Khaled. It also seems to have been a prelude to the Israeli invasion of Lebanon in 1982: it seems unlikely that Israel would have mounted such a massive offensive in the north without the Camp David treaty, since this would have left the Egyptian border undefended.[116] The Israelis originally claimed that their invasion of Lebanon was purely defensive: Ariel Sharon called it Operation Peace for Galilee. Its avowed aim was to protect Israelis from PLO terrorist attacks.[117] But this so-called peace operation led to an escalation of the conflict: the Israelis' aggressive and brutal behavior in Lebanon also provoked a new Shiite offensive in the area that was reminiscent of the *jihad* of the medieval Shiite Assassins in its terrifying suicide bombings. In the Middle Ages we have seen that one holy war led to another, but today it seems that even peace initiatives have acquired an aggressive dimension and lead to new holy offensives.

Indeed, at the time of writing the prospects of a peaceful settlement in the Middle East seem more remote than ever. No leader can ignore the new wave of religious extremism, which has helped to create a climate that makes peace impossible. President Hosni Mubarak still has to be extremely careful of Islamic radicals in Egypt, who watch him like hawks to make sure that he does not go the way of his predecessor. Nevertheless, Mubarak has tried to remain true to Camp David, despite Israel's behavior in Lebanon and the savage Israeli attempts to put down the *intifada* in the occupied territories. It was in the spirit of Camp David that Mubarak made his cautious peace initiative in September 1990. He offered to host talks between Israel and the Palestinians in Cairo and proposed a ten-point plan to ensure that the Palestinians in the territories would be able to choose their representatives in free elections. Israelis in the peace parties and on the left welcomed these proposals with enthusiasm, but the religious parties and the far right insisted that Israel must not accept Mubarak's conditions. Geula Cohen of Tehiya warned that Egypt's initiative foreshadowed a further Israeli capitulation, which she attributed to the primordial sin of the Camp David Accords.[118] In the United States, James Baker based his own proposals for Middle East peace talks between Israel and the Palestinians on Mubarak's plan. We have seen that Shamir rejected this plan outright on June 27, 1990, just three weeks after he had formed his coalition government with the religious and the far right parties.

It also seemed extremely unlikely that the Arab world would have accepted Mubarak's proposals. For years after Camp David, Egypt was in disgrace and was isolated from the Arab world, to the great detriment of the region as a whole. Mubarak has performed the delicate feat of bringing Egypt back into the Arab family, without reneging on Camp David. But his task seems impossibly difficult. He has to satisfy his colleagues in the Arab league *and* the Muslim extremists in Egypt while forging his own special relationship with the United States. Relations between the Muslim world and the West have become increasingly strained since the Islamic revolution in Iran. The assassination of Sadat was provoked by his Westernizing policies as much as by his peace initiative with Israel.

It is important to note that Islam is a universal religion and is not opposed to the West per se. But the stories of both Shah Mohammad Reza Pahlavi and President Anwar Sadat show that many Muslims now consider the West to be their enemy. The creation of the state of Israel seems, as we have seen, to be yet another assault of Western imperialism to the people of the Middle East. Years of humiliation and exploitation have resulted in an enmity and distrust of the western world which is quite new in Islamic history. Indeed, relations between Islam and the West have deteriorated to such an extent that it seems horribly possible that by the end of this century, the cold war that existed between the West and the Communist world will have been replaced by a cold war with Islam. It was intoxicating for the West to watch the peoples of Eastern Europe throwing off their shackles to embrace the democratic ideal in the last months of 1989. But there is unlikely to be such a dramatic reversal in the Muslim world. Western support for the oppressive regime of the Shah in Iran, to name just one example, has made the ideals of Western freedom and democracy a bad joke in the Middle East.

It is no accident that Muslim extremists in Egypt call Western imperialism *al-Salibiyya*, the Crusade: during the Crusades, the Muslim world suffered its first gratuitous Western invasion. In Chapter 11, we shall look at the way the West has unconsciously continued to cultivate crusading attitudes toward the people of the Middle East. We find it very difficult to accept this Muslim view of Western behavior in the Middle East, because we naturally have our own prejudice that can make us blind to realities that seem crystal clear to outsiders. Thus President Jimmy Carter did not see himself as a Crusader or an imperialist when he organized the Camp David meetings. He is a devout Christian Baptist and has continued to be committed to the cause of peace in the Middle East: he must have been horrified by the tragedy of Sadat. Indeed, he personally preferred Sadat to Begin, rather to the latter's chagrin. But in his public addresses in Israel, Carter made it very clear where his own sympathies lay. In 1978, at the time of the accords, he showed that his Baptist reading of the Bible had indelibly colored his outlook: "Israel is a return at last to the Bible land from which the Jews were driven so many hundred years ago, the establishment of the nation of Israel is the fulfillment of Biblical prophecy and the very essence of fulfillment."[119] These words could easily have been spoken by a member of Gush Emunim. Carter could only see Palestine as the land of the Bible, and so he completely ignored some twelve hundred years of Arab and Muslim history in *Falastin*. He could not attain to the perspective that I have called "triple vision," because he could only see the Middle East from the Judaeo-Christian point of view.

But Carter's successor, Ronald Reagan, proved to be even blinder to the perspective of the Arab and the Muslim world. Like Carter, Reagan liked to describe himself as a man of peace, but his peace-keeping contribution included the brutal bombing of Libya in April 1986 as part of his Crusade against international terrorism. The raid, which killed seventy-one Libyans, civilians as well as soldiers, was intended as a reprisal for a recent wave of Arab terrorism, which Reagan assumed to have been masterminded by Colonel Qadaffi. In fact it seems that he may have been overly hasty, since the terrorists concerned were most probably backed by Syria. Reagan's most serious mistake was the Irangate affair, when his government made overtures to what it was pleased to call "Iranian moderates"; this led to the scandal of the Iranian arms deal with the consequent deflection of the money to the Contra terrorists of Nicaragua. Reagan made it quite clear that he could not countenance an independent Palestinian state[120]: after the outbreak of the *intifada*, he and Secretary of State George Shultz preferred what was called the Jordanian option for the occupied territories, an option that was aborted on July 31, 1988, when King Hussein relinquished all claim to the West Bank. The last thing Hussein needed were two million highly politicized Palestinians in his Bedouin Kingdom.

At the time of writing, it is still too early to see how President George Bush will compare with his predecessors. At first it seemed as though there was a possibility of a significant change. The Bush administration responded to Arafat's recognition of the state of Israel by setting up talks with PLO officials. On May 22, 1989, Secretary of State James Baker addressed the formidable American Israeli Political Action Committee and delivered the toughest words that Israel had heard from Washington since the Suez crisis. He told his highly partial audience that the status quo could not continue:

Now is the time to lay aside, once and for all, the unrealistic vision of a Greater Israel. Israeli interests in the West Bank and Gaza, security and otherwise, can be accommodated on a settlement based on 242. Forswear annexation. Stop settlement activity. Allow schools to reopen. Reach out to Palestinians as neighbors who deserve political rights.

Baker also spoke sternly to the Palestinians, urging them to speak "with one voice for peace," to amend the PLO charter to meet the new Palestinian position and to abjure violence: "Reach out to Israelis and convince them of your peaceful intentions. You have the most to gain from doing so, and no one else can or will do it for you."[121] Baker's words created a sensation in Israel: it seemed clear that America did not want to see Israel on the West Bank.

Baker's speech to AIPAC did seem to mark a new direction and to approach the perspective of triple vision. He was not siding blindly with Israel and was trying to admit the Palestinian point of view. But by June 1990 the Middle East peace process had stagnated, the talks with the PLO had become a farce and finally collapsed, and Shamir showed more *chutzpah* toward the United States than any previous Israeli Prime Minister when he categorically and totally rejected Baker's peace proposals. It remains to be seen how the United States will respond to the Shamir coalition, which is committed to policies which Baker had described as unrealistic and unproductive in his AIPAC speech a year earlier: Shamir and his new allies are absolutely committed to the vision of the Greater Israel; they have made it quite clear that they have no intention of reaching out to the Palestinians as neighbors. Indeed, important members of Shamir's cabinet would be quite happy to deprive the Arabs under their rule of their political rights. If the United States continues to support the Shamir government, this will not merely betray those more moderate Israelis who deplore what is happening in their country, but it will also convince many Arabs and Muslims that Western ideals of freedom and democracy are indeed a bad joke.

We have now examined the new religious movements in Israel and the Muslim world today. We have looked at their strengths, weaknesses, and dangers. It is now time to examine in more detail the Western contribution to the problems of the Middle East. In the next two chapters I return to the story of the medieval Crusades. The Crusades of the thirteenth centuries showed that crusading was changing radically and dramatically and this would have important implications for the Western spirit. Though there was a détente between Muslims and Christians in the Middle East after Richard the Lionheart and the Third Crusaders failed to recover Jerusalem, crusading had become firmly embedded in the Western identity and sought new channels and new outlets. It has remained an important part of our Western view of the world. Politicians like Reagan still tend to use the word "Crusade" very readily to describe their policies, with no sense of shame and apparently very little appreciation of the dubious and cruel nature of the whole crusading enterprise. Indeed, the word and concept of "crusading" has been drained of its horror and we do not find it strange to use it to describe any idealistic campaign, even peaceful ones. In order to understand why the notion of crusading became central to the Western identity and how the term came to describe projects and ideals that had nothing whatever to do with a war for the Holy Land, we need to go right back to the thirteenth century, when this attitude first appeared in Europe.

# PART THREE

# Crusading and the Western Identity

# 1199–1221

## Crusades Against Christians and a New Christian Peace

T he central thesis of this book is that there is a strong connection between the medieval Crusades in the Holy Land and the con-flict between Arabs and Jews in the Middle East today. Indeed, we have already seen that since the conflict began Arab historians have developed an entirely new interest in crusading and that they see the Crusaders as the first Western imperialists and the Zionists as either new Crusaders or as tools of Western imperialism. Similarly crusading studies flourish in the Hebrew University of Jerusalem: wherever Is-raelis travel in their small country they see the great castles, churches and cities built by the Crusaders some nine hundred years ago. These ruins are eloquent reminders of another colonizing movement which had powerful Western backing and which tried to establish itself in the hostile Muslim world of the Near East. In particular, the Battle of Hittin between the Christian army of the Kingdom of Jerusalem and Saladin has been seen as significant by both Jews and Arabs. The Arabs naturally see this as an encouragement: poets and leaders call for a new Saladin to rise up and fight these latter-day "Crusaders." In their turn, some Israelis see an almost uncanny resemblance between their own situation today and that of the Christians on the eve of Hittin. They see that Israeli society is riven by deep, passionately maintained divisions, just as the Christians were in the Kingdom of Jerusalem. They also see that a minority of religious extremists has risen in their own midst and fear that this could be just as dangerous as a similar fanatical Christian minority had been to the Crusader Kingdom. In the last two chapters we have examined the revival of the holy war mentality on both sides of the Arab-Israeli conflict. We have seen that on both sides Jews and Arabs have been inspired by passions and enthusiasms that are very similar to the crusading emo-tions of the Christians and the Muslim *jihad* of Saladin.

But I have argued that there is more than an analogical link between crusading and the modern conflict: there is also a causal connection. Before Pope Urban II summoned the First Crusade at the Council of Clermont in 1095 there had been relative harmony between Jews, Christians and Muslims. Jews and Muslims had been quite prepared to live alongside Christians in peace. Christians had formed good relations with the Jews of Europe during the Dark Ages and, although they had been awed by the mighty Islamic empire, they were both incurious and ignorant about the religious beliefs and status of Muslims. But all this changed forever when the armies of the Cross responded to Urban's summons and marched eastward to liberate the Holy Sepulchre of Christ in Jerusalem. At the start of their journey the first Crusaders massacred the Jewish communities in the first European pogroms. At their journey's end they had massacred the Muslim inhabitants of Jerusalem with horrible savagery when they conquered the city in 1099. From the time of the First Crusade, Western Christians would never again regard Jews and Muslims as normal human beings. They saw them as inhuman monsters and developed fantasies about them which bore no relation to the truth but which actually reflected the insecurities of the people of Europe. Every time a Crusade was summoned against the Muslims there was a new outbreak of anti-Semitism in Europe, which became an indelible Western habit. Today the two victims of the Crusaders are locked in a deadly conflict, which in important ways has also involved the Christian West.

The crusading habit of anti-Semitism continued unabated in Europe, as we shall see, and found its fullest and most hideous expression in the Nazi crusade of Adolf Hitler. Without Western anti-Semitism, it is unlikely that there would have been a Jewish state in the Middle East today. But the habit of Western hostility toward Muslims also continued unabated in Europe and today some Muslims in the Middle East call Western imperialism *al-Salibiyya*, the Crusade, seeing colonialism and Western intervention in their affairs as performed in the same spirit of aggressive righteousness as had inspired the first Western offensive against them. Up to this point we have considered the viewpoint of both Jews and Arabs in some detail, but we have not yet put the West under the microscope. Are there really a connection and a tradition that link our current Western policies and prejudices with the Crusades? This is the question I want to consider in the third and final part of this book.

To do this, we need to look in some detail at the development of the crusading ethos in Europe after the disaster of Hittin and the failure of the Third Crusade. It will be recalled that the First Crusade of 1095–99 had been the first cooperative and self-conscious act of the newly emerging Europe, which was beginning to crawl out of the period of obscurity and impotence known as the Dark Ages. Crusading had made life impossible for the Jews of Europe and the Muslims of the Near East. But it had also been a bid to put Europe back on the map and to make Christendom a world power. In this it had been a brilliant success, and that was considered infinitely more important than Muslim or Jewish casualties. It was during the Middle Ages that the particular Western spirit was created that animates Europeans and neo-Europeans alike. As the Italian scholar and novelist Umberto Eco persuasively argues, all our major preoccupations and passions were forged at this time.[1] But crusading was inextricably entwined with these new enthusiasms. The Crusades were not a minority cult but were central to the developing Western identity and I wish to argue that this continued to be the case long after expeditions stopped going to the Holy Land and that crusading is still important to us today at a very deep level. If it were deprived of old outlets, crusading just found new forms: we have already seen how it was involved with courtly love, which would ultimately become our cult of romantic love. But this meant that a powerful and irrational hatred of Jews and Muslims was also central to the Western identity. In the next three chapters we shall be looking at this in more detail, examining the development of crusading after Hittin and the strong Western commitment to crusading that developed, enduring in buried and distorted forms to the present day.

Given the importance of the crusading ideal to medieval Europe, the Christian defeat at the hands of Saladin was an absolute catastrophe. It was far more than a mere military and political disaster. It raised terrible doubts and unanswerable questions. Why had God allowed his enemies to triumph? Could it be that God had deserted his new chosen people as he had formerly, so Christians believed, deserted his old chosen people, the Jews? Even more terrible to contemplate was the loss of Jerusalem, which was no ordinary city but a center of holiness and spiritual power which was now in the hands of the heinous infidel. In 1190 hopes were high when the Third Crusade sailed to the Middle East to fight Saladin but even the heroic Richard the Lionheart had been unable to recover Jerusalem for Christendom. The Christians in the Middle East had now only a precarious toehold in the Holy Land in their long thin state along the coast, stretching from Beirut to Jaffa. In Europe, Crusaders began to consider a new campaign: it was unthinkable that Jerusalem and the Holy Land should remain a part of Saladin's Muslim empire.

But it will also be recalled that in the Near East itself enthusiasm for the holy war had waned on both sides. The disaster of Hittin had taught the Franks of Palestine a much-needed lesson. They realized too late that their own religious extremism had been largely responsible for their defeat. They were now very anxious to appease the Muslims, because they knew full well that they would never sustain a new Muslim attack. On the Muslim side, too, enthusiasm for the *jihad* did not survive Saladin, who died in 1193. When his brother al-Adil eventually succeeded him, he was keen to normalize relations with the Christians. The *jihad* had not had time to put down strong roots in the Muslim world of the Near East. The practice of the holy war had been dead for centuries and Nur ad-Din and Saladin had revived it only with considerable effort. Once the Franks were no longer a real threat to the people of the area, the new passion for the *jihad* died a natural death. It was simply not as important to the Muslims as crusading was to Western Europe. In Christendom at the end of the twelfth century Crusaders were sharpening their swords but in the Middle East there was a new détente: Muslims and Christians settled down to live alongside one another in peace. After Hittin, therefore, crusading was only important in Europe.

I want to emphasize this point. One of the fantasies that Christians created about Islam at the time of the Crusades was that it was an essentially violent, intolerant religion. This was not true. The *jihad* was a forgotten practice that was revived only in response to the Western crusading initiative: in our own day a new *jihad* has arisen, caused at least in part by what has been perceived as Western aggression and interference. Crusading, which was so crucial to the development of Europe, made scarcely a ripple in the Muslim world. Certainly it had obsessed Nur ad-Din and Saladin and their supporters in the Near East, who were the unfortunate neighbors of the Crusader states. But in the rest of the vast Muslim empire the Crusades seemed like unimportant border incidents. The Islamic empire had much greater problems, which troubled most Muslims far more than the Crusaders did. These were major internal upheavals that transformed Muslim and Arab life in the House of Islam during the eleventh and twelfth centuries. First, it will be recalled that in the eleventh century the Seljuk Turks, new converts to Islam in Central Asia, had invaded the Arab Middle East and Byzantine Anatolia. They had ousted the old Arab leaders in that part of the Islamic empire and in effect taken control: the main opponents of the Crusaders were Turks, not Arabs. Next Arab Bedouin tribes from Upper Egypt invaded what is now Libya and Tunisia, causing immense devastation, and during the twelfth century fanatical, fundamentalist Berber Muslims had seized power for a period in Morocco and al-Andalus in Spain. Hitherto North Africa had been prosperous and a major center of civilization but it never recovered from these disasters. As the great fourteenth-century Arab historian Ibn Khaldun wrote: "all the plains were ruined; whereas formerly from the Negro-lands to the Mediterranean all was cultivated, as is proved by the traces remaining there of monuments, buildings, farms and villages."[2]

Thus the eleventh and twelfth centuries were a time of grave crisis in the Islamic empire that had nothing whatever to do with the Crusades. The Turkish sultans, atabegs and emirs in the Middle East created a feudal system in place of the old Arab monetary system: fiefs were given to chieftains of the armies to ensure loyalty and service. The system prevailed until our own century when it was replaced first by the Western protectorates and then by the Arab national states. Landowners suffered because of these nonresident landlords and there was widespread consternation at this social and economic transformation of society. This brought a new desire for security: during the twelfth and thirteenth centuries the first madrassas were established, first in Baghdad and then in other places of the empire. These Muslim colleges became bastions of orthodoxy. Hitherto Islam had encouraged a free spirit of inquiry and Muslim scholars had been in the intellectual vanguard of the world. It would take a long time for the new traditionalism to take root but this marked the first step in a process which ended the speculative, rationalist era. The process was naturally accelerated when, as we shall see in the next chapter, the Mongol hordes attacked the House of Islam during the thirteenth century, devastating major cities like Baghdad and destroying libraries, manuscripts and universities as well as slaughtering the population. The Mongol disaster was far more destructive in the long term than the invasions of the Crusaders. Henceforth Muslim scholars became anxious to recover what had been so tragically lost and to conserve what remained instead of experimenting with new ideas. This conservatism, which Western observers often scorned, was not endemic to Islam, which saw learning and discovery as religious duties,[3] but was due to major historical catastrophes. While the West was soaring ahead to new achievements, the Arab and Muslim world was looking back to the past, gradually entering into what could be called their own Dark Age. Muslims were told that the gates of *ijtihad* (independent reasoning) had been closed and that they should practice *taqlid*, emulation of the experts in Islamic holy law.

With all this going on, it was not surprising that most Muslims saw crusading as a minor problem. Not until a new wave of Western colonialism occurred did the Crusades became important in the Arab world, as we have seen. Neither was there any hatred of Christians and Jews comparable to the Western hostility toward Jews and Muslims. Again, this needs to be emphasized. The Christians of the West were fascinated by Muslims once the crusading project had got under way. We have seen that European scholars translated the Koran and wrote treatises on "Mohammadanism" that bore little relation to the truth but were almost fanatically intent on the rival religion. In Palestine the historian William of Tyre wrote a history of Islam which has unfortunately been lost. But during the Middle Ages there was absolutely no Muslim interest in either Western Christianity or Western culture. Of the many prolific Arab writers of the Middle Ages, only three give Western Christians a mention.

This is not very surprising. The Franks were a great military threat to the people of the Near East but in cultural terms they were no match for the Muslims, who regarded them as barbarians. Usama Ibn Mundiqh, the Syrian diplomat who spent some time in the Crusader Kingdom of Jerusalem, regarded the Franks as poor primitives, with good reason. Some of them had adopted a Muslim lifestyle, he conceded, and had therefore greatly improved. But in general they were extraordinarily ignorant and superstitious.[4] The Arabs regarded Europe as a poor, savage backwater that had nothing to offer them. We see this clearly in Usama's horror and embarrassment when a Frank offered to have his son educated at his expense in Europe: "A truly cultivated man would never be guilty of such a suggestion," Usama commented; "my son might as well be taken prisoner as go off into the land of the Franks."[5] Even though Europe had made huge strides since the First Crusade and was in the process of creating a new and exciting culture, she was still far behind Islam in the late twelfth century. The great Arab traveler Ibn Jubayr, who was writing at about the time of the Third Crusade, described a visit to Frankish Acre: "a land of unbelief and impiety, swarming with pigs and crosses, full of filth and ordure, all of it filled with uncleanness and excrement."[6] Some of the Franks were learning about hygiene from their Muslim neighbors but it took a long time before they discovered the virtues of cleanliness and reached the standard of the Arab world. Even though Islam was going through a period of great crisis, Western culture was assumed to be of no conceivable interest and this superior attitude persisted in the Muslim world long after Europe had in fact caught up with the Arabs. Thus even as late as the fourteenth century we find Ibn Khaldun remarking doubtfully: "We have heard of late that in the lands of the Franks, that is, the country of Rome and its dependencies on the northern shore of the Mediterranean, the philosophic sciences flourish . . . and their students are plentiful. But God knows best what goes on in those parts."[7] There was no feeling that this new information should be followed up. At the time of the Crusades this lofty indifference was understandable but later it would be dangerous and mean that the Arabs would fall behind in the march of progress.

It will be recalled that the Muslims only felt contemptuous of Western Christianity: they had a great respect for the Christian empire of Byzantium, which had not fallen into a Dark Age as the Western province of the Roman Empire had. Similarly, Islam had a policy of coexistence: Jews and Christians, the People of the Book, were allowed full religious liberty in the Islamic empire. It is true that they were second-class citizens but as the orientalist Bernard Lewis insistently points out, this was not the unacceptable state of affairs that it would be today.[8] At that time in the Middle East, one's first loyalty was to one's religious grouping; the secondary loyalty was to the state or the ruling dynasty. There was as yet no idea of a nation-state with equal rights for all citizens in either Islam or Christendom. Further, Muslims had less complex, tortured feelings about other religions than Western Christianity. The Middle East had always been an area of religious pluralism. The *Dar al-Islam*, the House of Islam, the official term for Muslim polity, contained people of many different races and many different religions: there were Arabs, Egyptians, Indians, Persians, Syrians, Phoenicians, Berbers, Turks and Kurds; there were also Christians, Jews, Buddhists and Hindus as well as Muslims. This was seen as a normal state of affairs, and by contrast the uniformity of faith and belief for which Western Christendom increasingly yearned would have seemed alien and monotonous to a Muslim.

It was also true that, because Islam regarded the two older Peoples of the Book as faiths which had partially revealed truth but which had been superseded in favor of Islam, she found them less threatening. Western Christians, on the other hand, could only reject Islam as a false religion because there *could* be no subsequent revelation after Christ.[9] Islam also had a simpler approach to Judaism: Muslims, of course, did not see the Jews as God-slayers. In contrast, the developing Christian fantasies about Jews showed deep complexity: the horrible images of the Jews devouring little children have been seen, in the modern idiom of psychoanalysis, as oedipal fantasies about the parent faith, and this modern interpretation puts an interesting interpretation on the crusading pogroms.[10] However that may be, Muslims had no

such neurotic fantasies about Jews. We have seen that when he conquered Jerusalem from the Christians Saladin invited the Jews to return
to the city from which they had been excluded by the Crusaders. In
the old medieval system the state did not have to be your enemy: it
could be your best friend. In the twelfth century Jews said public
prayers for Islamic rulers. Jews were not unruly subjects: after the
destruction of the Temple, survival was seen as an important Jewish
duty, and that meant that inflammatory revolutionary activities were
frowned upon. In their turn Muslims responded favorably to Jews,
seeing them as exceptionally law-abiding and also, because of their
financial ability, as wealth-producing citizens who were an asset to a
city.[11] We shall see that, despite the constant persecution Jews endured
in Europe, individual rulers were usually prepared to give them a
home for the same reason.

The Crusades were making life intolerable for Jews in Europe. But
we must remember that in the Middle Ages the vast majority of Jews
lived in Muslim countries: in Spain, in North Africa and in the Middle
East. European Jewry did not become a majority in the Jewish world
until the end of the nineteenth century.[12] Thus, while the Ashkenazic
Jews of Europe were quite understandably regarding Gentiles with
fear and distrust, the Crusades had made no real impression on the
majority of Jews, who were Sephardim living peacefully in the House
of Islam. It is important to make this clear because we have just been
considering the modern conflict in which Muslims and Jews in the
Middle East are deadly foes. In 1170 the Jewish traveler Benjamin of
Tudela visited Baghdad and found 40,000 Jews living there in full
security with twenty-eight synagogues and ten *yeshivoth*.[13] In the West
it was increasingly the case that the Jews were forced into the profession of moneylending, which was forbidden by Christianity. This
profession inevitably made people hate them even more. But in Islam
many different professions were open to Jews. They were frequently
doctors and civil servants. They were also traders and merchants and
were in this capacity often middlemen between East and West, Muslim
and Christian. Thus Kairouan in Tunisia, an important Islamic center,
was also a great center of Jewish scholarship as well as being an
important link in East-West trade.[14]

Jews certainly suffered at the hands of fanatical, fundamentalist Muslims. In Spain, for example, the fanatical Berber sects that overran
Morocco and al-Andalus for brief periods during the twelfth century
persecuted Jews. But Jews who fled this persecution usually moved
to another part of the Islamic empire and did not consider the option
of anti-Semitic Christendom. Thus the great Maimonides had left

Cordova at the age of thirteen in 1148 and had eventually settled in Egypt. In the classical period of Islam there was nothing to equal the anti-Semitic diatribes uttered by religious leaders and philosophers of Christendom; nor were there anti-Semitic portraits of Jews in Arab literature until our own century. The Jews of Islam were not surrounded by an aura of dread. They were often indeed seen as rather unimportant politically.[15] Unlike the Christians, they had no great empire behind them, as the Christian *dhimmis* had in Byzantium. Like the Christian *dhimmis*, they were not allowed to bear arms: defending Islam was seen as an exclusively Muslim privilege. Muslims knew that there were Christian armies in other parts of the world but that there were no Jewish armies. In the main Jews were treated with the lofty condescension that we have seen characterizing the Muslim approach to the Franks. But, as Bernard Lewis points out, this was considered normal: quite different from the dehumanizing myths that surrounded Jews in Christendom.[16] At the time of the Crusades, Jewry throve in the House of Islam: there were substantial and prosperous Jewish communities in forty-four towns of Muslim Spain, for example, and many had their own *yeshivoth*.[17] Apart from the period of Berber persecution in the twelfth century, Spain gave the Jews the best home they had ever had in the diaspora.

Thus, despite the cruelty that Crusaders had shown to both Jews and Muslims, at the end of the twelfth century most Jews and Muslims were uninterested in crusading. They were not smoldering with hatred of the Franks; they were not obsessed with a holy war ideology. Both had problems and preoccupations of their own. The great project of crusading, which had been so crucial to Western Christendom, left the vast majority of Jews and Muslims in the Islamic empire unmoved. Indeed, even Saladin's successors had abandoned the *jihad* and were beginning to normalize relations with the Westerners in the crusading states. From this point, trade with the West was far more important to the Muslims and Jews of the Middle East than a holy war against it. Traders and merchants either traded directly with European mercantile cities that were beginning to develop or else they conveyed goods from Europe to the Far East and vice versa. The Middle East was at the center of a mercantile nexus; it provided at this date the only path to India and it depended socially, intellectually and economically on the contacts with the outside world that trade demanded.

Trade was important to Europeans too. At the end of the twelfth century the maritime cities of Venice, Genoa and Pisa depended upon Muslim markets, ports and caravans. They had always found the crusading states useful in this respect and had established their own quarters in the main ports in Outremer, the name by which Christendom referred to her colonies "overseas." They certainly did not share the religious visions of the Crusaders, however. They saw the Muslims as normal colleagues who were essential business partners. We shall see that this secular attitude would have fateful consequences in the next crusading venture.

But crusading was far from dead in Europe. Pope Innocent III had come to power and was about to lead the Western Church into a new era of might. He was a fervent Crusader and was already planning a new Crusade to win Jerusalem back from the Muslims. But although the ideology of crusading was still central to the Western identity, the failure of Richard the Lionheart's Third Crusade had been deeply discouraging. The lure of Jerusalem had always been important: thousands of Crusaders had felt the pull of the powerful attraction of the Holy Land and had risked their lives for the Holy City. But the loss of Jerusalem and the difficulty that even the great Richard had experienced against Saladin had deprived crusading of a lot of its glamour. Richard had suggested that the next Crusade should be fought in Egypt: Christians should establish a base there from which to recover the Holy Land. But somehow the thought of fighting for Egypt, even though this was regarded as only a stage in the liberation of Palestine, was just not the same as setting out directly for the Holy Land itself. In the thirteenth century, we shall see, people continued to go on Crusades in the old way: there were five major expeditions in just under seventy years. But crusading was changing. We shall see that none of the Crusades discussed in *this* chapter got to the Holy Land. Crusading was finding new forms. Some of these directly contradicted the old ideals of the First Crusaders. But Europe was changing and growing and crusading changed to meet her new needs in the thirteenth century. So deeply embedded was crusading in the Western identity that, when the old crusading expeditions became less viable, crusading simply found new and sometimes very surprising forms indeed. We shall discover what some of these new forms of crusading were like in this chapter.

In 1199 a group of French and Flemish barons decided to lead a Fourth Crusade. They felt that the Third Crusade, which had been led by the three greatest rulers in Europe—Richard, Philip Augustus of France and the Emperor Frederick Barbarossa—had been too worldly. They wanted to take crusading back to the vintage days of the First Crusade, which had been led by barons. Their leader approached Innocent III with the idea. The Pope was delighted, feeling that a baronial Crusade would be more amenable to his control. He dispatched two popular preachers to summon the soldiers of God into the crusading army but the numbers of laymen who responded were disappointing. In 1201 Boniface of Montferrat took command of the project. He was of good Crusader stock. His father had settled in the Holy Land at the end of his life; his brother William had fathered the little King Baldwin V of Jerusalem, who had died shortly before the Battle of Hittin. His other brother Conrad had led the Christian resistance at Tyre after Hittin. In August 1201 Boniface held a conference which decided that the Fourth Crusade would attack Cairo, according to Richard the Lionheart's plan. This was a very ambitious and expensive project: a fleet would be necessary to take the Crusaders across the Mediterranean and already negotiations with Enrico Dandolo, the blind Doge of Venice, had begun in the hope that Venice would provide such a fleet.

After the meeting Boniface went to Germany to stay with his old friend Philip of Swabia, who was the son of former Crusader Frederick Barbarossa and the brother of the Emperor Henry VI.[18] Henry had died in 1197 but Philip shared many of his ambitions and now he made a suggestion to Boniface that would ultimately change the direction of the Crusade.

When Henry VI had conquered Sicily from the Norman dynasty in 1195, one of his prisoners of war was Irene Angelina, the daughter of the Emperor of Byzantium, who was also the widow of Roger, the dispossessed Crown Prince. Henry had married Irene to Philip and the arranged marriage developed into a love match, which naturally involved Philip in the affairs of the Emperor Isaac Angelus of Constantinople. The sons of Barbarossa were deeply hostile to the rival dynasty in the East, and Henry had long planned to lead a Crusade against Constantinople so that he could be the Emperor of the East and the West. In 1201 a new opportunity presented itself. A few months after the marriage of Philip and Irene, the inept Emperor Isaac had been unseated in a coup led by his brother, who became Emperor Alexius III. The ex-Emperor Isaac was blinded and he and his son, also called Alexius, were thrown into prison. In 1201, however, Prince Alexius managed to escape and he sought the protection of his brother-in-law in Germany. Philip introduced Alexius to Boniface at the end of the year and made a very interesting suggestion. He was anxious to help Alexius to recover the throne, because this would make the Eastern Emperor a client to his rival in the West. He pointed out that Byzantium could be a valuable detour on his way to Egypt. By unseating the Emperor Alexius III and installing the young Prince Alexius, he would have a grateful Emperor obliged to support the crusading effort. Boniface did not immediately commit himself. There were too many other necessary plans to be made before the Crusade got off the ground.

In April 1202 the Crusaders made a treaty with the Venetians, who hoped to make a considerable profit out of the holy enterprise. Enrico Dandolo agreed that for the sum of 85,000 marks he would provide transport and food for 4500 knights, 9000 squires and 20,000 infantry. Innocent was not happy about this arrangement, which let the entirely secular and materialistic Venetians play such a key role in the Crusade, and he deeply distrusted Dandolo. He was quite right to do so: Dandolo had no intention of fighting any Muslims because this would ruin his profitable markets in the East. At the very time he was making his treaty with the Crusaders, his agents had been making another treaty with the Sultan al-Adil, who had not retained his brother's enthusiasm for the *jihad* and preferred a profitable peace with Christians. Dandolo promised the Sultan that he would not countenance any attack on Cairo: he hoped to use the Crusade for his own nefarious purposes. An opportunity soon presented itself. By June 1202 the Crusaders had assembled in Venice, but unfortunately only half the number they had expected had taken the Cross and only two thirds of the money they owed Dandolo had been collected. When Dandolo found that they could not pay him in full, he took control. He crammed the Crusaders onto the tiny island of St. Niccolo di Lido and threatened to cut off their food supplies unless they paid up or else helped him in a project of his own before they went to the East. Venice had recently been in conflict with Hungary for the control of the Dalmatian trade routes, and the Hungarians had just seized the key port of Zara in modern Yugoslavia. Dandolo wanted the Crusaders to capture Zara for him with their huge army. To their credit, some of the Crusaders were disgusted by the idea of attacking a perfectly innocent Christian city and they left the Crusade, but those who stayed on to cooperate with Dandolo were probably more confused than wicked. Like many modern Crusaders, they would have felt, when they turned their Crusade into a Crusade against Christians, that the end justified the means.

On November 8, 1202, the Crusade sailed out of Venice and arrived in front of Zara three days later. There was a battle and the city surrendered on November 15 and was sacked by the Crusaders and Venetians. Innocent was very distressed and at first excommunicated the whole Crusade—an unprecedented disgrace—but then he relented, realizing that the Crusaders had been exploited. Dandolo remained under the ban but was entirely unperturbed, especially as Philip of Swabia had approached the Crusaders again with a very interesting offer. If the Crusaders put Prince Alexius back on his father's throne, Alexius would pay the money to the Venetians, would send 10,000 imperial troops to Cairo with the Crusaders and supply them with food and money. Finally he promised to make the Greeks submit to the Pope and the Latin rite. This was a very attractive idea: to restore the Greeks to the true faith would justify an attack on Constantinople and would be a great victory for the Crusade, which was now definitely under a cloud. Dandolo was delighted with the scheme, not because he cared a jot about the heresy of the Greeks, but because he saw a great opportunity for Venice. He hated Byzantium, which offered him very poor trading terms, and could never forget that it was during a brawl in Constantinople that he had lost his sight. The Crusaders approached Innocent and, though the Pope was very doubtful about any project managed by Dandolo and Philip of Swabia, he could not resist the idea of a newly united Christendom with himself at its helm. The First Crusade had been summoned partly to heal the rift with the Greek Orthodox, and if Alexius did force them to submit to the papacy the Crusade would at last have fulfilled this important objective.

After spending the winter in Zara, the Crusaders and Venetians sailed eastward in April 1203, occupying some important ports on their way to Constantinople. They found the country largely undefended, for the position of the usurping Emperor was very weak indeed. The imperial army now consisted mainly of mercenaries, many of whom were Franks whose loyalty clearly could not be trusted in this instance. The Emperor was not a man to inspire great personal loyalty and, when he saw the crusading fleet sailing up the Bosphorus, he realized that all was over and fled from the city with his family. The young Prince Alexius had assured the Crusaders, most unrealistically, that the Byzantines would greet them as liberators, but the Byzantines had bad memories of Crusaders and were outraged by this new Western interference in their affairs. They firmly closed their gates to the Crusaders and brought the blind former Emperor Isaac out of prison and reinstalled him as Emperor. Now that his father was back on the throne, they told Alexius, there need be no more trouble. Up to this point Alexius had behaved as though his father did not exist, but he could not very well quarrel with this. But the Crusaders were not satisfied because they needed Alexius to be in a position of power to accomplish their grand design. They insisted that Alexius should be a coemperor and on August 1, 1203, Alexius was solemnly enthroned in St. Sophia as his father's colleague.

But once he was on the throne Alexius discovered that he could not keep the promises he had made to the Crusaders. Naturally the Greeks refused to submit to Rome and the Latin rite. Neither could Alexius pay the Venetians: his father had been a very extravagant ruler and the Empire was in financial straits. He also found that he needed the Crusaders to stay on in Constantinople simply to keep him on his throne, so the Crusade was grounded again. An intolerable situation developed in Constantinople that winter. The Greeks hated to see the Franks strolling arrogantly through their city as though they owned it; drunken Crusaders often pillaged the villages of the suburbs and there was a very dangerous fire in the city when the Crusaders piously set fire to a mosque which had been built for visiting Muslim traders. The new Emperors proved to be quite inadequate and were hated because of their connection with the Franks. Finally in February 1204 there was a palace revolution: Alexius was strangled and Isaac died of grief a few days later, helped on, no doubt, by ill treatment in prison. Alexius Musuphlus, the son-in-law of Alexius III, ascended the imperial throne as Alexius V.

The revolution was a direct challenge to the Crusaders. For some time Dandolo had been trying to persuade them that the only way out of the mess was a full-scale assault on the city and now they decided to follow this advice and put a Frankish Emperor on the imperial throne. Any pretense that this Crusade was going to get back on course and fight Muslims in Egypt was abandoned, and the Fourth Crusade became a holy war against Greek Orthodox Christians, who had been the first official "enemy" of the West ever since the distant days of Charlemagne.

The Crusaders attacked the city on April 6. At first the Greeks fought back energetically but they were demoralized by the years of internal revolution within their empire and the mercenaries quickly became exhausted and could fight no more. Within ten days the city had submitted to the Crusaders, who entered the city in triumph. Boniface and the Doge were installed in the imperial palace and gave their troops permission to loot and pillage Constantinople, which for centuries had filled the Christians of Europe with envy and a burning sense of inferiority. The sack of Constantinople was one of the great crimes of history. For three days the Venetians and Crusaders rushed through the streets, raping, killing and pillaging with a horrible eagerness. Women and children lay dying in the streets and nuns were raped in their convents. The Venetians knew the value of the treasures that they carefully purloined to adorn their own cities, churches and palaces, but the Crusaders from northern Europe simply went on the rampage. In the great basilica of St. Sophia drunken soldiers tore down the silk hangings and trampled the sacred books and icons underfoot, and a prostitute sat on the Patriarch's throne singing bawdy songs. Palaces and hovels alike were vandalized. The chronicler Geoffrey Villehardouin wrote that never since the creation of the world had so much booty been taken from a city: no one could possibly count the piles of gold, silver and jewels or the bales of precious materials.[19] Nothing could have better illustrated the deep hatred which had always filled Crusaders when they confronted the magnificent capital of the Eastern empire that belonged to the Greeks, whom they had so often accused of treachery, effeminacy and cowardice, but who had really made them feel their own weakness too acutely for comfort.

After the carnage the Crusaders and Venetians appointed Count Baldwin IX of Flanders and Hainault (a compromise choice) to be the Latin Emperor of Byzantium and he was crowned with great pomp in the pillaged St. Sophia. For fifty-seven miserable years there was a Western Emperor in Constantinople and a Western empire in the East which the Latins called Romania. It seemed to the exultant Crusaders that the whole of the East was about to submit to the Roman Church and that the power of Western Christendom had been dramatically enlarged. With such a magnificent new power base in Byzantium, the reconquest of Jerusalem and the Holy Land would surely be only a matter of time. The Crusaders had always coveted the great relic collection in Constantinople and had considered the Greeks unworthy of this spiritual treasure, but now the Crusaders had captured this holy power for the West and many priceless relics were taken back to Europe. The Crusade seemed to have enriched Christendom spiritually and materially. Pope Innocent III, who had been horrified when he heard about the sack of Constantinople, still could not conceal his satisfaction when he contemplated this victory over the Eastern Church which had for so long refused to submit to the ever more powerful Western Pope.[20] Now the Greeks had been brought to heel and their humiliation would surely hasten their conversion. For a hundred and fifty years there had been tension and hostility between the Eastern and Western Churches, but now there would be a newly united Christendom.[21] But later, when he heard that his papal legate had absolved the Crusaders of their vow to journey to the Holy Land, he began to have serious misgivings.[22] The Crusaders now wanted to divide up their new territories among themselves into fat fiefs, on the European model. They wanted to enjoy the spoils that they had stolen and take the relics home to their grateful fellow Christians, who would be spiritually enriched by their powerful presence. The Crusade had shown itself to be an expedition whose only aim was to conquer Christian territory and would do nothing to win back Jerusalem.

As Innocent realized only too well subliminally, the Fourth Crusade was a travesty and a crime, which completely negated all the old idealism. Its leaders had wanted to return to the spirit of the First Crusade but had in fact flouted some of the most essential aims of Pope Urban, when he had summoned that first expedition. Urban had told the Franks that it was criminal and shameful for Christians to fight other Christians. This had always been Christian teaching from the time of St. Augustine. Urban had wanted the knights of Europe to stop fighting one another and expend their murderous energies on the Muslims. Further, the Crusade was to have been an act of love: the Crusaders were going to *help* the Greeks to recover their land from the infidel and to liberate these fellow Christians from the Muslim scourge. Now this Crusade had killed Christians, robbed them and destroyed the Greek Empire. It was, therefore, a dramatic abandonment of the early crusading idealism, similar to the moral and religious reversals we have seen in the new holy wars today.

The Latin empire of Romania did not survive the century. In 1261 the Greeks managed to fight the Latins, drive them out and put a Greek Emperor on the throne of Byzantium once more. But the ancient empire had been fatally wounded during this alien occupation. By parceling up portions of the great united state into fiefs as they would have done in Europe, they undermined the strength of the country in such a way that it was very difficult for the Greeks to recover it later.[23] Further, during their occupation the Europeans were just not sophisticated enough to understand the complex role that the Greeks had been playing for years in fending off the Muslim advance. Crusaders had always been angered and scandalized by the way the Byzantine emperors played off one Muslim ruler against another and had preferred to negotiate when war could be avoided. But in this way the Byzantines had been able to conserve their internal strength instead of indulging in bloody and wasteful wars, as well as weaken the strength of the various Muslim empires. They had thus been a bulwark between Islam and Western Christendom. This subtlety was quite lost on the Latins and it may be that their conquest of Constantinople gravely weakened the Greek Empire and hastened her final defeat by the Ottoman Turks in 1453. If this is so,[24] the Crusade would have actually helped the cause of Islam and in this it certainly reflected the feelings of some past Crusaders who had often hated "the Greeks" more than the Muslims.

Byzantium can be seen as one of the greatest casualties of the Crusades.[25] The Crusaders had helped to destroy a great and noble empire, which had remained far truer to the spirit of the gospels than the Western Church. The Greeks had never abandoned the ideals of pacifism, had never indulged a cult of war and, though they had sometimes made serious mistakes, they had survived for centuries living side by side with other great cultures in the East. Byzantium had lived alongside the Zoroastrian pre-Islamic Sassanid empire of Persia, beside the ancient non-Christian cultures of the Near East and had finally coexisted in relative harmony beside Islam, as a respected and powerful neighbor. The Greeks had been enriched by these contacts with other cultures and had developed a tradition of learning, art, scholarship and love of the intellect that was peculiarly their own. During the long and bloody history of the Crusades it is often refreshing to read of the forbearance and good sense of the Greek Emperors in not only putting up with but actually trying to help the churlish Crusaders from Europe. Now the Latins had deprived themselves of all this Greek wisdom. Instead of living side by side with other cultures, the Crusaders had opted for a far narrower perspective and demonstrated graphically that they not only wanted no contact or coexistence with Islam; they did not even want to live side by side with their fellow Christians. The sack of Constantinople, of course, put paid to any hopes of unity between the Eastern and Western Churches, which both sides had confidently expected until this date, whatever the tension. The Greeks could never forgive the Fourth Crusade and the West had caused the scandal of a permanently divided Christendom. The hatred of the Latins for the Greeks still survives in our use of the adjective "byzantine" to describe a frame of mind or type of behavior that prefers pointless and arcane subtlety for its own sake to plainer, more straightforward dealings. This is clearly a distortion that has come down to us from the Crusaders themselves.

The next Crusade was an even more shocking flouting of the rule that Christians should not kill other Christians. It is as though Christian aggression was frustrated, now that the new Muslim power made crusading less desirable, and so needed new outlets, nearer to home. It was another example of the way that a holy war mentality tends to turn inward upon itself and create either a civil war or serious religious conflict and division. This new type of Crusade was instigated by Pope Innocent III, and here we see a new type of Western leader, who turns a blind eye to inconvenient realities and manipulates events to further his own projects. Innocent uses language that is perhaps alien to us, who may not be so familiar with Catholic or biblical imagery. But he is also a very familiar figure indeed in his organization of this infamous diversion of crusading from Jerusalem to Europe. This Crusade was called to fight not the Muslims in the Near East but Christians in the south of France. It has been suggested that Innocent continued to feel very guilty about the sack of Constantinople and that this prompted him to summon the new Crusade in 1209 against "heretics,"[26] who lived a devout Christian life but who held different beliefs from the Catholics. However strongly Innocent felt about this heresy, two wrongs do not make a right. He could not absolve his own conscience for the crimes done to the Greeks by this new crusading initiative which slaughtered hundreds of other Christians and also led to a long and painful civil war in which many orthodox Catholics were killed.

From the middle of the twelfth century[27] missionaries had traveled from Eastern Europe and had preached to Westerners a different form of Christianity which they claimed to be the true religion of Jesus. They found a particularly receptive audience in the region of Toulouse and Languedoc and there was soon a thriving rival Church down there, which continually attracted new converts. Languedoc had never been much affected by the Cluniac reform and the clergy there tended to be too complacent to encourage spiritual fervor in the laity.[28] The courtly culture of the south had developed independently of the Church and had made the region more secular in spirit, but the southerners were a deeply religious people and the new religion satisfied a strong spiritual hunger.

These new Christians called themselves the Cathari or the Pure Ones. None of their writings survived the Crusade, so our only source of knowledge about their faith is the polemic of their Catholic enemies, who may have distorted their teaching.[29] It seems that Catharism was another form of a dualistic religion that went back to the very first days of Christianity. It had inspired the Gnostic Christians of the second and third centuries and also the Manichaeans, who had come from Persia and converted many Christians during the fifth and sixth centuries. St. Augustine had been a Manichaean before his conversion and had fought the religion bitterly for the rest of his life. The Church has always tried to suppress this religion but has never succeeded in stamping it out entirely: there are still Manichaeans in parts of Eastern Europe today. Like the Gnostics and Manichaeans, the Catharists believed that God was engaged in a constant battle with an Evil Principle who was not divine himself but who had created the world. The world was, therefore, essentially evil, but God had sent Jesus to save mankind from the world of evil matter. The Cathars did not believe that Jesus was God. He was an angelic figure who had not really taken a tainted human body, of course, but had only appeared to do so.

Because he could not therefore suffer and die, he had only seemed to die on the Cross and had redeemed the world not by his Crucifixion but by being a spiritual teacher or missionary from above.

The Catharists spent their lives trying to purify themselves from the physical and seeking the spiritual world. They were not baptized because water was matter and evil, but they had a sacrament which they called the *consolamentum*, which severed a man or woman absolutely from the world.[30] Once you had received this sacrament you had to live a life of such exceptional purity that most Catharists received it only on their deathbeds. There were, therefore, two ranks in the Catharist Church. First there were the elite, who had received the sacrament and who were called the Perfect.[31] They lived lives of complete chastity, great austerity and strict evangelical poverty. Because food was evil, many of them were said to fast to death in a martyrdom called the *endura*.[32] The Perfect did not lock themselves away in rich monasteries but toured the countryside in pairs, begging their bread, like the apostles. Even those southerners who were not converted by the Catharist missionaries were most impressed by their holy lives, which certainly put the orthodox Catholic clergymen to shame.[33] Less heroism was demanded of the Followers, who formed the second rank and the majority. They worshiped with the Perfect in a liturgy of repentance and lived according to the moral precepts of the Catharist Church, preparing for death and the final purification. They were not expected to be celibate, but marriage was forbidden as it was felt to give a hypocritical holy veneer to something inherently evil.[34]

Despite their obvious differences, the Catharist and the Catholic Churches were very much alike. The Catholics also believed in a struggle between God and a very powerful evil spirit, whom they called Satan or the Devil. They renounced the world and the flesh, like the Catharists. The Church may have preached that marriage was a holy state but most Catholics *felt* that sex was evil, whatever the dogma. Heloise's letters to Abelard deplored their marriage as being worse than their previous fornication for reasons that were pure Catharism. In the Catholic Church ascetics were encouraged to fast themselves into a dangerous emaciation and some women saints actually ruined their heath and died owing to this fasting. The orthodox also divided themselves into two ranks, with monks and nuns living the full Christian life and the laity living a diluted version.

Yet in very important ways Catharism opposed the whole ethos of crusading Christianity. Crusading was based on the cult of the Cross and the Holy Sepulchre, but the Catharists did not believe that Jesus had died on the Cross. Pilgrimage to the tombs of saints and veneration of relics had been crucial to Crusader piety, but a Catharist would not venerate either a tomb or a relic, because the dead body was a shameful husk, which the purified spirit had left behind. Because the world was evil, the idea of a holy land or a holy city were contradictions in terms. But even more basically than this, Catharists were strictly pacifist and nonviolent. They were also very tolerant people and seemed to have enjoyed disputing with the Catholics in open debate, and instead of spreading their religion by the sword they relied on peaceful missionary work.[35]

The Catharists were not the only heretics in Europe. In the north of France there was a similar return to basic Christian principles and a denial of the rich, powerful Church of Innocent III. The Waldensians and the Poor Men of Lyons also practiced strict evangelical poverty and roamed the countryside preaching to the common people. The particular danger of Catharism was that, unlike these northern "heretics," Catharism was not a disorganized, popular movement but had actually succeeded in creating an alternative Church in the south of France. Catharists had their own bishops and dioceses and their religion was not confined to poor people on the margins of society but had penetrated many of the great southern families and households and was accepted and even respected by the Catholic nobility.[36] This state of affairs could not be allowed to continue and at first Innocent tried to fight it by sending the Cistercians to preach against the heretics, but the Cistercians had changed since the vintage days of St. Bernard; having abandoned their former austerity, they had become very rich and were now identified with the establishment. The southerners were simply not impressed and thought that the Catharists were far more Christlike. Then Innocent tried to provide a Catholic alternative to the Catharists. A young Spaniard called Dominic Guzman had recently founded an order to fight against heresy by peacefully preaching to the people, instructing them in the truths of the faith so that they would be proof against the blandishments of the heretics. Dominic and his followers lived lives of evangelical poverty as the Catharists did and his Dominicans toured the countryside as mendicants, barefoot and begging for bread. This was the new Christian ideal of the thirteenth century, which would replace the old Cistercian elite. The Dominican was a new kind of monk who called himself a friar, a brother. Instead of seeing himself as part of an elite that was separate from the people, he saw himself as one with them and his way of fulfilling the gospel precepts was quite different from the way that monks had traditionally followed. Instead of making an exodus into a monastery or into the wilderness to pray, the friar went out to the people. Instead of taking a vow of stability and living in one monastery all his life like the Cluniac or the Cistercian, the friar was constantly on the road, sharing the lot of the poor laymen. The Dominicans showed a new thirteenth-century desire to imitate the life of Christ more closely and literally than the Cluniacs had done, and it was this desire that was also attracting people to the Waldensians, the Poor Men of Lyons and the Catharists. Dominic seemed the perfect answer to the Catharists, but though his Order of Preachers was accepted in Languedoc more readily than the Cistercians had been, and though the Dominicans were able to put up a good fight against the heretics in public debate, they actually made little impression.[37] There were very few converts from Catharism to orthodoxy, and the heresy continued to spread.

Innocent now felt that there was no other solution to the problem but the sword, and on November 17, 1207, he wrote to King Philip Augustus urging him to take an army to fight the heretics in the region of Languedoc, offering him indulgences that were similar to those given to people who went on a Crusade to the Holy Land to fight the Muslims.[38] For the first time in Europe, a Pope was calling upon Christians to kill other Christians: Innocent was setting a precedent for a new kind of holy war that would become an incurable disease in Europe. It looked forward to the wars and persecutions waged by Catholics and Protestants against one another, to the wars of religion in the seventeenth century and to the bitter, endless struggle in Northern Ireland today. It is important to understand how Innocent tried to justify his Crusade against Christians.

The letter to Philip is not a calculated, rational response to a political threat, but Innocent had recourse to the same imagery that we have seen used by Arab writers to describe the state of Israel today: the Catharist Church in the region of Toulouse was an abomination of nature and a rampant cancer in the body of Christendom. The heresy of Catharism, he wrote, "gives birth continually to a monstrous brood, by means of which its corruption is vigorously renewed, after that offspring has passed on to others the canker of its own madness and a detestable succession of criminals emerges."[39] This hysterical description bore no relation at all to the devout Catharists, but Innocent seemed unable to be rational. He responded to them in language that others have used later to describe an alien presence in their own lands that is threatening and traumatic in a way that defies rational analysis. Innocent could not see that the heretics had a point of view of their own. Even the Catharists' virtuous lives and wise arguments were satanic traps to entice the hapless Christians into a pit of bottomless evil.[40] This alien growth, gnawing away at the body of Christendom, he explained, could not be cured by means of a poultice but only by the knife, so Philip must arm himself strongly and "eliminate such harmful filth."[41] The great difference between the Arab polemic against Israel and Innocent's polemic against the Catharists is that Innocent is writing not about people who belong to a different race or religion but against his own fellow Europeans who profess to be Christians. Hitherto in crusading jargon "filth" had meant only Muslims: in 1207 other Christians had become "filth," meet only for extermination. A new paranoia was surfacing in thirteenth-century Europe, which narrowed the circle of what was acceptable and which introduced a new level of intolerance against coreligionists.

Philip Augustus was a hardheaded man who was not likely to be moved by such fantasies, but he was not averse to strengthening his hold over his vassals in Languedoc by a show of force. Many of his barons, however, were very responsive to this rhetoric and, at a time when the enthusiasm for a Crusade against the Muslims in the Holy Land seemed to be on the wane, frustrated Crusaders were eager to exterminate the heretics of Languedoc. Chief among these was Earl Simon of Montfort, who had joined the Fourth Crusade but had left when Boniface decided to attack Zara, disgusted by the prospect of Crusaders killing other Christians. Yet he had no doubt that the Christians of Languedoc were inhuman filth. Despite this eagerness, there was no holy war in 1207. Philip asked the Pope for guarantees that the Pope was in no position to give, so the campaign was deferred for the time being.

At the same time the Pope also instructed Count Raymund VI of Toulouse and Count Raymund-Roger of Béziers and Carcassonne to root out the heretics in their lands, but to his horror both refused to do so. Neither of them was a Catharist himself, but they respected the devotion of their fellow countrymen and certainly they were not going to slaughter them to satisfy some whim of Pope Innocent. Southern integrity seemed to be at stake, and when the two superpowers of the papacy and the King of France seemed to unite against the Catharists of Languedoc, many Catholic southerners rallied behind their leaders. Feelings ran very high and the holy war was precipitated by an act of terrorism. On January 13, 1208, Count Raymund invited Peter of Castelnau, the papal legate, to Toulouse for discussions. At first he seemed to waver but then adamantly refused to accede to Innocent's demands and he threatened Peter and his colleagues with death as long as they remained in his lands. The next day one of his supporters stabbed Peter in the back after Mass and the legate died of his wounds. It was a clear warning to the papacy, and naturally Innocent saw this as a sign of the growing cancer in the south.

It is at this point that Innocent reminds us forcibly of modern leaders and statesmen denouncing "terrorists" as inhuman monsters who are a peril to humanity and must be annihilated, but completely ignoring the part that they or their clients have played in producing the situation that made some people desperate enough to resort to terrorism. On March 28, 1208, Innocent wrote to the faithful Catholics of the south, telling them the story of Peter's death and presenting him as a martyr.[42] Raymund, he said, had quite clearly colluded with this murder. He had not only threatened the legate publicly but had also received the murderer with great warmth. This was very flimsy and circumstantial evidence on which to build such a serious charge, which had fateful consequences.[43] Innocent blithely drew the conclusion that the Cathars were not simply a threat to truth but were also a direct threat to the peace of the region. "For if pestiferous men of this sort are trying not only to ravage our possessions but also to annihilate us ourselves," he explained, "they are not only sharpening their tongues to crush our souls but they are also in reality stretching out their hands to kill our bodies: the perverters of our souls have also become the destroyers of our flesh."[44] Yet if anybody was perverting truth here it was not the Cathars but Innocent himself. The Cathars, we know, had no such murderous intentions but were strict pacifists. Yet this did not seem to matter to Innocent, which reveals another flaw in his position: either he did not think truth mattered "in a good cause" and that the end justified the means if it stirred up hatred against the Cathars in the south, or he did not know much about the Cathar doctrines. If this latter was the case, then the only "heresy" he could legitimately accuse them of was a failure to submit to Rome and not, strictly speaking, a matter of "truth" at all. Either way, Innocent was cynically manipulating the realities of the situation to suit his own ends. Having "proved" that the Cathars were a danger to the faithful, Innocent summoned his Crusade for Peace: clearly it was his duty to annihilate this enemy, because the Catholics were going about in terror of their lives. The Church would move in to defend the faithful and, as a first step, he would excommunicate Count Raymund and his supporters, which meant that the Catholics were now released from their feudal oaths to him. But if this mild sanction failed, Innocent warned, "we will make it our business to take more serious action against him."[45]

It is quite true that the assassination of Peter of Castelnau was an immoral and dangerously provocative act. But the Pope was patently ignoring the obvious fact that he had *himself* threatened the peace of the region four months before, when he wrote to Philip Augustus urging him to invade the south. The terrorist may have killed one man, but the Pope had earlier urged Raymund to kill hundreds of southerners. Again one cannot help comparing this myopia of Innocent's with the one-sided view of participants in today's holy wars. Further, in Innocent we see the new, coldly manipulative Crusader, who is the first great aggressive "peacemaker" of the West. In his letter he mounts a ruthless, lying attack on the Cathars, who are about to "annihilate" his powerful Catholic Church:

> Since the Church in that region sits in sadness and grief with no one to comfort her after the death of that just man and it is said that the faith has disappeared, that peace has perished, that the plague of heresy and the fury of the enemy have grown stronger and stronger and that, unless she is strongly supported against such a new attack, the ship of the Church will seem to have been wrecked in that place almost completely, we advise all of you most urgently, encourage you fervently and in so great a crisis of need enjoin you confidently in the strength of Christ, granting you remission of sins, not to delay in making haste to combat so many evils and to make it your business to bring peace to those people in the name of him who is *the God of peace and love*.[46]

The new paranoia in the West caused the most powerful institution in Europe to feel deeply threatened by a sect of men and women who refused to touch a sword. These people, Innocent declared, were now "worse than the Muslims," and must be treated as ruthlessly.[47] Innocent prepared his violent reprisal.

In 1209 the Crusade was ready. Philip Augustus, who was having difficulties with the English at this point, was unable to lead the Crusade so Arnauld-Amalric, the Abbot of Citeaux, rode at the head of the large army of Crusaders. The south watched the advance with dread and Count Raymund tried to free himself from the catastrophe at the last minute by submitting to the Pope, but the Pope was unforgiving. "Once he is isolated and dependent on his own forces alone," he said to Arnauld-Amalric, "we can deal with him last of all and strike him down without much difficulty."[48] On July 22 the army surrounded the city of Béziers and demonstrated the deadly determination of these new Crusaders, who were prepared to wipe out this southern vermin as cruelly as they had exterminated the Muslims and the Jews. When the city surrendered and the Crusaders went to deal out the judgment of God, it is said that the soldiers asked the abbot how they could distinguish the heretics from the Catholics and that

Arnauld replied: "Kill them all; God will know his own."[49] Every single inhabitant of the city was massacred. The terror this inspired meant that the Crusade met with no further resistance until it reached Carcassonne in August. To save his people Count Raymund-Roger gave himself up to the Crusaders, was thrown into prison and his fief was given to Simon of Montfort. In November Raymund-Roger conveniently died in prison, and in a letter Innocent hinted that he had been murdered.[50] Simon, who was clearly anxious to establish himself as a legitimate ruler, exhibited the body to the people and had it buried with great ceremony. He then continued the Crusade, capturing one Catharist center after another, burning the heretics, and replacing the local aristocracy with a northern nobility. The Crusade was becoming an efficient army of occupation and when in 1212 it began to attack the area north of Toulouse the southerners appealed to Peter of Aragon to come to their aid, preferring his rule to the rule of these cruel, ruthless northerners.

Simon had become one of the richest and most powerful landowners in France during the Crusade. Every time he conquered a city he automatically became its overlord and gave it as a fief to one of his dependents. Yet it would be a mistake to see him as a secular Crusader, who made use of the Crusade to further his own worldly ambitions. He was a Crusader of the old type who certainly considered this war against French Christians to be just as holy as a war against the Muslims. Before he fought and defeated Peter of Aragon at the Battle of Muret, the chronicler Pierre des Vaux-de-Cernay described him praying with real crusading piety:

> Having prayed at length and with great devotion, he grasped the sword hanging by his side and laid it on the altar, saying "O good Lord, O Gentle Jesus! You have chosen me to wage your wars in spite of my unworthiness. It is from your altar that I receive my arms today, so that in the moment of fighting your battles I may receive my weapons from you."[51]

But however holy Simon's motivation, the southerners increasingly saw him as an invader who was taking their land away from them and threatening their own peculiarly southern identity. There had always been some tension between northern and southern France; southerners had always prized their own sophisticated courtly culture and tended to see the northerners as crude and uncivilized. After Simon's victory over Peter of Aragon at the Battle of Muret the southerners began to fight back on their own behalf. To talk about nationalism is anachronistic, but there was certainly an element of a nationalistic war here.[52] It could be argued that the first spontaneous nationalistic movement in Europe arose in response to the new Crusade. For nearly twenty years southerners fought against the northern representatives of their King, even though their struggle was hopeless. It would be 1229 before a later Crusader brought "peace" to France and took the Crusade against Christians into a frightening new phase.

Innocent's dealings with the Catharists had shown the hidden insecurity of the thirteenth-century Church, which was at the zenith of its power during his pontificate. This neurosis meant casualties and the Catharists had shown how dangerous pacifism and nonviolence could be in a world dominated by the habit and paranoia of a holy war. But the Catharists were not the only poor people taking to the road during these years. At the beginning of the thirteenth century Europe was undergoing economic and agrarian upheavals which were bringing her into a new period of prosperity and power, but this inevitably meant that some weaker people went to the wall. In some parts of northern France and Germany many poorer peasants could no longer make their farms sufficiently productive or else found that they lacked the capital to bring them up to the working standards of this newly efficient Europe. Many of these were forced to sell their farms to better-off peasants and found themselves homeless and reduced to beggary. During these years a new class appeared. Whole families of men, women and children were forced to live wandering, mendicant lives on the margins of society.[53] Often they would be drawn to the new heretical sects that stressed the value of holy poverty, which told these poor people that their suffering had a value: it was *they* who were truly imitating Christ, not the rich monks and clerics of Innocent's Church. From this point, sects like this mushroomed throughout Europe, often becoming increasingly belligerent toward the establishment, which was indifferent to their plight.[54]

When they first took to the roads, these wandering bands of poor people were often called the *pueri* (the children) in rather the same spirit as black servants are often called "boy" by white South Africans, and in the year 1212 the *pueri* formed a religious protest movement of their own.[55] A young French *puer* called Stephen had a vision of Jesus, who appeared to him in the guise of a poor pilgrim begging for bread. He gave Stephen a letter for Philip Augustus, in which he pleaded the case of the poor. There was a sudden surge of hope and excitement: it seemed that Christ had not forgotten the poor after all. He had shown that he was a poor man too and identified with them; he was ready to plead their cause against the rich and the powerful.

At about the same time a similar movement sprang up spontaneously in Germany, led by a *puer* called Nicholas. In each country about 30,000 *pueri* formed massive processions, carried large wooden crosses and tramped through the countryside and through the towns and villages. They transformed their enforced wandering into a holy journey, following the Cross of the poor and suffering Jesus. These processions were also a powerful demonstration of the plight of the *pueri* and a dramatic way of pointing to their identification with Christ, who had had nowhere to lay his head. The chroniclers of the time tell us that as they marched they sang: "Lord God, raise up the Christian people and give us back the True Cross."[56] But these holy journeys were not a prelude to a holy war. At the end of the summer the *pueri* disbanded peacefully and seemed to disappear from history. Many doubtless joined some of the new and more belligerent heretical sects like the Waldensians who also preached a return to apostolic poverty, and as a distinct class the *pueri* disappeared.[57]

Yet they rose to a posthumous new life thirty years later when they became Crusaders. When later chroniclers read about these strange processions, they naturally translated the word *pueri* as "children," without understanding its special social significance, and the strange story of the Children's Crusade was born.[58] In these later versions of their story, Nicholas and Stephen were children whom Jesus had inspired to lead Crusades to the Holy Land: they would succeed where their elders had failed, because Christ preferred their weakness to the arrogant, worldly strength of the older Crusaders who seemed unable to recover the Holy Land. Nicholas promised that he would conquer Islam by a peaceful missionary campaign. The children should march through Europe, cross the Alps and continue until they reached the Mediterranean. Then the waters of the sea would open for them as they had opened for the Israelites, and they would cross the sea dry-shod, conquering the Holy Land miraculously by divine power alone. Of course it didn't work out like that. The children suffered tremendous hardship on the journey, the later chroniclers related. Many died and many dropped out. Only about a third of the children survived and, when they rushed down to the Mediterranean, the sea did not open for them. The German children began their miserable journey back from Genoa but most died during their return home. Some of the French children stayed on in Marseilles, still desperate to get to the Holy Land. They were picked up by unscrupulous merchants who promised to transport them to Acre but actually sold them as slaves to the Muslims in North Africa and Egypt. Years later one of them returned home to tell their sad story.[59]

The tale of the Children's Crusade is probably one of the most fascinating and popular of all the crusading stories and this recent explanation does make very good sense. Perhaps the creation of the myth is as interesting as the story itself. It shows how deeply embedded crusading was in the consciousness of Europe. When the later chroniclers read about the great processions of *pueri* who carried crosses and prayed for the return of the True Cross, which had been lost at the Battle of Hittin, they automatically assumed that they must have been Crusaders who were marching to Jerusalem. In some respects, the chroniclers saw these "children" as fundamentalist Crusaders who were returning crusading to the pious days of Peter the Hermit. Stephen and Nicholas both presented themselves as prophets who had been divinely inspired, and Stephen actually had a letter from Christ as Peter was said to have had. Like Peter the Hermit's Crusaders, the "children" had a tragic fate. But in other ways this myth showed a longing for a Crusade that depended upon God, as earlier Crusaders had done. There was also a new pacifism in this myth of the children: Nicholas wanted to convert the Muslims by preaching to them, which was quite a novel idea in 1212.[60] The miraculous journey to the Holy Land would be a prelude not to a holy war but to a peaceful preaching campaign. At a time when people were becoming more and more disillusioned with conventional crusading, they were still not prepared to abandon the holy war but were seeking an alternative Crusade, which would bring God back as the focus and which made peace instead of war. But the fate the chroniclers dreamed up for their child Crusaders in the 1250s showed that there was little thought then of any such alternative being really viable.

There had been a similar dissatisfaction and frustration with crusading in 1212 and people had tried to imagine a different kind of holy war. The Crusade against the Catharists had been one of these new alternatives, but other Christians were imagining peaceful Crusades instead of a Crusade for Peace. Peter of Blois, the secretary of Eleanor of Aquitaine, wrote of the great hope and enthusiasm he had felt when the Third Crusaders left Europe. It seemed impossible that this mighty show of Christian force could fail to conquer Islam and regain the Holy Land. But when he heard of the disaster that had befallen Barbarossa's army and of the military stalemate that made it impossible for Richard to recover Jerusalem, he had been convinced that a new solution must be found: in the future it would be the poor people, not the rich and powerful kings and emperors, who would conquer Jerusalem. They would rely on the power of God instead of their own worldly power.[61] At this time also the preacher Alan of Lille argued that in future a Crusade would only succeed if it were inspired by poor people, who like Jesus had nowhere to lay their heads.[62] Alan and Peter both thought that the new Crusades would somehow take Jerusalem peacefully and not by the sword. There was a link between this kind of thinking and the peaceful demonstrations of the *pueri*, who had instinctively turned to the imagery of the pilgrimage and the Crusade to express their plight. Originally crusading had been a poor man's movement and had given the poor their first real sense of power during the First Crusade. The *pueri* would not be the last poor people to seek to change their lot in the context of a Crusade. The transformation of the story of the *pueri* into the legend of the Children's Crusade shows that people were beginning to dream of a peaceful Crusade and to seek an alternative Christianity which was closer to the life Jesus had lived on earth than the powerful Church of Pope Innocent.

There may have been no child Crusaders in Germany in 1212, but in that year Europe did witness the almost miraculous journey of an eighteen-year-old boy who quickly became known as Puer Apuliae (the Boy of Apulia) or simply Puer Noster (Our Boy). Frederick Hohenstaufen, the only son of the Emperor Henry VI, had been born in the south of Italy to Queen Constance, the Norman heiress of Sicily, on December 26, 1194. From the very beginning this child had been a controversial figure. The poet Geoffrey of Viterbo prophesied that the boy was destined to be the Last Emperor, who would unite the East and the West and establish a lasting peace,[63] but the Cistercian prophet Abbot Joachim of Fiore foretold that Frederick would prove to be Antichrist, who would wage war upon the Christians and be the scourge of the world.[64] Yet for the first years of his life Frederick lived in danger and obscurity. His father died in 1197 and Philip of Swabia rode south to collect the little Emperor and bring him back to Germany, but there was a revolution in northern Italy against the hated German rule which made him turn back, and Frederick passed his childhood as the King of Sicily, protected by Pope Innocent III. In Germany Philip of Swabia fought with Otto the Welf for the throne of Germany and the Germans forgot about Frederick; though the Pope had promised to protect Sicily, he did not push his ward's imperial claims.

But in 1210 some Germans remembered Sicily to further their own ambitions and Kaiser Otto IV, who had managed to gain the ascendancy, set off to conquer the kingdom for the house of Welf. As he watched the imperial army march through northern Italy and approach his own domain in the south, Frederick was convinced that he was finished. He had neither the army nor the support necessary to sustain such an attack but suddenly, at the eleventh hour, he experienced a salvation. Pope Innocent, who had been watching Otto's progress with considerable anxiety, suddenly excommunicated the Kaiser who was attacking his ward and gave encouragement to the anti-Welf faction in Germany. In September 1211 the German nobles, egged on by Philip Augustus, deposed the excommunicated Emperor and elected Frederick in his stead. When Otto heard the news he panicked and, instead of pressing ahead to destroy his rival, he turned back and rushed home to Germany to save his throne.[65]

Frederick was saved. Within a matter of days he had been rescued from certain destruction and elevated to the pinnacle of power. Not surprisingly, he regarded this salvation as a miracle, which proved that he was the chosen one of God, and to the end of his life he remained convinced that he had a special divine destiny.[66] His advisers urged him to refuse the imperial title: he could realistically rely only on the papacy for support and most of the Germans still supported Otto. Naturally Frederick waved aside such human fears and in mid-March 1212 he set out on a journey to Aachen, accompanied by a small band of retainers and trusting only in the power of God.[67] Europe watched the progress of this sunburned and raggedly dressed youth with astonishment. In April he arrived in Rome, where Innocent solemnly blessed his young ward, and then he set off for the dangerous imperial land in the north of Italy. At Pavia, the story goes, the Milanese tried to assassinate the young Emperor, but he simply jumped onto his horse and swam across the river. The people of Cremona saw his survival as miraculous and greeted him ecstatically as the Angel of the Lord.[68] From that moment his safety in Italy was assured but the real test lay in Germany. Otto had journeyed southward to meet his rival, and his servants, who had ridden ahead of him, were actually preparing a meal for him in Constance when suddenly Frederick appeared before them and demanded their support. His dramatic arrival seemed another miracle,[69] and when Otto arrived three hours later he found the city barred against him. By this time the people of southern and central Germany were ecstatic about this astonishing child, who seemed to be able to defeat the rich and powerful by trusting only in the Lord, and in December 1212 he was crowned King of the Germans in Mainz. Innocent himself called him a David, who had defeated the giant Otto the Welf, and the people of Germany were convinced of his divine election. "The child has conquered the Welf with heavenly rather than with earthly might,"[70] one poet wrote, and another troubadour sang "Behold the power of the child" in his rhymed chronicle:

Now comes the Pulian Child along—
The Kaiser's sword is twice as strong,
Whom yet the Child did overthrow
Without a single swordsman's blow:
The people's love towards him did flow.[71]

It was certainly true that the people of Germany took the child to
their hearts; he had an irresistible glamour and yet at the same time
he seemed one of themselves.[72] His homely face and clothing offset
his foreignness, which could have been a fatal disadvantage, and the
people remembered that, despite his southern blood, he was the grandson of the great Frederick Barbarossa.

It was this connection that finally persuaded the people of the imperial city of Aachen to open their gates to Frederick in mid-July 1215
and the young Boy of Apulia was solemnly crowned in the cathedral
and sat on the great throne of Charlemagne. He then amazed his
people again: immediately after he had received the imperial diadem
from the Archbishop, Emperor Frederick II suddenly and unexpectedly took the Cross.[73] The effect was magical. The child's miraculous
rise to power, his apparent divine election and his relationship to
Barbarossa, who had lost his life during a Crusade, raised everybody's
hopes. Frederick was already a young David who had cast the mighty
from their thrones: would he now become King David who conquered
Jerusalem?[74]

Yet in fact it proved more difficult to draw a Fifth Crusade together
than anybody had expected. After the great Lateran Council in 1215,
Innocent had sent traveling preachers all over Europe to preach a
Crusade and had been quite confident of a success. He had actually
written to al-Adil to warn him of the wrath to come and to advise
him to hand over Jerusalem peaceably.[75] But though the common
people were eager to take the Cross, the nobles seemed even more
reluctant to sail to the East than they had in 1202. It really did seem
as though conventional crusading was a dying enthusiasm and an
anachronism. When Innocent died in May 1216 his successor Pope
Honorius III found it very difficult to organize a Crusade: only a few
nobles set out that year with King Andrew of Hungary. Honorius
was also disturbed by a report he had recently received from the
Kingdom of Acre, which seemed very worrying.

The popular preacher James of Vitry had recently become Bishop
of Acre and he was dismayed by what he found in the Holy Land.
The Franks did not want a Crusade, he told the Pope. They were wary
of endangering the security of their tiny state and were afraid that a

holy war would destroy the excellent trading arrangements they were currently enjoying with the Muslims.[76] The Muslims were also enjoying the new trade with the West, and their passion for the *jihad* had died a natural death after Saladin's death in 1193. Al-Adil had no desire to call for a holy war, though he was taunted for this by a few of the officers in his army, and his son al-Malik al-Kamil, the viceroy of Egypt, fully shared his views: he had excellent relations with the 3000 Pisan, Venetian and Genoan merchants and traders who lived and worked in Cairo.[77] It seemed that this secular contact had made it possible for Christians and Muslims to live together in peace to their mutual advantage, but it seemed quite immoral to the newcomer, Bishop James of Vitry. He was also disturbed by the Franks' oriental lifestyle and seemed to equate the Franks' abandoning of a Western cultural identity with a denial of the Christian faith itself. The Franks had gone native, he wrote in disgust: they were fitter for the baths than for battle; they did not let their wives go to church more than once a year but would send them to the baths three times a week; the knights had love affairs with Muslim women, wore soft, effeminate clothes and were completely given over to lust and idleness.[78] They were very worried that a provocative Crusade from the West would ruin all this.

At first there seemed little danger. In 1217 Duke Leopold of Austria brought an army to the East to join the Hungarians, but nothing was achieved beyond a few desultory raids in Galilee. Most of the time the Crusaders wandered around collecting relics, and early the following year the Hungarians went home. Muslims and Franks both relaxed. But in 1218 three fleets from Frisia, France and England arrived in Acre and decided to revive the old plan of capturing Egypt. In May they sailed for Damietta, taking the Muslims there quite by surprise, and in August they actually managed to capture the city. The shock of the loss of Damietta was too much for the aging Sultan, who died a few hours afterward of a heart attack. To try to prevent a quarrel about the succession, he had arranged for the Ayyubid Empire of Saladin to be divided among his three older sons: al-Kamil was to take Egypt, al-Ashraf was to have Gezira and al-Mu'azam would take Damascus and Jerusalem. But there was still dissatisfaction, and while al-Kamil was away defending Egypt from the Franks, some Cairenes took advantage of his absence to put one of his younger brothers on the throne. Al-Kamil had to abandon the defense of the country and rush back to Cairo to put down the coup. The Crusaders had arrived in Egypt at an opportune moment and there was panic in the Muslim world. Sultan al-Mu'azam sent a message to Baghdad asking the Caliph for help and a vast army was promised, though it never arrived.

In September the Spaniard Cardinal Pelagius arrived in Damietta as the papal legate and he provided the leadership that the Crusade desperately needed. He found that morale was low despite their initial success: the Crusaders were dying of an epidemic that turned their skins black and killed one sixth of the soldiers. Pelagius insisted that action was the best remedy, and in February the Crusaders managed to occupy the city of al-Adilya. The Muslims were now becoming desperate. They had heard that the Emperor Frederick was on his way to the East, once he had settled his affairs in Germany. Al-Mu'azam began dismantling the walls of Jerusalem and other forts in Palestine in case he was forced to hand them over to the Christians, but in fact morale was still low in the Christian camp. After the Battle of al-Adilya there was a military stalemate and the epidemic continued to rage in both armies.

When Pelagius addressed the troops before the victory at al-Adilya he had made a suggestion that was quite new to crusading. Once they had conquered the Muslims, he said, it might be possible to convert the "perfidious and worthless people" to the true faith.[79] Hitherto no Crusader had ever thought of trying to convert Muslims; they had previously thought that the only solution was massacre, as St. Bernard of Clairvaux had written a hundred years earlier in his treatise on the Templars. But we have seen that in the thirteenth century there was quite a new enthusiasm for preaching in Europe. This was largely due to the heretics like the Cathars. The Cathars had traveled around preaching to the ordinary people, who were still so ignorant that they were very vulnerable to the heretics. They naturally saw these Cathar or Waldensian preachers, who preached a return to poverty, as much more concerned with them than the official Church, which had been content to leave them in ignorance, and it had been to counteract this that Pope Innocent encouraged St. Dominic to found his Order of Preachers, to instruct the poor laymen as the heretics were doing. But not all the preachers went to the poor. Some started preaching to the rich and to the middle classes and gained quite a following. One of the most popular of these charismatic preachers was James of Vitry, who had now come out to Acre, with the idea of preaching to the Muslims. It was an adventurous idea but, as we have seen already, James did not see this as a substitute for the Crusade, which he regarded as essential, as did Pelagius. Preaching could only be enforced by the sword. James had, however, managed to convert two Muslims and, though he had never been permitted to enter Muslim territory, he used to preach sometimes on the borders of the Christian Kingdom, taking the word of God to the front line of the holy war. Occasionally he sent letters in Arabic over the border, to explain the Christian religion to Muslims, and when children had been taken as hostages in the raids made by the Crusaders in Galilee in 1217, James had baptized them and sent them home over the border: by filling them with the life of Christ by means of the sacrament he had made them Christian infiltrators in enemy territory.[80]

Preaching and conversion were in the air, therefore, but suddenly a new arrival in Damietta took a much more radical approach. During the stalemate after the Battle of al-Adilya one of the most famous popular preachers in Europe asked Pelagius for permission to cross the enemy lines and preach to the Sultan al-Kamil. Most people would probably consider Francis of Assisi, who made this startling sugges-tion, as one of the most perfect Christians who ever lived. The gentle saint who wandered around Italy wedded to absolute poverty and preaching to birds and trees seemed to have broken through the hatreds of institutional religion and made peace with the whole world. He would seem to be far in spirit from the violence of crusading and yet it was no accident that he happened to be present in Damietta in 1219. Francis was devoted to the Church, unlike most of the other European Christians who were returning to the practice of absolute poverty and an exact imitation of Christ. This had enabled Pope In-nocent to make Francis' Friars Minor an official religious order, bring-ing the poverty movement within the established Church. Francis had made the "heresy" legitimate and when the greatest Poor Man of Europe had joined the Crusade in Egypt, he had been a powerful reminder that crusading should really be a poor man's movement. Like King Tafur, Francis had voluntarily renounced his wealth and joined the ranks of the poor. Like the very first Hospitalers and Templars, Francis and his disciples devoted themselves to the service of the poor, while they practiced a strict poverty themselves. Francis was simply the most recent expression of the reverence for holy poverty which had inspired the most fervent Crusades and there is no reason to suppose that he disapproved of the Crusades. Indeed there is a story that records his praise of the "holy martyrs" Roland and Oliver, who had died in Charlemagne's wars against the Saracens.[81] Like any fervent Templar, Francis dreamed of conquering "all peoples, races, tribes and tongues, all nations and men of all countries."[82] He intended his friars to do this by preaching and missionary work and he had devoted a whole chapter of his rule to the mission to Islam, but he probably saw the Crusade as having a useful role to play in this offensive. The first major Christian missionary approach to the Muslims took place in the context of a Crusade, and Francis seems to have found this quite appropriate.

Once he had been given permission for his brave peace initiative, Francis went into the enemy territory quite unarmed, but "strong in possession of the buckler of his faith," wrote James of Vitry.[83] The Muslims seized him on his way to the Sultan's tent and seem to have been rather impressed by this ragged and dirty fellow who had come on this impossibly brave mission. Provided that Francis did not insult Mohammad or Islam, al-Kamil would have had no objection to listening to him expound the gospel message, and it seems that he listened to Francis for three days and offered him precious gifts at the end of his visit. Francis naturally refused, even when the Sultan urged him to give them to the churches and the poor Christians, and he told the Sultan that God would look after the needs of the poor. When Francis left, al-Kamil is reported to have said: "Pray for me, that God may deign to show me the law and the faith that are most pleasing to him." Then he sent Francis back to the Christian camp, "with every mark of respect and in complete safety."[84] Needless to say, the Sultan was not converted, but the story does make a peaceful oasis in the story of the holy war.

The Fifth Crusade dragged on and al-Kamil was ready to make peace. Egypt was threatened with famine that year and could not withstand a long campaign, and both al-Kamil and al-Mu'azam were worried about the activities of their brother al-Ashraf in the far north. At the end of October the Sultan sent two Frankish prisoners of war to Pelagius with extraordinary generous terms: if the Crusaders would leave Egypt, he would return Jerusalem, all central Palestine and Galilee.[85] It is a sign of how very dead the lust for *jihad* was at this point. Al-Kamil saw Jerusalem purely in political terms, not as a holy city. Naturally King John of Acre urged Pelagius to accept these terms, but just as naturally Pelagius refused. At a time when Christians in Europe had begun to hound other Christians to death, it was not likely that they would make peace with the infidel. The military orders agreed with Pelagius for strategic reasons: the forts in Jerusalem and Galilee had all been dismantled and it would be impossible for the Christians to maintain them once the Crusaders had gone. The holy war was resumed and Pelagius waited confidently for the arrival of the Emperor Frederick.

Yet the Emperor never arrived. He fully intended to leave for the East but was not prepared to leave Europe until his empire was absolutely secure. Pope Honorius, who had once been his tutor, began to wonder whether this former papal client was really going to be as amenable as Innocent had hoped. Meanwhile the Crusader army was grounded in Damietta; bored Crusaders began to return home and there were bitter disputes between Pelagius and King John about the management of the campaign. In February 1220 John and his army returned to Acre and spent the rest of the year fending off Sultan al-Mu'azam, who had invaded the Christian Kingdom: the new Crusade had put an end to the peaceful coexistence of Muslims and Christians in the Middle East. In Egypt, none of the troops would fight without John, because he was the only leader whom all nationalities would obey. By July 1221 Pelagius could not wait any longer for Frederick and planned an attack on Cairo. King John arrived with troops from Acre, full of gloom but not wishing to be accused of cowardice. On July 12 the Crusaders set out with 630 ships, 5000 knights, 4000 archers and 40,000 infantrymen.[86]

The Egyptian army had come to meet the Christians but when they saw the size of their army they hastily retreated and many of the citizens tried to escape from Cairo. But al-Kamil was now very confident. Both his brothers had sent armies to help him, and they blocked the Crusaders' line of retreat to Damietta. As he watched the Crusaders march ever nearer to Cairo, the Sultan smiled to himself, hardly able to believe his luck. The Westerners did not notice that the waters of the Nile were rising. By mid-August the ground was so soggy and slippery that the Crusaders had to halt their advance and finally make a retreat. As soon as the retreat began, the Muslim soldiers demolished the dikes, troops moved to cut off the exit routes and within a few hours the Christian army was ignominiously imprisoned on an island of mud.[87] Pelagius had to sue for peace to save his army from annihilation, and naturally this time al-Kamil's terms were far less generous. The Crusaders must sign a truce for eight years and leave Egypt immediately; in return they could sail home unmolested.

The Fifth Crusade had been a humiliating failure and the prospect of the reconquest of Jerusalem seemed even further out of reach than it had thirty years earlier. In the same way the Crusade at home against the Catharists was proving ineffective: even though heretics were still burned in large numbers, the heresy continued to spread and seemed ineradicable. Indeed by making the heretics into martyrs for their cause (and in some sense for their country) the Crusaders were actually encouraging the heresy. Crusading did not seem to work anymore but this did not mean that the idea could be abandoned, because the habit was now an indelible part of the Western identity. In fact the holy war had diversified and discovered new forms and outlets. In the Middle East today, the Jewish and Islamic holy wars began as offensives against the Godless enemy, but then diversified so that today Jews are fighting holy wars against other Jews as well as against Muslim Arabs, and Muslims are fighting other devout Muslims as well as Jews and *munatiqeen*. This is precisely what happened in the Middle Ages in Europe, where a new habit of internal holy war had been created which would prove to be incurable. Nor could people abandon the conventional Crusade: after the failure of the Fifth Crusade, people looked for a scapegoat and found one ready to hand in the Emperor Frederick, who would be pressured to lead a Sixth Crusade to the Holy Land eight years later.

At the time of the Fifth Crusade a new movement toward the Muslim world had begun that at first sounds very positive. Before Francis of Assisi left Europe for Egypt, he had sent a party of Friars Minor to preach to the Muslims in Spain and Africa. After the Fifth Crusade other Franciscans went to the Holy Land to preach to the Muslims there. More encounters like the meeting between Francis and al-Kamil would probably have been a very good idea and we are so accustomed to the notion of spreading the faith by means of missionary activity that it seems incredible that nobody thought of this before. A missionary campaign which seeks to explain and share the truth sounds the obverse of the military campaign that seeks to conquer and kill. Yet in fact this peaceful project proved to be a new type of Crusade. The Franciscans went into Islamic lands not to save the souls of the Muslims but to achieve martyrdom. As soon as the first group of friars arrived in Seville, they resorted to the tactics of the Martyrs of Cordova. They tried to break into a mosque during Friday prayers, and when they were driven away they stood outside the Emir's palace and shouted abuse against Mohammad and Islam. They were not reaching out to the Muslims in peace and love but mounting an aggressive assault. The Muslim authorities were forced to arrest them, even though they were reluctant to do so. To avoid publicity, they moved the friars around from one prison to another and eventually had them deported to Morocco. Here the Franciscans went straight into a new offensive, behaving in exactly the same way, and were deported from one area to another on two more occasions by the embarrassed authorities. On one occasion the local Christian community pressured the Muslims to get rid of the friars, because they did not want to be associated with these fanatics and naturally feared that this might cause trouble for them. Finally the authorities were forced to execute the Westerners who were so flagrantly breaking the law of the land. They tortured the friars and offered them wealth and honor if they would repent of their behavior and convert to Islam. Finally they were executed.[88] When Francis heard of their "martyrdom" he is said to have cried: "Praise be to Christ! I know now that I have five Friars Minor!"[89] It seems that even though his peaceful embassy to al-Kamil had not been aggressive he did not disapprove of this other violent missionary offensive. This would prove to be the way the Franciscans would continue to preach to the Muslims. James of Vitry noticed these methods in the Holy Land:

> The Saracens listen willingly to the Friars Minor when they speak of the faith of Christ and the teaching of the Gospels. But when their words openly contradict Mohammad, who appears in their sermons as a perfidious liar, they strike them without respect, and if God did not protect them marvellously, would almost murder them and drive them from their cities.[90]

It was, therefore, wholly appropriate that the first mission to the Muslims occurred in the context of a Crusade, for missionary activity was a child of crusading and part of the war of the West against the East.

It seems that the aggression that inspired these missionaries was not always confined to a moral assault on the Muslims. Instead of seeking to save the souls of the Muslims they "preached" to, the Franciscans actually sought to compound their damnation. In 1227 a group of seven Franciscans who had preached their way into prison in Ceuta, Morocco, wrote home to say that the main object of their mission had been "the death and damnation of the infidels."[91] Jesus had said that anyone who rejected the faith would be damned: "He who believes and is baptised will be saved; he who does not believe will be condemned" (Mark 16:16). By ensuring that the Muslims were not only forced to reject the faith that was presented to them so insultingly but also to imprison, torture and kill Christ's ambassadors, the missionaries saw to it that they were damned indeed. None of the first missionaries seems to have been concerned with real conversion.

The Dominicans followed the Franciscans in preaching missions to Muslim countries, but they did not go there to seek voluntary martyrdom, did not insult Mohammad and confined themselves to preaching the word of God. Yet it seems that actually converting Muslims was not their first object. When Raymund of Peñafort, the great thirteenth-century Dominican missionary, was asked to justify his missionary initiative by churchmen in Europe, he gave five benefits that could accrue from his work. Missionaries, he said, can take care of the spiritual welfare of the knights engaged in a Crusade; they can preach to the oriental Christians; they can reform Christian apostates; they can prove to the Muslims that Christians do not worship idols and so improve their position in the Muslim world. Finally, very much at the bottom of the list and almost as an afterthought, Raymund suggests that his preaching might make a good impression on the Muslims and there just might be one or two conversions.[92] In other words, his mission was not for the Muslims but for the Christians. It is interesting that Raymund should have been asked to "justify" going into the House of Islam. Today most Christians would assume that this was a laudable enterprise but, as I shall show in the next chapter, during the late twelfth and throughout the thirteenth century Christians in Europe were being told to have no contact at all with either Jews or Muslims and this was being enshrined in rigid Church legislation. In this climate, Raymund's missionary initiative could only be viewed with suspicion because it brought him into dubious and perhaps unnecessary proximity to the infidel.

This very strange, aggressive and exclusive attitude was obviously born of the Crusades and it is therefore fitting that the most spectacular crusading venture—that of St. Francis—should have happened in the context of a military campaign against Islam. It is surely one of the ways that crusading has survived right up to the present day. We have seen that radical Egyptian Muslims call Western imperialism *al-Salibiyya*, the Crusade. They also give this name to Christian missionary work. The connection is obvious. When Europeans began their colonizing ventures during the eighteenth, nineteenth and early twentieth centuries, missionaries followed in their train and were encouraged by the colonialists, some of whom had no religious beliefs, as a valuable part of the Westernizing process. I am not decrying the work of all these missionaries, of course. Many were brave and committed men and women, but it must be said that trying to impose Western Christianity and morality on people who had quite different religious and cultural traditions was impertinent in that it often showed very little respect for local traditions. The missionaries believed that they were bringing "the truth" to these lost people; they saw *their* way as right and the religions and traditions of the people they were evangelizing as wrong. This meant that they were "saving" them. There is an arrogance in this assumption and even an aggression when one remembers the colonial context, with the Europeans' obvious contempt

for the "natives." There is in this view much of the spirit of the first
Franciscan and Dominican missionaries. European colonialists tended
to force their cultural wares on the "natives" whether they wanted
them or not, rather like the Franciscans, and were as indifferent to
their real needs as the Dominicans, seeking only to advance the cause
of their own country and its traditions. The French call the secular
version of this spreading of the good news of Western values *mission
civilisatrice* and we have seen that in the Middle East today many people
have been traumatized and put into cultural shock by this spreading
of Western "progress" among people who had venerable and distinguished civilizations of their own. The United States has taken on the
"mission" of spreading the gospel of Western culture today, and backs
it up by bribes of "aid" and "arms," rather as the religious missionaries
offered the benighted natives beads, medical aid and education. In the
West we have shown a missionary zeal to force our way of life on
other people whether they want it or not and have often shown great
insensitivity when we have done so.

The early years of the thirteenth century, therefore, reveal quite a
new trend in crusading. At a time when the conventional Crusade to
the Holy Land seemed difficult to achieve, crusading took new forms:
it was deeply bound up with many other movements and enthusiasms
that had nothing whatever to do with liberating the Holy Sepulchre
from the Muslims. It informed the struggle of poor against the rich,
as it had done from the very earliest days of the First Crusade. From
this point, it would be quite hard sometimes to distinguish a Peasants'
Revolt from a Crusade because the poor instinctively expressed their
struggle in the idiom of crusading. It inspired what might be called
the first spontaneous nationalist uprising in Europe, which took the
form of a counter-Crusade. It even informed apparently benevolent
activities like missionary work, and peace movements expressed themselves in the imagery and ideology of a Crusade. As I have already
said, this habit is still with us: we still talk about crusades for justice
or even, a supreme irony, a crusade for peace. We know intellectually
that the Crusades were ruthless and cruel activities: there is no way
that we can justify the bloodshed and intolerance that they caused.
But at another level we use the word "crusade" quite happily to describe a benevolent and noble campaign based on principle and idealism. We ought to pause and examine this habit because in itself it
could indicate that somewhere, somehow, we still endorse a crusading
spirit and that, way below the conscious rational self, there lurks a
potential Crusader in each one of us.

The Crusades of the early thirteenth century also show a new tragic intolerance of Christians against other Christians. Neither Jews nor Muslims have ever persecuted their coreligionists to this degree and they are quite understandably shocked at this Christian habit. Such persecution and intolerance were, of course, not a completely new departure. Christians had fought what they call heresy bitterly, ever since the early fourth century. Indeed, Christian discomfort about this sad trait has manifested itself in some remarkable projections and denials. Thus it is commonly believed that in the seventh century the Caliph Omar ordered the Muslims to burn down the great library of Alexandria but in fact this was one of the myths developed by Christians in the crusading period about Islam. The library was actually burned down generations earlier in the course of a violent struggle in the city between factions of warring Christians. Christians have long had a strange yearning for ideological conformity: maybe it is because the Christian creed is so complex. Jews and Muslims hold that beliefs about God are private affairs and would condemn the very concept of "heresy" as idolatry, because it raises essentially man-made beliefs to an unacceptably high level. But the commitment to intellectual conformity and uniformity has continued in the West in purely secular ways: an obvious example is McCarthy's crusade against Communism in the 1950s. This habit was burned into the Western spirit at the time of the Crusades; intolerance of other Christians reached new heights in the sack of Constantinople and the Crusade against the Cathars. Western Christendom was closing its doors to outside influence and to anything that challenged orthodoxy. From this point Westerners would develop a horror of foreign influence: they would renew themselves not by contact with other cultures but by revolutions and reformations from within. At the same time as these new Crusades against other Christians, we have seen that Muslims were beginning to retreat from their former openness and take refuge in conservatism: a process hastened by the Mongol invasions that I shall discuss in the next chapter. Similarly, the persecution of the Jews in Europe made them cut themselves off more firmly and decidedly than ever before from Gentile influence. All three faiths, therefore, which were so deeply related and had so much to offer one another, were retreating into intellectual ghettoes, into worlds hermetically sealed off from one another.

But despite this new type of crusading, the old notion of a campaign for the Holy Land was by no means dead. The last three Crusades of the thirteenth century returned to the old ideal of the recovery of the Holy Sepulchre. Yet we shall also see that because of major changes in the Middle East the old kind of Crusade no longer worked. These last Crusades to the Holy Land actually tell us more about Europe, however, and its new crusading morality. They were led by two very different men who presented Europe with a choice. Was Christendom to commit itself to the crusading spirit or would it adopt a more open attitude and reach out to Muslims and Jews?

# 1220–1291
# The End of the Crusades?

W hen the armies of the Sixth Crusade began to assemble in southern Italy in August 1227 there was a man in Europe who was a committed Christian but who also spoke fluent Arabic, corresponded with Muslim scholars and made it clear all his life that some of his best friends were Muslims. Through his Muslim friends abroad, he brought the first giraffe into Europe and sent the first polar bear into the Middle East. At a time when most people spoke at best only three languages, he spoke nine and wrote in seven. When to be a layman was, almost by definition, to be unlearned, this layman was a student of mathematics, jurisprudence, philosophy and natural history. When most Christians were encouraged to accept the "Truth" blindly, he never stopped asking difficult and disturbing questions. Yet this man was not an obscure intellectual eccentric. He was Frederick II, the Boy of Apulia, who had become the Holy Roman Emperor of the West and ruler of Sicily and Germany. His contemporaries, who had been stunned by him as soon as he appeared on the international scene, called him Stupor Mundi, the Wonder of the World.[1] It was on Frederick that all the hopes of Europe were centered in 1227 when he finally fulfilled his crusading vow and set off to the East to win back Jerusalem from his friend, the Sultan al-Kamil.

Frederick was a man born out of his time and in the wrong place. In Europe people were quite unable to understand him, because they had no category in which to place him. He seemed prodigious to his contemporaries, even monstrous. Some people saw his exceptional linguistic talent as a mark of the inspiration of the Holy Spirit, who had descended upon the apostles in tongues of fire and enabled them to speak strange languages, but others saw this gift as a mark of Satan, who had inspired the confusion of languages at the Tower of Babel.[2] Terrible stories circulated about Frederick's behavior which seemed scarcely human, let alone Christian. It was said that on one occasion, when he was having an argument with a priest about the immortality of the soul, to prove his point he had nailed one of the priest's disciples into a barrel. When the unfortunate man died, Frederick pointed out that his spirit must have died with him, because it could not have escaped from the vat. One of the most distressing aspects of this story, for a medieval, would have been the fact that Frederick could question the idea of the immortality of the soul at all, which was believed implicitly as absolute truth by the vast majority of Europeans. Frederick's insatiable curiosity was thought to be very threatening. Another story said that Frederick had once wanted to prove whether Hebrew, Greek, Latin or Arabic had been the original tongue given by God to Adam and Eve in the Garden of Eden. This was a question that would have had grave theological implications if Arabic, the sacred tongue of Islam, should have proved to be the original tongue. He had a number of children brought up in absolute solitude by nurses who were forbidden to speak to them, because he was curious to see if and when the children did speak they would use the language of their parents or the original tongue. The experiment failed because all the children died; as the contemporary historian Adam of Salimbene said, they were starved of affection.[3]

These stories may or may not have been true, but they do tell us important things about Frederick. First, he was a man who inspired these kinds of tales because he confounded basic assumptions and seemed a law unto himself. Second, although Frederick has often been hailed, quite rightly, as the first man of the Renaisssance and although his learning was astounding by the usual standards in Europe at that time, in fact he was a crude, amateur scholar. Certainly the Muslim scholars he consulted considered him so, though they were impressed by his open, inquiring mind. Third, Frederick was ready to exploit anybody. It is important not to sentimentalize his friendship with Muslims: Frederick would exploit Muslims as he would exploit anybody else. The story of his "experiment" with the children shows that his interest was entirely self-indulgent and often ruthless. But that he was able to see Muslims as normal and often admirable human beings was a great achievement, for he was living in a period of great intolerance.

For the past fifty years European Christians had been commanded by the Church to have nothing whatever to do with Muslims or Jews, the two victims of the Crusades, and legislation was made which linked the two together explicitly as a common foe. In the next chapter I shall show how important this attitude would continue to be. The Lateran Councils of 1179 and 1216 issued directives which cut people off from Muslims and Jews and forbade normal contact or coexistence. Any Christian who took service in the house of a Muslim or a Jew was to be excommunicated, as was anybody who looked after their children; anybody who traded with Muslims, who took merchandise to Islamic countries and sailed in their "piratical" ships was to be excommunicated and his property confiscated. Only missionaries, whose activities we have seen to be regarded suspiciously, were allowed to eat with Muslims and Jews. Pope Gregory IX, the cousin of Innocent III, who succeeded to the papacy in 1227, issued decretals which added some new prohibitions and reissued the old Lateran decrees. Muslims and Jews living in Christian countries were to wear distinctive clothing to distinguish them clearly from the Christian population. It was a way of isolating and stigmatizing the enemy and looked forward to the yellow star that Jews were forced to wear during the Nazi regime. On Christian holidays Muslims and Jews were not to appear in the street lest they contaminate the holy day and offend the faithful; they must not hold public office in a Christian country and Muslims were not allowed to assail the ears of the faithful by the call of the muezzin.[4]

But not everybody had succumbed to this group view. By an accident of history, Frederick had been brought up in the Mediterranean world, where a very different attitude prevailed. The merchants of Venice, Genoa and Pisa, for example, had no intention of obeying the Lateran decrees; for a long time they had been trading with Muslims and making treaties and agreements with them. In cities like Cairo, Muslims and European merchants enjoyed excellent relations to their mutual profit. Frederick had been brought up in Sicily where Muslims, Greeks, Normans and Germans lived side by side in reasonable harmony. The Norman conquerors of Sicily had actually encouraged the Muslims and made great use of their superior intellectual talents. Many Muslims held important positions at court. The court Arabs were allowed to pray in the direction of Mecca at the proper times and keep the Ramadan fast, even though the Normans had destroyed the most important mosque in Palermo. The policy had been to make war against Islam but to live in peace with Muslims. Muslim presence naturally meant that many scholars had come to Sicily during the late twelfth century and a good deal of useful translation work had been done. Frederick had grown up in a cosmopolitan atmosphere, therefore, which made it impossible for him to believe in only one point of view. Most royal children in Europe had a strictly monastic education, but Frederick was left very much to his own devices. Wandering around Palermo as a child, he came into contact with Arab and Byzantine scholars, who opened his naturally inquiring mind to ideas and concepts that were quite alien to the narrow scholastic intellectual world of the rest of Europe. Frederick was always convinced that ultimately Christianity was the true religion, but that did not mean that he hated the Muslims or the Byzantines nor did he consider them infidels and heretics. When he had left Sicily in 1212 for Germany, he encountered an intolerance and ignorance there that were quite alien to him and which he would despise all his life. This would make him feel more at home in the Muslim East than in Christendom, because the Muslims valued learning and scientific inquiry as he did, and his difference from the vast majority of his fellow Christians in Europe would naturally increase his sense of being specially singled out by God.

But there were signs that paranoid intolerance was about to take hold of Sicily. Toward the end of the twelfth century the great Arab traveler Ibn Jubayr had noticed that, although Muslims were very successful in the court of Palermo, they seemed frightened and uneasy.[5] They had good reason. At the beginning of the thirteenth century the Sicilian population declared open war on the Muslims: they expelled them from the cities and settlements, and then drove them from the fertile plains into the mountains where they lived as virtual outlaws.[6] When Frederick returned to Sicily from Germany in 1221, he knew that he had to deal with these enemies of the state, who were now waging guerrilla warfare from their mountain strongholds, and his solution was brilliant but callous. Frederick wanted the Muslims out of Sicily but he also wanted to use them for his own purposes, so he would not wage a war of extermination against them, although in the end that was what his policy would ultimately mean for the Arabs of Sicily. He began to force them down from the mountains, and by 1223 he wrote that most of the Muslims of Sicily had been forced into internment camps on the plains,[7] though in fact the fighting continued until 1245. From the camps the Muslims were shipped across to the mainland and were interned in the old fortress city of Lucera in Apulia. Here they were allowed to build their own independent city-state. They had their own amir, their own qadis, sheikhs and imams. They built mosques and the muezzin sounded loudly and freely. Within the city, Frederick built a scientific institute for the study of all branches of speculative science, and he made the Muslims of Lucera his favored court officials. "Most of his officials and courtiers were Muslims," wrote the Arab historian Jamal ad-Din Ibn Wasil, "and in his camp the call to prayer and even the canonic prayers themselves were openly heard."[8] The Arabs themselves were fanatically loyal to Frederick and called him their sultan.

Lucera and Frederick's private Muslim army were a scandal in Europe; they seemed a blot of godlessness on the face of Christendom. Yet though Frederick certainly enjoyed Lucera and his Arab friends there, this was a policy not of toleration but of exploitation. Lucera was certainly a city where Islam was tolerated and protected: Frederick would not allow papal missionaries there to harass the Muslims. But Lucera was also a refugee camp and a reservation. The Muslims *had* to live there and had no choice but to be loyal to Frederick because he was their only protector. Events proved that, by concentrating his Muslims in one place, Frederick had taken the first step to their final extermination.[9] They were safe during his reign and during the reign of his son Manfred, but when his territories were taken over by the French King Charles of Anjou at the end of the century they did not survive. When Charles spoke of Lucera, he used the imagery that we have seen used in our own day to describe an intolerable alien presence: it was "a nest of pestilence . . . lurid in pollution . . . the stubborn plague and filthy infection of Apulia."[10] In 1301 the French attacked the city, massacred its Muslim inhabitants, turned the mosque into a church and renamed Lucera the City of St. Mary.

Most people found Frederick's association with Muslims blasphemous and disturbing, but others found this breaking of a strong taboo fascinating and even liberating. Frederick inspired a great devotion all over Europe in people who felt that all was not well there. The establishment of Muslim Lucera and the blasphemous tales of his intellectual and scientific experiments made him a living legend and put him above ordinary mortals in the imagination of many people. But nothing excited such awe and fascination as the great processions of his imperial court that followed Frederick around Europe as he traveled from one of his castles to another. Nobody in Europe had ever seen anything like this unbelievably opulent and exotic spectacle. It was far more like the cortege of the oriental caliphs and sultans, who were denounced as *munafiqeen* by devout Muslims because of their un-Islamic splendor. Poets and chroniclers in Europe wrote of these processions in a state of stupefaction, unable to believe their eyes. First there was Frederick's famous menagerie, a collection of strange and exotic beasts that always traveled with him. This was not just a publicity stunt: Frederick was passionately interested in natural history and indeed once wrote a book on the Arabic sport of falconry. Lynxes, leopards and lions were borne through the streets in gilded cages or were led by slaves on silken ropes. Then came the famous giraffe, which must have been a shocking sight to people who had never conceived of such a peculiar animal. Brunetto Latini, the Florentine politician and man of learning, wrote in astonishment of the huge elephant that he saw picking up an ass in its trunk and dashing it to pieces.[11] People stared in fascination at this monstrous beast, waiting for its bones to change to ivory before their very eyes.[12] This spectacular and, perhaps, frightening procession of animals naturally stirred the imagination of the awed crowds. Some people said that these were the strange beasts that were prophesied to accompany Antichrist, for many of his contemporaries thought that Frederick was a man of such evil that he must be Antichrist. It seemed the only explanation for this extraordinary man. But other people claimed that these beasts represented the first sign of the messianic era, foretold by the prophet Isaiah when all manner of strange animals would live together in peace, the wolf lying next to the kid.[13] In this view, Frederick was a Messiah figure and a savior. He seemed lifted above the common human lot onto a plane between God and man. People also convinced themselves that he must be the Last Emperor, who would arrive at the End of Days and establish God's Kingdom on earth. When Frederick announced his intention of going to Jerusalem in 1227, it is easy to imagine the excitement that must have prevailed. His presence in Jerusalem, be he Messiah or Antichrist, would surely be an event of profound significance for the whole world.

There was a second aspect of these imperial processions that contributed to Frederick's myth. The elephant had come to Frederick as a gift from the Sultan al-Kamil and indeed the whole court had an oriental appearance. This brazen display of coexistence with the infidel was disturbing but also obscurely thrilling to many people because it flirted with the forbidden. In particular the veiled Muslim girls aroused avid speculation. Did Frederick keep a harem?[14] The popes certainly believed that he did and so did many of his supporters. Frederick, on the other hand, always insisted that these girls were just kept in the court because they worked as domestic slaves; their skills in needlework or dancing and singing were useful and entertaining, in the same way as the rope dancers, jugglers and snake charmers who were also part of the court. The fact that nobody ever knew for certain whether this harem existed made the idea of it even more tantalizing. Other members of the household were eunuchs and Arab male slaves, exquisitely and splendidly dressed, leading camels, laden with treasures and riches. This was an emperor whom many Europeans could be proud of. At last they had a ruler who was the equal of the sophisticated Muslim rulers or of the Greek Byzantine emperors, who had scorned European Christians for so long. The procession was also a sign that Islam could be dealt with and controlled. These Muslims were Frederick's slaves and his Arab army was under his control. At a time when the Muslims seemed frighteningly powerful, Frederick's court seemed somehow reassuring to his supporters.

It was also true, as we have seen, that many people at this time were far from happy with Innocent III's powerful Church, and those who did not want to go so far as to join one of the heretical sects that were springing up at that time hailed Frederick with enthusiasm because he was offering an alternative. Innocent III had taught that the fullness of power (*plenitudo potestatis*) resided in the papacy and that kings and emperors received their power from God through the mediation of the Pope. That was the meaning of the symbolic imperial coronation, when the Pope or his delegate placed the crown on the head of the new Holy Roman Emperor. This meant that the Pope was the temporal and spiritual head of Christendom and could remove a ruler from power if that king or emperor behaved in a way that was displeasing or detrimental to the Church. Frederick would have none of this. We have seen that he believed that he had a special divine mission; that meant that he received his power straight from God and certainly did not need the mediation of the Church. He had made this clear at his coronation, even though he had been the ward of Innocent III. It will be remembered that he caused great excitement in 1215 when, after receiving the crown, he had unexpectedly taken the Cross and summoned a new Crusade. This was actually a direct challenge to Innocent, because hitherto the only people who could officially summon a Crusade were the popes, but Frederick had made his Crusade not only a lay enterprise but a lay initiative. Throughout his life he continued to challenge the Pope and many people all over Europe supported Frederick, however awesome and bewildering his behavior. Pope Honorius had already found that he could not control the young Emperor and one of the most flagrant signs of Frederick's cool refusal to obey the Church was that the Pope could not force Frederick to fulfill his crusading vow and join the Fifth Crusade. When Honorius died in 1227 he was succeeded by Pope Gregory IX, who would issue the legislation ostracizing Muslims and Jews. Clearly he would have found Frederick's consorting with Muslims frankly blasphemous. He was very much of the same mind as his cousin Innocent III, and was determined to quash Frederick's claim to be the temporal head of Christendom, leaving the Pope as ruler only in spiritual affairs.[15] He decided to use Frederick's unfulfilled Crusader vow as a weapon and

said that if the Emperor did not take an army to the Holy Land
forthwith he would be excommunicated and this meant that his subjects could withdraw their allegiance from him.

In fact Frederick was himself eager to go to the East, for his own
reasons. He wanted to be the new Alexander the Great, who had made
himself lord of the world by gaining an empire in the East and the
West. It was for this that he had been called by God, he believed.[16]
This motive marks Frederick out at once from previous Crusaders,
because there was not a shred of the usual religious desire to liberate
Jerusalem. Even as secular a Crusader as Richard the Lionheart had
been convinced that Jerusalem belonged by right to the Christians,
but Frederick did not see Muslim presence in the Holy City as contaminating. His desire to go to the East was simply part of his own,
divinely inspired career. It must be remembered that, if his contemporaries could only explain Frederick in terms that were larger than
life, it was equally difficult for Frederick to explain to himself why he
was so very different from anyone else in Europe: his isolation led
him to see himself as God's chosen one.

Frederick had already been making preparations for his Crusade for
some time. He had rewritten the constitutions of the Teutonic
Knights, the German military order founded by Barbarossa.[17] Where
other military orders were directly dependent upon the Pope, the
Teutonic Knights were now dependent only upon the Emperor, as
befitted Frederick's imperial theory. In 1226 he sent them into pagan
Prussia to conquer it for Christendom and wrote a constitution that
would put the country under the direct control of the knights and
hence of the Emperor. This again was a direct challenge to the Pope,
who was planning a papal state in Prussia and to this end had sent
the Cistercians to make settlements there for some years.[18] Frederick's
Crusade, manned by his Teutonic Knights, would be an Emperor's
Crusade, not a papal Crusade.

The year before, Frederick had made another move that naturally
thrilled crusading Europe and that gave him once again a legendary
aura. He had married Princess Yolanda, the heiress to the throne of
Acre and Jerusalem. The fate of this poor sixteen-year-old girl shows
Frederick's cool, ruthless cruelty. Yolanda left Syria for the strange
world of the West, weeping bitterly, and was married to her frightening husband at Brindisi on November 9, 1225. On the wedding
night Frederick seduced Yolanda's cousin, and eventually sent the girl
off to Palermo, where she lived pining for her home in the East until
on November 25, 1228 (while Frederick was in the East), she gave
birth to a son, Conrad, who became heir to the throne of Jerusalem

and the light of his father's life. Having done her duty, Yolanda died six days after the birth. Most people in Europe, however, would have shed few tears for Yolanda, who, as a member of the despised caste of women, did not merit much attention. But the marriage itself greatly enhanced Frederick's status.[19] When he went to the East, he would go as the King of Jerusalem, so many people believed that this proved he was the long-awaited Last Emperor. But Frederick's conviction of his divine vocation did not blind him to practical reality: he knew that no Crusade had been successful since 1099 and that his chances of conquering Jerusalem militarily were slim. Then, however, shortly after his marriage to Yolanda it appeared that there was another way he could proceed.

During the Fifth Crusade the Sultan al-Kamil had heard a lot of talk about the powerful Emperor from the West who was hourly expected to arrive in Egypt, and naturally he was anxious to know how serious a threat Frederick presented. The reports he was getting back from his informants in Sicily seemed astonishing: here was a Christian Emperor who allowed the muezzin to summon Muslims to prayer, whose most powerful officers and court officials were Muslims, and who spoke fluent Arabic. When he heard of Frederick's marriage to Yolanda, he felt that it was time to look into the matter more closely and he sent the learned Emir Fakhr ad-Din al-Shaykh to Palermo. The Emir reported back in astonishment that all the rumors were true. Frederick spoke Arabic fluently, his courtiers and bodyguards were all Arabs, and the muezzin sounded freely in Palermo. The Emperor was full of contempt for the barbarous Europeans, especially for the Pope of Rome. This sounded very reassuring and al-Kamil began to correspond with Frederick. They discussed Aristotle, jurisprudence, the immortality of the soul and astronomy, and the Sultan sent animals as gifts for the menagerie. It transpired that neither Frederick nor the Sultan had any time for the useless and fanatical practice of the holy war and in 1227 the Sultan suggested that Frederick come out to the East. He had recently quarreled with his brother al-Mu'azam, ruler of Damascus and Jerusalem, and told Frederick that he would be very happy to help him conquer Jerusalem from his brother. A friendly buffer state between al-Kamil's Egypt and al-Mu'azam's Syria seemed highly desirable. Al-Kamil had no passionate feelings about the Holy City, unlike his uncle Saladin. Provided that it did not affect public opinion, al-Quds was only of military or political importance.[20] This was excellent news to Frederick, who had just been threatened by Gregory with excommunication for failing to fulfill his crusading vow. The conquest of Jerusalem would be a pure formality, he thought, but his coronation as King of Jerusalem would give him a prestige in the West that would greatly enhance his position against the Pope.

These arrangements were kept a closely guarded secret, of course, and when the crusading army gathered together in August it was assumed that this was a perfectly conventional Crusade. Of course when people saw that Frederick was taking some of his Muslim soldiers from Lucera to fight alongside his Teutonic Knights, many people—clerics and laymen—were scandalized and it increased their fear that Frederick must be Antichrist: there were ancient prophecies which said that the Muslims would be the attendants of Antichrist when he enthroned himself in Jerusalem. It also seemed to make a mockery out of the whole idea of a Crusade and was yet another example of Frederick's prodigious behavior that trod mercilessly on people's most cherished beliefs and prejudices.

The Crusade set sail with 3000 knights and 10,000 pilgrims but the heat and the press of crowds led to an outbreak of malaria. Frederick himself became ill and was forced to disembark at Otranto, while the rest of the Crusade sailed on to Acre without him. Pope Gregory was furious when he heard that Frederick had left the Crusade and was convinced that this illness was simply a ruse and another delaying tactic. He promptly excommunicated Frederick and prepared to invade his lands in the south of Italy in a "Crusade"—a disgraceful debasement of the ideal and one which put the people of southern Italy firmly behind Frederick. Frederick, however, remained untroubled. He assumed that the excommunication was just a routine matter and apologized humbly, offering to do penance. But Gregory was determined to press his advantage. He would lift the ban of excommunication only if Frederick accepted him as overlord of Sicily and southern Italy. This Frederick naturally refused to consider, but he was in a difficult dilemma. As an excommunicate, he was technically forbidden to go on a Crusade, but if he delayed any longer he would look absurd and lose face. He decided to put Gregory very subtly in the wrong and wrote a calm and dignified circular letter to the rulers of Christendom, apologizing for the delay and hinting—with the greatest possible respect—that Gregory was holding up the Crusade by refusing to lift the ban of excommunication simply to further his own territorial ambitions. It was imperative, he concluded, that he join his army in Acre and not hold up the work of God, so he would set sail immediately, trusting confidently that the Pope would lift the ban. Early in 1228 he set sail from Brindisi, putting Gregory in a very embarrassing position. "We have just left Brindisi for Syria," he wrote piously to the kings of Europe, "and are speeding along before a favourable wind with Christ for our leader."[21] Gregory reacted furiously by excommunicating the Emperor again—a pointless act, because it was like sentencing a man to death twice. He also actually invaded his Italian lands, a move which aroused a great deal of support for Frederick all over Europe, even though he was in the unique and grotesque position of leading a Crusade as an excommunicate.

When he arrived in Acre, Frederick expected the recovery of Jerusalem to be a mere formality, but the situation had changed since he had made his arrangement with Sultan al-Kamil, who was now very embarrassed by Frederick's arrival. While Frederick had been ill, al-Mu'azam had died, leaving Damascus to his very young and inexperienced son al-Nasir. It now looked as though al-Kamil would be able to conquer the whole of Palestine and Syria without making an unpopular treaty that would give al-Quds back to the Christians. But he was a man of honor and continued to feel obliged to keep his word to Frederick if he possibly could. Frederick, for his part, was desperate. His lands at home were in danger and he badly needed the coup of recovering Jerusalem to give him popular support in his struggle with the Pope. But he had arrived in Palestine with a modest army that was quite insufficient to liberate Jerusalem by force of arms. "I am your friend," he wrote to al-Kamil. "It was you who urged me to make this trip. The Pope and all the kings of the West now know of my mission. If I return empty-handed, I will lose much prestige."[22] It was a very frank expression of Frederick's uniquely selfish reasons for wanting to conquer Jerusalem.

The Sultan, however, was touched by Frederick's letter and realized the justice of Frederick's claim upon him. He sent Fakhr ad-Din to the Emperor with gifts and a message: he too had to take account of public opinion, he explained. To give up Jerusalem without a fight would be politically dangerous, because of the devotion the Muslims felt for the Holy City.[23] But he did not want to fight a wasteful war with his friend, which in terms of loss of life would be damaging to both of them and would delay his own conquest of his nephew al-Nasir's territory. Like Frederick, al-Kamil had his own selfish and entirely unreligious reasons for wanting to make a settlement. Fakhr ad-Din hinted that if it could be made to appear that a treaty concerning Jerusalem would stave off a bloody war between Christians and Muslims, that might solve everybody's problems. Frederick smiled and took the hint, thanking his friend for the good advice.[24] At the end of November 1228 he and the Christian army of Acre marched down the coast toward Jaffa. It was not a very threatening force and the army was ludicrously vulnerable. Because Frederick had been excommunicated, the Templars of Acre could not ride with him, so they took a parallel route: they were not really following Frederick, they just happened to be riding in the same direction. Al-Kamil, however, played his part with great conviction and warned the Muslims to prepare for a long and terrible war with the Christians. When, therefore, Frederick asked the Sultan for peace talks, al-Kamil was naturally bound by the principles of the Koran to negotiate for peace, if that was possible. Negotiations began in strict privacy, a privacy which was highly offensive to the Franks of Acre because they felt that Frederick should consult them instead of autocratically acting on his own initiative. Frederick and Fakhr ad-Din took no notice of this Christian objection and worked out the terms of a treaty, which they signed on February 29, 1229.

The treaty must be one of the most extraordinary diplomatic achievements of all time. Without fighting a single Muslim, Frederick had managed to win back Jerusalem; by means of peaceful cooperation he had achieved what no other Western Crusader had managed with mighty armies. There would be a truce between Muslims and Christians for ten years and the Christians would take back Jerusalem, Bethlehem and Nazareth, together with the western part of Galilee that adjoined Acre. The Muslims would evacuate Jerusalem, but they would keep the Dome of the Rock and al-Aqsa and a small group of imams and ulema would remain there. Muslims would be able to pray at these shrines and visit the city as unarmed pilgrims.[25] Frederick and al-Kamil were offering the solution of peaceful coexistence. Instead of fighting a series of pointless, destructive wars, Christians and Muslims should share the Holy City. Yet the howl of protest on both sides showed that they had gone to the limits of what was possible, as we have found in our own day. The Franks of Acre had not wanted a holy war with the Muslims at the time of the Fifth Crusade and had learned to form normal relations with their Muslim neighbors in secular matters. But once they were within reach of the Holy City, old, intolerant mechanisms at once went to work. The idea of a Christian monarch on a Crusade making friends with Muslims—and indeed feeling more obviously at home with them than with his own coreligionists—and allowing the Muslim filth to pollute the Holy City with their presence seemed an obscenity. In vain did the master of the Teutonic Knights point out that the Muslims who remained behind were a few old men who were closely surrounded by the imperial guard. The Franks replied that it was abominable that a holy Christian shrine should be contaminated by a pagan presence. Nobody seemed to understand that the two mosques had never had any Christian significance. It was generally believed that the Dome of the Rock was the old Jewish Temple, where Jesus had been presented to God and blessed by Simeon and where he had taught every day during the last week of his life. When the Christians had owned Jerusalem, the mosque had been a church called the Temple of the Lord, and had been the seat of a Christian patriarch. Now it was the seat of Mohammad, and Christian ears would have to listen to the sound of the muezzin and to the chanting of Muslim prayers without being able to object.[26] Muslims and Christians might be able to live together anywhere else and make compromises about any other matter, but not about the Holy City.

Al-Kamil had an even more difficult time. As soon as the treaty was announced, says Ibn Wasil, "the lands of Islam were swept by a veritable storm."[27] The people poured onto the streets in Baghdad, Mosul and Aleppo and at meetings in the mosques denounced al-Kamil as a traitor to Islam. The Sultan explained to the people that this was only a temporary measure. All they had given to the Franks were "some churches and some ruined houses" but the mosques remained in Muslim hands. Once he had sorted out the political situation in Palestine and Syria, he could easily "purify Jerusalem of the Franks and chase them out."[28] These rational justifications were of no avail and in Damascus al-Kamil's nephew and rival al-Nasir made political capital out of the general dismay and ordered Sheikh Sibt al-Jauzi to preach a sermon in the Great Mosque lamenting the loss of Jerusalem. The whole population of the city crammed into the mosque and the crowd wept and groaned aloud. "On that day one saw nothing but weeping men and women,"[29] wrote Ibn Wasil. In his prolix history *Mir'at azZaman* (*The Mirror of the Times*), Sheikh al-Jauzi wrote that his sermon dwelled on the grief and shame that al-Kamil had inflicted on the Muslim people: "O shame upon the Muslim rulers!" he cried, as the sobbing in the mosque rose to a crescendo. "At such an event tears fall, hearts break with sighs, grief rises on high!"[30] Some forty years earlier, Richard and al-Adil had been able to sit down together to negotiate and both had been honored by their contemporaries. Saladin had not been castigated for signing a treaty with Richard because that treaty had not sullied the integrity of al-Quds. It seems that once the habit of the holy war has been established it is impossible for either side to make any concession at all about a holy city or a holy land. That is a sobering thought for us today.

Undismayed by these lamentations, Frederick marched to Jerusalem for his coronation, accompanied by the Teutonic Knights and the largely Arab imperial guard. More absurdities ensued. The Bishop of

Caesarea was horrified that Jerusalem should open its gates to an excommunicate emperor, so he rushed there in Frederick's wake and put the holiest city in the world under an interdict. Frederick marched straight to the Holy Sepulchre Church and, because no priest or prelate would crown him, strode to the high altar, seized the crown and placed it on his own head.[31] It was a superb affirmation of his position: he received his power from God and did not need the mediation of the Church. But the coronation of a Western emperor in Jerusalem was an event that was surrounded with a nimbus of hopes, fears and yearnings. *Was* Frederick really the Last Emperor and had he succeeded in establishing the Kingdom of God, as he claimed when he cried: "Behold, now is the day of salvation!"[32] in his coronation speech? Or was Frederick the Antichrist, who had allowed Islam, the abomination of desolation, to establish itself in the Temple and who had made a mockery of the Pope of Rome? Nobody could decide.

Muslims were just as puzzled by Frederick as Christians were and this again tells us something important about the holy-war mentality. Tolerance is not prized or appreciated, even if this means the enemy treating the true religion with respect. After the coronation, Frederick went to the Temple Mount to visit the Muslim shrines, an event that was as shocking to the sensibilities of *both* sides as if President Sadat had prayed at the Wailing Wall during his visit to Jerusalem, or if Prime Minister Begin had joined him in prayer at al-Aqsa. Frederick seemed to feel no tension at all and assumed that these Muslims were as warmly disposed to him as his friends Fakhr ad-Din or the Luceran Muslims. He jested with them in Arabic and spent a long time admiring the mosques, being particularly delighted with the pulpit in the Dome of the Rock, which he climbed to the very top. When he came down, he affectionately took the hand of Shams al-Din, the Qadi of Nablus, who was acting as the official guide, and walked with him toward al-Aqsa. When he saw a priest entering the mosque with a New Testament, Frederick beat him up: "By God, if one of you dares to step in here again without permission, I will pluck out his eyes!"[33] That night the Qadi had ordered the muezzin to be silent as a mark of respect for the Christian Emperor, and Frederick was bitterly disappointed. The only reason he had wanted to sleep in Jerusalem, he said sadly the next morning, was to hear the muezzin in the Holy City.[34] This was neither appreciated nor understood by the Muslims. In a society in the throes of a holy war, toleration is not respected. Sheikh Ibn al-Jauzi, who had preached the inflammatory sermon in Damascus and who deeply disapproved of the treaty, had a very low opinion of Frederick during this visit. He was red-faced and undistinguished to look at, he wrote disdainfully. "Had he been a slave he would not have been worth 200 *dirham*."[35] The only way that the Sheikh could explain his attitude was by deciding that he was a cynic: "his Christianity was merely a game to him."[36] A secularly minded political Muslim like al-Kamil could appreciate an exchange of views and could respect and like Frederick. But these Muslim clergymen on the Temple Mount, whose lives were dominated by religion in the Holy City liberated by Saladin, could find toleration only incompatible with true religion. The question of Jerusalem was such a sensitive religious issue that on both sides most Christians and Muslims believed that their religious integrity demanded an absolute rejection of the enemy, who became the "other."

Frederick and al-Kamil had offered the Franks in Palestine their last chance; but on neither side was there any real will to peace, once the identity of Jerusalem was in question, an issue made fraught by one hundred and forty years of holy war. Where secular interests could unite Muslims and Christians, religious obsessions convinced both sides that it was impossible for them to share a society. Like President Sadat in our own day, Frederick learned how dangerous it was to make peace with the enemy and to meddle with religious issues. While he was making a private visit to the Jordan Valley, the Templars contacted al-Kamil, told him that the Emperor would be unguarded and suggested that he have him assassinated. Al-Kamil was absolutely disgusted and warned Frederick, who decided that he should go home as soon as possible. He returned to Acre and tried to leave the city early in the morning before anybody was about. But the butchers were already in the market cleaning the meat and they followed the Emperor down to the harbor, pelting him with entrails and excrement.[37] The peace treaty that he had made had revived the old religious chauvinism that had helped to destroy the Kingdom of Jerusalem in 1187. This would prove suicidal, and when Frederick sailed away from the Holy Land, rejected and covered in filth, the fall of the Kingdom of Acre was only a matter of time.

Yet Frederick was not rejected by everybody in Europe, even though he remained a deeply controversial figure until he died in 1250 at the age of fifty-seven. To his supporters, his coronation in Jerusalem naturally added to his glamour, even though Frederick never returned to the East, and when his son Conrad came of age he preferred to stay and rule under his father in Germany. Frederick managed to sort out his difficulties with Pope Gregory when he returned to Europe, and signed the Treaty of San Germano with him in 1230. But he continued to provide an alternative to papal Europe and battled with the popes for the secular leadership. He was seen by discontented Christians who hated the popes as a liberator and their champion against Rome, which was unnaturally refusing to admit the supremacy of this new Caesar. His struggle with the popes assumed almost cosmic proportions, and he was hailed by prophetic poets as an apocalyptic figure:

> Fate is still as the night. There are portents and wars
> In the course of the stars, and the birds in their flight.
> I am Frederick, the Hammer, the Doom of the World.
> Rome, tottering long since, to confusion is hurled,
> Shall shiver to atoms and never again be Lord of the World.[38]

The passion that Frederick inspired meant that, even though he fulfilled none of these hopes, shortly after his death in 1250 a belief developed that he would return and save the world. He would be a Christian Messiah, who would fight in the name of the poor, cast the mighty from their thrones and overthrow the Pope and the rich clergy who were a scandal to Christendom, because they oppressed poor Christians. People in the Holy Roman Empire prayed to him after his death as though he were indeed an almost divine figure: "Our forefathers looked no more eagerly for the coming of Christ than we do for thine," wrote a governor whose troops were in danger. "Come to free and to rejoice us. Show us thy countenance and we shall find salvation!"[39] Frederick had stirred the imagination of Europe so deeply that the belief in his Second Coming became very popular among the disenchanted people in Europe, who wanted a different kind of Christian identity. They made him the symbol of their own longings and, inevitably, produced a highly idealized portrait of this difficult and frequently cruel man.[40] Frederick had been as ready to exploit the poor as he was everybody else and would have put down any revolution in his own territory very brutally. But to his devotees he became the champion of the poor and in the next chapter I shall show that this belief in the Second Coming of Frederick was one of the ways that crusading was kept alive long after Crusades had stopped going to the Holy Land; it produced ideas of which Frederick would not have approved, but which had sinister repercussions in the twentieth century.

It is important not to idealize and sentimentalize Frederick, as his supporters did. But it is important, as we leave him, to notice that he offered an alternative that could have involved more than throwing off papal and Church supremacy in Europe. He showed that it was possible to respect and live with Muslims. Admittedly he was willing to exploit them when it suited him, but while Europe was grimly shunning all contact with Islam, Frederick saw Muslims as ordinary human beings with whom he frequently felt more at home than with his narrow-minded, fanatical fellow Christians back home. This was not because he was a freethinker. Frederick was a convinced Christian, and when he heard of al-Kamil's death in 1238 he mourned that his friend had never been converted to the true faith. He scoffed at religious superstition, but as a despot he would not allow heresy in his empire and persecuted heretics fiercely for their heterodox beliefs.[41] He understood the relation between heresy and revolution very well. But he could see the nobility and beauty of Islam and had no time at all for the absurd fantasies of "Mohammadanism" that were believed implicitly by his contemporaries. Neither was he an anti-Semite. Frederick once wanted to carry out a survey to prove that the anti-Semitic myths of cannibalism, the blood libel, ritual murder and the like were all false. He thought that Jews who had converted to Christianity should be questioned about these matters. They would have no reason to lie, because they had now abjured Judaism, and the myths would be scotched once and for all.[42] Frederick was as cruel as the popes and their crusading Church, but at least he was free of the terror that made Europeans conceive of Muslims and Jews as the enemies of God. Had this view prevailed in the West and the cold light of rationality been allowed to fall on the emotional mythologies surrounding Jews and Muslims, much tragedy might have been spared, not only in the Middle Ages but also today, as I want to argue in the following chapter.

But by this time most people were already staunchly committed to a deep loathing of both Jews and Muslims, and Frederick's extraordinary Crusade filled the popes and their supporters, who constituted the majority, with disgust. Frederick had been regarded as Antichrist for years, but his contact and treaty with Muslims gave a new force to this belief. He was now surrounded with much of the aura of horror that surrounded "Mohammadans." In 1239 Pope Gregory wrote to the Archbishop of Canterbury, quoting Revelation: "A beast arose out of the sea, filled with the names of blasphemy . . . it opened its mouth to utter blasphemies against God." This specter of evil lurking in the depths of the Christian subconscious which would emerge and destroy the world was now seen to be Frederick.[43] Matthew Paris, who had once been the English secretary of Eleanor of Aquitaine, wrote that Frederick felt closer to Islam than to Christianity. He wrote in horror of Lucera, of Frederick's "harem," and in 1247 wrote that he had made a treaty with the Sultan, who was his close friend, "to the confusion of all Christendom."[44] This was not true of course but people were not ready for Frederick's vision of coexistence with Islam.

They were already irrationally convinced that Islam was poised ready to wipe out Christian Europe.

In the years that followed his death Frederick's supporters became heretics and rebels, but his enemies became the establishment and intolerance of Muslims became an indelible habit in Europe. More scholars wrote about Islam and the Prophet Mohammad during the thirteenth century, which drove this hatred home. They built on the work of the twelfth-century Cluniac authors and Peter the Venerable, to produce ideas that would be considered self-evident facts well into the nineteenth century and which many people in the West would not find strange today. They claimed to be accurate and authoritative experts on Islam. Thus the thirteenth-century Spanish scholar Mark of Toledo produced a translation of the Koran that was indeed a considerable improvement on the work of Robert of Ketton. Other scholars, like Roderick of Toledo, who wrote *Historia Arabum* and the *Cronica de Espagna*, and the Dominican Ramon Marti, who wrote the *Fourfold Condemnation*, also claimed to be serious, objective works of scholarship. But the title of Ramon Marti's work shows their attitude: they were not writing to understand but to condemn.[45] They wanted to induce a certain emotional response in their readers and create a state of mind which would lead Christians to see Islam as an absolute evil and an unmanageable danger.

These new works on the religion that they insisted on calling "Mohammadanism" repeated all the old myths and added some of their own. They often relied on Christian and Muslim legends which bathed the Prophet and his religion in a bizarre and disreputable light. The picture of Islam that they created bore no relation to the reality but was a purely Western fantasy, which had already acquired the status of absolute truth. Thus at the end of the century the Dominican scholar Riccoldo da Monte Croce traveled in Muslim countries and was impressed and edified by the devotion and sincerity with which Muslims prayed and conducted their lives. They put Christians to shame, he wrote. But when he came to write his *Disputatio contra Saracenos et Alchoranum*,[46] he simply repeated the old myths recounted by Ramon Marti years earlier. The Christian image of Islam had an authority that easily overcame any objective contact with real Muslims. Riccoldo's absurdly prejudiced and inaccurate account of Islam would be used and implicitly believed by Western scholars until the very end of the seventeenth century.

The Christian scholars were at a loss to understand how Mohammad had managed to inspire such a loyal following in the Arab world, and so they presented him as an impostor or a fraudulent magician, who concocted false "miracles" that took in the simple-minded Arabs. Thus there was a story about the Koran miraculously appearing between the horns of an ox or a cow, straight from heaven. Again, Mohammad was said to have trained a dove to sit on his shoulder and pick peas from his ear. To his poor deluded countrymen, it looked as though the dove was whispering in his ear and they thought that the dove was the Holy Ghost. The scholars explained Mohammad's ecstasies during his revelations by claiming that he was an epileptic, which was at that time tantamount to saying that he was possessed by the Devil. He was also presented as a sexually obsessed pervert who attracted his followers into a religious cult that pandered to man's basest instincts.[47] The Muslim practice of polygamy was held to be purely bestial and was said to have reduced all Muslims to the level of animals,[48] and the Koranic description of paradise as a place of sensual delights was claimed to prove definitively that the religion was a cult of licensed self-indulgence.[49] It was by now implicitly believed to be an absolute truth that Mohammad had set himself up as a prophet in order to conquer the world and that most of his closest friends and followers had known that he was an impostor but had kept quiet about it because of their own base ambition.[50] This meant therefore that every Muslim was essentially a hypocritical, untrustworthy aggressor and sexual pervert, and somebody like Frederick who had serious and friendly dealings with them was tainted by the same evil and suspected of the ultimate betrayal.

These new critics of Islam simply could not break free from their Christian limitations and view the religion objectively. They could not see, for example, that it would be very easy for somebody who was anti-Christian to see Jesus as an impostor and to view his miracles as fakes. They could not see that to accuse "Mohammadanism" of being essentially violent and aggressive laid *Christians* open to a charge of hypocrisy and bad faith during the period of the Crusades. The thirteenth-century scholars were quite unable to see Islam outside the Western Christian context. They were still convinced, for example, that Mohammad was a Christian heretic who had founded a new Christian sect. They recounted a legend of a heretic called Sergius, who had fled orthodox Rome in the early years of the seventh century and had taken refuge in the Arabian desert. There he had met Mohammad, instructed him in his faith and coached him to be a prophet.[51] In this view, pre-Islamic Arabia was not a place in the Middle East with its own problems and preoccupations. In this imaginary geography, the Arabian Peninsula was seen as a region in the outskirts of the *Christian* world of Europe and the haunt of Christian schismatics and heretics who had to flee from the center of Christendom. So immersed were these scholars in Christian history that they were compelled to see Mohammad as a part of this history. They knew about the great heresies that had flourished in the Eastern empire in places like Alexandria and Ephesus. They had met the descendants of some of these heretics in the Middle East. From the third to the fifth centuries the orthodox Church had been involved in a series of bitter political and theological disputes with the Arians, the Monophysites, the Monothelites and the Nestorians, and when scholars encountered Islam, whose teaching about Jesus, for example, was not dissimilar to that of a heretic like Arius, they assumed that it was the last of these heresies.[52] They called it after its founder, just as they had in the case of Arianism, and ignored the name that Mohammad and Muslims used. Indeed, even though Muslims find it offensive, it is still common for people in the Western world to call Islam "Mohammadanism."

At the same time there was a development in the European hatred of the Jews during the thirteenth century. In 1243 near Berlin, the Jews were for the first time accused of stealing the Eucharist from churches and tearing the wafer to shreds. At once this became another standard charge against the Jews, and came up with the same regularity as the charges of child murder and cannibalism. The Jews were accused of a dedicated and murderous desire to wound Christ anew. To have crucified him once in Jerusalem had not been enough for them; they had constantly to lacerate his body again in the Eucharist. Nobody was able to reflect rationally that, since the Jews certainly did not believe that Jesus was present in the Eucharist, they would have very little interest in breaking into churches and desecrating the Host.[53] The devotion to the real presence of Christ in the Eucharist was new, and so automatically did people consider the Jews to be the enemies of Christ and of religion that they spontaneously made them the enemies of this new devotion. The accusation also expressed the Christian conviction that the Jews really "knew" perfectly well that Jesus was God and was present in the Eucharist, but that they maliciously and perversely refused to submit to the truth. This made them worthy of persecution, and pogroms sprang up all over Europe when Christians believed that the Jews had committed this new eucharistic crime. Pope Gregory did not approve of the pogroms but we have seen already that he had no love of the Jews and put them on a par with the Muslims. In 1240 he condemned the Talmud, a book as heinous to the Christians as the Koran. On the first Sunday of Lent he sent a letter to all the kings of Europe, telling them to seize the copies of the Talmud, which was now a forbidden book in Christendom, while the Jews were in the synagogue on the Sabbath. The books should be put in the custody of "our dear sons, the Dominican and Franciscan friars." There was not much response to this appeal. The Emperor Frederick, as one might expect, completely ignored it. But the King of France sprang to the task zealously. He ordered a certain Nicholas Donin, who was a convert from Judaism and was now a fervent Franciscan, to interrogate Rabbi Jehiel, a learned rabbi who was to represent the Talmud and the Jews in a public "debate," which was really a trial of Judaism. This was a horrible perversion of Frederick's plan to use the Jewish converts to Christianity in order to *help* the Jews. But Frederick had reckoned without the irrational nature of Christianity, which could so powerfully affect the imagination as to convince even converted Jews of the evil of their former faith. Because Donin knew the Talmud well, he was able to take the rabbi through all those passages which were insulting to Christians, even though he knew that they represented only a tiny portion of the whole and could not possibly be said to be representative of Talmudic Judaism. Thus he managed to produce a distorted picture of the Talmud, as a work that was wholly intent on a dedicated hatred of Jesus and his followers.[54] In 1242 the Talmud was condemned and the books were burned in the presence of the King. This action of the King of France was typical of the man who was to be the last great Crusader.

King Louis IX of France could not be a greater contrast to Frederick. He was considered by the vast majority of people in Europe to be a perfect type of Christian king and was an example of the ideal Christian of the thirteenth century. It is significant that, while Frederick's supporters became heretics and outcasts after his death, Louis was regarded as a saint by popular acclaim and was canonized by the official established Church. Even though he often behaved in a cruel, simple-minded, petty way, he is still called "St. Louis" today. He has a feast day on August 25 each year when a special Mass is celebrated in his honor. The readings from Scripture that have been chosen for this Mass include a reading from the Book of Wisdom (10:10–14) in the Old Testament, which is usually read on the feast day of a martyr, and we shall see that Louis did indeed die a pointless death on an extremely ill-conceived Crusade. The gospel reading (Luke 19:12–26) is the long parable of the talents where Jesus explains how a Christian should use his gifts fruitfully in this life, and the final prayer after the communion still celebrates Louis as a Christian soldier: "O God, You gave Your blessed confessor Louis renown on earth and glory in heaven; we pray You, appoint him a defender of Your Church."[55] Other prayers during this Mass recall St. Louis's utter dedication to the values of heaven, his holy contempt of this life and his love of Christ. My missal quotes with approval the praise of the seventeenth-century Catholic writer Jacques Bossuet: "He was the holiest and most just king who ever wore the crown."[56] Louis therefore is still venerated by millions of Catholics all over the world as an example to all kings and rulers, and also as a man who made the best possible use of his life and who died a holy death. Yet Louis was an anti-Semite and a cruel persecutor of heretics, and he was so consumed with loathing of Muslims that he led not one Crusade but two. There could scarcely be a more telling example of the way crusading values are still upheld subliminally by the official Church.

Where Frederick had presented himself as a rich and exotic ruler, Louis had a much simpler style. He used to sit cross-legged under a tree in his court at Vincennes, with his advisers around him, and encourage the people to bring their problems and difficulties to him.[57] In fact, even though he hated Jews, he thought of himself as one of the old kings of Israel. He judged his people like Solomon and, like Solomon, he was also a great builder. Churches and monasteries built in the new Gothic style sprang up all over France. The most spectacular of his building achievements was La Sainte Chapelle in the royal palace, which he began to build during the early 1240s when he was also organizing his campaign against the Talmud. As in King Solomon's day, building went hand in hand with warfare. La Sainte Chapelle was very much like Solomon's Temple in that it was built to enshrine the holiness of God. Louis had bought the important relic of the Crown of Thorns from the Latin Emperor of Constantinople, along with a large piece of the True Cross, some fragments of the holy spear, the robe worn by Christ, the holy sponge and the holy shroud. The Emperor of Constantinople could not manage the economy of the empire he had seized from the Greeks during the Fourth Crusade and so had to sell these priceless relics which the West had long coveted. Louis was able to profit from the crime of the Fourth Crusade and build a new holy place in the West.[58] The Crusades had violently wrested the "holiness" of the East and carried it in triumph to Europe, making a new holy place there. When we look at the almost miraculous beauty of La Sainte Chapelle, which was actually built to look rather like a reliquary and a crown, we should remember that it is one result of the Crusades. Without the bloodshed, violence and destruction of a Crusade, the chapel would never have been built.

Here it is important to recall the importance of relics in the piety of Western laymen. They were a physical contact with heaven and a source of valuable power. Holiness was still locally conceived and bound up with the physical and tangible, rather than a spiritual and pious state of soul. A good Christian king was not expected to have Solomon's proverbial wisdom and religious insight, but he was expected to build beautiful churches to enshrine relics. When a Christian like Louis went to pray at La Sainte Chapelle, he was probably not engaging in contemplative, internal prayer of the sort we automatically associate with Christian devotion today. That type of interior devotion or mysticism would not become common among laymen until the fourteenth century, the age of Julian of Norwich, Richard Rolle of Hampole and Walter Hilton. Christians of the period of the Crusades went into churches to encounter the holy power of the relics and expose themselves to the presence of God that was concentrated in a special place. It is in this light that we should view the new devotion to the Eucharist. At a time when the Christian possession of Jerusalem was problematic, it was important to have holy places at home, and the new celebration of the Real Presence made each church as holy as Solomon's Temple had been.

Louis's friend and biographer John of Joinville gives us some insight into what it meant to be a Christian in Louis's court. Since the Cluniac reform in the eleventh century, the religious experience of the layman had been shaped by performing certain external rites, like the pilgrimage or indeed the Crusade, which were supposed to form certain attitudes and values. By the middle of the thirteenth century we see in Joinville's account that these values had "taken," especially the value of poverty. He records long debates in the court about the type of clothes a Christian should wear, the merit of washing the feet of the poor and the importance of almsgiving.[59] When Joinville describes Louis's daily Christian regime, he simply lists the number of monastic offices he attended throughout the day.[60] Laymen were still encouraged to live the monastic life as far as they could. But this piety remained an external matter. Joinville does not show the Christians of Louis's court as being at all concerned with spirituality or with an inner attitude. Religion was still a matter of performing certain external gestures and rites in honor of Christ.

During our story we have seen that some religious orders had been making Christianity an inner mystical quest. The Cistercians had given the lead here in the early twelfth century and the Franciscans had also introduced a more affective, interior religious life, where the practice of holy poverty went hand in hand with an intensive prayer life. This was also the case with some of the heretical sects that were springing up in Europe during the thirteenth century. But to read Joinville's biography of Louis makes one aware that this was still not the case with most laymen, and I think that this will give us some idea of the mentality of many of the Crusaders. When Joinville writes about Louis's "charity" we see very clearly that he is not talking about a state of mind whereby Louis was filled with affective love toward his fellow man, nor was he engaged in a struggle to suppress "uncharitable thoughts." For Joinville and Louis "charity" meant practical almsgiving and care for the poor. He always had "six score poor persons fed in his house with bread and wine and meat and fish,"[61] wherever he traveled. Every day he had some "old and decrepit men"[62] dine with him at his table, and he daily gave "countless generous alms"[63] to poor religious, hospitals, fallen women and distressed gentlefolk. This is all very laudable, of course, but when Christians today talk of "charity" they usually mean more than generosity to the poor; they mean a state of mind, which must be cultivated by constant interior attention. Louis and his court do not seem to have arrived at this degree of moral sophistication. Indeed the moral discussions in the court are at a very basic level: Louis will spend some time explaining to Joinville that Christians must learn to repent and set their lives in order, because otherwise they will not gain such a great reward in heaven.[64] Although monks and friars were clearly aware of the interior implications of Christianity, this was not yet the case for the layman. His religious emotions and "mystical experiences" were very clearly tied to a visit to important places like La Sainte Chapelle or, pre-eminently, Jerusalem. They were not cultivated by a daily regimen of disciplined contemplation. Mystical vision was often experienced in emergencies, as we have seen. But a layman's daily Christian life was still largely a matter of exterior practice.

Indeed, serious thought of an independent nature was actually discouraged. This was because one of the most severe battles a Christian had to fight was a war against Satan, who constantly tried to destroy his faith. Louis told his men that they must suppress any doubts they had very violently, because these came from the Devil. One must cry: "Be off! You shall not tempt me from my firm belief in all the articles of the faith, even though you were to have all my limbs cut off!"[65] Faith was often a fearful struggle in which a man sometimes had to do violence upon himself because he saw his own natural thoughts as satanic if they questioned articles of faith. In this battle for the faith, a Christian could come to distrust and fear his own mind. Judaism and Islam are also religions of practice but they have simple creeds and Muslims and Jews do not have to do themselves such violence to believe them. But Christians were asked to accept very irrational dogmas, as, for example, that Christ was truly, physically present in a piece of bread. Joinville tells us of a knight who went in despair to the Bishop of Paris, unable to control his tears because he was losing his faith. Try as he would, he said to the bishop, "I cannot force my heart to believe in the Sacrament of the altar as Holy Church teaches."[66] He knew this was a temptation from the Devil and it made him absolutely miserable. It is not surprising that he found it difficult to believe that the body of Christ was truly present on the altar. Such a belief throws all rationality aside; it is contrary to the way we learn to understand the world and the laws of nature. It is noteworthy that the bishop did not attempt to convince the knight intellectually. He simply told him that, whereas he personally had no doubts at all on the matter (a fact which is a telling indication of the simplicity of the bishop's own state of mind), the knight's struggle was more pleasing to God. Interestingly, he illustrated this by means of a military simile. It was as though, during a war, he, the bishop, were defending a safe castle, while the knight was defending a castle on the front line that was continuously under assault. Holding on to the faith was, therefore, "a woeful struggle."[67] Christians who "forced" their minds to submit to these irrational doctrines had to do so on very flimsy grounds. Joinville tells a story of Louis's somewhat simplistic advice:

> He asked me a question: "What was my father's name?" I told him, "Simon." He then asked me how I knew. I answered that I thought I could be certain of it and believe it, since my mother had been my witness. "Then," he said, "you should believe no less firmly in all the articles of the faith, of which the apostles are your witness, as you hear sung every Sunday in the Creed."[68]

Louis also liked to tell the story of Simon of Montfort, the crusading hero who fought the Catharists. When he also encountered people of southern France who did not believe in the Eucharist, the count replied that, because he believed implicitly, he would have a richer crown than the angels when he got to heaven, because they did not need to have faith; they saw everything for themselves.[69]

Joinville gives quite a lot of space to the problem of faith; he shows that it was a difficulty and that people were, not unnaturally, finding it a struggle. I think that this tells us two important things. First, Christians who forced their minds to accept, without question, basically irrational and incredible doctrines were doing their minds no good at all. A person who accepted without a qualm that the bread of the Eucharist was the body of Christ was denying the evidence of his senses and the ordinary laws of nature. He was putting his religion into quite a separate category, and not only was he learning to repress doubt violently, he was also learning not to relate the natural with the supernatural or to make potentially dangerous connections and comparisons. When, therefore, he heard in the gospel that Jesus told him to love his enemies, a Christian like Louis would not connect this with the Church's view that he should kill them. Such lack of connection was part of his Christian makeup. The second important lesson we learn about this view of faith was that it was a very fragile state of mind. We have seen that such insecurity very often leads into a holy war.

Louis himself gives us an insight into the way this insecurity led to an instinctive belligerence. He liked to tell a story about a debate that had been planned at Cluny between Jews and Christians. Staying in the monastery as a guest was a knight who had recently been wounded. He asked the abbot if he might open the debate, and the abbot agreed, with some misgivings. The knight then asked the chief rabbi if he believed that the Virgin Mary was the Mother of God. Not surprisingly, the rabbi replied that he did not. The knight then simply hit him on the head with his crutch and knocked him out. That was the end of the debate. In terror, the Jews picked up their unconscious leader and fled, much to the annoyance of the abbot, who rebuked the knight, telling him that he had been extremely foolish. The knight replied that in his view the abbot had been a much bigger fool for arranging the debate in the first place. Many good Christians might have been deceived by the Jews' lying arguments.[70] Louis entirely agreed: "No one who is not a very learned clerk should argue with Jews," he commented. "A layman, as soon as he hears the Christian faith maligned should defend it by the sword, with a good thrust in the belly as far as the sword will go."[71] The kind of faith that requires an unnatural suppression of normal reasoning processes is inherently fragile. If a Christian hears doubt cast on essential but unnatural doctrines like the Incarnation, he may well feel the "dread" that we have seen in our story to arise from a deep threat to personal integrity and identity. We have seen in other circumstances that a person feeling this threat cannot understand the "other" point of view. A Crusader like Louis, whose mother had seen that he was brought up surrounded only by religious men,[72] would respond to Jews with violent aggression, as a reflex. It would also lead him to be prepared to fight the specter of "Mohammadanism."

In 1244 Christendom heard the dreadful news that the Christians had lost the Kingdom of Jerusalem once again. The Khwarazmian Turkish dynasty had been dislodged from Central Asia by the Mongol hordes and ran amok, fleeing westward to get as far as possible from the terrifying Mongols, destroying cities in their panic. When they arrived in Syria, 10,000 of them attacked Damascus and then rushed on to Jerusalem, occupied the city and drove out the Franks, before sweeping on to Gaza where, together with an Egyptian army, they defeated the Christians of Palestine in a decisive battle. The loss of Jerusalem was the usual trauma and threat to the integrity of Christendom. That year Louis fell ill in Paris, and Joinville relates that he was so bad that one of his nurses thought that he had died and wanted to cover his face, but the other stopped her, certain that the King's soul had not yet left his body. At that moment, wrote Joinville, God intervened: "Our Lord worked in him and soon sent him back his health. He had lost the power of speech, but as soon as he was again fit to speak he asked for the Cross to be given him, which was done."[73] He had been reprieved from death in order to recover Jerusalem.

Hopes were high and Louis's three brothers and most of the nobles also took the Cross. With an accredited saint at the head of God's army, it was felt that the Seventh Crusade could not possibly fail. Louis wanted to take crusading right back to its fundamental principles. There would certainly be no fraternization with the infidel and his army would be as pious as the First Crusaders. Frederick watched the organization of this new crusading initiative with deep cynicism and wrote to Louis, warning him that the enterprise was hopeless, but of course Louis completely ignored this advice. Frederick then wrote to his friend, Sultan as-Salih Najm ad-Din Ayyub, who had succeeded al-Kamil as Sultan of Egypt, warning him to prepare for this Seventh Crusade.[74]

Yet though Louis was a fundamentalist Crusader, returning crusading to its roots, his would also be a modern Crusade making use of the latest technology. It would be another four years before the Crusade was ready to leave because of all the elaborate preparations. He began by building a great harbor in the previously uninhabited bay at Aigues Mortes, where he gathered an enormous fleet. In his army were skilled engineers and bridge builders, who played a crucially important part in some of the battles, so that this Crusade has been called the Engineers' Crusade.[75] At Cyprus Louis began to collect huge supplies of wheat to ensure that the Crusade would be adequately provisioned, and Joinville described the towering wheat mountain that had been grassed over on top.[76] In this sense too Louis was returning to the spirit of the First Crusaders, who had prayed as though everything depended upon God, but had fought and planned with every human skill they could muster. Eventually the preparations were com-

plete and the fleet sailed for Egypt on August 28, 1248. Louis put in
at Cyprus on September 18 and was advised by the barons of Acre
to spend the winter there to avoid the storms and the treacherous
winter conditions in Egypt. They also hoped to persuade Louis to
take advantage of the quarrels among the Muslims to try to negotiate
the return of Jerusalem. As one might expect, Louis would have nothing to do with any diplomatic initiative with the infidel, and urged
the Templars, who had begun negotiations, to break them off immediately.

Yet Louis was quite prepared to consider another diplomatic initiative to the murderous Mongols, who were threatening the Muslims
in the East. Already in 1245 Pope Innocent IV had sent two missions
to the Khan, trying to ward off the coming destruction by suggesting
that they convert to Christianity. He had heard that some of them
were Nestorian Christians. The first embassy had returned discouraged, and told the Pope that the Mongols were not interested in
conversion but only in conquest. But the second returned with Nestorian envoys from the Mongol general Baichu, who was planning to
attack Baghdad and was quite happy to encourage the Christian Crusade to distract the Muslims of Syria. But no permanent alliance
seemed forthcoming and the two envoys were sent back to Baichu in
November 1248. A month later another two Nestorians arrived in
Cyprus, as envoys of another Mongol general, Aljighidai. They told
Louis that the Mongols were deeply interested in Christianity, and
Louis was delighted.[77] He sent two Dominicans on a mission to the
Khan, bearing gifts. One of these presents was a little portable altar,
with relics,[78] decorated with pictures that illustrated gospel scenes.
Louis was bitterly disappointed three years later when the Dominicans
returned with the sad news that the Mongols showed no signs of
sympathy for Western Christianity, but that they were prepared to
consider an alliance with the French King. Louis should send further
gifts as tribute.[79]

At first this strange episode seems rather refreshing. At last crusading
Europe was reaching out sympathetically toward another culture—a
culture which was entirely alien to Christians because it did not derive
from any of the three religions of Abraham. In fact the Dominican
and Franciscan envoys were very interested and excited by what they
saw of the Mongols and seemed able to describe these strange people
quite objectively, without any of the solipsistic fantasies that distorted
the Christian view of Judaism and Islam.[80] Yet this new quest for
contact was really inspired by the desperate needs of the holy war
against Islam. At the time of the Crusade the Mongols were drawing

nearer and nearer to the Islamic empire. Muslims had seen and suffered from the panic of the Khwarazmian Turks, in their headlong flight from these terrifying foes, who massacred and devastated wherever they conquered. With the Mongols to the East and Louis's Crusaders to the West, the Muslims felt caught between Scylla and Charybdis, and Louis's missionary initiative was, as usual, part of a deadly war against Islam.

Louis and the Pope were both so cheered by the thought of a new way of getting rid of Islam that they could not see that the Mongols were far more of a threat to Christendom than the Muslims had ever been. So deeply ingrained was the Western paranoia that the revelation of a far more ferocious race of Orientals did nothing to modify Western fantasies about "Mohammadanism," which people seemed to need as emotional ballast for their own view of themselves. In the eighteenth century we shall see that a similar revelation of a new Orient made absolutely no difference to the way people saw Islam. The old medieval prejudice flourished unchanged, while people enthusiastically and appreciatively studied an Orient that was far more challenging to the Christian world view.

In May Louis's beautifully equipped, modern army sailed from Cyprus to Damietta in Egypt. As soon as the banner of St. Denis had been carried ashore, Louis pushed past the papal legate, leaped into the water, which came up to his armpits, and waded to the beach, lance in hand. When he saw a host of Saracens on the beach, Joinville recalled, "he couched his lance under his arm and put his shield before him, and would have flung himself upon them had not his wiser companions held him back."[81] Instinctively Louis presented himself in a posture of unthinking aggression toward Muslims, just as he had with Jews. It was exactly the same response. But this gesture was also a deliberate harking back to the days of vintage crusading in *The Song of Roland*, and there would be a good deal of this dangerous and irresponsible chivalry during this Crusade, which might work all right in an eleventh-century poem but was impossible in the real world of the thirteenth century. Yet a Crusader like Louis, like many holy warriors today, could deliberately close his eyes to rationality and common sense in an absurd and dangerous gesture. In fact he had arrived in Egypt at a favorable moment. The Sultan was dying and his son and heir Turanshah was far away in Gezira. There was a very good chance, therefore, of a palace revolution and this could be very beneficial to the Crusaders. The Muslims were so lacking in confidence at this bad period that the citizens and the garrison simply fled Damietta and the Crusaders could occupy the city without a battle. The news of the loss of Damietta spread fear and consternation throughout the Muslim world; their position seemed hopeless. The dying Sultan made the same offer as his father al-Kamil had made thirty years earlier: he would give Jerusalem back to the Christians if Louis would evacuate Egypt. Naturally Louis refused to deal with the infidel and confidently waited for the Nile waters to subside before he continued his campaign. Yet this confidence would prove to be as ill founded in reality as the heroic gesture of flinging himself upon the Muslims single-handed.

Their new desperation gave the Muslims a grim determination, realism and political astuteness that would ultimately prove superior to the rather old-fashioned crusading heroics. This was a terrifying new world for the Muslims and they could no longer afford the chivalrous generosity of Saladin in their fight for survival. When a strong detachment of Crusaders marched on Mansurah on November 20, the Muslims braced themselves for the coming struggle, and when the Sultan finally died three days later, the Sultana Shajar ad-Durr acted swiftly and efficiently and kept his death a secret. By the time the news leaked out Fakhr ad-Din was firmly in control of events and Turanshah was already on his way to Egypt. Louis still hoped that a government led by a woman and an old man would shortly collapse and began to plan an offensive. On the night of February 8, 1250, the Crusaders managed to ford the canal that separated them from the Egyptian camp, make a surprise attack and put the enemy to flight. They were now in a strong position to take the city but threw away their victory in one of those anachronistic acts of foolish chivalry. The attack had been made by a vanguard, led by Louis's brother Robert of Artois and a contingent of Templars, and the Grand Master of the Templars strongly advised Robert not to attack the city until Louis and the main army had managed to ford the canal. But Robert would not wait and charged once more through the fleeing Egyptians and into the city, followed reluctantly by the Templars. Fakhr ad-Din, who had been in his bath, had rushed out into the streets without his armor and was set upon by the Templars and killed. But the Turkish Mamluk troops led by the slave officer Rukn ad-Din Baibars quickly organized themselves and caught the small crusading force in an ambush. Robert and the Templars were massacred: there were only five survivors.[82] Louis and the main army managed to hold back the Muslims and establish themselves in the former Egyptian camp but were not strong enough to take the city, which was equipped with better war engines than their own. The Crusaders sat for a further eight weeks outside Mansurah and the campaign seemed to be falling into the same pattern as the Fifth Crusade. On February 11 the Muslims attacked the camp and inflicted grave casualties; Turanshah arrived and there was no palace revolution; an Egyptian fleet cut off the food supplies and there was famine in the Crusader camp which was quickly followed by disease. The glamorous expedition had become a nightmare.[83]

Now that he had come face to face with reality, Louis offered to negotiate with Sultan Turanshah, but it was too late because the Egyptians knew very well how precarious his position really was. The situation was hopeless and at the beginning of April Louis and his officers decided to retreat. The sick were sent by ship up the Nile to Damietta and the army began to return along the road they had traveled so hopefully a few weeks earlier. But the Muslims followed the army, harassing them on all sides, and the Crusaders were too exhausted and ill even to resist them. When Louis himself succumbed to the sickness, his officers took the responsibility and surrendered to the Muslims. The whole army was taken into captivity.

It was a unique and difficult situation for both Muslims and Crusaders. The Egyptians were embarrassed by the vast numbers of prisoners, whom they could not afford to feed, and every day a hundred of the weaker soldiers were killed off. Yet, while both sides negotiated for the conditions of the ransom, they had a chance to look at one another at close quarters. To Joinville the Muslims seem to have become human beings. He recalled the kindness of an old Muslim soldier who used to carry one of the sick Crusaders to the latrines every day on his back;[84] he remembered the kindness of the emir with whom he was billeted: Joinville had eaten meat on Friday by mistake and the emir was at pains to reassure him that God would not punish him for this accident.[85] For their part the Muslims were impressed with the behavior of many of their prisoners and especially by the bearing of Louis himself. They even suggested, no doubt in jest, that he should be their next sultan. Louis seemed to have taken this seriously and told Joinville that he would have accepted the position.[86] Joinville wrote that the emirs said

> that the King was the most steadfast Christian you could find. They gave as an example of this that when he came out of his lodging he used to lie on the ground in the form of a cross and so made the sign of the Cross with his whole body. They said too that had Mahomet allowed such misfortunes to befall them they would never have kept their faith in him; and that if their people made him their Sultan, either they would have to become Christians or he would put them to death.[87]

If this really is accurate, it would seem that the emirs had summed up Louis's Christianity rather well—a religion of gesture and simple acts of devotion, which had very little to do with the love and pacifism of Christ. Louis most certainly would have forced any Saracen subjects to convert at swordpoint.

Eventually terms were agreed: Louis's wife Queen Margaret (who had remained with the garrison at Damietta) and the Templars managed to raise a million besants for the release of the King and most of the prisoners. But on May 2 there was a setback, when the palace revolution that the Crusaders had longed for actually happened. The Turkish Mamluks or former slaves, who had played such an important part in the defense of Mansurah, now demanded a greater say in the government, and when this was refused they assassinated Turanshah and took control. From this point the Mamluks would be the principal enemy of the Crusaders in the Holy Land. After the assassination, the emirs rushed to their Christian prisoners with the blood still on their hands and swords and threatened to put them to death.[88] In fact, however, the Mamluks had absolutely no intention of losing the enormous ransom and on May 6 Damietta was handed back to the Muslims and the sick and weary Crusaders sailed back to Acre. For two more years Louis and a number of the French barons remained in the Holy Land, building and repairing fortifications. The Crusade of the Engineers had ended as a building project; the complete fiasco of the Seventh Crusade made it clear to many people that it was impossible to conquer Jerusalem from Islam and that crusading should be abandoned. Joinville was one of these: after 1250 crusading seemed to him a useless, self-indulgent exercise, actually damaging the kingdom of France, which had been gravely weakened by the absence of the King and most of the knights. But one knight of Christ never gave up. After his return from the Holy Land in 1254 Louis led a devout life of penance, so that never again would he wear fine clothes and he was always very moderate at table. The failure of his Crusade, he was convinced, could only be explained by God's wishing to teach him humility,[89] a characteristically simple-minded explanation of a disastrous campaign which had cost thousands of Christian lives. He was determined to lead an army to the East again, even if he waited another twenty years. It was his duty to fight the Muslims, who were an absolute danger to the Christian people.

But in fact the Muslims of the Middle East were at that time in very great danger themselves. In 1257 the Mongol army led by Hulegu, the grandson of Genghis Khan, began to march toward Baghdad. Before this vast army Caliph al-Mustasi'un had no choice but to surrender on February 10, 1258, but the city was sacked and the population exterminated. It seemed as though Louis's hopes were to be realized and that the Mongols really would destroy Islam; there was great rejoicing in the Crusader states. In January 1260 Aleppo was destroyed, Damascus was taken and occupied and in March the Mongols swept into Palestine and took Nablus and Gaza. As the horrified Muslims watched the destruction of one city after another, they naturally associated these destroyers with the Christian menace, which had attacked them relentlessly for nearly two hundred years. Hulegu himself had Nestorian Christian connections and Damascus was now ruled by three Christian Mongols. But the Christian rejoicings were entirely misplaced and were based on a quite fictitious view of the Mongols. The Mongolian conquests were always accompanied by total devastation and extermination, unless the cities surrendered immediately and unconditionally; Hulegu would have made short work of Acre and Antioch and might even have gone on to invade Europe. Instead of neurotically inventing fantasies of Muslim conspiracies to conquer Europe, the Europeans should have been worrying about a far more dangerous enemy.

After the Mongols had conquered Gaza, they naturally looked toward Egypt and an envoy was dispatched to the Mamluk Sultan to order his capitulation. After the envoy had finished speaking, the Sultan simply struck off his head.[90] There was now a new harshness in the Muslim spirit and throughout the devastated Islamic empire people began to look to the tough Mamluks as their only hope. Sultan Saif ad-Din Qutuz seized the first chance that offered. Hulegu had to return to Persia after the death of his brother Möngke, the Supreme Khan, in order to cope with the inevitable problems of the succession, leaving only a few thousand horsemen in the country under the command of his lieutenant Kitbuga. In July 1260 Qutuz invaded Palestine, realizing that this was Islam's last chance. By this time some of the barons in Acre, though not in Antioch, were becoming thoroughly alarmed by the Mongols' ruthless brutality, and although they would not fight alongside a Muslim army they agreed not to attack the Mamluks from the rear. When a revolt broke out in Damascus at the end of August, Qutuz had time to deploy his troops very carefully at Ain Jalut in Galilee, and on September 3 the two armies met. By a brilliant ambush tactic, the Mamluks defeated and massacred the whole Mongol army, and this battle, which truly changed history, marked the end of Mongol supremacy.[91] It was an ironic reversal of Louis's hopes. Instead of the Mongols saving Christianity from Islam, it was the Muslims who saved Christendom from the Mongols, and instead of the Mongols converting to Christianity they would finally settle in Persia and Palestine and become Muslims.

Only two months after the great victory at Ain Jalut, Baibars, the hero of the Battle of Mansurah, assassinated Qutuz and became the Mamluk Sultan. It seems a sad reflection on the Mamluks, but many of them had always considered Baibars to be their natural leader. Baibars could not forgive the Franks at Antioch for colluding with the Mongols and in 1265 when Hulegu died he took advantage of Mongol quarrels to invade their territory in Palestine and establish a new base there. In 1268 he conquered Beaufort Castle near Acre and on May 1 he rode on to Tripolis. The ruler Count Bohemund, who was also Prince of Antioch, prepared for a long siege. But instead Baibars traveled swiftly northward and on May 14 his army surprised the city of Antioch, massacred the population and reduced the great and ancient city to ruins. He then sent a letter to Bohemund, telling him what had happened: "Be glad that you have not seen your knights lying prostrate under the hooves of horses, your palaces plundered, your ladies sold in the quarters of the city, fetching a mere dinar apiece—a dinar taken, moreover, from your own hoard!"[92] This was quite a new Islam. The trauma of recent years had produced a new cool ruthlessness and desperate determination to survive. Now that he had effectively destroyed Bohemund's power, Baibars was prepared to make a treaty with him. But still the Franks did not seem fully to have understood the precariousness of their position. Baibars had sent his chronicler Abd-al-Zahir to Acre to draw up the treaty. During the negotiations, when the Mamluks were proving to be quite inflexible, the King of Acre told Abd-al-Zahir to turn around. When he did so, he saw the whole Frankish army drawn up in battle array. Unperturbed, he said to the interpreter: "Tell the king that there are fewer soldiers in his army than there are Frankish captives in the prisons of Cairo." The King nearly choked and the terms of the treaty were quickly agreed.[93]

Yet Baibars was not simply a destroyer. The Battle of Ain Jalut had made him master of Damascus, Aleppo and Cairo, which meant that for the first time since Saladin the Ayyubid empire was united under a single ruler, and it represented a rebirth and a new power after the Mongol trauma. Like Louis, Baibars was a great builder, and there was a cultural renaissance under the Mamluks so that Egypt and Syria became centers of art and learning once more.[94] But to preserve the security of this revived Muslim empire required constant vigilance. Baibars knew that he had nothing to fear from the Franks in Palestine any longer, but there was always the possibility of a new Crusade from the West. Indeed shortly after the destruction of Antioch he heard some terrible news. King Louis of France had set out for the East at the head of a huge army. This time, to the Muslims' astonishment, he had made for Tunisia, an entirely new location for Crusaders. The Sultan Abu Abdullah Muhammad al-Mustansir bi-Ilah, ruler of Tunisia, prepared to meet this Christian attack and offered 8000 dinar for peace: his whole country was at this point weakened by plague and famine.[95] Baibars waited in Palestine with trepidation. If Louis succeeded in establishing a base in Tunisia, he was certain that he would then attack the Mamluks in the Near East, who were themselves also weakened by their long struggle, caught in a frightening vise between East and West. Anxiously Baibars watched the progress of the Crusade from Palestine. The Christians took the money the Sultan offered them but did not make peace and started their Crusade. They had, the Egyptian historian Taqi ad-Din al-Maqrizi tells us, 6000 cavalry and 30,000 infantry. "The Muslims kept up the fight until mid-Muharram, the end of August, with violent battles in which many of both sides died."[96] The Muslims of Tunis were almost defeated, when God suddenly seemed to step in and liberate them, and the Mamluks and the Tunisians could breathe again. Louis's army succumbed to the plague that was rife in Tunisia and on August 25, 1270, King Louis himself died. The King of France, wrote Maqrizi, as an epitaph, "was an intelligent man, cunning and deceitful."[97] That was one Muslim view of the most Christian King.

We have noted that in fact intelligence was not Louis's strong point and nowhere do we see his simple-minded irresponsibility more clearly than in the story of this last Crusade. When he had set off from Paris, against the advice of many of his barons like Joinville who were furious about this last Crusade, he was a very sick man. He was indeed so ill that Joinville had to carry him on the first leg of his journey in his arms.[98] Joinville himself had refused to take the Cross this time because he knew that he, like the King, was badly needed in France.[99] Had Louis stayed at home he might have lived a few years to do much useful work but, with an obstinate, almost pathological refusal to face reality that we have so often seen during the Crusades, he set out to endure the rigors of a hard campaign in an unhealthy climate, where there was already a major pestilence. It must have been obvious, even to Louis, that he would not live long, but it seems that he wanted to fight the Muslims to his very last gasp. Nothing, I think, illustrates his fanatical hatred of the Muslims more clearly than this suicidal expedition. The fall of Antioch must have filled Louis with such sickening dread that he was ready to make himself in effect a voluntary martyr to ward off the horror of an encroaching Islam.

Certainly Western Christians at once acclaimed Louis as a martyr and he was deeply lamented and revered as a Crusader, even though both his Crusades had been such dreadful failures. It was impossible for the crusading army to survive in Tunisia, once it had been decimated by the plague, which appears to have been a chronic form of dysentery. Scarcely able to believe their luck, the Muslims of Tunisia watched the Christians making their preparations to go home, and sent the good news to Baibars, who could also relax. Yet the local people were charitable enough to erect a small shrine in Louis's memory, for they could see that, even though he hated them to his last breath, he was a genuinely religious man. Louis would not have reciprocated this gesture. He was not of course buried in Muslim territory, and Louis, who had brought so many relics home from the East, now returned from the House of Islam as a relic himself. Because the Crusaders were afraid that the body would decompose, they boiled the flesh off the bones, which they enshrined in a casket which they buried as soon as they arrived in Christendom. By a strange irony, this meant that Louis was buried in the same Church of Monreale in Palermo as Frederick, his crusading predecessor.

That was the last Crusade. Small armies did cross the Mediterranean, as we shall see, to try to save the Kingdom of Acre, but as a mass movement the project was now dead and seen to be impractical. This Christian failure called into question the whole integrity of the faith and we can see some of this fear and dread in a poem written at about this time by a Templar in Acre:

> Rage and sorrow are seated in my heart, so firmly that I scarce dare stay alive. It seems that God wishes to support the Turks to our loss. . . . Ah, Lord God! Alas the realm of the East has lost so much that it will never rise up again. . . . Anyone who wishes to fight the Turks is mad, for Jesus Christ does not fight them any more. They have conquered, they will conquer. For every day they drive us down, knowing that God, who was awake, sleeps now, and Mohammad waxes powerful.[100]

Had God deserted his chosen people? The success of the early Crusaders had been a glorious affirmation of the faith, and it had led to Christians regarding Muslims as polluting filth, who could be exterminated like vermin. But what did their new success mean? Muslims began to pose a terrible unanswered question to Europeans and were surrounded with a new aura of dread.

Yet ultimately the Christians in the East proved to be their own worst enemies. In 1271 Baibars had conquered the great Krak des Chevaliers in Syria, which not even Saladin had been able to overcome. The little Christian Kingdom of Acre and County of Tripolis now consisted of only a few cities along the coast and their position was obviously precarious. But when Baibars died, Sultan Qalawun, his successor, seemed to go out of his way to befriend the Franks.[101] In 1183 he renewed the treaty that Baibars had made with the Franks, and Acre, Athlit and Sidon were at peace with their Muslim neighbors. But Tripolis stood aloof and still preferred to side with the Mongols, who were themselves trying to make a comeback during these years. Hulegu's grandson Il-Khan Arghun approached the Pope and the rulers of Europe in 1287 with a new offer of an alliance and proposed a joint offensive against the Mamluks in January 1291. When news of this reached Qalawun, he realized that the presence of the Franks was a permanent threat to Muslim security, but he still refused to break the truce. Instead he decided to make an example of Tripolis, which paraded its Mongol sympathies,[102] and which he besieged in March 1289; he took the city by storm on April 27. The historian Abu l-Fida described the events tersely: the civilians fled to the harbor and a few managed to take refuge on a small island just off the coast, "but most of the men were killed and the children taken captive."[103] The city was looted and razed to the ground and the Muslim troops then swam out to the island on horseback to kill those who had taken refuge there. For months it was impossible to land there, because of the stench of putrefying corpses.[104] The whirligig of time had brought its revenge. Desperation had reproduced in the Muslim soldiers the ruthless spirit of the Crusaders who conquered Jerusalem in 1099.

Yet even though many of his officers urged Qalawun to attack Acre, the Sultan refused to dishonor the truce. He urged Muslims to make use of Acre as a trading port and the city had never been so busy and even prosperous. Everybody had been able to benefit by this secular cooperation, and many of the more realistic barons were delighted with this turn of events. Perhaps Acre would be able to survive after all. But there was an aggressive party of religious chauvinists in Acre in 1289 as there had been in the Kingdom of Jerusalem a hundred years earlier and they urged King Henry to ask the Pope for another Crusade. In the summer of 1290 a crusading fleet from Italy sailed into the port of Acre. The Crusaders were feted in an extremely alcoholic banquet and then they rushed drunkenly through the streets of the city, attacking merchants from Damascus and any man who wore a beard, which meant that some Christians were killed.[105] Qalawun was appalled by this fresh assault, yet he was still unwilling to destroy the city and offered to make a new treaty. But Acre had been overtaken by a crusading madness and refused to make peace, so Qalawun, driven beyond further endurance, swore on the Koran that he would not lay down his arms until he had thrown the Franks into the sea.

As the Christians watched the huge army assembling in Cairo, they woke up to the reality of their position. But it was too late. The army left Cairo on November 4, 1290, but on the following day Qalawun, who was now an old man of seventy-seven, died and the army had to turn back and deal with the succession. Qalawun was succeeded by his son al-Ashraf Khalil, who continued his father's offensive. In March 1291 the army set out again and this time reached Acre, camping outside the city walls at the beginning of May. There was a siege of a few weeks but finally on June 17 the Muslims broke into the city and once again Christians experienced the Muslim intransigence that they seemed to have gone out of their way to create. There were terrible scenes in the city. Prisoners who had surrendered in good faith were mercilessly beheaded; the men were all killed and, in the light of the burning buildings, women could be seen running and weeping through the streets. The Muslim soldiers killed babies at their mothers' breasts and slaughtered pregnant women. During a truce, some Muslims rounded up a group of women and massacred them like vermin.[106]

The contemporary Muslim historians saw a vicious circle in these events, which they interpreted as a manifestation of the justice of God. Abu l-Mahasin ibn Taghribirdi points out that, according to the Muslim calendar, the Franks had conquered Acre from Saladin on Friday 17 Junada II at the third hour of the day in the Muslim year 587. After terms had been agreed, Richard the Lionheart had massacred the Muslim prisoners whom he had undertaken to spare. By a strange coincidence the Muslims had conquered Acre from the Christians on 17 Junada II, and the Sultan al-Ashraf also massacred the prisoners he had undertaken to spare. "Thus Almighty God was revenged on their descendants,"[107] he concludes. There was a coincidence too in the Christian calendar, for the Franks at Acre were defeated almost a hundred years to the day since they had defeated Saladin at the siege of Acre. We have noticed the uncanny coincidences about the dates of events during the story of the holy war. If this coincidence means anything it must surely throw up the frightening cycle of religious violence, which eventually in the Middle Ages came round full circle. The Franks had invaded Palestine in 1099 and there they had slaughtered thousands of Muslims who had done nothing to harm them, except that they were living in Jerusalem. So aggressive was the Frankish assault that eventually the *jihad* of Nur ad-Din and Saladin arose as a response to this Christian holy war. One holy war continuously led to another for a hundred years, until finally it looked as though the Christians had reproduced the murderous cruelty and hatred that they had felt for the Muslims in the hearts of the Muslims themselves. This was perhaps one of the most tragic consequences of the Crusades. The Crusaders' violence in 1099 had horrified the Muslim world in the Near East; now at Acre the Christians experienced the new Muslim violence that they had implanted in the area.

Yet another Muslim chronicler puts a slightly different emphasis on the events of 1291. Abu l-Fida writes:

> With these conquests the whole of Palestine was now in Muslim hands, a result that no one would have dared to hope for or to desire. Thus the whole of Syria and the coastal zones were purified of the Franks, who had once been on the point of conquering Egypt and subduing Damascus and other cities. Praise be to God![108]

In this view, the Muslim purging of Palestine was not a mechanical cycle but a matter of cause and effect. The Koran, we have seen, teaches that a war of self-defense is a Muslim duty when faced with oppression and aggression. The Franks had wanted to throw the Muslims out of their cities and conquer their lands. Therefore the Muslims had had to fight them back until the peril was eliminated. In rather the same way Western aggression in our own day has also produced a fresh round of Muslim intransigence and some religious Muslims have used the most desperate means of ejecting the current Western invaders from their lands. This is not just because "history repeats itself" in a deterministic cycle of fate. It is because there has been a similar Western aggression which has produced a similar effect in Muslims of the Middle East in our own times.

The Crusades also had an effect on the Jews, which is likewise very familiar to us today. They had made life intolerable for the Jews in Europe and we have seen that this led some Jews to dream of a return to Zion. Ever since Saladin had invited the Jews to come back to Jerusalem there had been large Jewish migrations there from Europe. These people did not just see themselves as refugees, but they regarded their return as a positive religious duty. Throughout the thirteenth century there had been mass migrations, from Normandy, England, Provence and Languedoc.[109] One group from Paris led by Rabbi Jehiel at the time of Louis's Crusade had intended to rebuild the Temple in Jerusalem.[110] In 1268 Rabbi Meir of Rothenburg was moved by the dramatic failure of the Crusades to reclaim the land for the Jews and tried to lead a great exodus from Germany but he was captured and imprisoned by Rudolph of Habsburg: at this time the Germans were finding the Jews too useful to their economy to allow them to leave. Rabbi Meir died in prison in 1293, an early martyr for the return to Zion.[111] We get some idea of what these Jews were feeling and thinking in the writings of the great Rabbi Nachmanides, who made the *aliyah* in 1267, after he had been exiled from Spain. He wrote that settlement in Eretz Yisrael was an absolute religious duty "incumbent upon *each* generation, binding upon *every* one of us, even in time of exile."[112] The land, he wrote, was beautiful but was now a desert: the Christians and Muslims had devastated it in their brutal wars. Eretz Yisrael, therefore, would not accept any other people but her rightful owners, the Jews: "For ever since we departed from it, it had not accepted a single nation. They all try to settle it but it is beyond their power."[113] It might even be the case that to fight a holy war for this land would also become an absolute religious duty and the Gentiles would only be allowed to stay on in Eretz Yisrael on carefully defined terms.[114] One of Nachmanides' disciples saw the fall of Christian Acre as the birth pangs of the Messiah but was convinced that the redemption could not occur while there were any *goyim* left in Eretz Yisrael: "Let no man think that the King Messiah will appear in an impure land; and let him not be deluded either into imagining that he will appear in the Land of Israel among Gentiles."[115] It is obvious that this religious Zionism is identical to the current extremist fervor for Eretz Yisrael today. In the next chapter I want to suggest that, like the medieval version, modern Zionism might also be a response to a crusading West.

The great crusading adventure was over. The dream took a long time to die and for another two hundred years there would be crusading projects. The last Crusader was Pope Pius II in 1464.[116] But none of these projects came to anything and there would be no Western hegemony in Jerusalem until the establishment of the British mandate in 1920. For almost two hundred years, as the West found her soul, crusading had been a central passion. Millions of Jews, Christians and Muslims had died in these savage holy wars; it is probably impossible to estimate exact numbers. Crusaders had massacred and driven Jews and Muslims from their homes, had carved themselves an empire in the Islamic wilderness, but were eventually ejected through their own fanaticism. The Muslims now owned the whole of the Near East and a significant part of Anatolia had been conquered from the Christians of Antioch. In 1261 the Greeks had managed to oust the Latins from Byzantium and so Constantinople was now in Greek hands, but Byzantium had been severely wounded in the struggle with the West. In Europe there were still some Muslims left. In Spain the Christian wars of reconquest had proved very successful during the thirteenth century: the Christians took Cordova in 1236 and Seville in 1248, but there was still a small Muslim kingdom in Granada. In 1301, as we have seen, Charles of Anjou would exterminate the Muslims of Lucera. Christendom was now striving to purge herself of Muslims as Muslims had striven to purge Syria and Palestine of Christians and was making life so unbearable for Jews that some of them were trying to leave Christendom too.

During the thirteenth century it seems that Europe made a decisive choice and the two last important Crusaders give us some idea of what that choice involved. There was the path offered by the Emperor Frederick that envisaged an acceptance of Jews and Muslims and the setting up of normal relations with them. Sometimes these relations might be exploitative or even antagonistic, but they were governed by the ordinary rules that shape human relations. There could also be a possibility of great friendship. The other way was the way epitomized by "Saint" Louis: this saw Jews and Muslims in a manner that was quite different from the way Western Christians judged every other people (even one as savage as the Mongols) and put them in a separate category. Louis saw Jews and Muslims as the essential enemies of religion and civilization and could only approach them in a spirit of absolute antagonism. Neither Frederick nor Louis was perfect and neither were their methods: both were cruel, ruthless men. But the story of the last three Crusades makes it clear that Europe had opted for Louis's way and violently rejected Frederick's. Even though Frederick had many supporters, these people were more truly in sympathy with his struggle against the papacy than with his policies of coexistence, though some may have been stirred by them on the level of fantasy. But Europe had committed herself to Louis's way since the First Crusaders responded to the call of Pope Urban and two hundred years of holy war had burned an absolute hatred of Jews and Muslims into the Western identity. In the last chapter I want to argue that this abnormal way of regarding Muslims and Jews is still a Western habit and is a legacy from the Crusades.

After the Crusades stopped going to the Holy Land, Europe still followed the path of "Saint" Louis, even when Europeans became more sophisticated and more spiritually aware. A single example makes this clear. Most of us would agree that one of the most evil of all Christian institutions was the Inquisition, which was an instrument of terror in the Catholic Church until the end of the seventeenth century. Its methods were also used by Protestants to persecute and control the Catholics in their countries. These methods were that "heretics" should be hunted out by a panel of inquisitors, who in the Catholic Church were usually Dominicans. This gave them a new nickname, for they were called *Domini canes*, the hounds of the Lord. These bloodhounds of orthodoxy sniffed out the heretics in the community and people who held unacceptable views or were accused of "unchristian" practices were arrested and flung into prison. There they would be tortured with unbelievable cruelty and made to "confess" their crimes. Frequently they were also accused of far more than heterodox opinions: they were forced to confess that they worshiped the Devil or took part in monstrous sexual orgies; once they had been tortured beyond endurance, they had no further strength to deny the charges. The inquisitors themselves were genuinely convinced that these abominable practices really were committed by "heretics" and this shows that Europe was still haunted by the same inner demons as had inspired Christians to make the Muslims and Jews monsters of evil in the Middle Ages. Four hundred years after the Crusades, sophisticated Europeans felt a sickening dread when they contemplated a challenge to their faith which impelled them to annihilate this threat. Once the heretic had confessed his error he might be released, but that was not always the case. After confession, the heretics were handed over to the secular authorities and were then either hanged or burned at the stake. Sometimes they were so badly injured that they could not walk to the pyre and the executioners tried to hide their dreadful wounds from the spectators.[117]

This obscene institution was the creation of that most saintly Christian king, "Saint" Louis. In 1229, when he was only fifteen, Louis organized the first Inquisition to eliminate the heresy of Catharism in the south of France. The military Crusade of Simon of Montfort had not proved as effective as had been hoped and the heresy continued to flourish, so Louis instructed the Dominicans, who had originally been created to preach peacefully to the heretics, to persecute them instead by inquisitorial methods.[118] The Inquisition continued to operate in the south until 1247 when Louis and his army massacred the last remaining Catharists in cold blood at Montségur. But once Catharism had been wiped out, there were many other heresies to extinguish and the Inquisition continued, as we have seen. It was not surprising that this noxious offspring of the Crusades was eventually used to persecute Muslims and Jews living in Christian territory, who had been forced to convert to Christianity. In the early part of the next chapter we shall examine this next phase of crusading activity against Jews and Muslims in the Christian West.

# 1300 to the Present Day
## New Crusaders in the West

The year 1492 is often seen as a symbolic watershed—as the beginning of the modern period. That year three very important things happened in Spain. In January, King Ferdinand and Queen Isabella brought the Christian wars of reconquest to a triumphant conclusion when they conquered the Muslim kingdom of Granada, the last stronghold of Islam in Europe. With deep emotion, crowds watched the Christian banner being ceremonially raised on the city walls, and throughout Europe church bells pealed joyfully. For four hundred years Europeans had been engaged in a desperate struggle against Islam and now they had finally purged Christendom of this "filth," as they called the Muslims. Three months later the Jews of Spain were given a terrible choice: they had to convert to Christianity or leave the country. Many were so attached to Spain that they chose baptism but about 100,000 Spanish Jews began a new period of exile and the Jews of Europe mourned the loss of Spanish Jewry as the greatest disaster to have befallen their people since the destruction of the Temple. But the year 1492 is primarily famous for another reason. Present at the liberation of Granada was a man whose name was Christopher Columbus. It seems that he may well have come from a family of Jewish origin: the name Colon was common among Italian Jews, he used to boast of his connection with King David, observed Jewish superstitions and sought out the company of Spanish Jews. In August 1492 he sailed across the Atlantic, hoping to arrive in India, but accidentally discovered the New World instead. In India Columbus had hoped to establish a Christian base from which Christendom could launch a new Crusade against Islam: his diaries show that years later he was still preoccupied with the conquest of Jerusalem.[1] As Europe sailed into the modern period, she was still motivated by the old crusading enthusiasms and the dreams and fears of crusading were to be entangled with those of the modern West. With Columbus they crossed the Atlantic and took root in America.

In this last chapter I want to trace the survival of crusading habits in the modern period, examining in particular the convoluted Western view of Islam and Judaism. But it will also be important, from time to time, to turn to the experience of Jews and Muslims to see how they were affected by this strange Western hostility. Spain's purge of Jews and Muslims at the very beginning of the modern era is most significant. We have seen that for a long time the popes had been trying to force the Christians of Europe to sever all relations with Muslims and Jews, the two victims of the Crusaders who seemed somehow fused in the European mind. But Muslim Spain had been the one place in Europe where Jews, Christians and Muslims had been able to live side by side and to build a rich culture together, which had transformed the intellectual experience of Europe. It will be recalled that during the latter half of the twelfth century scholars had congregated in Toledo from all over Europe to enjoy the fruits of Spanish scholarship and that Jews and Muslims had cooperated with Christian scholars in a translation project which restored to Europe the learning she had lost during the Dark Ages. But in 1492 Spain had been "purified" of the contamination of Jews and infidels and from this point the Spanish Inquisition would become an iniquitous byword of orthodoxy: it was as if Spain wished somehow to atone for her former tolerance, which she now regarded as unchristian.

Anti-Semitism had been growing in Spain since the end of the fourteenth century. Virulent preaching and punitive government measures had pressured the Jews of Spain to convert to Christianity. The rabbis had warned their people against conversion: they would find no rest among the Christians. They proved to be right. Many of the converted Jews, who were called *marranos*, became sincere Christians but others probably remained true to their old faith in secret and this caused a fresh terror among the Christians. They developed a horror of the very notion of crypto-Jews, lurking unseen and spreading their poison throughout society. In 1483 Ferdinand and Isabella had established the Spanish National Inquisition to hunt out these secret Jews. Dominican and Franciscan inquisitors rounded up suspects among the *marranos*, tortured them and forced them to confess their adherence to Judaism and to denounce other secret Jews. Within twelve years 13,000 people, most of them Jews, had died as victims of the Inquisition. The expulsion of the Jews, as might be expected, provoked a new terror of crypto-Jews and the new converts were arrested and watched keenly for signs of deviance. Up to this time the Inquisition had been unable to lay a finger on Muslims: its business was solely with faithless Christians. But in 1499 the Muslims who had stayed on in Spain after the conquest of Granada were given the same choice as the Jews seven years earlier: baptism or expulsion. Many left Christendom for the House of Islam but some were so attached to Spain, which had been their home for nearly eight hundred years, that they were baptized. Because these Muslim converts, who were known as *moriscos*, were given absolutely no instruction in their new faith, many of them remained true to Islam in secret and this naturally gave rise to a new Christian fear of crypto-Muslims. The Inquisition now began to hound and persecute *moriscos* together with *marranos*.

This new persecution was no longer, strictly speaking, based on religion. The hatred of Jews and Muslims had acquired a racial element: these *moriscos* and *marranos* were Christians and some of them were sincere Christians but they were always regarded with suspicion. As early as 1449 the Strictures of the Purity of Blood had been promulgated in Spain to define exactly who was a racially pure "Old" Christian and who was a tainted, suspect "New" Christian of Moorish or Jewish extraction. Centuries before a racist attitude became common in Europe, it had become part of the outlook of the Spanish people. New Christians remained suspect and vulnerable to the Inquisition for centuries. Many of the problems of St. Teresa of Avila, the sixteenth-century Carmelite mystic who was in constant trouble with the authorities, may have sprung from the fact that her family were New Christians of Jewish origin. As late as 1628 we find the Spanish inquisitor Juan Escobar de Caro explaining: "By *converso* (convert) we commonly understand any person descended from Jews or Saracens be it in the most distant degree. . . . Similarly a New Christian is thus designated not because he has recently been converted to the Christian faith but rather because he is a descendant of those who first adopted the correct faith."[2]

The long survival of this murderous suspicion and hostility shows how deeply the old crusading habit had penetrated the world view of Christendom, especially in Spain. It is also important to notice how hatred of Jews and Muslims was connected and followed the same pattern: the two victims of the Crusaders were still fused together in people's minds. *Marranos* and *moriscos* could both be rounded up for practices that had no religious significance whatever but which made them immediately suspect. Both, for example, could be denounced to the Inquisition for refusing to eat pork—a habit that is commonly retained after conversion or assimilation. *Marranos* would be arrested for lighting a candle on Sabbath eve and *moriscos* were burned to death for refusing to drink wine, for throwing sweets at a wedding or using henna. The smallest sign of a connection with Jewish or Muslim culture or religion, however neutral, was extremely dangerous.[3] Spaniards were deeply, fiercely resistant to the notion of assimilating people of Jewish or Moorish stock into their society: like the rest of Europe, they had discovered that they could not live alongside people of other religions and were taking this aversion to a fanatical extreme.

But the rest of Europe was no more tolerant than Spain. Indeed, the end of the crusading period marked a new era of intransigence. During the Black Death, which had struck Europe in 1348, people instinctively turned against the Jews and blamed them for this catastrophe. They were rounded up, tortured and made to confess that they had poisoned the wells and caused this terrible plague in order to wipe out the people of Christendom. The Pope and the bishops tried to stop the pogroms: they could see that the Jews were suffering from the Black Death as badly as everybody else. But the masses were quite beyond logic and reason. Killing Jews seemed to be the only way that they could cope with their fear and grief. By the end of 1349 there were hardly any Jews left in Germany or the Low Countries. The persecutions continued during the fifteenth century: one city after another found that it could not bear the presence of the Jews. Paul Johnson lists the shameful and constant expulsions and deportations of Jews "from Vienna and Linz in 1421, from Cologne in 1424, Augsburg in 1439, Bavaria in 1442 (and again in 1450) and from the crown cities of Moravia in 1454. They were thrown out of Perugia in 1485, Vicenza in 1486, Parma in 1488, Milan and Lucca in 1489 . . . and all Tuscany in 1494."[4] The expulsion from Spain must be seen in the context of this larger European trend.

Granada had been the last Muslim city in Europe and it is possible that when Muslims ceased to be a constant physical presence the people of Europe might have felt their fanatical hatred of Islam abating slightly. But it is also true that the failure of the Crusades had made "Mohammadanism" frightening in a new way because the Muslim victory had threatened the integrity of Christendom: the very thought of Islam had evoked a terrible dread that God might have deserted his people. In 1453 this terror was compounded when the Ottoman Turks conquered Byzantium and brought Islam to the very gates of Europe. Without the rampart of Christian Byzantium, the people of Christendom seemed more vulnerable than ever. It seemed as though the old medieval nightmare was about to come true: Islam was about to swallow up poor little Europe. In this climate there could be no new understanding of Islam, and the monstrous Muslim was known henceforth as "the unspeakable Turk." "Mohammadanism" now posed a threat and evoked a fear that were too dreadful to be voiced aloud.[5] For over a hundred years the frontiers of Europe moved alarmingly backward and forward while the Europeans grappled with the Ottomans until the Christian victory of Lepanto in 1571 put a stop to further Turkish conquests. But the shadow of this mighty Muslim empire still hung over Europe. A cool political look at the Ottoman regime would have shown Christians that it had grave internal flaws: for all its imposing military strength, there was no way that it could have conquered the whole of Europe. But faced with the Islamic peril, Europeans were incapable of this kind of detachment. Their vision of Muslims as the absolute enemies of Christendom had had too long to sink in; it had become an essential part of the way they saw the world.

After the crusading period, therefore, Jews and Muslims were both objects of irrational dread: both were seen to be capable of destroying Europe. They could not be seen as normal foreigners or ordinary military enemies but were synonymous with evil itself. During the Middle Ages the Western world had established its unique identity; by the end of the fifteenth century it was on the brink of future formidable achievements. But this Western mentality was not healthy: it was haunted by inner demons and by bogeys that it had created as images of its worst anxieties. The West would learn to control the world more successfully perhaps than any other culture but this fearful instability shows a central weakness. Crusading had been integral to the building of the new Western self during the Middle Ages but it had demanded a massive psychological denial, for right up to the very end of the crusading period nobody had ever seriously questioned the morality of these wars of extermination. Crusaders had sincerely believed that crusading was an act of the love of God. This must have involved serious repressions which, in turn, must have helped that process of projection whereby Jews and Muslims became everything that Christendom thought it was *not* (or, perhaps, feared that it *was*). In this chapter I want to show how this habit of projection continued. At each stage of Europe's development, as the West redefined itself, the images of "the Jew" and "the Muslim" were adjusted so that they could once again become the exact opposite of "us."

This characteristic was at first unique to Christianity: the people of Western Europe had become obsessively interested in their enemies —or rather with the images of these enemies that they had created.

But the Jews and Muslims themselves seemed quite uninterested in their powerful enemy, Western Christendom. This lack of interest was not always healthy either but it would be a mistake to imagine that Jews and Muslims were busily building their own unhappy and distorted stereotype of "the Christian" or "the Frank." In fact the people of all three faiths were walled off from one another. At the same time as Christians were sometimes quite literally pushing Jews and Muslims away from them, they, in their very different ways, were retreating from Western Christendom.

The Arabs, for their part, continued to be quite uninterested in Western Christendom. It will be recalled that during the crusading period the Franks of Europe had nothing to offer the Islamic world, which was far more advanced. But by the time Columbus discovered America, Christendom had more than caught up and was about to conquer whole new worlds. To consider, as the Arabs seem to have done, that nothing had changed in Europe since the Crusades was a serious misconception. But we have to remember that so far the West had made little impression on the Muslim world as a whole. The Crusaders had affected only those people of the Near East who had the misfortune to live in the vicinity of the Crusader states. The rest of the Islamic empire was not troubled by the Crusades and had other serious problems that had nothing whatever to do with the Franks. Within the Islamic empire, Christianity was regarded as a superseded religion: the Christian *dhimmis*, like the Jews, were second-class citizens. They were tolerated and accepted as part of the Arab family but the religion was inevitably regarded as imperfect and incomplete, and the inferior status of Christian Arabs emphasized this point. It seems that the Arabs identified the West entirely with inferior Christianity and therefore may have rejected its Christian culture in advance as inherently unsatisfactory. Indeed even in the early eighteenth century we find the famous Ottoman scholar Naima comparing the European states of his day to the medieval Crusaders and concluding that they were not worth his attention.[6]

There was nothing in Islam which encouraged this closed attitude. We have seen that in the early days Muslims had eagerly assimilated other cultural traditions and had been willing to learn from people who were more advanced than they were. But the Mongol invasions had brought about a new conservatism and in the early sixteenth century two new disasters struck the Arab world. First, on May 17, 1498, the Portuguese Vasco da Gama had followed up Columbus' triumph by sailing around Cape Horn and landing in India. Columbus had hoped to found a new crusading base in the subcontinent but

Vasco da Gama's achievement inflicted a far more crippling blow on the Middle East as a whole than any of the Crusaders' initiatives. This new sea route to the Far East was much cheaper and safer for Europeans, who could now bypass the Middle East altogether. The old trade routes to the Far East had been vital to the Muslim economy, and from this point the Middle East, which had been outflanked, became rather a backwater. This was compounded when the Ottomans conquered the Mamluk empire in 1517 and absorbed Syria, Egypt, Tunis and Algiers into their vast empire. The Arabs were now insulated by the Ottoman wall, which had much the same effect as an iron curtain. Cut off from profitable trading contacts with the outside world and transformed into a subjugated people, the Arabs suffered a crisis of confidence. In their new situation it was natural that they should be more preoccupied with the Ottoman Turks than with the distant West.

In one sense there was nothing new about the Ottoman regime: we have seen that Arabs had been led by the Turks ever since the eleventh century. But this was in effect a completely new departure: instead of the old confederation of Seljuk or Mamluk sultans and emirs, the Ottomans had created a highly centralized state, ruled from afar in Constantinople (which now became Istanbul). Increasingly, Turkish replaced Arabic as the official language and Arabic was retained only for worship, in rather the same way as Latin and Hebrew were used by Catholics and Jews. Arabs felt that they were losing their identity, and to this day the real triumphs of the Ottoman Muslims are not important to Muslim Arabs.[7] Harvard professor Wilfred Cantwell Smith, an expert on Islam and comparative religion, points out that the Arabs' sense of shame was increased by their sense of past greatness:

> The Arab sense of bygone splendour is superb. One cannot begin to understand the modern Arab if one lacks a perspective feeling for this. In the gulf between him and, for instance, the modern American, a matter of prime significance has been precisely the deep difference between a society with a memory of past greatness and one with a sense of present greatness.[8]

This is something, perhaps, that a British person can understand more easily than an American, because today the British also have a sense of a great past which is gone forever. It is not easy to adjust to permanent second-class status.

Today Arabs feel a twofold resentment about the Ottoman period, which they see as their Dark Age. First, the Ottoman Empire was a military autocracy that had a decaying feudal social system. Its initial strength inevitably gave way to a long miserable decline, and the Arabs inevitably declined within it. Second, when the Empire finally collapsed in 1918, the Arabs came under Western non-Muslim rule. This was not a sudden coup: a new kind of Western invasion had begun as early as the sixteenth century when the Ottomans gave Britain, France and Holland special concessions that allowed them the same rights in the Middle East as the native Christian *dhimmis* (or *millets* as the Turks called the protected minorities). The Europeans instantly established a network of trading posts and consular missions which proved to be the Trojan horse that brought Western cultural and social influence into the area.[9] These foreigners lined their pockets at the expense of local trade and at the same time established the West ever more firmly in the region so that it was not difficult for them to take over when the Empire finally collapsed. The Arabs were having to adjust to a painful political and social change; Ottoman supremacy hastened the process of decline that had begun after the Mongol invasions, and for the first time in Islamic history the Arabs had closed their minds somewhat to foreign influence in order to preserve what they could. It was, for these complex reasons, not easy for them to form any opinion of the West from the Ottoman ghetto. They had too many problems nearer home.

The Jews of Europe, of course, were also ghetto-bound and this was as much by their own desire as because of the intolerance of Europe. Sometimes Jews protested, as the Venetian Jews protested about the building of the new ghetto during the sixteenth century, which they felt combined minimum social contact with *goyim* and maximum economic exploitation. But in general the Jews felt that the ghetto was expressive of reality: it afforded some measure of protection and also made it easier for them to observe the Torah. During the Dark Ages, Jews had made a separate quarter, surrounded by a wall, a condition of their settlement in a town. Within the ghetto Jews studied their own Scriptures and writings and were not interested in the culture of their Christian neighbors. It was this enclosed life that helped them to preserve their own unique identity. Many of the rabbis of the sixteenth century would have liked the ghetto walls to be higher, so that no Gentile ideas penetrated Jewry.[10] Again, there was, of course, nothing intrinsic in Judaism that demanded such self-absorption. It is true that God had said that his chosen people was to be holy, like himself; that is, set apart, separated. It is also true that the Torah's strict dietary and other laws imposed some degree of segregation. But this has not always meant that Jews have shut themselves off from the Gentiles in this extreme way. We have seen that Philo of

Alexandria was influenced by Gentile ideas and that during the first century C.E. the diaspora Jews were very accepting of the *goyim*. Similarly in Muslim Spain, Jews had cooperated with Muslim and Christian scholars in the great translation project and in the Islamic world generally they had lived more integrated lives. They were regarded as part of the Arab people and took part in business, government and administration. The harsher conditions of Europe doubtless led to a closing of the doors of the ghetto against the murderous *goyim*.

But it is also true that, since the loss of the Temple, Jews had confined their scholastic and intellectual endeavors to the study of the Torah: they had stopped writing narrative and history—and this makes it difficult for us to find out much about Jewish attitudes. Maimonides, for example, had firmly opposed the writing of history: it was held that history had stopped when the Temple was destroyed and would be resumed when the Messiah came.[11]

Nevertheless Solomon Ibn Verga (d. 1525), a Spanish exile, did write the first Jewish work of history since Josephus had described the fall of Jerusalem. His *Shevet Yehuda* (*The Rod of Judah*) attacked the ghetto mentality of the Jews. Self-criticism had been a remarkable characteristic of Jewish historical writing since biblical times and Ibn Verga concluded that the Jews were partly responsible for their own misfortunes. They were brought up to hate and were educated too narrowly. Because they had neither political nor military education, they were very vulnerable in Europe. Jews should learn a greater balance and preach toleration of the *goyim*, who were not *all* bad.[12] He has a wise man say:

I have never seen a man of reason hate the Jews and there is none who hates them except the common people. For this there is a reason—the Jew is arrogant and always seeks to rule: you would never think that they are exiles and slaves, driven from people to people. Rather they seek to show themselves lords and masters. Therefore the masses envy them.[13]

No Christian writer would have been capable of such objectivity about his own people's failing toward his enemies at that time; nor would he have preached toleration of the "other." But Ibn Verga was most unusual: most Jews retained their hostility and refused to take any interest in the *goyim*. Ibn Verga was right when he claimed that the Jews had some friends in Christian Europe. Individual rulers had been happy to have Jews in their cities ever since the Dark Ages because they were such efficient producers of wealth. Their constant enforced wanderings had made them expert settlers and financially mobile, and from the sixteenth century onward the Jews contributed greatly to the growing capitalist identity of Europe. This debt is insufficiently acknowledged and capitalism is usually seen as an achievement of the Protestant ethic but there is no doubt that the Jews' contribution to the Western economy has proved to be crucial and formative to the present day.

The Jews' expulsion from Spain naturally encouraged their separatist spirit. We have seen that the distress endured by Jews during the crusading period led many to the Zionist solution. During the thirteenth century hundreds had made *aliyah* to Palestine. But the loss of Spain led to a different development that is most important in our story: there was a new and popular enthusiasm for the mysticism and ideology of Kabala. Hitherto Kabala had been esoteric, a mystical discipline for the chosen few, but after the expulsion from Spain it became a folk mythology and gradually became a central Jewish ideal. It provided an answer to the agonized questions: why did God not help his people? what did the endless exile mean?

Enthusiasm for Kabala was largely due to the charismatic and holy Spanish exile Isaac ben Solomon Luria (d. 1576). He taught a method of gaining access to God by meditating on the letters of the Divine Name, but more important for our purposes was his theory of the exile of the *Shekinah*. He taught that God himself had gone into exile when he created the world: he had vacated a space which had formerly been filled by his Presence (the *Shekinah*) in order to make room for the world. He had continued to dwell in certain parts of the cosmos but the vessels of the divine Presence had been unable to contain him. They had collapsed, the sparks of divine light had fallen to the earth and the whole cosmos was breaking down. The Jews' exile was a most important symbol of this universal and divine exile. But the Jews had a mission: by meticulous observance of the Torah they could release the sparks of divine light from the matter in which it was trapped. When this process had been completed, the exile of the *Shekinah* would end and the Messiah would return to achieve the redemption of the Jews. This idea gave the Jews hope and consolation: it encouraged them to feel that they could themselves help to end their exile.[14] After the loss of Spain, Luria taught that the exile of the *Shekinah* was nearly at an end and the coming of the Messiah was nigh. These apocalyptic hopes flared high, particularly after an anti-Semitic disaster. But Lurianic mysticism, which soon became widespread throughout Europe, meant that in the future Jews no longer believed that they would hasten the redemption by settling in Palestine. They envisaged a more mystical process and believed that they must wait until the Messiah appeared before they returned to Eretz Yisrael to end the exile. This view prevailed until it was challenged by the secular Zionists at the end of the nineteenth century.

Thus during the sixteenth century the Jews and Arabs were both, in very different ways, turning away from the intellectual rationalism that had previously characterized both the Jewish and the Islamic tradition. Hitherto, the Christians had been the ones who were prey to emotional and irrational mysticism on the one hand and to an insecure conservatism on the other. But now the position was reversed. The Arabs were succumbing to an intellectual Dark Age, born like the Dark Age in Europe of destructive invasions and social upheaval. The Jews were beginning to abandon the pragmatic rationalism and intellectual austerity of Maimonides. Instead they were turning to a more emotive and unrational faith. Neither had any interest at all in the ideas of the Christian West, which was at one of the most important turning points of its history.

The Protestant Reformation, which was followed by the Catholic Counter-Reformation, was not just a theological dispute. The new ideas about religion were symptoms of a far deeper change in the consciousness of Europe. It was a period when the West was re-forming or reshaping its identity and transforming the way it looked at the world. This was chiefly marked by a greater individualism: each Christian was now exhorted to be responsible for his own salvation and to interiorize his or her religious beliefs at a deeper level. It is easy to see that this would unleash a new type of dynamism in the West, one which would be characterized by greater efficiency and by private initiative. In both the Reformation and the Renaissance, man came to the center of the picture and that would encourage greater confidence in human potential.

But though this new Western consciousness would make the West more formidable and successful than before, it would be a mistake to think that Christianity was about to become a humane and tolerant religion. It was certainly true that Protestantism opposed practices which had been crucial to crusading, such as relics, pilgrimage and devotion to saints and holy places. But Protestantism had its own aggression. Luther, for example, believed that all rebellious peasants should be massacred and that the Pope was Antichrist.[15] Protestants would organize their own Crusades of great cruelty against Catholics and nonconformists. Further, Luther and the reformers saw "Moham-madanism" as a power that was as evil as the papacy: Rome was the head of Antichrist and "Mohammadanism" was his body. Zwingli and other reformers put forward similar ideas.[16] This fantasy of an alliance between Islam and the Catholic Church contradicted the whole history of the Middle Ages but that did not worry the reformers because they did not really see "Islam" as a religious, social or political entity but more as a state of absolute evil. The dehumanization of "Mohammadanism" had eventually been interiorized in the Western mind and become a symbol of absolute evil in people's emotional landscape. As Norman Daniel explains, the reformers "introduced the idea of Islam as an interior state which may be imputed to the enemies of pure doctrine (however the writer may define it). In doing so they in effect admitted the interiorization of Islam as the 'enemy' (undifferentiated) which it had been for so long in the European imagination."[17] Although Protestantism was striving for a less superstitious form of religion, it was still haunted irrationally by inner demons.

Luther was just as hostile to Jews. He told the Jews of Germany that, because he had reformed Christianity and made the Scriptures central, they could now become Christians: they would find their own Scriptures venerated, free of Romish error. This monstrous piece of impertinence showed absolutely no appreciation of the strong objections Jews have to the main Christian message. It arrogantly continued the old tradition of seeing Judaism as a mere prelude to and subsection of the "higher" religion of Christianity. When the Jews replied that they found a closer approximation to their Scriptures in the Talmud, Luther became aggressive. In his pamphlet *On the Jews and Their Lies* (1524) he looked forward to Hitler: Jews should be absolutely segregated from Christians, their homes must be demolished and they must live under one roof and do forced labor. Synagogues and prayer books should be burned. In 1537 Luther had already had the Jews expelled from Lutheran cities and they were also thrown out of Calvinist cities, even though Calvin sometimes spoke positively of Jews. It is significant that the Lutherans used this apparent appreciation of Judaism to discredit their Calvinist rivals and called them "Judaizers," associating them automatically with the "other."[18]

This is important. Europe was redefining itself and both Catholics and Protestants identified Jews and Muslims with the "other side." Lutherans linked Rome with Islam and Calvinism with Judaism. Catholics blamed the Jews, particularly the *marrano* converts, for secretly aiding and abetting the reformers: how else, they asked, could one explain the Protestant encouragement of Hebrew in the schools?[19] The tendency to seek culprits in enemies hidden in society had entered the West via crusading in the thirteenth century and was now an established habit that is still with us. Jews, for example, have always been linked with the current enemy of society: with Anabaptists, nonconformists, revolutionaries, homosexuals and Communists. Muslims were also brought in to discredit the "other side." Thus in the seventeenth century we find the Catholic missionary M. Febvre describing Muslims as "Mohammadan Protestants," who believed in justification by faith: "they hope for the remission of all their sins, provided they believe in Mahomet."[20] Just as absurd was the attempt of the Protestant travel writer L. Rauwolff to describe Muslims as "Mahommedan Catholics" believing in justification by works: "they go after their own invented devotion to good works, alms, prayers, fasting, redeeming of captives etc., to make satisfaction to God."[21] It is natural to explain another culture in terms of one's own but these ludicrous remarks are not so dissimilar in spirit from the popular distortions of "Islam" that are current in our own day, which tell us rather more about our own Western preoccupations, prejudices and anxieties than they tell us about Islam itself. It is common in the media or the popular press to see "Islam" stigmatized for being an excessively and essentially violent religion or for being inherently opposed to rationality and progress. If challenged, it is not unusual for people to look rather puzzled or bemused because accuracy is still not exactly the point at issue when talking about "Islam." It is still to some degree an interiorized symbol that reflects a Western state of mind and an image of everything that we in the tolerant and progressive West believe (or hope) that we are not. Western women, for instance, seem to want to believe that in Islamic law a man "owns" his wife and remain incoherently unconvinced, even after chapter and verse are quoted to them in refutation by angry Muslim women, who have been brought up in the West and who find this attitude prejudiced and offensive. This is an entrenched cultural habit, well established in the medieval Catholic tradition, that survived the upheaval of the Reformation period intact. From that time it became common to compare the Shiite-Sunni division in terms of the Catholic-Protestant split,[22] with approval or disapproval, depending on the writer's own bias. Shiites are usually seen to be "like" Catholics, with their cult of saints, and the severer Sunnis are held to be more "like" Protestants.

But in the early sixteenth century older and more traditional crusading myths were also circulating and would resurface horribly in the twentieth century. For years German Catholics had expected Frederick II to return as the Last Emperor and during the fifteenth century the belief in the Second Coming of Frederick was seen as a dangerous heresy. In the early years of the Reformation a Catholic known as the Revolutionary of the Upper Rhine produced a book called *The Book of a Hundred Chapters*. It is important not for the influence it exerted directly but for the influences it had absorbed and which persisted as part of the German sense of self until the Nazi era. The Revolutionary was a racist: he rewrote history and claimed, like the Crusaders, that *his* people, not the Jews, were the chosen people: the Jews had misled the world and robbed the Germans of the respect that was their due. The Germans, he claimed, had long ago "lived together like brothers on this earth, holding all things in common." They were the descendants of Noah's son Japheth and had settled in Europe after the flood, founding an empire with Trier as their capital. They had ruled the whole of Europe in a golden age but their empire had been destroyed by the Romans. To this day the Latins (the Italians and the French) had continued to oppress the German people. Fortunately Frederick would soon return. He would subjugate the Latins and purge Europe of the wicked in huge massacres, riding at the head of an army of the poor. Then he would re-establish the German Reich at Mainz, which would last a thousand years and usher in the Last Days. Once he had achieved this, Frederick would ride east, crush the Ottoman Empire and march to the Holy Land. He would destroy "the society of Muslims" and liberate Jerusalem, in further purges and massacres. Thenceforward the Germans would rule the world, re-establish their pure culture and everybody would acknowledge that they were the chosen race.[23] This was a direct continuation of a crusading tradition that first manifested itself in the twelfth century, when the Emperor Frederick Barbarossa rode east, presenting himself to his people as the Last Emperor. In fact the real Frederick II would have been astounded at the role he was expected to play, but historical accuracy was not important to his fifteenth- and sixteenth-century followers: whatever he had been in reality, he had become for them an interior symbol of the German spirit that was struggling to achieve its destiny. It is surely not accidental that the most exuberantly enthusiastic biography of Frederick was written by Ernst Kantorowicz, a patriotic German scholar who published his *Frederick the Second* in 1931.

But during the seventeenth century an entirely new attitude toward the chosen people and the Promised Land appeared which would prove to be extremely important. In this respect Protestantism really did reform old crusading notions. This new tendency appeared first in England, where some Protestants wanted to abolish the ritual and hierarchy of the Anglican Church and return to a simpler religion of direct intimacy with God, without the intervention of priests and ritual. They were called "Puritans" by their Anglican and Catholic opponents, because of their concern for moral and religious purity. The Bible is always crucial in any extreme Protestant sect that refuses to conform to the established Church, because it is the Word of God, the chief way in which he has communicated with man, and people usually interpret it quite literally. The Puritans were particularly drawn to the stern ethics of the Old Testament and took St. Paul very seriously when he wrote that Christians were the New Israel. Like the Crusaders before them, they insisted that they were God's new elect, the new chosen people. Unlike the Crusaders, the Puritans felt not that they had to slaughter Jews but that it was their duty that God's clearly expressed wishes for them in the Old Testament be carried out. They also applied to their own experience the lessons that God had given to the Jews in the days of the Old Covenant. Christians had always done this, but the Puritans took the logical step of identifying with the Jews of the past and gave themselves a rather Jewish identity: they gave their children Jewish names like Samuel, Amos, Sarah or Judith. Further they believed that they were living in the Last Days and St. Paul had said that before the Second Coming the Jews would be converted. The Jews would, therefore, not be Jews for very much longer.

During the seventeenth century it became increasingly dangerous to be a Puritan in England. They rejected the authority of bishops, so the establishment feared that this made them a political threat: soon they might also rebel against temporal authority. King James and Archbishop Laud became very hostile indeed, and James vowed that he would harry the Puritans from the land. It seemed to the Puritans that James and Archbishop Laud would shortly reintroduce Catholicism in England. In 1618, for example, James issued a *Declaration of Sports* which encouraged revels when planting and harvesting was over, instead of honoring the Sabbath and enforcing church attendance. This shocked the Puritans, who saw such revels as godless and many attacked the government angrily. Some were imprisoned and others were threatened with persecution. One of these was Thomas Shepard, who recorded a meeting with Laud in 1618 that gives some idea of the intensity of feeling.

[Laud] looked as though blood would have gushed out of his face and did shake as if he had been haunted with an ague fit, to my apprehension by reason of his extreme malice and secret venom. I desired him to excuse me. He fell then to threaten me and withal to bitter railing, calling me all to naught, saying, You prating coxcomb! Do you think all the learning is in your brain? He pronounced his sentence thus: I charge you that you neither preach, read, marry, bury, or exercise any ministerial function in any part of my diocese, for if you do, and I hear of it, I will be upon your back and follow you wherever you go, in any part of the Kingdom, and so everlastingly disenable you.[24]

There was naturally a good deal of debate among the Puritans about what they should do. Some Puritans had already fled the contamination of England and taken themselves off to Amsterdam where they formed a tight community, living according to their own ideals. But this seemed a cowardly solution to many: "Shall we leave [God's] subjects and children," asked the great Puritan preacher Richard Sibbes, "for this or that fear? Let our condition be never so uncomfortable, he can make it comfortable."[25] But Puritans were getting more and more angry and increasingly articulate. "To suffer imprisonment and disgraces for good causes, this is a good work," said John Preston in his sermons on *The Breast-Plate of Faith and Love*. But he also made it clear that Puritans should not just sit back and wait for deliverance from on high. They would have to take their destiny into their own hands and rebel against this oppression. "Let us not say we must be moderate . . . we must be men of contention."[26]

As so often in Christian history, this experience of trauma led most Puritans in England into a new holy war. They formed a fighting force called the New Model Army under Oliver Cromwell, which was also a spiritual way of life and a means of disciplining the self.[27] In this army the soldiers of God began to prepare their hearts for the reception of grace. Even though Cromwell would have condemned the Catholic Crusaders, it is clear that he and his new soldiers of God had a good deal in common with them. The Crusade had also originally been designed to create a new self and, ultimately, to fight the enemies of God. During the 1640s the army was strong enough to fight against the monarchy in the Civil War and the conduct of the army was again similar to the Crusades. There was much public reading of Scripture and prayer; Cromwell was also very careful to listen attentively to the seers and prophets who believed themselves inspired by God with political or military messages, for Puritanism was an exalted faith, encouraging extreme visionary states not dissimilar to those of the medieval holy wars.[28]

But a minority felt that this was not the answer and instead of joining the army took a decision that would change the course of history and also have important consequences in the conflict in the Middle East today. As early as 1620 the first band of Puritans left England in the *Mayflower* and sailed to the New World; from that date more and more settlers joined them in the new settlement that they called the Plymouth Plantation. Every year Americans remember this crucial moment in their history at Thanksgiving and the story and experience of the Pilgrim Fathers has been crucial in shaping the American identity. The very fact that they called themselves "Pilgrims" like the Crusaders and the early Zionist settlers shows how closely allied the Puritan migrations were to the spirit of other religious migrations that we have considered in this book. It also shows that a crusading enthusiasm is not only embedded deeply in the American identity and crucially formative in American history but also that there is a natural American affinity with Zionism. Let us examine this more closely.

First, it is important to say that, like the Zionists, the Pilgrim Fathers were fleeing oppression in Europe. Familiarity with the story of the *Mayflower* can lead us to see this as a rather romantic episode, perhaps not dissimilar to the glamorous way in which some people see the Crusades. But the emigration was painful and dangerous. The voyage was long, perilous and acutely uncomfortable. Some people actually died on the long journey across the Atlantic and when they arrived many more died of disease and hunger. It was in its own way as traumatic as crusading. The country seemed inhospitable and the settlers spoke of it as "a vast and empty chaos."[29] They were more impressed by the desolation of the New World than by the beauties of which Americans are now so rightly proud. The whole experience was a struggle to achieve a new, independent identity in a new world, not at all dissimilar to the aims of the early Zionists. Like other émigrés that we have met in this book, the Pilgrim Fathers would have denied that they were *merely* fleeing persecution and would have stressed their positive hopes. They were very sensitive to the charge leveled against them by their English brethren that they were running away.[30] But the fact remains that had they not been persecuted by the English establishment none of them would have considered this drastic uprooting. John Winthrop, the governor of the colony, wrote a list of reasons for "the Plantation in New England" (1629) in which the second was this:

All the other churches of Europe are brought to desolation, and our sins, for which the Lord begins already to frown upon us, do threaten us fearfully, and who knows but that God hath provided this place to be a refuge for many whom he means to save out of the general calamity; and seeing the church hath no place to fly into but the wilderness, what better work can there be than to go before and provide tabernacles, and food for her, against she cometh thither.[31]

The corruption they had seen and the dangers they had endured in England had given them an apocalyptic sense of an impending catastrophe, not unlike that experienced by Herzl, who rightly sensed an imminent anti-Semitic calamity. This sense of extremity and fear and desperate search for a refuge was as strongly felt by the New England settlers as all their more positive hopes for the country. America has prided itself on being a nation of refugees and for providing a haven for immigrants who have fled oppression and persecution in Europe. The giant Statue of Liberty in New York Harbor must have been a moving sight to all the persecuted, downtrodden Europeans who later made the dangerous and uncomfortable voyage over the Atlantic. America, like Israel later, was a country born out of suffering in Europe.

Yet there are closer similarities. Like the Crusaders, the Pilgrim Fathers and their followers turned spontaneously to the experience of the old chosen people, the Jews, when they were setting up their colony, and as was their wont they interpreted their struggle in the light of the ancient Jewish experience. Indeed they called their colony the "English Canaan"[32] and gave their settlements in the American wilderness biblical names: Hebron, Salem, Bethlehem, Zion and Judea. The Zionists too, secular as they were, turned back to the Bible in their colonizing effort. In making a Christian presence an "established fact" in the New World, the Americans also had to grapple with the problem of the native American Indians, whose land they proposed to take away. They came up with the same justification that the Zionists would make use of later when defending their claim against the Palestinians: America was an "empty" country, a barren wilderness, which the natives were too primitive to develop properly. As early as 1622 Robert Cushman, the business agent of the colony, wrote of the Indian problem, significantly referring to the Old Testament.

[They] do but run over the grass, as do also the foxes and wild beasts. They are not industrious, neither have art, science, skill or faculty to use either the land or the commodities of it, but all spoils, rots and is marred for want of manuring, gathering, ordering, etc. As the ancient patriarchs therefore removed from straiter places into more roomy, where the land lay idle and waste, and none used it, though there dwelt inhabitants by them (as Genesis 13:6, 11, 12, and 34:21 and 41:20) so it is lawful now to take a land which none useth to make use of it.[33]

When they found that gentle persuasion was insufficient to allay Indian hostility, the Puritans turned their migration into a holy war, on the ancient Jewish paradigm in the early books of the Bible. Like the Crusaders and like the Zionists, they resorted to extreme and ruthless methods in their holy war against the Pequot Indians during the 1640s. They naturally compared these enemies with the Amalekites and the Philistines "that did confederate against Israel,"[34] and massacred the Pequots with a truly Joshuan zeal. Yet ironically some eminent settlers like John Eliot, Thomas Thorowgood and Samuel Sewall took the opposite view: they believed that the Indians were of Jewish origin and that their conversion would be a step toward Christ's Second Coming.[35]

Puritans were generally convinced that they were living in the Last Days and many of the settlers saw their migration as a prelude to the Second Coming. In this they were obviously very much of the same mind as the early Crusaders, when they migrated to Jerusalem at the end of the eleventh century, and also of the early Labor Zionists, who confidently expected the socialist millennium and looked forward to creating a model society in Palestine, which would be a light unto the Gentiles. In 1654 the Puritan settler Edward Johnson published his *Wonder-Working Providence of Sion's Savior in New England*, a history of the colony, and expressed a common feeling among the Puritans, who were living in what they called the "new" world for a very special reason:

> Know this is the place where the Lord will create a new heaven and new earth in, new churches, and a new commonwealth together. Verily if the Lord be pleased to open your eyes, you may see the beginning of the fight, and what success the armies of our Lord Jesus Christ have hitherto had. . . . Further know these are but the beginning of Christ's glorious reformation and restoration of his churches to a more glorious splendor than ever. He hath therefore caused the dazzling brightness of his presence to be contracted in the burning glass of these his people's zeal, from whence it begins to be left upon many parts of the world.[36]

In 1654 it seemed very unlikely that the struggling little colony would one day be the center of Christianity but today, even though Johnson's fervent apocalyptic hopes have come to nothing, it is perhaps true that the leadership of the Christian world has passed from Europe to the pioneers in America.

When Johnson wrote his book it would have seemed to most Puritans that the first fruits of the millennium had been manifested not in America but in England, for Cromwell had led his New Model Army to victory against the royalists in 1649, had beheaded King Charles I and established a Puritan republic in England with himself as "Lord Protector." He did not think that New England was important in the least and wrote of America as a "poor, cold and useless"[37] place. But in Cromwell's Puritan England there were two events that showed the shape of things to come. In the heady days of his victory in 1649 Cromwell had received a petition from the Puritan colony that had been established in Amsterdam, headed by Anne and Ebenezer Cartwright, urging him to hasten the Second Coming of Christ. In the Bible it was prophesied that the Jews would be scattered "to the ends of the earth" (Deuteronomy 28:64; Daniel 12:17) but that prophecy had not been fulfilled, for there had been no Jews in England (a country that Jews at that time called Kezar ha-Aretz: the end of the earth)[38] since King Edward I had expelled them from the country. Cromwell, the Cartwrights urged, should hasten the coming redemption by bringing the Jews back to England. In the new Puritan republic the Jews would surely be converted to Christianity and this would also hasten the Second Coming of Christ. Secondly, the Cartwrights asked

> That this nation of England, with the inhabitants of the Netherlands, shall be the first and readiest to transport Israel's sons and daughters on their ships to the land promised to their forefathers Abraham, Isaac and Jacob for an everlasting inheritance.[39]

The Cartwrights' petition shows how close the Puritans were in spirit to the Crusaders and to extreme religious Zionists today. Instead of waiting passively for the redemption, the Puritans believed that they should hasten it by fulfilling the prophecies themselves.

The prospect of being conveyed to Eretz Yisrael by the British government would prove to be very attractive to many Jews at the time of the Balfour Declaration. But in 1649 the Jews did not want to go: Kabalistic messianism was now normative and most Jews felt that they should wait until the Messiah summoned them to the Promised Land. But many were very interested in the first part of the petition: that the Jews be allowed to settle in England. Apocalyptic hopes were as high among Jews as among Puritans at this time. They often flared up after a catastrophe and in 1648 there had been dreadful pogroms and massacres of Jews in the Ukraine. This was a particular disappointment: the Jews had become very numerous in Poland and, as expert settlers, they had proved invaluable as middlemen to the Polish government who were attempting to colonize the Ukraine:

they acted as tax collectors, bailiffs and stewards, and it seemed as though they had found a new home. But they were also dangerously exposed and precisely because they *were* middlemen they became the focus of Ukrainian and peasant hatred of the Poles. In 1648 as part of their revolt against the Polish government, the Ukrainian Cossacks massacred about 100,000 Jews, destroyed their homes and forcibly deported the rest. As usual, the Jews searched their souls to discover the meaning of this crisis and some were convinced that the Messiah was at hand. Like the Puritans, the Jews considered the year 1666 an apocalyptic year and many waited confidently for the imminent redemption.

Many of the refugees from the Ukraine had settled with the Jewish community in Amsterdam, the home also of the Cartwrights and their Puritan sect. The Dutch government had been happy to welcome a colony of Jews because they knew they would be valuable to the economy but this new influx was too much: a sudden increase in the Jewish population of a city very often inspired a new bout of anti-Semitism and this was greatly feared by Manasseh ben Israel, an Amsterdam Jew whose family had come from Spain. Manasseh was anxious to reach out to the *goyim*. He wanted to win acceptance for the Jews and he wrote books for Christian readers, showing that Christianity and Judaism had more in common than people thought. He was in this respect a most unusual Jew, who insisted that the *goyim* could become friends of the Jewish people:

> Hence it may be seen that God hath not left us; for if one persecutes us, another treats us civilly and courteously; and if this prince treats us ill, another treats us well; if one banisheth us out of his country, another invites us with a thousand privileges, as diverse princes of Italy have done, the most eminent King of Denmark and the mighty Duke of Savoy in Nissa. And do we not see that those Republiques do flourish and much increase in trade who admit the Israelites.[40]

When the Ukrainian refugees arrived in Amsterdam, Manasseh sought help from the Puritan community. He agreed with them that the redemption of 1666 could not occur unless the Jews were settled in the Kezar ha-Aretz and he also saw this as a solution to the current problem: let the surplus of Jews leave Holland and settle in England. In 1650 he published *Spes Israeli* (*The Hope of Israel*), which argued his case and was read by many Puritans with enthusiasm. Manasseh himself presented a petition to Cromwell and had discussions with him about the feasibility of the Jews coming to England. Cromwell had not responded to the Cartwright petition but he was interested in developing a British Jewry because he could see that it would help the ailing economy of the country, which had been badly damaged by the Civil War. But nothing seemed to come of these discussions and in 1655 Manasseh died, a disappointed man. But the following year some London Jews who had been living incognito declared their true Jewish identity and asked permission to build a synagogue. Cromwell was happy to agree and the Jews in England became the first in Europe to receive full citizenship. Jewish immigrants began to arrive in the Kezar ha-Aretz.[41]

This started a tradition in Protestant Britain, which proved to be prepared to use the Jews for its own convenience: Cromwell was interested in their economic value and the Cartwrights saw the Jews as part of the plan for a Christian redemption. We shall see that from this date there were constant calls from English Protestants that the Jews be returned to Zion. They had been brought up on a diet of Bible stories and saw Palestine as a Jewish country. They were usually totally unaware of the centuries of Arab Palestine and left the Arabs out of their vision. They also seemed to see Judaism as a subsection of Christianity, the higher religion, and to see Jews as tools of British and Christian aims. This attitude, we know, had fateful consequences and culminated in the Balfour Declaration of 1917.

But Cromwell's admission of the Jews as full citizens also had another most important corollary. In 1654 the first Jewish settlers arrived in America on the French privateer *St. Catherine*. They settled in the Dutch colonial town of New Amsterdam but the Dutch did not allow them to build a synagogue, forced them to live separately from Gentiles and gave them no rights. But when the town fell to the English Puritan settlers of New England in 1664 and became New York, the Jews were given the full citizenship that they had in England. American Jewry had been born. The Jews were deeply compatible with the Puritans and fitted perfectly into the American congregational system. They had, after all, been congregationalists for centuries! Like the Puritans, the Jews had also long renounced clericalism and preferred religious government by the congregation: Jews had maintained the primacy of the individual conscience for over a thousand years. In America the Jews were just another congregation rather than a special and exotic community. They went to their particular, chosen synagogue as a Protestant went to his chosen church. Without abandoning their faith, the Jews would achieve full integration in America. America would replace the home they had lost in Muslim Spain and from this point there was another Jewish center in their vision of the world: it was no longer divided into Eretz Yisrael and the *herut*, the exile. There were Eretz Yisrael, the diaspora and America.[42]

When the apocalyptic year 1666 finally arrived, the Jewish world in Europe as well as in the Ottoman Empire was shaken when a Messiah *did* appear in Palestine and summoned the tribes of Israel. Shabbtai Zvi, an unbalanced young man, had long been convinced that he was the Messiah and in 1666 his claim was supported by the influential and charismatic Kabalist Nathan of Gaza and by the local rabbis. The Jews were urged to hasten Zvi's success by means of prayer and scrupulous observance of the Torah, as Lurianic messianism enjoined. There was immense excitement; in Turkey enthusiastic riots broke out when it was known that Zvi was coming to Turkey to convert the Sultan. The Ottoman authorities became alarmed and when Zvi arrived he was arrested and taken into the Sultan's presence. There he was given the choice of death or conversion to Islam. To the immense scandal and distress of all the Jewish communities throughout the world which had supported him, Zvi denied that he was the Messiah and converted to Islam. From this point Jews in both East and West became most suspicious of anybody who claimed to be the Messiah; the idea of a physical interpretation of messianism, including settlement in Eretz Yisrael, became even more discredited. A more spiritual observance of Kabalistic messianism became normative: it was observance of Torah and prayer alone which would end both the exile of the *Shekinah* and the exile of the Jews.

The Shabbtai Zvi affair shows how far the Jews had diverged from the old medieval Jewish rationalism: Maimonides had been very wary indeed about how Jewish belief in the Messiah should be interpreted. Lurianic ideas, which stressed the inadequacy of reason and a mystical transcendent prayer, were now central in Jewish life. Previously, ancient superstitions and belief in magical legends had been kept firmly in check but now they were rife in the ghetto. Particularly widespread was the enthusiasm for the *golem*.[43] The *golem* story had many variations but always followed the same pattern. Certain very holy men were believed to have the power to breathe life into an artificial man, the *golem*, who thus acquired a life of his own. He avenged the Jews by attacking the Gentiles, eye for eye, tooth for tooth. But always, in the end, the *golem* became a Frankenstinian monster who got out of control and ran amok. The legend could be seen as a telling indication, perhaps, of what Jews might like to do to the *goyim* if they had the chance. He was an objectified projection of Jewish hostility. But the story also revealed the dangers of Jewish retaliation: it could get out of hand and rebound on the Jews themselves. In the intensely emotional world of the ghettos by the late seventeenth century, the *goyim* were associated with the "other," just as Jews and Muslims were in Christian thought. They were linked with what was known as the demonic *"Otra Sitra"* or the "other side," which was everything God was not. But, unlike the Christians, the Jews did not create detailed stereotypical fantasies of the *goyim*: they preferred to leave them well alone.

At about the same time as the Shabbtai Zvi fiasco another event had made just as painful an impression on European Jewry and this had confirmed Jews in their policy of avoidance of all aspects of the Gentile world. In 1656 the brilliant philosopher Baruch Spinoza had been excommunicated, cast out of the synagogue of Amsterdam and sent over to the "other side." While the edict of excommunication was read out, the lights of the synagogue were gradually extinguished until the congregation was left in total darkness, experiencing themselves the darkness in Spinoza's soul:

> Let him be accursed by day and accursed by night; accursed in his lying down and his rising up, in going out and in coming in. May the Lord never more pardon or acknowledge him! May the wrath and displeasure of the Lord burn against this man henceforth, load him with all the curses written in the book of the Law, and raze out his name from under the sky. . . . Hereby, then, are all admonished that none hold converse with him by word of mouth, or communication by writing, that no one do him any service, abide under the same roof with him, approach within four cubits' length of him, or read any document dictated by him or written by his hand.[44]

The terrifying words remind us that by this date Judaism could be just as fiercely aggressive as Christianity in abhorring heresy and deviation; they also reveal the huge gulf that existed between the nation of Israel and the world outside the safe orthodoxy of the ghetto. Spinoza, who was then aged twenty-four, was also cast out of his father's house and from Amsterdam. Until his death in 1677 he lived among the *goyim* but never became a Christian. As a young student he had become dissatisfied with the study of the Torah and the Talmud and had joined a circle of Gentile Freethinkers. This had led him into a philosophical position that bordered on atheism. A century later his view of religion based on reason and the rejection of the concept of revelation would be commonplace during the Enlightenment, but in his own day Spinoza was a revolutionary thinker.

During the eighteenth century Gentile philosophers like Voltaire looked back to Spinoza with admiration but the rabbis saw him as a terrible example of what could happen to a Jew who toyed with the ideas of the *goyim*: the Gentile world could lead to the loss of the Jewish faith. This confirmed many in the policy of ignoring and avoiding the Gentiles and also in the trend away from rationalism.[45] A reaction against rationalism also led to the Jewish religious revolution or reformation that is known as Hasidism. Like the Christian sects of the American Great Awakening on the Methodism of John Wesley in England, this was a successful attempt to wrest Judaism away from the control of the establishment. It was a people's religion, teaching that even simple people could experience direct contact with God without the rabbis or the scholars. Its great apostle, Israel ben Eliezer, who is most often known as the Baal Shem Tov (Master of the Good Name) taught a method of prayer based on Lurianic contemplation of the letters of the Divine Name which led to the Hasidim being possessed by a form of the divine spirit. Hasidic meetings were noisy, charismatic affairs: the Hasidim shouted aloud, danced and sang, horrifying the Orthodox establishment. In addition, the Baal Shem Tov replaced the discredited cult of an imminent Messiah with the figure of the *zaddick*, the holy man whose piety and charisma could lead the masses to God. The Hasidim may have shared many of the characteristics of charismatic Christian movements of the eighteenth century, but they were quite uninterested in the Christians. After the death of the Baal Shem Tov in 1760, the movement continued and thrives to the present day. Hasidim continue to live as though the surrounding world of the *goyim* did not exist and they are not interested in the cult of Eretz Yisrael: they already meet God in Torah observance and mystical prayer. Even though it began as an anti-intellectual movement, Hasidism has attracted the admiration of eminent Jewish scholars like Martin Buber, Gershon Scholem and Louis Jacobs.

During the eighteenth century there was also a religious revolution in which we can see the first stirrings of the Arab Awakening. By this time the essential weaknesses of the Ottomans had led to misrule, corruption, anarchy and stagnation throughout the Empire. The intellectual decline meant that Muslims still studied according to the principles established in the great medieval universities. The mediocrity and conservatism of the Middle East would lead Western observers to blame Islam for encouraging obscurantism and intellectual conformity but, as we know, that was another inaccuracy. Islam had a strong rationalistic and speculative tradition and Muslim scholars had once been in the intellectual vanguard of the world. But in most of the Middle East there was now an inward-looking attitude that was still unable to take in the new achievements of Western Europe. In the Arabian Peninsula the Arabs produced their own Puritan revolution. Mohammad ibn Abd al-Wahhab (d. 1792), a jurist of Najd, founded a sect that claimed to return to the original spirit of the Prophet Mohammad. Like Luther, he wanted to strip away all later accretions, particularly those introduced by the Sufis, the mystics of Islam, and restore Islam to the splendor of purity that it had enjoyed in Medina in the seventh century. He condemned popular belief in the power of saints as intercessors and the Shiite cult of the tombs of the imams. He refused to accept the authority of any of the classical schools of Muslim law and declared that the gates of *ijtihad* (independent reasoning) had been reopened. *Taqlid* (emulation of the masters of the Sharia) was condemned.

Wahhabism tended to be iconoclastic, like English Puritanism. In 1744 Ibn Abd al-Wahhab had infuriated the Muslim establishment by attacking local shrines and was given asylum by Mohammad ibn Sa'ud, ruler of the small principality of Diriya in Central Arabia. The two men then formed a coalition and Ibn Sa'ud accepted the responsibility of becoming a true Islamic ruler, under the guidance of Ibn Abd al-Wahhab. They began a reform that centered on the same issues as those of the Prophet Mohammad's revolution against the establishment of Mecca. They attacked the oppression of the poor, indifference to the plight of widows and orphans, immorality and idolatry. Wahhabism emphasized the brotherhood and equality that should prevail among all Muslims, irrespective of tribe or rank. They also insisted that the Arabs, not the Turks, should control the Muslim *umma* and Ibn Sa'ud called a *jihad* against those Arab sharifs who ruled in the Hejaz in the name of the Ottoman Turks. Again, this Arab revival had nothing to say as yet about the West: it was a revolution against the Turks and the religious establishment. It was extremely successful, for the Wahhabis managed to wrest a large portion of Central Arabia away from the Ottomans. The sect also proved enduring. The Wahhabis threatened the provinces of Syria and Iraq: in 1803 they attacked the shrine of Imam Husain at Karbala, on the grounds that this cult was superstitious idolatry. In 1813 a Turkish-Egyptian alliance defeated the Wahhabis but the sect revived during the nineteenth and twentieth centuries and is the form of Islam practiced today in the kingdom of Saudi Arabia, which was established in 1932. Later Arab movements, as we shall see, would be inspired by their contact with the West at the very end of the eighteenth century. New Western ideas would prove to be a revelation. But many of them also looked back to the spirit of Wahhabism, which had been the first sign that the Arabs were about to shake off the stagnation of their Ottoman Dark Age and attempt to take their destiny into their own hands.

Since the Reformation a new phenomenon had appeared in Western Christianity, which consisted of violent reactions against religion, succeeded by an intense return to fundamentalist belief and practice. These periods also coincided with another phenomenon which is unique in world history: periods of religiosity coincided with extreme sexual repression and these were succeeded by frenetic permissiveness during the more secular periods. This lurching to and from religious belief suggests a certain imbalance that is not evident in other cultures. Thus the intense religiosity of the sixteenth and seventeenth centuries was followed by the reaction of the skepticism of the Enlightenment. We can learn a lot from the Enlightenment because our own century claimed that man had outgrown religion, rather as the eighteenth-century philosophers had done. This proved to be an inaccurate forecast then and has been a false prediction today. The eighteenth-century Age of Reason was a reaction to the extremism of the Reformation period, when thousands of people had been persecuted for their beliefs. But the Enlightenment proved that people needed more than reason and science: it led to the revival of a charismatic and fundamentalist form of Christianity in the nineteenth century on both sides of the Atlantic. In our own day a period of secularism and skepticism has been succeeded by a new type of Christian fundamentalism in Europe and America that is usually dependent upon a literal interpretation of Scripture and is often very aggressive toward other religions. It is unrealistic to try to batten down the religious need and expect it to disappear. The religious instinct is as impossible to suppress as the sexual instinct; indeed in both cases repression is likely to lead to a more extreme and uncontrollable form of passion. It is also true that during an age of unbelief people continue to be influenced by the habits of faith. The old religious prejudices and myths continue to assert themselves, even though our minds *know* that we are being bigoted and irrational. The eighteenth century shows this clearly, especially as regards the view of Jews and Muslims.

In 1704, for example, Nathaniel Crouch edited and published a volume of essays called *Two Journeys to Jerusalem*. The contributors are not Pilgrims; there is a new coolness toward the Holy Land which is discussed as objectively and scientifically as though it were any other country. They comment on population and on flora and fauna. Again, the old crusading hatred of Judaism seems to have vanished: there are accounts of Manasseh ben Israel and the Shabbtai Zvi fiasco that take an intelligent and detached interest in these events. Crouch, using the pseudonym Robert Burton, wrote one of the travel diaries in the book. Again, it is clear that he is not a religious man but it is also clear that he had been influenced by the Bible to see Palestine as the country of the Jews. Here his scientific objectivity seems to desert him. His Bible reading had suggested to him that Palestine was a populous, thriving place and he was shocked to see that the country did not live up to his idea of a land flowing with milk and honey. It was from Burton that the English people first heard that Palestine was a barren desert. Without considering any other option, Burton irrationally concluded that the past fertility of the country was due entirely to the Israelites, who, he said, had terraced and fertilized the land and wasted none of it.[46] He did not seem to recall that the land had been flowing with milk and honey *before* the Israelites conquered it, as the Bible itself makes clear, nor did he reflect that he had personally seen only a very small bit of the country: the land between Jaffa and Jerusalem has never been very fertile.

But there was one objection to Burton's thesis that only the Jews had been able to make Palestine prosper that was staring him in the face. Jerusalem is full of the architectural relics of civilizations that had been established in the country *after* the fall of Jewish Jerusalem in C.E. 70. The Romans, Byzantines, Arabs, Mamluks and Crusaders had all established societies there and some had been very prosperous. They had left many imposing buildings and works of art behind them. Burton ignored all this and narrowed the entire history of the country to the relatively short period of Jewish occupation. In particular, he failed to see the significance of the Dome of the Rock, which still dominates the Old City. It did not seem to remind him that the Muslims had been established in Palestine for over a thousand years and had made their own unique contribution to its beauty at a time when the British had been primitive barbarians. Burton ignored all this and decided that if the prosperity of the country was entirely due to the industrious Jews its decay had been caused by the "want of culture and tillage among the barbarous Infidels . . . who by their continuous wars and ravages have made it almost desolate and like a desert . . . a place forsaken by God."[47] Even the new man of reason could not interpret the facts before him without referring to a biblical tradition that, in his more rational moments, he might dismiss as an obsolete myth.

There was clearly a very great change in the attitude toward Islam. What had happened to the "unspeakable Turk" and the monstrous

Muslim who sought the overthrow of Christendom? By the eighteenth century Europe was far more confident and rising to new power. The eighteenth century marked a new period of expansion and broadening horizons, as France and Britain fought each other for the control of India until Britain established hegemony in 1767. The Ottoman Empire, on the other hand, was obviously in decline: "Mohammadanism" seemed to be a spent fire and no longer haunted the imagination of Europe. Muslims could easily be dismissed now as the "barbarous infidel" and the former achievements of Islam were no longer a threat and could be ignored. But it is a mistake to imagine that, because *we* think something is no longer a problem because *we* don't see it, it no longer exists. The Arabs had failed to "see" Christianity and imagined that Europe had developed little since the period of the Crusades: at the end of the century they would get a severe shock when they encountered the new West. In our own century we in the West were shocked by the new outbreak of revolutionary Islamic activity and realized belatedly that Islam had been alive and well all along but we had not "seen" it. The eighteenth-century Wahhabi revolution was just one sign of its continued survival.

Burton was developing the "double" vision that we shall see to be characteristic of British Zionism, which saw the Jews and ignored the Arabs. We see this again in a prayer of Joseph Priestley, the Unitarian minister and distinguished chemist. Priestley urged the Jews to convert to Christianity because he saw the two religions as complementary. Again, Priestley was not taking Judaism seriously as an independent religion and was failing to apply to this religious issue the scientific virtues of detachment that he needed in his work. He urged the Jews to acknowledge Jesus as Messiah: that

> the God of Heaven, the God of Abraham, Isaac and Jacob whom we Christians as well as you worship, may be graciously pleased to put an end to your suffering, gathering you from all nations, resettle you in your own country, the land of Canaan, and make you the most illustrious of all nations on the earth.[48]

Priestley cannot seem to see that although *he* graciously acknowledges the Jewish patriarchs the Jews are not going to be able to acknowledge Jesus as the Messiah. He does not appear to realize that, though Christians need the Jewish Scriptures, the Jews have no need of the New Testament. Priestley's Christianity demands the conversion of the Jews but we know that the Jews themselves had very different religious aspirations at the time. Priestley's attitude is an improvement on the old habit of seeing unbaptized Jews as worthy of annihilation but he does wipe out the Jewish view of religion. Similarly he appears to have no vision of Islam at all. The Islamic experience is completely ignored. Muslims also venerate the Jewish patriarchs and acknowledge that Jesus was the Messiah but for Priestley they are not worth a plea or a prayer. They seem not to exist. Like Burton, he left Islam out of the picture and saw only two religions in the tradition of historical monotheism.

Later in the eighteenth century other British Zionists called for a return of the Jews to Palestine. Nobody considered the fact that the Jews themselves at this point had quite different religious aspirations and would not wish to be deported to Palestine. The existence of the Arab Muslims was ignored as was the Islamic claim to Jerusalem. But the British were beginning to look greedily at the decaying Ottoman Empire and were ready to use the Jews for their own political convenience. Thus in 1790 James Beere, Rector of Sandbrook, submitted a petition to William Pitt asking him to assist in hastening the Second Coming by bringing about the "final restoration of the Jews to the Holy Land." Beere also shrewdly pointed out that this would be economically advantageous to the British. Once the Jews were settled, they would "stand in need of many manufactured articles, of the necessities of life . . . especially woollens and linens."[49] The return of the Jews would be of benefit to the British trade outposts in the Middle East and would also make the British an important political presence in Palestine. In 1800 James Bicheno published *The Restoration of the Jews—The Crisis of the Nations*, which also argued that the return of the Jews would not only hasten the millennium but would also strengthen the British claim to Palestine.

In the eighteenth century, therefore, people were trying to be fair and objective. But the old received ideas of Europe continued to influence them. In some ways it is certainly true that the Age of Reason did broaden the outlook of Christendom. Previously the whole of the Orient had been equated with Islam in the popular mind. But during the Age of Reason a far more venerable and challenging Orient was discovered. In 1759 the French orientalist Abraham-Hyacinthe Anquetil-Duperon translated the *Avesta*, the Zoroastrian Scriptures of ancient Persia, and followed this with a translation of the Hindu *Upanishads*. A new religious world was opening up which was quite outside the experience of the three religions of Abraham. Surely this would mean that the threat of Islam would be neutralized and seen more objectively in this wider context? Indeed, the eighteenth century fostered a new "love" of the Orient. Orientalists like Sir William Jones made this new world available to the general reader, and painters, composers and writers started to meditate on the exotic, mysterious East. This, of course, was no more accurate than the old hostile image of "Islam" had been. It was a similar expression of Western dreams: the "exotic East" bore no relation to the real Orient and travelers there often felt disappointed and cheated when they discovered this. The new cult of the Orient was simply another projection, this time of Western longings for commodities not available at home. It was also a way of taming the challenge of the East and making it a province of the Western imagination. Egotism always rears its ugly head: we have seen that selfish political and religious dreams influenced the way people saw Palestine. Similarly, when they contemplated the newly discovered Orient they were dominated by fantasies that completely lacked the objectivity of the ideal of reason.

It may well be impossible to understand another culture fully. Our thoughts are shaped by language and institutions that color our attitudes at a very deep level, and perhaps this makes it impossible to appreciate something founded on quite different cultural and linguistic norms. It may also be impossible to rid ourselves of inherited habits of prejudice. The least we can do is to make ourselves aware that these exist. At the very beginning of the period one important scientific study proved that old habits died hard. In 1697 the *Bibliothèque orientale* of Barthélmy d'Herbelot was published posthumously. It remained an important and authoritative reference book in Europe and Britain until the beginning of the nineteenth century and was a major source of Western knowledge about the Orient. D'Herbelot seemed to have made a great effort to break out of the old prejudices of Christian scholarship. He had actually used Arabic, Turkish and Persian sources and presented his reader with a history of the world that took in the traditions of non-Christian religions. He gave alternative accounts of the creation of the world, for example, in an attempt at objectivity. It is rightly claimed that there is a certain arrogance in this attempt to reduce the vast and alien complexity of the East into a neat, alphabetical Western scheme[50] but it could be argued that at the outset we need some kind of familiar system when we approach an entirely foreign culture. Despite this objective and scientific outlook, and despite the use of sources that would certainly have contradicted him, D'Herbelot simply reproduced the old medieval picture of Islam. Under the section "M" we find "Mohammad" described as "the famous imposter" and "founder of a heresy which has taken the name of religion, which we call Mohammadan. See entry under *Islam*."[51] Although D'Herbelot was aware of the real name of the religion, the important thing was that *we* prefer to call it "Mohammadan." D'Herbelot also compared this "heresy" to other Christian heresies like Arianism. It was a faithful repetition of the medieval view. Despite his massive and impressive researches, D'Herbelot simply transmitted the old received opinion about Islam and, as he was such an authority, he impressed it indelibly on the minds of most orientalists until the early nineteenth century. He was not being deliberately perverse: he probably could not look at Islam in any other way. But this confident Western intellectual had codified, defined and cut the Prophet down to size according to the European scheme of things. Islam was presented as an eccentric deviation from mainstream Western thought, which had no power to challenge or threaten "our" point of view.

In the same year the English orientalist Humphry Prideaux published *Mahomet: the True Nature of Imposture*. The title alone shows that he had unquestioningly accepted the medieval prejudice. Indeed, he cited Riccoldo da Monte Croce as his major source. But the important thing is that Prideaux presented himself as a man of reason and one could therefore have expected him to take a more objective view. He claimed that not only was Islam a mere imitation of Christianity, it was a clear example of the idiocy to which all religions, Christianity included, could sink if they were not based firmly on the rock of reason. In effect, Prideaux was doing here what Europeans had always done: he was using a fictional image of "Islam" as a foil against which the new, rational Europe could measure itself. The Age of Reason was attempting to break free of the religious prejudice which had oppressed the people of the West for so long. But Prideaux makes no attempt to free himself from the old prejudice against Islam but swallows the whole medieval tradition without a qualm. The strength of received ideas is even more strikingly manifest in the *Vie de Mahomed* by Henri, Comte de Boulainvilliers (Paris, 1730; London, 1731). The count also repeated all the medieval fantasies but turned the whole tradition on its head. The medievals claimed that Mohammad had made up his religion to make himself master of the world: the count agreed that this was so and found it admirable. Unlike irrational Christianity, Islam was a natural, not a revealed, religion and the Prophet a great military hero like Caesar or Alexander the Great. The count must have been one of the first Europeans to speak positively about Islam but his natural religion of reason is a travesty and based on the same old lies. However rational or unbiased people claim to be, received ideas are stronger than our more consciously sought views and if accepted uncritically can make nonsense of our liberal theories.

So entrenched was the old medieval view that it appeared even when eighteenth-century historians of Islam were trying to dispute the received opinion. As early as 1708 Simon Ockley distressed many of his readers when he published the first volume of his *History of the Saracens* because he did not reflexively present Islam as a religion of the sword but tried to see the seventh-century Islamic *jihad* from the Muslims' point of view. Yet even though Ockley was striving for accuracy and was meticulous in his research (Volume II did not appear until ten years later) he was still subject to the ancient prejudice. Mohammad, he said, was "a very subtle and crafty man, who put on the appearance only of those good qualities, while the principles of his soul were ambition and lust."[52] It would be hard to find a more succinct summary of the medieval view. What is perhaps more significant is that the introduction to the *Cambridge History of Islam* (1970) hailed Ockley's work together with D'Herbelot's *Bibliothèque* as "highly important" in broadening "the new understanding of Islam."[53] If Islamic scholars in our own day praise D'Herbelot and Ockley, who had no hesitation about denouncing "Islam" as a depraved heresy, it is no wonder that many of us lesser mortals are still so confused.

A more distinguished and influential historian of Islam also seemed to praise and understand the religion and yet at the same time reverted to the old hostile prejudice. In his fiftieth chapter of *The Decline and Fall of the Roman Empire*, Edward Gibbon sonorously praised the "lofty monotheism" of Islam but also wrote that Mohammad was either a fraud or an enthusiast (a bad word in Enlightenment rationalism), a religious fanatic beyond the reach of reason, who was able to convert the barbarous Arabs by the most unworthy means:

> From all sides the roving Arabs were allured by the standard of religion and plunder; the apostle sanctioned the licence of embracing female captives as their wives and concubines; and the enjoyment of wealth and beauty was a feeble type of the joys of Paradise prepared for the valiant martyrs of the faith.[54]

Gibbon allowed that, despite this unfortunate start, Muslims did manage to attain to a certain nobility in their religion; sometimes, he felt, it was a little too stark in its lack of understanding of human failings (unlike Christianity, is the implied comparison). But Gibbon really showed his colors when he dealt with the Koran. He began by referring to the Muslim belief that the beauty of the Koran shows that it came from God:

> This argument is most powerfully addressed to a devout Arabian whose mind is attuned to faith and rapture, whose ear is delighted

by the music of sounds, and whose ignorance is incapable of comparing the productions of human genius. The harmony and copiousness of style will not reach, in a version, the European infidel; he will peruse with impatience the endless incoherent rhapsody of fable and precept and declamation, which seldom excites a sentiment or an idea, which sometimes crawls in the dust, and is sometimes lost in the clouds.[55]

This is self-congratulation indeed: "we" are discerning, civilized and rational enough to see through the preposterous claim of the Prophet, but "they" are incapable of any such insight, because they are childish barbarians. Writing at the end of the century, Gibbon had absorbed the Western self-confidence and sense of superiority that brought with it an arrogant blindness: because *he* cannot understand the Koran, he assumes that there is nothing in it and that the "devout Arabian" does so because he is an inferior human being. It would seem from reading Gibbon's chapter that the old irrational terror of "Mohammadanism" was well and truly dead and had been replaced by a calm, slightly amused contempt for a religion that cannot be taken too seriously. This new Christian superiority is not at all dissimilar to the Arab attitude toward the poor benighted Franks at the time of the Crusades. Some fifty years later Thomas Carlyle wrote one of the first European eulogies of Mohammad in his essay "The Hero as Prophet" and for the first time denounced the old medieval lies, but even he balked at the Koran, which he described as "a wearisome, confused jumble, crude, incondite; endless iterations, long-windedness, entanglement; most crude, incondite, insupportable stupidity in short."[56] Apart from the obvious comment that Carlyle's own style in this sentence is not above criticism, there is no doubt that the Koran does present a problem to Westerners.

For centuries Europeans had relied upon the old medieval translations of the Koran, which had really been translations of Christian prejudice, as we have seen. But in 1734 George Sale had published his translation of the Koran which gave readers like Gibbon and Carlyle an accurate English translation for the very first time. This translation is one of the finest achievements of the Age of Reason and represented a considerable advance. It must be said, alas, that Sale was not perfect. He wrote an introduction which aired old medieval prejudice: "It is certainly one of the most convincing proofs that Mohammadanism was no other than a human invention, that it owed its progress and establishment almost entirely to the sword." He does follow this by admitting that Mohammad's right to take up arms in self-defense against the Meccans "may perhaps be allowed."[57] There was still a deep need to belittle or explain away the strongly compelling power of the religion. But despite this ingrained prejudice, Sale's actual translation was an enormous improvement on the old versions of the crusading period. He used proper Muslim and Arabic commentators instead of prejudiced Christian sources, and if people criticize the translation today it is not because they consider it inaccurate but because they find the style rather heavy. Nevertheless giving people in Europe an accurate translation should have meant that people would have had no excuse for propagating the old fantasies about Islam as a depraved religion, particularly the scholars of the Enlightenment. The translation should have aroused a new interest. Yet this did not happen.

However technically accurate Sale's version of the Koran was, it suffered from one unavoidable defect: it was not in Arabic. Had he been able to achieve a livelier style, this insurmountable problem would still have remained. Muslims claim that the Koran is untranslatable, for the beauty of the Arabic is an essential part of its meaning. They point to this beauty as proof of its divine origin. Indeed the beauty of the Koran is one of the reasons for the spreading of the Arabic language from the Arabian Peninsula throughout the Middle East and North Africa. When people in these countries converted to Islam they had to learn the Koran in Arabic and they then went on to change their language. That even the ordinary, uneducated people were inspired to make this linguistic change is a tribute to the extraordinary emotional and intellectual attraction of the sacred book of Islam. It is very striking to watch even unreligious Arabs listening to the Koran when it is broadcast on the radio, sung to a special chant. They are clearly enthralled and find it very difficult to express exactly why these words give them such pleasure. Perhaps the Koran is comparable to some of Shakespeare's songs or to certain well-known passages of the King James Bible in English. The language has an absolute beauty that is enhanced by emotional associations. Obviously nothing of this can come out in translation.

For a non-Arabic speaker, the Koran is not very accessible. It is always true that other people's holy books are difficult to penetrate; it is an indication of the great difficulty of truly understanding another culture. Anglicans who are loyal to the King James Bible would probably not be so moved by the Hebrew words if they could read them because, beautiful as the English is, it has transformed the Hebrew into something very different and quintessentially English. Hebrew versions of the psalms, for example, are a lot less sonorous and mellifluous and more brutal and direct than a King James devotee might expect. To attach ourselves to the Jewish Scriptures, we have had to translate them into another idiom and have turned them into something else. It is possible that some great stylist might be able to do something similar with the Koran, but then it would not be the Koran anymore. Part of the difficulty is that Arabic has a different logic from European languages and words have a far wider and more complex range of meaning and association, which makes a translation an impoverishment. Without the beauty, the complexity and associative power of the Arabic, an English translation of the main "sense" of the words, however careful and accurate, is bound to be a distortion. I myself have found that constant reading of the Koran in an English translation does familiarize one with a certain dynamic and beauty, but I am quite aware that this is probably entirely different from the experience of reading the Arabic original. Even though I am in the early stages of learning Arabic, I have to recognize that I shall probably never be proficient enough to appreciate the beauty and the complexity of the Koran as a native speaker does.

Therefore, though Sale's version was undoubtedly an important and essential contribution to Western knowledge of Islam, the Koran still remained a very difficult book for English people to read and understand. It was not likely to make people suddenly aware of the power of the book and the religion. In the West today we have a number of accurate and more attractive translations of the Koran but this has not helped us to approach the religion more sympathetically. The power of received ideas about Islam still tends to be stronger than the Muslim holy book, which few people have actually read. Unlike the people of the eighteenth century, we are living at a time when Muslims feel great hostility toward the West and this makes it more difficult to be objective in our judgments. But since we pride ourselves on our liberal Western traditions (and often blame modern Muslims for their intolerance) it is surely important that we do not descend to the level of the Muslims we criticize and that we try to live up to our own values.

Reason therefore proved inadequate as a means of acquiring an objective and balanced understanding of Islam in the eighteenth century. The *philosophes* of the French Enlightenment show this most clearly. They were rightly critical of the religious prejudices which had terrorized so many of the people of Europe and had encouraged vicious persecution of so-called heretics. But in their own writings they tacitly condone prejudice toward both Jews and Muslims. Voltaire, for example, wrote in the *Dictionnaire philosophique* that the Jews were a "totally ignorant nation, who for many years have combined contemptible miserliness and the most revolting superstition with a violent hatred of all those nations which have tolerated them."[58] This judgment, uttered by the apostle of pure reason, discounts centuries of Jewish intellectual history but he was simply repeating the old Christian inherited prejudice he professed to despise. For centuries people had accustomed themselves to seeing the Jews as the murderous enemies of Christians and of every Western aspiration, which meant that they had suffered from religious persecution more than anybody else in Europe. Voltaire vehemently condemned prejudice and persecution yet never questions his own anti-Semitism. But there was one major difference between Voltaire's image of the Jew and the old Christian prejudice: Christians had always claimed that the Jews were the enemies of religion but, since Voltaire believed that religion was a bad thing, he turned the old stereotype on its head and denounced the Jews *because* they were slaves to superstition and religion. Taking it at some deep and subrational level for granted that the Jews were against "us," he had simply adjusted the stereotype to make it conform to the paradigm. Now that Europeans were assuming a rationalist identity, the Jews were accused of being irrational.

He was also prejudiced against Islam. Voltaire wrote a tragedy on the life of Mohammad which he called *Fanaticism* (1742). The title itself indicates his attitude. Voltaire differed from the medievals in that he found their fantasies about the Prophet insufficiently scurrilous, so he made up some more of his own. Mohammad was a common impostor, like the founders of all other religions. Like them, he had resorted to common conjuring tricks which his followers preferred to see as miracles. Much was made of Mohammad's passionate and erotic nature. We have seen that writers like Prideaux and Boulainvilliers had used their distorted version of "Islam" to denigrate Christianity, and Voltaire also used the Prophet to denigrate religion, showing that he had been a cynical impostor who yet managed to lead his people to a glorious victory by means of these fairy tales. Like Gibbon, Voltaire looked at the early Arabians with disdain and found some extenuating circumstances for Mohammad's behavior: living, as he did, among such barbarous and crude people, Mohammad had had to resort to these tricks to make any impression on them. Again, when Voltaire wanted to show how tolerant *he* was and how intolerant Christianity was in his *Essai sur les moeurs*, he praised Islam for its toleration. But his conclusion there remained that its founder had been "regarded as a great man even by those who knew that he was an impostor and revered as a prophet by all the rest."[59] The medievals had presented Mohammad in a disreputable light because it was the only way that they could understand and interpret the extraordinary power of his religious thought: to acknowledge this would have been too threatening. Voltaire made use of the medieval prejudices that he was committed to despise because he was similarly unable to accept the compelling religious vision of Islam, religion in his book being an execrable and outmoded activity.

The old hysterical view of Islam prevailed, however. Right at the end of the eighteenth century, in 1799, a life of Mohammad was published in England which seems scarcely sane: Mohammad was worse than Caligula, Domitian or Judas Iscariot. "Many millions of rational human beings," the author cried in anguish, "are degraded to the rank of brutes by the consummate artifice and wickedness" of the Prophet.[60] The very idea that Muslims believe that their "religious farrago" is a valid form of ritual and spiritual experience seems to drive the author into a state of frenzy.[61] These absurd distortions reveal a deep dread lurking beneath the skeptical, rational facade of society. Similarly, the celebrated French philosopher of the Enlightenment Baron Paul Henri Holbach wrote in his L'Ésprit du judaïsme (1770) that Moses had founded a bloodthirsty religion, which had corrupted Christian society and made the Jews "the enemies of the human race. . . . The Jews have always displayed contempt for the clearest dictates of morality and the law of nations. . . . They were ordered to be cruel, inhuman, intolerant, thieves, traitors and betrayers of trust. All these are regarded as deeds pleasing to God."[62] A cursory reading of the Bible would have contradicted this view but the Jewish Scriptures were no more able to counter Holbach's prejudice than the Koran had been able to counter Voltaire's. The Enlightenment had been a great intellectual adventure and had produced important results. But Europe was no more rational or healthy than she had ever been. People were still haunted by inner demons that reason was powerless to control and by a fear which it could not assuage. The imbalance revealed itself in the violent reaction against the Enlightenment that sprang up on both sides of the Atlantic during the nineteenth century and which took the form of a fundamentalist Christianity that was plagued with sexual terror and repression. In our own century, despite our cool, secular rationalism, we are well aware that Western society is still afflicted by irrational fears that exist far below the cerebral self and which emerge in enthusiastic religion, violence, drug addiction and nihilism.

Nevertheless, for all its inadequacy, the Enlightenment did seem at the time to herald a brave new world and this had important consequences for the Jews of Western Europe. After the French Revolution of 1789, during which the Goddess of Reason had been enthroned in Notre Dame, the Jews of France were given full citizenship and equal rights; other countries followed suit and from this point Jews began to leave the ghettos and to take a greater part in the life of Europe. The anti-Semitic and antireligious tenor of the French Enlightenment had made it unattractive to Jews but the German Enlightenment seemed to attempt a new understanding of the religious experience. It was in Germany that the *haskalah*, the Jewish enlightenment, was born, and sadly this gave many Jews the idea that there was a deep affinity between Jewish and German culture. The leading light of the *haskalah* was Moses Mendelssohn (d. 1786), who was introduced to the salons by Gotthold Lessing. Mendelssohn had a much more positive idea of the *goyim* than most of his fellow Jews at that time. He wanted to win acceptance for Jews and he fought anti-Semitism but he also attacked the conservatism and intolerance of the ghettos, which were still haunted by the shade of Spinoza. He wanted Jews and Germans to share a society, for in his view religion was a matter of private conviction. He saw Judaism as an ethical, rational religion that was free of some of the worst irrational excesses of Christianity but which had not been revealed: he denied that the Jews were a chosen people and that Eretz Yisrael had a sacred character. But most Jews could not accept this idea because Mendelssohn's rational religion was simply not Judaism.[63]

But increasingly young Jews left the orthodoxy of the ghetto and tried to assimilate with Western culture. These *maskilim*, as they were called, were unsatisfied with an intellectual diet that consisted solely of Torah. They made a great impact in letters, art, politics and philosophy. One could say that the twentieth century has in some important respects been the creation of the three great *maskilim* Marx, Freud and Einstein. The *maskilim* wanted to identify with Western culture but often found that the only way to achieve full assimilation and preferment was to accept baptism. Most of these *maskilim* were, in the spirit of the Enlightenment, hostile to all religion so they did not all see this as a religious betrayal. The German Jewish poet Heinrich Heine called baptism "the entrance ticket to Western culture"[64] but he showed that he had great ambivalence about his own baptism when he attacked friends for being baptized. The *maskilim* tried to accept baptism in the spirit in which many people learn English today as a way of participating in mainstream culture. But it was not surprising that they felt ambiguous about this very complex step. They assumed, as we saw in Chapter 3, that residual anti-Semitism would gradually wither away but with hindsight we can see the necessity of baptism as a sign that anti-Semitic values, though muted in expression, were still alive and well. They had simply gone underground for a time and, like the religious impulse, would erupt again even more fiercely for this period of repression.

We have seen that throughout the eighteenth century people had been gathering information about the Orient and in 1798 Napoleon's famous expedition to Egypt showed the start of a new phase: Europe would now use this knowledge to control and dominate the East. Napoleon wanted to challenge the British hegemony in India by establishing his own Eastern empire and he revived the old crusading project of founding a base in Egypt from which to launch an attack on the Muslim lands of Palestine and Syria. The expedition, therefore, caused great excitement because it tapped a powerful old Western dream. With the fleet sailed scores of orientalist scholars from the Institut d'Égypte, founded by Napoleon, as advisers to the occupying forces. As soon as the fleet landed, Napoleon sent them off on what we should call a fact-finding mission and he gave his officers strict instructions to follow their advice. For the first time the Arabs of the Middle East were presented with the new, powerful Europe, of which they were ignorant but which seemed to know all about them. At Alexandria, Napoleon had announced to the people: *"Nous sommes les vrais musulmans."*[65] He had the sixty sheikhs of al-Azhar in Cairo brought into his quarters with full military honors, whereupon he praised the Prophet, discussed Voltaire's *Fanaticism* and seemed able to hold his own. Nobody took Napoleon very seriously as a Muslim but the scholars had been right: this sympathetic knowledge of Islam did allay the hostility of the people to a degree. From henceforth, Europeans would use their knowledge not primarily for the purposes of understanding but for power and control of the East. But this expedition was not only a landmark for Europe: it had a profound effect on the Arab world. Arabs looked at this new, knowledgeable and technically advanced West and wondered how these former Crusaders had got so far ahead. Where had the Muslim countries gone wrong?

Napoleon also courted the Jews of Africa and Asia, urging them to rise up against the Turks to gain possession of their ancient homeland. They were the "Rightful Heirs of Palestine," he declared in the spring of 1799.

Israelites, unique nation, whom, in thousands of years, lust of conquest and tyranny were able to deprive of ancestral lands only, but not of name and national existence!

Attentive and impartial observers of the destinies of nations, even though not endowed with the gifts of seers like Isaiah and Joel, have also felt long since what these, with beautiful and uplifting faith, foretold when they saw the approaching destruction of their kingdom and fatherland: that the ransomed of the Lord shall return, and come with singing unto Zion, and the enjoyment of henceforth undisturbed possession of their heritage will send an everlasting joy upon their heads (Isaiah 35:10).

Arise, then, with gladness ye exiled![66]

Although he was more flattering to both Jews and Muslims than the Crusaders, Napoleon shared the essential crusading attitude of seeking his own Western fulfillment in the Middle East and making the Jews and Muslims subordinate to that vision. His plan was to conquer Palestine from the Ottomans, establish himself in Jerusalem and hand the country over to the Jews, who, he was sure, would guard it for him against all comers. He would go on to establish his own capital in Damascus. But a month after this dramatic proclamation he was defeated by a combined army of British and Turks. Napoleon's army sailed back to Europe but not before it had sown the seeds of Western revolutionary ideas in the Middle East.

The Egyptian historian al-Jabarti was an eyewitness of the Napoleonic invasion. He tells us that the French fleet had been preceded by the arrival of the English fleet in the port of Alexandria. The British told the notables of the city that they would help them to drive the French away, but the notables replied: "This is the sultan's country; neither the French nor any other people have any rights in it. Please go away."[67] They had not answered the British as Egyptian nationalists but as loyal members of the Ottoman Empire. But Napoleon's invasion was an eye-opener for many thoughtful Arabs of the Near East. They were not much impressed by the French claim to be "true Muslims" but they were very impressed by the free, confident bearing of the French soldiers of this post-Revolutionary army. It was a chink in the great wall that the Ottomans had erected around their empire through which Western ideas could penetrate.[68] Many Arabs responded eagerly. In the early days of the Islamic empire Arabs had responded gladly to the challenge of the ideas of other cultures, and this first contact with the West was a very creative encounter. Many asked what they could take from Western culture to revitalize the countries of Islam. This was highly displeasing to the Ottoman ruling class but, aware that the watchful eye of the powerful West was upon them, they could not prevent the spread of these radical, modernizing ideas. For centuries the Arabs had dismissed Western culture as essentially beneath their notice and the period of Turkish rule had encouraged an inward-looking mentality in the Ottoman ghetto. But many were quick to see that things had changed drastically, once they were exposed to the new Europe.

One of the first young Arabs to praise European culture was the Egyptian writer Rifa al-Tahtawi (d. 1873). He lived for years in Paris and became a Francophile, writing enthusiastically of the cleanliness, industry and intellectual curiosity of French society. But he was also aware that the Arab people themselves had once had a similar dynamism: they should go back to the golden age of Arab civilization. In particular, al-Tahtawi saw the importance of education. He had been much impressed by the French concern to educate their children, so he urged the people of the Middle East to return to the study of the rational sciences and insisted that everybody should receive a political education so that they could criticize social abuses constructively. These had once been important Arab values but the people had forgotten them and fallen into a dark age of ignorance and passivity. Al-Tahtawi's ideas were revolutionary at this particular point in time. But there is a leisurely, relaxed quality in his work. The necessity for change did not seem urgent.[69] But as time passed, the West showed that it was not just a neutral power from whom the Arabs could learn. Nor would future Western invaders be as easy to repel as Napoleon had been.

During the nineteenth century Western presence increased in the Middle East as the Ottoman Empire, "the sick man of Europe," sank wearily toward its inevitable demise. From the sixteenth century, trading posts and consular missions had been established but now Europeans were concerned no longer solely with trade but with development and control. The activity seemed benevolent: Europe was bringing the good news of technical progress and building hundreds of miles of roads and railways; these ribbons of communication actually had little impact on the people of the countries through which they passed but did make European presence more mobile and efficient. The most spectacular of these engineering feats was the building of the Suez Canal in which French engineers cooperated with the Pasha and people of Egypt. But this Western involvement simply led to increased Western control: in 1875 Britain took advantage of the financial troubles of the Pasha to buy 44 percent of the shares and thus became part owner of the canal. As we know, this became a symbol of unjust colonial exploitation. At the beginning of the nineteenth century the Romantic movement had stressed religious themes

like liberation, redemption and salvation and there is no doubt that
the Westerners presented themselves as bringing salvation and liberation of sorts. It was a message that was underlined by the influx of
missions and missionary schools into the area. These inevitably tended
to undermine Middle Eastern culture at the same time as they offered
"salvation." As in India, the Western colonialists encouraged this missionary activity, seeing that it would back up their own work. But in
fact these missionary schools had another effect that would help the
new Arab awakening. They translated textbooks and tracts into Arabic;
these were intended for their Arab Christian students but were read
by Muslims too. Unwittingly the missionaries had helped the Arabs
to revive their own language for more widespread daily use.

But we know too that during the nineteenth century Europe established colonies right across North Africa. It began as early as 1830
when the French colonized Algiers and the British colonized Aden in
1839 in what is now the Yemen. The countries of Western Europe
then colonized between them Tunisia in 1881, Egypt in 1882 and
the Sudan in 1898. In 1912 Libya and Morocco would be occupied
and then the great powers turned their attention to the Middle East.
The colonialists would have argued that they were bringing progress
into the region at the same time as they were increasing their own
power and that this justified their venture. But it must also be remembered that this benevolent activity was accompanied by a certain
amount of force and violence. It may be instructive here to recall the
pacification of Algeria, which took many years because the French
aimed at total control of the country. Any retaliation was put down
brutally in reprisal raids, masterminded by the celebrated General
T. R. Bugeaud. The contemporary French historian M. Baudricourt
gives us an idea of what one of those raids was like:

> Our soldiers returning from the expedition were themselves
> ashamed . . . about 18,000 trees had been burnt; women, children
> and old men had been killed. The unfortunate women particularly
> excited cupidity by the habit of wearing silver ear-rings, leg-rings
> and arm-rings. These rings have no catch like French bracelets.
> Fastened in youth to the limbs of girls they cannot be removed
> when they are grown up. To get them off our soldiers used to cut
> off their limbs and leave them alive in this mutilated condition.[70]

Algeria was a particularly obnoxious occupation. Except for the colonization of Libya by the Italians, no other colonial power attempted
such total domination. Later imperialism became more sophisticated

and gave way to quasi-colonialism, whereby the West retained the real power and control but left native institutions intact in such a way as to ensure the physical domination of the country. Nevertheless, there were shameful incidents in British Egypt, for example, just as there were in British India. Colonialism is a form of violation or even rape because it is usually carried out by a stronger power against the will of the weaker indigenous population. However benevolently it is presented, colonialism shows itself in its true colors in such violent incidents and it is not surprising that the colonialists have left bitterness behind.

But the West managed to maintain the high-minded view of their *mission civilisatrice*, as we see in the writings of the French Christian apologist, François René de Chateaubriand. Chateaubriand had been enormously impressed by Napoleon's expedition. He saw him as a Crusader-pilgrim, "the last Frenchman who left his country to travel in the Holy Land with the ideas, the goals and the sentiments of a pilgrim of former times."[71] Chateaubriand also bathed the Crusades in a glamorous light. The nineteenth century tended to look back at the Middle Ages in a most idealized way: in the poems of Tennyson or the novels of Walter Scott medieval stories become quite different from the grim reality. Throughout this book we have seen how people return to the past to find inspiration for the present, and at the start of the colonial venture Chateaubriand had already seen the creation of the first French colonies in the Middle East as a liberation. The Crusaders, he argued, had tried to bring Christianity to the East, a cult "which had caused to reawaken in modern people the genius of a sage antiquity and had abolished base servitude."[72] Of all religions, Christianity was the one "most favourable to freedom." But the Crusaders had clashed with Islam, "a cult that was civilization's enemy, systematically favourable to ignorance, to despotism and to slavery."[73] In the early nineteenth century the crusading venture had become a benevolent spreading of the gospel of freedom; it had been drained of its violence and horror and become a liberation movement. In the process Islam had become once again the opposite of everything the new West stood for in the heady days after the French Revolution. In the hierarchical Middle Ages, Islam had been stigmatized as an antinomian religion, which gave too much liberty to menials. Now the image of "Islam" had been completely reversed in order to become the opposite of "us."

This view of a despotic and unenlightened Islam justified the crusading venture. It is not surprising that, when Chateaubriand visited

Palestine himself, he applied his crusading fantasy to the reality in front of him. In his best-seller, *Journey from Paris to Jerusalem and from Jerusalem to Paris* (1810–11), he wrote that the Arabs "have the air of soldiers without a leader, citizens without legislators, and a family without a father." They were crying out for the benevolent intervention of the civilized West because they were an example of "civilised man fallen again into a savage state."[74] We have seen that the Ottoman period had been a Dark Age for the Arabs but we have also seen that they had themselves been impressed with Napoleon and were about to try to apply Western ideas to their own traditions. But Chateaubriand waved aside the idea that the Arabs were able to redeem themselves. In the Koran there was "neither a principle for civilisation nor a mandate that can elevate character." Islam preaches "neither hatred of tyranny nor love of liberty"[75]—another Western myth about the Muslim holy book. When Chateaubriand entered the Holy Sepulchre, at the climax of his pilgrimage, he saw himself as the representative of God's new chosen people, rather as the Crusaders had done, who had been anointed with the task of saving the world. At about the same time Alphonse de Lamartine saw the Orient yearning for the colonial intervention of Europe during his trip to the Middle East. He saw it as a place of "nations without territory, *patrie*, rights, laws on security . . . waiting anxiously for the shelter" of Western colonialism:

> This sort of suzerainty thus defined and consecrated as a European right will consist principally in the right to occupy one or another territory, as well as the coasts, in order to found there either free cities of European colonies or commercial ports of call.[76]

When the French looked back on the period of the Crusades they highlighted its benevolent aspects. Today, however, when the Arabs call Western imperialism *al-Salibiyya* (the Crusade) they are recalling some of the more ruthless and violent aspects of colonialism.

One of the most interesting visitors to Palestine during the nineteenth century was Benjamin Disraeli, the future Jewish Prime Minister of Britain. It was he who would acquire part ownership of the Suez Canal in 1875. Disraeli had been baptized as an infant and brought up as a Christian but he remained true to his Jewish origins and liked to see himself as "the missing page between the Old Testament and the New."[77] He blamed Christians for not recognizing their debt to Judaism and Jews for not realizing that Christianity was "completed Judaism." In 1829 he made a passionate speech in the House of Commons:

What is your Christianity if you do not believe in Judaism? On every altar we find the table of the Jewish law. All the early Christians were Jews, every man in the early ages of the Church by whose power or genius the Christian faith was propagated was a Jew. If you had not forgotten what you owe to this people, you as Christians would be only too ready to seize the first opportunity of meeting the claims of those who profess the religion.[78]

He was deeply moved by a visit to Palestine and, like Chateaubriand, he also returned to the Middle Ages. He at once began work on his novel *Alroy*, which tells the story of the revolution of David Alroy, the twelfth-century Iraqi Jew, against the Muslim Caliph. At one point in the novel it seems as though Disraeli, whose perspective is clearly different from Chateaubriand's, is envisaging the Zionist solution. Alroy's Jewish mentor gives voice to his secret dream:

You ask me what I wish: my answer is, national existence, which we have not. You ask me what I wish: my answer is Jerusalem. You ask me what I wish: my answer is the Temple.[79]

At this point it must be recalled that there were as yet no *Jewish* Zionists: Zionism would not become a factor in Jewish life for another fifty years. The Jews of Europe were either seeking assimilation, like Disraeli himself, or were holding firm to the Kabalistic messianism of the ghettos. Disraeli was himself far more committed to the imperialist policy of Great Britain, as we see in *Tancred* (1847), another novel set in the Middle East but during the contemporary period. Interestingly, in that novel Disraeli sees the *Arabs* as the people who will help the British to found their colonies.[80]

Other British travelers returned to the principles of non-Jewish Zionism, which seemed firmly established. A few years after Disraeli's trip, Lord Lindsey published his *Letters from Egypt, Edom and the Holy Land* and revived the old idea that the decay into which the land had fallen was due to the departure of the Jews. The land would be renewed by the "return of her banished children and the application of industry commensurate with her agricultural capacities to burst once more into universal luxuriance and be all she was in the days of Solomon."[81] In 1844 Eliot Warburton published his popular *The Crescent and the Cross*, which also saw the Crusades as a paradigm for the new colonialism, even if he expressed this less exquisitely and more bluntly than Chateaubriand. He discovered in himself a "sort of patriotism for Palestine."[82] As he wandered around the Holy Land, visiting places that had become so familiar to him in the Bible, he reflected that it was Britain's *duty* to take possession of Egypt and Palestine, which were already really hers by right. Thus she would secure her right of way to India, and to this end there must be a new and more successful crusading effort: "the interests of India may obtain what the Sepulchre of Christ has been denied."[83] Wherever he went, he managed to convince himself that the people were expecting the British to liberate them and bring them into that happy state enjoyed by the Indians of the subcontinent. Egotistic and selfish visions can easily blur our view of the reality in front of us. None of these writers was bothering to look at the Arabs clearly, nor were they at all heedful of what the Jews themselves really wanted at that moment in time. The same year the Reverend A. Bradshaw published *A Tract for the Times, being a Plea for the Jews*, urging the government to grant the Jews four million pounds to hasten their return to the Promised Land, while Dr. Thomas Clarke lumped Jewish interests together with those of Great Britain in *India and Palestine: Or the Restoration of the Jews Viewed in Relation to the Nearest Route to India*. The Jews, he argued, were people like "us": "brave, independent and spiritual people, deeply imbued with the sentiment of nationality."[84] Shortly afterward a committee was convened in London to work for the return to Zion and the inaugural address given by one Reverend Tully Crybbace called for a state that stretched "from the Euphrates to the Nile and from the Mediterranean to the Desert."[85] These dreams and images of the Jews and a Jewish homeland were as much projections as the old anti-Semitic fantasies had been. This time, instead of being images of Western fears and anxiety, they were crude projections of what the British wanted.

But the return to Zion was not just the pipe dream of private individuals. Thus in 1838, the year before the British colonized Aden, Prime Minister Lord Palmerston had decided to establish a new viceconsular mission in Jerusalem and sent William Young to fill the post. His instructions were to afford protection to the Jews. The Jews had not asked for this: colonies of devout religious Jews had, as we have seen, lived for centuries in Eretz Yisrael, either in Jerusalem or Safed. They were *millets* of the Ottomans and needed no extra protection. Advisers warned Palmerston that he had no business setting himself up as the champion of the Jews in this way, but Palmerston saw this as a new means of establishing a strong British presence in the Middle East. The colonial powers were making great use of the *millets* precisely for this purpose: the French were claiming to be the "protectors" of the Catholics and the Russians were zealously defending the "rights" of the Orthodox Christians. Britain had no natural clients among the millets: there were no native Arab or Turkish Protestants, so the Jews seemed an obvious choice, given the British interest in Zionism.

This initiative had been suggested to Palmerston by the great philanthropist Ashley, Lord Shaftesbury, who was his stepfather-in-law and also the mentor of William Young. Shaftesbury had more traditional apocalyptic hopes. He had long been interested in the project of converting the Jews to Christianity, not out of loving concern for their salvation (he was actually rather anti-Semitic and voted against Jewish emancipation in 1861) but in order to hasten the Second Coming. He was also convinced that returning the Jews to Zion was an important step toward the millennium and considered Young's consular mission had brought the fulfillment of that hope a little nearer. In his diary he wrote: "What a wonderful event it is. The ancient city of the people of God is about to resume a place among the nations and England is the first of the Gentile Kingdoms that ceases to tread her down."[86]

Two years later, again under the influence of Shaftesbury, Palmerston wrote an extraordinary letter to John, Viscount Ponsonby, his ambassador in Istanbul, telling him to work for the return of the Jews to Palestine.

There exists at present among the Jews dispersed over Europe a strong notion that the time is approaching when their nation is to return to Palestine. . . . Consequently their wish to go thither has become more keen, and their thoughts have been bent more intently than before upon the means of realizing that wish. It is well known that the Jews of Europe possess great wealth; and it is manifest that any country in which a considerable number of them might choose to settle would derive great benefit from the riches they would bring into it.[87]

It is important to stress once again that this was a complete fantasy, because the Jews of 1840 were either seeking to assimilate or would have considered a return to Eretz Yisrael without the Messiah as an impious aping of redemption. But the Jews' real wants and needs were a matter of total indifference to Palmerston, who saw a colonial opportunity for Great Britain in the Zionist scheme. Exactly a week later, on August 17, 1840, Lord Shaftesbury got the editor of *The Times* to publish a leading article which disclosed a plan "to plant the Jewish people in the land of their fathers," which was now under "serious political consideration." It hoped that the Turkish Sultan would consent to receive the Jews into Palestine and would assure them of law, justice and safety, which would be secured to them under the protection of a European power. The editorial caused a great stir. "The newspapers teem with documents about the Jews," Shaftesbury recorded in his diary. "What a chaos of schemes and disputes on the horizon. . . . What violence, what hatred, what combination, what discussion. What stir of every passion and every feeling in men's hearts."[88]

Perhaps the most remarkable of these British Zionist visions is George Eliot's *Daniel Deronda*, which was published in 1879 on the eve of the First Aliyah. Deronda, the hero, shows some of the complications in this British vision. He is fortunate enough not to discover his Jewish blood until he is quite grown up and has received an impeccable education as an English gentleman. He is, therefore, really one of "us" and in a perfect position to carry out the Zionist project on Britain's behalf. Throughout the novel Daniel is described in Christlike terms and as a redemptive presence, who is constantly rescuing the other characters from failure, despair or temptation. As a savior and redeemer, Deronda will rescue the Middle East. Daniel's mentor Mordechai discusses the Zionist idea most fully. He is a Jewish Zionist, whose vision looks forward to the imperialistic Zionism of Herzl. The Jews, Mordechai argues, will "redeem the soil from debauched and paupered conquerors"; the polity of the Jewish state will be "grand, simple, just like the old" Jewish Kingdom, which at the time of the Bible had established

> more than the brightness of Western freedom amid the despotisms of the East. And the world will gain as Israel gains. For there will be a community in the van of the East which carries the culture and the sympathies of every great nation in its bosom; there will be a land set for a halting place of enmities, a neutral ground for the East as Belgium is for the West.[89]

There is no hope that the East will be able to reform and redeem itself: it needs Daniel as the representative of Great Britain.

Yet there are hints in the novel of that latent anti-Semitism which was often inherent in the British Zionist vision, as we saw in Lord Shaftesbury. Daniel is really more of an Englishman than a Jew; Mordechai, the real Jewish visionary, cannot possibly be the representative of Britain: he is suffering from an incurable disease and this makes him physically repellent. He is also made to speak throughout in an archaic biblical style. The implication is that Judaism is a moribund, anachronistic faith that needs a healthy infusion of life from Britain.

Mordechai's sister Mira, who eventually marries Daniel, is portrayed with a sentimentality which the mature Eliot does not usually allow herself with her heroines. Mira's diminutive size and her exquisite singing voice, which is too soft to fill a concert hall, also seem to cut Judaism down to size and belittle it. Her father is as classically evil as Dickens' evil Jew Fagin, and when Deronda is searching for Mira's family he has many worrying hours rehearsing over and over again in his mind what he will do if the family turns out to be as common and vulgarly Jewish as he fears.

But Eliot's vision was not a total fantasy. Not only was *Jewish* Zionism (as opposed to Gentile forms of Zionism) about to begin its complex history but in his civilized urbanity Deronda looks forward to Herzl, whom he even resembles physically. Further, as we have seen, many Jews at this period were willing to throw in their lot and identify with the new, liberal Europe. They felt that she had a mission to civilize the world. Thus at the time *Daniel Deronda* was written, French Jews were praying in the synagogues for France as the new chosen nation:

> Almighty Protector of Israel and humanity, if of all religions ours is the most dear to you, because it is your handiwork, France is of all countries the one which you seem to prefer because it is the most worthy of you. . . . Let France not keep this monopoly of tolerance and justice for all, a monopoly as humiliating for other states as it is glorious for her. Let her find many imitators and as she imposes on the world her tastes and her language, the products of her literature and her arts, let her also impose her principles, which it goes without saying, are more important and more necessary.[90]

The ambivalence that Eliot displays toward Judaism was also felt by many assimilated Jews themselves. We have already considered the complex feelings of the German Jewish poet Heinrich Heine (d. 1856). Throughout his life he was contemptuous of Orthodoxy and the Talmud but at the end of his life he suffered a debilitating disease that kept him almost bedridden for ten years. At that time he returned to Judaism and used to say that he was no longer a liberated and assimilated Hellene but "a poor, deathly-sick Jew."[91] It is a perception of Judaism that reminds us of Eliot's Mordechai. But Heine, the poet of freedom, also praised France and, by implication, Christianity. Freedom was

> the new religion, the religion of our time. If Christ is not the god of this new religion, he is nevertheless a high priest of it, and his

name gleams beautifully into the hearts of the apostles. But the French are the Chosen People of the new religion, their language records its first gospels and dogmas. Paris is the New Jerusalem, the Rhine is the Jordan that separates the consecrated land of freedom from the land of the Philistines.[92]

For many assimilated Jews, Europe had replaced Eretz Yisrael and many of them would not have found Chateaubriand's idealistic vision of the new colonial French Crusaders at all exaggerated. It is sad to recall these hopes. Theodor Herzl remained committed to the colonial ideal but he had been a passionate assimilationist before he was converted to Zionism at the court-martial of Captain Dreyfus.

But not all *maskilim* endorsed the colonial ideal. Karl Marx hated the British policy in India but even he was ambivalent. He sympathized with the suffering of the native Indians but had a deterministic view of history which meant that everything was tending toward the socialist millennium. It was a deeply Jewish vision (although Marx hated religion), being reminiscent of the providential view of history that culminated in the messianic redemption: in Chapter 3 we saw how swiftly the Labor Zionists of the Second Aliyah were able to fuse Marxism with the Zionist ideal. Marx felt, therefore, that in implementing her repulsive colonial policies Britain could be "the unconscious tool of history."[93] The ruthlessness of imperialism could force the Indian communities to save themselves, do a good Marxist analysis of their situation and join in the revolutionary struggle.

Marx was attempting an entirely new vision of the world and was redefining mankind. Still, even though he was Jewish himself, he saw "the Jew" as the enemy of progress according to the old paradigm. The problem was economic, he wrote in his two anti-Semitic essays of 1844. "Let us consider the real Jew," he urged. "Not the *Sabbath Jew* . . . but the *everyday Jew*." This was not religious Judaism: "What is the worldly cult of the Jew? *Huckstering*. What is his worldly god? *Money*." Jewish commercial ability had enabled many Jews to survive in anti-Semitic Europe but jealousy of Jewish success had led the *goyim* to see a conspiracy behind it and, in a vicious circle, this had led to new hatred and paranoia. Marx believed that the Jews had corrupted all mankind by making money the God of the world and infecting Christianity with this poison. In order "to make the Jew impossible" therefore, Marx concluded, the whole economic order had to be changed. Once that had happened, all "religious consciousness would evaporate like some insipid vapour in the real, life-giving air of society."[94] By getting rid of the money-Jew the world would save itself.

In *A History of the Jews*, Paul Johnson has argued that Marx's anti-Semitism gave birth to his later militant socialism.

> His mature theory was a superstition, and the most dangerous kind of superstition, belief in a conspiracy of evil. But whereas originally it was based on the oldest form of conspiracy-theory, anti-Semitism, in the late 1840s and 1850s this was not so much abandoned as extended to embrace a world conspiracy-theory of the entire bourgeois class. Marx retained the original superstition that the making of money through trade and finance is essentially a parasitical and anti-social activity, but he now placed it on a basis not of race and religion, but of class.[95]

Even while Marx was struggling to get away from religion, he was still impelled by the old religious prejudice to make the Jews the enemy of the world.

This is also the case with Ernest Renan, the influential French philologist, who conformed more completely to the old prejudiced crusading paradigm by fusing Jews and Arabs together as the obverse of all "we" stand for. Both Renan and Marx were rewriting history and offering a new interpretation of the past which claimed to liberate man from religion by means of science. Philology was not an obscure outmoded academic discipline in the nineteenth century. It offered a new, alternative vision of world history to replace the old history of salvation. Instead of seeing language as a gift that God had given to man in the Garden of Eden, as the medievals had imagined, philologists saw it as a human invention. In place of the original sacred tongue that fascinated the medievals, the philologists posited an original Indo-European language which had been developed by the Aryans of Asia and Europe and which gave birth to the later Aryan languages. They believed that they could reconstruct this original tongue by applying their scientific rules. In fact they created some new myths. Renan turned to philology when he lost his Christian faith, and later he would reinterpret the early Christian past in the new "scientific" way, writing the lives of Jesus and St. Paul and explaining them in human, natural terms instead of theologically. He wanted to show the natural basis of religion. These widely read books caused great consternation. When Renan became a philologist, he had turned to the study of Hebrew and Arabic, the Semitic languages. He argued that Hebrew and Arabic were degraded forms, which had deviated from the Aryan tradition and become irredeemably flawed. The languages could only be studied as an example of arrested development because they lacked the progressive and developmental qualities that were inherent in "our" Aryan linguistic systems. It will be obvious to the reader how this complemented the current colonial vision. For Renan, too, Jews and Arabs were *une combinaison inférieure de la nature humaine.*"

> Therefore we refuse to allow that the Semitic languages have the capacity to regenerate themselves, even while recognising that they do not escape—any more than other products of human consciousness—the necessity of change or of successive modifications.[96]

From this philological fantasy developed the new racial theory which opposed Semites to Aryans.

Renan translated the old religious prejudice with uncanny accuracy into a secular, scientific idiom. The concept of the inferior Semitic languages made Jews and Arabs once again a distorted mirror image of the enlightened and progressive West. Because their languages could not develop as "ours" could, Jews and Arabs themselves were flawed human beings.

> One sees that in all things the Semitic race appears to us to be an incomplete race, by virtue of its simplicity. This race—if I dare use the analogy—is to the Indo-European family what a pencil sketch is to a painting; it lacks that variety, that amplitude, that abundance of life which is the condition of perfectibility. Like those individuals who possess so little fecundity that, after a gracious childhood, they attain only the most mediocre virility, the Semitic nations experienced their fullest flowering in their first age and have never been able to achieve true maturity.[97]

The old religious fantasies had been tranlated into a new racial myth which had been scientifically "proved."

These dangerous theories of race became crucial at the end of the nineteenth century when, as I pointed out in Chapter 3, nationalism became a new enthusiasm and people started to define themselves anew in national or racial terms. In Germany the cult of the *Volk* was perhaps most fully seen in the operas of Richard Wagner, which later had such a profound influence on Hitler and his followers. The pure, noble German race, the source of all goodness and beauty, was celebrated in a musical form that made it larger than life. This cult of the Aryan race went hand in hand with a virulent anti-Semitism. As Wagner wrote in 1881:

> I regard the Jewish race as the born enemy of pure humanity and everything that is noble in it; it is certain that we Germans will go

under before them, and perhaps I am the last German who knows how to stand up as an art-loving man against the Judaism that is already getting control of everything.[98]

Friedrich Nietzsche hated Christianity. In *Antichrist* he argued that it had "waged a war to the death against every feeling of reverence and distance between man and man." He urged Germans to throw off its puling values and return to the pagan Aryan values: pride, severity, strength, hatred, revenge. Christianity had corrupted the world but this was the fault of the Jews, because the Christian was "that *ultima ratio* of the lie, is the Jew once more, even thrice more."

One cannot read these Gospels too warily. . . . One is among Jews: *first* consideration if one is not to lose the thread completely—Paul and Christ were little superlative Jews. . . . One would no more associate with the first Christians than one would with Polish Jews—they both do not smell good. . . . There is only one solitary figure one is obliged to respect: Pilate, the Roman governor. To take a Jewish affair *seriously*—he cannot persuade himself to do that. One Jew more or less—what does it matter?[99]

Nietzsche became mad in 1889, the year that Adolf Hitler was born, and his ideas, which were widely disseminated in Germany, were ready to hand when Hitler began to shape the Aryan identity once more. In Chapter 3 we discussed the different reactions among the Jews to this new late nineteenth-century explosion of anti-Semitism.

But the Arab Semites were also being discussed at the same time. Expert orientalists began to produce an equally racist fantasy of the "Arab mind." Unlike the Jews, who were present in Europe, the Arabs were a distant and unthreatening reality. As Europe prepared to colonize the Middle East it was consoling to hear the scholarly myths present the Arabs as primitives desperately in need of Western redemption. These theories were different from Chateaubriand's poetic musings earlier in the century because they claimed to be objective, scientific studies. In 1881, for example, the orientalist William Robertson Smith toured the Hejaz during the course of his research into early Islam. His basic assumption was that nothing had changed since the time of Mohammad and that it was, therefore, perfectly possible to see what the first *umma* was like by looking at modern Arabs. There is an uncanny similarity between this nineteenth-century Western view and the old Arab view of the West, which had assumed that nothing had changed since the Crusades. The difference was that, where the Arab theory remained a tacit assumption, the new Western view of the Arab world was documented and dogmatically expounded as scientific truth. Robertson Smith concluded that the problem with Islam was that it was too Arab; it was, therefore, constitutionally incapable of development.

> The prejudices of the Arab have their roots in a conservatism which lies deeper than his belief in Islam. It is, indeed, a great fault of the religion of the Prophet that it lends itself so easily to the prejudices of the race among whom it was first promulgated, and that it has taken under its protection so many barbarous and obsolete ideas, which even Mohammad must have seen to have no religious worth, but which he carried over into his system in order to facilitate the propagation of his reformed doctrines.[100]

Robertson Smith did not consider the historical reasons why the Arabs might have become so conservative; a student of Islam, he does not compare past dynamism with the present situation nor does he consider the movements for Arab reform which were eagerly being debated throughout the Muslim world. He simply makes them the opposite of the dynamic, progressive West.

In his important book *Orientalism: Western Conceptions of the Orient*, Edward W. Said points out: "Smith's vision of the world is binary, as is evident in such passages as the following:

> The Arabian traveller is quite different from ourselves. The labour of moving from place to place is a mere nuisance to him, he has no enjoyment in effort [as 'we' do], and grumbles at hunger or fatigue with all his might [as 'we' do not]. You will never persuade the Oriental that, when you get off your camel, you can have any other wish than immediately to squat on a rug and take your rest (*isterih*), smoking and drinking. Moreover the Arab is little impressed by scenery [but 'we' are]."[101]

Robertson Smith has no respect for what he chooses to call "the jejune, practical and . . . constitutionally irreligious Arabic mind,"[102] without reflecting that this might be just as fictional a portrait as his image of "us," who never cease striving purposefully onward to even greater heights of achievement. Said goes on later in the same chapter to discuss the work of another famous orientalist, Duncan Black Macdonald, who was often sought out by colonialists for advice about how to manage the Orientals. Macdonald was committed to the old medieval view that Islam was a Christian heresy rather than an independent faith, which instantly makes the Muslim Arab a failed version of "us." In *The Religious Attitude and Life in Islam* (1909) he gives what he sees as the self-evident definition of the oriental mind. He begins by saying that "it is plain" that the conception of the Unseen is much more real to the Oriental than to Western people: the "large modifying elements which seem, from time to time, almost to upset the general law" do not upset this apprehension of the Unseen. But "the essential difference in the Oriental mind is not credulity as to unseen things but inability to construct a system as to seen things."[103] The Oriental has "no sense of law" and therefore the implication is that he cannot fruitfully organize his existence in the way that Western people can. The oriental mind is so lawless that "it is evident that anything is possible to the Oriental."

> *Inability*, then, to see life steadily, and see it whole, to understand that a theory of life must cover all the facts, and *liability* to be stampeded by a single idea and blinded to everything else—therein, I believe, is the difference between East and West.[104]

This hopeless creature, lost in a metaphysical fog (quite unlike the practical, level-headed British), was clearly not capable of taking command for his own destiny. It was, therefore, up to "us."

But not all travelers in the Middle East came to these conclusions. In 1884, Denis de Rivoyre, a Frenchman, who traveled from one end of the Arab-speaking world to the other, wrote:

> Everywhere I came upon the same abiding and universal sentiment: hatred of the Turks. . . . The notion of concerted action to throw off the detested yoke is gradually shaping itself. . . . An Arab movement, newly-risen, is looking in the distance and a race hitherto downtrodden will presently claim its due place in the destinies of Islam.[105]

In fact the Arab world was not sitting back fatalistically but was trying to mobilize itself, first against the dead hand of the Ottomans and secondly against the West, which was increasingly revealing its naked colonial ambitions. But this did not mean that the Muslim reformists were rabidly anti-Western and rejecting of Western culture.[106] On the contrary, they knew that they needed Western progress and particularly Western science but they also knew that they could not become Westerners themselves. If they were to fight the colonial West, they must graft this European expertise onto their own traditions. All the nineteenth-century reformists were concerned to return to their own Arab traditions, before the disaster of Turkish hegemony, all wanted to mobilize the resources of Islam effectively, and all tended to look back in various ways to the principles of the eighteenth-century Wahhabi revolution.

Perhaps the most important of these reformers was Jamal ad-Din al-Afghani (d. 1897). Most of the Muslim movements of the twentieth century look back to his theories. Born a Persian Shiite, he called himself "the Afghan," claiming to be a Sunni so that he could address the majority. In fact, throughout his remarkable career al-Afghani showed an extraordinary ability to become all things to all men. He toured Iran, Afghanistan, Egypt and India, presenting himself in different guises as circumstances required. At different times he presented himself as a revolutionary, a secular freethinker, a Shiite martyr and a parliamentarian. He seems to have been a skeptic but as a boy he had been a "*talabeh*," a seeker, and student in a *madrassa*, and he had also been trained in the mystical discipline of *erfan* practiced by the Sufis. This early training proved crucial. In particular *erfan* teaches the mystic to transcend himself and become one with the world in front of him; he experiences a liberating loss of the normal boundaries around the self. In the West this kind of mysticism tends to be quietist but the Sufis have a long tradition of political commitment. The Sufi's love of the *umma* is central to his religion and if he sees it threatened he will fight a *jihad*: thus Sufis fought with Saladin's army against the Crusaders. *Erfan* teaches the adept fearlessness and indifference to death. In particular, he should have no fear of the political powers-that-be. It has been suggested that al-Afghani's own recklessness and adoption of different roles was influenced by the mystical habit of *erfan*, with its enlarged concept of self.[107]

Al-Afghani wanted the Muslims to band together to face the threat of the West and to take their destiny into their own hands. His early contact with the *ulema* had convinced him that they would be worthy leaders of the Muslims but he wanted the new Islam to be a civilization and an allegiance rather than a religious faith. It was al-Afghani who introduced, as a revolutionary idea, the Western notion of secular politics into the region. Though many Muslims would quite understandably see this as an unacceptable innovation in Islam, it was a remarkable achievement. Al-Afghani knew that the Muslims would have to use Western ideas if they were to prevail against the colonialists. He was adamantly opposed to any collaboration with the colonial authorities and urged the *ulema* to stand up against them but the task was impossible to implement in a short time. Al-Afghani underestimated the immense amount of internal work and rethinking that would be necessary before the people would be ready to strip Islam of its corruptions and build a new Islamic civilization on classical Arab foundations. It was certainly too great a task for the demoralized *ulema* of the period. But al-Afghani was also possessed by a realistic sense of urgency: if the Muslims were to close their doors against the colonial domination of the West, there was very little time left.

His disciple, Mohammad Abduh (d. 1905), had a different outlook, even though he was basically in sympathy with al-Afghani. Instead of his mentor's broad theater of operations, Abduh concentrated his activities in his native Egypt. Indeed, the word *watan* (homeland), a word not previously used in political Muslim or Arabic discourse, occurred more and more frequently in his writing. Abduh had also had some mystical training and was committed to his own Islamic culture but he was also a great admirer of the West. He had been deeply influenced by Tolstoy and Herbert Spencer, whom he knew personally. Abduh never adopted a Western lifestyle but he frequently visited Europe to refresh himself spiritually. His ideas were more realistic in some respects than those of al-Afghani: he was convinced that the latter's policy of concerted opposition to the colonialists would simply anger them to no good purpose. In 1888 he had made the decision to return to British Egypt and work under Lord Cromer. He was appointed Mufti, the interpreter of Islamic law in the courts. He was committed to the liberating principles of *maslaha* (public interest), which allows the law to be modified to meet modern conditions, and also to *ijtihad* (independent reasoning). He knew that Arabs must have intellectual freedom if they were to catch up with the West and take their place beside the European nations in the modern world. Hence he was opposed to the practice of *taqlid* (emulation of authority) which, as we have seen, had prevailed since the Mongol invasions. The power of the West was largely due to its overwhelming scientific and technological superiority and Abduh founded nonreligious schools in Egypt, where Arabs could study the secular sciences.

But, like any reformer, Abduh wanted to return to fundamentals. He was convinced that the rot had set in after the Muslims submitted to Turkish authorities in the Middle Ages. Arabs must return to the spirit of the Prophet and the Rightly Guided Caliphs, the golden age when Arabs had been their own masters and had made Islam a world power. Accordingly, he applied the principle of *talfiq* (literally, "piecing together"): rulings could be formulated by looking at the teaching of all four Islamic schools of jurisprudence in an attempt to grasp the basic principle; then the matter could be referred back to the Koran, the *hadith* and the Rightly Guided Caliphs.[108] But though Abduh was a fundamentalist, he was certainly not opposed to progress. He simply felt that the Arabs could only make true progress if their journey into the modern world was undertaken in the spirit of their great past. Abduh was convinced that there was no opposition between religion and science, between God's word in the Koran and God's word uttered in nature.

But, again, other Muslims would disagree. Indeed during the nineteenth century many Europeans had found great difficulty in reconciling the discoveries of Lyall and Darwin with the Bible. In Islam the problem was accentuated by the fact that God had revealed himself precisely *in a text*: some Muslims would see any criticism of the text as a reflection on the integrity of Islam. But Muslims did not need to apply the principles of the new biblical science that was helping some Christians with this problem. There was a long and perfectly reputable Islamic tradition of interpreting the Scriptures symbolically. The rationalist philosophers had led the way as had the great twelfth-century theosophist Ibn al-Arabi. Some of the esoteric *batini* sects like the Druzes and the Alawis had long used the natural sciences as a means of meditating upon God's work in the world and had used mathematics as a discipline which weaned the mind away from the concrete. (Interestingly, the *batinis* have been able to adjust more easily to new scientific developments than any other Muslim group.) But not all Muslims would agree. Henceforth in Arab countries there would sometimes be a split between orthodox, traditional Muslims and secular Arabs educated in the new schools founded by Abduh and his followers in other countries. The West had got used to the ideal of the secular by slow degrees but it was an immense—and in some ways an unavoidable—upheaval in the Middle East and has probably still not been wholly assimilated. There was also the problem of how to interpret the legislation given in the Koran. It is important to be clear that this constitutes only about 10 percent of the whole Koran: the other 90 percent is about God's work in nature and history. But such as it was, it applied to the conditions of seventh-century Arabia. Could a Muslim, for example, drink alcohol and remain true to his faith? There were difficult problems to be addressed that could not be solved by one or two men but would take time. To accept the superficial trappings of Western culture without relating them to Arab experience would be dangerous. It was unfortunate that their colonial masters were in general not disposed to understand or appreciate this Arab desire for a deep reform.

The great Syrian journalist Rashid Rida (d. 1935), who was Abduh's disciple, was also concerned to make that creative journey to the past in order to move forward into the future. This has, of course, been a major theme in our story. Rida was also convinced that the acceptance of the Turks as leaders had been disastrous for the Arab Muslims. He was very close in spirit to many of the ideas of the Wahhabis: he was a devoutly religious man who lived according to ascetic ideals. He was more concerned with the revival of Islam than with the emergence of Arab nationality, as were all these early reformers: Rida even wanted to restore the Arab caliphate. He was also mystically inclined and a member of the Naqshbandi Sufi order, which believes that a good Muslim should be active in the world rather than retreat into contemplative withdrawal. A Naqshbandi is duty-bound to be politically active if he sees disorders in the *umma*: if necessary, he can cooperate with the authorities but sometimes he also has a duty to rebel. Rida was a product of the radical strain in Islam, whereas Abduh was a fine example of a more conservative Muslim who was ready to work with the status quo. But Rida and his followers were also helping to raise Arab consciousness. None of these reformers wanted to break up the Muslim empire; though they all wanted to be rid of the Ottomans, they certainly had not envisaged the Western vision of nation-states. Nevertheless future Arab nationalists, in the new Arab states, would later draw on these earlier Pan-Islamic ideas of a return to Arab roots. During the 1950s and 1960s the Nasserites and the Syrian *Ba'ath* (Renaissance) Party took this old ideal and developed the Pan-Arab idea. They wanted to preserve the old unity of the *umma* in the new diversity. Religion and politics were separate on the Western model but they saw Islam as a great civilization as well as a religion that was coextensive with the Arab peoples. This vision of Arabism was not racist: people of very many ethnic groups belong to the Arab nation just as they had been since the Middle Ages. Pan-Arabism was a reversed mirror image of our Western nationalism. The colonial powers had created the modern nation-states and had divided the unity of the old *umma*: Pan-Arabism sought to discover the values that all these Arab states had in common. In Europe, nationalism had been the breaking down of a community into smaller groups who felt bound together by a shared experience.

We have seen that the Jews had been considered part of the Arab family for centuries, just as the Berbers and Egyptians had been and in rather the same way as somebody can consider himself Jewish and American today. The *dhimmis/millets* had been protected minorities but during the nineteenth century their second-class citizenship had become unacceptable. We have seen that the Western nations were exploiting their position in order to increase their own power in the region. To meet this pressure from the West, in 1857 the Ottomans declared Jews and Christians to be the equals of the Muslim subjects of the Empire. As one might imagine, there was rejoicing among the former *millets* and a certain amount of grumbling among Muslims. But the move was welcomed in some of the Arab provinces because they felt that this would give the Arabs greater strength and unity. But there were problems: the foreign traders and consuls in the region tended to favor the former Christian *millets* over the Muslims and this caused resentment; to deflect Muslim hostility away from themselves, the Turkish and Arab Christians often stirred up anti-Jewish feeling. There was as yet no racist element in this. It was a hostility based entirely on the relative strengths and weaknesses of the three groups within the Ottoman polity and economy. The resident Europeans, however, began to import dangerous Western ideas into the region. Thus in 1840 the first European-style pogroms broke out in Damascus where reports of the old Western myth of the blood libel had been spread by a Capuchin monk and fanned by an anti-Semitic French consul. This set an important trend: the anti-Semitic ideas were introduced by the European or Russian residents, especially those who belonged to religious communities or churches.

In 1869 the first anti-Semitic text was published in the Middle East: it was a translation into Arabic of a very popular forgery purporting to be the confessions of a former Moldavian rabbi who had converted to Christianity, which had been influential in Europe. The Ottoman authorities stopped the circulation of this tract. During the 1890s there were translations by Arab Christians of three French and German anti-Semitic tracts; they made little impact and were in fact denounced by many Turkish and Arabic journalists. These translations had been promoted by the resident French, whose anti-Semitism had flared high after the Dreyfus scandal. Some of the Arabs were sympathetic to Dreyfus and others were delighted to have the opportunity to jeer at the enlightened Europeans who had presented themselves to the Middle East in such a liberal guise. In particular Rashid Rida pointed out that this new anti-Semitism was racist rather than religious: the French, as anybody could see, were not religious people. The accusations they were at present hurling against the Jewish captain could just as easily be leveled against the people of the Middle East. Before 1948 and the Arabs' humiliation by the Israeli army, there was no anti-Semitism in the Middle East comparable to the European mania. But two of the texts published in the 1890s, which had a small readership and much criticism when they first appeared, were reprinted in Egypt during the 1960s and became very popular: a sad comment on the growth of Western anti-Semitism in the Middle East.[109] In the early days of the

Arab-Israeli conflict, however, the Arabs were not influenced by anti-Semitism. Before the creation of the state of Israel they could distinguish very clearly between the former Jewish *millets* and the Russian Zionists, who were their political enemies.

The new Arab Awakening in the Middle East had little chance against the colonialists, who preferred the new racist, scientific theories which justified their taking control and which insisted that the Arabs were incapable of regenerating their own society. Thus Lord Cromer contemptuously dismissed Abduh's ideas: Islam, he declared, could not reform itself. He insisted that the Arabs were irredeemably illogical and too childish to know what was good for them. Cromer had worked in Egypt and India and in his view "Orientals," be they Egyptian or Indian, were really all the same. In his magisterial two-volume work, *Modern Egypt*, Cromer fell into the long-established habit of putting "the Oriental" in complete opposition to "us": "somehow or other the Oriental generally acts, speaks, and thinks in a manner exactly the opposite to the European."[110]

> Sir Alfred Lyall once said to me: "Accuracy is abhorrent to the Oriental mind. Every Anglo-Indian should always remember that maxim." Want of accuracy, which easily degenerates into untruthfulness, is in fact the main characteristic of the Oriental mind.
>
> The European is a close reasoner; his statements of fact are devoid of any ambiguity; he is a natural logician, albeit he may not have studied logic; he is by nature sceptical and requires proof before he can accept the truth of any proposition; his trained intelligence works like a piece of mechanism. The mind of the Oriental, on the other hand, like his picturesque streets, is eminently wanting in symmetry. His reasoning is of the most slipshod description. Although the ancient Arabs acquired in a somewhat higher degree the science of dialectics, their descendants are singularly deficient in the logical faculty. They are often incapable of drawing the most obvious conclusions from any simple premises of which they may admit the truth.[111]

With this view of the Arab mind (which is identical to the "Indian mind"), Britain was unlikely to respect the Arabs' desire for independence and self-reformation. Nor would she feel bound to keep any of the promises or pledges she had made the Arabs about their political independence.

European contempt for both Arabs and Jews was demonstrated in the series of secret pacts and agreements made between 1915 and 1918. Perhaps the clearest proof of that contempt was the British hijacking of the Arab revolt against the Turks, via T. E. Lawrence of Arabia. Lawrence himself shows a racist contempt for the Arabs throughout *The Seven Pillars of Wisdom* but was ashamed when the British broke their pledge to the Arabs and took control after their conquest of Damascus. But the McMahon-Hussein correspondence of 1915 was, of course, followed by the Sykes–Picot agreement in 1916, the modification of Sykes–Picot by the British and the Balfour Declaration in 1917, and the Anglo-French Joint Declaration of 1918. All these secret agreements made contradictory pledges to Jews and Arabs and, as Lord Balfour himself made clear in the cynical remark I quoted earlier, as regarded Palestine the powers did not intend to keep a single one of their promises. The other Arab states got their independence but found that their freedom was constantly neutralized by the great powers by means of treaties and countertreaties; in recent years the British and the French have been replaced by the United States and the USSR. The orientalist Bernard Lewis comments that three invaders have successfully penetrated the Arab world—the Crusaders, the Mongols and the Western powers; of these the last has proved to be the most humiliating and the most enduring.[112]

But given this fundamental contempt for both Jews and Arabs during the First World War, what made the British, against all the odds, stand by the Balfour Declaration during those crucial years of 1920–28? The answer must surely lie in the long and complex tradition of British Zionism, which touched a deep nerve in the English Protestant identity. In 1917, of course, Lord Balfour could be seen as a typically manipulative politician: he hoped that the Declaration would win international Jewish support for Britain during the First World War and he was conscious of the strategic importance of Palestine. But he was also inspired by the Christian Protestant tradition. He had been brought up in the Scottish Church and the biblical image of a Jewish Palestine affected him powerfully: he imagined that there would be a cultural renaissance in the new Israel that would be a light unto the Gentiles.[113] Like all Zionists, he was completely indifferent to the claim of the Palestinian Arabs, who had long been regarded by the British as barbarous and unworthy caretakers. As he said with astonishing bluntness in his *Memorandum Respecting Syria, Palestine and Mesopotamia*:

> For in Palestine we do not propose even to go through the form of consulting the wishes of the present inhabitants of the country, though the American Commission has been going through the form of asking what they are. The Four Great Powers are committed to

Zionism. And Zionism, be it right or wrong, good or bad, is rooted in age-long traditions, in present needs, in future hopes, of far profounder import than the desires and prejudices of the 700,000 Arabs who now inhabit that ancient land.[114]

Like a true Crusader, Balfour was convinced that "our" view of the Holy Land put him above ordinary moral considerations. Zionism was by now so firmly established as self-evidently right that it was impossible for Balfour to see that the Arabs had any claim at all to the land they had inhabited for twelve hundred years.

Balfour was also a typical Zionist in an uneasy anti-Semitism. In 1905 he had introduced the Aliens Bill in Parliament in order to limit Jewish immigration. He may have wanted Jews to be in Palestine, but he did not want them in his own country, and these anti-Semitic feelings disturbed him.[115] He was aware of the shameful tradition of persecution in Europe and may well have felt that the enthusiastic support he gave to Zionism in some way atoned for his instinctive anti-Semitism. It is significant that his strongest opponents in England were Jewish. Lord Montagu, one of the leaders of British Jewry, opposed Zionism from the beginning and he accused Balfour and his colleagues of promoting a Jewish homeland in Palestine simply to get the Jews out of England. During the discussions leading up to the Balfour Declaration, he submitted a memorandum stating that "the policy of His Majesty's Government is anti-Semitic in result and will prove a rallying ground for anti-Semites in every country of the world."[116] But his Gentile colleagues were as blind to Jewish objections as they were to Arab objections. As had always been the case, what mattered was what Europeans wanted in the Holy Land.

Balfour could rely on the support of a generation of Zionist politicians who included Prime Minister David Lloyd George, Mark Sykes, Leopold Amery, Lord Milner, Lord Harlech, Robert Cecil and C. P. Scott. They could all see the political advantages of the Zionist idea, but they were also compelled by the old Protestant view of a strictly Jewish Palestine. Lloyd George, for example, had been brought up by his uncle, who had been a preacher in a fundamentalist Welsh Baptist sect with a tradition of interpreting the Bible quite literally. When Lloyd George listened to Weizmann talking about Palestine he was naturally stirred and excited by these very early associations: the places that Weizmann mentioned were more familiar to him, he said, than places on the Western front.[117] He could only see Palestine in Jewish terms, as he explained in a speech to the Jewish Historical Society in 1925:

I was brought up in a school where I was taught far more about the history of the Jews than about the history of my own land. I could tell you all the kings of Israel. But I doubt whether I could have named half a dozen of the kings of England, and not more of the kings of Wales. . . . We were thoroughly imbued with the history of your race in the days of its greatest glory, when it founded that great literature which will echo to the very last days of this old world, influencing, moulding, fashioning human character, inspiring and sustaining human motive, for not only Jews, but Gentiles as well. We absorbed it and made it part of the best of the Gentile character.[118]

There could hardly be a clearer statement about the Western habit of interiorizing Judaism, absorbing it and making it part of the Christian, European self. A Jewish Palestine was in an important way a British Protestant projection in the Middle East. But Lloyd George was well known for making anti-Semitic remarks, despite his love of the Jewish Scriptures.[119] Although British Zionism seemed to deny crusading anti-Semitism, there was really no fundamental change. Such Zionists, in a convoluted way, still wanted Palestine for themselves and were still either anti-Semitic or blind to the real power and independent integrity of Judaism.

British Catholics responded differently. Mark Sykes, for example, who had had a Catholic upbringing, confessed that he had a strong "distaste for Jews" and at first opposed the Zionist project for precisely this reason. He was, however, an ardent nationalist and colonialist and one of the architects of the notorious 1916 Sykes–Picot agreement. When the full colonial implications of Zionism were explained to him, he became an enthusiastic convert. He would now see the "Jew" as "our" representative in the barbarous Middle East who was taking possession of Palestine in "our" name. He also saw Zionism as a solution to the Jewish problem. Instead of a hybrid, assimilating Jew living disturbingly in the heart of Christian Europe, there would be a new Hebrew nationalist in his own country, reassuringly distant and distinct.[120] Zionists like Balfour and Sykes were still opposed to the idea of absorbing and assimilating Jews into European society, in much the same way as fifteenth-century Spanish Catholics had been. Zionism was a way of deporting Jews without giving way to overt anti-Semitism and banishing them from Europe by offensive persecution. Gentile support for the state of Israel in the West was from the beginning complex and neurotic, molded not simply by political and humanitarian reasons, but by millennial Protestant and biblical ideas, crusading colonialism and crusading anti-Semitism. Non-Jewish Zionists were in a very real sense neo-Crusaders, even if they were no longer inspired by the old passion for the tomb of Christ.

This becomes very clear when we consider the Gentile Zionists' attitude to the "Arabs." Yet again the old prejudice came into play, and because the Arabs really were, quite understandably, opposed to the Zionist scheme, they were made into the distorted enemy of true civilization yet again. But this time they were juxtaposed and measured against "our" new representative, the "Jew." Richard Meinertzhagen, chief political officer for Palestine and Syria on General Allenby's staff, was deeply anti-Semitic. He confessed in his diary that he was "imbued with anti-Semitic feelings."[121] He feared Jewish presence in his own country as a threat to the British identity; the Jews could, he thought, easily gain too much influence "in professions, in trades, in universities and museums, in finance and as landowners."[122] He was ready for a radical if not for a final solution. If the Jews became too powerful, he decided, "then of course we shall have to act against them, but it will not take the form of a concentration camp."[123] But the Zionist solution, which proposed a convenient way of getting rid of this threat, was attractive in other ways. Meinertzhagen felt a "great sentimental attraction" to the idea of the persecuted Jews returning to their ancient land.[124] The old biblical vision was linked to the new colonial vision: "Jewish brains and money" would redeem the barren wilderness that was Palestine.[125] A friendly Palestine was "vital" for the future strategic security of the British government and Meinertzhagen was convinced that this would be impossible if it was in Arab hands.[126] As had long been a British habit, Meinertzhagen was ready to split his anti-Semitism and make the "Arab" the opposite of the "Jew." This mythical bifurcation appears constantly in his diary. "Intelligence was a Jewish virtue," he wrote antithetically, "and intrigue was an Arab vice."[127] The Jews were "virile, brave, determined and intelligent" while the Arabs were "decadent, stupid, dishonest and producing little beyond eccentrics influenced by the romance and silence of the desert."[128] If the Jews took over in Palestine there would be "progress" and the "up-setting of modern government," but an Arab government would mean "stagnation, immorality, rotten government, corrupt and dishonest society."[129] These new fictional stereotypes now set the two old crusading enemies off against one another:

The Palestine Arab will never reach the Jewish standard of ability in any sense. The Jew will always be on top and he means to be there. He looks forward to a Jewish state in Palestine with sovereign rights, a real National Home and not a sham Jewish–Arab confederation.[130] . . . The Jew, however small his voice, however mild his manner, will in the end be heard and he will succeed. The Arab will trumpet and bluster, others in Europe and America will sing his praises if the local orchestra breaks down, but he will remain where he is and has for ever been, an inhabitant of the east, nurturing stagnant ideas and seeing no further than the narrow doctrines of Mohammed [sic].[131]

The old blind prejudice against "Islam" had modulated into the new secular prejudice against the "Arab," who was the obverse of everything "we" stood for. But Meinertzhagen's ineradicable Jewish anti-Semitism is also revealed in this paragraph, not least in his use of the reductive term the "Jew." Like the "Arab," the "Jew" is a monolithic fantasy created by "us." There is no such thing as *the* "Jew" or *the* "Arab" and it is dangerous to suppose that there is. There are rather millions of Jewish and Arab individuals with an infinitely varied combination of talents, enthusiasms, hopes, fears, faults, neuroses, defects and ambitions. But since the time of the Crusades fantasies were created that had no reality outside European people's views of themselves. The "Jew" that Meinertzhagen contemplated was simply a flattering portrait of "us" in endless opposition to his and our equally fantastic enemy the "Arab." The antithesis is a rhetorical ploy that gives the conflict an elegant logical and literary but not objective reality.

It was because of the fantasy of the "Jew" that six million Jews were exterminated by the Nazis in the ultimate secular Crusade. This has naturally given people a very healthy fear of Jewish anti-Semitism and has led to an increased support for the state of Israel in the West. But it would, I fear, be unrealistic to think that there is no longer any European anti-Semitism. Gentile support for Zionism was from the start bound up with a stubborn anti-Semitism or, at least, with a willingness to annihilate the Jews' plans and religious vision in favor of the Christian ideal. Europeans are still filled with complex feelings about their history of anti-Semitism which culminated in the Holocaust. Support for Israel has often been inspired by a natural desire to make amends. Very often, in Europe and Britain, it has made a scapegoat of the Palestinians. It is certainly true that many Palestinians today feel that they have been made to suffer for the crimes committed by Europeans against Jews. There is, on the other hand, absolutely no squeamishness about Arab anti-Semitism, which sometimes seems to be the one form of acceptable racism left in a country like Britain. Biased and prejudiced remarks are bandied about in public and in private, and people look genuinely astonished if it is pointed out that they would quite properly be shocked if the same remarks were directed against blacks or Jews.

In Britain we have had particular difficulties in coming to terms with the Arabs which do not apply in the United States. At a time when our British economy seems incurably sick and there is increasing hardship and unemployment, it has been very hard to see the newly rich Arabs from the Gulf states pour into London and virtually take over districts like Park Lane or Earls Court. The resentment we used to feel about rich Jews now seems to have been transferred in toto to the rich Arabs. In the 1970s anti-Semitic Arab jokes became common: there was talk of stewed goat being served at the Hilton and camels being parked outside the Playboy Club. Arabs were buying up our stately homes! There was an ugly and belligerent edge to the delivery of these not so amusing jokes. It seemed as though this new Arab invasion had revived the old buried phobia of the Arab *jihad*: Arabs seemed all set once again to take over the world. It is, however, also true that there has been a dramatic change since the Palestinian uprising in the occupied territories. The *intifada* has won the Palestinian Arabs many supporters in Britain and alienated many people against Israel. The more positive approach to the Arab people is to be welcomed: what is not so good is the threat of a new bout of anti-Semitism as a consequence of Israeli policy. It is essential that the people of Europe stop lurching from one exaggerated and irrational extreme to another. It has been an entrenched habit ever since the Crusades and a recognition of this unhealthy trait could be a first step toward demythologizing our response toward Arabs and Jews today.

The leadership of the Christian world has, however, passed from Europe to the United States. America's approach toward Arabs and Jews is bound to be different. Many of the old crusading attitudes certainly passed to America together with the immigrants from Europe. We have seen that, for example, there is a gulf between America's experience of present greatness and the Arab sense of past splendor. American attitude to Arab oil wealth has been different from the British reaction. Edward Said comments that in American eyes the Arabs have none of the moral qualifications that justify this wealth, which seems an affront to decent values and civilization. At the time of the OPEC oil crisis of 1973, he recalled cartoons and posters which depicted Arabs leering beside petrol pumps:

These Arabs, however, were clearly "Semitic": their sharply hooked noses, the evil, mustachioed leer on their faces, were obvious reminders (to a largely non-Semitic population) that "Semites" were at the bottom of all "our" troubles, which in this case was principally a gasoline shortage. The transference of a popular anti-Semitic animus from a Jewish to an Arab target was made smoothly, since the figure was essentially the same.[132]

This is a precisely observed example of the old crusading habit of linking Arabs and Jews as a common threat to society. There has been anti-Semitism in the United States, though it never reached anything like the severity of European hostility to Jews.

But America has also developed quite a different attitude. From the days of the *Mayflower*, Americans actually identified with Jews and gave the new Canaan a quasi-Jewish identity. America has provided a refuge for millions of Jews who fled persecution in Europe. Today American Jews maintain that America has replaced the home they found in Muslim Spain. Emma Lazarus, the Jewish-American poetess, was inspired by the sight of the Ashkenazic refugees from Russia flooding into New York in 1883 to write these lines that have ever since been associated with the Statue of Liberty:

> Give me your tired, your poor,
> Your huddled masses yearning to breathe free,
> The wretched refuse of your teeming shore,
> Send these, the homeless, tempest-toss't, to me:
> I lift my lamp beside the golden door.

This identification of Jewish and American interests and idealism has persisted. Today some American Jews argue either that New York is the new capital of Judaism or that, together with Israel, American Jewry "will create something new for themselves and the world," which will replace the Jewish culture that was lost in Europe.[133] Americans can rightly be proud of this achievement. They have established a strong emotional bond and even an identification with a people whom Europeans have persecuted and massacred ever since the Crusades.

This American identification with the Jewish people was shown very early in the history of Zionism. The Balfour Declaration was most enthusiastically received. President Woodrow Wilson gave it unqualified support, even though it was against the spirit of his famous Fourteen Points, which condemned private agreements about territory and proclaimed the principle of the self-determination of peoples.

Point 12 had even insisted that the non-Turkish nationalities of the Ottoman Empire should be assured an unmolested opportunity for autonomous development. But Wilson, who had been brought up in the American Protestant tradition, was a natural Zionist.[134] The Jews were a special case. Many congressmen thought so too. Senator Henry Cabot Lodge, for example, made a classic Zionist statement which he worded very strongly.

> It seems to me that it was entirely becoming and commendable that the Jewish people in all portions of the world should desire to have a national home for such members of their race as wished to return to the country which was the cradle of their race and where they lived and laboured for several thousand years [sic]. . . . I never could accept in patience the thought that Jerusalem and Palestine should be under the control of the Mohammedans . . . that Jerusalem and Palestine, sacred to the Jews . . . a land profoundly holy to all the great Christian nations of the West, should remain permanently in the hands of the Turks, has seemed to me for many years one of the great blots on the face of civilization that ought to be erased.[135]

His identification with the Jews made Jewish Palestine sacred to his own identity and blinded him to the claim of the "Mohammedans." He had a double but could not achieve a triple vision, like so many Gentile Zionists before him. Non-Jewish Zionism is a form of Protestant crusading and Senator Lodge felt as great a sense of outrage at the thought of Muslim occupation of Jerusalem as any medieval Catholic Crusader. Americans have continued to feel strongly about Israel and this fervor has increased with the rise of a new wave of American Christian fundamentalism which is aggressively Zionist. Fundamentalists have become very powerful in America; Jerry Falwell's Moral Majority has had to be courted as a power bloc during presidential elections. They have given strong support to the Jewish lobby, though they do not feel the same sense of identification with the Jews as the more secular American Zionists. Like the Puritans, they believe that the Last Days are at hand and that the Jews will either have to be converted or suffer in hell. But they also passionately believe that the Jews must live in Israel to fulfill biblical prophecy. They have returned to a classical and extreme religious crusading.[136]

For those millions of Americans who are not fundamentalists, however, there is another reason for this identification with the Zionists, which I have already referred to. From the earliest days of Labor Zionism, Americans found themselves naturally identifying with the

Jewish pioneers. In 1929 the Protestant minister John Haynes spontaneously made this connection when he met the *chalutzim* during a visit to Palestine:

> As I met and talked with these toilers on the land, I could think of nothing but the early English settlers who came to the bleak shores of Massachusetts, and there amid winter's cold in an untilled soil, among an unfriendly native population, laid firm and sure the foundations of our American Republic. For this reason I was not surprised later, when I read Josiah Wedgewood's "The Seventh Dominion," to find this distinguished Gentile Zionist of Britain speaking of these Jewish pioneers as "the Pilgrim Fathers of Palestine."[137]

Pioneering Zionism was praised in glowing terms during the congressional debate at the time of the Balfour Declaration. Thomas J. Lane, Representative for Massachusetts (the home of the Pilgrim Fathers), spoke in words which at once recall the words of the Founding Fathers of America:

> To build the Kingdom of God, the Jews must not be dissipated among other nations. Always ineffective as minorities, as the Prophets preached, they must have their own nation—there to work and develop the ideal social order, as a model and example from which other nations may learn.[138]

He was a religious Zionist before most Jews were. In 1937 Senator Alben W. Barkley visited Palestine and proclaimed that there was a "natural link" between the Jews and their land, which was responding and flowering at their hands. He sounds not dissimilar to Nachmanides in the twelfth century. At the same time Senator Champ Clark produced the old argument about the Jews making the desert bloom: "Their coming converted a barren land into a literal Biblical land of 'milk and honey.' . . ." A barren country, desolate and forsaken for centuries."[139]

But there is another important aspect of this pioneering attachment, which President Jimmy Carter touched upon when he made his speech before the Knesset in 1979:

> Seven Presidents have believed and demonstrated that America's relationship with Israel is more than just a special relationship. It has been and it is a unique relationship. And it is a relationship which is indestructible, because it is rooted in the consciousness and the morals and the religion and the beliefs of the American people themselves. . . .

Israel and the United States were shaped by pioneers—my nation is also a nation of immigrants and refugees—by peoples gathered in both nations from many lands.[140]

Like the Jewish Zionists, the American settlers were not just pioneers but refugees who fled oppression in Europe. Both America and Israel are in this sense creations of Europe. For Americans and Israelis the bond is strong because each recognizes the other at a deep level. People who have suffered oppression have a strong bond and empathy that others, who have not suffered in this way, cannot understand. Yet this does not mean that either of these countries of refugees should be able to oppress other people and drive them into permanent exile.

A strong identification, such as America feels for Israel, means that objectivity can be very difficult. A threat to Israel could be seen as a threat to the identity of America itself and as a wound in her integrity. Certainly the United States sees Israel as her alter ego in the Middle East. On October 3, 1987, Congressman Gerry Sikorski wrote an open letter to the editor of the Jerusalem *Post* defending the massive amount of aid given to Israel, which in his view is cheap at the price. In the past United States aid to Israel was a "feel good," sentimental item in the budget. Not any more:

> The Pentagon classifies Israel as a "major non-Nato ally." Our relationship is one of strategic cooperation that cannot be exaggerated.
>
> The American Sixth Fleet now makes regular port visits to Haifa. The US carrier-based aircraft practise on Israeli firing ranges in the Negev desert. Joint anti-submarine exercises have become a matter of routine. US and Israeli military planners meet every few months, and US material is now being pre-positioned in Israel.
>
> Israel aids us in our intelligence-gathering operations, and recently initiated special participation in the development of an Anti-Tactical Ballistic Missile system.

Israel and America are, therefore, fighting a war together. Doubtless Congressman Sikorski would describe all this activity as "peacekeeping" but it has often taken aggressive forms. The American bombing of Tripoli in Libya in April 1986, for example, in the war against "international terrorism" caused considerable revulsion throughout Europe and actually occasioned some Arab sympathy for Qaddafi, who had hitherto been seen as rather a maverick in the Arab world and had not been taken very seriously. When moderate Arab leaders like President Mubarak of Egypt and King Hussein of Jordan heard that America had been selling arms to Iran, the archterrorist state in the region, they felt outraged and insulted. They had put themselves in some danger in their own countries by trying to curb extremism and supporting American policies and felt this dubious Irangate initiative as a slap in the face, though it must be said that their response was restrained and controlled. On July 3, 1988, Iran Air Flight 655, a civilian flight, was by mistake shot down by the American peace-keeping fleet in the Gulf. It is, perhaps, not surprising if the Arab and Muslim population of the Middle East sometimes feel that the American peace mission in the area is double-edged and aggressive.

Congressman Sikorski summarized the values that America saw in Israel in his letter to the Jerusalem *Post*. Israel "provides a model for democratic developments in an area of the world that is not very familiar with the concept of democracy. It aids us in deterring Soviet-backed radicalism in the Middle East. It helps us in our continuous battle against terrorism." We have, however, seen that some Israelis fear for the future of democracy in their country and are embarrassed by the terrorism undertaken by members of the Israeli far right. Israel has long been the alter ego of the United States in the Middle East, but we have also seen that there are signs, at the time of writing, that the Bush administration will work more than previous administrations for the principle of triple vision, seeing the point of view of all three participants in the conflict: the West, Israel and the Arabs.

Throughout our story we have seen wars and battles being fought for feelings that are so deeply entwined with our sense of self that logic and reason cease to function. The wars in the Middle East today are becoming more like the Crusades in this respect, especially in the religious escalation on both sides of the conflict. They are "holy" wars because they are fought on issues that are felt to be sacred by all three participants and they could be seen as the last round in a long and bitter process which began when the European Crusaders attacked Muslims and Jews at the period when the West was finding its soul. The issues are complicated for Arabs and Jews, but we must not forget that they are frequently tortuous and difficult for "us" in the West in both Europe and the United States. If there is to be a peaceful solution, it is not only Arabs and Jews who must sort out their feelings and demythologize the struggle. We in the West must come to terms with our own inner demons of prejudice, chauvinism and anxiety, and strive for a greater objectivity.

# EPILOGUE
# Triple Vision

There is a popular postcard on sale everywhere in Israel that never ceases to astonish me. It shows an "artistic" shot of the Shepherds' Field outside Bethlehem and there are real live shepherds, watching their flocks there today, just as they did on the first Christmas night. They look very biblical shepherds, for they are wearing the traditional headdress that all Christians have seen in countless Nativity plays. These *keffiyehs* hide the men's faces, which is just as well because these are Arab shepherds of the West Bank, posing as first-century Jewish shepherds in the Christian story. There could scarcely be a more ironic and distorted expression of triple vision. It shows the confused and troubled bond that links Jews, Christians and Muslims together and completely ignores the frightening realities of the present conflict. The card is obviously designed for Christian pilgrims to send home to show their friends that everything in the Holy Land is "just the same" as it was in the time of Christ. But, as we know, things are very different. In the first century the Jews were struggling against an unwanted occupation which resulted in a holy war that lost them their land. Today it is the Jews who are the brutal occupiers of Bethlehem and the other towns in the occupied territories, and some of their methods would have shocked even the Romans. But Christian pilgrims do not want to see this and they buy the card as intended. The Holy Land is still a mythical land to many of them, who show a ready willingness to suspend their disbelief as they tour the country in their air-conditioned buses, insulated from the troubling contemporary realities. When they visit Kfar Kana in Galilee they look with reverence at the large water jugs which Jesus is supposed to have used when he worked his first miracle and turned the water into wine at the wedding in Cana. There is a postcard of these too. If the pilgrims actually notice that Kfar Kana is an Arab town, they probably see the Arabs in their *keffiyehs* as merely providing local color and ignore the complexity of their position as Arabs in the Jewish state.

Of course not all pilgrims swallow everything they are told so gullibly but the very fact that in the twentieth century the mythical reality of that small strip of land between Egypt and Syria is more real to thousands of Christian pilgrims than the political reality is an important reminder. The people who make these pilgrimages are educated men and women, who do not believe in Father Christmas but who are prepared to kiss the gold star in the Church of the Nativity in Bethlehem which marks the spot of Christ's birth. When they go to the Holy Sepulchre Church in Jerusalem, they want to pray at the slab of stone on which Jesus is said to have been laid after the Crucifixion and at the ornate tomb of Christ, whence Jesus rose from the dead. The physical connection with Jesus makes these places in some way "holy" and people want to believe in their authenticity.

Religious faith is not an obsolete passion. Nor is it a delusion which people cannot help because they lack the brains or the education to disprove the articles of the creed. People choose to believe what cannot be rationally proved one way or the other, because they need this larger mythical dimension in their lives. We are now in a position to see that religion is not something that we can get rid of once we have progressed to a more "enlightened" state. The eighteenth-century Age of Reason gave way to a strong and fundamentalist resurgence of Christianity in the nineteenth century. Similarly, the secularism of the twentieth century has given way to a renewed religious passion. People need to tell themselves stories about the world and their life in it, so that they have a sense of meaning and purpose. It is very hard to live according to the bleak light of the atheistic or agnostic day, which has rationally disposed of religious faith. In Judaism, Christianity and Islam, which all insist that their myths are historically true, people have a religious geography which gives them a sense of their place in the world and a tangible connection with the unseen. So strong is this desire to believe in the holy place that the political reality under the pilgrim's nose inevitably fades from view.

Throughout this book we have seen that a devotion to the holy place can make people act in a violent and irrational way. I am reminded of an occasion on which I filmed in the Holy Sepulchre Church during the production of a television series. It was a dark, gusty evening and while the electricians and the cameramen were setting up the lights around the tomb of Christ, I was standing outside the church with some members of the Israeli crew. Opposite us was the small mosque which was built to commemorate the spot on which the Caliph

Omar prayed when he conquered Jerusalem for Islam in 637. It will be remembered that he had been invited by the Greek Patriarch to pray inside the Holy Sepulchre, but he declined so that the Christian holy place could be preserved intact. The mosque was lit brightly and in the surrounding darkness it looked far more dramatic than it does during the day. The only other lights were in the Holy Sepulchre: Christianity and Islam faced each other. Suddenly the conversation I was enjoying with the crew was shattered by the earsplitting call of the muezzin, summoning the faithful to prayer. The call to prayer is a long and passionate-sounding chant and I found it particularly exhilarating that night. In the dark, with no modern buildings visible, we could have been back in Jerusalem at the time of Saladin.

But my Israeli colleagues had a very different reaction. My rational and kindly companions of a few minutes ago were transformed into crude boors, who made obscene gestures at the mosque, gave exaggerated imitations of the muezzin with distorted, angry faces, and jeered at the Arabic sounds. I had seen this before during the filming. Sometimes we had had to stop shooting and wait for several minutes until the call to prayer was over, and this seemed to reduce the Israeli crew to particular fury. As I watched them I could not but be reminded of the medieval decrees that forbade the muezzin to give the call to prayer in Europe because this strident reminder of the presence of Islam was too disturbing to be permitted. My Israeli friends seemed to be afflicted by the "dread" that we have seen impelling people to irrational violence throughout our long story. I could see why it was disturbing for them. The muezzin in Israel today is far louder than he was in medieval times, because his voice is recorded and amplified to great—sometimes excessive—volume. It sometimes seems deliberately aggressive: a reminder to the Israelis that Islam and the Arabs are still a strong presence in their Jewish state and that they will not go away. When Israelis are awakened at dawn by the muezzin, have their conversations interrupted, or are forced to suspend their activities until the sometimes deafening call to prayer is over, they are being regularly reminded of a fact which many would prefer to forget. It is right that they have this incessant reminder. Problems will not disappear just because we choose to forget about them. The muezzin pierces the Holy Sepulchre too and I watched a passing Franciscan friar shaking his head impatiently at the sound as he left the church. It is important that Christians and Jews should be reminded of the Muslim presence in a land where Arabs are treated as second-class citizens. But it is saddening if the muezzin had in fact issued a war cry. All three of the traditions of historical monotheism are dedicated to peace and benevolence; all three have, at different times of their history, been committed to the ideal of toleration. But it is particularly sad that the Mosque of Omar, which was built in memory of Omar's courteous act and his vision of the continued coexistence of the three religions in Jerusalem, should now make the call to prayer a defiant reminder. It is a symbol of the bad relations that have existed between the three religions ever since the Crusades.

Once the last echoes of the muezzin faded away, my Israeli companions became recognizable human beings once more. The reason we were standing outside the church was that very soon we were going to be locked up in it for several hours and we wanted to enjoy the fresh air beforehand. Ever since the Ottoman time, the key to the church has been in the keeping of a Muslim. The Turks were driven to this measure, not because they wanted to control the Christians in Jerusalem, but because the different Christian sects who had chapels in the huge complex of the Holy Sepulchre Church were in a constant state of war. One sect was continually locking the others out, and eventually the Turks decided that this intolerable state of affairs must cease: none of the Christian sects should have the key; instead a neutral Muslim would supervise the locking of the church. Because we wanted to have the church to ourselves while we were filming, we went inside at seven o'clock, when it was closed to the public. We watched the great doors swing to and heard the Muslim custodian turn the key in the lock. Until he came back at midnight there was no way to get out.

Because of the terrible acrimony that still exists between the different Christian denominations, each sect has a time during the night when it has exclusive control of the church, on a rota basis. We always preferred to film when the Greek Orthodox were having their turn, because they were far more tolerant than the Latins, who were represented by the Franciscans. In this respect things have not really changed much since the time of the Crusades, except that the Greeks now truly loathe the Latins, instead of merely despising them. There had already been a collision earlier in the evening, when a Franciscan brusquely told our locations manager that the Greeks had had no right to give us permission to film: he was clearly very suspicious indeed about this production, which he sensed would be critical of the Catholic Church. Fortunately, after a sharp exchange, the Franciscan was worsted and he stomped away muttering and shaking his head. That the holiest shrine in the Christian world should be the scene of such bitter hostility between Eastern and Western Christians is an indication that the irrationality and hatreds of crusading are far from dead.

We finished filming at ten o'clock and then had two hours to wait before we were let out. I prowled around the vast church, which looked extremely sinister in the dim light. Indeed, though I am not usually sensitive to "vibrations" of this kind, I always have a strong sense of evil in the Holy Sepulchre, probably because I am so conscious of the blood that has been shed for the sake of this building. Occasionally I came across the slumbering forms of the Israeli crew, who had chosen to sleep the last two hours away.

Eventually at midnight I went upstairs to the Golgotha chapel, which overlooks the front doors, to get a good view of the unlocking. As soon as they heard the knocking on the door, the Israelis woke up and waited to be liberated by a Muslim from this Christian insanity. The sensible Greek Orthodox priest, who had been looking after us that night and who told me that he considered this ceremony a sacred duty, passed a ladder through a hole in the door that had been cut precisely for this purpose. The Muslim took it, placed it against the door on the outside, climbed up it to the lock (which is high up in the door) and with deep and grateful joy we heard the key turn. Slowly the great doors swung open and it was an immense relief to see the outside world again: the dark square, the starry sky with the crescent moon—and the Mosque of Omar opposite.

It seems extraordinary that such a ridiculous and cumbersome arrangement should still be necessary in the twentieth century. The fact that a group of well-educated, religious men cannot sit around a table and find some reasonable *modus vivendi* in the Holy Sepulchre shows the depth and power of this crusading hatred. A holy place inspires a frightening irrationality and intransigence, and if Christians, who all believe that this is the holiest place in the world, cannot find it in them to live together in peace, then there is little hope that Muslims and Jews will find a means of peaceful coexistence in the holy city and the Holy Land. It is no use expecting a rational and logical solution. People are blinded by fierce religious vision, which locks them into old exclusive prejudice.

When President Jimmy Carter, Prime Minister Menachem Begin and President Anwar Sadat signed the Camp David treaty in 1979, many of us thought with relief that the Arab–Israeli problem might be solved. Now we realize how wrong we were. President Carter lost office because he could not force the Ayatollah Khomeini's regime to return the American hostages. President Anwar Sadat was assassinated by Muslim extremists in his own country, largely because of the Camp David treaty. Menachem Begin, a religious man himself, was condemned by religious and secular Jews in Israel for handing back the

Sinai Peninsula to Egypt. The problem cannot be solved by ordinary territorial agreements. Too many deep religious emotions are involved and they make the idea of sharing a country impossible. We are not wholly rational beings. We are illogical, emotional creatures, clinging to myths that are fundamentally sacred to our identity. We can make compromises on all kinds of pragmatic matters, but once these beliefs are threatened we close our eyes entirely to reason and common sense; they no longer apply. We cannot even see facts that stare us in the face, nor can we see how illogically we are behaving.

What will happen in the future? It would be a mistake to make ordinary political predictions, because too many unpredictable emotional factors are involved. Just how unpredictable was shown dramatically in February 1989 while I was preparing this book for publication in the United States. In recent months relations between Britain and Iran had been steadily improving: diplomatic relations had been re-established and it seemed as though we could confidently expect the release of Roger Cooper, a Briton imprisoned in Teheran on spying charges. The Islamic revolutionary fervor seemed to have burned itself out and people were predicting that there would soon be a more moderate government in Iran. But on February 14 the world was shocked to hear that the Ayatollah Khomeini had issued a *fatwa* which sentenced to death the British novelist Salman Rushdie, together with his publishers, Viking Penguin, because his novel *The Satanic Verses* was "against Islam, the Prophet and the Koran." At once Mr. Rushdie went into hiding, the *fatwa* was condemned all over the West for its illegality in threatening the life of a British subject and for its denial of freedom of speech, and later in the month diplomatic relations between Britain and Iran were broken off again. At the time of writing, it is impossible to see how this crisis can be resolved.

The affair of *The Satanic Verses* is a frightening warning: we must not take these religious passions lightly or dismiss them as the crazed fantasies of an eccentric minority that cannot long survive in our enlightened world. There is no purely rational explanation or solution to this problem. It appears that the Ayatollah was not acting purely from theological zeal but that he recognized that the novel had aroused an extemity of emotion in the Muslim world that he could exploit for his own purposes in his political struggle with the moderates in Iran. The book had already been ceremonially burned for its alleged blasphemy by the Muslim community of Bradford in England and people had actually died in riots which had exploded in protest against the novel in India and Pakistan. Mr. Rushdie could not have foreseen the violence of this reaction. Indeed, his stated political stance is one of opposition to Western imperialism and to Zionism, two issues that were paramount in the Ayatollah's own world view. Even though Mr. Rushdie is no longer a believing or practicing Muslim, he is known to have been disturbed by Western prejudice against Islam. Nevertheless, his novel has touched a raw nerve. The pain and distress of the Muslims who are protesting against its publication erupted spontaneously and is undoubtedly a reality which we ignore at our peril. There has long been a tendency in the West to deny the presence or the integrity of Islam and it is now clearly dangerous for us to do so. We are absolutely right to defend the principle of liberty of expression. This is precious to us and an essential part of our Western identity at the present time. We had to fight for it during centuries of oppressive bigotry and we must not lose it now. But it would be wrong to dismiss this Muslim anger loftily and patronizingly: this will only exacerbate the situation. Instead we have to respect it as a fact of life—however bizarre and inexplicable it may seem to "us"—and realize that we are partly responsible for this unhappy mess.

Indeed, the crisis of *The Satanic Verses* appears to be yet another distorted instance of "triple vision": some of the Muslim demonstrators have emphasized the fact that Mr. Peter Mayer, the head of Viking Penguin, is Jewish. In this view, Judaism and the West have once more teamed up to humiliate the Islamic world; it is another instance of the paranoid stereotyping that has poisoned relations between Jews, Christians and Muslims ever since the Crusades. But we must remember that *The Satanic Verses* is only the latest of a long line of books written in the West, supported and, indeed, even promoted by the establishment, which have presented Islam and its Prophet in a distorted light. Throughout the world Muslims are now telling us that they will not accept this tradition of prejudice any longer. They will not be soothed by rational arguments, as, for example, that the book is "only" a work of fiction and that the views expressed by its characters are not necessarily Mr. Rushdie's own. The emotions aroused are too deep to be assuaged by logical arguments and the fact that Mr. Rushdie was born a Muslim himself is simply, in their view, another cruel twist in this long history of hatred. True, few of these protesters have actually read *The Satanic Verses*, any more than they read the learned tomes of those Western writers who have attacked Islam ever since the Crusades. Latterly, as we have seen, some of these writers have been advisers on colonial and foreign policy and the Western contempt for Islam has been transmitted to them through their experience of Western colonialism and Western foreign policy in the Middle East.

Crusáding Christianity developed as a response to a long period of humiliation and impotence during the Dark Ages. It was a radical new departure, having nothing whatever to do with the pacifist religion of Jesus, but it provided the people of Europe with an ideology that restored their self-respect and made the West a world power. The Iranian Revolution, with its theme of hatred of the Western world, was born of the humiliation and impotence of the colonial period, when Britain and America were felt to have exploited the people of Iran and to have supported the tyrannical regime of the Shah. Like crusading in some ways, the Iranian experience has been a radical departure from established Muslim tradition: In January 1988 the Ayatollah Khomeini had issued a *fatwa* which shocked the mullahs of Qum: he claimed that his regime had the same authority as the Prophet Mohammad and that it had the power to stop "any religious law if it feels that it is correct to do so," even religious practices like prayer, fasting or the *hajj* pilgrimage.[1] No Muslim leader has ever claimed parity with the Prophet or claimed the power to abolish any of the five "pillars" of Islam. Like the Crusaders, the Ayatollah had departed dramatically from the spirit of the religion for which he had fought. When the Rushdie affair broke out, it was noticeable that the official Muslim response in the Arab world was far more restrained and had more in common with the cautious policies of Saladin. Saudi Arabia's state-approved theologians asked that Mr. Rushdie be brought to trial: this might take the form of a show trial *in absentia* in a Muslim country or a lawsuit in Britain to press for the application of the blasphemy laws to Islam. Clerics of al-Azhar in Cairo denied the Ayatollah's right to apply Islamic law outside the Muslim world. It seems, therefore, that in the Arab Sunni world Muslims were anxious to confine their response to gestures of disapproval and did not wish to incite illegal violence. In some ways the Ayatollah's form of Islam had over the years of his rule acquired a tendency that had more in common with the Crusaders than with mainstream Islam. This is an irony that we should not be too swift to deride.

Obviously the religious passions of the Middle East are no longer always amenable to rational control. The area has become a tinderbox that could ignite into a nuclear holocaust, if this extreme spirit were allowed to get out of control. It appears that Israel might have a nuclear bomb and experts have predicted that some of the Arab states could also acquire bombs within the next ten years.[2] Peace in the area is an urgent priority and we in the West must ensure that we personally do nothing to precipitate this ultimate catastrophe. Feeling against us runs high in the region; it sometimes assumes horrible forms. Nevertheless we have a responsibility to remain calm and perhaps to be more careful of attitudes of prejudice or carelessness, which, as the Rushdie affair shows, we can no longer afford.

The Jews and the Arabs have their own problems with each other and they both have a long way to go before a peaceful solution becomes a real possibility. It is not sufficient for us in the West to support or condemn either side. We are also involved in the conflict and must make our own attitudes our prime responsibility. Over the years our relations with both peoples have been influenced by powerful myths and enthusiasms that have been written deeply into our identity. Crusading is not a lost medieval tradition: it has survived in different forms in both Europe and the United States and we must accept that our own views are as likely to be blinkered and prejudiced as either the Arabs' or the Jews'. It is probably impossible for us to change these old crusading attitudes overnight. The prophets of Israel, the parent of the two younger faiths, proclaimed the necessity of creating a new heart and a new soul, which was far more important than external conformity. So too today. External political solutions are not enough. All three of the participants in the struggle must create a different attitude, a new heart and spirit. In the Christian West we must try to make the painful migration from our old aggressions and embark on the long journey toward a new understanding and a new self.

# NOTES

**CHAPTER ONE** In the Beginning there was the Holy War. Why?

1. Robert the Monk, *Historia Iherosolimitana*, quoted by August C. Krey, *The First Crusade: The Accounts of Eye-Witnesses and Participants* (Princeton and London, 1921), p. 30. There are no exactly contemporary accounts of Urban's speech and these quotations come from works written shortly after the success of the Crusade and reflect a later view than Urban's, at a time when crusading ideology had developed.

2. Fulcher of Chartres, *A History of the Expedition to Jerusalem, 1095–1127*, trans. and ed. Frances Rita Ryan (Knoxville, 1969), p. 66.

3. Modern scholars give various figures. It is very difficult to assess the medieval accounts accurately. The chroniclers had no means of counting these vast hordes.

4. Alexiad, ed. and trans. B. Leib, 3 vols. (Paris, 1937–45), x, v, 7; Vol. II, p. 208.

5. These early stories were handed down in an oral tradition and first committed to writing in about the ninth century B.C.E.

6. The Sea of Reeds was obviously not the Red Sea but was probably a marshy part of the Nile Delta. As I shall have to refer to this event later, I shall continue to use the traditional name, Red Sea.

7. The giving of the Ten Commandments or the Decalogue to Moses is described in Exodus 20. The other commandments are found in Leviticus, Numbers and Deuteronomy and in other chapters of Exodus. These first five books of the Bible are therefore also called the Torah.

8. II Samuel 7; I Chronicles 17.

9. I Chronicles 22:5–10, an account written by the sixth-century priestly tradition; abhorrence of spilled blood is a feature of the priestly writings for ritual as well as for humanistic reasons.

10. Solomon's kingdom extended into what is now the Negev, Jordan and Syria. It included cities that are today Damascus and Amman.

11. For the pagan elements in Solomon's Temple, see I Kings 7:15–22 and

Chaim Potok, *Wanderings: A History of the Jews* (New York, 1978; 1983), pp. 157–58.

12. Deuteronomy 7:3. See p. 8 of this chapter.

13. See in particular I Kings 18:20–46, where Elijah slays the 450 prophets of Baal, the fertility god.

14. For the reform of Josiah, see II Kings 22 and 23.

15. See, for example, Isaiah 1:11–20.

16. Jeremiah 31:31–37.

17. For Original Sin, see Glossary.

18. See Exodus 19:6. God will make Israel a "holy" people, which can also be translated "set apart," or even "who dwell alone." The idea of separation is very important in Judaism, which celebrates the "holiness" of things by separating them from one another.

19. Ezekiel 34:25. Tel Aviv is Hebrew for the Hill of Spring, and if this is translated the point of the prophecy is lost.

20. Isaiah 2:2–5, 11:6–16.

21. Zion was the name of the ancient citadel which King David had captured from the Jebusites when he conquered Jerusalem.

22. See Potok, *Wanderings*, pp. 213–14.

23. See Ezra 4:1–4, and Potok, *Wanderings*, p. 241.

24. Paul Johnson, *A History of the Jews* (London, 1987), p. 147.

25. For scriptural accounts of the redemption, see Daniel 7:9–14 and Zechariah 12; for the Messiah, see Zechariah 9.

26. In the Acts of the Apostles 5:36–38 Rabbi Gamaliel gives an account of two of these Messiahs.

27. For the Essenes, as for other first-century sects like the Sadducees, the Pharisees and the apocalyptists, see Hyam Maccoby, *Judaism in the First Century* (London, 1989), pp. 11–37.

28. Josephus, *The Jewish War*, trans. G. A. Williamson (Harmondsworth, 1959), p. 367.

29. Mark 1:15. The Greek is stronger: "The Kingdom of God has already arrived."

30. See the story of Zacchaeus (Luke 19:1–10), who was a sinner because he collaborated with the Romans by collecting their taxes and cheated his own people.

31. Mark 11:10; Mathew 21:12; Luke 21:37.

32. The episode of the expulsion of the moneylenders could be a relic of an account of a much larger demonstration. After it the chief priests "were afraid of him because the people were carried away by his teaching" (Mark 11:19). Mark then goes on to give an account of Jesus' teaching in the Temple, where he had spent some days (14:48).

33. Matthew 5:39; Mark 15:1–6.

34. See Hyam Maccoby, *Revolution in Judaea: Jesus and the Jewish Resistance* (London, 1973), pp. 151–205.

35. Acts of the Apostles 2:40, 5:27–42.

36. The dispute is toned down in the interests of presenting a picture of Church unity in Acts 15, which was written about fifty years after the event. Paul himself was writing only seven years later and his is a much harsher account (Galatians 2:1–14).

37. For the teaching of Paul, see Karen Armstrong, *The First Christian: St. Paul's Impact on Christianity* (London, 1983), passim.

38. Galatians, passim, I Corinthians 10:1—13; II Corinthians 5:1–10; Romans 4:18–25, 6:1–4, 9:1–11.

39. Revelation 19:19 and Daniel 11:31, 12:12, which people also applied to the Beast.

40. II Thessalonians 1:4–8.

41. This appears as early as the second century in I John 2:14–19.

42. See W. H. C. Frend, *Martyrdom and Persecution in the Early Church: A Study of a Conflict from the Maccabees to Donatus* (Oxford, 1965), passim.

43. Matthew 16:24, Luke 14:27.

44. Foundation Charter of King Edgar for New Minister, Winchester, quoted by R. W. Southern, *Western Society and the Church in the Middle Ages* (London, 1970), pp. 224–25.

45. For a discussion of Byzantine attitudes to war, see Zoé Oldenbourg, *The Crusades*, trans. Anne Carter (London, 1966), pp. 70–71.

46. See Jonathan Riley-Smith, *The First Crusade and the Idea of Crusading* (London, 1986), pp. 6, 17, 27, 133, 165.

47. See Maxime Rodinson, *Mohammed*, trans. Anne Carter, 2nd ed. (London, 1981), pp. 1–36, for a study of pre-Islamic Arabia.

48. Genesis 16:7–16; 17:20; 21:15–21.

49. This tradition of the *hanifs* has been incorporated into the Koran: 2:126–30, 3:97, 14:38.

50. Rodinson, *Mohammed*, p. 71.

51. Muhammad Zafrulla Khan, *Islam: Its Meaning for Modern Man* (London, 1962, 1980), p. 25.

52. A *hadith* (tradition) of the seventh-century Muslim Bukhari, quoted by Rodinson, *Mohammad*, p. 74. For *hadith*, see Glossary.

53. Khan, *Islam*, pp. 26–27. See also Koran 42:52–3.

54. For Bukhari's mid-seventh-century account of how the Koran was collected and compiled, see Bernard Lewis, *Islam from the Prophet Mohammad to the Capture of Constantinople*, 2 vols., Vol. II: *Religion and Society* (New York and London, 1976), pp. 1–2.

55. See Rodinson, *Mohammed*, pp. 84–89.

56. Koran 2:46, 145; 13:11; 53:39–40.

57. See Khan, *Islam*, pp. 42–4, for this early account of the battle.

58. Rodinson, *Mohammed*, p. 171.

59. Khan, *Islam*, p. 164.

60. Ibid., p. 158.

61. Koran 8:62–3; 16:95.

62. Rodinson, *Mohammed*, p. 171. *Al-Furqan* is also another name for the Koran (25:1).

63. Koran 17:1.

64. Rodinson, *Mohammed*, p. 286.

65. For a fuller discussion, see W. Montgomery Watt, "Islam and the Holy War," in T. P. Murphy, ed., *The Holy War* (Columbus, 1974); Bernard Lewis, *The Jews of Islam* (New York and London, 1982), pp. 17–45.

66. *The Decline and Fall of the Roman Empire*, Ch. 52:16, quoted by Bernard Lewis, *The Muslim Discovery of Europe* (New York and London, 1982).

67. Lewis, *The Muslim Discovery*, p. 19.

68. Lewis, *The Jews of Islam*, pp. 25–45 and passim. Also *Semites and Anti-Semites: An Inquiry into Conflict and Prejudice* (London, 1986), pp. 117–40.

69. Steven Runciman, *A History of the Crusades*, 3 vols., Vol. I (London, 1984 ed.), p. 3.

**CHAPTER TWO**  Before the Crusade; the West Seeks a New Christian Soul

1. R. W. Southern, *Western Society and the Church in the Middle Ages* (London, 1970), pp. 56–57; 53–72 for a fuller description of the position of Eastern and Western Church.

2. Eddius Stephanus, *Vita Wilfridi*, quoted in ibid., pp. 57–58.

3. Migne, *Patrologia Latina*, Vol. 89, columns 520, 524, quoted in ibid., p. 59.

4. Einard and Notger the Stammerer, *Two Lives of Charlemagne*, trans. and ed. Lewis Thorpe (London, 1969), pp. 131, 142, 148, 153.

5. Ibid., pp. 143–46.

6. Ibid., pp. 103, 124–25.

7. Quoted by R. W. Southern, *The Making of the Middle Ages* (London, 1987 ed.), p. 34.

8. Jonathan Riley-Smith, *The First Crusade and the Idea of Crusading* (London, 1986), p. 4.

9. Southern, *Western Society and the Church*, pp. 27–35.

10. For the penitentials, see Karen Armstrong, *The Gospel According to Woman: Christianity's Creation of the Sex War in the West* (New York, 1987), pp. 35–36.

11. P. A. Sigal, "Et les marcheurs de Dieu prirent leurs armes," *L'Histoire*, 47 (1982), 60–61 and passim. Also Ronald C. Finucane, *Miracles and Pilgrims: Popular Beliefs in Medieval Europe* (London, 1977), passim.

12. Peter Brown, *The Cult of the Saints: Its Rise and Function in Classical Antiquity* (London, 1982).

13. Finucane, *Miracles and Pilgrims*, p. 26.

14. Southern, *Western Society and the Church*, pp. 30–31.

15. Barbara Tuchman, *Bible and Sword: How the British Came to Palestine* (London, 1982 ed.), pp. 13–21.

16. Francesco Gabrieli, "Islam in the Mediterranean World," in Joseph Schacht and C. E. Bosworth, eds., *The Legacy of Islam* (2nd ed., Oxford, 1979), p. 91.

17. Riley-Smith, *The First Crusade*, p. 21.

18. Geneviève Bresc-Bautien, "L'An prochaineau Saint-Sépulchre!," *L'Histoire* 47 (1982), 74–79.

19. Georges Duby, "The Peace of God," in *The Chivalrous Society*, trans. C. Postan (London, 1977); and H. E. Cowdrey, "The Peace and the Truce of God in the Eleventh Century," *Past and Present* 46 (1970).

20. Quoted in Henri Focillon, *The Year 1000* (New York and London, 1952), p. 67.

21. Quoted in Finucane, *Miracles and Pilgrims*, pp. 114–15.

22. Quoted by Sigal, "Et les Marcheurs de Dieu prirent leurs armes," pp. 60–61.

23. Norman Cohn, *The Pursuit of the Millennium: Revolutionary Millennarians and Mystical Anarchists of the Middle Ages* (London, 1970 ed.), pp. 30–35.

24. Riley-Smith, *The First Crusade*, p. 5.

25. Ibid., pp. 5–8, 16–17.

26. *Gesta Tancredi*, quoted in ibid., p. 36.

27. Jonathan Riley-Smith, "The First Crusade and St. Peter," in B. Kedar, H. E. Meyer, and R. C. Smail, eds., *Outremer: Studies in the History of the Crusading Kingdom of Jerusalem, Presented to Joshua Prawer* (Jerusalem, 1982), pp. 45–48.

28. *The Song of Roland*, trans. Dorothy L. Sayers (London, 1957), stanza 260, p. 105.

29. Ibid., stanza 72, p. 87.

30. Ibid., stanza 87, p. 94.

31. Ibid., stanza 173.

32. Riley-Smith, *The First Crusade and St. Peter*, p. 45. Also *The First Crusade*, p. 25.

33. Riley-Smith, *The First Crusade*, pp. 17–22 for the Cluniac ideal of liberation.

34. Ibid., p. 19.

35. Ibid., pp. 22–25.

36. Steven Runciman, *A History of the Crusades*, 3 vols. (London, 1984 ed.), vol. I, p. 108.

37. Riley-Smith, *The First Crusade*, pp. 48–49.

38. Quoted in Runciman, *A History of the Crusades*, vol. I, p. 113.

39. Jonathan Riley-Smith dissolves the legend of the "Peasants' Crusade" and explains that these were proper armies not fanatical hordes of peasants in *The First Crusade*, pp. 51–52.

40. Regine Pernoud quotes the twelfth-century historian William of Tyre,

who attributes the crusading initiative to Peter in *The Crusaders*, trans. Enid Grant (Edinburgh and London, 1963), p. 24.

41. *The First Crusade*, pp. 53–58.

42. For the position of the Jews in Europe before the Crusades, see Paul Johnson, *A History of the Jews* (London, 1987), p. 205.

43. "Chronicle of Rabbi Eliezer bar Nathan" in Schlomo Eidelberg, trans. and ed., *The Jews and the Crusaders: the Hebrew Chronicles of the First and Second Crusade* (London, 1977), p. 80.

44. "The Narrative of the Old Persecutions or Mainz Anonymous" in ibid., pp. 99–100.

45. See "Chronicle of Solomon bar Simson" in ibid., p. 62.

46. See ibid., p. 28. Emich "concocted a tale that an apostle of the Crucified had come to him and made a sign on his flesh to inform him that when he arrived in Magna Graecia, he [Jesus] himself would appear and place the kingly crown upon his head and Emich would vanquish his foes." Emich was claiming to be the new Holy Roman Emperor: Magna Graecia is Italy. His crusade would fulfill the old myths.

47. Romans 11, passim.

**CHAPTER THREE**   The Present Conflict: Jews and Arabs Seek a New Secular Identity

1. The armies of Lebanon, Syria, Jordan, Iraq and Egypt.

2. The UN figures were 656,000 Palestinian refugees; Israel's figures range from 550,000 to 600,000; 750,000 is the figure quoted by people sympathetic to the Palestinian cause. In any event, there are now 4,000,000 people who call themselves Palestinians today, and apart from the 700,000 living as a minority in Israel, the others are either in exile or living under Israeli occupation in the Gaza Strip and the West Bank.

3. Forty-nine people died; 495 were injured (95 percent seriously) and there were many cases of rape and mutilation. There was massive devastation: 1500 homes and workshops were looted and destroyed and a fifth of the population rendered homeless. The violence had been inspired by semiofficial anti-Semitic propaganda. (Conor Cruise O'Brien, *The Siege: The Saga of Israel and Zionism* (London, 1986), p. 96.

4. For *Volk*-style anti-Semitism, see Paul Johnson, *A History of the Jews* (London, 1987), pp. 392–94.

5. I will discuss these later in Chapter 11, p. 508.

6. Quoted by Amos Elon, *The Israelis, Founders and Sons*, 2nd ed. (London, 1981), p. 70.

7. "We are duty bound to take courage, to rise; and to see to it that we do not remain for ever the foundling of the nations and their butt." *Autoemancipation*, quoted in O'Brien, *The Siege*, p. 46.

8. As Pinsker attended the meetings, he was slowly converted to the idea that the Jewish state must be in Palestine, because it was the "instinctive" wish of the people (Elon, *The Israelis*, p. 71). This instinctive, subrational feeling for Palestine will be a key factor in our story, medieval and modern.

9. "The Road from Motol," quoted in O'Brien, *The Siege*, p. 46.

10. Johnson, *A History of the Jews*, p. 38.

11. *A Jewish State* (London, 1896), p. 38.

12. *Protocols of the Fourth Zionist Conference* (London, 1900), quoted in Regina Sharif, *Non-Jewish Zionism: Its Roots in Western History* (London, 1983), p. 74.

13. Quoted in O'Brien, *The Siege*, p. 78.

14. The young Zionist Vladimir Jabotinsky was at the Congress and, though he admired Herzl, he voted against even looking at an alternative to Palestine. "I don't know why," he said later, "simply because this is one of those 'simple' things which counterbalances thousands of arguments." Ibid., p. 102.

15. Ibid., p. 103.

16. Weizmann shared Herzl's urgency and sense of impending disaster. He expressed it starkly: "One fundamental fact—that we must have Palestine if we are not going to be exterminated." Ibid., p. 132.

17. Text provided by Walter Lacqueur and Barry Rubin, eds., *The Israel-Arab Reader: A Documentary History of the Middle East Conflict*, 4th ed. (London, 1984), p. 17.

18. O'Brien, *The Siege*, p. 130.

19. At the time of the Balfour Declaration the Jewish inhabitants of Palestine constituted only 11 percent of the whole population; the rest were Arab. Indeed the Jewish population had declined from 85,000 in 1914 to only 66,000 in December 1918. Ibid., p. 133.

20. Elon, *The Israelis*, p. 81.

21. Schlomo Avineri, *The Makings of Modern Zionism* (London and New York, 1981), p. 200.

22. Elon, *The Israelis*, p. 134.

23. Ibid., p. 75.

24. Ibid., p. 98.

25. Ibid., pp. 105, 326.

26. Quoted in Johnson, *A History of the Jews*, p. 403.

27. Ibid.

28. Quoted in Eliezer Schweid, *The Land of Israel: National Home or Land of Destiny*, trans. Deborah Greniman (New York, 1985), p. 48.

29. Elon, *The Israelis*, p. 77.

30. Ibid., p. 112.

31. Schweid, *The Land of Israel*, p. 158, Kabalistic terms in italics.

32. Ibid., p. 143.

33. O'Brien, *The Siege*, p. 133.

34. Elon, *The Israelis*, p. 338.

35. Ibid., p. 155.

36. *Documents on British Foreign Policy* (1919–1939), First Series, Vol. IV, p. 345, quoted in O'Brien, *The Siege*, p. 144.

37. Elon, *The Israelis*, p. 110.

38. Schweid, *The Land of Israel*, p. 139.

39. Ibid., p. 140.

40. Khalid A. Sulaiman, *Palestine and Modern Arab Poetry* (London, 1984), p. 18. The poem was read aloud at a reception in Government House in Jerusalem on December 24, 1918, celebrating the anniversary of the occupation of Palestine by the British.

41. Ibid., p. 21. Al-Bustani had seen a door plate of a room in Government House in Jaffa which read: "The Jewish Society Lieutenant Macrory" and this inspired the poem.

42. Ibid., p. 53. The Banu Fihr were the Qureish, the ruling clan in Mecca at the time of the rise of Islam. Mohammad was of the Qureish tribe.

43. Ibid., p. 199.

44. Ibid.

45. Ibid., p. 45.

46. O'Brien, *The Siege*, p. 140.

47. Ibid.

48. Ibid., p. 146.

49. Ibid., pp. 163–64.

50. Paul Johnson, *A History of the Jews*, pp. 437–39.

51. O'Brien, *The Siege*, p. 140.

52. Ibid.

53. Sulaiman, *Palestine and Modern Arab Poetry*, pp. 35–36.

54. Ibid., p. 36.

55. O'Brien, *The Siege*, p. 120.

56. "The Iron Wall: We and the Arabs," quoted in Lenni Brenner, *The Iron Wall: Zionist Revisionism from Jabotinski to Shamir* (London, 1984), p. 75.

57. Ibid, p. 77.

58. Ibid.

59. Quoted in Michael Palumbo, *The Palestinian Catastrophe: The 1948 Expulsion of a People from Their Homeland* (London, 1987), p. 1.

60. Ibid., p. 2.

61. Ibid.

62. Ibid., p. 4.

63. O'Brien, *The Siege*, p. 230.

64. Palumbo, *The Palestinian Catastrophe*, p. 32.

65. O'Brien, *The Siege*, p. 230.

66. Palumbo, *The Palestinian Catastrophe*, p. 32.

67. O'Brien, *The Siege*, p. 733.

68. Johnson, *A History of the Jews*, p. 29.

69. Brenner, *The Iron Wall*, p. 143.

70. See Rosemary Sayigh, *Palestinians: From Peasants to Revolutionaries* (London, 1979), passim., and Palumbo, *The Palestinian Catastrophe*, passim.

71. Schweid, *The Land of Israel*, p. 204.

72. Quoted in Edward W. Said, *The Question of Palestine* (London, 1980), p. 14.

73. *Ha'aretz*, April 4, 1969.

74. Quoted in Elon, *The Israelis*, p. 281.

75. Ibid., pp. 280–81. Elon calls archaeology a "popular movement. It is almost a national sport. Not a passive spectator sport, but the thrilling active pastime of many thousands of people."

76. Sigmund Freud, "A Disturbance of Memory on the Acropolis," *Character and Culture* (New York, 1963), p. 311, and Freud's *Letters to his Fiancée, December 1883* (London, 1960).

77. Elon, *The Israelis*, p. 281.

78. Ibid., pp. 232–35.

79. Quoted and translated in ibid., p. 277.

80. Ibid., Yizar's italics.

81. Amos Oz, *My Michael*, trans. Nicholas de Lange (London, 1984 ed.), p. 215.

82. Ibid., p. 219.

83. Ibid., pp. 219–20.

84. Elon, *The Israelis*, p. 107.

85. Oz, *My Michael*, pp. 223–24.

86. Ibid., p. 224.

87. "An Argument on Life and Death (B)" in *In the Land of Israel*, trans. Maurice Goldberg-Bartura (London, 1983), p. 144.

88. Peter Mansfield, *The Arabs*, 3rd ed. (London, 1985), pp. 254–55.

89. He shouted at his junior minister Anthony Nutting: "But what's all this nonsense about isolating Nasser, of 'neutralising' him, as you call it? I want him destroyed, can't you understand?" Anthony Nutting, *No End of a Lesson* (London, 1967), quoted in Mansfield, *The Arabs*, p. 250.

90. O'Brien, *The Siege*, Chapter 7, "The Second Israel," pp. 333–62.

91. Elon, *The Israelis*, pp. 219–21.

92. Y. Harkabi, *Arab Attitudes to Israel* (Jerusalem, 1972), pp. 70–72.

93. Sulaiman, *Palestine and Modern Arab Poetry*, p. 134.

94. Ibid.

95. Ibid., pp. 134–35.

96. Ibid., p. 145.

97. Jonathan Raban, *Arabia Through the Looking Glass* (London, 1983 ed.), pp. 329–30.

98. Bernard Lewis, *The Jews of Islam* (New York and London, 1982), passim.

99. Bernard Lewis, *Semites and Anti-Semites: An Inquiry into Conflict and Prejudice* (London, 1986), p. 273.

100. Harkabi, *Arab Attitudes to Israel*, pp. 229–37.

101. E. Sivan, *Modern Arab Historiography of the Crusades* (Tel Aviv, 1973), passim.

102. "We Muslims possess a glorious revolution, proclaimed fourteen [*sic*] centuries ago in order to restore to humanity its proper sentiment and dignity and to give man his proper due." Nasser in a Friday sermon at al-Azhar, Cairo, quoted in Edward Mortimer, *Faith and Power: The Politics of Islam* (London, 1982), p. 273.

103. Ibid., p. 274.

104. Ibid., pp. 273–74.

105. A refugee in Nahr al Bared camp speaking to Rosemary Sayigh, *Palestinians*, p. 85.

106. Ibid., p. 5.

107. O'Brien, *The Siege*, pp. 469–70.

108. Ibid., p. 470.

109. Sayigh, *Palestinians*, p. 12.

110. Ibid., p. 111.

111. Ibid., pp. 10–11.

112. Sulaiman, *Palestine and Modern Arab Poetry*, pp. 123–24.

113. Ibid., pp. 119–20.

114. Ibid., p. 121.

115. Ibid., p. 122.

116. Ibid., p. 198.

117. Ibid., pp. 202–4.

118. Johnson, *A History of the Jews*, p. 333.

119. Elon, *The Israelis*, p. 234.

120. Sayigh, *Palestinians*, p. 110.

121. Ibid., p. 111.

122. For the text of Resolution 242, see Lacqueur and Rubin, *The Israel-Arab Reader*, pp. 365–66. It is against international law to extend frontiers by means of war.

123. Alain Gresh, *The PLO: The Struggle Within, Towards an Independent Palestinian State*, trans. A. M. Berrett (London, 1985), p. 33.

124. Ibid.

125. Interview with the Algerian paper *Monjahid* in late 1969, quoted in ibid., p. 30.

126. Article 20. For the text of the PLO charter, see Lacqueur and Rubin, *The Israel-Arab Reader*, pp. 366–72.

127. In an interview with the *Sunday Times*, June 15, 1969.

128. Sayigh, *Palestinians*, p. 146.

129. Ibid., p. 166.

130. Ibid., p. 167.

131. Edward W. Said, *The Question of Palestine (London, 1980)*, p. 135. See also pp. 139–40.

132. Sulaiman, *Palestine and Modern Arab Poetry*, p. 146.

133. Ibid., p. 147.

134. For the text of the speech, see Lacqueur and Rubin, *The Israel-Arab Reader*, pp. 504–18.

135. Maxine Rodinson, *Israel and the Arabs*, trans. Michael Perl and Brian Pearce, 2nd ed. (London, 1982), p. 286.

136. Uri Avnery, *My Friend the Enemy* (London, 1986), p. 334.

137. Ibid., p. 197.

138. Jonathan Kuttab, "The Children's Revolt," *Journal of Palestine Studies*, 68, Summer 1988, pp. 26–35; Daoud Kuttab, "The Palestinian Uprising: The Second Phase, Self-Sufficiency," in ibid., pp. 36–45.

**CHAPTER FOUR**   1096–1146: The Crusade Becomes a Holy War and Inspires a New *Jihad*

1. Jonathan Riley-Smith, "The First Crusade and St. Peter," in B. Z. Kedar, H. E. Mayer and R. C. Smail, eds., *Outremer: Studies in the History of the Crusading Kingdom of Jerusalem* (Jerusalem, 1982), p. 46.

2. *Gesta Francorum*, or *The Deeds of the Franks and the Other Pilgrims to Jerusalem*, trans. Rosalind Hill (London, 1962), p. 37.

3. Ralph of Caen, *Vita Tancredi*, quoted in Jonathan Riley-Smith, *The First Crusade and the Idea of Crusading* (London, 1986).

4. Riley-Smith, *The First Crusade*, pp. 44–45.

5. Ibid., p. 112.

6. Walter Porges, "The Clergy, the Poor and the Non-Combatants on the First Crusade," *Speculum*, 21 (1946), quotes Anna, who makes a clear distinction between the Eastern and Western views of war: "For the rules concerning priests are not the same among the Latins as they are with us. For we are given the command by the canonical laws and teaching of the Gospels: Touch not, taste not, handle not! For thou art consecrated, whereas the Latin barbarian will simultaneously handle divine things and wear his shield in his left arm and hold his spear in his right hand, and at one and the same time, he communicates the body and blood of God and looks murderously and becomes a man of blood. . . . For this barbarian race is no less devoted to sacred things than it is to war."

7. Steven Runciman, *A History of the Crusades*, 3 vols. (Cambridge, 1954; London, 1965), vol. I, p. 153.

8. *Gesta Francorum*, pp. 33–34.

9. Riley-Smith, *The First Crusade*, p. 85.

10. Porges, "The Clergy, the Poor and the Non-Combatants," quotes Adhémar: "Not one of you can be saved unless he honours the poor and

relieves them. Just as you cannot be saved without them, so they cannot live without you." It shows the conscious desire to return to the spirit of the first Christians in Jerusalem who lived as one and held all things in common. Acts 2:44–45.

11. The phrase is coined by Riley-Smith in *The First Crusade*, p. 2.

12. Ibid., p. 63.

13. Fulcher of Chartres, *A History of the Expedition to Jerusalem, 1095–1127*, trans. and ed. Frances Rita Ryan (Knoxville, 1969), p. 85.

14. Ibid., p. 86.

15. Ibid.

16. Raymund of Aguilers, quoted in August C. Krey, *The First Crusade: The Accounts of Eye-Witnesses and Participants* (Princeton and London, 1921), p. 116.

17. Riley-Smith, "The First Crusade and St. Peter," pp. 54–55.

18. *Gesta Francorum*, p. 27.

19. Ibid., p. 23.

20. Riley-Smith, *The First Crusade*, p. 100.

21. *The Expedition to Jerusalem*, p. 80.

22. *Gesta Francorum*, p. 22.

23. Runciman, *A History of the Crusades*, Vol. I, p. 91.

24. Raymund of Aguilers, *Liber*, quoted in Krey, *The First Crusade*, p. 125.

25. Fulcher of Chartres, *The Expedition to Jerusalem*, p. 96.

26. Riley-Smith, *The First Crusade*, p. 91.

27. Riley-Smith, "The First Crusade and St. Peter," pp. 59–62, for the numerous religious titles they gave to themselves and their army.

28. Fulcher of Chartres, *The Expedition to Jerusalem*, p. 102.

29. *Gesta Francorum*, p. 39.

30. Ibid., p. 40.

31. Riley-Smith, *The First Crusade*, p. 115.

32. Ibid., p. 116.

33. Ibid., p. 117.

34. Ibid., pp. 117–18.

35. *The Expedition to Jerusalem*, p. 226.

36. Riley-Smith, *The First Crusade*, p. 112.

37. Ibid., p. 113.

38. Porges, "The Poor, the Clergy and the Non-Combatants," p. 13. He suggests that the nucleus of this group may have been survivors from Peter the Hermit's Crusade, who afterward recruited poor Crusaders into their ranks.

39. Ibid.

40. Quoted by Norman Cohn, *The Pursuit of the Millennium: Revolutionary Millenarians and Mystical Anarchists of the Middle Ages* (London, 1957, 1970), p. 66.

41. Ibid.

42. Ibid.

43. Ibid., p. 67.

44. Ibid.

45. See Runciman, *A History of the Crusades*, vol. I, pp. 241–46, 257, 258, 259, 260, 273, for a clear account of Peter's visionary career.

46. Fulcher of Chartres, *The Expedition to Jerusalem*, devotes a whole chapter to these visions: pp. 100–1. One soldier who was actually climbing down the walls to safety on the other side saw his dead brother, a crusading martyr, who urged him to return.

47. For Stephen's vision, see *Gesta Francorum*, pp. 56–58.

48. Fulcher of Chartres says that when the Crusaders conquered Antioch "many of them had at once commingled with unlawful [pagan] women," and they thought that Kerbuqa's arrival with his confederacy was God's punishment: *The Expedition to Jerusalem*.

49. Ralph of Caen, *Vita Tancredi*. He comments that Bohemund was "no fool." "When did Pilate ever come to Antioch?" he asked. Quoted by Krey, *The First Crusade*, p. 33.

50. The verse from the Office that Christ had told Stephen should be sung daily by the Crusaders was Psalm 47:5:

> There was a rallying, once, of kings advancing together
> along a common front;
> they looked, they were amazed, they panicked, they
> ran.

It was obviously a reference to Kerbuqa's confederacy and a prayer that this victory of the chosen people should be repeated.

51. *Gesta Francorum*, p. 59.

52. Ibid., p. 67.

53. "When our men saw the host of warriors on white horses they did not understand what was happening or who these men might be, until they realized that this was the succour sent by Christ and that the leaders were St. George, St. Mercury, and St. Demetrius. (This is quite true, for many of our men saw it.)" (*Gesta Francorum*, p. 69.) An interesting insight into the visionary consciousness of these desperate men.

54. *The Expedition to Jerusalem*, p. 106.

55. Izz ad-Din ibn al-Athir, quoted and translated by Francesco Gabrieli, ed., *Arab Historians of the Crusades*, translated from the Italian by E. J. Costello (London, 1984), p. 8.

56. *The Expedition to Jerusalem*, p. 117.

57. Riley-Smith, *The First Crusade*, p. 97.

58. Ibid., for this exalted mood of fervor, p. 98.

59. Zoé Oldenbourg, *The Crusades,* trans. Anne Carter (London, 1966), p. 132.

60. "We could achieve nothing, so that we were all astounded and very

much afraid." *Gesta Francorum*, p. 90. This incident was a severe check to their mounting confidence in their supernatural abilities, and perhaps this "dread" contributed to the final atrocity.

61. *Gesta Francorum*, p. 91.
62. Ibid., p. 262.
63. Krey, *The First Crusade*, p. 261.
64. Ibid., p. 262.
65. Ibid.
66. Ibid.
67. Riley-Smith, *The First Crusade*, pp. 124–25.
68. Ibid., pp. 122–23.
69. Ibid., p. 122.
70. Ibid., p. 121.
71. Ibid.
72. Ibid.
73. In the account of Urban's speech that Guibert of Nogent wrote in his *Gesta Dei per Francos* (*c.* 1104) he made Urban say that unless Christians were in Jerusalem Antichrist would not appear and the Last Days would be delayed. Quoted by Krey, *The First Crusade*, p. 38.
74. Riley-Smith, *The First Crusade*, pp. 120–34.
75. Ibid., p. 143. See also account of Urban's speech, p. 1.
76. Robert the Monk, "Apart from the mystery of the healing cross, what more marvellous deed has there been since the creation of the world than was done in modern times in the journey of our men to Jerusalem?" Ibid., p. 140.
77. Ibid., p. 141.
78. Ibid.
79. Ibid., p. 149.
80. R. W. Southern, *Western Society and the Church in the Middle Ages* (London, 1970), p. 225.
81. Riley-Smith, *The First Crusade*, p. 119.
82. Riley-Smith, *The Knights of St. John in Jerusalem and Cyprus, 1050–1310*, (London, 1967), p. 40.
83. Norman Daniel, *The Arabs and Medieval Europe* (London and Beirut, 1975), p. 40.
84. Oldenbourg, *The Crusades*, p. 208.
85. Ibn al-Athir in Gabrieli, *Arab Historians of the Crusades*, p. 11.
86. Amin Maalouf, *The Crusades Through Arab Eyes*, trans. Jon Rothschild (London, 1984 ed.) pp. 2–3.
87. Ibn al-Athir in Gabrieli, *Arab Historians of the Crusades*, p. 11.
88. Maalouf, *The Crusades Through Arab Eyes*, p. 82.
89. Gabrieli, *Arab Historians of the Crusades*, pp. 54–55.
90. Maalouf, *The Crusades Through Arab Eyes*, p. 82.
91. Gabrieli, *Arab Historians of the Crusades*, p. 55.
92. Ibid.

93. Maalouf, *The Crusades Through Arab Eyes*, p. 137.

94. Gabrieli, *Arab Historians of the Crusades*, pp. 52–53.

95. Ibid., p. 53.

96. Maalouf, *The Crusades Through Arab Eyes*, p. 143.

97. Ibn al-Athir in Gabrieli, *Arab Historians of the Crusades*, p. 65.

98. From the "Ode to Zion," trans. T. Carmi in *The Penguin Book of Hebrew Verse* (London, 1984 ed.), p. 348.

99. Eliezer Schweid, *The Land of Israel: National Home or Land of Destiny*, trans. Deborah Greniman (New York, 1985), pp. 59 and 47–60 for a fuller account of Halevi's theory of the holiness of Eretz Yisrael.

100. T. Carmi, *The Penguin Book of Hebrew Verse*, p. 335.

101. Quoted in Schweid, *The Land of Israel*, p. 67.

**CHAPTER FIVE**    1146–1148: St Bernard and the Most Religious Crusade

1. Bernard of Clairvaux, Letter to the Duke and people of Bohemia, in Jonathan and Louise Riley-Smith, *The Crusades: Idea and Reality, 1095–1274* (London, 1981), p. 97.

2. Ibid.

3. Quoted in Henri Daniel-Rops, *Bernard of Clairvaux*, trans. Elizabeth Abbot (New York and London, 1964), p. 40. Source not given.

4. Quoted in Steven Runciman, *A History of the Crusades*, 3 Vols. (Cambridge, 1954, London, 1965), Vol. II, p. 254.

5. Jonathan and Louise Riley-Smith, *The Crusades*, p. 97.

6. Ibid.

7. Letter to the Eastern Franks and to the Bavarians, ibid., p. 95.

8. Ibid., p. 97.

9. Ibid.

10. Ibid., p. 95.

11. R. W. Southern, *The Making of the Middle Ages* (Oxford, 1953, London, 1987), p. 158.

12. In England he was called "Hearding" and in France "Stephen" but never both together.

13. Daniel-Rops, *Bernard of Clairvaux*, p. 45.

14. R. W. Southern, *Western Society and the Church in the Middle Ages* (London, 1970), pp. 258–65, for Cistercian colonizing.

15. Ibid., pp. 257–58.

16. The knights had become a military aristocracy and formed what we might today call a "class"; many young knights who felt the need for this new spiritual quest were recruited by Bernard.

17. Southern, *Western Society and the Church*, p. 257.

18. Ibid., p. 258.

19. This was still the generally accepted view, though Bernard's was probably

the last generation to hold it. In the next chapter I shall show a new secular spirit at work in Europe.

20. Bernard of Clairvaux, Epistle 64, quoted in André Vauchez, "Saint Bernard, un prédicateur irrésistible," *L'Histoire*, 47 (1982), 28–29.

21. Ibid., p. 29.

22. Southern, *The Making of the Middle Ages*, p. 20.

23. *Gesta Regum*, quoted in ibid., p. 69.

24. Quoted in Stephen Howarth, *The Knights Templar* (London, 1982), p. 70. Source not given.

25. From *De Laude Novae Militiae* (In Praise of the New Chivalry), quoted in Zoé Oldenbourg, *The Crusades*, trans. Anne Carter (London, 1966), p. 289.

26. Ibid., quoted in Ernst Kantorowicz, *Frederick the Second, 1194–1250*, trans. E. O. Lorimer (London, 1931), p. 87.

27. Ibid., quoted in Jonathan and Louise Riley-Smith, *The Crusades*, p. 102. Bernard is alluding to a passage in St. Paul's letter to the Romans 8:31–39, celebrating the love of Christ.

28. Ibid.

29. Vauchez, "Saint Bernard, un prédicateur irrésistible," 27–28.

30. Quoted in Watkin W. Williams, *St. Bernard of Clairvaux* (Manchester, 1935), p. 290.

31. Quoted in Henry Adams, *Mont Saint-Michel and Chartres* (London, 1986 ed.), p. 296.

32. Vauchez, "Saint Bernard, un prédicateur irrésistible," p. 27.

33. Williams, *St. Bernard of Clairvaux*, pp. 271–73.

34. Ibid., p. 273.

35. Jean Markale, *Aliénor d'Aquitaine* (Paris, 1983), p. 26.

36. Georges Duby, *The Knight, the Lady and the Priest: The Making of Modern Marriage in Medieval France*, trans. Barbara Bray (London, 1985 ed.), p. 196.

37. Odo of Deuil, *De profectione Ludovici VII in orientem, The journey of Louis VII to the East*, ed. and trans. Virginia G. Berry (New York, 1948), pp. 17, 19. (The English version is on pages marked with odd numbers only.)

38. Ibid., p. 29.

39. Ibid., p. 41, but the charge is leveled with great frequency throughout.

40. Ibid., p. 55.

41. Ibid., p. 129.

42. Ibid., p. 57.

43. Ibid., pp. 57, 59.

44. Ibid., pp. 73–76. Odo tries to gloss over the King's desertion of the army.

45. Duby, *The Knight the Lady and the Priest*, pp. 190–8, for the part this incident played in the divorce proceedings between Louis and Eleanor.

46. Especially from Usama ibn Mundiqh, whose comments are quoted and

translated by Francesco Gabrieli, trans. and ed., *Arab Historians of the Crusades*, trans. from the Italian by E. J. Costello (London, 1978, 1984), pp. 73–84.

47. *De Consideratione*; John and Louise Riley-Smith, *The Crusades*, pp. 61–62.

48. Giles Constable, "The Second Crusade as seen by Contemporaries," *Traditio*, 9 (1953), p. 268.

49. Quoted in Adams, *Mont Saint-Michel and Chartres*, p. 101.

50. Ibid. Adams comments: "Such deep popular movements are always surprising and at Chartres the miracle seems to have occurred three times, coinciding more or less with the dates of the Crusades and taking the organization of a Crusade."

51. See Norman Daniel, *The Arabs and Medieval Europe* (London and Beirut, 1975), Chapter 10, "Arab Scientific Literature in Europe."

52. Ibid., pp. 269–72.

53. Dante Alighieri, *The Divine Comedy: Hell*, trans. Dorothy L. Sayers (London, 1949), Canto IV, lines 112–51, pp. 44–45.

54. Southern, *The Making of the Middle Ages*, pp. 39–40.

55. Benjamin Z. Kedar, *Crusade and Mission: European Approaches Towards the Muslims* (Princeton, 1984), p. 123.

56. Ibid., p. 102

57. Ibid., pp. 104–5.

58. Ibid., pp. 106–7.

59. Norman Daniel, *Islam and the West: the Making of an Image* (Edinburgh, 1960), p. 124.

60. Kedar, *Crusade and Mission*, p. 99.

61. Daniel, *Islam and the West*, p. 124.

62. Ibid.

63. In an interview with Raphael Mergui and Philippe Simonnot, *Israel's Ayatollahs: Meir Kahane and the Far Right in Israel* (London, 1987 ed.), p. 113.

64. See Abelard's account in "The Story of My Calamities," in *The Letters of Abelard and Heloise*, trans. and ed. Betty Radice (London, 1974), pp. 70–74.

65. Roger Boase, *The Origin and Meaning of Courtly Love: A Critical Study of European Scholarship* (Manchester, 1977), passim.

66. Daniel, *Islam and the West*, p. 154.

67. Ibid., p. 154.

68. Paul Johnson, *A History of the Jews* (London, 1987), pp. 209–10.

69. Norman Cohn, *The Pursuit of the Millennium: Revolutionary Millenarians and Mystical Anarchists of the Middle Ages* (London, 1970 ed.), pp. 76–86.

70. Amin Maalouf, *The Crusades Through Arab Eyes*, trans. Jon Rothschild (London, 1984), p. 151.

71. Ibid., pp. 152–53.

72. Bernard Lewis, *The Assassins* (London, 1967), passim.
73. Ibid. p. 5.

CHAPTER SIX    1168–1192: A Religious *Jihad* and a Secular Crusade

1. Amin Maalouf, *The Crusades Through Arab Eyes*, trans. Jon Rothschild (London, 1984), p. 159.
2. Ibid.
3. Ibid., p. 169.
4. Ibid.
5. Stanley Lane-Poole, *Saladin and the Fall of Jerusalem* (London and New York, 1898), p. 99.
6. Francesco Gabrieli (trans. and ed.) *Arab Historians of the Crusades*, trans. from the Italian by E. J. Costello (London, 1978, 1984), pp. 86–96.
7. Ibid., pp. 89–90.
8. Lane-Poole, *Saladin*, p. 99.
9. Gabrieli, *Arab Historians of the Crusades*, p. 106.
10. Ibid., p. 98.
11. Maalouf, *The Crusades Through Arab Eyes*, p. 172.
12. Baha ad-Din in Gabrieli, *Arab Historians of the Crusades*, p. 107.
13. Ibid., p. 111.
14. Ibid., p. 98.
15. William, Archbishop of Tyre, *A History of Deeds Done Beyond the Sea*, trans. E. A. Babcock and A. C. Krey, 2 vols. (New York, 1943), Vol. II, pp. 505–6.
16. Steven Runciman, *A History of the Crusades*, 3 vols. (Cambridge, 1954; London, 1965), Vol. II, pp. 440–42.
17. Lane-Poole, *Saladin*, p. 272.
18. Runciman, *A History of the Crusades*, Vol. II, p. 453.
19. Ibid.
20. Ibn al-Athin in Gabrieli, *Arab Historians of the Crusades*, p. 119.
21. Ibid., p. 120.
22. Ibid.
23. Quoted in Marshall Whithed Baldwin, *Raymund III of Tripolis and the Fall of Jerusalem* (Princeton, 1936), p. 113.
24. Runciman, *A History of the Crusades*, vol. II, p. 457.
25. Gabrieli, *Arab Historians of the Crusades*, pp. 131–32.
26. Maalouf, *The Crusades Through Arab Eyes*, pp. 192–93.
27. Ibid, p. 193; also Gabrieli, *Arab Historians of the Crusades*, pp. 112, 124, 133–34.
28. Gabrieli, *Arab Historians of the Crusades*, pp. 138–39.
29. Muhammad Zafrulla Khan, *Islam: Its Meaning for Modern Man* (London, 1962, 1980), p. 182.
30. Gabrieli, *Arab Historians of the Crusades*, p. 140.

31. Ibid., p. 153 (pp. 151–53 for the whole sermon).

32. Maalouf, *The Crusades Through Arab Eyes*, p. 196.

33. Ibid., p. 196–97.

34. Ibid., p. 196.

35. Ibn al-Athir in Gabrieli, *Arab Historians of the Crusades*, p. 141.

36. Ibid., pp. 141–42.

37. Ibid.

38. Ibid., pp. 142–44.

39. Maalouf, *The Crusades Through Arab Eyes*, p. 200.

40. Ibid., pp. 203–4.

41. Gabrieli, *Arab Historians of the Crusades*, pp. 144–46.

42. One such inscription can be seen in the Church of St. Anne in Jerusalem, which was the royal chapel of the Crusader Kingdom but which was turned into a madrasah by Saladin.

43. Joshua Prawer, *The Latin Kingdom of Jerusalem: European Colonialism in the Middle Ages* (London, 1972).

44. Gabrieli, *Arab Historians of the Crusades*, p. 101.

45. Maalouf, *The Crusades Through Arab Eyes*, p. 205. See also Baha ad-Din, who also describes another such "poster" depicting a Muslim knight whose horse is urinating on Christ's tomb: "This picture was carried abroad to the markets and meeting places; priests carried it about, clothed in their habits, their heads covered, groaning 'O the shame!' In this way they raised a great army." Gabrieli, *Arab Historians of the Crusades*, pp. 208–9.

46. Gabrieli, *Arab Historians of the Crusades*, p. 215.

47. Paul Johnson, *A History of the Jews* (London, 1987), pp. 210–11.

48. Gabrieli, *Arab Historians of the Crusades*, p. 213.

49. Ibid., p. 214.

50. Maalouf, *The Crusades Through Arab Eyes*, p. 213.

51. Gabrieli, *Arab Historians of the Crusades*, p. 226.

52. Ibid.

53. Ibid., pp. 226–27.

54. Runciman, *A History of the Crusades*, vol. III, p. 58.

55. Gabrieli, *Arab Historians of the Crusades*, pp. 225–26.

56. Ibid., p. 91.

57. Ibid., p. 92.

58. Ibid.

59. Runciman, *A History of the Crusades*, vol. III, p. 68.

60. Ibid., p. 72.

61. Norman Daniel, *The Arabs and Medieval Europe* (London and Beirut, 1975), pp. 182–83.

62. See B. B. Broughton, *The Legends of Richard I, Coeur de Lion: A Study of Sources and Variations to the Year 1600* (The Hague and Paris, 1966), passim.

CHAPTER SEVEN   1967: Zionism Becomes a Holy War

1. Speech at UAR Advanced Air Headquarters, May 25, 1967, quoted in Walter Lacqueur and Barry Rubin, eds., *The Israel-Arab Reader: A Documentary History of the Middle East Conflict*, 4th ed. (London, 1984), p. 174.

2. Conor Cruise O'Brien, *The Siege: The Saga of Israel and Zionism* (London, 1986), pp. 413–14.

3. Harold Fisch, *The Zionist Revolution: A New Perspective* (London and Tel Aviv, 1978), p. 87.

4. "The Right of Israel," in Lacqueur and Rubin, *The Israel-Arab Reader*, p. 231.

5. Fisch, *The Zionist Revolution*, p. 89.

6. *Israel: An Echo of Eternity* (New York, 1969), quoted in ibid., p. 21.

7. Amos Elon, *The Israelis, Founders and Sons*, 2nd ed. (London, 1981) p. 262.

8. An abridged edition was translated in English by Henry Near, ed., *The Seventh Day: Soldiers Talk About the Six Day War* (London, 1970).

9. Quoted by Amos Elon in *The Israelis*, p. 246.

10. Eliezer Schweid, *The Land of Israel: National Home or Land of Destiny*, trans. Deborah Greniman (New York, 1985), passim but especially pp. 202ff.

11. Amos Elon, *The Israelis*, p. 263.

12. Ibid.

13. Trans. T. Carmi, *The Penguin Book of Hebrew Verse* (London, 1984), p. 571. This is a prose translation, which I have ventured to reline. "The Locking of the Gates" is the *neila*, the evening prayer at the end of Yom Kippur.

14. Oz quotes this in "An Argument on Life and Death (A)" in *In the Land of Israel*, trans. Maurie Goldberg-Bartura (London, 1983, Flamingo ed.), p. 120.

15. A. Cohen, *Everyman's Talmud* (New York, 1975), p. 65.

16. Quoted in Paul Johnson, *A History of the Jews* (London, 1987), p. 545.

17. The remarks of Eshkol and Dayan are both quoted in Bernard Avishai, *The Tragedy of Zionism: Revolution and Democracy in the Land of Israel* (New York, 1985), p. 244.

18. Ibid., p. 245.

19. Raphael Mergui and Philippe Simonnot, *Israel's Ayatollahs: Meir Kahane and the Far Right in Israel* (London, 1987), p. 218.

20. Fisch, *The Zionist Revolution*, p. 73.

21. Ibid., p. 77.

22. Avishai, *The Tragedy of Zionism*, pp. 252–53.

23. O'Brien, *The Siege*, pp. 504–5.

24. Ibid., p. 408.

25. Ibid.

26. Avishai, *The Tragedy of Zionism*, p. 94.
27. Ibid.
28. Fisch, *The Zionist Revolution*, p. 63.
29. Avishai, *The Tragedy of Zionism*, p. 97.
30. Schweid, *The Land of Israel*, p. 172 and pp. 171–88 for a fuller discussion of Kook's ideas.
31. Ibid.
32. Mergui and Simonnot, *Israel's Ayatollahs*, p. 125.
33. Ibid., p. 123.
34. Oz, "An Argument on Life and Death (B)" in *In the Land of Israel*, p. 132.
35. Ibid., p. 133.
36. Mergui and Simonnot, *Israel's Ayatollahs*, pp. 123–28.
37. Ibid., p. 128.
38. Amnon Rubinstein, "Policing the Settlers," *Ha'aretz*, April 14, 1988.
39. Rija Shehadeh, "Occupier's Law and the Uprising," *Journal of Palestine Studies*, 67, pp. 24–37.
40. Oz, "An Argument on Life and Death (A)" in *In the Land of Israel*, p. 121.
41. Mergui and Simonnot, *Israel's Ayatollahs*, p. 114.
42. John King, "Why They Are Not So Keen to Return," *Middle East International*, 329, p. 17.
43. Mergui and Simonnot, *Israel's Ayatollahs*, p. 131.
44. Ibid., p. 124.
45. Oz, in "An Argument on Life and Death (A)" in *In the Land of Israel*, p. 118.
46. "The Finger of God" in ibid., pp. 60–61.
47. O'Brien, *The Siege*, Chapter 7, "The Second Israel," passim.
48. Johnson, *A History of the Jews*, p. 546.
49. Ibid., pp. 535–36.
50. Ibid., p. 536.
51. Mergui and Simonnot, *Israel's Ayatollahs*, p. 101.
52. Ibid., p. 114.
53. Liebowitz is quoted in Alan Schonfield's famous film *Courage Along the Divide*, (1987).
54. Mergui and Simonnot, *Israel's Ayatollahs*, p. 115.
55. Ibid., p. 51.
56. Ibid., Chapter 2, "An Interview with Rabbi Meir Kahane," pp. 29–89 passim.
57. Ibid., pp. 49–50.
58. From a speech recorded by Alan Schonfield in the film *Shattered Dreams* (1987).
59. Mergui and Simonnot, *Israel's Ayatollahs*, pp. 22–23.
60. Ibid., pp. 78–82, for Kahane's plans to segregate Arabs from Jews in Israel.

61. Ibid., p. 45.
62. Ibid.
63. Ibid., p. 44.
64. Ibid., p. 141.
65. Peretz Kidron, "Resurgence of a Racist," *Middle East International*, 307, p. 11.
66. Ibid.
67. Ibid.
68. Charles Richard, "The Banning of Kahane," *Middle East International*, 336, p. 10.
69. Quoted in Kidron, "Resurgence of a Racist," ibid., 307, p. 11.
70. Amnon Rubinstein, "Policing the Territories," *Ha'aretz*, April 14, 1988.
71. Daoud Kuttab, "Violent Deeds and Words," *Middle East International*, 313, pp. 12–13.
72. Peretz Kidron, "Israel after Beita," *Middle East International*, 323, pp. 7–9.
73. Quoted in ibid., p. 8.
74. Peretz Kidron, "Revival of the Peace Movement," *Middle East International* 327, p. 9; Gideon Spiro, "The Israeli Soldiers Who Say 'There Is a Limit,'" ibid., 333, pp. 18–20; Israel Shahak, "Israel's Army and the *Intifada*," ibid., 354, pp. 16–18; Mordechai Bar-On, "Israeli Reactions to the Palestinian Uprising," *Journal of Palestine Studies*, 68, pp. 46–63.
75. Charles Richards, "Shamir Tries to Calm Anti-Arab Fury," *The Independent*, July 10, 1989.
76. Quoted in ibid.
77. Edy Kaufman, "The *Intifadah* and the Peace Camp in Israel," *Journal of Palestine Studies*, 68, pp. 66–80.
78. Lamis Andoni, "Hussein Throws Out a Multiple Challenge," *Middle East International*, 331, pp. 3–4; Donald Neff, "Shultz's Wishful Thinking," ibid., p. 4; Peretz Kidron, "An End of Peres's Options," ibid., pp. 4–5.
79. Israel Shahak, "Why Shamir rules Israel: the deeper reasons," *Middle East International*, 379, pp. 15–16.

**CHAPTER EIGHT**     1981: The Death of President Anwar Sadat—Holy War and Peace

1. Desmond Meiring, *Fire of Islam* (London, 1982), pp. 5–8.
2. Ibid., p. 31.
3. Mohamed Heikal, *Autumn of Fury: The Assassination of Sadat* (London, 1983; 1986 ed. used), pp. 17–19. He points out that Sadat preferred to forget this and presented his childhood as idyllic: a much-loved child leading a simple village life in the village of Mit Abu el-kom, where he had in fact spent his very earliest years with his grandmother. Heikal

says he would have won much more sympathy if he had told the true story. Mohamed Heikal is probably the greatest journalist in the Arab world, was a close friend of Nasser, a member of his government, and helped Sadat in the early years of his presidency. Even though he was eventually imprisoned by Sadat and publicly denounced by him, this is a fair and compassionate assessment of Anwar Sadat.

4. Ibid., p. 20. In his autobiography, *In Search of an Identity* (London, 1978), Sadat preferred to dwell on his studious days at Mit Abu el-kom: "I see it so clearly that I have the impression of leaving it yesterday. I owe a great deal to the excellent teacher I had there, Sheikh Abdul-Hamid, recently deceased; it is he who inculcated in me my love of knowledge and spirit of true faith. I remember my lessons with emotion: I sat on the ground with my comrades, holding on my knees my small slate and rustic reed pen, which served me for writing." Quoted by Meiring, *Fire of Islam*, p. 41. Given the mawkish tone of this work, it seems more charitable to Sadat to rely on Mohamed Heikal. The oversimplistic and unself-critical nature of the work does reveal an essential flaw in Sadat's mind, which contributed to his tragedy. He was not a bad man so much as a simple-minded one.

5. Heikal, *Autumn of Fury*, pp. 20–35. Sadat, he says, had become submissive as a child in his miserable home, but had retreated into a private world of fantasy that had a streak of violence.

6. He was at first not told about the Free Officers because of this opposition. Ibid., p. 35.

7. Ibid., p. 37.

8. Ibid., p. 40.

9. Ibid., p. 42. Nasser appointed him to the post when he was leaving to go to the Arab summit conference at Rabat and had heard of a CIA plot against his life. "If anything did happen to him, said Nasser, Sadat would be all right for the interim period. People in the Socialist Union and the army would look after the real business and Sadat's job would be largely ceremonial." (Heikal reporting his conversation with Nasser on the subject; ibid.).

10. Ibid., p. 70.

11. Ibid., p. 51.

12. Sadat on Nasser in *In Search of an Identity*: "We had hoped for the arrival of a benevolent dictator, a just tyrant: when we had him, we understood that this system, however seductive it might appear from the outside, was built on sand; naturally then it would crumble in a short time. But the most annoying thing about this experience wasn't the complete ruin of our economy, nor our humiliating military position: it was the mountain of hate that had accumulated during this attempt to build a community founded on power. Because of the absence of human values in such a community, people only worried about their external success and tried to make the biggest material profit

possible, legally or not, and even if this meant the destruction of our next-door neighbour." (Quoted by Meiring, *Fire of Islam*, p. 74.) This is a classic example of projection: every word of it could apply to his own regime.

13. Caption under a photograph of Sadat and the Shah, opposite p. 157 of Heikal, *Autumn of Fury*.

14. Edward Mortimer, *Faith and Power: The Politics of Islam* (London, 1982), pp. 286–87.

15. Asaf Hussain, *Islamic Iran: Revolutionaries and Counter-Revolution* (London, 1985), p. 55.

16. This was a Koranic term: the *munafiqeen* in the Koran are those people in Medina who converted to Islam not out of conviction but for political expediency.

17. Luke 18:25–30; Mark 10:41–45.

18. Shiites trace the succession from Ali differently. Thus "Sevener Shiism" recognizes only seven legitimate Imams; "Twelver Shiism," practiced in Iran, has twelve Imams: Twelver Shiites claim that in 874 the Twelfth Imam went into hiding or into "occultation" and that when he died in 917 there were no further descendants of Ali. Many believe that this "Hidden Imam" is a Messiah figure: he will return to inaugurate a golden age at the end of time. This concern with physical succession (*al-nass*) sees the holiness of God as connected physically with the Prophet's family.

19. Seven of the Imams of Twelver Shiism died in this way.

20. Hussain, *Islamic Iran*, pp. 59–60.

21. In fact, other groups who were not radical Muslims joined the mullahs' struggle. Kurds, leftists and secular guerrilla groups fought alongside the Muslims. These seculars constituted a minority but provided invaluable military support and expertise. They did not want an Islamic Iran but they felt that Khomeini offered the only hope of overcoming the Shah, which was their priority, because he alone had the support of the masses.

22. Rodinson published three articles in *Le Monde* on December 6, 7 and 8, 1978. These have been translated. Rodinson, "Islam Resurgent?" *Gazelle Review* 6, Roger Hardy ed. (London, 1979).

23. Hussain, *Islamic Iran*, p. 110.

24. Ibid., p. 20. Also Roy Mottahedeh, *The Mantle of the Prophet: Religion and Politics in Iran* (London, 1985; 1987 ed. used), pp. 287–336.

25. Hussain, *Islamic Iran*, p. 75.

26. Quoted in Gregory Rose, "*Velayat-e Faqih* and the Recovery of Islamic Identity in the Thought of Ayatollah Khomeini," in Nikkie R. Keddie, ed., *Religion and Politics in Iran: Shiism from Quietism to Revolution* (New Haven and London, 1983), p. 181.

27. Hussain, *Islamic Iran*, pp. 69–71.

28. Mary Hegland, "Two Images of Husain: Accommodation and Revo-

lution in an Iranian Village," in Keddie, *Religion and Politics in Iran*, pp. 221–25.

29. Mottahedeh, *The Mantle of the Prophet*, pp. 144–85.

30. Hegland, "Two Images of Husain," p. 229.

31. William O. Beeman, "Images of the Great Satan: Representations of the United States in the Iranian Revolution," in Keddie, *Religion and Politics in Iran*, pp. 191–217.

32. Shahrough Akhari, "Shariati's Social Thought," in Keddie, *Religion and Politics in Iran*, pp. 125–44, and Hussain, *Islamic Iran*, pp. 75–85.

33. Heikal, *Autumn of Fury*, pp. 73–74.

34. Ibid., pp. 179–182.

35. Gilles Kepel, *The Prophet and Pharaoh: Muslim Extremism in Egypt*, trans. Jon Rothschild (London, 1985), pp. 113–14.

36. Abraham Rabinovich, "A Split in the Golden Path," Jerusalem *Post International*, December 19, 1987, pp. 113–14.

37. Karen Armstrong, *The Gospel According to Woman, Christianity's Creation of the Sex War in the West* (London, 1986), passim.

38. Blu Greenberg, *On Women and Judaism: A View from Tradition* (Philadelphia, 1981), pp. 107–8, though the author does quote other, more negative traditions also (ibid., pp. 114–15). She also suggests that in Spain contact with Christianity produced new prohibitions (ibid., p. 116).

39. Ibid., pp. 117–18.

40. See Geoffrey Parrinder, *Sex in the World's Religions* (London, 1980), pp. 162 and 155–76, for an account of sexuality and Islam.

41. Ibid., pp. 160–61. Circumcision of either sex is not mentioned in the Koran, but it later became a law for all men because it was said to be founded on the customs of the Prophet, and some authorities thought it also obligatory for women.

42. H. R. Hays, *The Dangerous Sex: The Myth of Feminine Evil* (London, 1966); see p. 57 but also passim for an account of Western misogyny. For a convenient summary see also D. S. Bailey, *The Man-Woman Relation in Christian Thought* (London, 1959).

43. I have discussed this more fully in *The Gospel According to Woman*, pp. 2–4.

44. Parrinder, *Sex in the World's Religions*, pp. 162–63. He also quotes the sixteenth-century Sheikh al-Nafzawi of Tunis, who opens his book *The Perfumed Garden for the Soul's Delectation*: "Praise be to God, who has placed man's greatest pleasure in the natural parts of man to afford the greatest enjoyment to woman." The famous *Thousand and One Nights* is a clear instance of the Muslim appreciation of sex, which is equally pleasurable to men and women. Judaism is also enthusiastic about love and sex, as can be seen by the inclusion of the Song of Solomon in the Jewish Scriptures. See Parrinder, *Sex in the World's Religions*, pp. 192–93; he quotes a rabbi saying: "Every man needs a woman and

every woman needs a man and both of them need the Divine Presence"
(p. 191).

45. See, for example, St. Jerome: "If we abstain from coitus we honour
our wives but if we do not—well, what is the opposite of honour but
insult" (*Adversus Jovinian*, 1, 7) quoted in Bailey, *The Man-Woman
Relation in Christian Thought*, p. 44. Luther took the same prejudice
into Protestantism. He saw marriage as a "hospital for sick people" to
which a man was driven against his will by uncontrollable lust, and
that "the greater part of married persons still live in adultery" because
of their unruly imaginations. Ibid., p. 118.

46. Greenberg, *On Women and Judaism*, passim.

47. Muhammad Zafrulla Khan, *Islam: Its Meaning for Modern Man* (London, 1962, 1980), p. 28.

48. Parrinder, *Sex in the World's Religions*, pp. 173–76.

49. For conditions in the universities, see Kepel, *The Prophet and Pharaoh*,
pp. 135–38.

50. Ibid., pp. 142–46.

51. Ibid., pp. 139–40.

52. Ibid., pp. 47–49, 62–63.

53. Ibid., pp. 37–59.

54. Ibid., p. 74.

55. Ibid., pp. 75–76.

56. Ibid., pp. 7–105, for an account of Shukri Mustafa and the Society of
Muslims.

57. Ibid., p. 84.

58. Ibid., pp. 87–89.

59. Heikal, *Autumn of Fury*, p. 138.

60. Kepel, *The Prophet and Pharaoh*, pp. 94–95.

61. Ibid., p. 95.

62. Ibid., pp. 96–98.

63. Ibid., pp. 98–99.

64. Heikal, *Autumn of Fury*, p. 98.

65. He was giving an interview to a Lebanese journalist in his rest house
and suddenly noticed a column of smoke rising from the town. "What's
that?" he asked. "Perhaps the rioting from Cairo has spread here," the
journalist replied. "What riots?" asked the astonished Sadat. (Heikal,
*Autumn of Fury*, p. 99.)

66. Conor Cruise O'Brien, *The Siege: The Saga of Israel and Zionism* (London, 1986), pp. 571–73.

67. Ibid., pp. 569–70.

68. Ibid., p. 573.

69. Heikal, *Autumn of Fury*, p. 105.

70. Arafat had been summoned to Egypt especially to hear an "important"
announcement and was furious about the peace initiative and the trick
that had been played upon him. Ibid., p. 106.

71. O'Brien, *The Siege*, p. 575.

72. *The Battle for Peace* (New York and London, 1981), quoted in Meiring, *Fire of Islam*, pp. 88–89.

73. Abridged text of the speech in Walter Lacqueur and Barry Rubin, eds., *The Israel-Arab Reader: A Documentary History of the Middle East Conflict* (4th ed., revised and updated, London, 1984), p. 592.

74. Ibid., p. 598.

75. Ibid.

76. Ibid., pp. 594–95.

77. Ibid., p. 595: "In the absence of a just solution of the Palestinian problem, there will never be that durable and just peace upon which the entire world insists."

78. Ibid., p. 599.

79. Quoted in O'Brien, *The Siege*, p. 577.

80. Ibid., p. 588.

81. Heikal, *Autumn of Fury*, pp. 114–15.

82. Ibid., p. 116.

83. Ibid.

84. Ibid.

85. Menachem Begin, "Autonomy Plan for the Occupied Territories" (December 28, 1977), in Lacqueur and Rubin, *The Israel-Arab Reader*, p. 615.

86. O'Brien, *The Siege*, p. 583.

87. Ibid.

88. Ibid., pp. 583–96.

89. "Camp David Frameworks for Peace" (September 17, 1978), in Lacqueur and Rubin, *The Israel-Arab Reader*, pp. 609–14.

90. For Begin's position, see O'Brien, *The Siege*, pp. 600–2.

91. Lacqueur and Rubin, *The Israel-Arab Reader*, p. 620.

92. Ibid., pp. 61–67.

93. Heikal, *Autumn of Fury*, pp. 106–7, 221–22.

94. Ibid., p. 183.

95. Ibid., pp. 182–83.

96. Ibid., pp. 184–85.

97. Kepel, *The Prophet and Pharaoh*, p. 112.

98. Ibid., pp. 112–13.

99. Ibid., pp. 117–18.

100. Ibid., p. 112.

101. Ibid., pp. 119–24.

102. Ibid., pp. 150–51.

103. Ibid., p. 251.

104. Ibid., pp. 172–90.

105. Ibid., pp. 194–204.

106. Ibid., p. 197.

107. Heikal, *Autumn of Fury*, p. 253.

108. Ibid., pp. 118–19.
109. Ibid., p. 250.
110. Ibid., p. 251.
111. Ibid.
112. Ibid., p. 252.
113. Ibid., pp. 256–64.
114. Ibid., p. 263.
115. Peter Kemp, "Terrorists in Cairo," *Middle East International*, 302 (1987), 12.
116. Heikal, *Autumn of Fury* pp. 284–86.
117. Ariel Sharon, "Israel's Security" (December 15, 1981), in Lacquer and Rubin, *The Israel-Arab Reader*, pp. 355–69.
118. Peretz Kidron, The Thunderbolt from Cairo, "*Middle East International*, 359, p. 4.
119. Speech delivered on May 1, 1978, quoted in Regina Sharif, *Non-Jewish Zionism: Its Roots in Western History* (London, 1983), p. 136.
120. O'Brien, *The Siege*, pp. 637–39, 644–46.
121. The text of Baker's speech is quoted in Donald Neff, "Baker Grasps the Nettle," *Middle East International*, 351, pp. 6–7.

**CHAPTER NINE**   1199–1221: Crusades Against Christians and a New Christian Peace

1. Umberto Eco, "The Return of the Middle Ages" in *Travels in Hyperreality*, trans. William Weaver (London, 1987), p. 64. He argues that both Americans and Europeans have inherited the legacy of the Middle Ages, which bequeathed to us all our modern problems. He lists merchant cities, capitalist economy, modern armies, the national state and a supernatural federation, class struggle, the concept of heresy or ideological deviation, our concept of love as a "devastating unhappy unhappiness," conflict between church and state and technological transformation of labor in inventions like the windmill and the acceptance of Arab mathematics.
2. Quoted in Bernard Lewis, *The Arabs in History* (London, 1950), p. 146.
3. Thus the Hadith (tradition) attributed to the Prophet: "Angels spread their wings for the seeker of learning as a mark of God's approval of his purpose." Quoted in Peter Mansfield, *The Arabs* (3rd ed., London, 1985), p. 93.
4. "There are some Franks who have settled in our land and taken to living like Muslims. These are better than those who have just arrived from their homelands, but they are the exception and cannot be taken as typical." In Francesco Gabrieli, *Arab Historians of the Crusades*, trans. E. Costello (London, 1978, 1984), p. 78. Usama's wry account shows a mild, controlled consternation at the Franks' admittedly barbarous treat-

ment of their women, primitive medical practices and intense religious intolerance.

5. Ibid., p. 82.

6. Quoted in Bernard Lewis, *The Muslim Discovery of Europe* (New York and London, 1982), p. 98.

7. Lewis, *The Arabs in History*, p. 61.

8. Bernard Lewis, *Semites and Anti-Semites: An Inquiry into Conflict and Prejudice* (London, 1986), p. 123.

9. Lewis, *The Muslim Discovery of Europe*, p. 61.

10. Norman Cohn, *The Pursuit of the Millennium: Revolutionary Millenarians and Mystical Anarchists of the Middle Ages* (London, 1970 ed.), pp. 86–87.

11. Paul Johnson, *A History of the Jews* (London, 1987), p. 199.

12. Lewis, *Semites and Anti-Semites*, p. 66.

13. Johnson, *A History of the Jews*, p. 176.

14. Ibid., p. 177.

15. Lewis, *Semites and Anti-Semites*, p. 126.

16. Ibid., p. 123.

17. Johnson, *A History of the Jews*, p. 177.

18. Henry VI, who enters our story only through his brother and his son Frederick II, was more formidable than any ruler in Europe since Charlemagne. He had a high sense of the office of emperor and almost succeeded in establishing it on a hereditary basis. This led him to see the Byzantines as absolute enemies, as Charlemagne had. In 1197 he laid careful plans for a Crusade against Byzantium but died as he was amassing his armada, or he could well have succeeded in making himself master of Christendom. After his death Philip and Otto the Welf were engaged in a dispute for the succession, and Philip clearly wanted to use the Crusade to further his imperial ambitions.

19. Steven Runciman, *A History of the Crusades*, 3 vols. (Cambridge, 1954; London, 1965), vol. III, p. 124.

20. He wrote an ecstatic letter to the Emperor Baldwin, giving him his approval without reserve. Ibid., p. 128.

21. Hymns were sung to celebrate the downfall of *Constantinopitana, civitas diu profana*. Ibid.

22. Ibid., pp. 128–29.

23. R. W. Southern, *The Making of the Middle Ages* (Oxford, 1953; London, 1987), p. 60. He speaks of the "homely conceptions" of the Franks of Byzantium, who "laid more stress on personal rights than on large, strategic designs." They were "baffled" by the Eastern empire and by dividing it up they produced a "disjointed mechanism."

24. Southern (ibid., p. 61) is doubtful that it did. Runciman is convinced that it was "the Crusaders themselves who wilfully broke down the defence of Christendom and thus allowed the infidel to cross the Straits

and penetrate into the heart of Europe." *A History of the Crusades*, vol. III, p. 477.

25. As it is by Runciman, ibid., p. 474.

26. Jacques Madaule, *The Albigensian Crusade: An Historical Essay*, trans. Barbara Wall (London, 1967), p. 63.

27. Though the wave of missionaries arrived in France at about the time of the Second Crusade, there had been Cathars in Europe since the middle of the eleventh century and we hear of them dying for their faith. Zoé Oldenbourg, *Le Bûcher de Montségur* (Paris, 1959), p. 55.

28. When Bernard preached the Second Crusade in 1146 he had found the churches empty and had been able to get very little support, but the Catharist missionaries attracted large audiences and enthusiastic converts. Ibid., p. 44, and Madaule, *The Albigensian Crusade*, p. 50.

29. Oldenbourg, *Le Bûcher de Montségur*, pp. 37–49, for a summary of Catharist belief.

30. Ibid., pp. 49–50.

31. Ibid., p. 54.

32. Zoé Oldenbourg (ibid.) discounts this as one of the distorted myths of the Catholics about the Cathars, who were against violence of any kind. They would not have approved of this suicide. It seems that this fantasy of the *endura* was a projection of a Christian disturbance about the body, for many ascetics starved themselves into emaciation for the love of Christ.

33. Ibid., p. 61.

34. Ibid., pp. 63–67.

35. Madaule, *The Albigensian Crusade*, p. 53. He points out that the Cathars were very different from some "heretics" in the north, like the Hussites and the Lutherans, who were very pugnacious and bellicose in their attitude to the Catholic Church. I shall touch on Lutheran aggression in Chapter 11.

36. Ibid., p. 52.

37. Oldenbourg, *Le Bûcher de Montségur*, pp. 96–105.

38. Jonathan and Louise Riley-Smith, *The Crusades: Idea and Reality, 1095–1274* (London, 1981), pp. 78–80, for a text of the letter.

39. Ibid., pp. 78–79.

40. Innocent accuses the Cathars of "abstaining from certain vices in order that men should think them pious" but in reality they are "the worst of men," given over to "many-sided deceit." Ibid., p. 79.

41. Ibid., p. 80.

42. Ibid., pp. 80–85. The events are not related as a normal crime but as a battle between good and evil in the manner of the holy war. The followers of Raymund are "attendants of Satan" (ibid., p. 81) and Peter is a martyr, who, like Christ and St. Stephen, died "lovingly" forgiving his enemies, saying " 'May God forgive you because I forgive you,' repeating over and over again this phrase, so full of love and forbearance" (ibid.).

Innocent is slightly embarrassed that this holy martyr does not seem to be working any miracles but puts this down to the "incredulity" of the southerners, who are blocking the south off from God (ibid., p. 82).

43. Ibid., p. 85.
44. Ibid., p. 83.
45. Ibid., p. 84.
46. Ibid., p. 85.
47. Ibid.
48. Madaule, *The Albigensian Crusade*, p. 65.
49. This is the popular legend. What probably happened is that the Catholics were urged to leave the town to save their lives but refused to leave their fellow citizens and died fighting for their sakes. From the start this Crusade was a confrontation between north and south. Oldenbourg, *Le Bûcher de Montségur*, pp. 115–16.
50. Madaule, *The Albigensian Crusade*, p. 68.
51. Ibid., pp. 73–74.
52. After the Battle of Baucaire in 1217, when Raymund defeated Simon and the Crusaders, the people of Toulouse greeted him ecstatically and cried that he had rescued their way of life from the northerners. Their courtly values, which "were in their grave, have found again their life and their strength and their health-giving capacities; our children and our children's children will be enriched." Quoted in ibid. p. 83.
53. Georges Duby, "Les pauvres des campagnes dans l'Occident médiéval jusqu'au XIII siècle," *Revue d'Histoire de l'Église de France*, 52 (Paris, 1966), pp. 23–32.
54. Umberto Eco (trans. William Weaver) shows how far this connection between the poor, heresy and revolution had gone by the fourteenth century throughout *The Name of the Rose* (1983).
55. Peter Raedts, "La Croisade des enfants a'-t-elle eu en lieu?" trans. Jacques Bacalu, *L'Histoire*, 47 (Paris, 1982), 32. This important article has transformed our view of the so-called Children's Crusade and I repeat its findings here.
56. Ibid., p. 30.
57. Ibid., pp. 30–31.
58. Ibid., p. 32.
59. This later version of the Crusade is followed by Runciman, *A History of the Crusades*, vol. III, pp. 139–44.
60. Ibid., p. 141.
61. Raedts, "La Croisade des enfants," p. 35.
62. Ibid.
63. Ernst Kantorowicz, *Frederick the Second, 1194–1250*, trans. E. O. Lorimer (London, 1931), p. 3.
64. Ibid., p. 4.
65. He said that he had had a dream: a young bear had got onto his bed and grown larger and larger until it pushed him off. Ibid., p. 53.

66. Frederick said it was a sign from heaven "against all probabilities of men." Ibid.

67. God, he said, "contrary to human knowledge, had miraculously preserved him for the governance of the Roman Empire." Ibid., p. 55.

68. Ibid., p. 57.

69. Ibid., pp. 58–59.

70. Ibid., p. 61.

71. Ibid.

72. Ernst Kantorowicz romantically says that he looked less like an emperor "than a fairy prince or an adventurer in tatters." Ibid., p. 55.

73. He declared that it seemed to him "both reasonable and seemly to follow the example of the Great and Holy Charles and my other ancestors" (ibid., p. 73). He had clearly absorbed his ancestor Barbarossa's view of the Empire as a German institution and of Charlemagne as the ancestor of the Germans, not of the Franks. This may be why he appeals to the German scholar Kantorowicz, who was writing in the early 1930s.

74. Ibid.

75. He had noticed that "the 666 years allotted in Revelation to the Beast were nearly spent. It was indeed nearly six and a half centuries since the birth of Mahomet." Runciman, A History of the Crusades, vol. III, p. 145. It was not only poets and the poor who had apocalyptic dreams. Please note that the Muslims are now figures of absolute evil.

76. Ibid., p. 146.

77. Amin Maalouf, The Crusades Through Arab Eyes, trans. Jon Rothschild (London, 1984), pp. 219–22.

78. Norman Daniel, The Arabs and Medieval Europe (London and Beirut, 1975), p. 206. Daniel says that in Vitry's view the Franks were "de-Latinised Latins, deEuropeanised colonists ... cultural defectors" (ibid.).

79. Benjamin Z. Kedar, Crusade and Mission: European Approaches Towards the Muslims (New Jersey, 1984), p. 73.

80. Ibid., p. 120.

81. Ibid., p. 130.

82. Ibid., p. 123.

83. Quoted by Régine Pernoud, The Crusaders, trans. Enid Grant (Edinburgh and London, 1963), p. 221.

84. Ibid.

85. Runciman, A History of the Crusades, vol. II, p. 161.

86. Ibid., p. 167.

87. Maalouf, The Crusades Through Arab Eyes, p. 226.

88. Norman Daniel, Islam and the West: The Making of an Image (Edinburgh, 1960), p. 121.

89. Pernoud, The Crusaders, p. 221.

90. Ibid., pp. 222–23.

91. Kedar, *Crusade and Mission*, pp. 125–26.
92. Daniel, *Islam and the West*, p. 121.

CHAPTER TEN  1220–1291: The End of the Crusades?

1. Ernst Kantorowicz, *Frederick the Second, 1194–1250*, trans. E. O. Lorimer (London, 1931), p. 356.
2. Ibid., pp. 396–97.
3. Norman Daniel, *The Arabs and Medieval Europe* (London and Beirut, 1975), p. 161.
4. Ibid., pp. 254–58.
5. Ibid., p. 148.
6. Ibid., pp. 150–53.
7. Ibid., p. 154.
8. Francesco Gabrieli, trans. and ed., *Arab Historians of the Crusades*, trans. from the Italian by E. J. Costello (London, 1978, 1984), pp. 277–78.
9. Daniel, *The Arabs and Medieval Europe*, pp. 154–55.
10. Ibid., p. 156.
11. Kantorowicz, *Frederick the Second*, p. 311.
12. Ibid.
13. Ibid., p. 358.
14. Ibid., pp. 310–11.
15. Ibid., p. 171.
16. Ibid., p. 168.
17. Ibid., pp. 88–90.
18. Ibid., pp. 93–95.
19. Steven Runciman, *A History of the Crusades*, 3 vols. (Cambridge, 1954; London, 1965), vol. III, pp. 175–77.
20. Amin Maalouf, *The Crusades Through Arab Eyes*, trans. Jon Rothschild (London, 1984), pp. 226–27.
21. Kantorowicz, *Frederick the Second*, p. 176.
22. Maalouf, *The Crusades Through Arab Eyes*, p. 226.
23. Ibid.
24. Ibid., but Steven Runciman, using Western sources, says that Frederick was trying to "hasten matters by a military display" and that al-Kamil was eventually forced to come to terms because of the deterioration in his own political position in the area.
25. Runciman, *A History of the Crusades*, vol. III, p. 187.
26. Daniel, *The Arabs and Medieval Europe*, p. 157.
27. Maalouf, *The Crusades Through Arab Eyes*, p. 230.
28. Gabrieli, *Arab Historians of the Crusades*, p. 271.
29. Ibid., p. 273.
30. Ibid., p. 274.
31. Runciman, *A History of the Crusades*, vol. III, pp. 188–89.
32. Kantorowicz, *Frederick the Second*, p. 200.

33. Gabrieli, *Arab Historians of the Crusades*, p. 274.

34. Ibid., p. 275.

35. Ibid.

36. Ibid.

37. Runciman, *A History of the Crusades*, vol. III, p. 192.

38. Kantorowicz, *Frederick the Second*, p. 519.

39. Ibid., p. 253.

40. Norman Cohn, *The Pursuit of the Millennium: Revolutionary Millenarians and Mystical Anarchists of the Middle Ages* (London, 1957, 1970), pp. 113–19.

41. Kantorowicz, *Frederick the Second*, pp. 264–65.

42. Ibid., p. 414. But again, as with his relations with Muslims, it is important not to idealize this. Frederick made the Jews wear special clothing, as Pope Gregory did, but he would often take the side of the Jews against the Church, in order to further his own ends. Jews were just more people to exploit when it suited him. Ibid., p. 268.

43. Daniel, *The Arabs and Medieval Europe*, p. 158.

44. Ibid., p. 164.

45. Ibid., pp. 238–39.

46. Ibid., pp. 243–45.

47. Norman Daniel, *Islam and the West: The Making of an Image* (Edinburgh, 1960), pp. 79–108.

48. Ibid., pp. 135–40. In fact Mohammad's introduction of polygamy had nothing to do with sexual self-indulgence but arose out of concern for Muslim women. During the wars with Mecca, many women were widowed and they and their children were left without protectors, so in order to provide for them Muslim men married the widows and took them under their protection. No one was allowed to have more than four wives, and the Koran is very strict indeed about fairness and equality. "If you fear you will not be able to deal justly with them, then marry only one" (4:4). The man must make identical provision for each wife and spend the same period of time with each and must show no extra affection for any of them. Because of this stringency, modern Muslim apologists argue that polygamy was allowed only under special circumstances, like those which pertained in Medina during the Prophet's life. Because it is impossible for any man to treat more than one wife with the equity that the Koran demands, they quote it as being in favor of monogamy. Geoffrey Parrinder, *Sex in the World's Religions* (London, 1980), p. 516.

49. Daniel, *Islam and the West*, pp. 148–52.

50. Ibid., pp. 289–90.

51. Ibid., p. 84.

52. Arius did not believe that Jesus was God, conceived in the womb of Mary, but that he was promoted to special status during his lifetime.

53. Paul Johnson, *A History of the Jews* (London, 1987), p. 211.

54. Ibid., pp. 217–18.

55. Dom Gaspar Lefebvre OSB, ed., *Saint Andrew Daily Missal, with Vespers for Sundays and Feasts* (Bruges, 1961), pp. 1423–24.

56. Ibid., p. 1421.

57. John of Joinville, *The Life of St. Louis*, trans. René Hague and ed. Natalie de Wailly (London, 1955), pp. 37–38.

58. Michel Dillange, *The Sainte-Chapelle*, trans. Angela Moyon (Paris, 1985), p. 9.

59. John of Joinville, *The Life of St. Louis*, pp. 29–32.

60. Ibid., p. 36.

61. Ibid., p. 209.

62. Ibid.

63. Ibid.

64. "He asked me whether I wished to be respected in this world and enjoy Paradise after my death. When I answered that I did, 'Take care, then,' he said, 'not consciously to do or say anything which, if all the world were to know it, you could not acknowledge' " (ibid, p. 27). This is a typical example of Louis's simple morality. Joinville's refreshing honesty is worth quoting. When St. Louis asked him whether he would rather be a leper or commit a mortal sin, Joinville promptly replied (for "I could never tell him a lie") "that I would rather commit thirty mortal sins than become a leper" (ibid., p. 28) and when Louis asked him if he washed the feet of the poor, he was even more vehement: "God forbid, sir! . . . No, I will not wash the feet of those brutes." Louis replied, "That was a poor answer," but could only explain the desirability of this practice by saying that "you should not despise what God did as a lesson to us" (when Jesus washed the feet of his disciples at the Last Supper) (ibid., p. 29).

65. Ibid., p. 33.

66. Ibid., p. 34.

67. Ibid., p. 35.

68. Ibid., pp. 33–34.

69. Ibid., p. 35.

70. Ibid., pp. 35–36.

71. Ibid., p. 36.

72. Blanche of Castille, a formidable lady who acted as his regent when Louis was a minor, "chose for him the company only of men of religion. Child though he was, she made him hear all the hours of the Office and listen to the sermons on feast days. He used to recall that his mother had sometimes told him that she would rather he had died than that he committed a mortal sin." (Ibid., p. 41.) Reading this, one has to feel sorry for Louis.

73. Ibid., p. 51.

74. Maalouf, *The Crusades Through Arab Eyes*, pp. 236–37, and Runciman, *A History of the Crusades*, vol. III, p. 257. Frederick's letter of warning to the Sultan must have inspired Matthew Paris' accusation.

75. Régine Pernoud, *The Crusaders*, trans. Enid Grant (Edinburgh and London, 1963), pp. 247–48.

76. *The Life of St. Louis*, p. 56.

77. Norman Daniel, *The Arabs and Medieval Europe*, p. 244, for a discussion of these conversion fantasies.

78. John of Joinville, *The Life of St. Louis*, p. 57.

79. Ibid., p. 144.

80. Ibid., pp. 144–45.

81. Ibid., p. 64.

82. Ibid., pp. 77–78.

83. Ibid., pp. 96–97. Joinville describes the horrible disease graphically: "The skin became covered with black and earth-covered spots, just like an old boot ... the flesh on our gums began to rot away." Ibid., p. 97.

84. Ibid., p. 105.

85. Ibid., p. 196.

86. Ibid., p. 116.

87. Ibid.

88. Ibid., p. 113.

89. Ibid., p. 196.

90. Maalouf, *The Crusades Through Arab Eyes*, p. 44.

91. Ibid., pp. 246–47.

92. Ibid., p. 250.

93. Ibid., p. 251.

94. Mamluk buildings are much in evidence in Israel.

95. Gabrieli, *Arab Historians of the Crusades*, p. 303.

96. Ibid.

97. Ibid., p. 304.

98. John of Joinville, *The Life of St. Louis*, p. 213.

99. Ibid. Joinville goes so far as to say that all those who encouraged Louis to take the Cross again had committed a mortal sin.

100. Quoted by Stephen Howarth, *The Knights Templar* (London, 1982), p. 223.

101. Maalouf, *The Crusades Through Arab Eyes*, pp. 250–54.

102. They had actually fought alongside the Mongols during a fresh attempted invasion in 1281.

103. Gabrieli, *Arab Historians of the Crusades*, p. 342.

104. Ibid.

105. Maalouf, *The Crusades Through Arab Eyes*, pp. 256–57.

106. Gabrieli, *Arab Historians of the Crusades*, pp. 344–50; and Daniel, *The Arabs and Medieval Europe*, pp. 208–9.

107. Gabrieli, *Arab Historians of the Crusades*, p. 349.

108. Ibid., p. 346.

109. "Thirteenth-century contemporary documents convey an impression that all the long-repressed yearning of the Jews for the Holy Land— kept alive by persecution, faith and daily prayer—suddenly found an outlet in a movement of return. Pilgrimage and migration acquired a new and particular character." Joshua Prawer, *The Latin Kingdom of Jerusalem: European Colonialism in the Middle Ages* (London, 1972), p. 244.

110. Ibid., p. 250.

111. Ibid.

112. Ibid., p. 248.

113. Ibid., p. 247.

114. Nachmanides quotes God's commandments to Joshua to slaughter the Canaanites and denies vehemently that this command was confined to the original "holy war" for the Promised Land: "This is not so, for we were enjoined to destroy the nations if they make war upon us. But if they wish to make peace, we shall make peace with them and let them stay on, upon certain terms. But we shall not leave the land in their hands or those of any other nation at any time whatsoever!" Ibid., p. 248.

115. Ibid., p. 251.

116. Runciman, *A History of the Crusades*, vol. III, p. 467.

117. Norman Cohn, *Europe's Inner Demons* (London, 1975), passim, for an account of the inquisitorial process.

118. Gregory IX followed this initiative by calling a *general* Inquisition against other heretics in 1233. Jacques Madaule, *The Albigensian Crusade: An Historical Essay*, trans. Barbara Wall (London, 1967), pp. 95–96.

**CHAPTER ELEVEN**   1300 to the Present Day: New Crusaders in the West

1. Paul Johnson, *A History of the Jews* (London, 1987), p. 230; Friedrich Heer, *The Medieval World, 1100–1350*, trans. Janet Sondheimer (London, 1962), p. 318.

2. Quoted in Bernard Lewis, *Semites and Anti-Semites, An Inquiry into Conflict and Prejudice* (London, 1986), p. 83.

3. Johnson, *A History of the Jews*, pp. 221–29; Norman Daniel, *The Arabs and Medieval Europe* (London and Beirut, 1975), pp. 313–14.

4. Johnson, *A History of the Jews*, pp. 230–31.

5. Edward W. Said, *Orientalism: Western Conceptions of the Orient* (London, 1978; 1985 ed.), p. 74.

6. Bernard Lewis, *The Muslim Discovery of Europe* (London and New York, 1982), pp. 61–66; 312.

7. Peter Mansfield, *The Arabs* (3rd ed., London, 1985), pp. 65–67.

8. W. C. Smith, *Islam in Modern History* (Princeton, 1957), p. 95.

9. Malise Ruthven, *Islam in the World*, (London, 1984), pp. 292–93.

10. Johnson, *A History of the Jews*, pp. 234–36.

11. Ibid., p. 148.

12. Encyclopaedia Judaica, VIII, 1203–5.

13. Quoted in Johnson, *A History of the Jews*, p. 234.

14. Chaim Potok, *Wanderings: A History of the Jews* (New York, 1983 ed.), p. 447.

15. Norman Cohn, *The Pursuit of the Millennium: Revolutionary Millenarians and Mystical Anarchists of the Middle Ages* (London, Paladin ed., 1970), pp. 80, 248.

16. Norman Daniel, *Islam and the West: The Making of an Image* (Edinburgh, 1960), pp. 280–81.

17. Daniel, *The Arabs and Medieval Europe*, p. 302.

18. Johnson, *A History of the Jews*, pp. 242–43.

19. Ibid., p. 241.

20. Daniel, *Islam and the West*, p. 284.

21. Ibid., p. 285.

22. Ibid., p. 284.

23. Cohn, *The Pursuit of the Millennium*, pp. 119–25.

24. Quoted in Alan Heimert and Andrew Delbanco, eds., *The Puritans in America: A Native Anthology* (Cambridge, Mass., 1985), p. 21.

25. Ibid., p. 19.

26. Ibid., pp. 19–20.

27. Ibid., p. 20.

28. Keith Thomas, *Religion and the Decline of Magic* (London, 1971), pp. 163–64.

29. Robert Cushman, "Reasons and Considerations Touching the Lawfulness of Running Out of England into Parts of America" (1622), in Heimert and Delbanco, *The Puritans in America*, p. 44.

30. For example Thomas Shepard, "The Sound Believer" (c. 1633): he argued that it was "their zeal to preach the word, not cowardice, that led them to emigrate to a place where they could preach without danger of imprisonment." Ibid., p. 33.

31. Ibid., p. 71.

32. Thus Thomas Morton in his open letter, "New English Canaan," ibid., pp. 49–50.

33. "Reasons and Considerations," ibid., p. 44.

34. Quoted in Regina Sharif, *Non-Jewish Zionism: Its Roots in Western History* (London, 1983), p. 90, source not given.

35. Heimert and Delbanco, *The Puritans in America*, p. 278.

36. Ibid., pp. 115–16. Johnson also imagines Christ summoning the Pilgrims into his army through his herald-at-arms: "Oh yes! oh, yes! All you people of Christ that are here oppressed, imprisoned and scurrilously derided, gather yourselves together, your wives and little ones,

and answer to your several names as you shall be shipped for his service in the Western world, and more especially for planting the United Colonies of New England, where you are to attend the service of the King of Kings," ibid., p. 114.

37. Ibid., p. 7.
38. Johnson, *A History of the Jews*, p. 276.
39. Quoted in Sharif, *Non-Jewish Zionism*, p. 24.
40. Johnson, *A History of the Jews*, p. 246.
41. Ibid., pp. 275-77. The Jews in England were full citizens and subject only to those restrictions that later applied to English Catholics and nonconformists who refused to submit to the 39 Articles of the Church of England and, like them, were emancipated from these disabilities during the latter half of the nineteenth century.
42. Ibid., pp. 278–82.
43. Gershom Scholem, "The Golem of Prague and the Golem of Rehevot," in *The Messianic Idea in Judaism* (New York, 1971), pp. 335–40.
44. Quoted in Johnson, *A History of the Jews*, p. 290.
45. Ibid., p. 288.
46. Barbara Tuchman, *Bible and Sword: How the British Came to Palestine* (New York, 1956; London, 1957, 1982), pp. 153–54.
47. Ibid., p. 154.
48. Quoted in Sharif, *Non-Jewish Zionism*, p. 37.
49. Ibid., p. 40.
50. Said, *Orientalism*, pp. 64–67.
51. Quoted in ibid., p. 66.
52. Quoted in Daniel, *Islam and the West*, p. 297.
53. P. M. Holt, Introduction to the *Cambridge History of Islam*, P. M. Holt, Anne K. S. Lambton and Bernard Lewis, eds., (Cambridge, 1970), p. xvi, quoted in Said, *Orientalism*, pp. 63–64.
54. Quoted in Daniel, *Islam and the West*, p. 291.
55. Edward Gibbon, *The Decline and Fall of the Roman Empire*, Dero E. Saunders, ed., abridged in one volume (London, 1980), p. 651.
56. "The Hero as Prophet," *On Heroes and Hero-Worship* (London, 1841), p. 63.
57. Quoted in Daniel, *Islam and the West*, p. 300.
58. Quoted in Johnson, *A History of the Jews*, p. 309.
59. Quoted in Daniel, *Islam and the West*, p. 290.
60. Ibid., p. 287.
61. Ibid., p. 384.
62. Quoted in Johnson, *A History of the Jews*, p. 309.
63. Potok, *Wanderings*, pp. 486–89.
64. Johnson, *A History of the Jews*, p. 343.
65. Said, *Orientalism*, p. 82.
66. Quoted in Sharif, *Non-Jewish Zionism*, p. 50.
67. Mansfield, *The Arabs*, p. 134.

68. Ibid., p. 105.
69. Ibid., pp. 137–38.
70. M. Baudricourt, *La Guerre et le gouvernment de l'Algérie* (Paris, 1853), p. 160.
71. Quoted in Said, *Orientalism*, p. 171.
72. Ibid.
73. Ibid., p. 172.
74. Ibid., p. 171.
75. Ibid., p. 173.
76. Ibid., p. 179.
77. Johnson, *A History of the Jews*, p. 324.
78. Tuchman, *Bible and Sword*, p. 220.
79. Ibid. p. 222.
80. Ibid., p. 223.
81. Ibid., p. 213.
82. Ibid., p. 212.
83. Ibid.
84. Ibid., p. 214.
85. Ibid., pp. 214–15.
86. Ibid., p. 191.
87. Ibid., p. 175.
88. Ibid., p. 176.
89. *Daniel Deronda* (Panther ed., London, 1970), p. 486.
90. Quoted in Johnson, *A History of the Jews*, p. 381.
91. Potok, *Wanderings*, p. 491.
92. Johnson, *A History of the Jews*, p. 346.
93. Karl Marx, *Surveys from Exile*, ed. and trans. David Fernbach (London, 1973), p. 306.
94. Marx, two essays "On the Jewish Question" (1844), quoted in Johnson, *A History of the Jews*, pp. 351–52.
95. Ibid., p. 352.
96. Quoted in Said, *Orientalism*, p. 142.
97. Ibid., p. 149.
98. *Religion and Art* (1881), quoted in Johnson, *A History of the Jews*, p. 394.
99. *The Antichrist*, trans. R. J. Hollingdale (London, 1968), pp. 157–62.
100. Quoted in Said, *Orientalism*, p. 236.
101. Ibid., p. 237.
102. Ibid., pp. 236–37.
103. Ibid., pp. 276–77.
104. Ibid., p. 277.
105. Quoted in Mansfield, *The Arabs*, p. 151.
106. There were attempts in North Africa to fight the colonial powers on the old religious *hijra/jihad* model but these were easily quashed. The most famous and successful of these archaic movements was the Mahdist

uprising led by Mohammad Ahmad, who declared himself to be the *mahdi* (messiah) in 1881, went into voluntary exile with his companions and fought the British with some success; his most famous victory was against General Charles George Gordon at Khartoum in 1885: the Mahdist regime in the Sudan was put down in 1898. These old-style movements needed a new ideology and this was provided by the reformers; the ideas of the reformers still today inform Islamic movements that return to the older paradigm. It will be noticed that, in an attempt to confine my argument to the Middle East, I have not discussed important Indian Muslim reformers like Sayyid Ahmad Khan (d. 1898), Mohammad Iqbal (d. 1938) and, more recently, Abual Ala Maududi (d. 1979). These writers had a strong influence on the Arabs of the Middle East, however.

107. Roy Mottahedeh, *The Mantle of the Prophet: Religion and Politics in Iran* (London, 1985), pp. 183–84.
108. Ruthven, *Islam and the West*, p. 305.
109. Lewis, *Semites and Anti-Semites*, pp. 127–31.
110. Quoted in Said, *Orientalism*, p. 39.
111. Ibid., p. 38.
112. Lewis, *Semites and Anti-Semites*, p. 125.
113. Conor Cruise O'Brien, *The Siege, the Saga of Zionism and Israel* (London, 1986), p. 29.
114. Quoted in Sharif, *Non-Jewish Zionism*, p. 78.
115. O'Brien, *The Siege*, pp. 28–29.
116. Ibid., p. 26. See also Claude Montefiore in a letter to the War Cabinet, October, 1917, in an effort to avert the Balfour Declaration: "It is very significant that anti-Semites are always so sympathetic to Zionism," ibid, p. 27.
117. Sharif, *Non-Jewish Zionism*, p. 80.
118. Ibid., p. 79.
119. Ibid.
120. Ibid., pp. 3–4.
121. Richard Meinertshagen, *Middle East Diary 1917–56* (London, 1960), p. 67.
122. Ibid., p. 183.
123. Ibid.
124. Ibid., p. 49.
125. Ibid.
126. Ibid., p. 203.
127. Ibid., p. 8.
128. Ibid., p. 17.
129. Ibid., p. 12.
130. Ibid., p. 161.
131. Ibid., p. 167.
132. Said, *Orientalism*, pp. 285–86.

133. Potok, *Wanderings*, p. 522, and Bernard Avishai, *The Tragedy of Zionism: Revolution and Democracy in the Land of Israel* (New York, 1985), pp. 358–59.
134. Sharif, *Non-Jewish Zionism*, pp. 93–97.
135. Ibid., p. 108.
136. David Turner and Robert Olson, "Praise the Lord and Save Israel," *Middle East International*, 306, pp. 15–16.
137. Sharif, *Non-Jewish Zionism*, p. 135.
138. Ibid., p. 110.
139. Ibid.
140. Ibid., p. 135.

## EPILOGUE  Triple Vision

1. Quoted by Godfrey Janson, "Khomeini's Heretical Delusions of Grandeur," *Middle East International*, 317, p. 18.
2. Frank Barnaby, "The Nuclear Arsenal in the Middle East," *Journal of Palestine Studies*, 17:1.

# GLOSSARY OF TERMS

**Alem.** *See* Ulema.

**Aliyah** (Hebrew: ascension, immigration.) Originally the word was used to describe the ascent of the Temple Mount by Jewish pilgrims to Jerusalem, and thus by extension it meant "pilgrimage." The word has also acquired connotations of rising to a more exalted spiritual state and to a higher level of being. The Zionists chose to describe immigration into the land of Israel as an *aliyah* and it is still used today to denote the act of emigrating from the diaspora (q.v.) and becoming a citizen of the state of Israel. The word "Aliyah" is also used in Zionist history to describe the five great waves of Jewish immigration into Palestine before the Second World War. Thus:

> First Aliyah: 1882–1903
> Second Aliyah: 1904–14
> Third Aliyah: 1919–23
> Fourth Aliyah: 1924–28
> Fifth Aliyah: 1929–39

These Aliyahs correspond with new waves of anti-Semitic persecution in Europe.

**Amir** (Arabic: one who commands.) This came to describe either a military commander or a prince. In Turkish, the word became emir.

**Antichrist** This was a figure which haunted the imagination of European Christians. From certain prophecies in the New Testament, they evolved a belief in a figure who would rise to power at the end of time. His coming would herald the Last Days. He was the opposite of a Messiah, because he was the enemy of Christ and of all Christians. (*See* Messiah, Last Emperor, Hidden Imam.) Antichrist would deceive many people and attract a large following, but he would also persecute the faithful and fight God's champions. Eventually he would be crowned in Jerusalem (q.v.) and establish himself on the site of the Jewish Temple. He would appear to rule in triumph but eventually God would send down the Archangel Michael to fight him and Christians would flock to join the last terrible battle. Then the Second Coming of Christ would occur and an era of peace and glory would begin. It was generally believed that Antichrist would be an ordinary human being, though a person of absolute evil. The Protestant reformers did not jettison the belief in Antichrist but added fantasies of their own. Instead of seeing Antichrist as an individual, they tended to see him as a whole evil institution, like the Church of Rome or Islam.

**Apocalypse** (Greek: revelation.) All three religions have developed an apocalyptic tradition, relating to the events that will occur at the end of time, when God's power and justice will be finally revealed. In each tradition the city of Jerusalem (q.v.) plays a crucial part. In Jewish apocalyptic writing, the Messiah will appear on the Mount of Olives to fight a terrible battle with the enemies of the Jewish people, after which he will reign triumphantly from Jerusalem and bring peace to the whole world. The Gentile nations will pay tribute to God's chosen people. (*See* Messiah, Redemption.) In Christianity, Antichrist will be crowned in the Temple, will fight the Christians there and a New Jerusalem will descend from heaven, ushering in a new world order, where suffering and injustice are no more. (*See* Antichrist, Last Emperor.) In Islam, God's Last Judgment will finally punish the evildoers and Islam will triumph over the world. Mohammad will descend from heaven onto the Mount of Olives and lead the faithful into the city, walking on a giant sword that acts as a bridge, and the Prophet Jesus will descend from heaven into the Great Mosque of Damascus. All three traditions envisage a final world victory for the true religion. People still believe in these future events today in all three religions, and this naturally affects their attitude to the political status of Jerusalem.

**Ark of the Covenant** This was a portable shrine which the ancient Israelites carried with them during their forty years' wandering in the Sinai Peninsula. It contained the tablets of the law and also localized the Presence of Yahweh (q.v.), which rested upon it in the form of a cloud.

**Ashkenazim** Originally a corruption of the German *allemagne*, it was used to describe the Jews of Germany, but later was extended to refer to the Jews of Eastern, Central and Western Europe, as opposed to the Sephardim (q.v.).

**Atabeg** (Turkish: literally prince–father.) Originally an atabeg was a guardian appointed to act as a regent and protector to minor princes in the Seljuk clan; later atabegs became *de facto* rulers in their own right, even governors and founders of dynasties.

**Ayatollah** (Persian: Miraculous Sign of God.) In Iran it is a term used to describe those scholars of Islamic law who have attained a sufficient knowledge and authority to give rulings on matters of Islamic practice. This authority has not, until recently, extended to matters of belief or theological opinion. The faithful choose an ayatollah on whom they can model themselves and so feel confident that they are keeping the holy law of Islam. They consult him or his more learned followers about finer points or abstruse matters, to make sure that they are living a truly Muslim life. They also follow their ayatollah in political matters, because they trust that his knowledge of Islamic law will guide them to make a correct assessment of a given situation and show them how true Muslims should act, if they face oppression and persecution for example.

**Ba'ath** (Arabic: renaissance.) This is the name given to the socialist party of President Hafez al-Assad of Syria.

**Benedictine** This is a religious order that follows the rule of St. Benedict of Nursia. It became the dominant form of Western monasticism during the Dark Ages and was a major force in the Christianization and recovery of European culture and power after the destruction of the Roman Empire. The Cluniacs and the Cistercians were eleventh- and twelfth-century forms of Benedictine monasticism. Even though they differed from one another sharply, both would have argued that they were living according to the spirit of St. Benedict and living lives of poverty, stability and celibacy, and both centered their lives on the singing of the divine office (a daily service of psalms and readings from Scripture) which they called the *Opus Dei*, the work of God.

**Betar** (an acronym for the Hebrew *Brit Trumpeldor*: the Covenant of Trumpeldor.) An activist and military youth movement of Revisionist Zionism (q.v.), founded by Vladimir Jabotinsky and Joseph Trumpeldor, a one-armed Jewish hero of the Russo-Japanese War.

**Black September** Refers originally to September 1971, when King Hussein of Jordan turned against the Palestine Liberation Organization (q.v.) and expelled them from the country. A Palestinian terrorist group calling itself Black September was responsible for the killing of eleven Israeli athletes at the Olympic Games of 1972.

**Blood Libel** A Christian anti-Semitic myth dating from the twelfth century, which claimed that Jews needed to consume Christian blood each year and so were impelled to murder Christian children by means of a blasphemous crucifixion and to use their blood to make Passover bread.

**Caliph** (Arabic: successor, deputy.) The caliph was the successor and deputy of the Prophet Mohammad and was recognized as the supreme authority of the Muslims by the Sunni (q.v.) until the Mongolian invasions in the late thirteenth century. According to the Sharia (q.v.), the caliph exercised full authority in both spiritual and political matters, but in fact his position was weak. After the period of the *rashidun*, the first four Rightly Guided Caliphs, and the rise of the sultans and amirs (q.v.) throughout the huge Islamic empire, the caliph lost credibility and became a figurehead. When Saladin and Shirkuh occupied Egypt in 1169, the Shiite caliph ruling there was believed to be a descendant of Ali and his wife

Fatima, the daughter of the Prophet Mohammad. He too was a mere cipher and the real power had passed to the vizier (q.v.).

**Chalutz** (Hebrew: pioneer; plural: *chalutzim*.) Literally the word means "vanguard" and the Zionist settlers who called themselves *chalutzim* in the first years of the twentieth century saw themselves as vanguards of a new socialist era. The biblical term *chalutz* had connotations of liberation, rescue and exaltation and also had an aggressive dimension. It meant "to pass over armed before the Lord into the land of Canaan" (Numbers 32:32) (Amos Elon, *The Israelis, Founders and Sons*, 2nd ed. (London and Tel Aviv, 1981, 1983), pp. 111–12).

**Chansons de Geste** (French: the Songs of Deeds.) Refers to those songs which began to be composed at about the time of the First Crusade, celebrating the glorious achievements and heroism of the age of Charlemagne and exalting the military prowess of the Franks. The most famous of these was *The Song of Roland*.

**Chivalry** (from the French *chevalier*, horseman, knight.) The word expressed different values at different times and different places. Basically, it denoted the knightly code or the manner in which knights were supposed to fight and live. In *The Song of Roland* chivalry is seen as very aggressive and brutally masculine. The knight was meant to be a fierce warrior of absolute courage and massive physical strength, and was not expected to be wise or spiritual. The Church tried to reform this chivalry and Christianize it during the eleventh century, and churchmen taught the knights that they must protect the poor and destitute, according to biblical values. This Christian chivalry was important during the Crusades. Finally, the courtly love tradition tried to civilize Western chivalry. A knight was supposed to be engaged in a quest for virtue ·and for beautiful, courtly behavior, inspired by a lady whom he loved from afar. The Muslims also had a chivalric code, which shared most of the values of Christian chivalry.

**Cluny, Cluniac** The Benedictine monastery at Cluny in Burgundy initiated a reform which attempted to Christianize Europe and teach the people true Christian values. At the end of the tenth and throughout the eleventh century Cluny and the other Benedictine houses which joined this reform movement constituted the most powerful and influential institution in Europe.

**Covenant** (translation of the Hebrew *brit*.) This is a vital concept in Judaism. When God called Abraham he made a covenant agreement with him and as a sign of this covenant Abraham circumcized himself and all the male members of his household. At eight days old each Jewish male undergoes circumcision (*brit*) and enters into this covenant agreement between God and the descendants of Abraham, who are his chosen people. By this covenant, God promises that the Jews will be his people above all others, provided that they obey him and keep the Torah (q.v.), the law of Moses. They must not worship any other God but him and must obey his commandments absolutely.

**Dhimmi** From the Arabic *Dhimma*, which was a pact between the Muslim state and, in Europe, the Jews and Christians living under Muslim rule and, in the Middle East and Asia, the Hindus, Zoroastrians and Buddhists. They were afforded full religious liberty and were given military and civil protection, on condition that they respected the supremacy of Islam. The people who came under the *Dhimma* were known as *dhimmis*, which by extension came to mean "protected minorities."

**Diaspora** This is the name given to the dispersal of the Jewish people throughout the world and to those Jews who live outside the Land of Israel.

**Dinar** (Greek: denarion.) The unit of gold currency used by Muslims.

**Dirham** (from Greek: *drakme*.) The unit of silver currency used by Muslims until the Mongol conquests.

**Emir** (Turkish.) *See* Amir.

**Faqih** (Arabic.) A Muslim jurisprudent, who is deemed capable and sufficiently knowledgeable to give a *fatwa* (q.v.).

**Fatah** (Arabic: opening.) Refers to the conquest of Mecca by Mohammad and to the Islamization of any city or country. Yasir Arafat has called his party Fatah, even though it is a secular party. It seems that he wanted to reassure the religious Arab states of the Gulf that he would not adopt foreign ideologies like communism or socialism in his struggle to return the Palestinian people to their homeland. Fatah is the largest party in the Palestine Liberation Organization (q.v.).

**Fatwa** (Arabic.) An opinion or a ruling given by an appropriate Islamic authority that interprets a point of holy law in a way which will be binding on those Muslims who accept him as their guide.

**Fedayeen.** *See Fida'i.*

**Feudalism** A defensive network of dependent loyalties that grew up in Europe during the Dark Ages. A man would bind himself to his lord and both would mutually swear to be loyal to one another: the vassal (q.v.) promised to fight for his lord's rights and to protect his patrimony and honor, and in his turn the lord promised to defend his vassal from a mutual enemy. In his turn, the lord would have a more powerful overlord, and so on. At the head of this feudal pyramid was the King.

**Fida'i** (Arabic plural: *fedayeen*.) Literally "one who sacrifices himself" and by extension a freedom fighter, who is prepared to risk his life for the sake of the people.

**Fief** This was the name given to the land owned as patrimony and which was at the heart of feudalism (q.v.). A vassal held his patrimony or fief from his lord, who was duty-bound to come to his aid if it was attacked, just as the vassal was bound to fight for the fief of his lord.

**Fundamentalism** This word is generally applied to any extreme religious movement, but I think that this is misleading. When Christians use the term "fundamentalism" they mean a movement that is going back to the fundamentals of the faith and to what they see as the spirit of the gospels. Such Christian movements tend to be very literal-minded and aggressive in their interpretation of the Bible. This aggressive literalness is certainly manifest in some extreme Jewish movements today. Christian fundamentalists tend to be backward-looking and to cast off what they see as later accretions of the faith, and this too could be true of some Jewish "fundamentalists" in Israel. But it is not true of modern extreme Islamic groups and to use the word "fundamentalist" of the Iranian revolution raises certain expectations in a Western environment that are not applicable.

**Gospels** These are four documents that were chosen by the Church to be authentic accounts of the life and teachings of Jesus Christ. The earliest, that attributed to St. Mark, was written about C.E. 70, some fifty years after the death of Christ. The gospels of Matthew and Luke were written during the 80s and that of St. John in about C.E. 100. The gospels reflect the teaching of St. Paul, which was radically different from the teaching of the apostles, who had intended to remain fully observant Jews and saw Christianity as a Jewish sect.

**Goyim** (Hebrew: singular, *goy.*) The name given by Jews to denote non-Jews or Gentiles.

**Gush Emunim** (Hebrew: the Bloc of the Faithful.) A religious–political group formed in Israel in 1974 to Judaize the occupied territories by means of illegal settlement there and by encouraging Jews in the diaspora (q.v.) to emigrate to Israel and join them in Gaza or the West Bank.

**Hadith** (Arabic.) A tradition handed down orally through a reliable train of sources relating a saying or deed of the Prophet Mohammad for the guidance of Muslims. These were gathered together during the ninth century. The whole corpus of the *hadith* is one of the major sources of Islamic law.

**Haganah** (Hebrew: defense.) The Jewish Defense Force formed in Palestine to protect Zionist interests under the British mandate, which became the base of the Israeli army after the state of Israel was established in 1948.

**Hajj, hajji** (Arabic: pilgrimage.) The pilgrimage to Mecca, Arafat and Mina which was originally made by pagan Arabs to pagan shrines there in pre-Islamic Arabia. Mohammad reinterpreted these ancient pagan rites and made the *hajj* one of the five pillars of Islam, an obligatory practice for all Muslims. Every Muslim is required to make the pilgrimage to Mecca at least once in his or her lifetime if circumstances permit. A Muslim who has made the *hajj* is given the title *hajji.*

**Hajji.** *See Hajj.*

**Halakah** (Hebrew.) The part of the Talmud (q.v.) concerned with legal matters, as opposed to the Haggadah, which comprises tales and folklore.

**Hanif** (Arabic: infidel.) This was the derisive name given by the pagan Arabs in pre-Islamic Arabia to the Arabs who had become monotheists, worshiping only Allah, and who claimed that he was the God of the Jews and the Christians.

**Herut** (Hebrew: freedom.) A political party founded in 1948 by Menachem Begin and the Irgun to perpetuate the ideals of Vladimir Jabotinsky and the Revisionist Zionists (q.v.). Herut is the major party in the right-wing bloc that was formed later and which is called the Likud.

**Hidden Imam** In what is known as Twelver Shiism, the Hidden Imam is an Islamic Messiah figure. The Shiites would not accept the political authority of the caliphs (q.v.) but took as their leader (imam) the direct descendants of Ali, the cousin and son-in-law of the Prophet Mohammad. There were twelve of these imams and because they set up a rival dynasty they were often murdered by the caliphs of the Sunni tradition (q.v.). Eventually the Twelfth Imam went into hiding in 874 and died in 920. After that there were no more direct descendants of Ali and the Shiites claim that there can be no more legitimate authority in the absence of this Hidden Imam, who they say is in a state of "occultation." They believe that one day the Twelfth Imam will return and inaugurate a golden age.

**Hijra** (Arabic: migration.) Often misspelled *hegira*. The migration of Mohammad from Mecca to Medina in 622. It has been used by later Muslims to describe a migration from the community in order to live a more truly Islamic life. Such a *hijra* is seen as a positive protest and a move for revolution and reform.

**Holy, holiness** This is a crucial term. When we use the word "holy" today we usually refer to a state of spiritual purity, but the word has more concrete meanings in all three traditions.

> (1) In Judaism, the notion of holiness is bound up with the notion of a physical separation: the holiness of things is celebrated by setting them apart from one another: Sabbath from the rest of the week, milk from meat and Jews from Gentiles. The Holy Land is the place where the Jews must live as a holy or consecrated people, set apart (Exodus 19:6). Today radical religious Jews in Israel claim that the Jews must be a nation "which dwells alone" and some even want to purge the land of Gentile presence.

> (2) In medieval Christianity holiness was popularly conceived as a tangible power inherent in certain physical objects and was, therefore, intensely localized. Relics of the saints provided a physical link with heaven. The Holy Land was the most holy relic of all because it was saturated with this holy force by means of its physical connection with Jesus.

(3) In Islam there would be no such veneration of anything physical, because this would be considered idolatry. But the "sanctuary" of Mecca is a consecrated area and, as in Judaism, this means that it is set apart. Certain things are forbidden (Arabic: *haram*), notably violence, and there must be no non-Muslims in Mecca and its environs.

**House of Islam** (translation of the Arabic: *Dar al-Islam.*) This is the name given to Muslim territory in the Islamic holy law.

**House of War** (translation of the Arabic: *Dar al-Harb.*) In the Islamic holy law this describes the non-Muslim world beyond the Islamic frontiers. In Islamic legal theory, there must be a perpetual state of war until all the world submits to the supremacy of Islam and the true religion. Until that time the state of war may be suspended by truces but cannot be ended by a permanent peace. In practice, Muslims abandoned this notion in the eighth century, accepted that Islam had reached its territorial limits and had normal trading and political connections with the non-Muslim countries.

**Ijtihad** (Arabic.) Literally, like many Muslim terms, this means "exerting oneself." Later it came to mean "individual reasoning" about the revelation of God to Mohammad. One who was expert enough to develop Islamic tradition by means of individual reasoning was called a *mujtahid* (q.v.) (one who exercises *ijtihad*). Many Muslims believe that only the great masters of early Islam had the right to use *ijtihad* and that after the ninth century the gates of *ijtihad* had been closed. Muslim scholars could only reason by analogy when applying Islamic law to contemporary conditions. In Iran, however, another Muslim tradition *does* allow *mujtahids* of sufficient standing to exercise individual reasoning and to make a contribution to the Islamic tradition.

**Imam** (Arabic: leader.) Generally the word is used to describe any leader of the Muslim community or a Muslim who leads the prayers in the mosque. In the Shiah (q.v.) the word was applied to the descendants of Ali, whom Shiites believed to be the only legitimate rulers of Muslims; Shiites also expect the Hidden Imam (q.v.) to return as an Islamic Messiah to inaugurate a golden age. Consequently the word "imam" has much greater force and authority.

**Indulgence** This is a complex Catholic practice that was important during the Crusades. By performing certain actions, the popes granted Catholics a means of remitting the temporal punishment they must endure for their sins in this world and also in purgatory, where they purge themselves of their sins before getting into heaven. A pilgrimage to Jerusalem or Compostela or, later, a Crusade ensured that a Christian was absolved of all the punishment that was awaiting him, and if he died during it he would go straight to heaven.

**Irgun** The underground military and terrorist wing of the Revisionist Zionists (q.v.) which operated in Palestine and in Israel from 1931 to 1949, led by Menachem Begin, who became Prime Minister of Israel in 1977.

**Islam** The correct name for the religion of Muslims. It means submission to God and a Muslim is "one who submits."

**Jerusalem** This city is holy to all three religions:

(1) When King David conquered this Jebusite city in about 1000 B.C.E. he wanted to make it the center of his kingdom and of Judaism; to house the Presence of God, David's son Solomon built a temple, which was destroyed by the Babylonians in 589. But Jews continued to pray facing Jerusalem, wherever they happened to be, and the city became central to the Jewish identity.

(2) The city was holy to Christians because it was the scene of the death and resurrection of Christ and housed the holiest relic of all, the tomb of Christ (*see* Holy). Although Jerusalem was always venerated by the Greek Orthodox and by oriental Christians, the Western Christians had the most fanatical devotion to the holy city because of their physical interpretation of holiness. Protestants abolished practices like pilgrimages to shrines and relics and would regard excessive devotion to Jerusalem, as expressed by the Crusaders, to be idolatry.

(3) In Islam, Jerusalem is holy because Muslims believe that in the early days of his prophetic period Mohammad traveled there by night in a mystical flight. He alighted on the Temple Mount and thence ascended to heaven, where he spoke to Jesus and Moses. The vision expresses the connection between Islam and the two older religions, and the two mosques that commemorate this event are built on the site of the Jewish Temple, which is regarded by Muslims as the third holiest place in the Islamic world, after Mecca and Medina.

**Jihad** (Arabic: striving, effort.) Usually used in this book to mean "holy war" against unbelievers or against Christians, who oppressed and persecuted Muslims in their Crusades.

**Ka'aba** (Arabic.) The most holy shrine in Islam. It is a small square building in the center of the Great Mosque in Mecca, which Muslims believe to have been built by Abraham and his son Ishmael to the one God. From Ka'aba we get our word "cube."

**Kabala** (Hebrew.) The system of Jewish mysticism.

**Kibbutz** (from the Hebrew *kibbush*: conquest.) A Jewish agricultural settlement where property is owned in common.

**Koran** (Arabic: recitation.) The name given to the holy book of Islam, which Muslims believe was dictated to Mohammad by God himself. Mohammad, who could not write, was told to recite the words after the divine voice. These utterances were written down by those of his disciples who were literate and were collected by his disciples by the middle of the seventh century. As the revelations came to Mohammad, he passed them on to the Muslims, who had to learn them by heart and place each new revelation in the place that the Prophet prescribed.

**Labor Zionism** This is the school of Zionists led by David Ben-Gurion, who became the first Prime Minister of Israel in 1948. Labor held undisputed sway in Israel until 1977, when the right-wing Zionists led by Menachem Begin came to power. Labor Zionists were secular socialists who originally believed that they would create a model, equal society in Palestine. They also believed that labor (*avodah*) on the land of Israel would save the Jews from the weakness they had acquired in the diaspora and that this labor would give the Jews a claim to Palestine. Hence they called their colonizing effort the "Conquest of Labor."

**Last Emperor** This was the Emperor whose coming was predicted by the Sibylline prophets (q.v.) and who was eagerly expected by lay Christians in Europe during the Middle Ages. This Emperor was expected to unite the East and West, slaughter the enemies of Christ, march to Jerusalem to be crowned, inspire the coming of Antichrist (q.v.) and so inaugurate the Last Days and the glorious era of the Second Coming of Christ. In effect this hoped-for Emperor was a Christian Messiah. (*See* Messiah and Hidden Imam.)

**Lehi** (Hebrew; an acronym for *Lohana Herut Israel*: Fighters for the Freedom of Israel.) This was a terrorist, militant Zionist organization that fought the British and the Arabs in Palestine before the establishment of the state of Israel. It was founded by Avraham Stern and was called the "Stern Gang" by the British. Later it was led by Yitzhak Shamir, who became Prime Minister of Israel in 1986.

**Madrassa** (Arabic.) A seminary or college of Islamic learning, which is often, though not always, attached to a mosque.

**Mamluk** (Arabic: literally "owned.") The word was at first used to describe a white slave who had been trained to be a soldier. This was a way for slaves to acquire freedom and eminence in the Muslim world. Some Mamluks, who converted to Islam and won their freedom, even became military commanders and founded dynasties. The most famous of these Mamluk dynasties was that founded in Egypt in 1250 at the time of the Seventh Crusade, which eventually drove the Christians from the Crusader states. The Mamluk dynasty survived until 1517.

**Marranos** The name given to the Spanish Jews who converted to Christianity under pressure and who many Spaniards believed were practicing their old religion secretly.

**Martyr** (Greek: witness.) In the early Church a martyr was seen as witnessing to Christ in a pagan world by dying for him. The Arabic *shaheed* (martyr) also has this connotation of witnessing to the truth and power of the faith. In all three religions of Judaism, Christianity and Islam, martyrs who voluntarily expose themselves to the dangers of death for the sake of their religion are venerated. In the holy wars of all three religions, people who die in the struggle are venerated as martyrs, even though they have met their deaths by fighting other people aggressively.

**Messiah** (Hebrew: anointed one.) The Messiah foretold by the prophets was expected to deliver the Jewish people from their suffering and oppression at the hands of the Gentiles. He would also ensure the final triumph of the chosen people, establish them gloriously in Jerusalem and vanquish their foes. All the Gentile nations would be forced to pay tribute to the Jewish people and a golden age of cosmic peace and harmony would begin. It must be emphasized that there was no thought of the Messiah's being a divine being. St. Paul taught his converts that Jesus had been the Messiah (Christ is simply a Greek translation of the Hebrew: *Messhiach*), and later Christians developed the belief that Jesus had been God and assumed that the Jews had expected him to be the Son of God. But in the Jewish Scriptures the phrase "Son of God" means a perfectly normal human being, who is very close to God. Such a man was King David, whom God had anointed as king. Many Jews believed that the Messiah would be a descendant of King David at the time of Christ. Today the Jews who are expecting the imminent advent of the Messiah and the redemption (q.v.) are not expecting a divine being to arrive, though some of them are expecting catastrophic and miraculous events to accompany him.

**Mizrachi** (abbreviation of Hebrew *Mercaz Ruhani*: spiritual center.) This was a religious Zionist movement whose members wanted to form a religious state in Israel, rebuild the Temple and rule according to the Torah (q.v.). They did not want a secular democracy run on modern lines.

**Mohammadanism** This is the name that Christians and Western people often incorrectly give to Islam. Similarly they call Muslims "Mohammadans." This habit is offensive to Muslims, because it implies that Mohammad is the equivalent of Christ in Christianity. Medieval Christians believed that Muslims thought that Mohammad was pretending to be God, like Christ, but this idea would have been considered blasphemous by Mohammad, who never claimed to be anything other than a normal, albeit privileged human being. Further, the word "Mohammadan" was originally always used in a pejorative sense in the polemic against Islam, which produced a very distorted image of the religion in the West. Consequently, it has the same offensive connotations for Muslims as Yid or Zhid has for Jews.

**Monotheism** The worship of only one God, the central tenet of Judaism, Christianity and Islam.

**Moriscos** The name given to the Spanish Muslims (Moors) who converted to Christianity and were believed to be practicing their former religion in secret.

**Mortal sin** This is a Catholic concept. Catholics have traditionally believed that there are two types of sins committed by Christians: mortal and venial. A venial sin is a lesser sin, like telling a lie, and it can be forgiven by means of a prayer of contrition. A mortal sin is a major sin like murder or adultery. As its name suggests, it causes the death of grace in the soul, because it severs a Christian from God absolutely and can only be forgiven by means of the sacrament of penance, when a Catholic confesses it to a priest and receives absolution from God. If a person dies with unconfessed mortal sin on his soul, he or she will go to hell for all eternity. To qualify as mortal, the sin must be a grave one and must be committed knowingly and deliberately and with a clear knowledge of the spiritual consequences.

**Mufti** (Arabic.) An expert in Islamic law. Unlike the Qadi (q.v.), his status is usually private and voluntary rather than an official appointment. It is bestowed on a Muslim who is renowned for his scholarship and personal reputation. That is what was scandalous about the British promotion of Hajji al-Husseini during the mandate.

**Mujahid** (Arabic, plural: *mujahideen*.) A freedom fighter who takes part in a *jihad* or struggle for the liberation of his people from tyranny and persecution. Not to be confused with:

**Mujtahid** (Arabic, plural: *mujtahideen*.) An Islamic scholar qualified to exercise *ijtihad* (q.v.) or independent judgment in all matters pertaining to Islamic practice. This means he can issue authoritative opinions on the basis of his knowledge of Islamic law and this can also be a political judgment. A *mujtahid* is not supposed to issue judgments relating to doctrine or theological belief, which is considered a private matter for each Muslim, provided, of course, that he acknowledges the two articles of the Muslim creed: There is only one God and Mohammad was his Prophet.

**Mullah** (Arabic.) An Islamic preacher.

**Munafiq** (Arabic: hypocrite; plural: *munafiqeen*.) In the Koran (q.v.) the word refers to people in Medina who had converted to Islam but were not totally committed to the faith and worked to undermine Mohammad's political supremacy. It has since been applied to people who only pretend to believe in Islam, or who pay lip service to Islam while denying essential principles like justice and equality. Hence too, by extension, the term can mean any bad ruler who denies Muslims human rights that are their due and who is cruel and oppressive.

**Muslim calendar** This is strictly lunar and each year consists of 354 days. The months do not therefore correspond to fixed seasons. The Muslim era began on the first day of the year in which Mohammad migrated from Mecca to Medina, in *our* year 622.

**Oley** (Hebrew: pilgrim; plural: *olim.*) This is the word applied by Zionists to Jews who emigrated to the land of Israel and it is still used of immigrants today. The word *olim* is a near mystic term supercharged with emotion, ancient faith and historical associations. Besides meaning "those who ascend," referring to the ascension of the Temple Mount, it also means to rise above earthly desire to a nobler state of mind. Compare *Aliyah, Chalutz* (q.v.).

**Original sin** This is a doctrine peculiar to Christianity and is not part of either the Jewish or the Muslim faith. It teaches that when Adam and Eve sinned in the Garden of Eden all their descendants were doomed to hell and perpetual estrangement from God. Furthermore, man had "fallen" from a state of primeval innocence and was permanently impaired, spiritually and even physically. Fortunately God promised that he would send a redeemer, who was of course Jesus Christ. Jesus rescued men from this separation from God, provided that they entered into his death and resurrection by means of the sacrament of baptism. But even after baptism Christians feel the effects of Original Sin. They still get sick and die, which was not part of God's original intention, and, however hard they try, they still have a tendency to go on committing sins. The state of Original Sin, therefore, means a displacement from one's best self, an exile from God and a state of weakness and disability.

**Orthodox** (Greek: the right opinion.) During the first five centuries of Christianity there were many disputes about doctrine, particularly about the very difficult question of how Jesus could have been both God and man. In the Greek world particularly, which had always loved debating this kind of philosophical nicety, the argument was very acrimonious and many teachers and their followers were branded as "heretics," who believed a false doctrine, as opposed to the Christians, who remained loyal to the teaching of the official Church, which alone had the "right opinion." The Greek Church today still calls itself the Orthodox Church, to distinguish it from those Churches which have abandoned the correct interpretation of the faith. In Judaism the term is used to distinguish those Jews who practice a strict and literal interpretation of the Torah (q.v.), as compared to Conservative or Reform Judaism which have both modified the law to meet modern conditions. It must be stressed, however, that Orthodox Jews distinguish themselves from the Conservative and Reform Jews solely in matters of practice and not, like the Christians, in matters of belief.

**Palestine Liberation Organization, the PLO** This is the organization led by Yasir Arafat to restore the Palestinian people to their homeland. It is an alliance of several parties, the largest of which is Arafat's Fatah. The PLO has a charter which declares that Judaism is not a nation but a religion and that the enemy of the Palestinians is not Judaism but

Zionism. The PLO is a secular movement, which is working to establish an independent Palestinian secular state in which Jews, Christians and Muslims will all enjoy equal rights. Some extreme members of the PLO have formed terrorist groups.

**Pentateuch** (Greek.) The first five books of the Bible (Genesis, Exodus, Leviticus, Numbers and Deuteronomy), which Jews also call the Torah (q.v.), because it contains the law of Moses.

**Pillars** (translation of Arabic *rukn.*) These are the five practices which every Muslim must perform. First he or she has to make profession of the Muslim faith, which is expressed in the simple proclamation: There is only one God and Mohammad was his Prophet. The other "pillars" are prayer at the appointed times, almsgiving, fasting during the Muslim month of Ramadan (q.v.) and the *hajj* (q.v.), or the pilgrimage to Mecca. It will be clear that, like Judaism, Islam is a religion of practice rather than a religion of theological orthodoxy, like Christianity, which requires assent to many quite abstruse *doctrines* but does not have a codified law that is comparable to either the Torah or the Sharia (q.v.).

**Pogrom** (Russian: destruction.) An organized massacre which is directed toward the annihilation of any one body or class of people, particularly Jewish communities.

**Polytheism** The worship of many gods.

**Prophet** (Latin: to speak on behalf of.) We often use this word to mean a person who foretells the future. But in all three religions of Judaism, Christianity and Islam that is not a prophet's first task, though predicting future events may be one of his functions. A prophet is a person who speaks on behalf of God; God has communicated his will to him directly. He is an intermediary between God and man, who will correct, guide and lead a community to a closer approximation of God's will.

**Qadi** (Arabic.) A judge who officially administers the Sharia (q.v.).

**Rabbi** (Hebrew: master.) A Jewish religious teacher.

**Ramadan** (Arabic.) During this month in the Muslim calendar (q.v.) Muslims fast, and keeping Ramadan is one of the five pillars of Islam (q.v.). It is equivalent to the Christian Lent, but with one crucial difference. In Lent, the emphasis is on suffering and penance. A Christian who fasts during the six weeks leading up to Easter is particularly mindful of the suffering of Christ on Good Friday and often wants to suffer "with" him. But Ramadan is not meant to be a suffering experience. Muslims rise before dawn and eat a large meal that will get them through the day. After sundown they eat another large meal. Sometimes people put on weight during Ramadan! The point of the fast is not penance but a means of remembering God in a special way each year.

**Redemption** Christians call the death and resurrection of Christ their redemption because they believe that by this means he saved the world. When Jewish people speak of redemption, they usually refer to the coming of the Messiah (q.v.) and the dawning of a new era of peace and harmony, when God's chosen people will live in their land according to the Torah (q.v.), and the whole world will acknowledge the truth of Judaism and be redeemed through this recognition.

**Reform Judaism** has modified the law or Torah (q.v.) to meet modern conditions.

**Revisionist Zionism** This was an ideology propounded by Vladimir Jabotinsky, which broke away from Labor Zionism (q.v.). Revisionists denied that peaceful colonizing would be sufficient to obtain Palestine for the Jews and advocated a military struggle. Revisionists also tended toward an extreme nationalism and were affected by the racial chauvinism that had filled Europe at the end of the nineteenth century. Jabotinsky believed that Jews could only fulfill themselves if they had a land of their own and kept their race pure by not mixing with other nations. Menachem Begin, who became Prime Minister in 1977, was an ardent disciple of Jabotinsky; and President Yitzhak Shamir, who became Prime Minister in 1986, was also a Revisionist.

**Rum** (Arabic: Rome.) Commonly used by Muslims in the crusading period to refer to Christian Byzantium, which was the eastern part of the old Roman Empire. It was also the name given to the territory in Anatolia and Asia Minor which the Seljuk Turks had conquered from Byzantium during the late eleventh century, and the Turkish Sultan was called the Sultan of Rum.

**Sabra** (Hebrew.) The name given to Jewish Israelis who are born in the land of Israel. Literally it is the name of an Israeli fruit, which is tough and prickly on the outside but soft and sweet inside, and this is meant to be an image of the Sabra personality.

**Salvation** This word has been used in this book to describe those events in which God's elect are rescued from an impending and apparently inevitable destruction by a sudden reversal of fortune that seems miraculous and can only be explained by positing divine intervention. This experience has befallen Jews, Christians and Muslims throughout the story of the holy wars.

**Saracen** (Greek *Sarakenoi* and Latin *Saracenus*: the people that dwells in tents.) This was the word used by Greeks and Romans and by Greek and Latin Christians to describe the people of the Arabian Peninsula, who lived in tents that were much the same as those still used by Bedouins today. The "Saracens" never referred to themselves like this: they just called themselves "Arabs," but in the Christian world the name stuck, long after the "Saracens" had stopped living in tents. The word came to be used by Western people to describe all Muslim people, no matter what their ethnic origin, until relatively recently. Arabs, Berbers, Turks and Kurds were all called "Saracens."

**Sephardim** A Jewish tradition that originated in Spain. In Israel today the term is usually used to describe the Jews who came to Israel from the Arab countries after 1948. The Ashkenazim (q.v.) tended to look down on the Sephardic Jews and reduced them in effect to the status of second-class citizens, which the Sephardim bitterly resent.

**Sharia** (Arabic). The Holy Law of Islam, which was compiled and codified by the great Muslim jurists of the eighth and ninth centuries, who applied the principles of the Koran and the *hadith* (q.v.) to the smallest details of everyday life, and which was flexible enough to give a distinct identity to Muslims all over the Islamic empire. Where the West inherited Roman law as a secular legal system, Islam developed its own code of religious law, so that there is no equivalent of either the Sharia or the Torah (q.v.) in Christianity. The word "Sharia" means the road or way to a watering hole, which must always be followed. In a desert society such a path would be a literal lifeline, and deviation from it was possibly dangerous.

**Sheikh** (Arabic: old man, elder.) The word used in a number of contexts A sheikh can be a religious, a chief or a tribe or a man who has wor respect and renown in the community.

**Shiah** (Arabic, *Shiah i-Ali*: the partisans of Ali.) Originally this was a political movement of a minority of Muslims in the community, who believed that the Prophet Mohammad had wanted Ali ibn Talid, his cousin and son-in-law, to succeed him instead of Abu Bakr, the first Caliph. After the period of the four Rightly Guided Caliphs (*see* Caliph), the descendants of Ali offered an alternative to the rule of the caliphs, who had ceased to govern according to Islamic principles. In claiming to be the imam (leader) of the Muslims they were accepting a revolutionary responsibility. After Ali's line died out, most Shiites declared that the twelfth and last imam would return as a Messiah. (*See* Hidden Imam.) Shiites developed different devotions and religious practices from the Sunni Muslims (q.v.) but there is no difference in the essentials of the faith in the two traditions: Shiites and Sunnis all uphold the five pillars of Islam (q.v.).

**Shtetl** A small Jewish town or settlement in Russia and Eastern Europe.

**Sibylline oracles** Hellenistic Judaism produced books, preserved in Rome, which claimed to be the utterances of inspired prophetesses. Christian Sibylline texts began to appear in the fourth century and were believed by many Christians in Europe to be gospel truth. They foretold the coming of an emperor who would unite the East and West, slaughter the enemies of God and be crowned in Jerusalem (q.v.). Antichrist (q.v.) would then appear, the Archangel Michael would destroy him and Christ would return in glory.

**Sultan** (Arabic: originally government.) The Sultan wielded military and political authority over a group of Muslims, but theoretically he was subservient to the Caliph (q.v.).

**Sunna, Sunni** (Arabic, *Sunna*: the way.) The Sunna is the way of the Prophet Mohammad and includes everything he said, did, caused, ordered or allowed to happen. A Sunni is a Muslim who follows this way. The word is, however, most commonly used to distinguish the majority of Muslims from the Shiite minority. *See* Shiah.

**Suzerain** A medieval feudal overlord. *See* Feudalism, Fief.

**Talmud** The body of Jewish civil, ceremonial and traditional law, which developed from the Torah (q.v.) and from the oral and written commentary upon it by the great rabbis.

**Taqlid** (Arabic: emulation.) This Muslim practice teaches the faithful to emulate the *mujtahideen* in their observance of the Holy Law of Islam, because they are not equipped to do this themselves. They are not professionally intent on the study of the law and cannot appreciate all the complexities involved. There are Muslims who object to this and say that it is an un-Islamic practice because it creates an elite. *See* Ayatollah, *Ijtihad, Mujtahid*.

**Tefillin** Small leather boxes containing words from the Torah (q.v.) which proclaim the essence of the Jewish faith: "Hear, O Israel, the Lord is our God, the Lord is one." In the Torah, Jews are commanded to bind these words to themselves, and during prayer a Jewish man will attach the *tefillin* to his arm and forehead with leather thongs (Deuteronomy 6:4–9).

**Torah** (Hebrew: the Law.) The whole of the Torah comprises the 613 commandments that bind observant Jews. The commandments regulate the conduct of everyday life, yet they are felt not as a burden but as a privilege and a joy. Jews believe that the Torah enables people to live a rich and healthy life, because it is the expression of the will of God. On Simchat Torah, which celebrates the gift of the law to the Jewish people, Orthodox Jews dance joyfully, holding the Torah scrolls aloft. The Psalms in particular dwell on the precious gift of the Torah. There is no equivalent to the Torah in Christianity.

**Ulema** (Arabic, singular: *alem*.) The learned men who devote their lives to the study of the Holy Law of Islam.

**Umma** (Arabic.) The community of Islam.

**Vassal** In the feudal system, the term referred to one who held his land from his lord on condition that he remained faithful to his lord's interests. (*See* Fief.) A vassal was bound to his lord in a relationship that was as strong as his relationship with his kin.

**Vizier** (From the Arabic *wazir*: minister.) Under the Shiite dynasty in Egypt, conquered by Saladin and Shirkuh, the Vizier was in charge of the administration of the realm, under the nominal authority of the Caliph (q.v.). When Saladin abolished the caliphate, the Vizier became the supreme power in Egypt.

**Yahweh** This is the name that God gives to himself in the Jewish Scriptures. When Moses asks him for his name, God replies: "*Ehyeh esher ehyeh*: I am what I am" (Exodus 3:14). God is refusing to reveal his name because he can never be defined or summed up by man. On this principle, devout Jews never mention this name of God. In English versions of the Bible, Christians often translate Yahweh as "Jehovah."

**Yeshiva** An institute for Talmudic learning.

**Yishuv** The Jewish community in Palestine, before the creation of the state of Israel in 1948.

**Yom Kippur** The Jewish Day of Atonement.

**Zion** Zion was the name of the ancient citadel of the Jebusites in Jerusalem (q.v.), which King David conquered from them in about 1000 B.C.E. It is often used as a synonym for Jerusalem. The Zionists, who wanted to return the Jewish people to the land of their fathers, naturally looked back to the old religious dream of a Jewish return to Zion.

**Zemiros** Religious Hebrew songs sung at meals on feast days and on the Sabbath.

**Zoroastrianism** The official religion of the Persians before they converted to Islam. It was a dualistic religion, in which a good spirit fought an evil spirit in a constant battle.

# BIBLIOGRAPHY*

Abelard, Peter, with Heloise, *The Letters of Abelard and Heloise*, ed. and trans. Betty Radice (London, 1974).

Adams, Henry, *Mont Saint-Michel and Chartres* (London, 1986 ed.).

Akhari, Shahrough, "Shariati's Social Thought," in Nikkie R. Keddie, ed., *Religion and Politics in Iran: Shiism from Quietism to Revolution* (New Haven and London, 1983).

Arberry, A. J., *Sufism: An Account of the Mystics of Islam* (London, 1950).

Armstrong, Karen, *The First Christian: St. Paul's Impact on Christianity* (London, 1983).

————, *The Gospel According to Woman, Christianity's Creation of the Sex War in the West* (London, 1986; New York, 1987).

Auerbach, Erich, *Mimesis: The Representation of Reality in Western Literature* (New Jersey, 1953).

Avineri, Schlomo, *The Makings of Modern Zionism* (London and New York, 1981).

Avishai, Bernard, *The Tragedy of Zionism: Revolution and Democracy in the Land of Israel* (New York, 1985).

Avnery, Uri, *My Friend, the Enemy* (London, 1986).

Bailey, D. S., *The Man-Woman Relation in Christian Thought* (London, 1959).

Bakhash, Shaul, *The Reign of the Ayatollahs: Iran and the Islamic Revolution* (London, 1986).

Balard, Michel, "Des châteaux forts en Palestine," *L'Histoire*, 47 (Paris, 1982).

Baldwin, Marshall Whithed, *Raymund III of Tripolis and the Fall of Jerusalem* (Princeton, 1936).

Barkun, Michael, *Disaster and the Millennium* (New Haven and London, 1974).

Beeman, William O., "Images of the Great Satan: Representations of the United States in the Iranian Revolution," in Nikkie R. Keddie, ed.,

*Periodicals referenced in the text and notes have not been included in the Bibliography.

*Religion and Politics in Iran: Shiism from Quietism to Revolution* (New Haven and London, 1983).

Bellow, Saul, *To Jerusalem and Back: A Personal Account* (London and New York, 1976).

Ben-Ami, Aharon, *Social Change in a Hostile Environment: The Crusaders' Kingdom of Jerusalem* (New Haven, 1969).

Bendt, Ingela, and James Downing, *We Shall Return, Women of Palestine* (London, 1982).

Berque, Jacques, *Arab Rebirth: Pain and Ecstasy*, trans. Quinton Hoare (London, 1983).

Boase, Roger, *The Origin and Meaning of Courtly Love: A Critical Study of European Scholarship* (Manchester, 1977).

Brenner, Lenni, *The Iron Wall: Zionist Revisionism from Jabotinski to Shamir* (London, 1984).

Bresc-Bautier, Geneviève, "L'An prochain au Saint-Sépulchre!," *L'Histoire*, 47 (Paris, 1982).

Broughton, B. B., *The Legends of Richard I, Coeur de Lion: A Study of Sources and Variations to the Year 1600* (The Hague and Paris, 1966).

Brown, Peter, *Religion and Society in the Age of St. Augustine* (London, 1972).

———, *The Making of Late Antiquity* (Cambridge, Mass., and London, 1978).

———, *The Cult of the Saints: Its Rise and Function in Classical Antiquity* (London, 1982).

Buber, Martin, *On Zion: The History of an Idea* (London, 1973).

Burman, Edward, *The Assassins: Holy Killers of Islam* (London, 1987).

Burns, Robert Ignatius, SJ, *Islam Under the Crusaders: Colonial Survival in the Thirteenth-Century Kingdom of Valencia* (Princeton, 1973).

Burr, G. L., "The Year 1000 and the Antecedents of the Crusades," *American Historical Review* 6 (1900).

Calkins, Robert G., *Monuments of Medieval Art* (Ithaca and London, 1979).

Carlyle, Thomas, *On Heroes and Hero-Worship* (London, 1841).

Chrétien of Troyes, *Arthurian Romances*, ed. and trans. W. W. Comfort (London, 1975).

Cobban, Helena, *The Making of Modern Lebanon* (London, 1985).

Cohen, A., *Everyman's Talmud* (New York, 1975).

Cohen, Geula, *Woman of Violence: Memoirs of a Young Terrorist, 1943–1948* (London, 1966).

Cohn, Norman, *The Pursuit of the Millennium: Revolutionary Millenarians and Mystical Anarchists of the Middle Ages* (London, 1957, 1970).

———, *Europe's Inner Demons* (London, 1975).

Collins, Roger, *Early Medieval Spain: Unity in Diversity, 400–1000* (London, 1983).

Comnena, Anna, *Alexiad*, 3 vols., ed. and trans. B. Leib (Paris, 1937–45).

Constable, Giles, "The Second Crusade as Seen by Contemporaries," *Traditio*, 9 (1953).

Contamine, Philippe, "Une Guerre pour le Royaume des cieux," *L'Histoire*, 47 (Paris, 1982).

Cowdrey, H. E. J., "The Peace and the Truce of God in the Eleventh Century," *Past and Present*, 46 (1970).

——, "Pope Urban's Preaching of the First Crusade," *History*, 55 (1970).

Daniel, Norman, *Islam and the West: The Making of an Image* (Edinburgh, 1960).

——, *The Arabs and Medieval Europe* (London and Beirut, 1975).

Daniel-Rops, Henri, *Bernard of Clairvaux*, trans. Elizabeth Abbot (New York and London, 1964).

Duby, Georges, "Les Pauvres des campagnes dans l'Occident médiéval jusqu'au XIII siècle," *Revue d'Histoire de l'Église de France*, 52 (Paris, 1966).

——, *The Chivalrous Society*, trans. C. Postan (London, 1977).

——, *The Knight, the Lady and the Priest: The Making of Modern Marriage in Medieval France*, trans. Barbara Bray (London and New York, 1983, 1985).

Dufourcq, Charles-Emmanuel, "L'Impossible Voyage en terre sainte," *L'Histoire*, 47 (Paris, 1982).

Duncalf, F., "The Peasants Crusade," *American Historical Review*, 26 (1921).

EAFOD and AJAZ, eds., *Judaism or Zionism: What Difference for the Middle East?* (London, 1986).

Eco, Umberto, trans. William Weaver, *Travels in Hyper-reality* (London, 1986).

Edbury, P. W., ed., *Crusade and Settlement* (London, 1985).

Eidelberg, Shlomo, trans. and ed., *The Jews and the Crusaders: The Hebrew Chronicles of the First and Second Crusades* (Wisconsin and London, 1977).

Einard and Notger the Stammerer, *Two Lives of Charlemagne*, trans. and ed. Lewis Thorpe (London, 1969).

El-Asmar, Fouzi, *Through the Hebrew Looking Glass: Arab Stereotypes in Children's Literature* (London and Brattleboro, Vermont, 1986).

Eliot, George, *Daniel Deronda* (London, Panther ed., 1970).

Elon, Amos, *The Israelis, Founders and Sons*, 2nd ed. (London and Tel Aviv, 1981, 1983).

Evans, G. R., *The Mind of Bernard of Clairvaux* (London, 1983).

Falk, Richard, "Iran: Human Rights and International Law," in D. H. Albert, ed., *Tell the American People: Perspectives on the Iranian Revolution* (Philadelphia, 1980).

Favier, Jean, "Les Templiers, ou l'échec des banquiers de la croisade," *L'Histoire*, 47 (Paris, 1982).

Finucane, Ronald C., *Miracles and Pilgrims: Popular Beliefs in Medieval Europe* (London, 1977).

Fisch, Harold, *The Zionist Revolution: A New Perspective* (London and Tel Aviv, 1978).

Fleming, Gerald, *Hitler and the Final Solution* (Oxford and London, 1985, 1986).

Focillon, Henri, *The Year 1000* (New York, Paris and London, 1952).

——, *The Art of the West in the Middle Ages*, 2 vols., 3rd ed., trans. Donald King (Oxford, 1980).

Frend, W. H. C., *Martyrdom and Persecution in the Early Church: A Study of a Conflict from the Maccabees to Donatus* (Oxford, 1965).

Freud, Sigmund, *Character and Culture* (New York, 1963)

——, *Letters to his Fiancée, December 1883* (London, 1960).

Fulcher of Chartres, *A History of the Expedition to Jerusalem 1095–1127*, trans. and ed. Frances Rita Ryan (Knoxville, 1969).

Gabrieli, Francesco, trans. and ed., *Arab Historians of the Crusades*, trans. from the Italian by E. J. Costello (London, 1978, 1984).

——, *Muhammad and the Conquests of Islam*, trans. Virginia Luling and Rosamund Linell (London, 1968).

——, "Islam in the Mediterranean World," in Joseph Schacht and C. E. Bosworth, eds., *The Legacy of Islam* (2nd ed., Oxford, 1979).

Gauvard, Claude, "La Chase aux hérétiques," *L'Histoire*, 47 (Paris, 1982).

Geoffrey of Villehardouin and John of Joinville, *Chronicles of the Crusades*, trans. and ed. M. R. B. Shaw (London, 1963).

Gibbon, Edward, *The Decline and Fall of the Roman Empire*, abridged in one volume, ed. Dero E. Saunders (London, 1980).

Gilmour, David, *Lebanon: The Fractured Country* (London, 1983).

Gordon, A. D., *Selected Essays* (New York, 1938).

Greenberg, Blu, *On Women and Judaism: A View from Tradition* (Philadelphia, 1981).

Gresh, Alain, *The PLO: The Struggle Within, Towards an Independent Palestinian State*, trans. A. M. Berrett (London, 1985).

Grunberger, Richard, *A Social History of the Third Reich* (London, 1971).

Harkabi, Y., *Arab Attitudes to Israel* (Jerusalem, 1972).

——, *Israel's Fateful Decisions* (London ed., 1988).

Havighurst, Alfred. F., ed., *The Pirenne Thesis* (Boston, 1965).

Hays, H. R., *The Dangerous Sex: The Myth of Feminine Evil* (London, 1966).

Heer, Friedrich, *The Medieval World, 1100–1350*, trans. Janet Sondheimer (London, 1962).

Hegland, Mary, "Two Images of Husain: Accommodation and Revolution in an Iranian Village," in Nikkie R. Keddie, ed., *Religion and Politics in Iran: Shiism from Quietism to Revolution* (London, 1983).

Heikal, Mohamed, *Autumn of Fury: The Assassination of Sadat* (London, 1983, 1986).

Heimert, Alan, and Andrew Delbanco, eds., *The Puritans in America: A Narrative Anthology* (Cambridge, Mass., 1985).

Herrman, Klaus, "Politics and the 'Divine Promise,' " in EAFOD and AJAZ, eds., *Judaism or Zionism: What Difference for the Middle East?* (London, 1986).

Herzl, Theodor, *The Jewish State* (London, 1896).

————, *The Complete Diaries of Theodor Herzl*, ed. Raphael Patai (New York, 1960).

Hess, Moses, *Rome and Jerusalem* (New York, 1943).

Hill, Rosalind, trans. and ed. *The Deeds of the Franks and the Other Pilgrims to Jerusalem* (London, 1962).

Holt, P.M. ed., *The Eastern Mediterranean Lands in the Period of the Crusades* (Forest Grove, Oregon, 1977).

Howarth, Stephen, *The Knights Templar* (London, 1982).

Hussain, Asaf, *Islamic Iran: Revolution and Counter-Revolution* (London, 1985).

John of Joinville, *The Life of St. Louis*, trans. René Hague, ed. Natalie de Wailly (London, 1955).

Johnson, Paul, *A History of the Jews* (London, 1987).

Josephus, *The Jewish War*, trans. G. A. Williamson (London, 1959).

Kantorowicz, Ernst, *Frederick the Second, 1194–1250*, trans. E. O. Lorimer (London, 1931).

Kaplan, Michel, "Le Sac de Constantinople," *L'Histoire*, 47 (Paris, 1982).

Kedar, Benjamin Z., *Crusade and Mission: European Approaches Towards the Muslims* (Princeton, 1984).

Kedar, B. Z., H. E. Mayer and R. C. Smail, eds., *Outremer: Studies in the History of the Crusading Kingdom of Jerusalem. Presented to Joshua Prawer* (Jerusalem, 1982).

Keddie, Nikkie R. ed., *Religion and Politics in Iran: Shiism from Quietism to Revolution* (New Haven and London, 1983).

Keneally, Thomas, *Schindler's Ark* (London and New York, 1982).

Kepel, Gilles, *The Prophet and Pharaoh: Muslim Extremism in Egypt*, trans. Jon Rothschild (London, 1985).

Khan, Muhammad Zafrulla, *Islam: Its Meaning for Modern Man* (London, 1962, 1980).

Kobler, Franz, *The Vision Was There* (London, 1956).

————, *Napoleon and the Jews* (New York, 1976).

Krey, August C., *The First Crusade: The Accounts of Eye-Witnesses and Participants* (Princeton and London, 1921).

Lacqueur, Walter, *A History of Zionism* (New York, 1972).

Lacqueur, Walter, and Barry Rubin, eds., *The Israel–Arab Reader: A Documentary History of the Middle East Conflict*, (4th ed., revised and updated (London, 1984).

Lane-Poole, Stanley, *The Moors in Spain* (London and New York, 1890).

————, *Saladin and the Fall of Jerusalem* (London and New York, 1898).

Lawrence, T. E., *Seven Pillars of Wisdom: A Triumph* (London, 1926, 1935).

————, *The Letters of T. E. Lawrence of Arabia*, ed. David Garnett (London, 1964).

Lecler, J., *Tolerance and the Reformation* (London, 1960).

Leslie, S. Clement, *The Rift in Israel: Religious Authority and Secular Democracy* (London, 1971).

Lewis, Bernard, *The Assassins* (London, 1967).

———, *The Arabs in History* (London, 1950).

———, *Islam from the Prophet Mohammad to the Capture of Constantinople*, 2 vols, vol. I: *Politics and War*; vol. II: *Religion and Society* (New York and London, 1976).

———, *The Muslim Discovery of Europe* (New York and London, 1982).

———, *The Jews of Islam* (New York and London, 1982).

———, *Semites and Anti-Semites: An Inquiry into Conflict and Prejudice* (London, 1986).

Lyons, M. C., and D. E. P. Jackson, *Saladin: The Politics of the Holy War* (Cambridge, 1982).

Maalouf, Amin, *The Crusades Through Arab Eyes*, trans. Jon Rothschild (London, 1984).

Maccoby, Hyam, *Revolution in Judaea: Jesus and the Jewish Resistance* (London, 1973).

———, *The Sacred Executioner: Human Sacrifice and the Legacy of Guilt* (London, 1982).

Madaule, Jacques, *The Albigensian Crusade: An Historical Essay*, trans. Barbara Wall (London, 1967).

Mâle, Émile, *The Gothic Image: Religious Art in France of the Thirteenth Century*, trans. Dora Nussey (London and New York, 1913).

Mansfield, Peter, *The Arabs*, 3rd ed. (London, 1985).

Markale, Jean, *Aliénor d'Aquitaine* (Paris, 1983).

Marx, Karl, *Surveys from Exile*, ed. and trans. David Fernbach (London, 1973).

Meinertzhagen, Richard, *Middle East Diary: 1917–1956* (London, 1960).

Meiring, Desmond, *Fire of Islam* (London, 1982).

Mergui, Raphael, and Philippe Simonnot, *Israel's Ayatollahs: Meir Kahane and the Far Right in Israel* (London, 1987).

Metzger, Jan, Martin Orth and Christine Sterzing eds., *This Land Is Our Land: The West Bank Under Israeli Occupation*, trans. Dan and Judy Bryant, Janet Goodwin and Stefan Schaaf (London, 1983).

Micheau, Françoise, " 'Jihad': L'Islam relève le défi," *L'Histoire*, 47 (Paris, 1982).

Migne, J. P., *Patrologia Latina*, 383 vols. (Paris, 1864–84).

Mitchell, R. P., *The Society of the Muslim Brothers* (Oxford, 1969).

Morrisson, Cécile, "La Grande Rupture avec l'Orient," *L'Histoire*, 47 (Paris, 1982).

Mortimer, Edward, *Faith and Power: The Politics of Islam* (London, 1982).

Mottahedeh, Roy, *The Mantle of the Prophet: Religion and Politics in Iran* (London and New York, 1985, and London, 1987).

Murphy, Thomas Patrick, ed., *The Holy War* (Columbus, 1974).

Musurillo, Herbert, ed. and trans., *The Acts of the Christian Martyrs* (Oxford, 1972).

Nasir, Sari J., *The Arabs and the English*, 2nd ed. (London, 1979).

Near, Henry, ed., *The Seventh Day: Soldiers Talk about the Six Day War* (London, 1970).

Nicholson, R. A., *The Mystics of Islam* (London, 1914).

O'Brien, Conor Cruise, *The Siege: The Saga of Israel and Zionism* (London, 1986).

Odo of Deuil, *De profectione Ludovici VII in orientem: The Journey of Louis VII to the East*, ed. and trans. Virginia G. Berry (New York, 1948).

Oldenbourg, Zoé, *Le Bûcher de Montségur* (Paris, 1959).

——, *The Crusades*, trans. Anne Carter (London, 1966).

Ovendale, Ritchie, *The Origins of the Arab–Israeli Wars* (New York and London, 1984).

Oz, Amos, *My Michael*, trans. Nicholas de Lange (London, 1972, 1984).

——, *The Hill of Evil Counsel*, trans. Nicholas de Lange (London, 1978).

——, *Where the Jackals Howl*, trans. Nicholas de Lange and Philip Simpson (London, 1980).

——, *In the Land of Israel*, trans. Maurice Goldberg-Bartura (London, 1983).

——, *A Perfect Peace*, trans. Hillel Halkin (London, 1985).

Palumbo, Michael, *The Palestinian Catastrophe: The 1948 Expulsion of a People from Their Homeland* (London, 1987).

Parisse, Michel, "Godefroy de Bouillon, le croise exemplaire," *L'Histoire*, 47 (Paris, 1982).

——, "Les 'Profits' de la guerre sainte," *L'Histoire*, 47 (Paris, 1982).

Parkes, J. W., *The Jew and the Medieval Community* (London, 1938).

Parrinder, Geoffrey, *Sex in the World's Religions* (London, 1980).

Pastoureau, Michel, "La Coquille et la croix: les emblèmes des croisés," *L'Histoire*, 47 (Paris, 1982).

Patlagean, Evelyne, "Les Juifs, les 'Infidèles' de l'Europe," *L'Histoire*, 47 (Paris, 1982).

Peretz, Don, "The Semantics of Zionism, Anti-Zionism and Anti-Semitism," in EAFOD and AJAZ, eds., *Judaism or Zionism: What Difference for the Middle East?* (London, 1986).

Pernoud, Régine, *The Crusaders*, trans. Enid Grant (Edinburgh and London, 1963).

Pirenne, H., *Mohammad and Charlemagne*, trans. Bernard Miall (New York, 1939).

Porges, Walter, "The Clergy, the Poor and the Non-Combatants on the First Crusade," *Speculum*, 21 (1946).

Potok, Chaim, *Wanderings: A History of the Jews* (New York, 1978, 1983).

Prawer, Joshua, *The Latin Kingdom of Jerusalem: European Colonialism in the Middle Ages* (London, 1972).

——, *The World of the Crusades* (London, 1972).

Raban, Jonathan, *Arabia Through the Looking Glass* (London, 1979, 1983).

Raedts, P., "La Croisade des enfants a'-t-elle eu en lieu?," trans. Jacques Bacalu, *L'Histoire*, 47 (Paris, 1982).

——, "The Children's Crusade of 1212," *Journal of Medieval History*, 3 (1977).

Ranelagh, E. L., *The Past We Share: The Near-Eastern Ancestry of Western Folk Literature* (London, 1979).

Richard, Jean, "Vie et mort des États croisés," *L'Histoire*, 47 (Paris, 1982).

——, "La Bataille de Hattin: Saladin défait l'Occident," *L'Histoire*, 47 (Paris, 1982).

Riley-Smith, Jonathan, *The Knights of St. John in Jerusalem and Cyprus, 1050–1310* (London, 1967).

——, *The Feudal Nobility and the Kingdom of Jerusalem, 1174–1277* (London, 1973).

——, *What Were the Crusades?* (London, 1977).

——, "Crusading as an Act of Love," *History*, 65 (1980).

——, "The First Crusade and St. Peter," in B. Z. Kedar, H. E. Mayer and R. C. Smail, eds., *Outremer: Studies in the History of the Crusading Kingdom of Jerusalem. Presented to Joshua Prawer* (Jerusalem, 1982).

——, *The First Crusade and the Idea of Crusading* (London, 1986).

——, with Louise Riley-Smith, *The Crusades: Idea and Reality, 1095–1274* (London, 1981).

Rodinson, Maxime, *Israel: A Colonial–Settler State?* (New York, 1973).

——, *Mohammed*, trans. Anne Carter (2nd ed., London, 1981).

——, *Israel and the Arabs*, trans. Michael Perl and Brian Pearce, 2nd ed. (London, 1982).

——, *Cult, Ghetto and State: The Persistence of the Jewish Question* (London, 1983).

Rose, Gregory, "*Velayat-e Faqih* and the Recovery of Islamic Identity in the Thought of Ayatollah Khomeini," in Nikkie R. Keddie, ed., *Religion and Politics in Iran: Shiism from Quietism to Revolution* (New Haven and London, 1983).

Rothschild, Jon, ed. and trans., *Forbidden Agendas: Intolerance and Defiance in the Middle East. From the Journal Khamsin* (London, 1984).

Runciman, Steven, *A History of the Crusades*, 3 vols. (Cambridge, 1954; London, 1965).

——, *The Medieval Manichee: A Study of the Christian Dualist Heresy* (Cambridge, 1960).

Russell, Frederick H., *The Just War in the Middle Ages* (Cambridge, 1979).

Ruthven, Malise, *Islam in the World* (London, 1984).

Said, Edward W., *Orientalism: Western Conceptions of the Orient* (New York and London, 1978, 1985).

——, *The Question of Palestine* (London, 1980, 1981).

——, *Covering Islam: How the Media and the Experts Determine How We See the Rest of the World* (New York and London, 1981).

——, *After the Last Sky* (London, 1986).

Saunders, J. J., *A History of Medieval Islam* (London, 1965).

Sayigh, Rosemary, *Palestinians: From Peasants to Revolutionaries* (London, 1979).

Schacht, Joseph, and C. E. Bosworth, eds., *The Legacy of Islam*, 2nd ed. (Oxford, 1979).

Schiff, Ze'ev, and Ehud Ya'ari, *Israel's Lebanon War*, trans. Ina Friedman (London, 1985).

Scholem, Gershom, *The Messianic Idea in Judaism, and Other Essays on Jewish Spirituality* (New York, 1971).

Schweid, Eliezer, *The Land of Israel: National Home or Land of Destiny*, trans. Deborah Greniman (New York, 1985).

Shahak, Israel, "The Jewish Religion and Its Attitude to Non-Jews," *Khamsin*, 8 and 9 (1981).

Shahar, Shulamith, *The Fourth Estate: A History of Women in the Middle Ages*, trans. Chaya Galai (New York and London, 1983).

Sharif, Regina, *Non-Jewish Zionism: Its Roots in Western History* (London, 1983).

Sick, Gary, *All Fall Down: America's Fateful Encounter with Iran* (New York and London, 1985).

Sigal, P. A., "Et les marcheurs de Dieu prirent leurs armes," *L'Histoire*, 47 (Paris, 1982).

Sivan, E., *Modern Arab Historiography of the Crusades* (Tel Aviv, 1973).

Smith, Wilfred Cantwell, *Islam in Modern History* (Princeton, 1957).

Southern, R. W., *The Making of the Middle Ages* (Oxford, 1953; London, 1987).

———, *Western Views of Islam in the Middle Ages* (Cambridge, Mass., 1962).

———, *Western Society and the Church in the Middle Ages* (London, 1970).

Sulaiman, Khalid A., *Palestine and Modern Arab Poetry* (London, 1984).

Taheri, Amir, *The Spirit of Allah: Khomeini and the Islamic Revolution* (London, 1985, 1987).

Talbi, Mohamad, "Saint Louis: voir Tunis et mourir," *L'Histoire*, 47 (Paris, 1982).

Thomas, D. M., *The White Hotel* (London and New York, 1981).

Thomas, Keith, *Religion and the Decline of Magic* (London, 1971).

Toland, *Adolf Hitler* (London and New York, 1976).

Tuchman, Barbara W., *Bible and Sword: How the British Came to Palestine* (New York, 1956, and London, 1957, 1982).

al-Udhari, Abdullah, trans. and ed., *Victims of a Map, A Bilingual Anthology of Arabic Poetry* (London, 1984).

Usama Ibn Mundiqh, *An Arab–Syrian Gentleman and Warrior in the Period of the Crusades*, trans. P. K. Hitti (New York, 1929).

Vauchez, André, "Saint Bernard, un prédicateur irrésistible," *L'Histoire*, 47 (Paris, 1982).

Ward, Barbara, *Miracles and the Medieval Mind* (London, 1982).

Watt, W. Montgomery, *Muhammad at Mecca* (Oxford, 1953).

————, *Muhammad at Medina* (Oxford, 1956).

————, *Muhammad: Prophet and Statesman* (Oxford, 1961).

————, *A History of Islamic Spain* (Edinburgh, 1965).

————, *The Influence of Islam on Medieval Europe* (Edinburgh, 1972).

————, "Islam and the Holy War," in Thomas Patrick Murphy, ed., *The Holy War* (Columbus, 1974).

————, "The Significance of the Early Stages of Imami Shiism," in Nikkie R. Keddie, ed., *Religion and Politics in Iran: Shiism from Quietism to Revolution* (New Haven and London, 1983).

William, Archbishop of Tyre, *A History of Deeds Done Beyond the Sea*, trans. E. A. Babcock and A. C. Krey, 2 vols. (New York, 1943).

Williams, Watkin W., *St. Bernard of Clairvaux* (Manchester, 1935).

Wolff, Philippe, *The Awakening of Europe*, trans. Anne Carter (London, 1968).

Wood, Charles T., *The Age of Chivalry: Manners and Morals, 1000–1450* (London, 1970).

Wright, Robin, *Sacred Rage: The Crusade of Modern Islam* (London, 1986).

Yadin, Yigael, *Masada: Herod's Fortress and the Zealot's Last Stand*, trans. Moshe Pearlman (London, 1966).

Yehoshua, A. B., *A Late Divorce*, trans. Hillel Halkin (New York and London, 1984; London, 1985).

————, *The Lover*, trans. Philip Simpson (New York, 1977; London, 1985.

# INDEX